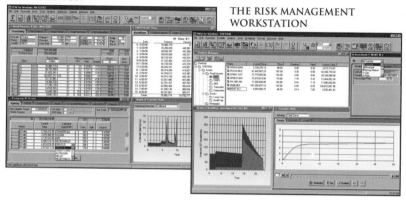

The Handbook of Nonagency Mortgage-Backed Securities

Edited by

Frank J. Fabozzi, CFA
Adjunct Professor of Finance
School of Management
Yale University

Chuck Ramsey
Managing Director
Structured Capital Management
and
CEO
Mortgage Risk Assessment Corporation

Frank R. Ramirez
Managing Director
Structured Capital Management

Michael Marz
Vice Chairman
First Southwest Company

Published by Frank J. Fabozzi Associates

© 1997 By Frank J. Fabozzi Associates
New Hope, Pennsylvania

This publication is designed to provide accurate and authoritative information in regard to the subject matter covered. It is sold with the understanding that the publisher is not engaged in rendering legal, accounting, or other professional services.

ISBN: 1-883249-19-8

Printed in the United States of America

TABLE OF CONTENTS

PREFACE

The dominant sector of the mortgage-backed securities (MBS) market is securities backed by Ginnie Mae, Fannie Mae, and Freddie Mac, popularly referred to as *agency securities*. Today, an equally important sector of the MBS market is developing: the market for *nonagency MBS*. These securities are issued by private entities. Unlike agency MBS, investors are exposed to credit risk. While investors in agency MBS have focused totally on prepayment risk, investors in nonagency MBS must concentrate on both prepayment risk and credit risk.

The nonagency MBS market has recently gone through some significant changes. In past years, the word "nonagency" was synonymous with "no way." Investors considered nonagency MBS securities not worth the risks. In reality, the market suffered from a complete lack of any means to evaluate risks. In the last few years, however, millions of dollars have been invested in solving that problem. The results can be measured by the tremendous increase in market participants. Today, the "credit sensitive" sector of the MBS market means opportunity.

Fundamental to this significant change is an investor's ability to calculate, and now even forecast, "loss severity." This ability to make educated guesses about an individual property value has never been greater than today. The future, however, has already been determined. Currently under development are significant analytical programs. The database for many of these models is over 60 gigabytes (45 million properties for those who don't like gigabytes). These models, along with far better loan-level information, will allow investors to do what they have the right to do, evaluate risk.

Current and potential investors in this market sector must have the skills to identify and then capitalize on the opportunities available. The purpose of the *Handbook of Nonagency Mortgage-Backed Securities* is to provide investors with the tools to effectively participate in this market.

The *Handbook* is divided into four sections. Section I covers whole-loan collateralized mortgage obligations (CMOs). The six chapters in Part A cover the unique investment characteristics of whole-loan CMOs. The six chapters in Part B provide a detailed explanation of how to assess the credit quality of whole-loan CMO structures. The state-of-the art databases available to analyze these securities are also described. The prepayment characteristics of whole-loan CMOs are documented in the three chapters in Part C.

Section II covers two types of asset-backed securities — home equity loan-backed securities and manufactured housing loan-backed securities. These asset-backed securities are included in our coverage of nonagency MBS since the loans are backed by residential property. Coverage includes an explanation of these securities, their default profiles, their prepayment characteristics, and techniques for analyzing them.

Commercial MBS is covered in the eight chapters in Section III. Commercial properties include multifamily residential buildings, retail shopping malls, neighborhood shopping centers, office buildings, hotels and motels, and industrial warehouses. Once again, there is coverage of the structures, prepayment characteristics, default profiles, and analytical issues. The sole chapter in Section IV covers municipal housing revenue bonds and discusses the complications associated with analyzing these securities.

To be effective, a book of this nature should offer a broad perspective. The experiences of a wide range of experts are more informative than those of a single expert, particularly because of the diversity of opinion on some issues. We have chosen some of the best known practitioners who have been actively involved in the evolution of this market to contribute to this book.

We are extremely excited about the future for nonagency MBS. We hope that if your investment objectives permit, this book will encourage you to participate in this asset class and provide insightful analysis to enhance investment returns.

Frank J. Fabozzi
Chuck Ramsey
Frank R. Ramirez
Michael Marz

CONTRIBUTING AUTHORS

William J. Adams, CFA	Conseco Capital Management, Inc.
Jesse M. Abraham, Ph.D.	Federal Home Loan Mortgage Corporation
Steven Abrahams	Morgan Stanley
Donald S. Belanger	Fitch Investors Service, L.P.
Douglas L. Bendt	Mortgage Risk Assessment Corporation
Eric Bruskin, Ph.D.	Deutsche Morgan Grenfell
Da Cheng	Wall Street Analytics, Inc.
Manus J. Clancy	The Trepp Group
Michael Constantino, III	The Trepp Group
Adrian R. Cooper, Ph.D.	Wall Street Analytics, Inc.
Joseph F. DeMichele	Conseco Capital Management, Inc.
Akiva Dickstein	Lehman Brothers
Pamela T. Dillon	Fitch Investors Service, L.P.
John N. Dunlevy, CFA, CPA	Hyperion Capital Management
Howard Esaki	Morgan Stanley
Frank J. Fabozzi, Ph.D., CFA	Yale University
Yizhong Fan, Ph.D.	Global Advanced Technology
Peter Fastovsky	Nomura Securities International, Inc.
Mark Feldman	Bear, Stearns & Co., Inc.
Joseph C. Franzetti	Duff & Phelps Credit Rating Co.
Thomas Gillis	Standard and Poor's
Laurie Goodman, Ph.D.	PaineWebber, Inc.
Cathy Hansen	Frank J. Fabozzi Associates
Kenneth Higgins	Fitch Investors Service, Inc.
Jason Huang	Wall Street Analytics, Inc.
David P. Jacob	Nomura Securities International, Inc.
Andrew Jones	Duff & Phelps Credit Rating Co.
Bruce Kramer	Bear, Stearns & Co.
Linda Lowell	PaineWebber, Inc.
Mary Sue Lundy	Fitch Investors Service, Inc.
Michael Marz	First Southwest Company
John Miller	Bear, Stearns & Co.
Michael Radocy	Hyperion Capital Management
Chuck Ramsey	Structured Capital Management and Mortgage Risk Assessment Corporation
Robert Restrick	Morgan Stanley
Pete Rogers	Global Advanced Technology
Peter Rubinstein, Ph.D.	PaineWebber, Inc.
Jennifer Schneider	Duff & Phelps Credit Rating Co.
Andrew Shook	Hyperion Capital Management, Inc.
David Sykes, Ph.D.	Deutsche Morgan Grenfell
H. Scott Theobald	Federal Home Loan Mortgage Corporation
Edward L. Toy	Teachers Insurance and Annuity Association
Dale Westhoff	Bear, Stearns & Co., Inc.
Michael D. Youngblood, Ph.D.	Chase Securities Inc.

INDEX OF ADVERTISERS

Section I:

Whole-Loan CMOs

Part A: Background

Chapter 1

The Nonagency Mortgage Market: Background and Overview

Eric Bruskin, Ph.D.
Director
Deutsche Morgan Grenfell

David Sykes, Ph.D.
Director
Deutsche Morgan Grenfell

INTRODUCTION: NONCONFORMING LOANS AND NONAGENCY SECURITIES

The three U.S. government-chartered mortgage agencies are the foundation on which the entire mortgage-backed securities (MBS) market is based: the Federal National Mortgage Association (FNMA or "Fannie Mae"), the Federal Home Loan Mortgage Corporation (FHLMC or "Freddie Mac"), and the Government National Mortgage Association (GNMA or "Ginnie Mae"). The constituencies they serve and the nature of their government sponsorship may differ somewhat, but the end result is the same: by issuing securities with their implicit (Fannie Mae and Freddie Mac) or explicit (Ginnie Mae) government guarantee, the agencies promote the availability of mortgage funding at the lowest possible cost to the vast majority of American home buyers. However, this policy-driven "agency advantage" applies only to loans that meet certain criteria, most significantly with respect to loan size and underwriting standards.

Only *conforming* loans are eligible to be purchased and/or guaranteed by one or more of the agencies; these are the loans that back (or "collateralize") agency MBSs, which are guaranteed against credit losses by the agency that issues them. As a part of the Department of Housing and Urban Development, Ginnie Mae is involved in securitizing *government sponsored* mortgages, primarily FHA-insured or VA-guaranteed mortgage loans. Fannie Mae and Freddie Mac securitize *conventional* mortgage loans that conform to their loan size and underwriting standards.

The authors wish to express their gratitude to Cathy Smiley for valued assistance in preparing this chapter.

Nonconforming conventional loans are traded in a parallel *nonagency* market which, to investors, primarily means that the mortgages do not carry an agency guarantee against credit losses. (The nonagency sector is also alternately referred to as the *private-label* market.) Thus, in order to qualify for a rating, securities backed by nonagency mortgages must carry alternative forms of credit enhancement.

Loan Size

To qualify for agency securitization or purchase programs, a conventional mortgage loan must have a "conforming balance." The maximum limit in 1996 was $207,000 for both Fannie Mae and Freddie Mac. Each agency decides independently, but historically their limits have been the same. Higher limits apply to 2-to-4 family properties, and lower limits apply to the FHA/VA mortgages collateralizing Ginnie Mae securities. Mortgage loans that exceed the conforming limits, generally termed "jumbos," make up a substantial majority of the raw material used in the creation of nonagency securities. These loans are geographically concentrated in metropolitan areas with high-cost housing: the Boston-to-Washington corridor on the east coast, and the San Diego, Los Angeles, and San Francisco regions on the west coast. Thus, a pool of jumbo loans will usually be more regionally concentrated than a conforming pool. For example, it is not uncommon for a jumbo pool to have a California concentration in excess of 50% as compared with a typical conforming pool's concentration of around 25%.

The conforming limit is based on the year-over-year average house price change as reported by the Federal Housing Finance Board (FHFB); however, it is reset based only on the value reported in October, which could represent a short-term spike. The agencies may, but are not required to, raise the loan limit if the index increases, and historically they have not lowered it in response to declines in the index. For example, between 1993 and 1995 the FHFB index declined nearly 5%, yet Fannie Mae and Freddie Mac held the loan limits fixed at $203,150. A flurry of controversy ensued, as the "conforming limit" defines the size boundary of the nonagency market, and lenders and conduits that depend on the jumbo market for business have seen their market eaten away in small slices as Fannie Mae and Freddie Mac have continued to raised their limits over time (see Exhibit 1). It has been estimated that the $3,850 increase in the 1996 loan limit shifted 1.5% (approximately $10 billion) in mortgage volume from the nonagency jumbo market to the agency mortgage market.

Exhibit 1: Conforming Loan Limits

Year	Loan Limit ($)	Year	Loan Limit ($)	Year	Loan Limit ($)
1985	115,300	1990	187,450	1995	203,150
1986	133,250	1991	191,250	1996	207,000
1987	153,100	1992	202,300	1997	214,600
1988	168,700	1993	203,150		
1989	187,600	1994	203,150		

The controversy surrounding conforming loan limits intensified in October 1996, when the FHFB index surged nearly 10%, making legally permissible a loan limit increase of almost $18,000. Such a change could have resulted in an estimated $17 billion loss of business for the jumbo nonagency market. Members of Congress joined the mortgage industry trade groups in calling for Fannie Mae and Freddie Mac to voluntarily limit their 1997 loan limit increases consistent with the spirit of their legal mandate: to serve low and moderate income housing needs. Fannie Mae and Freddie Mac conceded and increased their 1997 conforming loan limits to only $214,600, about $10,000 less than the legal limit, effectively netting out the prior decreases in the FHFB Index.

Underwriting Standards

The second major source of nonconforming loans is so-called "B/C quality" or "subprime" originations, which fall short of agency standards with respect to borrower characteristics (such as debt-to-income ratio and credit history) or loan characteristics (such as loan-to-value ratio). B/C refers to a grading scale that classifies loan credit quality on a scale from A (conforming) to D (equity-based lending without regard to borrower income). This category of nonconforming loans also includes "low-doc" and "no-doc" originations where the borrower's income and/or other credit information are inadequately documented, either unreported or unverified. It is assumed that these borrowers would not qualify for the loan under the more stringent agency guidelines.

Typically a weak borrower is required to make a larger down payment: thus, most B/C loans have lower loan-to-value ratios. Alternatively, a stronger borrower may be granted a loan with a very low down payment. This is often the case with first-time homebuyers who may be cash-poor but starting out in a career that pays well. The agencies increased their involvement with high-LTV loans in 1994 when origination volume dropped significantly after a nearly 3-year refinancing boom, during which lenders easily maintained more restrictive underwriting standards. Similarly, since 1994 nonconforming underwriters have dramatically increased their activity in the B/C sector in an attempt to curb the precipitous drop in refinancing-driven originations.

Thus a conventional loan backing a nonagency MBS may be nonconforming with respect to balance, underwriting, or both. A loan with a conforming balance in a nonagency pool almost invariably signals nonconforming underwriting. Loans conforming with respect to both will naturally be securitized through the agencies because the price execution is better. Jumbo loans have no other securitization outlet, and should thus reflect the industry's overall underwriting mix, which is predominantly "A" level. In response to investor preference, however, nonagency issuers rarely mix underwriting categories within a single MBS.

Risks in Nonagency Securities

Credit risk is the major story in nonagency MBSs. Agency securities are 100% guaranteed against credit losses by the U.S. government (explicitly or implicitly).

Nonagency MBSs almost always carry less than 100% loss protection, and in a form which is never as robust as a U.S. government guarantee. As a result, there are several ways in which credit problems on the underlying mortgage loans could affect investors. If enough borrowers default, and property losses are sufficiently high, aggregate losses may exceed the available credit support. Alternatively, severe economic stress could render insurance companies unable to pay claims. The rating agencies have established various criteria — levels of loss protection and legal/structural requirements for the mechanism that makes and keeps loss protection available — that render these possibilities sufficiently remote to satisfy investor demand for highly rated securities.

    Many structural options are available to protect investors against mortgage default risk, event risk, and timing risk. Throughout the 1980s, third-party supports such as pool insurance, bond insurance, letters of credit (LOCs), and corporate guarantees were frequently used. However, investors' heightened awareness of event risk (mostly due to corporate downgrades), combined with the withdrawal of many third-party providers in the aftermath of the Texas, New England, and California real estate debacles resulted in a decisive turn towards subordination and other "stand alone" credit enhancement techniques that are internal to the structure itself. We outline the mechanics of these techniques below in a discussion of the structuring process.

    Callability — the potential for the acceleration of principal payments — affects both agency and nonagency MBSs. The main issue here is whether nonconforming loans prepay any differently than conforming loans. But call risk can be mitigated — or exacerbated — by the way that prepayments are allocated among different classes of a multiclass security. Most of these techniques are familiar from agency securities, but two ("shifting interest" and "stepdown triggers," which are related to each other) are unique to nonagency securities. As detailed in our section on the structuring process, these structural mechanisms are creatures of the rating agencies: they respond to credit events, not prepayments, and need to be analyzed differently.

HISTORICAL HIGHLIGHTS

The Early Years: 1977-1986

The first rated, public-issue nonagency MBS was issued by Bank of America in 1977. Until the mid 1980s, though, issuance was sparse and inconsistent. During this period, the dominant players in the unsecuritized whole-loan sector were thrift institutions, whose traditional business was originating 30 year fixed-rate mortgages funded by short-term financing. As the yield curve inverted and competition for deposits intensified, the spread over funding costs disappeared and then turned negative. In response, a few of the more agile institutions (especially in California) turned to the secondary market to dispose of their nonconforming fixed-rate mortgage loans and shifted their focus from fixed-rate to adjustable-rate lending. At least one conduit was also established during this period to purchase nonconforming loans from institutions who lacked the "critical mass" to issue their own MBS. At that time, a $50-100 million issue was pretty respectable, but many private transactions were less than $25 million. Most issues were rated double-A by Standard and Poor's (then the only rating agency active in the nonagency MBS sector) on the basis of credit support provided, in most cases, by pool insurance or a letter of credit (LOC).

The nonagency market was slow to get started primarily because of high interest rates, resulting in low mortgage production and an ill-tempered bond market. Issuers who wanted to reach the public market were also inconvenienced by the need to register each new MBS separately. In fact, many early nonagency MBSs were private placements, but "pipeline" issuance programs require the size and liquidity of the public securities market to absorb the potential supply. The nonagency MBS market thus received a considerable boost from the Secondary Mortgage Market Enhancement Act of 1984 (SMMEA), which permitted shelf registration of nonagency MBSs rated double-A or higher. (The agencies were and are exempt from SEC registration requirements.)

The vast majority of nonconforming mortgages, however, still traded as unsecuritized "whole loans." In some of these transactions, the buyer had recourse to the seller for reimbursement of credit losses in the form of a 10% subordinated interest retained by the seller, who was generally the servicer as well. This prototypical senior/subordinated structure improved upon traditional recourse arrangements in one significant respect: the buyer had recourse to asset cash flow instead of the unsecured credit of the seller. Most mortgage seller/servicers were unrated or noninvestment grade entities, especially in the aftermath of a nationwide recession and a real estate debacle in Texas, the "oil patch" and the southwest.

The Advent of Senior/Subordinated MBSs: Mid 1980s

In the early 1980s, an attempt was made to use a senior/subordinated (or "A/B") structure in a publicly issued MBS, but the securities were never issued because of the unfavorable tax treatment then accorded to multiclass mortgage-backed securities. (The mechanics of the structuring technique is outlined below in our discussion of the structuring process.) The IRS removed this obstacle with an interim rule in 1986 and the REMIC (Real Estate Mortgage Conduit) legislation in 1987. As a credit enhancement technique, subordination could be applied to any type of mortgage including those which, for whatever reason, were rejected by the pool insurers; and subordination could be used by any issuer to create highly rated securities, regardless of the issuer's own credit rating (which in the late 1980s was not likely to be very strong). The rating agencies developed extensive criteria for senior/subordinated structures, and over the next few years a flood of senior/subordinated issuers entered the market, starting with Home Savings of America in July 1986. These issuers fell into one of three categories:

1. Banks and thrifts who were either "testing the waters" or selling assets to raise capital (recall that the late 1980s saw the final phase of the thrift crisis).

2. Larger originators of nonconforming loans who found third-party loss coverage to be uneconomic (in the case of ARM loans, which pool insurers were reluctant to cover) or unavailable (especially in California following the 1989 earthquake).

3. Mortgage banking and conduit operations who funded their nonconforming originations and loan purchases through securitization.

Origins of the "B-Piece" Market: Late 1980s

Issuers who used the pre-REMIC tax rule were required to retain the subordinated interest (or "B-piece"). REMIC issuers were permitted to sell the subordinated interest, although most chose initially to retain it, for three reasons: (1) they believed that their credit losses would be small; (2) the regulatory treatment was favorable, not yet fully recognizing the highly leveraged nature of a subordinated MBS; and (3) it was highly uncertain how investors would receive a subordinated MBS. Agency MBS investors were unaccustomed to credit risk, corporate high yield investors were unfamiliar with mortgage risk, and the size of the bonds was too small to entice either group to invest the time required to understand subordinated MBS. A few issuers did begin to sell their B-pieces as soon as the REMIC legislation permitted them to. The first such sale was by the Residential Funding Corporation (RFC) in the first half of 1987. In general, the early sellers of subordinated interests were conduits and mortgage banks, who were not portfolio originators and thus were uninterested in retaining their subordinated interests. However, the advent of various risk-based capital regulations and accounting rules in 1989 and the early 1990s made it much less attractive for regulated institutions to hold subordinated interests, and they began to release them into the market.

Early B-piece pricing was relatively crude. The securities were untranched shifting-interest subordinated classes, sized to provide double-A levels of credit support: generally 6% to 8% for fixed-rate loans and 8% to 12% for ARMs. Because they were in a first loss position, the B-pieces were unrated; but they were also large enough that *historical* loss levels (such as those being used by pool insurers, for example) might still leave them largely intact. At the time, however, investors had little or no *actual* data on anything other than the Great Depression and early reports from the developing debacle in Texas. Thus, most investors initially valued B-pieces too conservatively for the sale to make sense for most issuers, and many of the largest ones continued to hold back.

Pricing aside, the investor base for unrated subordinated securities with average lives in excess of 15 years (with 30-year mortgages) was vanishingly small. But if the B-piece was itself tiered into a senior "fast pay" and a junior "slow pay" class, the senior-subordinated (or "mezzanine") class could merit a

Baa rating from Moody's, which was the first rating agency to rate such classes in late 1988. The resulting investment grade security had an average life below 10 years, which increased its investor appeal (although many MBS investors were still restricted to double- and triple-A securities). However, the remaining first loss class was more highly levered and *extremely* long — essentially unsalable and less appealing to retain. Thus, for many issuers, triple-B mezzanines didn't significantly improve the economics of the overall transaction.

The Thrift Crisis and The Resolution Trust Corporation: Early 1990s

In response to the massive collapse of S&Ls in the late 1980s, Congress in 1989 created the Resolution Trust Corporation (RTC) as a corporation wholly owned by the U.S. government. Its primary function was to oversee the liquidation of the assets of savings institutions seized by regulatory authorities in order to minimize losses to the government's Savings Association Insurance Fund. In this capacity, the RTC was the largest issuer of nonagency residential MBSs in 1991 and 1992. Having then largely exhausted its inventory of performing residential mortgages, the RTC pioneered the securitization of nonperforming loans with its "N-series" transactions in 1993. With the shoring-up of the thrift crisis, the RTC was folded into the FDIC at the end of 1995. Nevertheless, its frequent issuance and large transaction size helped consolidate the nonagency MBS investor base and transform the nonagency MBS market into a major mortgage market sector.

One of the RTC's most important contributions to the development of the nonagency MBS market was in the area of investor reporting. Prior to 1991, private issuers were generally resistant to providing detailed information on the collateral backing their nonagency MBSs, primarily because of the forbidding amount of information processing involved. (Notable exceptions at the time were the Prudential Home Mortgage Company which provided loan-level updates on its nonagency pools, and Citicorp Mortgage Securities which provided summary updates on its MBS issues in a quarterly digest.) The RTC's actions greatly softened the private issuers' resistance by working actively with its Wall Street dealers to assure the marketability and liquidity of its securities. Part of its strategy was the coordinated distribution of information, raising the prevailing market standards for investor reporting. However, standardization was limited because many RTC transactions involved unusual or unique collateral. Nevertheless, the efforts of the RTC in providing collateral information effectively prodded the private issuers to provide detailed and updated data regarding collateral composition and performance.

Explosive Growth and Structural Evolution: 1991-1993

As discussed above, the pace of nonagency issuance began to accelerate with the advent of the senior/subordinated structure in 1986 (Exhibit 2), but the most dramatic growth came with the 1991-93 market rally. Annual issuance quadrupled between 1990 and 1993. More nonconforming loans were being originated, and a larger percentage of them were being securitized. As shown in Exhibit 4, in 1990 only about 27% of nonconforming loans went into MBSs; by 1993, this number had risen to about 46%. Nonagency MBSs represented 16.5% of all MBSs issued in 1992, up from 2.6% in 1986. In terms of total mortgage securities outstanding (see Exhibit 3), nonagency securities grew impressively from 5% in 1990, first achieving its current level of 11% in 1993. This is especially impressive given that the agencies were chipping away at size of the jumbo nonagency market via increases in their conforming loan limit requirements by more than 50% during this period, from $133,250 in 1986 to $203,150 in 1993 (see Exhibit 1 above).

Exhibit 2: Nonagency Issuance ($ million)

Year	REMICs	ARMs	Total Whole Loan Issuance	% Total Mortgage Market
1982	NA	NA	253	NA
1983	NA	NA	1,585	NA
1984	NA	NA	236	NA
1985	NA	NA	1,956	1.8%
1986	NA	NA	6,993	2.6%
1987	9,044	2,057	11,100	4.5%
1988	3,303	12,118	15,420	9.3%
1989	7,812	6,426	14,238	6.6%
1990	16,812	7,619	24,431	9.4%
1991	30,599	18,750	49,349	14.8%
1992	63,448	26,018	89,466	16.5%
1993	77,759	20,734	98,493	14.8%
1994	47,902	15,280	63,182	15.0%
1995	25,871	11,135	37,006	12.2%
1996 (11 months)	28,719	5,959	34,678	8.1%

Source: Inside MBS & ABS, Inside Mortgage Finance, Mortgage Market Statistical Annual.
Copyright 1996, Bethesda, MD, 301.951.1240

Exhibit 3: Securities Outstanding: Nonagency Versus Agency
($ million)

Year	Agency	% Total	Whole Loan	% Total	Total
1987	668,427	96%	27,800	4%	696,227
1988	745,183	96%	34,865	4%	780,048
1989	870,789	95%	43,325	5%	914,114
1990	1,017,470	95%	53,335	5%	1,070,805
1991	1,156,388	93%	84,000	7%	1,240,388
1992	1,272,009	91%	132,000	9%	1,404,009
1993	1,348,620	89%	164,000	11%	1,512,620
1994	1,441,933	89%	183,600	11%	1,625,533
1995	1,498,956	88%	194,700	12%	1,693,656
(Nov) 1996	1,657,106	89%	206,600	11%	1,863,706

Source: *Inside Mortgage Securities* and DMG
Copyright 1996, Bethesda, MD, 301.951.1240

Exhibit 4: Securitization Rates: Whole Loans Versus Agency
($ million)

Year	Agency		Whole Loans	
	Originations	Securitized	Originations	Securitized
1990	367,820	63.9%	90,620	27.0%
1991	449,660	59.6%	112,410	35.4%
1992	714,940	63.6%	178,730	41.6%
1993	818,000	69.5%	201,860	48.2%
1994	610,760	58.9%	162,360	38.7%
1995	489,540	54.4%	146,230	23.9%
1996 (9 months)	502,060	57.4%	149,960	20.2%

Source: *Inside Mortgage Securities* and DMG
Copyright 1996, Bethesda, MD, 301.951.1240

Investors were willing to absorb this vastly increased issuance for several reasons. A massive educational blitz by Wall Street dealers and the rating agencies (by now increased to four that were actively rating nonagency MBSs) significantly heightened investors' awareness of the product, their comfort level with its credit quality, and their understanding of the various cash flow structures involved. More frequent issuance, larger deal sizes and more uniform credit enhancement structures also improved the product's liquidity. Finally, and perhaps most significantly, most nonagency MBSs were now being issued as CMOs rather than as single-class passthroughs, thus accessing a much broader spectrum of fixed income investors.

This shift to CMO issuance was the outward manifestation of several underlying trends that were changing the structure of the entire nonagency MBS market:

1. A shift from adjustable-rate to fixed-rate originations in the nonconforming loan sector;

2. The related shift in loan origination market share from thrifts and other portfolio originators to mortgage banks and conduits;

3. Increased attention to nonagency loan prepayment trends (although with varying degrees of success), which facilitated investor acceptance of increasingly prepayment-sensitive principal allocation structures.

The shift to CMOs was also responsible for a change in the predominant rating level of new issue nonagency MBSs from double-A (which was customary for nonagency passthroughs) to triple-A (which is customary in the CMO sector). This in turn helped to establish subordination as the dominant credit enhancement technique, for several reasons:

1. By 1992, the traditional LOC banks had all been downgraded below triple-A, precluding them from playing a primary role in a triple-A rated transaction;

2. By 1992, only one pool insurance provider was still rated triple-A, and it was strictly limiting its exposure to California loans;

3. The triple-A bond insurers' pricing levels were uncompetitive for generic nonconforming mortgages;

4. The larger subordinated classes required to support a triple-A rated senior class were readily divisible into various subclasses with intermediate ratings, particularly in the double-A to triple-B range, thus accessing a much broader spectrum of fixed income investors.

The B-Piece Market Comes Into Its Own

The successive tiering and tranching of residential B-pieces had continued — spurred on by parallel innovations in the RTC's commercial MBS sector with its unprecedentedly large subordinated classes — and in 1992 a number of favorable trends combined to jump-start what could finally be called the B-piece market:

1. A move towards triple-A senior classes (for reasons discussed above) resulted in larger subordinated classes which could be divided into more different credit tiers — everything from double-A down to single-B on top of an unrated first loss class. Larger subordinated classes also increased the importance of favorable B-piece pricing to the economics of the overall securitization.

2. Credit portents were turning favorable: delinquency rates on residential fixed-rate mortgages and consumer credit lines were declining noticeably, and with the exception of California, home prices had demonstrably bottomed out in the southwest and the northeast. (California represented more of a speed bump than a genuine obstacle in the path of the securitized mortgage credit markets.)

3. The bond market rally began to force MBS investors to seek out new sources of yield enhancement. Double-A and even triple-A rated mezzanine classes enabled more conservative investors to get comfortable with subordinated MBSs (although ERISA regulations continued to prevent pension funds — significant buyers of long paper — from investing in subordinated MBSs regardless of the rating).

4. A number of large issuers had settled on a standard structure that included multi-tiered subordinated classes, enhancing the prospects for continued supply and liquidity. This was important because the structure and analysis had become quite complex, requiring a lengthy education process which could be justified only if the product was to remain available in significant amounts.

As a result, yield spreads on rated subordinated MBSs tightened dramatically during 1992 — by about 100 bps for triple-B classes and 200-400 bps for noninvestment grade classes.

The MBS Tidal Wave

Throughout 1992 and 1993, the nonagency MBS market was running on all cylinders. Loan origination and MBS issuance hit unprecedented levels, as did the offering spreads of most credit-sensitive tranches. Investors continued to absorb the continuing supply, despite growing disenchantment with the extremely high prepayment speeds being experienced by new issues. These speeds were *very* far above the rates forecasted by Wall Street prepayment models, largely because the mortgage origination market had undergone a structural change that went undetected by the model-fitters: no-point refinancings. On the other hand, there seemed to be few worries about credit quality (apart from California, where foreclosures were beginning to rise in response to a powerful recession that had begun in 1991). The traditional "A-quality" lenders could pick and choose among the huge volume of mortgage applicants, and fully underwritten loans once again became the rule after several years of "limited doc" and "no-doc" lending aimed at preserving market share. According to the rating agencies' loss curves, the newly originated loans backing new-issue MBSs would not be at significant risk of default for several years. In fact, even seasoned MBSs were believed to be better off as a result of the avalanche of prepayments, which prematurely depleted those pools of many loans which were still performing at the time but which could be expected (on statistical grounds) to default at some future time. The massive rally had apparently "cleansed" the national mortgage pool of much of its credit risk, further enhancing the appeal of subordinated classes from newly issued MBSs and seasoned deals with low California concentrations.

Retrenchment: 1994-1996

But then the music stopped. During the first six months of 1994 interest rates increased more than 200 basis points (bps), a resounding end to a remarkable 3-year rally. Refinancing activity dried up, causing total originations to drop by 36% from 1993 to 1995. Moreover, many investors lost confidence in some of the recent CMO structural innovations. For example, investors who had purchased prepayment-protected CMO classes saw their structural protection eroded by the massive prepayments of 1991-1993. Then in 1994, these same bonds that had experienced an unanticipated shortening came under threat of a dramatic extension as prepayments rates dropped precipitously. Confidence in structured fixed-income products was also shaken by several highly publicized interest-rate derivatives related failures such as Orange County (California) and the Askin funds. On the supply side, the profitability of CMO issuance was squeezed as the yield curve flattened 155 bps: the spread between the 10-year and the 1-year Treasury dropped from 220 bps at the beginning of 1994 to 65 bps by year-end. Consequently, agency CMO issuance collapsed from $324 billion in 1993 to $23 billion in 1995.

Over the next couple of years, MBS investors assimilated the lessons to be gleaned from the 1993-1994 turn in the market. Although the yield curve as of this writing is still relatively flat, renewed confidence and better understanding have substantially restored the demand for mortgage securities in general, and CMO products in particular. As of the third quarter of 1996, CMO production represented about 21% of total MBS production for the period. This is up from the single digit percentages of 1994-1995, but still a far cry from the early 1990s when the CMO market consumed as much as 70% of new security issuance.

Alternative Lending Programs

As interest rates backed up in 1994, mortgage originators scrambled to find ways to offset the dramatic drop in refinancing applications. Most originators focused on broadening their market base by developing or expanding not only the subprime (B/C) credit programs mentioned above, but also specialized B/C programs involving high LTV mortgages (some known informally as *"125s,"* referring to the maximum LTV percentage available), and other programs designed to accommodate "alternative" A-credit borrowers who seek loans either above or below the conforming limit but for various reasons do not fit the agency or standard jumbo underwriting criteria.

B/C-Credit Programs Many of these programs have had considerable success. As illustrated in Exhibit 5, B/C issuance approximately tripled between 1994 and 1996. However, much of this growth springs from the increased packaging of B/C mortgages as home equity loan-backed securities (HELs) which trade in the asset-backed securities market, despite their undeniable mortgage-like nature (long-term, fully amortizing, first liens).

This peculiar state of affairs turns on a prepayment story: B/C borrowers take on high rate mortgage loans because they are not eligible for anything else, and their loan amounts are typically lower than for A-quality loans. Thus, these borrowers are expected to be less sensitive to interest rates because of the restricted opportunities to refinance and the limited dollar reduction in their debt service. On the other hand, overall prepayment speeds (it is further claimed) are secularly fast because these borrowers are motivated to refinance into an A-quality loan as soon as their credit position improves. Under these prepayment assumptions, B/C MBSs appear to be shorter and yet less callable securities — precisely the characteristics sought by ABS investors. However, these assumptions are untested by experience, and could unravel, as conforming MBS assumptions did, if future product innovation provides appealing alternative financing for credit-impaired borrowers. For the present, though, established B/C lenders increasingly focus their B/C mortgage production on HELs which are funneled into the ABS market. In 1994, 56% of B/C MBSs were backed by HELs; by the third quarter of 1996, HELs accounted for 75% of all B/C issuance.

Exhibit 5: B/C Mortgage-Backed Issuance (millions)

Year	Issuance
1994	$11,051
1995	$18,466
1996 (3 Quarters)	$30,430

Source: *Inside MBS & ABS, Inside Mortgage Finance, Mortgage Market Statistical Annual,* Copyright 1996, Bethesda, MD, 301.951.1240

High LTV ("125") Programs Given the partially unsecured, consumer loan-like nature of 125% LTV loans, most originators have restricted their 125 lending to borrowers with at least A-quality credit. With LTVs above 100%, the usual protection afforded by borrower equity is no longer present; thus, the integrity of these loans depends entirely on the creditworthiness of the borrower. Consequently, borrowers in these programs typically pay consumer loan level interest rates of around 14%, or a 500-600 bps premium over conforming mortgage rates. Conservative estimates peg 125 loan originations for 1996 to be between $1.5 to $2.0 billion 1996. Citing the huge size of consumer debt (over $1.7 trillion), many believe the 125 loan market has tremendous potential for growth, with estimates for 1997 as high as $10 billion.

A Note on Credit Risk in Alternative Lending Programs Standardization of loan programs nationwide has been a key element facilitating the development and evolution of today's massive MBS market. However, as we have just seen, in their search to preserve market share and fully utilize existing servicing capability when loan originations slow down, lenders need to unearth borrowers who were previously undetected, underserved, or underqualified. In the jumbo loan sector, these have generally been borrowers who in one way or another fail to satisfy one or more of the standard underwriting guidelines. In the 1980s, these borrowers were attracted to the "limited doc" or "no doc" programs in which the lenders waived most of the documentation required to demonstrate the borrower's financial strength (in other words, "don't ask, don't tell") in return for a large down payment. "No doc" programs were also known as "equity lending" because the loan quality depended entirely on the value of the underlying real estate. Lenders believed that increased borrower equity would reduce the probability of default and mitigate losses in the actual event of a default.

Unfortunately, the lenders had miscalculated. "Limited doc" loans rapidly became the worst performing sector of the nonagency MBS market. The most spectacular failures were due to borrower fraud, particularly fraudulent appraisals (which misrepresented the LTV ratio) and "silent second" mortgages (i.e., second mortgages taken out simultaneously with the first mortgage, unbeknownst to the first mortgage lender, thus misrepresenting the borrower's debt ratios). However, even mainstream lenders experienced much higher-than-anticipated losses on their limited doc portfolios, for several reasons:

1. *Adverse selection:* The near-total lack of borrower disclosure attracted genuinely weak borrowers, rather than creditworthy ones who failed to qualify on a technicality.

2. *Payment-induced borrower default:* Most limited doc loans were ARMs because they were more likely to have to remain in the lender's portfolio; and the combination of deep teaser rates and rising interest rates caused payments to increase dramatically through the late 1980s.

3. *Decreased equity:* When the real estate market turned sour, prices on distressed properties dropped much faster than the overall average, which rapidly deflated the enhanced equity cushion

The mid 1990s vintage alternative lending programs described above — high LTV loans and loans to borrowers with poor credit histories — are admittedly risky, but they do avoid most of the errors of the 1980s' "limited doc" programs. All borrower information is fully disclosed, so lenders are dealing with "the devil they know."

Subperforming and Nonperforming Loans What might seem like the final frontier in mortgage securitization has now been reached with the development of an active market for the securitization and sale of delinquent and defaulted loans. This growing market sector was initially spawned by the fallout from the RTC's securitizations, and the key to its acceptance was the practice (also initiated by the RTC) of structuring the transactions around a "special servicer" with specific expertise in working out and disposing of troubled loans. In the RTC transactions, the special servicer was also required to take an equity interest in the transaction.

More recently, the main sources of product have been HUD and large institutional lenders looking to cleanse their balance sheets. If the securitization's purpose is to finance the acquisition of the loans, it will generally employ a "liquidating structure" in which the bonds are paid down by the proceeds from sale of the loans as they are resolved — either through foreclosure or a return to performing status. Otherwise, the loans are securitized *after* they are worked out using more traditional CMO structures. All of these securitizations were nonagency transactions until late 1996 when Freddie Mac guaranteed a large pool of reperforming loans from a HUD auction. However, a controversy has arisen (unresolved as of this writing) as to whether this type of transaction is consistent with the U.S. government's goal in the HUD auctions of disposing of troubled assets.

The Lessons of History: 1997–Present

Can we tentatively conclude that the nonagency MBS market has now experienced a complete business cycle since the early-to-mid 1980s?

- Interest rates have rallied and backed up twice (bond market crashes in early 1987 and 1994), with corresponding flows and ebbs in issuance volume.

- Underwriting standards have gone from agency-conforming down to no-documentation, back up to agency conforming, and now perhaps a sideways extension to riskier borrowers but with full documentation.

- Home prices have strongly peaked and troughed in the southwest, the northeast, and in California while continuing to advance more moderately in the midwest and southeast.

- Delinquency and default rates on nonagency mortgages have deteriorated and recovered strongly, with early indications of another moderate downturn in high-LTV and other "alternative" loans.

- Hundreds of insolvent Savings and Loan institutions went through a final spasm of loan activity before being flushed through the system by the RTC. In their wake, bank capital regulations fostered a more conservative attitude towards risk assessment which drastically reduced weaker borrowers' access to funding. As a result, more aggressive lending is now the province of specialized mortgage bankers and conduits that are, at this writing, amply funded by the capital markets, largely through securitization.

- Nonagency MBS structures underwent an efflorescence from simple pass-throughs to CMOs with 40 classes distributed among 6 or 7 rating levels, and then pulled back to somewhat simpler structures after the derivatives debacle of 1994.

If the nonagency market can be said to have "seen it all," or at least to have shaken out most of the kinks, then nonagency MBSs are well on their way to becoming commoditized portfolio staples, with adventurous yield-seekers advised to set their sights elsewhere. However, if history is any guide, then we expect that surprising developments are always lying in wait, creating the best opportunities for swift learners.

MARKET OVERVIEW

Investors

The sustained growth in the nonagency MBS market is a testimony to the investor appetite for whole-loan product. Virtually all major institutional categories are involved. In recent years, pension funds and insurance companies have each carried roughly between 25% to 30% of all institutional holdings; banks, thrifts, and mortgage funds each hold between 12% to 15%; and foreign investors carrying the balance of about 5%.

Attractive Spreads

For many investors, the appeal of nonagency MBSs arose out of a growing aversion to the "event" risk associated with corporate bonds. Rather than being concentrated on any single economic entity, the credit risk of nonagency MBSs is diversified across a pool of many individual borrowers. Thus many high-yield investors have been attracted to this market. This is especially true for buyers of subordinated classes, which as of this writing trade from 150 bps over Treasuries for triple-B classes to 1,000 bps and beyond for unrated first loss classes. The spread range reflects the range of credit quality available. For example, in the 10-year sector as of this writing, double-A mezzanine bonds trade at about 130 bps over the 10 year Treasury and single-A classes at about 150 bps over the 10 year. Senior tranches typically trade 30-40 bps cheaper than comparable agency securities, roughly decomposed as follows: 10-15 bps for liquidity, 5 bps for credit risk, 5 bps for risk-based capital weighting, and 10-20 bps for greater prepayment volatility. The spread advantage in subordinate tranches is, naturally, dominated by credit considerations.

In addition to minimizing event risk, multiclass nonagency MBS structures provide investors with a richer menu of options than is typically associated with high-yield corporate debt. The available bond types include most of the tranche types found in the agency market: sequential-pay bonds, planned amortization classes (PAC), targeted amortization classes (TAC), floaters, inverse floaters, principal only classes (PO), interest only classes (IO), PAC IO, PAC inverse IO, etc.

Issuers

The past few years of generally reduced loan origination volume has somewhat shifted the center of gravity in the nonagency MBS issuer community. Small and large originators now rely increasingly on whole-loan conduits for the distribution of their product. This has led to a relatively limited number of strong conduits and mortgage banks that have survived a variety of mergers and failures over the years. Three conduits — Residential Funding Corporation, GE Capital Mortgage Services, and Independent National Mortgage Corporation — were among the top four issuers in both 1995 and 1996. The largest mortgage bank, Prudential Home Mortgage (acquired by Norwest in 1996), slipped from first in 1993 to third in 1996. As can be seen from Exhibit 6 these four issuers alone accounted for fully 60% of total private-label MBS issuance in 1996. Also evident from Exhibit 6 are two large commercial banks who were historical top-10 issuers but have since "fallen off the map" in 1995-1996.

THE SECURITIZATION PROCESS

The process of securitizing residential whole loans can involve either seasoned or newly originated loans. The overwhelming majority of nonagency MBSs, however, are backed by newly originated mortgages. The process for securitizing new originations is outlined in Exhibit 7. In general, the primary components are:

1. Mortgage originator: mortgage brokers or loan origination offices or bank branches
2. Seller/Servicer (usually the same party)
3. Issuer (a special-purpose, bankruptcy-remote entity)
4. REMIC or Grantor Trust
5. Master Servicer (usually different from the servicer if securitized by a conduit)
6. Trustee/Bond Administrator
7. Investors

Exhibit 6: Top Private MBS Issuers in at Least Two Years from 1993 to 1996 (Bold Indicates Top 10)

1996 Rank	Issuer	Volume ($ billions)				Market Share (%)			
		1996	1995	1994	1993	1996	1995	1994	1993
1	Residential Funding Corp.	**$9.9**	**$6.1**	**$4.6**	**$13.0**	**25.8%**	**17.6%**	**7.3%**	**13.2%**
2	GE Capital Mortgage Services	**$4.8**	**$3.1**	**$10.5**	**$8.0**	**12.6%**	**8.9%**	**16.6%**	**8.2%**
3	Norwest Asset Securities Corp./ Prudential Home Mortgage	**$4.5**	**$2.5**	**$7.2**	**$27.2**	**11.9%**	**7.1%**	**11.4%**	**27.6%**
4	Independent National Mortgage/ CWMBS (Countrywide)	**$3.9**	**$4.4**	**$9.8**	**$6.2**	**10.2%**	**12.7%**	**15.5%**	**6.3%**
7	Salomon Brothers Mort. Sec. Corp	**$1.9**	$0.3	$2.4	$2.3	**5.0%**	0.8%	3.9%	2.3%
8	Merrill Lynch	**$1.8**	**$1.0**	**$2.5**	$1.7	**4.8%**	**3.0%**	**4.0%**	1.8%
9	Bear Stearns Mortgage Sec. Corp.	**$1.6**	$0.3	$0.3	**$2.9**	**4.1%**	0.8%	0.5%	**2.9%**
10	Donaldson Lufkin & Jenrette	**$1.2**	**$1.7**	$2.2	$1.7	**3.2%**	**4.7%**	3.5%	1.7%
14	Saxon Asset Securities Corp./ Ryland Mortgage Securities Corp.	$0.7	$0.4	**$4.5**	**$7.4**	1.8%	1.1%	**7.2%**	**7.6%**
15	Capstead Capital Corp.	$0.6	$0.5	**$3.4**	**$3.4**	1.5%	1.3%	**5.4%**	**3.5%**
23	Citicorp/Housing Securities Inc.	$0.3	$0.9	**$2.6**	**$4.3**	0.9%	2.5%	**4.1%**	**4.3%**
—	Chase Mortgage Finance Corp.	—	$0.3	**$2.5**	**$4.8**	—	0.9%	**3.9%**	**4.9%**
—	Securitized Asset Sales-Pru	—	**$2.6**	$1.4	**$2.5**	—	**7.4%**	2.2%	**2.5%**

Source: Deutsche Morgan Grenfell, *Inside MBS & ABS, Inside Mortgage Finance, Mortgage Market Statistical Annual,* Copyright 1996, Bethesda, MD, 301.951.1240

Exhibit 7: The Securitization Process

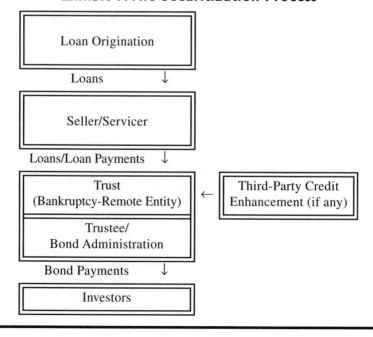

Mortgage conduits monitor both the lender and investor sides of the market, compiling a daily pricing sheet that informs the participating mortgage bankers and brokers of the levels at which new loans will be purchased. As the mortgage banks sell into the "warehouse," the individual loans are accumulated into pools which are sold to a special purpose, bankruptcy-remote entity. The special-purpose entity is a wholly-owned subsidiary of the issuer, essentially a legal vehicle that shields the integrity of the MBS from any future economic difficulties of the issuer's parent company. The master servicer often acts as the on-going servicer of the loans once they are securitized. Finally, when the issuer is an independent conduit such as Residential Funding Corporation, the master servicing is usually performed in-house. Investment bank conduits generally contract out the master servicing to an outside party.

The trustee acts on behalf of the investors. Its primary responsibilities include monitoring the integrity of the overall transaction and the monthly bond administration. This generally includes overseeing the servicing activity, receiving monthly cash payments from the servicer, forwarding the cash flows (as paying agent) to the investors, and maintaining any reserve accounts called for by the bond structure. In some instances, the trustee may subcontract with a separate party to carry out all or part of the bond administrative process. In any case, these details are transparent to the investor, just as they are with agency deals.

THE STRUCTURING PROCESS

Credit Structuring: General Principles

Rating agencies determine the level of credit support required for a structured MBS based upon the collateral characteristics, the rating of significant parties to the ongoing transaction, and the rating desired for the security itself. In general, the required levels and how they are allowed to vary over time are *independent* of how the credit support is provided (e.g., whether through a reserve fund, third-party guarantee, subordination, etc.). To get a triple-A rating, MBSs generally require 4% to 5% loss coverage for 15-year fixed-rate collateral, 6% to 8% for 30-year fixed-rate collateral, and 10% to 12% for ARM collateral.

The full amount of credit support must be available at or soon after the start of the transaction (the *Cut-Off Date*), and the initial requirement remains in force for an extended period of time: it is not reduced as the pool balance declines over time, at least for several years. Initially, the principal balance is reduced almost exclusively by prepayments (as opposed to amortization). However, the rating agencies take a conservative view that only good loans prepay, because weaker borrowers cannot qualify for a refinancing. Thus, although the pool balance has declined, the credit risk has not. This view of early prepayments and their negative effect on credit risk is called "adverse selection." To counteract the effects of adverse selection, rating agencies require that the initial loss coverage be maintained until the pools are sufficiently seasoned to ascertain their performance character. This period is generally 5 years for fixed-rate loans, 10 years for ARMs, and 15 years for negatively amortizing ARMs. During this period, the credit support grows *as a percentage* of the outstanding pool balance. After this period, the loss coverage requirement "steps down" over the next few years, provided that the delinquency and loss experience of the pool does not exceed certain levels, known as "triggers." During the stepdown period, the *amount* of credit support is gradually reduced, but may continue to grow as a percentage of the pool balance — it just grows at a slower rate. The stepdown schedule generally runs for 4 years, after which the credit enhancement requirement becomes simply a fixed percentage of the outstanding pool balance, which number varies depending on the structure and, in most structures currently in use, on the historical paydown experience of the pool.

Coverage for short-term delinquencies, also known as liquidity coverage, is now generally provided by a highly rated "backstop," most commonly the master servicer or trustee who provides this service for a fee. In older transactions or when the assets are particularly unconventional, this coverage more often comes from the same source as the loss coverage, which is then sized appropriately to include the liquidity requirement. The rating agencies generally require that any third party providing delinquency coverage be assessed no lower than one level below the desired rating on the security or alternatively, have a sufficiently high short-term credit rating.

Although the rating agencies vary in the methods in which they assign security ratings, all of their methodologies are based on a review of the risk characteristics of the underlying mortgage collateral and the security's structure.

Collateral Quality

The rating agencies review the aggregate pool characteristics in addition to each loan's individual characteristics. At the loan level, the contractual features of the loan and the underlying property securing each loan are examined. At the pool level, aggregate characteristics such as the number of loans in the pool and their geographic concentration are taken into consideration.

Loan-to-Value Ratio

The loan-to-value (LTV) ratio is the ratio of the loan balance to the lesser of the purchase price and the appraised value of the property. LTV is an important indicator of default potential because a financially troubled borrower should not need to default if the property can be sold to repay the mortgage, i.e. if the current LTV ratio (based on a realistic appraisal and adjusted for selling costs) is less than 100%.

Prospectuses report the LTV *at origination* of the loan, which loses meaning over time as the loan seasons and property values change. Also, LTVs can be artificially lowered by inflated appraisals. Investors in seasoned transactions (particularly the subordinate classes) use brokers' price opinions (BPOs) or home price indexes to obtain a *current* LTV. Loan amortization also affects the LTV, but amortization is negligible throughout the period when a loan is at highest risk of default. (This is less true of 15-year fully amortizing loans.) A high original LTV indicates a low down payment, which reflects poorly on a borrower's credit quality. As mentioned in the historical survey, however, high-LTV lending is currently an area of intense focus by loan originators.

Mortgage Type

Fixed-rate loans default less often than loans with variable payments. Rating agencies assign higher risk weightings for adjustable rate mortgages (ARMs) as well as buydown loans, tiered payment mortgages (TPMs) and other mortgages with contractual payment increases because of the risk of "payment shock" when the increase occurs. This risk is particularly high for borrowers who qualified for the loan on the basis of a discounted initial rate ("teaser"). ARMs with a more volatile underlying index, less restrictive interest rate caps, or payment caps that cause negative amortization or provide for periodic unlimited payment resets are especially at risk.

Mortgage Term and Coupon

Shorter amortizing terms and lower coupons cause a faster buildup in equity. They also have larger payments, which only a relatively strong borrower will voluntarily assume. Note that balloon loans have short maturities but longer amortizing terms, resulting in a lump sum payment due at maturity, making default highly likely if the borrower cannot refinance.

Documentation Standards

Full documentation standards for conforming loans require verification of income (VOI), verification of employment (VOE), verification of deposits (VOD) as the source of the down payment, credit reports, and property appraisals. The VOD and the property appraisal are especially important to the integrity of the LTV ratio, and the VOI validates the borrower debt-to-income ratio. Many loans are nonconforming simply because of inadequate ("limited") documentation.

Loan Purpose

Financing the purchase of a vacation home or investment property is riskier than financing the purchase of one's primary home, because the borrower can default on the second home and still have a place to live. Investment properties are particularly risky because the borrower is less committed to maintaining a property that he does not personally occupy and may depend on rental income to maintain the mortgage payments. Refinancing to a lower rate improves loan quality because it accelerates loan amortization and reduces the borrower's debt service. However, equity take-out (or "cash-out") refinancings increase the LTV ratio and, therefore, require additional credit support.

Loan Seasoning

According to Standard & Poor's (S&P), about two-thirds of losses generally occur by the seventh year of a pool's life, and 90% by the tenth year. By that time, the expectation is that property appreciation and loan amortization will have produced substantial borrower equity, and the borrower's long occupancy indicates financial stability. However, the record low mortgage rates in 1993 and the consequent wave of refinancings may actually have *increased* the risk in older mortgage pools because the loans that remain are presumably those that were unable to refinance because of poor credit, i.e. they have been adversely selected. On the other hand, Moody's has observed that many of the loans that were refinanced at a very early age would have defaulted later on; therefore, the refinancing wave actually *removed* some credit risk from the then-existing pools. If this is true, then the credit performance of MBSs backed by loans originated in 1991 and 1992 may be better than expected.

Property Type

The default risk is lower for loans secured by owner-occupied, detached single-family properties than those secured by multifamily dwellings, planned unit developments (PUD), condominiums, and townhouses. Although housing prices usually decline during a recession, there is more sustained demand for single-family detached homes. Townhouses, PUDs, condominiums, and especially 2-4 family dwellings generally experience sharper declines. As the property value declines, the LTV ratio increases and thus the risk of default increases.

Geographic Diversification

Economic diversification and regional special hazards must be considered when analyzing the default risk of a loan. More credit support is required when more than 5% of the loans are in one zip code, or just 1% per zip code in an area prone to special hazards like earthquakes. Loans originated in an area dominated by one industry are more susceptible to troubles in that industry, as demonstrated by the debacle in Texas and the surrounding "oil patch" states precipitated by the collapse of oil prices in the mid 1980s. On the other hand, special hazard-related fears failed to materialize in the aftermath of two serious earthquakes in California in 1989 (Loma Prieta, near San Francisco) and 1994 (Northridge in Los Angeles' San Fernando Valley), although the 1994 quake did temporarily exacerbate existing credit problems. Simple probabilistic arguments show that earthquake-related losses should not exceed rating agency-mandates for special hazard coverage unless the frequency and severity of property damage approach levels far in excess of anything observed even near the epicenters of the two recent California quakes.

Structural Issues

Once the quality of the collateral has been established, the rating agencies verify that the collateral cash flow adequately supports the deal structure. Scrutiny of the deal infrastructure provides the final element in assessing the credit enhancement required for a security.

Soundness of the Servicer and Trustee

Many of the servicer's functions are critical to the credit quality of a transaction. In addition to collecting the monthly payments and passing the cash flows to the trustee, the servicer handles delinquent loans, initiates foreclosure procedures, and liquidates properties when necessary. To maintain the timely payment of principal and interest to investors, the servicer typically advances missed payments due to delinquency and foreclosure, and is reimbursed as loans cure and properties are liquidated. If the servicer is rated (generally) more than one grade lower than the transaction, a backup servicer is required. Generally, however, the trustee must be at least double-A for any issue.

Interest Shortfall

Investors expect to receive interest based on a full 30 day month. However, borrowers who prepay between monthly payments only pay interest through the prepayment date. In most nonagency MBSs the servicer is required to pay compensating interest to cover the shortfall, but only up to a specified percentage of the monthly servicing fee. In the event that the interest shortfall is not fully compensated, the loss is shared on a pro-rata basis by all classes, regardless of their credit priority. As investors realized in 1992-1993, structures that do not pay compensating interest can result in significant yield impairment in a high prepayment environment.

CREDIT ENHANCEMENT TECHNIQUES

As we have seen, mortgage credit risk encompasses short-term delinquencies as well as unrecoverable losses due to borrower default. The agencies eliminate mortgage credit risk from the securities they issue by guaranteeing the timely payment of principal and interest (or ultimate payment of principal for Freddie Mac non-Gold PCs). Nonagency MBSs rely on a variety of credit enhancement techniques, which can be categorized according to whether they are internal or external to the security structure. External credit enhancement techniques are provided by either the issuer or a third party; internal credit enhancement techniques rely on reallocation of cash flow within the structure, thus avoiding "event risk" associated with third parties which can result in the downgrade of a MBS whose mortgage loans are performing flawlessly.

External Credit Enhancements

Prior to any structural considerations — before any decision is made as to whether a loan is to be retained, sold or securitized — all lenders require the borrower to provide standard hazard insurance, and most require primary mortgage insurance (PMI) if the LTV ratio is above 80%. PMI is usually written to cover 20% to 25% of the original loan balance. Normally, when the LTV ratio falls below 80%, PMI insurance is no longer required. Flood insurance is required in government-designated flood plains, but earthquake insurance is not required in seismic risk areas.

Pool Insurance

Pool insurance normally covers losses due to borrowers' economic circumstances, and specifically excludes ("carves out") losses that result from bankruptcy, origination fraud, and special hazards. The amount of pool insurance purchased for a transaction is determined by the rating agencies as described in the previous section.

A bankruptcy bond provides coverage against a court order that modifies the mortgage debt by decreasing the interest rate or reducing the unpaid principal balance. Such a reduction in mortgage debt is known as a "cramdown." Individuals can file for bankruptcy under Chapter 13 and Chapter 7 of the Internal Revenue Code. Chapter 13 bankruptcy filings allow individuals to retain their assets while restructuring or forgiving debts. Under Chapter 7 bankruptcy filings, personal assets are liquidated to pay debts; cramdowns are not allowed. In the 1993 case of Nobleman versus American Savings, the U.S. Supreme Court disallowed cramdowns under Chapter 13 filings as well. While cramdowns are allowed under Chapter 11 bankruptcy filings, Chapter 11 is primarily used by businesses. Thus, given the relatively unlikely event of bankruptcy, most rating agencies would normally require as little as $100,000 to $150,000 of loss coverage on a $250 million pool of high quality mortgages.

Because pool insurers will not cover losses stemming from fraud during the loan application process, rating agencies require fraud coverage of 1% to 3% of the original pool balance. Fraud coverage is allowed to decrease over the first six years of a transaction, because the risk of losses due to fraud declines as the loans season.

Sources of special hazard insurance have nearly dried up since the 1989 and 1994 earthquakes in California. This has become more or less moot, however, as subordination has now almost universally supplanted pool insurance in nonagency MBS transactions. In the period after 1989, however, many pool insured transactions included a small subordinated class specifically for special hazard loss coverage. These classes found a few willing buyers (and mostly did very well in the wake of the 1994 quake), and were thus arguably the first securitization of earthquake risk, predating the current cluster of state government-sponsored "earthquake bonds."

Letters of Credit

The issuer of a whole-loan security or a third party with a sufficient rating can provide a LOC in the amount required by the rating agencies to enhance the entire deal or in a lesser amount designed to complement or upgrade other forms of credit enhancement. To protect the investor from event risks, some LOCs are designed to convert to cash if the LOC provider is downgraded.

Bond Insurance ("Surety Bonds")

Traditionally insurers of municipal bonds, Capital Markets Assurance Corporation (CapMAC), Financial Guarantee Insurance Corporation (FGIC), Financial Security Assurance (FSA), and Municipal Bond Insurance Association (MBIA) are also active in the mortgage-backed securities arena. Typically, bond insurers will not take the first-loss position in the credit support structure and thus require at least one other form of credit support, usually subordination, to bring the underlying assets up to an investment-grade (usually triple-B) rating. Since surety bonds generally provide 100% coverage for all types of losses unconditionally, they are often used to "wrap" existing transactions that are extremely novel or otherwise off-putting to investors regardless of their structural enhancements. For a time in the early 1990s, several extremely conservative investors would demand (and pay for) a "surety wrap" around an already triple-A transaction.

Corporate Guarantees

Corporate guarantees cover all losses and can be used as stand-alone credit support or in conjunction with other forms of credit enhancement to provide the loss coverage required to obtain a particular rating. However, if the primary credit support is provided by a rated entity, the security is subject to reevaluation, and potentially downgrade, if that entity is downgraded. For example, when Citibank was downgraded in the early 1990s, all but the most highly seasoned of the MBSs guaranteed by Citibank were downgraded as well.

Because of concerns about the ratings of third-party credit support providers, and because of the more stringent capital treatment of issuer recourse for financial institutions, the use of external credit enhancement techniques has declined substantially since the 1980s. For example, in 1987 70% of nonagency MBSs were externally credit enhanced. As shown in Exhibit 8, this figure has dropped as low as 8% in 1994. However, in recent years, surety bond usage has increased, primarily as a result of the rapid growth in subprime and home equity loan-backed security issuance, which (as described above) are being classified as asset-backed securities, a market more accustomed to bond insurance. In the traditional A-quality jumbo market, however, the senior/subordinated structure is by far the most widely used credit enhancement technique.

Internal Credit Enhancement

Internal credit enhancement techniques allocate a portion of the collateral cash flow to provide the credit support needed to obtain a desired rating for the security. This self-insurance aspect of internal credit enhancement structures eliminates the event risks associated with external credit enhancement methods. The most popular form of internal credit enhancement is the senior/subordinated structure. Other internal structures include reserve funds and spread accounts, both of which are normally used in addition to a subordinate class.

Exhibit 8: Private Label Issuance by Credit Enhancement Type
(Percent of total issuance)

	1996	1995	1994	1993	1992	1991	1990
Total Issuance (Dollars in Billions	$38.4	$37.0	$63.2	$98.5	$89.5	$49.7	$24.4
Internal Credit Enhancement Methods:(%)							
Subordination	72	61	92	83	48	70	49
Reserve Fund	0	5	1	1	17	—	—
Super-Senior	0	—	—	2	3	11	—
External Credit Enhancement Methods:							
Pool Insurance	1	2	2	11	28	10	23
Surety Bonds	18	21	4	2	2	<1	5
Letter of Credit	0	—	—	—	1	5	15
Corporate Guaranty	0	—	—	—	—	<1	3
Multiple Support	4	2	—	1	1	4	5
Other/Resecuritization	4	9	2	1	—	—	—

Source: Inside MBS & ABS, Inside Mortgage Finance, Mortgage Market Statistical Annual
Copyright 1996, Bethesda, MD, 301.951.1240

Senior/Subordinated Structures

In this structure, one or more subordinate classes are created to protect the senior classes from the risks associated with whole-loan mortgages. The original senior/subordinated structures were composed of two classes. The senior ("A") class is protected against credit loss by the subordinate ("B" or "junior") class which assumes a first-loss position. If a loss is experienced on an underlying mortgage loan, funds that would normally be allocable to the subordinate class are redirected to the senior class. If these funds are insufficient to cover the loss (and no funds are available from a reserve fund, spread account or other form of credit enhancement), payments otherwise due to the subordinated class are diverted in subsequent months to pay off the shortfall. It is important to note, however, that the specific allocation of cash flow to accomplish this can vary considerably in different versions of the structure.

In current structures, the senior class is protected from losses until the subordinated B class is exhausted. In early senior/subordinated transactions, however, protection was limited to a prespecified "subordinated amount" which applied to the actual cash amount diverted from the subordinated to the senior class. In either case, prepayment makes the total amount of available *interest* cash flow uncertain, so the rating agencies have required the total amount of loss coverage in the form of principal. Thus the subordinate class size must be at least as large as the initial required coverage amount. For example, a $100 million 30-year fixed-rate pool which requires an initial 8% loss coverage would need a subordinate class of size $8 million to provide sufficient loss coverage to receive a triple-A rating on the senior class. Note, however, that in structures that exhaust the subordinated class, the total amount of credit support will equal the principal balance *plus* all interest payments diverted to the senior class, thus providing more than the required 8%.

In the early senior/subordinated transactions, the issuer was required by tax regulations to hold the subordinate class. This requirement was eliminated in 1987 by the REMIC regulations, but investors were not sufficiently comfortable with mortgage credit risk to take even a mildly leveraged first-loss position in a mortgage pool. In 1989 a three class senior/ subordinated structure appeared, which divided the subordinated class into a "senior subordinated" or "mezzanine" class which was investment grade (generally triple-B) and an unrated "junior subordinated" first-loss class. In 1991, in response to conservative investors' concerns about mortgage credit in a generally weak economic environment, the *senior* class was divided in the same way to produce a "super-senior" class *on top of* a regular triple-A senior class. This "belt and suspenders" structure was short-lived, however, and (as discussed above) the market soon settled on a structure with triple-A senior classes, double-A "mezzanine" classes, and a series of tiered subordinate classes rated from single-A down to single-B. The senior class is further structured into a variety of tranches familiar from agency CMOs, such as PAC-support structures or floater-inverse floater structures, suiting the needs of a diverse investor population.

The senior/subordinated concept can be implemented in many different specific forms, and for a while it seemed as if issuers and Wall Street dealers were intent on trying every one at least once. However, all of the structures can be understood in terms of a single general principle: the structure must preserve the availability of sufficient credit support to satisfy the general loss coverage requirements described under "Credit Structuring" above. This can be done with a subordinated class alone, or in combination with a reserve fund or spread account, third-party guaranties, etc. The earliest senior/subordinated transactions used a specific type of "reserve fund" structure, but since about 1989 the structure of choice has been the so-called "shifting interest" structure. An alternative structure that is sometimes used with high-margin collateral combines a subordinated class with a spread account that provides a measure of first-loss protection.

Reserve Fund Structure

Recall that (1) in all MBS transactions, the initial level of loss coverage must be maintained for the first 5 or 10 years for fixed-rate or adjustable-rate loans respectively; and (2) the rating agencies require credit support from a subordinated class to be available in the form of principal, because prepayments render the total amount of interest cash flow uncertain. Any principal amounts distributed to a subordinate class reduces its principal balance and thus reduces available credit support. For this reason, during the initial "fixed" period of the credit support requirement, the subordinate class' share of principal is directed to a reserve fund. Thus, the sum of the subordinated class balance and the reserve fund balance will satisfy the credit support requirement. As actually implemented, the subordinated class' share of both principal *and interest* are diverted to the reserve fund until an initial targeted balance is attained, because under normal conditions both amortization and prepayments are minimal at the outset of a transaction, and a certain amount of liquidity is desirable to cover early delinquencies or even losses. This requirement is relaxed as the pool seasons, in accordance with the "stepdown" principles outlined above. If the pool performs well, the accumulated funds in the reserve fund are released incrementally to the subordinated class starting at the beginning of the "stepdown" phase of the transaction.

Historically, the delinquency portion of the credit support requirement was deposited into the reserve fund by the issuer at the outset of the transaction. Once the reserve fund reached the initial required target, the issuer was reimbursed. The structure becomes fully self-insured once the issuer has been reimbursed.

The rating agencies require that amounts in the reserve fund can be invested only in short-term high-quality securities. Thus the owner of the subordinate class experiences a decline in yield without a corresponding decline in risk. This disadvantage led to the development of a structure without a reserve fund.

Shifting Interest Structure

Instead of diverting subordinate cash flows to a reserve fund, the shifting interest structure diverts subordinate cash flows to the senior class — in particular, during the initial phase of the credit support requirement, the subordinated class' share of *prepayment principal* is reallocated to the senior class instead. (The adverse selection theory can be used to argue that only the percentage of prepayments due to the subordinated class needs to be diverted to the senior class, since only prepayments reduce the pool balance without reducing the latent credit risk.) Since the senior class receives more than its *pro rata* share of principal, it is paid down disproportionately quickly and over time will constitute a progressively smaller percentage of the total ownership interest in the mortgage pool.

During this initial period, the subordinate class receives only its *pro rata* share of *principal amortization*, which is practically nothing at all in the early years of a transaction. Its balance remains nearly constant (near enough to satisfy the rating agencies), thus preserving the required amount of credit support. As the pool pays down but the subordinated class does not, its ownership interest in the pool increases over time. Thus, the ownership interest gradually "shifts" from the senior class to the subordinated class — hence the name "shifting interest." (Note that this reallocation of principal cash flows within a multiclass structure was not possible until the REMIC legislation took effect in 1987; thus, pre-1987 senior/subordinated transactions were required to use the reserve fund structure, as did many post-1987 transactions until the early issuers revised their legal documents accordingly.)

As with any MBS structure, the loss coverage requirement will eventually be allowed to decline if the pool seasons well. In the shifting interest structure, this is accomplished by reducing the percentage of the subordinated class' prepayment entitlement that is diverted to the senior class. For the first 5 or 10 years of the transaction, 100% of the subordinated class' share of prepayments is diverted to the senior class. During the next 4 years, this percentage is allowed to gradually "step down" to zero, at which point no further diversions are made and the two classes receive principal on a *pro rata* basis. From then on, the respective senior and subordinate percentages (i.e. their proportionate ownership interests in the pool) remain constant.

Because the senior class receives prepayments otherwise due to the subordinate class, the senior class has a higher effective prepayment rate than the collateral, while the subordinate class has a lower effective prepayment rate. In fact, during the initial phase of the credit support requirement, the subordinated class' effective prepayment rate is zero (unless the collateral prepays so quickly that the senior class is retired completely during this period). This causes the subordinate class to have the average life stability of a PAC or super PAC.

Although reserve funds are occasionally used for delinquency coverage, the whole point of the shifting interest structure was to eliminate the need for the reserve fund. Thus, delinquency coverage is usually external to the shifting interest structure, and has been customarily provided by the master servicer or trustee.

Spread Accounts

"Excess servicing" or "spread," i.e. mortgage interest in excess of that required to pay investors, the servicer or other fees, can be used to pay down bonds or deposited into a spread account. (Otherwise, it is returned to the issuer or residual holder and plays no part in the structure.) If the spread is used to pay down bonds, it can be shown that the result is a buildup of "overcollateralization." If the spread is deposited into a spread account, then the subordinated class can be paid down as the spread account builds up, so that the sum of the subordinated class balance plus the spread account satisfies the total credit support requirement. Of course, the subordinated class cannot be paid down by the spread itself! Instead, the subordinated class is permitted to receive appropriate amounts of principal which, in the absence of the spread account, would be diverted to the senior class as described above. In MBS transactions, spread accounts must be supplemented by another form of credit enhancement because (1) excess servicing is typically insufficient to provide the required levels of credit support by itself, and (2) even if it were, prepayments render unpredictable the ultimate amount of excess spread that will be collected over time.

Spread accounts are most often used to help support a senior/subordinated structure with high margin collateral such as ARMs or B/C loans, and are generally used to enhance the appeal of subordinated classes by providing first-loss protection.

PREPAYMENTS

Fannie Mae's and Freddie Mac's securitization programs require loans to meet guidelines that limit servicing fees, loan size, weighted average maturity (WAM) dispersion, and underwriting criteria. The homogenous nature of the collateral and an abundance of historical data have facilitated the creation of relatively sophisticated prepayment models for agency-conforming mortgages. However, nonagency prepayment rates are more difficult to model because the collateral is much less homogeneous than conforming loans.

In general, historical data on prepayments, defaults, and foreclosures are more difficult to come by; fortunately, however, many of the larger nonagency issuers have been providing some of this information to investors and dealers. Most of them provide the necessary prepayment information, and many also provide monthly loss and delinquency levels aggregated at the deal level. The current state of the art in this area is probably Norwest Mortgage's SecuritiesLink, which provides deal-level information on prepayments, delinquencies, losses, prepayment interest shortfalls and all other information pertinent to investor distributions, free to investors through a fax service, a computer bulletin board and, as of early 1997, a World Wide Web site, as well as complete loan-level payment histories on every nonagency loan ever securitized through Prudential Home Mortgage, SASI and NASCOR which are available electronically by subscription. This is especially valuable for studying prepayments and defaults because it includes loans that are no longer active, thus avoiding the statistical censoring problem.

When attempting to forecast nonagency prepayment rates, investors must consider the variables (loan rate, age, and seasonal effects) as well as the geographic concentration, term, LTV ratios, origination standards, and the loan sizes and types comprising the pool. As with conforming loans, whole-loan prepayment rates tend to increase when interest rates decline, and as the loans season. Typically, a greater variance in loan types results in higher prepayment rates for nonagency MBSs relative to similar coupon agency MBSs because pools with a given net coupon will include some mortgages with higher mortgage interest rates.

Since nonagency securities are frequently backed by a large number of jumbo loans, the collateral often has a relatively high regional concentration. Hence, the prepayment performance of a whole loan security is often tied to a particular region's economic circumstances. The earliest conventional wisdom was that jumbo borrowers were wealthier and thus more mobile and more likely to be "trading up" to larger homes; they were also more financially sophisticated, hence more likely to take advantage of refinancing opportunities. Recent prepayment theories frame the prepayment incentive more systematically, in terms of *dollar savings* in the monthly payment rather than *rate* reductions in the mortgage contract; in this view, even a small rate reduction can still produce substantial monthly savings on a high balance loan, which should result in faster prepayment speeds for nonconforming loans. More recently, however, with the collapse of most high-priced real estate markets and the advent of mortgage products for distressed borrowers, nonconforming loans are frequently observed to prepay more slowly than their conforming counterparts.

DEFAULTS

Default research on nonagency MBSs has been more sporadic than prepayment research because (1) detailed mortgage credit analysis under *expected* conditions (as opposed to the rating agency stress scenarios) wasn't critically important to investors until they began to look at lower rated subordinated classes, and (2) even when investors began to clamor for this information, it wasn't generally available from issuers. Academic research in the field has focused almost exclusively on conforming loans, and has produced little that can be usefully applied to investment analysis of nonagency MBSs. Most research has focused on the option theory of mortgage default, which views default as the borrower's exercise of an option to put the property to the issuer at a price equal to the unpaid mortgage balance. In this view, the option is "in the money" if the property value is less than the mortgage balance. However, people don't default on a mortgage simply because it is "under water." Clearly factors such as the legal, social and transactional costs of default, the preservation of a good credit record, and the cost of alternative housing affect the borrower's decision. These are variously accounted for in the theory as "transaction costs," but there is no agreement as to exactly how to do this to obtain successful predictions. Arguably, a pure or "ruthless" option-based theory of default is a failing paradigm.

A competing theory of mortgage default is the "ability to pay" theory, which focuses on the borrower's cash flow. Eclipsed for a while by the option theory, it is now in effect being revived by the recent focus on using borrower credit scores and credit reports as predictors of borrower default. In this view, a borrower will default if he cannot afford to pay the mortgage. However, it is clear that if the property value exceeds the mortgage balance (i.e. the option is "out of the money"), the distressed borrower should be able to sell the property and pay off the mortgage. Thus, default should only occur if *both* circumstances hold: insufficient cash flow *and* an "in the money" option. As with most economic processes, however, individual psychology acts as a source of "friction" or "inertia" that can result in "irrational" borrower behavior that doesn't obey the theory.

A few dealers and data vendors have constructed "default models," but these are primarily statistical fits of the rather sparse data that are actually available, not descriptive models. They involve more parameters than prepayment models do, and are based on far fewer observations. For that reason alone, on statistical grounds their predictions will be much less reliable than those of the prepayment models that have been around for years. Standard errors and out-of-sample historical validations are rarely reported, and in general the research, because of its proprietary nature, is not subject to the type of review typical of academic research. In addition, even when default is a certainty, loss severities are extremely sensitive to servicer practice, including workout strategies, short sales and, if all else fails, the efficacy of their foreclosure and REO departments. Thus, investors need to closely scrutinize the underlying data, assumptions, and methodologies to ascertain whether the "credit-adjusted spreads" from the current generation of default models are as useful to valuation of MBS credit risk as OASs have proved to be for prepayment risk.

SUMMARY AND OUTLOOK

In summary, nonagency MBSs afford a wide range of yield opportunities to investors willing to take *structured mortgage credit risk.* Investors can take simple mortgage credit risk by purchasing whole loans. *Structured* securities are created with ratings from triple-A to single-B (and occasionally lower), depending on leverage and credit support levels. Unrated securities generally exhibit extreme leverage and equity-like risk profiles. The underlying *mortgages* comprise familiar products such as 15- and 30-year fixed rate jumbo loans with well-characterized risk profiles, and newer, relatively untested products such as "B/C" mortgages. *Credit risk* is unique to nonagency MBSs; prepayment risk is common to the agency and nonagency sectors, and operates in much the same way in both. Historically, the nonagency sector has richly repaid investors who were willing to take the time to familiarize themselves with something new and "unconventional" (to coin a phrase). We expect this to continue to be the case as the market continues to mature and broaden its investor appeal.

Chapter 2

Nonagency Small-Balance Loans

Steven Abrahams
Principal
Mortgage Research
Morgan Stanley

Howard Esaki
Principal
Mortgage Research
Morgan Stanley

Robert Restrick
Associate
Mortgage Research
Morgan Stanley

INTRODUCTION

Since 1993 mortgage bankers have found a new niche in lending to borrowers who fall just outside the bounds of FNMA/FHLMC underwriting guidelines. These borrowers often want loans well below the agencies' current limits of $207,000, but the borrowers fail to meet agency guidelines on other counts. The steady flow of these loans into the securitized market has put them on many investors' radar screens but left some wondering exactly who the borrowers are and how they might prepay. That issue lies at the center of valuing the securities backed by these new small-balance nonagency loans.

More recently, credit analysis of small balance loans has come to play an important role, as senior-subordinated structures have started to replace third-party guarantees. In this chapter we review the general characteristics of nonagency small balance pools and present a prepayment analysis. We find that small balance pools have much less interest sensitivity than jumbo mortgage pools. Finally, we present evidence that the credit risk of mortgage pools decreases as loan size falls.

35

Exhibit 1: Key Originators' 30-Year Nonagency Loan Volume: 1/94-4/96

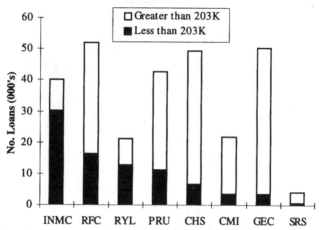

Note: All statistics based on a representative random sample of 5,000 30-year loans originated between 1/94-4/96 with balances less than $203,000. Originators included are Countrywide/INMC, RFC, Ryland, Prudential, Chase, Capstead, GE, Sears.

Source: Morgan Stanley

WHO IS THAT SMALL-BALANCE BORROWER?

The focus on small-balance, nonagency loans comes as production in the sector has surged since 1993. These loans helped originators stay busy after the refinancing booms of 1992 and 1993. Major originators have securitized nearly 85,000 small balance 30-year loans between January 1994 and April 1996 — more than 30% of their total securitized nonagency unit volume (Exhibit 1). Some originators have made these loans the bulk of their securitized origination. For example, these loans account for more than 75% of securitized 30-year nonagency originations coming from INMC since 1993. RFC, Ryland and Prudential also have originated heavily in the sector.

Low Balance, High Coupon Loans

Viewed in aggregate, the small-balance 30-year loans present a striking combination of small average size and high average gross coupon. The first would augur for less prepayment risk than jumbos, the second for more. Average small-balance nonagency loan size has hovered around $100,000 since 1994, nearly the same level as 30-year conventional 30-year loans but well below the $307,000 average size of traditional nonagency jumbos.

The average gross coupon on the small-balance nonagency loans, however, has run 75-150 bp higher than agency rates, and 50-100 bp higher than jumbo rates. The high interest rate on the smaller balance marks the prevailing par rate — the current coupon, as it were — for the unique borrowers that end up in these small, nonagency loans. Refinancing risk in these loans is best understood by focusing not on gross coupon relative to agency rates but on loan size and how much rates have moved since loan origination. Smaller loans stand to save fewer dollars by refinancing and are less likely to be solicited by commission-based mortgage brokers. Further, even if a small nonagency loan has a coupon 150 bp above agency rates, that loan may have no refinancing incentives if rates have stood still since origination.

Investors, Income Estimators, and Others

One key to the high rates on small-balance nonagency loans is the more-than-20% concentration of investor properties (Exhibit 2). Some originators show even higher investor percentages. The mortgage banks have taken advantage of FNMA/FHLMC's refusal to underwrite investor properties with LTV ratios greater than 70%. The banks step in and offer loans up to 90% LTV — but at a price. Some originators' underwriting guidelines require up to 25% mortgage insurance coverage, and liquid assets sufficient to cover up to six months of principal, interest, taxes, and insurance. Investor loan balances also tend to be small relative to non-investors'. (See Exhibit 3.) The banks also ask the investor to pay an interest rate that typically stands 75 bp higher than the rate paid by non-investors. In any pool of small-balance nonagency loans, investors' typically bear the highest rates by far.

Small-balance nonagency mortgages also show a 61% sample of low- or no-documentation loans. Some underwriters' guidelines allow these borrowers to report an income without offering any documentation, such as pay-stubs or tax returns. Some low- or no-documentation borrowers even forego an income statement altogether. The agencies, by contrast, require documentation of reported income.

Exhibit 2: Features of Recent Small Balance versus Nonagency Loans

Loan Feature	Less Than $203,000	Greater Than $203,000
Avg. Size	$103,200	$307,500
Documentation		
Full	39%	76%
Limited	50%	22%
None	11%	2%
Original LTV	75%	77%
Residence		
Investor	22%	1%
Primary	69%	90%
Other	10%	9%

Note: All statistics based on a representative random sample of 5,000 30-year loans originated between 1/94-4/96 with balances less than $203,000. Originators included are Countrywide/INMC, RFC, Ryland, Prudential, Chase, Capstead, GE, Sears.

Source: Morgan Stanley

Exhibit 3: Recent Small Balance Nonagency Investor and Non-Investor Loans

Loan Feature	Nonagency	
	Investor	Non-Investor
Average Size	$81,350	$109,900
Documentation		
Full	78%	28%
Limited	18%	59%
None	4%	13%
Original LTV	75%	69%

Note: All statistics based on a representative random sample of 5,000 30-year loans originated between 1/94-4/96 with balances less than $203,000. Originators included are Countrywide/INMC, RFC, Ryland, Prudential, Chase, Capstead, GE, Sears.

Source: Morgan Stanley

The low- and no-doc borrowers often are self-employed or own small businesses, and the income stated on their tax returns would fail to qualify them under agency standards for the loan they want. These are not B- or C-quality borrowers, however. For borrowers hoping to bypass full income documentation, underwriting guidelines can require a high credit score, proof of substantial liquid assets, and can limit LTV ratios to 80%. Borrowers unwilling even to verbally report incomes can be required to show an extremely high credit score, pay for the entire loan downpayment with their own cash, show substantial liquid assets, and an LTV of 70% or better. Of course, the low- and no-documentation 30-year loans also carry interest rates roughly 35 bp higher than fully documented small balance, nonagency loans. Just as they did in the investor properties, the banks have relaxed some underwriting standards, tightened others, and raised the borrowers' interest rates. Originators aim to produce loans that represent the same net credit risk embedded in any FNMA or FHLMC mortgage.

In some pools of small-balance nonagency loans, the investor properties and limited documentation loans account for nearly 80% of the mortgages. The remaining 20% comes from a variety of sources, including:

- Expatriots and foreign nationals without recent U.S. credit histories,
- Borrowers with excellent credit records that want a high LTV loan and would rather pay a nonagency rate than the mortgage insurance required by FNMA/FHLMC, and
- Borrowers who fail to meet agency standards for mortgage debt as a percent of income (28%) or total debt as a percent of income (36%).

PREPAYMENTS ON SMALL-BALANCE LOANS

Although the prepayment history is short, small-balance nonagency loans have shown much less interest rate sensitivity than jumbo loans and arguably less sensitivity than regular agency loans. Structures backed by small-balance collateral, nevertheless, have traded at spreads appropriate for much more negatively convex securities.

Less Negative Convexity Than Jumbos

The stability of these smaller loans relative to nonagency jumbos has been clear in the last year. As interest rates fell and created refinancing opportunities for borrowers, deals backed by small-balance loans prepaid only 20% to 75% as fast as deals backed by similarly aged jumbo collateral.

The historically better convexity of the smaller mortgages relative to jumbos shows even in analysis of individual loans. We analyzed prepayments in a sample of 7,500 nonagency loans — a third with balances under $203,000 and the remainder comprised of jumbos.[1] The analysis controlled for differences in loan age and seasonal effects — factors that could cloud a picture of loans' interest rate sensitivity. It also accounted for the tendency of the smaller loans to come out with relatively high interest rates.

Exhibit 4 shows a curve of estimated 1-month prepayment rates for seasoned small-balance and jumbo 30-year loans depending on their relative refinanceability. The small-balance loans respond more slowly as refinancing incentives rise, as indicated by WAC to 30-year fixed mortgage rate ratio values greater than 1.0. For instance, small-balance loans with gross coupons 10% higher than market rates have prepaid near 20% CPR, while jumbos with similar refinancing incentives have prepaid near 40% CPR.

Exhibit 4: Refi Response in Small Balance versus Jumbo Nonagency Loans

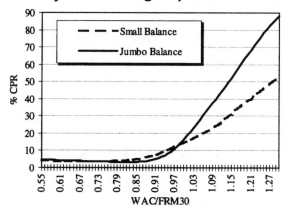

Source: Morgan Stanley

---

[1] The sample included 2,500 loans with original balances under $203,000 securitized by INMC between 3/94-8/95, and 5,000 loans with balances over $203,000 securitized equally by PHMS and RFMSI over the same period. INMC loans offered the longest available prepayment history.

Exhibit 5: Prepayment History on INMC versus Agency Collateral

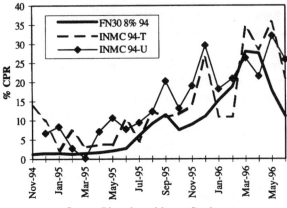

Source: Bloomberg, Morgan Stanley

The loan level analysis indicates that loan size plays a dominant role in determining prepayment risk, a role exceeded in importance only by refinancing incentive and loan age. Loan size determines the absolute savings available from refinancing, as well as the likelihood that the loan gets targeted by commission-based mortgage brokers. Other variables, such as designation as an investor property or limited documentation, play minor roles in the prepayment history of these loans. Some analysts have reported that investor loans have prepaid significantly more slowly than non-investors', but that may be because the former typically have smaller loan balances than the latter.

Faster Seasoning

Relative to conventional loans, the smaller nonagency mortgages have shown a faster rate of seasoning and comparable speed in refinancing. Limited prepayment history makes the precise pattern muddy.

The history of INMC 1994-T and INMC 1994-U offer the longest pictures of speeds in small-balance loans relative to agency collateral, although deals from RALI and other issuers would show roughly the same pattern (Exhibit 5). The INMC deals had underlying loans with average balances of $141,000 and $146,000 and gross weighted average coupons of 9.08% and 9.28%, respectively. It is important to note that at least 17% to 23% of the loans in these deals had jumbo balances. When these loans were originated in the summer of 1994, agency borrowers could get loans at roughly 8.5%, making conventional 8.0% pass-throughs a relevant prepayment benchmark.

Although prepayments in both the INMC deals and the benchmark pass-through slid as interest rates rose through the end of 1994, the small-balance nonagency loans still prepaid faster. This suggests faster seasoning in the nonagency loans. From the summer of 1995 until recently, as interest rates fell and the loans became refinanceable, speeds rose in both the small-balance nonagency and agency loans. Both the INMC and agency prepayments picked up at roughly the same rate. INMC speeds ultimately came in above the agency pace, but that probably was due to the higher base rate of seasoning in the INMC loans. Other comparisons of prepayments on small-balance nonagency collateral against agency passthroughs show a similar trend: faster seasoning but comparable refinancing.

The faster seasoning on small-balance nonagency loans likely comes from borrowers who eventually qualify for lower-rate, agency mortgages: investors, low- and no-documentation borrowers, and borrowers with short credit histories. With the rates on these nonagency loans historically standing 75 to 150 bp higher than rates on agency loans, borrowers have clear incentives to qualify for an agency loan. The factors that put these borrowers in the small-balance sector initially — high LTVs, erratic income, limited credit histories — can improve enough to allow an agency refinancing.

Impact on Valuation

The rough similarity of speeds in small-balance nonagency loans and conventional passthroughs has clear implications for relative value. Structures backed by the smaller loans still trade at nominal spreads comparable to structures backed by jumbo mortgages. The structures collateralized by the smaller loans should show less negative convexity than the jumbo securities, however, and consequently offer better relative value.

The small-balance structures also should offer better value then agency CMOs. The agency and small-balance securities likely deliver comparable negative convexity, but the nonagency structures — particularly with 5-year or longer average lives — have traded this summer at nominal spreads 35 to 40 bp wider. That nominal spread advantage should translate almost directly into an option-adjusted advantage too.

Securities from three transactions done in early 1996 show the potential advantage in the small-balance sector (Exhibit 6). RALI 1996-QS4 A8 is backed by nonagency loans with an average balance of $135,000 and an average gross coupon of 9.15%. FHLMC 1853 B is backed by TBA 30-year 7.5s. RFMSI 96-S4 A9 is backed by loans with an average balance of $294,162 and an average gross coupon of 7.75%.

Exhibit 6: Relative Value in Comparable-Duration New Issue Small-Balance, Agency and Jumbo Tranches as of July 23, 1996

Security	Collateral	Type	Coupon	7/23/96 Price	Projected Avg. Life	Yield	OAD	ZVol Spread	Option Cost	OAS
RALI 96-QS4 A8	Small-Balance	SEQ	8.0%	$98-08	11.1	8.31%	6.5	149	63	86
FHR 1853 B	Agency	SEQ	7.5%	$97-02	11.1	7.99%	6.5	114	58	56
RFMSI 96-S4 A9	Jumbo	SEQ	6.9%	$94-03	7.7	7.95%	6.8	107	66	41

Source: Morgan Stanley

Our valuation of these securities uses appropriate prepayment models:

- A model for the small-balance loans that uses 175% of the agency season-ing curve, and standard agency refinancing sensitivity,
- The Morgan Stanley Prepayment Model for agency collateral, and
- A model for the jumbo loans that reflects their historical tendency to season slower than agencies', but refinance faster.[2]

The small-balance security shows a 35 bp advantage in zero-volatility spread over the agency tranche, and a 42 bp advantage over the shorter-average-life jumbo tranche. After accounting for option costs,[3] the small-balance security shows a sig-nificant 30 bp OAS advantage over the agency tranche, and a 45 bp advantage over the jumbo tranche. All three securities show comparable option-adjusted durations.

Risks in Valuation

The clearest risks in valuing the small-balance nonagency sector are slower-than-expected seasoning and occasional inclusion of jumbo-balance loans in the under-lying collateral.

The short prepayment history of the sector makes the seasoning curve a little uncertain, but the uncertainty falls most heavily on the shorter, tight-window tranches of a typical structure. Slower-than-expected seasoning translates into significant extension risk in the shorter tranches, minor extension in the longer, wide-window cash flows. The yield curve through most of 1996 accentuates these risks — the steep front of the curve makes extension risk costly for shorter tranches, with the flat back end of the curve making extension risk relatively inexpensive on longer cash flows.

Some deals backed predominately by small-balance nonagency loans also contain some jumbo balances, and these jumbos stand to refinance quickly if rates drop. The resulting prepayment spike, however, should be short-lived.

NONAGENCY LOAN SIZE AND LOSSES

Although it is too early to have significant delinquency and loan loss data on new small balance programs, many outstanding nonagency deals contain a small per-centage of low balance loans. In 1994, several originators of nonagency mort-gages started to release loan level loss data.[4] (Significant loan level loss data do

---

[2] For a description of the jumbo model, see "Opportunities for Yield Buyers in Discount nonagency CMOs," *Mortgage Research Weekly,* Morgan Stanley, April 6, 1995.

[3] Estimated option costs are influenced not only by prepayment assumptions, but by dollar price as well. Lower priced securities show lower option costs, all else equal.

[4] Prudential Home Mortgage was the first issuer to release loan level loss data. In 1995, Chase Home Mort-gage, Securitized Asset Sales, Inc. (SASI), and GE Mortgage Capital have also started to provide these data.

not yet exist for RALI and INMC transactions.) In combination with previously released loan level delinquency data, this information allows us to analyze the impact of specific mortgage characteristics on defaults and losses in greater detail than before. These loan attributes include the loan-to-value ratio, mortgage type, loan purpose, documentation, and geographic location.[5] Based on this data, we find that loan balances less than $150,000 have significantly lower delinquency and loss rates than higher balance loans.

These lower loss rates occurred despite other negative credit characteristics of low balance loans such as high LTVs and higher than average concentrations of condos, limited documentation loans, and investor properties. These characteristics preclude many of these conforming size loans from being sold to FNMA and FHLMC, limiting securitization to nonagency pools.

Rating Agencies View High Balance Loans as Riskier

In assessing credit support for pools of nonagency loans, rating agencies treat higher loan amounts as more risky than lower balance loans. Standard and Poor's, for example, assigns a 1.2 risk weight to loans with a balance between $400,000 and $600,000. This means that a pool consisting entirely of loans with balances in this range would have a credit support requirement 1.2 times more than a prime pool to obtain a rating of AAA. (A prime pool has loan balances less than $400,000.) The credit penalty rises to 1.6 for loans between $600,000 and $1 million and 3.0 for loans above $1 million. Fitch has a similar penalty for large loan balances, while Moody's analyzes home price, a highly correlated variable to loan balance.

Low Balance Loans, Lower Delinquencies, and Lower Losses

Using loan level data, we analyzed delinquency and loss experience with finer loan amount gradations than rating agency guidelines. We analyzed the credit of loans segregated into six categories: (1) $75,001 to $150,000; (2) $150,001 to $250,000; (3) $250,001 to $500,000; (4) $500,001 to $750,000; (5) $750,000 to $1 million; and, (6) over $1 million. The number of loans below $75,000 was not large enough to be meaningful. We also divided the data into two cohorts: loans originated from 1986 to 1990 and from 1991 to 1995. Loans originated before 1991 have already passed through their peak loss period.

Exhibits 7 and 8 show that for 1986 to 1990 originations, the $75,001 to $150,000 category has the lowest delinquency statistics. For this loan amount category, 50 day plus delinquency levels (including foreclosures and REO) are 55% of the level for all loans originated from 1986 to 1990. The $750,001 to $1 million category has the highest delinquency rate, 183% of its age cohort average.

For more seasoned loans (1986-1990), the lowest balance category also has the lowest cumulative loss level. The $75,001 to $150,000 loans have cumula-

---

[5] The loss and delinquency data in this chapter are based on August 1995 remittance reports.

tive losses of 0.17% of their original balances, or 14% of the average for all loans in the cohort. Similar to the delinquency statistics, the $750,001 to $1 million category has the highest cumulative losses, more than double the average. The average cumulative loss for all loans in the seasoned category is 1.23% of original balances.

For more recent origination years, the delinquency rate dispersion is not as great, but still exhibits the general pattern of higher delinquency rates for larger balance loans. Loss rates monotonically increase with loan balance size, but have less extreme values than for more seasoned loans.

Exhibit 7: Loan Balance: 60 Day and 90 Day Delinquency, Foreclosure, and REO Data*
(Risk weights represent the ratio of delinquencies per category to the average for the entire sample.)

Loan Balance Range ($)	1986-1990 Originations			1991-1995 Originations		
	$ Originated (millions)	60+ Delinquency Rate (%)	Risk Weight	$ Originated (millions)	60+ Delinquency Rate (%)	Risk Weight
75,001 to 150,000	707	0.53	55	4,082	0.37	96
150,001 to 250,000	6,673	0.76	79	26,220	0.39	102
250,001 to 500,000	7,810	1.12	116	63,775	0.35	91
500,001 to 750,000	1,224	1.02	105	11,030	0.44	115
750,001 to 1,000,000	476	1.77	183	4,384	0.66	172
Over 1,000,000	82	1.46	151	693	0.62	160
Total	17,088	0.97	100	110,973	0.39	100

*Delinquency information for loans issued by SASI, Prudential Home Mortgage, GE Capital, Chase, Countrywide, and Residential Funding Corporation.

Source: Morgan Stanley

Exhibit 8: Loan Balance: Cumulative Loss Data*
(Risk weights represent the ratio of loss per category to the average for the entire sample.)

Loan Balance Range ($)	1986-1990 Originations			1991-1995 Originations		
	$ Originated (millions)	Cumulative Loss (%)	Risk Weight	$ Originated (millions)	Cumulative Loss (%)	Risk Weight
75,001 to 150,000	148	0.17	14	2,502	0.02	29
150,001 to 250,000	2,681	1.00	82	17,718	0.04	72
250,001 to 500,000	4,525	1.33	109	44,244	0.05	103
500,001 to 750,000	746	1.12	91	6,759	0.06	116
750,001 to 1,000,000	329	2.74	224	2,930	0.12	233
Over 1,000,000	73	0.00	0	538	0.13	246
Total	8,547	1.23	100	75,118	0.05	100

*Loss information for loans issued by SASI, Prudential Home Mortgage, GE Capital, and Chase. 0.00 may include losses less than 0.005%.

Source: Morgan Stanley

Low Balance Advantages Offset Other Risks

Although lower balance loans have good credit performance, they also have several risky loan characteristics, such as higher than average LTVs, concentrations of investor properties, condos, and limited documentation loans. In analyzing the loan level data, we discovered that loan-to-value ratios and loan balances were inversely correlated, implying that the superior credit quality of low balance loans is not a result of greater borrower equity. For example, for the 1986 to 1990 originations, the weighted average loan-to-value ratio falls from 71% for mortgages in the $75,001 to $150,000 to 62% for loans with a balance of over $1 million.

In addition, the concentration of investor properties and condominiums is much higher than average in the $75,001 to $150,000 category for both the 1986 to 1990 and 1991 to 1995 cohorts. 76% of the lowest balance loans originated between 1991 and 1995 were limited documentation, three times the average for all loans in that age cohort. In spite of this concentration, low balance loans had less than one-half the average cumulative loss and a slightly lower delinquency rate than for all loans.

Less Volatility for Lower Home Prices

We believe that the higher loss rates for large-balance loans are a result of the greater volatility of prices of expensive homes. In California and the Northeast, where 75% or more of the properties backing nonagency loans are located, high value home prices have fallen by as much as 30% since their peak in the late 1980s. During the same period, lower value home prices were stable to even rising in some areas. Prices for higher value homes tend to be more volatile because of the relative thinness of the market and the difficulty of evaluating the unique features of many expensive homes. For this reason, Moody's looks at home value as a better indicator of risk than loan value.

Exhibits 9 through 12 show that higher home values generally have greater delinquency and loss rates, although the correlation is not as strong as with loan amounts. For the 1986 to 1990 originations, the lowest delinquency rates are for the $150,001 to $250,000 category; the lowest losses are for the $75,001 to $150,000 loans. For newer originations, loans below $250,000 have thus far exhibited the lowest loss rates, although these categories also have the highest delinquency rates. Many of these loans are still too early in the credit risk cycle to draw definitive conclusions about lifetime loss performance.

CONCLUSION

With a likely refinancing sensitivity that matches agency collateral and a seasoning ramp that goes higher, small nonagency loans should show marginally better cash flow stability than agency loans. Deals backed by small nonagency loans, however, have traded recently at spreads close to jumbo-backed deals. Some *but not all* of that spread stands as a concession for nonagency credit risk and liquidity. Investors consequently stand to pick up option-adjusted spread relative to either agency or jumbo nonagency securities. Structures backed by small-balance loans should offer less negative convexity than jumbo deals, and more base-case spread than agency CMOs. In addition, the credit risk associated with low balance loans has historically been less than that for jumbo loans.

Exhibit 9: Loan Characteristics: 1986 to 1990 Originations (Percent of Category)

Loan Balance Range ($)	Documentation		Occupancy		Condo	Cashout	LTV
	Limited	None	Second	Investor			
75,001 to 150,000	32	1	3	1	8	14	71
150,001 to 250,000	28	1	1	0	5	16	71
250,001 to 500,000	38	1	2	0	5	22	69
500,001 to 750,000	42	1	2	0	4	26	66
750,001 to 1,000,000	38	1	4	0	4	32	63
Over 1,000,000	28	0	10	1	5	19	62
Total	34	1	2	0	5	20	69

0 may include less than 0.5%.

Source: Morgan Stanley

Exhibit 10: Loan Characteristics: 1991 to 1995 Originations (Percent of Category)

Loan Balance Range ($)	Documentation		Occupancy		Condo	Cashout	LTV
	Limited	None	Second	Investor			
75,001 to 150,000	76	7	5	6	8	20	67
150,001 to 250,000	24	2	2	0	4	13	73
250,001 to 500,000	20	1	2	0	3	15	71
500,001 to 750,000	21	1	2	0	3	16	67
750,001 to 1,000,000	21	0	2	0	2	17	61
Over 1,000,000	10	0	3	0	1	17	59
Total	23	1	2	1	3	15	71

0 may include less than 0.5%.

Source: Morgan Stanley

Exhibit 11: Home Prices: 60 Day and 90 Day Delinquency, Foreclosure, and REO Data
(Risk weights represent the ratio of delinquencies per category to the average for the entire sample.)

Home Price Range ($)	1986-1990 Originations			1991-1995 Originations		
	$ Originated (millions)	60+ Delinquency Rate (%)	Risk Weight	$ Originated (millions)	60+ Delinquency Rate (%)	Risk Weight
75,001 to 150,000	230	0.64	70	1,731	0.48	125
150,001 to 250,000	2,147	0.55	60	5,972	0.55	144
250,001 to 500,000	9,293	0.96	105	60,047	0.38	98
500,001 to 750,000	2,937	0.93	102	23,838	0.33	86
750,001 to 1,000,000	1,153	0.93	101	9,776	0.36	93
Over 1,000,000	992	1.31	143	9,445	0.48	124
Total	16,774	0.92	100	110,972	0.39	100

Source: Morgan Stanley

Exhibit 12: Home Price: Cumulative Loss Data
(Risk weights represent the ratio of loss per category to the average for the entire sample.)

Home Price Range ($)	1986-1990 Originations			1991-1995 Originations		
	$ Originated (millions)	Cumulative Loss (%)	Risk Weight	$ Originated (millions)	Cumulative Loss (%)	Risk Weight
75,001 to 150,000	85	0.13	12	1,056	0.00*	5
150,001 to 250,000	391	0.87	82	3,899	0.03	64
250,001 to 500,000	4,749	1.11	105	41,272	0.05	99
500,001 to 750,000	1,657	0.99	93	16,244	0.05	104
750,001 to 1,000,000	669	0.83	78	6,399	0.04	84
Over 1,000,000	670	1.37	129	6,174	0.08	153
Total	8,233	1.06	100	75,118	0.05	100

Source: Morgan Stanley

* Less than 0.005%

Chapter 3

Structural Nuances in Nonagency Mortgage-Backed Securities

Peter Rubinstein, Ph.D.
Senior Vice President
PaineWebber, Inc.

Nonagency residential mortgage-backed securities are incredibly complex. The usual risk present in all fixed income securities — the fluctuation of interest rates — is both amplified and distorted in whole loan passthroughs by features that hamper liquidity: credit risk, prepayment risk, a lack of data, and structural complexity. This chapter focuses on some of the least understood structural aspects of these securities — nuances that may appear small, but in fact significantly impact yield.

By nuance, we do not mean the way CMO tranches prioritize cash flows, or differences in credit structuring techniques. These are major issues that we assume the reader is familiar with. Instead, this chapter examines more subtle structural issues that are sometimes referred to in the prospectus, but often are fully disclosed only in the pooling and servicing agreement. These include: advances of delinquent principal and interest, claims adjustments for liquidated loans, compensating interest for prepayments, ratio stripping, and interest subordination (including potential payment delays to subordinated classes). While we discuss specific structures of certain issuers, these structures change over time, so all references to specific issuers and their policies describe some, but not necessarily all, of their transactions.

ADVANCES

Advances are funds servicers loan to the trust to allow the trustee to make timely payments of interest and principal to investors. Servicers advance only to cover homeowner delinquencies, not shortfalls for other reasons. For example, reduced

This chapter was written while the author was employed as Chief Mortgage Economist at Moody's Investors Service.

interest collections due to mid-month prepayments, the Relief Act, or "cramdowns," are not reasons for advancing because these are not events of default; homeowners are allowed in these circumstances to make reduced payments.[1] Nor do servicers advance principal to cover defaults in the final repayment of balloon loans.

In most nonagency MBSs, advancing is performed by the master servicer from its own funds. In some transactions, reserve funds may be used to support advancing, and occasionally subservicers have the primary obligation to advance. No interest is paid the servicer for advanced funds; instead, the servicer usually keeps all late penalties collected from delinquent borrowers as additional compensation. Virtually all transactions require a back-up servicer to provide advancing in case the primary servicer fails to advance; this function is usually performed by the trustee. Advanced funds are recouped by the servicer when either the homeowner pays delinquent interest and principal or when the property is foreclosed and sold. In either case, advances are repaid before cash is distributed to security owners.

Forms of Advancing

The obligation to advance in the private-label market is limited and varies substantially by issuer. The best and most common form of advancing offered in the nonagency market is called *mandatory* advancing.[2] Mandatory advancing calls for the servicer to advance both interest and principal on delinquent loans. Failure to advance is an event of default unless the servicer determines that there is no reasonable chance of recouping advanced funds from the ultimate disposition of the property.

A few issuers, such as Countrywide Funding Corporation and Countrywide Mortgage Conduit (now renamed Independent National Mortgage Corporation), offer a slightly weaker form of mandatory advancing. In deals sold under the "CWMBS, Inc." description, they advance interest but not principal for loans that have progressed to REO (i.e., loans that have completed the foreclosure process).[3]

Other issuers, such as Chemical Mortgage Securities, Inc., and PNC Mortgage Securities Corp., offer a slightly stronger form of mandatory advancing. They will advance even when advanced funds are not deemed recoverable from the specific loan that has gone bad so long as credit support is available to absorb any loss.

The next best form of advancing, found in a fair number of transactions, is called *optional* or *voluntary* advancing. In these transactions, the servicer intends to advance but is not required to do so. In other words, failure to advance is not an event of default.

---

[1] The federal Soldiers' and Sailors' Relief Act of 1940 allows certain military personnel to pay reduced interest rates on home mortgages during times of war. A cramdown is a reduction in either the mortgage interest rate or the principal amount imposed by a bankruptcy court.

[2] Servicers of pools with first-lien mortgages virtually always advance both scheduled interest and principal. Servicers of securities backed by second-lien mortgages (such as home equity transactions) traditionally do not advance principal.

[3] In this sense, CFC and CMC resemble Freddie Mac, which guarantees the ultimate return of principal rather than the timely payment of principal on most of its earlier transactions.

Generally, optional advancing works as well as mandatory advancing as long as the pool is performing well, but in some transactions optional advancing has stopped because of extremely high delinquencies. For example, in many ComFed transactions advancing has stopped.

A variation on optional advancing offered by Citicorp Mortgage Securities, has optional advancing by the master servicer but mandatory backup advancing by the trustee. Operationally, this arrangement is as good as normal mandatory advancing as long as the back-up servicer is highly rated and capable of servicing.

Although less common now, many older transactions offer even weaker forms of advancing. In transactions with *limited* advancing, the servicer must advance, but only up to some specified limit. The most common types of limits are: (1) a preset, fixed dollar amount; (2) a floating dollar amount, typically tied to the amount in the reserve fund; or (3) a maximum number of missed payments per loan.

In transactions with *partial* advancing, funds are advanced only to the extent needed to make up for missed payments to the senior classes. The weakest and most unusual form of advancing, of course, is no advancing at all. We are unaware of any publicly offered transactions that completely lack advancing.

THE IMPACT OF ADVANCING

The primary purpose of advancing is to smooth a pool's cash flow stream, but in doing so, advancing also shifts cash flows in time. With no advancing, a pool generates smaller monthly payments whenever homeowners fail to pay, followed by larger cash flows when homeowners cure or the property is liquidated. So advancing missed payments provides larger cash flows earlier in the deal, followed by smaller cash flows when the servicer reimburses itself, which, *ceteris paribus*, is a benefit because of the time value of money. On the other hand, advances increase pool losses because the proceeds from the liquidation of a loan are used first to repay all servicer advances, leaving a smaller recovery for the trust. Holding all else equal, this increases the loss suffered by the first loss bond, and increases the risk of loss to all other bondholders, particularly for the subordinates.

Ultimately, the impact of advancing on investors depends upon how the transaction is tranched. For transactions with internal credit support, advancing has a greater impact on the subordinated classes. Senior classes in modern senior-subordinated REMIC structures receive interest and principal first, so a lack of advancing will cause a payment delay to the senior class only if delinquency shortfalls exceed the total amount due the subordinate class.[4] Such events are rare in a two-class structure, although in a multi-class structure with many "skinny"

---

[4] Older grantor trust passthroughs first pay senior interest, then subordinate interest, followed by senior principal and then subordinate principal. In these structures interest and principal payments from homeowners retain their original character — principal cannot be used to pay interest and vice versa — so operationally the senior class is always paid first.

mezzanine classes, a lack of advancing would make payment delays to the mezzanine classes far more likely. Some subordinate bonds, on the other hand, would suffer payment delays without advancing, and as noted above, the subordinate bonds absorb most of the incremental risk caused by higher pool losses.

Advancing is an important benefit for transactions enhanced with only a pool policy. Without advancing, highly rated classes would experience payment delays, and could suffer significant payment delays. Note that the risk is twofold: (1) the investor would lose interest on delayed payments, a reinvestment risk, and (2) the maturity of the security would be extended by the payment delays, a duration risk.

Advancing has different effects in the case of CMO/REMIC cash flow tranching. Since a primary objective of these structures is to control maturity by sequentially allocating all pool principal to one tranche at a time, serious delinquencies coupled with no advancing could cause extension risk, particularly to the class receiving principal at the time of the delay. While the level of risk depends partly on the specific cash flow prioritization scheme used in the structure, a major portion of the risk also depends on how poorly the collateral is performing (i.e., the level of delinquencies) and on how quickly the collateral can be liquidated.

Exhibit 1: Advancing Policy

Issuers Typically Offering Mandatory Advancing
Prudential Home Mortgage Securities, Inc.
Residential Funding Corporation
SBMS, Inc. (Salomon Brothers Mortgage Securities, Inc.)
Housing Securities Inc.
Ryland (mandatory for subservicers, limited for Ryland as backup servicer)
Countrywide Funding Corp. (interest only on REOs)
Countrywide Mortgage Conduit, Inc. (interest only on REOs)
Merrill Lynch Prime First
Chase Mortgage Finance Corp.
PNC (will advance on non-recoverables if subordination is still intact)
Paine Webber
Sears
Chemical (will advance on non-recoverables if subordination is still intact)

Issuers That Have Transactions With Optional Advancing
ComFed (advancing has stopped on many transactions)
Citicorp Mortgage Securities Inc. (mandatory back-up advancing)
Republic Federal S&L Assn.
Glendale Federal S&L Assn.
California Federal S&L

Issuers That Have Transactions With Limited Advancing
Home Owners Federal S&L Assn.
Sandia
Columbia S&L Assn.

Issuers That Have Transactions With Partial Advancing
Imperial Savings Assn.

Exhibit 2: Investor Checklist for Advancing

Key questions

- Is there advancing?
  - Is the advancing mandatory, optional, limited, or partial?
  - What is the credit rating of the advancing party? Can it honor its commitment?

- Is there back-up advancing?
  - Is the backup advancing mandatory, optional, limited, or partial?
  - What is the credit rating of the advancing party? Can it honor its commitment?

Additional questions if advancing is optional, limited, partial, or non-existent

- What dollar volume of advancing is likely, given the collateral?
  - Are the loans from a fast or slow foreclosure state?
  - What level of delinquencies can be expected over the life of the pool? For example:
    - Does the pool have "A" quality credits or "B" & "C" quality credits?
    - Are the loans 30- or 15-year (15-year loans tend to have stronger borrowers)?
    - Are the loans fixed-rate or adjustable-rate? (ARMs tend to have weaker borrowers)?

- How will advancing interact with the credit and cash flow tranching?
  - How much cash is available from subordination to absorb a lack of advancing?
  - How sensitive is the tranche to extension risk if advancing fails?

In Georgia, for example, the foreclosure process is fast, typically three to six months, so delays will be minimal even if delinquencies are severe. In New Jersey and Massachusetts, on the other hand, the foreclosure process is slow, often taking two years. Because the impact of a delay in the receipt of principal can be funneled into just one tranche at a time, a lack of advancing could cause substantial extension risk to the currently amortizing tranche in a pool with high delinquencies (i.e., shortfalls beyond the amount that can be absorbed by subordinate classes) on collateral originated in slow foreclosure states.

Exhibit 2 provides an investor checklist for advancing.

Claims Adjustments

Between 10% to 20% of all nonagency mortgage-backed securities are enhanced with pool policies. Pool policies typically pay 100% of any loss due to borrower default, but only if the servicer "properly" manages the delinquency, which generally means that the servicer must manage the delinquency to minimize losses.[5] If the insurance company finds that the servicer has not properly managed the defaulted loan, it can reduce the amount of the claim paid.

---

[5] Standard pool policies cover 100% of each loan's loss up to the overall policy limit, with the exclusion of losses due to fraud, special hazard, or bankruptcy. A variation, called a modified pool policy, covers no more than 25% of each individual loan's balance. Note that in some foreclosures the insurance company manages the disposition of the property, in which case the problems that could cause a claim adjustment are mitigated.

Claims adjustments are common. For example, insurance companies have refused to pay for losses due to penalties imposed when the servicer failed to pay property taxes on time. Adjustments have also been made because of servicers' failure to notify the insurance company in a timely fashion of the default, in which case the adjustment is usually to deny coverage for interest during the period for which the notification was late. Other adjustments have been made because the servicer paid excessive legal fees or repair costs on liquidated REO property.

For investors, the key concern with claims adjustments is that most transactions enhanced with pool policies have no other form of credit support, so any loss due to an uncovered claim flows directly through to senior bondholders. Such losses have been small to date because most issuers and servicers have been willing to absorb claims adjustments in order to maintain the goodwill of investors, but no formal mechanism exists in servicing documents for covering these losses. This is an issue worth watching because it could become a problem in the future. In fact, in 1995 S&P placed 444 transactions on *CreditWatch* for possible downgrading because of this issue. To mitigate the chance of losses from claims adjustments, investors should look for pools managed by reputable servicers.

Note that losses from claims adjustments are a distinct, separate issue from the loss in yield that investors can suffer when pool policy claims are settled in the middle of the month. This is similar to the "compensating interest" issue in that pool policies pay for lost interest only up to the date of settlement. The balance of the month's interest is generally covered only if and to the extent that the transaction offers compensating interest for pool policy settlements.

Compensating Interest

Compensating interest is the payment by the servicer to investors of a full month's interest on loans for which only a partial month's interest has been collected because of prepayment during the month. Some transactions also offer compensating interest to cover the loss of interest from mid-month liquidations, mid-month pool policy settlements, and curtailments.

The financial impact of compensating interest, can be significant. Here we discuss only the variations of compensating interest offered in the nonagency market. Exhibit 3 lists typical compensating interest provisions for some issuers.

The most important distinction among issuers is that compensating interest is simply not offered on many transactions in the nonagency market. For example, virtually all RFC transactions before 1994 do not pay compensating interest. Similarly, GE transactions issued in the beginning of 1994 and earlier as well as some of the early SBMS Inc. transactions do not pay compensating interest.

Of the issuers that do offer compensating interest, none fully reimburses investors in all circumstances. Most issuers limit compensating interest to be no more than the master servicing fee. In some instances, only part of the master servicer fee is made available for compensating interest. Since the size of the master servicing fee varies substantially, a part of a large fee may actually be more than all of a small fee.

Exhibit 3: Compensating Interest Policies of Select Issuers

Issuer	Limits
Prudential	Cover full prepayments up to 20 bps master servicing fee on fixed rate products, and 25 bps on ARMs. Partial prepayment shortfalls borne by subordinate tranche. Starting with 1994-26, full prepayments received before the 17th of the month are passed through in current month without interest. Full prepayment after the 16th of the month receive compensating interest but are passed through in the following month.
RFC	Virtually never offered before 1994-13.
GE	None on transactions before 1994-26.
Countrywide Funding Corp.	Prepayments before the 15th of the month passed through in current month without interest; full prepayments after the middle of the month are covered up to half the master servicing fee (half of 25 bps=12.5 bps).
Countrywide Mortgage Conduit, Inc. (now called Independent National Mortgage Corporation)	Full and partial prepayments up to 12.5 bps of the master servicing fee.
Merrill Lynch Prime First	Full, partial, and liquidations covered up to master servicing fee (typically > 25 bps).
Citicorp Mortgage Securities Inc.	Full and partial prepayments up to servicing fee (typically 25 bps).
Sears	Full, partial, and pool policy settlements up to master servicing fee.
Paine Webber	Full and partial prepayments up to master servicing fee (typically +/- 29 bps).
Home Owners Federal S&L Association (older deals)	Full prepayments up to master servicing fee, but for senior class only.
Chase	Full prepayments, partial prepayments, and liquidations covered up to the master servicing fee.
Coast S&L (older deals)	None
Chemical	Full and partial prepayments up to the master servicing fee (fee varies)
Ryland	Full prepayments, partial prepayments, and liquidations covered up to the primary servicers' servicing fee (not master servicing fee)

Occasionally, subservicers must contribute all or part of their servicing fees to cover compensating interest, and some issuers allow their investment earnings on payments held for distribution (i.e., the float) to augment the amount available for compensating interest.

A second issue concerns what types of lost interest are covered. Whenever compensating interest is offered, prepayments in full are covered, but partial prepayments (i.e., curtailments) are often excluded. Payment of compensating interest on liquidations, mid-month pool policy settlements, and other loan terminations is uncommon.

A third aspect of compensating interest is how prepayment interest shortfalls (i.e., any partial month's interest that is not compensated for) are distributed among various cash flow tranches and credit classes. A common practice is to prorate any interest shortfall among various credit classes on the basis of the outstanding principal balance of each class, and then within each class, to distribute shortfalls to each cash flow tranche pro rata, according to the amount of accrued interest due.

Some issuers, such as Countrywide Mortgage Conduit, Inc., treat their excess master servicing spread as a class (whether securitized or not) and allow it to absorb a pro-rata share of any prepayment interest shortfall. Other issuers, such as Prudential, allocate prepayment interest shortfalls from full prepayments across all classes, but allocate shortfalls due to partial prepayments to only the subordinate classes. This effectively gives the senior tranches full protection up to the master servicing fee so long as the subordinate classes are in existence.

A last dimension of compensating interest concerns the timing of payments. Most issuers pass full prepayments on to investors in the month following receipt. Partial prepayments are usually passed through in the same month of receipt if received before the determination date (i.e., the date on which payment to certificate holders is calculated).

Countrywide Funding Corporation, some of the newer PNC transactions, and new Prudential transactions have introduced a variation allowing the passthrough of full prepayments received before the middle of the month in the same month received, but without interest from the first day of that month to the day of prepayment. This essentially causes the same 25-day delay an investor would get with full compensating interest. Prepayments received after the middle of the month for these issuers receive normal compensating interest, but the prepayments are passed through in the following month.

Exhibit 4 provides a checklist for investors to evaluate compensating interest.

Exhibit 4: Investor Checklist for Compensating Interest

- Is compensating interest offered?

- If compensating interest is offered, what types of loan terminations are covered:
    - full prepayments?
    - partial prepayments?
    - mid-month pool policy settlements?
    - other liquidations?

- What is the maximum amount available for compensating interest:
    - How large is the master servicing fee?
    - Are other funds available, such as float?
    - What percentage of the fee is made available?

- How are unsupported interest shortfalls allocated to investors?

- When are prepayments (or other terminations) passed through?

RATIO STRIPPING

Home mortgage rates vary substantially both over time and in different places, which makes it virtually impossible for issuers to assemble large, fixed-rate pools with homogeneous interest rates. Consequently, as individual loans prepay, the interest rate generated by the entire pool (i.e., the weighted average coupon or WAC of the pool) shifts, even if all the individual mortgages have fixed rates. To create large classes of securities with fixed interest rates, the pool cash flow must be modified.

A common method for creating a constant remittance rate is called *ratio stripping*. The procedure is quite simple. The issuer first picks the fixed remittance rate it wants to offer investors. Then, for all loans with mortgage rates above the chosen remittance rate, all interest above the remittance rate — called *stripped interest* — is assigned to someone else, typically either a separate tranche, a subservicer, or the master servicer. If the stripped interest is sold as a separate tranche, is often called a *WAC IO* (interest-only).

For loans with a mortgage rate below the remittance rate, on the other hand, the issuer "strips" off enough principal so that the interest on that loan in relation to the remaining principal equals the desired remittance rate. The right to receive the stripped principal is typically sold off as a separate tranche called a *WAC PO* (principal-only). The net result of this process is the creation of up to three classes; a large class that will always produce a fixed remittance rate, plus one or two strip classes. An example will illustrate this process.

Assume that a $30 million pool of new 30-year fixed-rate mortgages is composed of three groups of loans, each with a face value of $10,000,000. Assume the first group pays interest at 7%, the second at 8%, and the third at 9%; and assume that the current market rate is 8%. Suppose the issuer wants to offer as large a tranche as possible yielding 8%.

To accomplish this, 100 basis points of the interest stream from the 9% loans is stripped off and securitized as a separate WAC IO tranche, leaving a $10 million piece earning 8%. Similarly, $1.25 million face value of the principal from the 7% loans is securitized as a separate WAC PO tranche, leaving $8.75 million, which will effectively earn 8% because this remaining piece is entitled to 7% interest earned on the full $10 million ($7\% \times 10,000,000/8,750,000 = 8\%$). By stripping off the excess interest and principal, the issuer creates a $28.75 million tranche that will always generate an 8% interest rate regardless of prepayments, assuming full compensating interest, mandatory advancing, and no losses due to default.

This synthetic 8% pool, however is not the same as, and will not perform like, a real 8% pool. Similarly, the WAC IO and WAC PO stripped securities created by ratio stripping are different from pure IOs and POs created by separating the entire interest and principal streams as, for example, in the FNMA IO/PO program. The differences are caused by two factors: amortization and prepayments. Furthermore, the way prepayment rates are reported could mislead investors into overvaluing these securities.

Consider first the WAC IO. By definition, WAC IOs are created off relatively high-coupon collateral. High-coupon mortgages have two distinguishing characteristics: (1) they amortize more slowly than low-coupon mortgages, and (2) they prepay at a faster rate. The slower amortization means that WAC IOs will generate more cash flow each month (except for the first month) than pure IOs off any lower coupon pool as long as prepayments are comparable, because the balance on the underlying WAC IO pool is larger at any given time.

On the other hand, WAC IOs created out of relatively high-coupon collateral are likely to prepay faster than IOs based on current-coupon collateral. This means they will likely generate less cash flow, and should therefore be less valuable than "normal" IOs.

Usually the prepayment effect dominates. Unfortunately, however, prepayment rates are always reported for the entire pool. The pool contains a blend of low and high coupons, so the reported rate will understate the prepayment rate sustained on that portion of the pool underlying the WAC IO because the WAC IO is stripped off only the high-coupon mortgages. The risk is that investors could be misled into thinking that the collateral underlying the WAC IO is prepaying at a better (i.e., slower) rate than it really is.

At the same time, the WAC PO (like all POs) generates a fixed amount of aggregate cash flow over its life, regardless of amortization or prepayment rates. Only the timing of the cash flows is affected by these factors. By definition, WAC POs are created from relatively low-coupon mortgages. Lower-rate mortgages amortize faster than high-coupon mortgages. Since POs are similar to zero-coupon bonds purchased at a discount, the faster amortization makes the WAC PO more valuable than a "normal" PO stripped off an entire pool.

WAC POs created from relatively low-coupon collateral are, however, less likely to prepay than pure POs, which makes them less valuable. Usually, the prepayment effect will dominate. The amortization impact dominates only if rates rise sufficiently to choke off virtually all prepayments. As with the WAC IO, the reported pool prepayment rate will misstate (in this case, overstate) the prepayment rate experienced on the collateral subset underlying the WAC PO, so the investor could be misled into thinking the WAC PO is prepaying at a better (i.e., faster) rate than it really is.

Last, consider the large synthetic 8% tranche created by ratio stripping. Part of the tranche, $10 million, is composed of true 8% mortgages. These will amortize and prepay like any comparable group of 8% mortgages. Another $10 million (face value) of the collateral underlying the tranche will amortize and prepay like 9% mortgages, and the rest like 7% mortgages. Under most interest rate scenarios, the pool in this example will prepay more rapidly at first than a homogenous 8% pool as the 9% mortgages refinance, and more slowly later on as the 7% mortgages are likely to remain intact.

INTEREST SUBORDINATION AND PAYMENT DELAYS

The intent of interest subordination is to make a liquidation look like a prepayment from the senior bondhlders' point of view, which means that the senior bonds are to receive their pro rata share (based on their percentage ownership of the pool) of the *par* balance of each loan liquidated. In a non-interest subordinated structure, and particularly in the early years of a pool's life, this cannot be done because the typical liquidation does not generate enough recovery to pay the seniors their pro rata share. To make up for the shortfall, the interest subordination mechanism allows the trustee to reallocate all cash flows due to the subordinate bonds to the senior bonds (both interest and principal). Most transactions issued in the early 1990s were structured with some form of interest subordination. The mechanism fell out of use in 1994 after S&P announced that it would no longer rate deals with interest subordination.

The cash flow taken from subordinate classes is technically not lost; it is borrowed. Operationally, however, the pool may never generate enough cash in the future to repay the first-loss subordinate tranche. On the other hand, mezzanine classes are more likely to be repaid after some delay. A simple example will best illustrate how interest subordination works.

Assume a new transaction has three credit tranches: a $90 million senior class, a $5 million mezzanine class, and a $5 million first-loss class. Assume for simplicity that the pool is composed of $100 million of identical, new, 30-year fixed-rate mortgages with loan rates and net passthrough rates of 12% per year (1% per month). Assume that on the first payment date a loan with an original balance of $200,000 is liquidated, and assume that only $120,000 in cash is recovered from the disposition of the property net of all sales costs, generating an $80,000 loss to the pool.

Under most interest subordination programs, and assuming full advancing, the master servicer will attempt to pay the senior class $179,948.49 which is 90% of $199,942.77 (the original face value of the liquidated loan less $57.23 in principal already advanced). Most of the money ($120,000) is available from the liquidation proceeds. To make up the shortfall, the servicer will take interest and principal that would have been paid to the subordinated classes.

Each subordinate class would otherwise be entitled to 5% (their pro rata share) of 1% (the monthly interest rate) of $100 million (the principal balance), or $50,000 in interest, plus 5% of $28,612.60 (= $1,430.63) of scheduled principal repayments. Since this is more than enough to make up for the shortfall in liquidation proceeds, the senior class will receive a full, default-induced prepayment of $179,948.49, constructed as follows:

$120,000.00	liquidation sales proceeds
−2,057.23	advances that must be recouped by the servicer
+51,430.63	scheduled principal and interest due the first-loss class
+1,430.63	principal due the mezzanine class
+9,144.46	interest due to the mezzanine class
$179,948.49	reduction in senior balance

At the end of the month, the mezzanine class will still have a balance of $5 million, will receive the remaining $40,855.54 interest not taken for subordination, and will be owed $9,144.46 interest. The first-loss class will receive no cash flow and they will be owed $50,000 interest. In most transactions, the balance of the first-loss class will be adjusted such that the sum of all class balances equals the face amount of the pool. The senior class will receive a full interest payment of $900,000 and will have its balance reduced to:

$$\begin{array}{ccc} \text{Balance} & \text{Liquidation} & \text{Scheduled} \\ \text{beg. of Month} & \text{Principal} & \text{Principal} \\ \hline 90{,}000{,}000.00 & - \quad 179{,}948.49 & - \quad 0.9(28{,}612.60) \end{array} = 89{,}794{,}300.16$$

If the interest available from the subordinate classes had not been enough to cover the losses sustained, many transactions will take future months' subordinate interest until the senior class balance is reduced by its share of the full liquidated loan amount.

Interest taken from the first-loss class is rarely capitalized, which means that the delayed interest does not earn interest. Treatment of delayed interest on mezzanine classes varies. In Chase Mortgage Finance Corporation transactions, interest taken from the mezzanine class is capitalized, effectively earning interest on interest. Other issues (Prudential transactions, for example) typically do not capitalize mezzanine interest taken.

For the senior class, interest subordination is clearly a benefit. To the extent that losses are first absorbed by subordinate interest, the subordinate principal balance is higher, in theory offering greater protection against future losses. For the subordinate class, of course, interest subordination is bad. It forces subordinate classes to wait for their money, and exposes them to credit risk for a longer period of time, and few transactions pay the subordinate classes interest on delayed interest.

Despite the problems interest subordination can cause for junior classes, it was not an issue in the markets until late 1992. Up to that date, many first-loss tranches were held by the original issuers, and those that were sold were almost never rated, so they were typically purchased by investors with sufficient credit expertise to evaluate the potential loss due to payment delays.

In November 1992, Prudential started to resecuritize large groups of first-loss tranches it had been holding. In summer 1993, a mezzanine tranche in one of these resecuritizations experienced a payment delay because a sufficient number of the underlying subordinate securities had experienced payment delays.

The delay caught some investors off guard. In the world of corporate and municipal bonds, a delay in the receipt of interest or principal is an event of default; these issuers promise timely payments of interest and principal. In the world of agency (i.e., GNMA, FNMA, and FHLMC) mortgage-backed securities, a delay in the payment of *interest* is an event of default. With the exception of some FHLMC issues, a delay in the payment of principal is also an event of default, because the agencies also promise timely payments.

But in the world of nonagency mortgage-backed securities, payment delays (as opposed to a loss of principal or interest) are generally not an event of default because the transaction documents do not promise timely payment of interest and principal, but only the *ultimate* payment of interest and principal. The possibility of a delay is a fully disclosed feature of all interest subordination deals. Furthermore, as discussed earlier, virtually all other nonagency deals have some potential for delays because of advancing policies.

So interest subordination does pose some risk for junior tranches. For first-loss tranches, the impact can be substantial. For mezzanine classes, the expected timing, lower probability, short duration, and smaller size of any payment delays suggests that the impact on yield should be small.

It is worth noting that the effects of interest subordination go away over time. Consider a bond in which the senior percentage has been worked down to 30% of the deal. Since most recoveries from liquidations produce 60 to 70 cents on the dollar, it is unlikely that a liquidation will fail to produce enough cash to pay out the senior bond's entitlement. There will be no need for the senior bondholders to borrow the subordinate bondholders' cash flow. Furthermore, if the subordinate bond has built up an indebtedness from past borrowed interest, then the current subordinate bondholders at the time the need to borrow interest disappears will start to receive this extra cash flow on top of their normal principal and interest payments. This will effectively boost the yield on these bonds.

Exhibit 5 lists issues typically structured with and without subordination.

Exhibit 5: Issues Typically Structured With and Without Subordination

Issues typically structured with interest subordination
Prudential Home (prior to 1994-28)
Chase Mortgage Finance Corp.

Issue typically structured without interest subordination
Citibank, N.A.
Countrywide
GE Capital Mortgage Services, Inc.
Household Bank, f.s.b. (under SASI shelf)
Housing Securities, Inc.
Household Bank (under SASI shelf)
Paine Webber
PNC Mortgage Securities Corp.
RFC
Sears Mortgage Securities Corp.

CONCLUSION

In the nonagency mortgage-backed securities market, complexity is compounded by a lack of standardization. This chapter identifies some of the structural nuances that differentiate securities in the nonagency market, and explains their importance to the investor.

Not all structural issues are covered, and there are many non-structural issues that can have a significant impact on yield. The key lesson of this chapter is that the details of each transaction must be examined, because there is substantial variation across deals, and the differences can have a substantial impact on yield.

Chapter 4

A Risk-Return Framework for Evaluating Non-Investment-Grade Subordinated MBS

Laurie Goodman, Ph.D.
Managing Director
Mortgage Strategy
PaineWebber, Inc.

Linda Lowell
Senior Vice President
Mortgage Strategy
PaineWebber, Inc.

INTRODUCTION

Investors in non-investment-grade subordinated mortgage-backed securities (MBS) often focus exclusively on the delinquency history of an issuer in evaluating their holdings. In fact, however, this subordinated paper is more appropriately judged in a risk-return framework that looks at the price paid for the security in conjunction with its anticipated losses. Although delinquencies are highly correlated with mortgage defaults, they are not at all the same measure. But the attention given to delinquencies sometimes obscures the importance of other factors critical to analyzing this paper. Three we consider essential are: (1) the actual loss generated by each foreclosure (commonly known as the loss severity), (2) the timing of the defaults, and (3) the price paid for the security.

In this chapter, we demonstrate how to incorporate both defaults and loss severities into a yield analysis of non-investment-grade subordinated MBS. We compare relative value between different subordinated classes and take a close look at how home-price appreciation affects loss severity. We show that during a period of even very modest increases in housing prices, subordinated mortgage paper can withstand a substantial increase in defaults and still maintain yield.

Delinquencies Do Not Equate to Losses
On Credit Tranches

An important point mortgage-backed securities investors should bear in mind in evaluating subordinated issues: The vulnerability to *loss* of credit support tranches is not simply a function of delinquencies. Most mortgage delinquencies are cured before the loan is foreclosed. For example, in the fourth quarter of 1995, the MBA reported that 30-day delinquencies amounted to 2.15% of conventional loans; in the following quarter, the first quarter of 1996, 60-day delinquencies were a much smaller 0.42% of conventional loans. This makes sense. Mortgage borrowers have powerful incentives to avoid foreclosure: The home provides shelter and is the center of family life; in addition, equity in the home represents, if not the largest, a major investment for most households. Along with the down payment and regular amortization, home-price appreciation builds equity; borrowers in extreme circumstances who have equity to protect are far more likely to sell the house rather than allow the servicer to foreclose. (We are ignoring the value, as well, of good credit to most households.)

Owner's equity also serves as a buffer against loss to the investor if the loan does go into foreclosure. As a result, not every foreclosure need result in a loss. Once the servicer liquidates the property, proceeds are applied first to satisfy amounts owed to the servicer for advances, servicing compensation, foreclosure expenses and so forth; then to any accrued interest payable but not advanced to bondholders; and third to the outstanding principal balance of the loan. The realized loss is the remaining loan balance. Loss severity expresses the loss as a fraction or percentage of the outstanding loan amount. (Alternatively, we can speak of "recovery rate," or the fraction that is recovered. A loss severity of 20% would be equivalent to a recovery rate of 80%.)

Clearly, loss severity is a function (1) of the length of time from default to liquidation — this variable largely determines the amount of the servicers' advances and other foreclosure expenses — and (2) of the owner's equity. Owner's equity, in turn, is a function of the original down payment, or original LTV ratio, and the amount of home-price appreciation. The higher the rate of home-price appreciation, the lower the severity of any loss.

We can make this concrete with a simple example. Assume a borrower defaults on a remaining balance of $85,000 on a house originally purchased at $100,000, and the servicer incurs expenses of $17,000 — including advances to investors — in the course of foreclosing and liquidating the property (in other words, expenses amount to 20% of the remaining loan amount, an assumption slightly more conservative than the mid-point by state[1]). To break even, then, liquidation proceeds must amount to $102,000. If the property's market value remains unchanged, a loss of $2,000 will be realized. That equates to a loss sever-

---

[1] Clearly this is an artificial example for A-quality whole loan collateral. Private mortgage insurance (PMI) is required on loans with LTVs greater than 80%.

ity of 2%. On the other hand, if the house has appreciated by 5%, liquidation proceeds are $105,000 and no loss is realized. We would argue, in fact, that the homeowner would endeavor to liquidate (and thus prepay) before foreclosure to limit his own loss. Any home-price *depreciation,* on the other hand, would clearly *increase* the loss severity. For instance, 5% depreciation would result in a loss of $7,000, or a loss severity of 7%.

As a matter of fact, most housing markets performed very well in 1995, even in California and the Northeast, where jumbo conventional loans are concentrated. Exhibit 1 details, by state, rates of home-price appreciation as calculated by Freddie Mac from the joint Freddie Mac-FNMA Repeat Sales database for the period extending from first quarter 1995 to first quarter 1996.[2] For the United States as a whole, home prices appreciated 5.5% over the period. Moreover, the increases were very broad-based, ranging from a low of 3.8% in California to 10.4% in Utah. Although home prices appreciated more slowly in California and the Northeast, it is clear that, even in these regions, the rate of home-price appreciation for this period was on the order of 4.5%.

Exhibit 1: House Price Appreciation Rates — 1995:1 to 1996:1

---

[2] The figure was provided to us by FHLMC. It originally appeared in *SMM: A Freddie Mac Quarterly,* 13:2 (May 1996), p. 7.

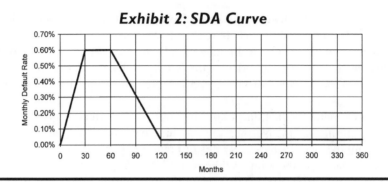

Exhibit 2: SDA Curve

SDA: Incorporating Defaults and Loss Severities into Yield Analysis

Clearly, the yield on lower rated or unrated credit tranches is subject to a number of factors, including default rates, loss severity, and the timing of the losses. To reflect these various parameters in cash-flow analyses of credit tranches in a consistent, standardized manner, the Public Securities Association adopted the Standard Default Assumption (SDA) in May 1993. The SDA provides for monthly default rates to rise (in linear fashion, by even steps) from 0 to a peak of 0.6% per month (annual rate) over the first 30 months. They remain at that peak rate for the next 30 months (month 30 to month 60). After month 60, defaults decline to a "tail" value of 0.03% per month over the next 60 months (month 61 to month 120). They remain constant at the tail value until the last month of the remaining life of the pool, when the default rate drops to 0. Default rates for a specific cash-flow calculation are expressed as a multiple of SDA — 245% SDA, for example — just as with the PSA prepayment standard. Exhibit 2, depicts 100% SDA. (Most readers familiar with the credit analysis of mortgage pools will recognize that this pattern is roughly analogous to the default assumptions made by the rating agencies. The agencies have determined that at least 80% of defaults occur in the first seven years of the life of a mortgage loan. In Moody's model, losses are concentrated in years 4 and 5; S&P assumes that defaults occur in the second through fourth years of the transaction.)

The SDA methodology requires that three additional factors be specified in order to incorporate loss-experience assumptions into cash-flow analysis: loss severity, time to liquidation, and whether principal and interest are advanced to the subordinate in question. Clearly, regardless of the assumptions made about these inputs, the number of defaults registered as losses will also depend on the prepayment experience of the pool (given a constant rate of default, if no loans prepay, the absolute number of loans). The SDA was intended to be used in conjunction with the PSA's prepayment standard. For example, assuming a loss severity of 20%, 12 months to liquidation, and advancing at 200% PSA, 100% SDA generates 2.5% cumulative defaults on new 30-year mortgages with a 7.5% gross WAC. Cumulative losses equate to cumulative defaults multiplied by the loss severity. For example, if 2.5% of the pool defaults, with a severity of 20%, then the loss rate is 0.5% ($0.025 \times 0.2 = 0.005$).

Exhibit 3: Details of Subordinate Tranches
in a Representative Structure
($500mm, 7.5% Coupon, 200% PSA)

Tranche	Rating	Amount ($mm)	Percent of Deal	Pricing
Senior	AAA	471.21	94.25	
Mezz	AA	11.26	2.25	
B1	A	6.26	1.25	
B2	BBB	5.51	1.10	
B3	BB	2.75	0.55	+500/10yr., Px = 71:10
B4	B	1.00	0.20	+1000/10yr., Px = 53:14
B5	Unrated	2.00	0.40	Px = 24:00
Total		500.00	100.00	

SDA Analysis of an Example Deal

To assess the relative impact on subordinate tranches of delinquency rates on the one hand and recovery rates on the other, we structured the simple deal shown in Exhibit 3. As can be seen, the senior bonds make up 94.25% of the deal and subordinate tranches the remaining 5.75%. The three investment-grade classes, mezzanine, B1 and B2, comprise 4.6% of the deal. The non-investment-grade classes B3, B4, and B5 — double-B, single-B, and unrated, respectively — comprise the remaining 1.15% of the deal. Tranche B3 is assumed to be priced at 500 basis points over the 10-year, corresponding to a dollar price of 71:10. (Pricing levels are as of June 26, 1996.) Class B4 is priced at 1,000 basis points over the 10-year, corresponding to a dollar price of 53:14. Class B5, the unrated first-loss piece, is assumed to be offered at a dollar price of 24:00. Note that the market prices assume no defaults and are based on the pricing speed of 200% PSA, for loans with a 7.90% gross WAC.

Yield/cumulative loss profiles for classes B3, B4 and B5, given various prepayment (PSA) and default (SDA) assumptions, are shown in Exhibits 4, 5, and 6 respectively. When applying the SDA, we assume a recovery rate of 80%, equivalent to a loss severity of 20%. (Later, we will examine the effect of different recovery rates.) We also assume a period of 12 months between default and liquidation, commonly referred to as the "lag." When a borrower is seriously delinquent on a loan (typically more than 90 days), the servicer will move to foreclose. At this point, the borrower gives over the deed, or the property is repossessed; this is the event that defines a *default*. The legal foreclosure process differs state by state; it lasts from three to six months in some states to over two years in others, after which the servicer can liquidate the property. The common reasonable assumption is of a 1-year lag between default and liquidation. A longer lag would raise the yield on the subordinated tranches, a shorter lag would lower it. We also assume that the servicer continues to advance delinquent principal and interest payments through foreclosure. In nearly all deals, this is the case.

Exhibit 4: Tranche B3 Default/Yield Matrix*
Price: 71.31

% PSA	Percent SDA									
	0	20	50	75	100	150	200	250	300	350
100										
Yield	11.46	11.47	11.52	11.28	10.65	5.58	−9.14	−16.43	−22.32	−27.34
Cumulative Loss	0.00	0.12	0.31	0.46	0.62	0.92	1.21	1.51	1.79	2.07
150										
Yield	11.71	11.72	11.76	11.78	11.61	7.52	−5.98	−14.27	−20.36	−25.53
Cumulative Loss	0.00	0.11	0.28	0.42	0.55	0.83	1.09	1.36	1.62	1.87
200										
Yield	11.93	11.94	11.97	12.00	12.01	9.04	2.38	−11.89	−18.31	−23.65
Cumulative Loss	0.00	0.10	0.25	0.38	0.50	0.75	0.99	1.23	1.46	1.70
250										
Yield	12.12	12.14	12.16	12.19	12.21	10.58	5.28	−9.07	−16.12	−21.67
Cumulative Loss	0.00	0.09	0.23	0.34	0.46	0.68	0.90	1.12	1.33	1.54
300										
Yield	12.30	12.31	12.33	12.36	12.37	11.71	7.33	−0.45	−13.72	−19.59
Cumulative Loss	0.00	0.08	0.21	0.31	0.42	0.62	0.82	1.02	1.22	1.41

* Recovery rate of 80%, lag of 12 months.

Exhibit 5: Tranche B4 Default/Yield Matrix*
Price: 53.44

% PSA	Percent SDA									
	0	20	50	75	100	150	200	250	300	350
100										
Yield	16.09	16.11	15.27	12.78	1.54	−10.06	−18.57	−25.31	−30.77	−35.35
Cumulative Loss	0.00	0.12	0.31	0.46	0.62	0.92	1.21	1.51	1.79	2.07
150										
Yield	16.54	16.56	16.63	14.42	5.93	−8.38	−17.13	−24.11	−29.78	−34.60
Cumulative Loss	0.00	0.11	0.28	0.42	0.55	0.83	1.09	1.36	1.62	1.87
200										
Yield	16.93	16.95	17.02	16.22	10.58	−6.58	−15.65	−22.82	−28.69	−33.63
Cumulative Loss	0.00	0.10	0.25	0.38	0.50	0.75	0.99	1.23	1.46	1.70
250										
Yield	17.27	17.30	17.34	17.40	13.33	−4.59	−14.05	−21.44	−27.46	−32.62
Cumulative Loss	0.00	0.09	0.23	0.34	0.46	0.68	0.90	1.12	1.33	1.54
300										
Yield	17.58	17.60	17.65	17.70	16.25	−2.28	−12.36	−20.00	−26.21	−31.43
Cumulative Loss	0.00	0.08	0.21	0.31	0.42	0.62	0.82	1.02	1.22	1.41

* Recovery rate of 80%, lag of 12 months.

Exhibit 6: Tranche B5 Default/Yield Matrix*
Price: 24.00

% PSA	Percent SDA									
	0	20	50	75	100	150	200	250	300	350
100										
Yield	36.26	32.89	24.72	16.18	9.88	0.13	−7.17	13.00	−17.86	−22.12
Cumulative Loss	0.00	0.12	0.31	0.46	0.62	0.92	1.21	1.51	1.79	2.07
150										
Yield	36.98	33.89	25.81	17.36	10.83	0.85	−6.65	−12.60	−17.57	−21.83
Cumulative Loss	0.00	0.11	0.28	0.42	0.55	0.83	1.09	1.36	1.62	1.87
200										
Yield	37.63	34.70	27.54	18.89	11.87	1.62	−6.07	−12.18	−17.25	−21.57
Cumulative Loss	0.00	0.10	0.25	0.38	0.50	0.75	0.99	1.23	1.46	1.70
250										
Yield	38.20	35.43	29.94	21.13	13.01	2.44	−5.42	−11.66	−16.90	−21.30
Cumulative Loss	0.00	0.09	0.23	0.34	0.46	0.68	0.90	1.12	1.33	1.54
300										
Yield	38.72	36.10	31.10	23.60	14.31	3.35	−4.72	−11.12	−16.41	−20.99
Cumulative Loss	0.00	0.08	0.21	0.31	0.42	0.62	0.82	1.02	1.22	1.41

* Recovery rate of 80%, lag of 12 months.

An SDA yield table is a matrix, with varying PSA assumptions on one dimension (the vertical on Exhibits 4, 5, and 6) and SDA assumptions on the other. For every PSA/SDA combination, two numbers appear in the cell. The top number is the yield and the bottom number is the cumulative losses to final maturity on the collateral, given the various assumptions. Thus, at 100% SDA and 200% PSA, Class B3 yields 12.01%, reflecting cumulative losses of 0.50%. Note the yield is approximately the same in this case as that of 0% SDA because the principal of this tranche is not hit. Instead, lower-rated tranches B4 and B5, representing 0.60% of the deal absorb the losses.[3]

Now let us look at what happens when defaults do begin to erode the principal of B3. At 150% SDA and 200% PSA, B3 yields 9.04%, given cumulative losses to the collateral of 0.75%, which eat into its principal. At 200% PSA and 200% SDA, the bond yields 2.38%, with cumulative losses of 0.99%, cutting deep into its principal. That is, cumulative losses of 0.99% take out more than half of B3's share of the principal; the first 0.60% would come from B4 and B5 and the remaining 0.39% from B3, which comprises 0.55% of the total deal. Thus, 70.8% (0.39/0.55) of B3's principal would be lost and only 29.1% would eventually be returned to investors.

There are several characteristics of SDA analysis investors should note. First, the faster the collateral prepays, the higher the yield for any given SDA

[3] Actually, the yield will be marginally higher at 100% SDA, 12.01%, than at 0% SDA, 11.93%, because if there are no principal losses on the B3 piece, the cash flows will be received a bit earlier at higher SDAs.

default rate. For example, at 100% SDA and 200% PSA, Class B3 yields 12.01%. At the same SDA and 300% PSA, the bond yields 12.37%. In general, the higher the prepayment rate for a given default frequency, the lower the cumulative defaults and hence losses. This occurs because faster prepayments reduce the principal balance faster; so that the same default rate is applied to smaller remaining balances to generate smaller dollar amounts of defaults.

Second, investors should notice how well the yields hold up as the bonds begin to absorb losses. For example, there is no combination of speeds between 100% and 300% PSA and defaults between 0% SDA and 100% SDA that can eliminate the 0.60% of the support below B3 (noted in Exhibit 3) and result in actual principal losses to B3. In the 150% SDA scenarios, the losses are high enough to take out a portion of B3's principal. As we pointed out above, at 200% SDA, B3 loses more than half its principal return.

What might surprise a number of readers is that despite the negative yield in scenarios in which a large portion or all of the tranche is eliminated by losses, the total rate of return may still be close to zero or positive. In the case of B3, at 200% SDA and 200% PSA, the total rate of return is 2.38%. The explanation lies in the timing of the losses. The bond pays a coupon of 7.5%. However, the coupon is based on the nominal, or face amount. The actual price of the security is 71.312 (71:10) so that the current yield on the security is 10.52%.[4] In other words, the investor earns 10.52% current yield on the bond until losses are realized (plus the difference between 71:10 and par as any principal is returned by regular amortization).

Timing of losses is even more significant in the case of B5, the first-loss piece (Exhibit 6). At 100% SDA and 200% PSA, cumulative loses of 0.50% on the collateral wipe out the bond's principal. However, the yield is still 11.87%. In effect, the investors earn a 7.5% coupon on the nominal amount, but that is returned against a purchase price of 24. The total return would reflect the fact that, while the entire principal was lost, the coupon payments still were more than sufficient to deliver a positive return. This can be seen intuitively by considering that, if the collateral has no losses for 3.2 years, while the bond pays a coupon of 7.5%, and then the tranche is wiped out, the return is effectively zero (7.5/24).

Relative Value Relationships
Between the Subordinated Classes

The relationship *between* the classes is quite interesting, as well, particularly in relative value terms. Exhibit 7 compares yields as a function of SDA, assuming 200% PSA, for Classes B3, B4 and B5. (The 200% PSA rows from Exhibits 4, 5, and 6, respectively). The first thing that stands out in the figure is that Class B3, rated BB, and in the third-loss position, has, generally speaking, less yield variability than B5, the unrated first-loss piece; when defaults are low, B3 yields less, when defaults are high, B3 yields more. Investors should conclude that if they

---

[4] Current yield is coupon/price.

expect losses to be lower, the unrated first-loss piece will perform better. In other words, at low SDAs, the first-loss piece is obviously more attractive. As the SDAs increase, Class B3 starts to look better than the first-loss piece; given prepayments speeds of 200% PSA, the crossover point is between 75% and 100% SDA. (Note that at very high default rates, there is another crossover point, between 250% and 300% SDA. At this point, cumulative loses are such that Classes B3, B4, and B5 are all wiped out. No investor who expected this kind of losses would consider this paper.) Ultimately, making a choice between B3 and B5 depends on what investors believe the cumulative losses will be. If lower SDAs are anticipated, the first-loss piece is preferable; if there is more uncertainty about the prospects for default, B3 is the better choice.

Interestingly, as Exhibit 7 demonstrates, Class B4, the B-rated second-loss piece looks extremely unattractive relative to the credit tranches on either side of it on the loss ladder. It is always dominated by B5 (assuming 200% PSA). It is easy to see intuitively why this is the least attractive bond of the three. It has little more protection than the first-loss piece. The first-loss piece absorbs the first 40 basis points of losses and this one the next 20 basis points. However, the dollar price of this piece is more than twice that of the first-loss piece — 53:14 versus 24:00. Quite frankly, we think that, at that price, investors are paying a great deal for little additional protection.

Investors who buy single-B paper — and who don't want to buy unrated paper — instead, may wish to consider a combination of unrated paper and BB-paper. A portfolio invested in 50% unrated paper and 50% in BB-rated paper actually provides more loss protection, a lower dollar price ((1/2 (71:10 + 24) = 47:21 versus 53:14 on the B4 tranche) and a considerably higher yield in all scenarios than the B-rated bonds. This comparison is illustrated in Exhibit 8. While a yield of 1,000 basis points over the 10-year may sound like a lot of yield, using small amounts of unrated paper in combination with more highly rated paper is a better strategy. During the time we were evaluating these securities, we did not believe that B-rated subordinates could tighten any further without the unrated paper doing even better.

Exhibit 7: Yield Profile of Subordinated Bonds

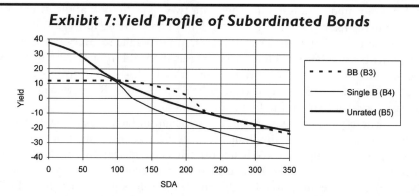

Exhibit 8: Yield Profile on Combination of BB and Unrated Tranche versus Single B

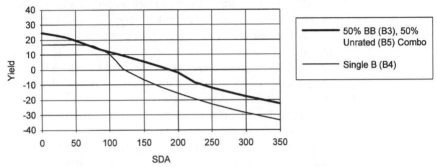

Exhibit 9: Yield Profile of BB (B3) Bond

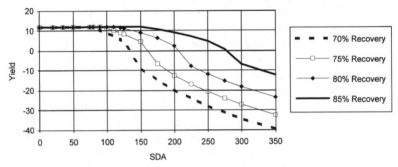

The Effect of Home-Price Appreciation

Assumptions about the recovery rate, or loss severity, have a major impact on the yield profiles of credit tranches. Home-price appreciation, as we have discussed, raises the recovery rate. Exhibits 9, 10, and 11 show the effects of various recovery rates on yield at 200% PSA for various SDA assumptions on Classes B3, B4, and B5 from our model transaction. There are two ways to look at the effect of an increase in the recovery rate. We can first look at the increase in yield as the recovery rate increases. For example, at 100% SDA, raising the recovery rate from 75% to 80% on B3 (the BB-rated tranche) increases the yield from 11.22% to 12.01%. The same change in recovery rate raises tranche B4's yield from −1.14% to 10.57%, and raises B5's yield from 6.05% to 11.86%. Readers can read the increase for other SDAs off Exhibits 9, 10, and 11.

These yield changes are quite significant. In fact, even if these increases in the recovery rate were simultaneously associated with increases in default rates, the investor might still be better off. This can be seen by simply drawing a horizontal line in Exhibits 9, 10, and 11 from one recovery curve to the next. We illustrate this procedure using B5, the unrated first-loss piece, in Exhibit 11. We initially pick a point, such as 100% SDA on the 70% recovery curve. The corresponding yield is 1.17%. We then drawn a horizontal line at this yield through the other recovery curves. From this, we determine, that, if the recovery rate were to improve to 75%, the SDA could be 121% in order to yield the same 1.17%. That is, this "breakeven SDA" is the intersection of the horizontal line in Exhibit 11 and the 75% recovery curve. Thus, raising the recovery rate from 70% to 75% raises the "break-even SDA" to 121% — a sizable increase. Raising the recovery rate from 75% to 80% means the collateral can default at a rate of 153% SDA and still yield the same 1.17%. These breakeven SDAs are shown in Exhibit 12 for all three tranches.

It is clear from the Exhibit 12 that, for given recovery rates, the breakeven SDAs are relatively similar across the three non-investment-grade tranches. In particular, an increase in the recovery rate on B5 from 75% to 80% would increase the breakeven SDA from 121% to 153%, similar to B3, where the breakeven SDA increases from 121% to 157%, and B4, where the break-even SDA increases from 121% to 154%.

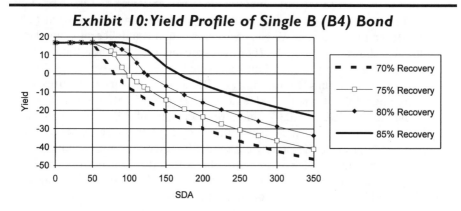

Exhibit 10: Yield Profile of Single B (B4) Bond

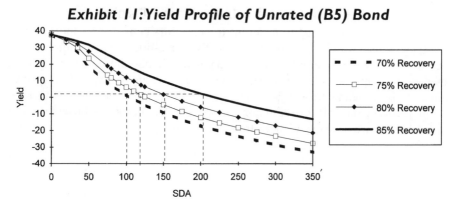

Exhibit 11: Yield Profile of Unrated (B5) Bond

Exhibit 12: Breakeven Yield SDAs at Various Recovery Rates

Bond	Yield (%)	SDA	Recovery Rate (%)	Cumulative Defaults
BB (B3)	8.98	100	70	2.51%
BB (B3)	8.98	121	75	3.03%
BB (B3)	8.98	157	80	3.91%
BB (B3)	8.98	184	85	4.56%
Single B (B4)	−7.40	100	70	2.51%
Single B (B4)	−7.40	121	75	3.03%
Single B (B4)	−7.40	154	80	3.83%
Single B (B4)	−7.40	211	85	5.21%
Unrated (B5)	1.17	100	70	2.51%
Unrated (B5)	1.17	121	75	3.03%
Unrated (B5)	1.17	153	80	3.81%
Unrated (B5)	1.17	207	85	5.12%

For most investors, saying the break-even SDA can increase from 121% to 153% doesn't mean much. We can easily translate this number into cumulative defaults, also shown in Exhibit 12. (For each recovery rate, we know the yield and cumulative losses. Cumulative defaults are simply the cumulative losses divided by the loss severity.) Thus, for example, on B5, a 70% recovery rate corresponds to a cumulative default rate of 2.51%, a recovery rate of 75% corresponds to a cumulative default rate of 3.03%, and a recovery rate of 80% corresponds to a cumulative default rate of 3.81%. The critical point is how much higher a default or loss rate can produce the same yield with a 5% increase in the recovery rate. Our point is that home-price appreciation has lifted the recovery rate, and this effect on non-investment credit tranches is far greater than any increase in delinquencies could have — especially on highest quality collateral.

Consequences for Investment Decisions

To recap, there is one important point for investors considering subordinated mortgage tranches to bear in mind. Nationally, home-price appreciation has been healthy. Even in those areas of the country where jumbo mortgages represent a more significant share of the market, home prices have enjoyed moderate appreciation. A rise in home prices raises the recovery rate. And even a modest increase in the recovery rate will offset major hikes in the default rate — hikes far larger than anything we have experienced thus far.

Chapter 5

Understanding Shifting Interest Subordination

Manus J. Clancy
Vice President
The Trepp Group

Michael Constantino, III
Assistant Vice President
The Trepp Group

INTRODUCTION

During the early years of the evolution of the collateralized mortgage obligation market, the challenge of securitizing pools of residential mortgages focused on providing greater average life stability to investors eager to reduce prepayment exposure. In fact, since the majority of securitizations of residential mortgages involved the packaging of government agency mortgage-backed securities, issuers and underwriters rarely had to concern themselves with credit risk at that time. Those issuers that did securitize "whole loans" (those not guaranteed by FNMA, FHLMC, or GNMA) used a potpourri of bond structures to mitigate credit risk. Letters of credit, pool insurance, corporate guarantees, and reserve funds were all used periodically to reduce credit risk from these issues.

Over time, the agency CMO and whole loan CMO markets became both more competitive and, not surprisingly, more efficient. In the pursuit of alleviating call risk and creating tranches that were appealing to investors, agency CMOs became increasingly complex. Seemingly, with each new issue came more intricate principal repayment rules and diverse bond types, all aimed at meeting the average life demands of the marketplace and providing greater prepayment certainty. Likewise, the whole loan CMO market evolved. Gradually, the whole loan market moved away from third-party guarantees and gave way to bond structures that could "stand alone." The result was the senior/subordinate bond structure combined with the shifting interest mechanism. This structure sought to combine the tranching common in agency CMOs with the creation of senior tranches, mezzanine tranches, and subordinate tranches to isolate and manage the risks arising from mortgage defaults and delinquencies. Today, the vast majority of whole loan CMOs utilize the senior/subordinate structure with shifting interest.

The introduction of "credit tranching" to bond structures added substantially to the complexity of securitization (as if the 128-tranche agency CMO was not complex enough). As mentioned earlier, the securitization of whole loans relies on the creation of senior and subordinate classes within the bond structure. Often these classes are paid principal and interest simultaneously over time. The percentage of principal each subordination level receives changes periodically based upon the credit history of the loans backing the CMO causing the subordination percentages to "shift" over time (hence "shifting interest"). This chapter will examine the intricacies of whole loan CMO senior/subordinate bond structures focusing primarily on the shifting interest rules of such structures. First, the differences between bond structures of agency CMOs and whole loan CMOs will be reviewed in greater detail. Second, shifting interest itself will be explained more thoroughly. Third, the various methods that are utilized to determine how principal is paid each period will be discussed. Finally, it will be demonstrated that the presence of these rules can have a significant effect on the yield and average life of a security.

COMPARING BOND STRUCTURES

Clearly, there are substantial differences between the bond structures that have emerged from issues backed by agency MBS and those of deals backed by whole loans. For agency CMOs in which prepayment or "call" risk has been the only concern, the structures have relied entirely on "horizontal" slicing and dicing: carving out different tranche types to meet certain average life demands by the marketplace and providing more prepayment stability. This involves the use of payment rules to allocate principal in different directions over time. The result has often been 30 or 40 tranche issues with PACs, TACs, VADMs, accrual bonds, and so forth. For traditional CMOs backed by whole loans in which both prepayment risk and credit risk are concerns, issuers must combine horizontal tranching to alleviate call risk with "vertical" credit support structuring. This has meant carving out senior tranches, mezzanine tranches, and subordinate tranches to isolate the risks arising from mortgage defaults and delinquencies. Exhibits 1 and 2 illustrate the differences between agency CMOs and whole loan CMOs.

Exhibit 1: Principal Distribution for Agency CMOs

A-1 PAC	A-2 PAC	A-3 PAC	A-4 PAC	A-5 COMPANION / A-6 COMPANION	A-7 COMPANION	A-4	A-3	A-2	A-1

Exhibit 2: Principal Distribution for Whole Loan CMOs

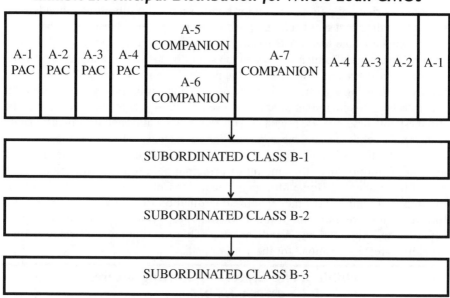

DEFINING SHIFTING INTEREST

The vast majority of whole loan CMOs that have been issued since 1992 utilize the senior/subordinate structure with shifting interest. The protection afforded to the senior classes of bonds against losses arising from mortgage defaults in these structures is the result of three features of the bond structure: (1) each period the senior bonds are given their allocation of principal and interest before any distributions are made to the subordinate bonds, (2) the losses from the liquidation of defaulted mortgage loans are first allocated to the subordinate bonds until they are retired before any losses are allocated to the senior bonds, and (3) the constantly changing allocation of prepayments and certain liquidation proceeds is disproportionately weighted toward the senior classes in the early years of the issue. The focus of this chapter is on the third component which will be referred to henceforth as shifting interest, so called because the disproportionate allocation of principal causes senior and subordinate percentages to shift over time.

The purpose of shifting interest is to manage, over the life of the CMO, the amount of subordinate bonds that remain outstanding each period to "absorb" losses and protect the senior bonds. The weaker the credit history of the loans backing a whole loan CMO, the greater the level of subordination that will be required to remain outstanding over time. Conversely the stronger the credit history, the lower the subordination requirement each period. In addition, because historical default rates are lower for newly originated mortgages, the level of protection that is needed at closing is usually less than the level of protection that is needed as a mortgage pool seasons. The percentage of subordination is managed by manipulating the amount of principal paid to the senior bonds versus the subordinate bonds each period according to a set of rules outlined in the prospectus. Generally, if the collateral backing a whole loan CMO has a weak credit history, these rules will direct a greater percentage of principal flows to the senior bonds so that a higher subordination percentage remains. Alternatively, the payment rules will "reward" strong credit history by allowing a greater percentage of the principal flows to go to the subordinate tranches. It is important to note that even for those whole loan CMOs with the strongest collateral history, principal will generally be allocated disproportionately to the senior bonds, causing the subordination percentage to grow over time.

The following examples demonstrate the effects on the subordination level of "manipulating" the amount of principal paid to the senior bonds each period for Prudential Home Mortgage Securities Company, Inc., Series 1995-7. Exhibits 3, 4, and 5 show the level of subordination (the "subordinate interest") for the first 15 years of the issue at various prepayment speeds assuming no defaults. As Exhibits 4 and 5 indicate, the subordination level grows over time providing greater "cushion" for the senior bonds.

Exhibit 3: The Effects of Shifting Interest
0% PSA, No Defaults

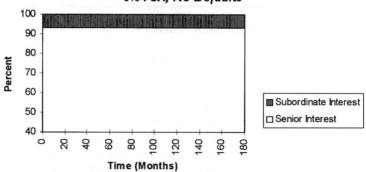

Exhibit 4: The Effects of Shifting Interest
250% PSA, No Defaults

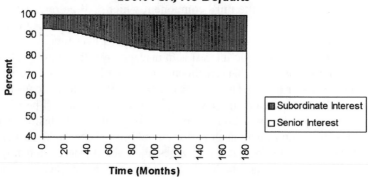

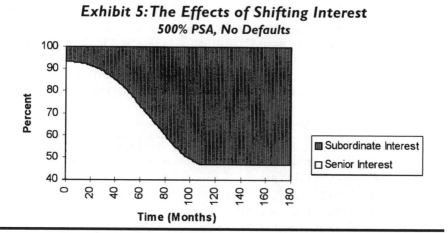

Exhibit 5: The Effects of Shifting Interest
500% PSA, No Defaults

Time (Months)

The percentages of the aggregate principal balance of the mortgage loans represented by the senior and subordinate bonds will, in all likelihood, fluctuate over time for two reasons. First, losses that are incurred on defaulted mortgages are allocated to the subordinate bonds prior to being allocated to the senior bonds. Because losses are allocated to the subordinate bonds first, the outstanding balance of the subordinate bonds is reduced thereby decreasing the subordinate percentage and increasing the senior percentage. Second, prepayments and other unscheduled payments on the mortgages are disproportionately allocated to the senior bonds for a defined period of time. Because prepayments and certain recoveries are disproportionately allocated to the senior bonds, the amortization of the senior bonds is accelerated thereby decreasing the senior percentage and increasing the subordinate percentage. Although the rules that govern the allocation of both losses and prepayments each alter the percentages of the classes, shifting interest refers to the mechanism that determines the ratio of the distributions of prepayments and other unscheduled payments of principal to the senior and subordinate bonds.

COMPARING PRINCIPAL ALLOCATION FROM ISSUE TO ISSUE

Payments of principal that are available to pay bonds are usually classified in the following categories: (1) scheduled principal, (2) prepayment principal, (3) recovery principal of liquidated loans, and (4) repurchase principal (the difference in the principal balance of loans that were repurchased due to substitution). In the principal payment rules of whole loan CMOs, the percentage of each category that is allocated to the senior bonds can differ significantly. The four categories listed above are all "cash flow items" (i.e., amounts that are part of available cash). In addition to these amounts, the senior bonds are sometimes allocated a portion of the "loss" amount. The loss amount is the difference between the balance of a defaulted loan and the amount recovered through the sale of the property which is categorized as "recovery principal." Clearly this is not a cash flow item. To the extent the loss amount is distributed as principal to the senior bonds, it must come from cash that would otherwise be paid to the subordinate bonds.

The following examples demonstrate two of the most common sets of principal distribution rules that are found in whole loan CMO bond structures:

Prudential Home Mortgage Securities Company, Inc., Series 1993-39

Principal Type	Percentage Allocated to Senior Bonds
1. Scheduled Principal	Senior Percentage (or "Senior Interest")
2. Prepayment Principal (Full and Partial)	Senior Prepayment Percentage
3. Repurchase Principal	Senior Prepayment Percentage
4. Recovery Principal	Senior Prepayment Percentage
5. Realized Losses (Principal Portion)	Senior Prepayment Percentage

Residential Funding Mortgage Securities, Inc., Series 1994-S13

Principal Type	Percentage Allocated to Senior Bonds
1. Scheduled Principal	Senior Percentage
2. Prepayment Principal (Full and Partial)	Senior Accelerated Distribution Percentage
3. Repurchase Principal	Senior Percentage
4. The lesser of	
a) Recovery Principal	Senior Accelerated Distribution Percentage
or	
b) Recovery Principal plus Realized Losses (Principal Portion)	Senior Percentage

The senior percentage is defined as the ratio of the balance of the senior bonds to the balance of the mortgage loans. This is also referred to in some transactions as the senior interest. If the mortgage loans experience neither prepayments nor defaults, the senior bonds will be paid their proportionate share of principal and the initial percentages that were evidenced by the senior and subordinate bonds at deal closing will remain constant throughout the life of the issue. In other words, since only scheduled principal payments are made by the mortgagors and because the senior bonds are entitled to only their pro rata share of these amounts, the senior percentage will never change. Exhibit 3 illustrates this point.

The senior prepayment percentage (or the senior accelerated distribution percentage as it is referred to in Residential 1994-S13) is defined as the senior percentage plus the product of (1) a declining percentage (the "shifting interest vector" for purposes of this chapter) and (2) the subordinate percentage, where the subordinate percentage is equal to the difference between 100% and the senior percentage. By allocating a portion (the shifting interest vector) of the subordinate bonds' pro rata share of certain types of principal to the senior classes, the senior classes will amortize more quickly and the subordinate interest in the mortgage loans will increase as a result.

The shifting interest vector normally equals 100% at deal closing and reduces over time according to a schedule of percentages specified in the prospectus (the vector specified in the prospectus will be referred to as the "base vector" — it will be described in greater detail below). In other words, in the early years of the transaction, the senior bonds will receive 100% of certain principal receipts that would otherwise go to the subordinate tranches if the deal was paying *pari passu*. As mentioned above, the presence of losses decreases the protection afforded to the senior classes by reducing the subordinate bonds, while the presence of prepayments has the effect of offsetting those losses by increasing the protection afforded to the senior classes by increasing the subordinate percentage. Normally, the base vector percentages diminish over time until reaching a point at which the senior and subordinate bonds begin paying pro rata based on their outstanding balances. However, because the future performance of a given portfolio of mortgage loans cannot be known with certainty at issuance, performance "triggers" are built into the principal payment rules which, if activated, will cause the shifting interest vector to vary from the base vector if certain criteria are not satisfied. These triggers will be referred to henceforth as shifting interest tests. In such cases, the shifting interest vector percentages may not reduce and the senior bonds will continue to receive a disproportionately high share of principal.

The analysis of how the shifting interest vector can vary from the base vector and the effect that changes to the shifting interest vector have on the performance of the bonds is one of the most difficult, as well as one of the most widely overlooked, challenges in analyzing whole loan CMOs. There is a multitude of different types of triggers as well as a host of differing methods for calculating each trigger. Furthermore, each type of test has a different effect on the shifting interest vector and can alter the yield on a given bond significantly. The following section will examine the structural nuances of shifting interest.

Base Vector

To help clarify the analysis of this topic, the term "base vector" will be used to distinguish the shifting interest percentages that are established in the prospectus at issuance from that which is calculated each period. The actual vector of percentages that is used each period for the purpose of calculating the principal distribution amount is referred to as the "shifting interest vector." It is important to remember that the base vector and the shifting interest vector will be identical each period unless the loans backing an issue fail to meet certain criteria. In such cases the shifting interest vector will vary from the base vector.

There are two base vectors that are commonly used in the payment rules of whole loan CMOs, one for issues backed by fixed-rate mortgages and one for issues backed by adjustable-rate mortgages. These vectors are shown below.

Issues Collateralized with Fixed Rate Mortgages		Issues Collateralized with Adjustable Rate Mortgages	
Base Vector	Period After Issuance	Base Vector	Period After Issuance
100%	First Five Years	100%	First Ten Years
70%	Sixth Year	70%	Eleventh Year
60%	Seventh Year	60%	Twelfth Year
40%	Eighth Year	40%	Thirteenth Year
20%	Ninth Year	20%	Fourteenth Year
0%	Thereafter	0%	Thereafter

It is important to add that the base vector for issues that are collateralized by loans that are not fully amortizing (i.e., balloon loans) always equals 100%. Moreover, some of these issues collateralized by balloon mortgages treat the balloon amount as scheduled principal while others treat it as a prepayment of principal.

Recall that these figures represent the percentage of the subordinate bonds' pro rata share of certain principal flows that will be redirected to the senior bonds. For example, assume that an issue is in its sixth year and is backed by fixed-rate mortgages. At closing, the ratio of senior to subordinate bonds was 94% to 6%. Assume further that losses have been modest and prepayments have been relatively high and as a result, the current ratio of senior bonds to subordinate bonds is 78% to 22%. In a particular month in the sixth year, scheduled principal flows equal $200,000 and prepayments total $500,000. In this example, assuming no triggers have been activated that would cause the shifting interest vector to differ from the base vector, the senior bonds would receive the following:

$$78\% \text{ of } \$200,000 \qquad \text{or} \quad \$156,000$$
$$\text{plus}$$
$$78\% \text{ of } \$500,000 \qquad \text{or} \quad \$390,000$$
$$\text{plus}$$
$$70\% \text{ of } 22\% \text{ of } \$500,000 \quad \text{or} \quad \$77,000$$

In the example above, 78% represents the senior percentage, 22% represents the subordinate percentage, and 70% represents the value of the shifting interest vector in the sixth year.

SHIFTING INTEREST TESTS

The base vector will be applicable for as long as the performance of the mortgage pool satisfies certain criteria. This criteria is evaluated through the use of a web of complex tests that are required to be completed at the beginning of each payment period before principal is distributed. Although there are many different tests that are used in the whole loan CMO universe of transactions, the majority of them can fit into three broad categories: balance tests, principal loss tests, and delinquency tests.

Balance Tests

The *balance test* is the most universally applied and homogeneous of all the shifting interest tests. Balance tests directly evaluate the current subordinate interest available to protect the senior bonds. In a deal with shifting interest, losses are allocated to the subordinate bonds first and thus have the effect of reducing the subordinate interest or percentage. However, if prepayment activity has existed at a sufficiently high rate, the senior interest may decrease since prepayments are allocated to the senior bonds in an accelerated manner. Even though losses may have taken place, the senior bonds may have more protection in percentage terms than they did at closing. The purpose of the balance test is to evaluate this ongoing relationship.

For example, assume that at bond issuance a deal has the following characteristics: the aggregate principal balance of the mortgage pool is $100 million, the principal balance of the senior bonds is $95.5 million, and the principal balance of the subordinate bonds is $4.5 million. If, at the end of five years, $19.5 million in principal has been prepaid and $500,000 of losses has been allocated to the bonds, are the senior bonds more at risk than they were at bond issuance? In other words, do the remaining senior bonds have as much protection (in percentage terms) as they did at issuance?

The balance test compares the current senior interest to the senior interest at closing. In the example above, the senior interest or senior percentage equals 95.5% at closing. If the test reveals that the current senior percentage is greater than 95.5%, it will evidence the fact that losses on the portfolio are outweighing the benefits to the senior bonds of prepayments. In such an event, the balance test trigger will be activated and the shifting interest vector will recalibrate to give the senior bonds an even larger share of certain principal revenues than called for in the base vector.

In our example, the principal balance of the senior bonds at the end of the fifth year is $76 million (assuming all principal paid, $19.5 million, is "prepayment" principal) and the principal balance of the subordinate bonds is $4 million. The senior percentage is 95% while the subordinate percentage equals 5%. Therefore, the subordinate interest has increased from 4.5% to 5% meaning the protection afforded to the senior bonds has increased as a percentage of the issue. In this case, the balance test is not triggered and the shifting interest vector will continue to mirror the base vector. If losses on the pool had been $1.5 million instead of $500,000, the senior and subordinate bonds would have been $76 million and $3 million, respectively. Thus, the senior percentage would have been approximately 96.2% and the test would have "failed." In such an event, the shifting interest vector would no longer mirror the base vector. Instead of reducing from 100% to

70%, this hypothetical issue would see its shifting interest vector continue to give 100% of all prepayments to the senior bonds.

Another type of balance test compares the current subordinate percentage with a different threshold percentage. Although the majority of issues have tests that only seek to identify a poor credit history for the pool, this balance test is intended to signify a strong history. If the current subordinate interest is greater than a multiple (usually two) of the subordinate interest at issuance, the balance test trigger will be activated and the shifting interest vector will begin to differ from the base vector. However, unlike the change to the base vector that would accompany a senior percentage trigger event, the change to the base vector that would accompany a subordinate percentage trigger event would increase the principal flows to the subordinate bonds rather than decrease them.

Principal Loss Tests

As a mortgage pool seasons, it will inevitably experience unscheduled events such as prepayments and liquidations, the latter being the focus of *principal loss tests*. Loans can be classified as either *performing*, those currently remitting scheduled payments each month, or *non-performing*, those that are not currently remitting scheduled payments each month. A loan that is delinquent may return to performing status. However, a delinquent loan that never begins remitting payments will enter the foreclosure process and will ultimately be liquidated.

The majority of whole loan CMOs are structured with liquidity provisions that require the servicer to make advances of scheduled principal and interest. Therefore, during the delinquency and foreclosure period, the cash flows to the bondholders are not interrupted. Upon the sale of a foreclosed property, the liquidation proceeds minus foreclosure costs and servicer reimbursements will most likely be less than the principal balance of the mortgage loan and thus will affect the cash flow to the bondholders. This amount represents the total loss on the property and, depending on the deal structure, is a close approximation of the loss that will be allocated to the bonds. A principal loss test trigger will be activated if the historical dollar amount of principal losses on the collateral exceeds certain threshold levels. Such an event would result in the shifting interest vector being altered.

There are two basic types of principal loss tests: a fixed structure and a variable structure. In a fixed structure, the principal losses of the mortgage pool that have been experienced up to and including the current period are compared with a fixed threshold balance that is defined in the prospectus. The fixed threshold balance is usually equal to the product of a given percentage and the initial principal balance of the subordinate bonds. Using the earlier example in which the principal balance of the subordinate bonds is $4,500,000, assume the principal loss test establishes that the shifting interest vector will be altered if losses exceed 10% of the original subordinate bond balance. In this case, the trigger event of the principal loss test will be activated as soon as cumulative losses exceed $450,000 (i.e., 10% of $4,500,000). If losses are less than $450,000, the event will not be triggered and the shifting interest vector will mirror the base vector (unless some other test has been triggered). If losses exceed $450,000, the trigger event will be activated and the two vectors will diverge.

In a variable structure, the principal losses of the mortgage pool that have been experienced up to and including the current period are compared with a threshold balance that increases over time. The computation of the balance is the same as under the fixed structure, however, the given percentage varies as the issue seasons. Using the previous example and a variable structure, the trigger event of the principal loss test will be activated as soon as cumulative losses exceed the threshold balance for the corresponding period. For instance, if cumulative losses equal $1,400,000 in the 65th period (the sixth year), the trigger event of the principal loss test will be activated as illustrated in the table below.

Loss Percentage	Period After Issuance	Threshold Balance
30%	Sixth Year	$1,350,000
35%	Seventh Year	$1,575,000
40%	Eighth Year	$1,800,000
45%	Ninth Year	$2,025,000
50%	Thereafter	$2,250,000

Delinquency Tests

Delinquency tests are by far the most complicated and have the most variations of all shifting interest tests. Delinquency tests, like principal loss tests, are created to evaluate the credit history of the mortgage pool. However, delinquency tests serve a purpose that is slightly different than principal loss tests. Principal loss tests track the severity of losses from the date of issuance through the current period, which provides the context for evaluating the entire history of the mortgage pool. In contrast, delinquency tests aim to evaluate the recent payment history of the mortgage pool (which, in turn, can be used to predict how the pool will behave in the future). Because a significant number of loans that are delinquent will ultimately be liquidated, the monitoring of delinquency levels helps to estimate the number of liquidations that will take place in the near future.

Unlike the two tests described earlier which are very similar from issue to issue, delinquency tests differ from one issue to the next. Although there are numerous variations in these tests, the basic structure is relatively consistent. Most delinquency tests compare, over a certain period of time, the average percentage of loans in the mortgage pool that have a specified delinquency status to a threshold percentage stated in the prospectus.

The basic structure of a typical delinquency test consists of four components:

1. Period of time tested
2. Severity of delinquency (*delinquency range*)
3. Delinquency calculation (*delinquency level*)
4. Threshold percentage

The period of time that is considered "recent" delinquency history is the most widely altered component from issue to issue. The "window" that is tested can vary from three months to a year. For instance, a prospectus may state that the test will fail if, during the previous six months, the average aggregate balance of loans that have been delinquent for 60 days or more each month exceeds 2% of the average aggregate loan balance during that same six month period. Alternatively, some issues use the same parameters but test a 12-month period.

Another component that is varied is the severity of the loan delinquencies that are tested. The delinquency severity refers to the length of time since a particular loan has last remitted a scheduled payment. For example, one delinquency test may consider, as a starting point, all loans that have been delinquent for 60 days or more. That subset, which would include loans 60, 90, 120 days, etc. delinquent, is the delinquency range. The most common delinquency range includes loans that are 60 days delinquent and beyond. However, 30-day and 90-day severities have been used as starting points for these calculations in certain issues. (Some variations of this test exclude delinquent loans that are classified as REO while others include loans that are classified as REO.)

The first component designates the period of time that will be analyzed while the second component designates the subset of loans that will be analyzed. The third component designates the formula that will be used to calculate the percentage that will be compared to the threshold percentage. Because the test compares the current delinquency level to a threshold percentage, the calculation must convert real numbers into percentage form.

The first step of the calculation is aggregating the balance (or payment) of the loans that are within the delinquency range each period (which will be used in the numerator), and aggregating the balance (or payment) of all loans each period (which will be used in the denominator). The ratio that will be calculated represents the *delinquency level* for each period. As alluded to above, there are two methods that are used to calculate this ratio: a balance method and a payment method. The *balance method* uses the sum of the individual balances of those loans that meet the specified criteria (delinquency range and period of time tested) for each month. For example, if the test is written to compare the average balance of loans that were delinquent for 60 days or more during the previous 12 months, the aggregate balance of loans that meet that criteria in each of the 12 months will be used in the numerator and the aggregate balance of all loans in each of the 12 months will be used in the denominator. In contrast, the *payment method* uses the sum of the individual scheduled payments of those loans that meet the criteria that would have been received on each loan had they not been delinquent and the sum of the individual scheduled payments of all loans.

Because the test evaluates a period of time rather than a single period, there is a delinquency level for each period. Delinquency tests compare the average delinquency level during this period of time to the threshold percentage. To determine the average delinquency level that will be compared to the threshold level, there are two methods. For example, suppose that the period of time tested is three months (i.e., the delinquency range includes loans that are delinquent for 60 days or more), and the balances of all loans and delinquent loans are as follows:

Time	Aggregate Balance of All Loans	Balance of Loans 60 days or More Delinquent
−3	$100,000,000	$9,000,000
−2	$98,000,000	$1,850,000
−1	$93,000,000	$1,000,000

Assuming that the balance method is utilized, some issues specify that the calculation should be as follows:

$$\frac{(d_3 + d_2 + d_1)}{3} \div \frac{(b_3 + b_2 + b_1)}{3}$$

$$\left[\frac{9,000,000 + 1,850,000 + 1,000,000}{3}\right]$$

$$\div \left[\frac{100,000,000 + 98,000,000 + 93,000,000}{3}\right] = 4.07\%$$

In contrast, other issues state that the calculation should be as follows:

$$\left[\frac{d_3}{b_3} + \frac{d_2}{b_2} + \frac{d_1}{b_1}\right] \div 3$$

$$\left[\frac{9,000,000}{100,000,000} + \frac{1,850,000}{98,000,000} + \frac{1,000,000}{93,000,000}\right] \div 3 = 3.99\%$$

Assuming that the threshold delinquency percentage equals 4.0%, it would be important to perform the calculation using the correct method. One method calculates the average delinquency level to be greater than 4% (which would cause the shifting interest vector to change) while the other method calculates the average delinquency level to be less than 4% (in which case there would be no change).

How the Shifting Interest Vector Changes

It has been mentioned throughout the chapter that the base vector is established at closing as a set of declining percentages that are used for the calculation of principal payment distributions. If a trigger from any performance test or group of performance tests is activated, the shifting interest vector will deviate from the base vector. The question is, how does it deviate? Each test or group of performance tests specifies how the shifting interest vector will change if the particular test fails. These changes are not necessarily the same from test to test. For instance, the triggering of one type of test may cause the shifting interest vector to "revert" to the original base vector value of 100%. The balance test, which is the most widely used test, normally uses this method. Other tests, by comparison, will hold the shifting interest vector as well as the senior prepayment percentage constant at the value that was registered in the period the trigger event of a test was first activated rather than reducing the percentages as scheduled in the base vector. The delinquency test and the principal loss test normally use this method.

EFFECT OF SHIFTING INTEREST TESTS ON YIELDS AND AVERAGE LIVES

A decline in the credit quality of a portfolio of loans collateralizing a whole loan CMO and the consequent triggering of shifting interest performance tests can have a dramatic effect on the yield and average life of a security. Residential Funding Mortgage Securities I, 94-S13 illustrates this effect. Cash flows were projected for this deal at issuance using summary collateral and prepayment speeds of 0%, 250%, and 500% PSA. Exhibit 6 shows the yields and average lives for Tranches A-4 and B-1 at those three speeds *assuming no shifting interest tests are triggered.*

Cash flows were then projected a second time for the same tranches using the same prepayment speeds. In the second projection, however, it was assumed that the shifting interest vector never reduces below 100%. The results of the second scenario can be seen in Exhibit 7.

In the first example, since no tests were triggered, the actual shifting interest vector mimicked the base vector (i.e., 100%-70%-60%-40%-20%-0%). In the second hypothetical example, the shifting interest vector remained locked at 100% and the subordinate tranches were not entitled to any of the prepayment principal received on the loans until all senior bonds (with the exception of the PO tranche) were retired. The results indicate sharp average life differences between the two examples, particularly at 250 PSA. Specifically, the average life on Tranche A-4 diminishes by over a year while the average life on Tranche B-1 increases by over six years.

Exhibit 6: Residential Funding, 94-513 Assuming No Shifting Interest Tests are Triggered

Tranche	Average Lives			Yields		
Prepayment Speed	0	250	500	0	250	500
A-4						
Price 98	23.63	10.88	5.89	7.18	7.27	7.39
B-1						
Price 94	20.04	11.91	9.63	7.69	7.87	7.97

Exhibit 7: Residential Funding, 94-513 Assuming the Shifting Interest Vector Never Falls below 100%

Tranche	Average Lives			Yields		
Prepayment Speed	0	250	500	0	250	500
A-4						
Price 98	23.63	9.76	5.51	7.18	7.28	7.40
B-1						
Price 94	20.04	18.14	10.79	7.69	7.71	7.91

As one would expect, the results assuming no prepayments are identical from one example to the next. Although the vector itself changes between the two scenarios, each vector is being multiplied by zero (the amount of prepayments) and, therefore, there is no effect.

To further illustrate the potential for average life and yield differences, cash flows were projected for the same issue using actual collateral, a settlement date of August 25, 1996, a prepayment speed assumption of 200% PSA, and a default speed assumption of 500% SDA with a loss severity of 50%. Prepayments have the effect of decreasing the senior interest and liquidations have the effect of increasing the senior interest. If the performance tests were ignored, prepayments and certain unscheduled collections of principal would be distributed according to the base vector. However, if the performance tests were modeled, the trigger of senior percentage test (balance test) would be activated and 100% of prepayments and other unscheduled collections of principal would be distributed to the senior classes as opposed to the percentages set by the base vector. The following table displays the difference in yield that would result if the performance tests were ignored versus if the performance tests were modeled.

Class	Price	Yield Modeling Performance Tests	Yield Ignoring Performance Tests
M-1	93.67	1.33	−0.47

CONCLUSION

Throughout the history of the CMO market, clearly the lion's share of research has been devoted to determining principal repayment expectations. The process of determining the value of a CMO security has evolved from simply choosing a prepayment speed based on historical data to the development of complex interest rate generators, prepayment models, and OAS. Not surprisingly, relatively little effort has been devoted to the understanding of how modest changes to the credit history of a set of loans backing a whole loan CMO can alter a security's cash flow. However, as demonstrated earlier, this element of analyzing whole loan

CMOs cannot be overlooked. Significant yield and average life differences can result from changes to the credit characteristics of a portfolio of loans collateralizing a whole loan CMO using a senior/subordinate bond structure once the intricate shifting interest rules are taken into consideration.

Chapter 6

Accounting for Whole Loans and Securitized Products by Investors

Cathy Hansen
Consultant
Frank J. Fabozzi Associates

INTRODUCTION

This chapter is to provide a profile of accounting guidelines set by the Financial Accounting Standards Board (FASB) for non-agency whole loans. Generally accepted accounting practices will be discussed for both securitized whole loan deals as well as non-securitized "packages" of loans. Issues to be explored include balance sheet placement, breakdown of cash flows into income and return of capital, and the FASB Statements and bulletins that support the methods.

The FASB has issued several Statements, exposure drafts, and reports that cover the topic of accounting for securities and/or the purchase of loans. Securitized, structured non-agency whole loans are viewed as a security by the FASB and are therefore identical in treatment to an agency issued CMO. Non-structured and non-securitized pools of loans purchased are treated as loans rather than securities and have a different set of accounting methodology. Applicable FASB documents include FASB Statement No. 91, "Accounting for Non-refundable Fees and Costs Associated with Originating or Acquiring Loans and Initial Costs of Leases," released in 1986; the Emerging Issues Task Force Issue 89-4, "Accounting for a Purchased Investment in a Collateralized Mortgage Obligation Instrument or in a Mortgage-Backed Interest-Only Certificate," released in 1989; and FASB Statement No. 115, "Accounting for Certain Investments in Debt and Equity Securities," released in 1993. FASB Statement 115 supersedes FASB Statement No. 12, "Accounting for Certain Marketable Securities" and alters other previous FASB pronouncements. FASB Statement No. 65 covers accounting practices for the purchase of pools of loans, unstructured and unsecuritized. A FASB special report was issued in February, 1996 on *Net Present Value Based Measurement*. It contains several proposals for changes to accounting methods that would affect both agency and non-agency products. The project is currently taking responses to the special report. All of these publications are available for purchase directly from the publications department of the FASB.

FASB 115

We will first look at the securitized non-agency whole loan. The initial accounting subject upon the purchase of this instrument is where to place it on the balance sheet. As previously stated, it is viewed as a security and is carried in the securities section of the asset side of the balance sheet. FASB 115 requires further classification. There are three categories from which to choose to place the security. They are: (1) Held to Maturity (HTM), (2) Available for Sale (AFS) and (3) Held for Trading (HFT). Valuation methods are determined by the decision of which category to place the security. The decision is to be substantially permanent; however, FASB allowed some leniency in moving bonds from one category to another under some circumstances in the initial period of conforming with FASB 115.

A security is classified as Held to Maturity (HTM) if the investor has the ability and the intent to hold it to maturity. Securities in this category use the amortized cost valuation method.

A security that is acquired for the purpose of earning short-term trading profits from market movements is classified as Held for Trading (HFT). Securities held in Held for Trading are valued based upon current market values, or the mark to market method. Unrealized profits and losses from market changes for this class are included in earnings and reflected on the income statement in the current period.

Securities classified as Available for Sale (AFS) are also valued by current market value. Securities are held in this category if they are not purchased for short-term trading and the investor does not have the ability and/or the intent to hold the security to maturity. Unrealized gains and losses for securities in this class are to be excluded from earnings until realized and are reported in a separate component of shareholders equity. Once the gains or losses become realized they are reported on the income statement.

There are two valuation methods for investments subject to FASB 115: (1) amortized cost and (2) mark to market. Securities in the HTM category may be carried at amortized cost. Those held in either AFS or HFT categories must be priced according to current market values at the end of each accounting period, typically monthly. Movement of a security from one category to another may cause the entire portfolio to be reclassified to a position requiring all securities to be marked to market.

Interest income, including amortization of premiums and discounts at purchase, are to be included in earnings for all three categories. No changes for calculation of premium/discount amortization and interest income are implemented by the issue of FASB 115.

Transfers between categories may call into question the investor's intent and ability to hold securities to maturity and subject the entire portfolio holding to mark to market accounting. Two conditions exist under which securities may be sold from the HTM category. Both conditions consider the security as matured. The first condition is that the maturity date is so near that interest rate risk is no longer a pricing factor. "So near" is defined in FASB 115 as within three months. The second condition is that a substantial portion of the principal outstanding at acquisition date has been returned prior to the sale of the security. "Substantial" is defined in FASB 115 as at least 85% of the par value purchased, not 85% of original par value of the security.

There are circumstances under which transfers are allowed without calling intent and ability into question. The circumstances are:

1. Significant deterioration in the issuer's creditworthiness.
2. Changes in tax law that reduces or eliminates tax-exempt status of interest on the security (but not a change in tax law that revises the marginal tax rates applicable to interest income.)
3. Major business combination or major disposition (such as sale of a segment) that necessitates the sale or transfer of held-to-maturity securities to maintain the enterprise's existing interest rate risk position or credit risk policy.
4. Change in statutory or regulatory requirements significantly modifying either what constitutes a permissible investment or the maximum level of investments in certain kinds of securities, thereby causing an enterprise to dispose of a held-to-maturity security.
5. Significant increase by the regulator in the industry's capital requirements.
6. Significant increase in the risk weights of debt securities used for regulatory risk-based capital purposes.[1]

There can be significant differences in income calculated from the amortized cost method to the mark-to-market method even though the actual cash flow is unchanged. Exhibit 1 shows the net effects on the balance sheet and income statement of the two valuation methods over a 5-year period. The exhibit displays a security with a par value of $1 million and a 7% coupon. For this illustration we assume the security is purchased at par.

Using the amortized cost method, the value of a security reported in the balance sheet reflects an adjustment to the acquisition cost only for the amortization of premiums and discounts. For a security acquired at a premium, the adjustment decreases the reported value; the amortization of a discount increases the reported value. If the security is held to the maturity date, the amortized cost method would report a balance sheet value equal to the par value at that date. In our example, the security is purchased at par and there is no adjustment.

[1] FASB 115, p. 3.

Exhibit 1: The Effect of Accounting Method on Income Statement and Balance Sheet

	Market Value	Held to Maturity Amortized Cost	Trading Mark to Market	Available for Sale Mark to Market
Assets				
Acquisition	$1,000,000.00	$1,000,000.00	$1,000,000.00	$1,000,000.00
Year End-1	$1,003,125.00	$1,000,000.00	$1,003,125.00	$1,003,125.00
Year End-2	$950,000.00	$1,000,000.00	$950,000.00	$950,000.00
Year End-3	$1,011,250.00	$1,000,000.00	$1,011,250.00	$1,011,250.00
Year End-4	$998,750.00	$1,000,000.00	$998,750.00	$998,750.00
Year End-5	$1,032,500.00	$1,000,000.00	$1,032,500.00	$1,032,500.00
Income Statement				
Year End-1		$70,000.00	$73,125.00	$70,000.00
Year End-2		$70,000.00	$16,875.00	$70,000.00
Year End-3		$70,000.00	$131,250.00	$70,000.00
Year End-4		$70,000.00	$57,500.00	$70,000.00
Year End-5		$70,000.00	$103,750.00	$70,000.00
Total		$350,000.00	$382,500.00	$350,000.00
Shareholder's Equity				
Year End-1		$0.00	$0.00	$3,125.00
Year End-2		$0.00	$0.00	($53,125.00)
Year End-3		$0.00	$0.00	$61,250.00
Year End-4		$0.00	$0.00	($12,500.00)
Year End-5		$0.00	$0.00	$33,750.00
Total		$0.00	$0.00	$32,500.00

The income statement in this method reflects the coupon interest adjusted for the amortization. Amortization of a premium reduces income while accretion of discounts increase income. Given the absence of a premium or discount in our exhibit, income is equal to coupon payments.

Using the mark-to-market method, the balance sheet reported value of a security is the current accounting period market value. Gains or losses are reflected in the income statement for securities classified as Held for Trading, or in shareholder's equity for those in Available for sale. Simply stated, gains or losses on securities that are in the Held for Trading category are immediately recognized on the income statement. Gains or losses on securities in the Available for Sale category are considered unrealized and carried in shareholder's equity until those gains or losses become realized.

ACCOUNTING FOR PERIODIC CASH FLOWS

Non-agency whole-loan CMOs produce periodic principal and interest payments to investors as do their agency issued counterparts. Typically those cash flows are received monthly. Some are quarterly while others are deferred until preceding classes in their structure have been retired. In any of these instances a portion of amounts received is income and another is to be applied to the asset as a return of investment. Only in the case of a security purchased at par is the amount of interest received income and the amount of principal received return of capital. Adjustments have to be made for securities purchased above or below par.

FASB No. 91 was issued in 1986. It was drafted to address accounting methods for non-refundable fees on loans originated or purchased and costs of leases. FASB 91 states that income is to be calculated based upon a constant effective yield. This yield is the internal rate of return of future cash flows projected from an assumption of prepayments. This calculated yield will determine the amount of income earned on the basis of each periods outstanding dollars invested. The remaining cash flows for the period are considered return of capital and are returned to the asset itself. FASB 91 further states that should actual prepayments differ from estimates, the yield is to be recalculated, and net investment amounts, as well as income, are to be adjusted to the amount that would have existed had the new yield been applied since acquisition.

There are three components necessary for FASB 91's interest method of calculating income (1) cost, (2) projected cash flow stream, and (3) yield. Upon the purchase of the security the steps for this exercise are as follows. A prepayment estimate is determined and cash flows are generated based upon the structure of the deal. Using original dollars invested as cost an internal rate of return (IRR) is calculated from the projected cash flows.

The beginning book value of the security is its cost at purchase. Income for each period is calculated by multiplying the derived yield (IRR) by the book value of the security for the current period. The difference between the periodic cash flow received and calculated income is considered the period's return of capital. Each period the book value is reduced by the amount of capital returned by crediting the asset, until the original cash investment is totally returned to the investor as the security is retired.

The same results can be achieved by determining the net present value of the projected cash flows for each period using the calculated yield as the discount rate. The change in each period's net present value (NPV) is the amount of capital returned to the investment. Remaining cash flow for the period is income, both interest and amortization. Each of the methods described will produce the same amount for income and return of capital given that prepayment estimates and discount rates are unchanged.

Simply, all monies received for a security in excess of the original cost of the investment are the investors earnings or income. Exhibits 2 and 3 show accounting schedules for both a premium and discount security purchase.

The book price of a security is the relationship between the investor's book value and the current par value of the security. All book prices will move from original cost toward par, except in the case of an interest-only class, whose unit cost will move toward zero.

Exhibit 2: FASB 91 — Interest Method — Discount — Year 1

Par Value:	1,000,000	Purchase Price:	96.5000
Coupon:	8.00%	Cost:	$967,222.22
Months to Maturity:	60	Yield (IRR):	9.81%
Prepayment Estimate:	250 PSA		

Total Principal Year 1	292,484.70	Total Return of Capital Year 1	279,538.14
Total Interest Year 1	68,881.45	Total Income Year 1	81,828.02
Total Cash Flow Year 1	361,366.15	Total Cash Flow Year 1	361,366.15

	Principal Balance	Principal	8.00% Interest	Total Cash Flows	Beginning Book Value	Income at 9.81%	Return of Capital	Ending Book Value	Book Price
	(1)	(2)	(3)	(4)	(5)	(6)	(7)	(8)	(9)
1	1,000,000.00	26,704.44	6,666.67	33,371.11	967,222.22	7,903.44	25,467.66	941,754.56	96.759
2	973,295.56	26,259.55	6,488.64	32,748.19	941,754.56	7,695.34	25,052.85	916,701.71	96.797
3	947,036.00	25,821.20	6,313.57	32,134.77	916,701.71	7,490.63	24,644.15	892,057.56	96.835
4	921,214.80	25,389.30	6,141.43	31,530.73	892,057.56	7,289.25	24,241.48	867,816.08	96.873
5	895,825.51	24,963.75	5,972.17	30,935.92	867,816.08	7,091.17	23,844.75	843,971.33	96.912
6	870,861.76	24,544.47	5,805.75	30,350.21	843,971.33	6,896.33	23,453.89	820,517.44	96.952
7	846,317.29	24,131.37	5,642.12	29,773.48	820,517.44	6,704.68	23,068.81	797,448.64	96.991
8	822,185.92	23,724.36	5,481.24	29,205.60	797,448.64	6,516.18	22,689.42	774,759.22	97.031
9	798,461.56	23,323.36	5,323.08	28,646.44	774,759.22	6,330.77	22,315.66	752,443.55	97.072
10	775,138.20	22,928.28	5,167.59	28,095.87	752,443.55	6,148.43	21,947.44	730,496.11	97.113
11	752,209.91	22,539.05	5,014.73	27,553.78	730,496.11	5,969.09	21,584.69	708,911.42	97.155
12	729,670.87	22,155.57	4,864.47	27,020.04	708,911.42	5,792.71	21,227.33	687,684.09	97.197

1 = Par Value of Security
2 = Principal payments
3 = Interest payments
4 = Total periodic cash flow
5 = First period: Bond cost
Subsequent periods = ending book value (8) of previous period
6 = Book value (5) × Yield/no. of periods in year
7 = Total cash flow (4) less income (6)
8 = Beg. book value (5) less return of capital
9 = Ending book value (8)/Par Value (1) after period payment

Paragraph 19 of FASB 91 states that should actual prepayments differ from estimates, a new yield is to be derived using actual payments received and future cash flows projected at a rate closer to current market activities. Adjustment must then be made as if the new rate of return had been used from the acquisition of the security. The carrying value is to be adjusted with a corresponding increase or reduction to interest income. No statement is made as to the frequency of these adjustments. However, to accurately report annual earnings on investments, annual adjustment should be considered at a minimum.

For certain CMO tranches, whether backed by agency product or whole loans, there may be no cash flow, or cash flows may be interest only for a period of time. Accrual bonds or Z bonds and inverse floater classes are examples. In these instances, there is either no cash flow or insufficient cash flow to cover the calculated income. Nevertheless, income is calculated and booked accordingly. The shortage creates a negative book value reduction which results in an increase to the carrying value of the security. The shortage of cash is covered by a debit to the asset itself. Income earned, but not received as cash, is considered phantom income and is taxable. Once the security begins to pay principal, entries to the asset become positive resulting in a reduction of book value until complete retirement.

Exhibit 3: FASB 91 — Interest Method — Discount — Year 1

Par Value:	1,000,000		Purchase Price:		103.2500	
Coupon:	8.00%		Cost:		$1,034,722.22	
Months to Maturity:	60		Yield (IRR):		6.19%	
Prepayment Estimate:	250 PSA					
Total Principal Year 1	292,484.70		Total Return of Capital Year 1		306,380.82	
Total Interest Year 1	68,881.45		Total Income Year 1		54,985.33	
Total Cash Flow Year 1	361,366.15		Total Cash Flow Year 1		361,366.15	

	Principal Balance	Principal	8.00% Interest	Total Cash Flows	Beginning Book Value	Income at 9.81%	Return of Capital	Ending Book Value	Book Price
	(1)	(2)	(3)	(4)	(5)	(6)	(7)	(8)	(9)
1	1,000,000.00	26,704.44	6,666.67	33,371.11	1,034,722.22	5,333.19	28,037.92	1,006,684.31	103.430
2	973,295.56	26,259.55	6,488.64	32,748.19	1,006,684.31	5,188.68	27,559.51	979,124.80	103.388
3	947,036.00	25,821.20	6,313.57	32,134.77	979,124.80	5,046.63	27,088.14	952,036.65	103.346
4	921,214.80	25,389.30	6,141.43	31,530.73	952,036.65	4,907.01	26,623.72	925,412.94	103.303
5	895,825.51	24,963.75	5,972.17	30,935.92	925,412.94	4,769.79	26,166.13	899,246.81	103.259
6	870,861.76	24,544.47	5,805.75	30,350.21	899,246.81	4,634.92	25,715.29	873,531.52	103.216
7	846,317.29	24,131.37	5,642.12	29,773.48	873,531.52	4,502.38	25,271.10	848,260.41	103.171
8	822,185.92	23,724.36	5,481.24	29,205.60	848,260.41	4,372.13	24,833.47	823,426.94	103.127
9	798,461.56	23,323.36	5,323.08	28,646.44	823,426.94	4,244.13	24,402.31	799,024.63	103.082
10	775,138.20	22,928.28	5,167.59	28,095.87	799,024.63	4,118.35	23,977.52	775,047.11	103.036
11	752,209.91	22,539.05	5,014.73	27,553.78	775,047.11	3,994.77	23,559.01	751,488.10	102.990
12	729,670.87	22,155.57	4,864.47	27,020.04	751,488.10	3,873.34	23,146.70	728,341.40	102.944

1 = Par Value of Security
2 = Principal payments
3 = Interest payments
4 = Total periodic cash flow
5 = First period: Bond cost
    Subsequent periods = ending book value (8) of previous period
6 = Book value (5) × Yield/no. of periods in year
7 = Total cash flow (4) less income (6)
8 = Beg. book value (5) less return of capital
9 = Ending book value (8)/Par Value (1) after period payment

DETERMINATION OF NON-EQUITY

The FASB's Emerging Issues Task Force Project 89-4 (EITF 89-4) addresses methods of application of income and capital for debt securities. The consensus reached by the task force is that accounting for investment in a CMO structure, whole loan-backed or not, needs to be consistent with the type of the investment. Certain CMO classes, namely residuals, are issued in the form of equity. Some of the equity classes consist only of future cash flows that will be collected under conditions existing at issue. A set of six criteria govern. An asset meeting all six criteria is accounted for according to the accounting method prescribed for non-equity investments. The criteria for non-equity classification of a CMO issued in equity form are as follows:

- The assets in the special-purpose entity were not transferred to the special-purpose entity by the purchaser of the CMO instrument.
- The assets of the special-purpose entity consist solely of a large number of similar high-credit monetary assets (or one or more high-credit-quality mortgage-backed securities that provide an undivided interest in a large number of similar loans) for which prepayments are probable and the timing and amounts of prepayments can be reasonably estimated.
- The special-purpose entity is self-liquidating; that is, it will terminate when the existing assets are fully collected and the existing obligations of the special-purpose entity are fully paid.
- Assets collateralizing the obligations of the special-purpose entity may not be exchanged, sold, or otherwise managed as a portfolio, and the purchaser has neither the right not the obligation to substitute assets that collateralize the entity's obligations.
- There is no more than a remote possibility that the purchaser would be required to contribute funds to the special-purpose entity to pay administrative expenses or other costs.
- No other obligee of the special-purpose entity has recourse to the purchaser of the investment.
- The ability of a purchaser of a CMO instrument to call other CMO tranches of the special-purpose entity generally will not preclude treatment of the purchaser's investment as a non-equity instrument provided all the above are met.

Additionally, the task force concluded that the level of risk of non-equity CMO instruments is required to be determined before accounting methods are determined. If a significant portion of the original investment is at risk because of (1) interest rate changes, (2) prepayment of underlying collateral or (3) reinvestment earnings of collected but not distributed cash flows, the instrument is declared high-risk. Interest-only certificates and/or tranches also fit the high-risk description in that their purchase price consists of only premium, and is subject to substantial loss of original investment due to prepayment risk. Therefore, IOs are to be accounted for in the same method as set forth for high-risk CMOs, the 89-4 method.

The 89-4 method for high-risk CMO classes is similar to FASB 91's interest method in that upon purchase an effective yield is derived on the basis of cost and projected cash flows. Cash flows are to be projected based upon prepayment assumptions consistent with those set by marketplace participants for comparable investments. The yield is then used to calculate income on the original dollars invested for the first accounting period. Cash flow received is first applied to the amount of income accrued, with any excess applied to the carrying value of the security.

The glaring difference between 89-4 and FASB 91 is that for each subsequent period, the yield must be recalculated on the basis of the amortized cost of the security and new projected cash flows. The new yield at each reporting period is used to determine income on outstanding dollars invested. These steps are repeated until the investment is completely retired.

Obviously, no "catch-up" method is necessary as with FASB 91's interest method that allows a constant yield for periods when prepayment estimates are close to real activity. With EITF 89-4, the carrying value of the security will equal the net present value of projected cash flows at the current yield for each accounting period. The yield must *not* be negative. In the event that the newly generated present value is less than the present value of the same projected undiscounted cash flows, the loss is to be taken in the current period, and income for that period will be zero.

Premiums and discounts for non-equity CMO classes are to be accounted for as prescribed in FASB 91.

WHOLE LOAN PACKAGES
(NON-STRUCTURED AND NON-SECURITIZED)

Investors may purchase packages of loans that have no securitization and in no way resemble a structured group of classes. Cash flows received from these packages of loans are paid to the investor exactly as they are paid by their makers. There is no credit enhancement or subordinated pieces, simply a package of debt. These packages of loans are still considered loans and accounted for as such by their purchaser. As for balance sheet placement, they are to be carried as loans, not securities, on the asset side of the balance sheet. FASB Statement No. 65 governs. Even though carried as loans, a determination must be made as to whether they are held for sale or not. The categories have no titles of their own, the loans are either to be resold or held. If the loans are to be held to retirement, they are to be carried at amortized cost. The method for determining amortized cost is still FASB 91. Premiums and discounts are accounted for using FASB 91's interest method. Loans that are held for sale are to be valued by the lower of cost or market method, known as LOCOM. Amortized cost is to be determined using the interest method and the market value is to be obtained for each reporting period. The more conservative of the two values, the lower of the amortized cost or the current market value, is to be the carrying value of these loans. The lower of the two will not necessarily be the same each period. Amortized cost may be lower than market value for one period and the reverse may be true for the next. It is always the lower of the two chosen for valuation for each reporting period.

Part B: Credit Analysis

Chapter 7

The Default and Loss Experience of Nonagency MBS

Thomas Gillis
Managing Director
Standard and Poor's

Private placements initially dominated the early years of the nonagency MBS market. These privately placed transactions (in the late 1970s and through the early 1980s), kept their loss experience confidential. As the public nonagency MBS market emerged, so did the reporting of loss information. Investors and analysts' appetite and demand for credit information on the loans underlying these transactions grew along with the whole loan market. Loss information, reported on only 43% of all outstanding publicly rated pools in 1994 has risen to approximately 77% in 1996.

The improvements made in the dissemination of credit information has been significant. However, further credit related disclosure is necessary and will only advance investor comfort with the product. Additional information about real estate owned (REO) would help predict future losses more accurately. A loan that goes from foreclosure to REO will have the effect of reducing reported foreclosures without increasing reported losses. These properties in REO are generally losses waiting to be incurred. Information with respect to estimated property value, location, and accrued interest to date would greatly enhance investor's ability to predict near term losses. Differences also exist in defining currently reported information. Nevertheless, the market is heading in the right direction, making more information available and accessible to the market. In this chapter, a review of loss information on 1,130 whole-loan pools selected from the Standard & Poor's data base is provided.

Since the market's inception, Standard & Poor's has rated approximately 2,600 issues, representing over $340 billion of nonagency mortgage securities. The loss analysis presented in this chapter focuses solely on pools of first-mortgage loans securing publicly issued nonagency mortgage-backed securities that were rated by Standard & Poor's. The sample was drawn from all transactions outstanding as of June 1996 and approximately 140 issues that have matured. Actual loss data are used where available. Otherwise, a loss is assumed to be the difference between the original credit support provided and the current credit support outstanding.

LOSS EXPERIENCE

CMO loss experience is a function of the foreclosure and loss experience on the loans securing the CMOs. If all of the mortgages pay, the CMO will pay. If mortgages default and losses are incurred, those losses will be covered by a third-party credit enhancement or allocated to the appropriate classes of the MBS.

Because credit protection and subordinated classes are barriers against loss to senior classes, the loss experience at the loan level can differ significantly from the loss experience of the securities supported. Since most senior classes are rated either AA or AAA, these classes receive the greatest amount of credit protection. Credit protection for senior classes rated by Standard & Poor's has averaged 9%, down from 10.5% in December 1993. Lower average loss coverage numbers reflect the high volume of lower risk mortgage pools issued as a result of the refinance boom in 1993 and 1994.

A simple rule of thumb for assessing credit protection is to convert it into the range of foreclosure and loss scenarios that it protects against. Credit protection of 9% translates into a range of potential default scenarios: from 100% of loans being foreclosed upon and incurring a 9% loss on average to a foreclosure rate of 9% and incurring a 100% loss. The typical loss incurred on a mortgage will approximate 30% to 40%. At an average loss of 40%, credit protection of 9% will guard against 22.5% of the loans in the pool being foreclosed upon.

LOSS ANALYSIS

Our analysis compares losses at the loan pool level and not the security level. Since securities often represent less than 100% of the unpaid principal balance of the loans securing the issue, the analysis would not be an accurate measure of losses at the security level. Most nonagency MBS are multi-class securities, with the subordinate class, which is in a first-loss position, generally retained by the seller.

The 1,130 pools of mortgages surveyed had approximately $254 billion in original principal amount. The pools had an average balance of $183 million. To date, losses total $1.6 billion, averaging $1,427,984 per pool, representing 63 basis points. These pools are protected with approximately $18.8 billion of credit support, an average of 9.0% per pool. Exhibit 1 provides a breakdown by year of security issuance.

Any loss analysis performed for mortgages needs to be conducted on the basis of the origination year. As Exhibit 1 indicates, mortgage losses are a function of time. The losses increase over time, with the newest pools experiencing the lowest losses. This is a normal occurrence, given the nature of mortgages. A foreclosure on average takes over a year to complete, making any losses in the first year unlikely.

Exhibit 1: Breakdown of Loan Pool Level ($ Millions)

Year	Number of Pools	Total $ Amount	Total Losses	Losses as % Initial $ Amount
1986*	91	7,474.2	91.3	1.22
1987	76	7,857.6	99.2	1.25
1988	92	8,527.2	148.3	1.74
1989	91	9,585.3	209.5	2.09
1990	71	10,180.7	294.2	2.79
1991	84	15,257.6	290.0	0.75
1992	160	53,503.1	321.7	0.54
1993	178	38,442.6	120.0	0.27
1994	199	41,090.6	30.7	0.07
1995	88	17,695.5	8.7	0.04
Total	1,130	209,614.4	1,613.6	0.64

* Includes transactions issued prior to 1986.

Exhibit 2: Residential Default Curve

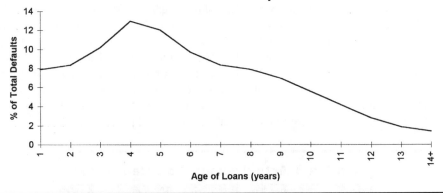

Likewise, as the mortgage amortizes, losses become more remote after a certain passage of time, generally five to seven years. This is commonly referred to as the *loss curve*. The losses, being reported in the 1995 transactions, are a result of including seasoned, and on occasion delinquent, mortgages in some of those transactions. Standard & Poor's surveillance of outstanding losses will measure a transaction's performance using as a proxy the default curve in Exhibit 2.

Using this curve, we can equate the losses experienced for pools originated over different years. If each pool's future losses follow this curve, a projection of the total losses that will be incurred over the life of these transactions can be made.

While the curve provides a useful way to compare pools originated in different years, it too has its shortcomings. Each pool has its own loss curve, which can vary substantially from another. Pools with little seasoning render the use of the curve less reliable. Likewise, the more years a pool has seasoned beyond its origination date, the more weight can be placed on the loss curve analysis. The loss curve is a conservative approach, pushing more losses out into the future than may actually occur.

Exhibit 3 tabulates losses projected for the life of the pools sold each year, assuming all the pools follow the same pattern of loss as determined by the default curve in Exhibit 2. As Exhibit 3 indicates, losses have been and are projected to be quite volatile from origination year to origination year. Losses are projected to average 2.0% of the initial principal balance for the 10-year period, with a standard deviation of 1.4.

The impact of the rolling recession can be seen as losses from 1988 through 1991 stand out as all being higher than average. The 1994 and 1995 book of transactions is less reliable, because there has not been enough time yet to judge the ultimate performance of these transactions. The volatility of the historical loss performance demonstrates the importance of the economic cycle in determining future losses. Mortgages originated at the peak, the Northeast in 1988-1989 and California in 1990-1991, are accumulating losses at a significant pace, in spite of little relative difference in their risk profile (excluding the RTC in 1991).

Exhibit 4 provides additional information about range of loss experienced by pool within an origination year. The exhibit segregates the number of pools by dollar loss into six categories. Two thirds of all pools have experienced equal to or less than $500,000 in losses, with only 6% exceeding $5 million in losses. However, looking at the peak loss years of 1988 through 1991 the distribution of losses changes considerably. In those years, pools that have experienced zero losses occur at less than half the rate of all outstanding transactions. Nonagency MBS that have experienced losses of $5 million or more during the 1988 through 1991 time period occur at almost twice the rate of the overall population.

Exhibit 3: Actual versus Projected Losses

Year	Actual Losses Dollar (000)	Actual Losses Percentage	Projected Losses Dollar (000)	Projected Losses Percentage
1986*	91,269	1.22	97,115	1.30
1987	99,161	1.25	117,685	1.50
1988	148,339	1.74	191,876	2.25
1989	209,520	2.09	301,728	3.15
1990	294,233	2.79	481,481	4.73
1991	290,000	0.75	564,312	3.70
1992	321,700	0.54	817,535	1.53
1993	120,000	0.27	454,718	1.18
1994	30,700	0.07	189,506	0.46
1995	8,700	0.04	110,546	0.62

* Includes transactions issued prior to 1986.

Exhibit 4: Pool Losses

Year	Number of Pools with Total Losses not Exceeding					
	Zero	$500,000	$1 million	$5 million	$10 million	>$10 million
1986*	37	26	10	14	2	2
1987	26	17	10	17	5	1
1988	19	27	10	31	3	2
1989	22	7	13	34	13	2
1990	21	5	4	22	10	9
1991	27	28	12	16	0	1
1992	59	16	10	60	10	5
1993	93	36	22	23	2	2
1994	138	52	5	3	1	0
1995	65	22	1	0	0	0
Total	507	236	97	220	46	24
% Total	45%	21%	9%	19%	4%	2%
1988-1991	26%	20%	12%	30%	8%	4%

* Includes transactions issued prior to 1986.

ABOUT THE DATA

Standard & Poor's data base, which is one of the most extensive in the industry, required some adjustments in order to produce this analysis. Reporting differences from one issuer to another and the complexity of the data make precise measurements not possible.

For purposes of this analysis, all loss comparisons are made on the pools backing the transactions and not the specific issues. Issuers offering one series backed by two distinctive pools of mortgages are treated as two pools. Similarly, multiple series backed by the same pool of mortgages are treated as one pool. All second mortgage and most bond insured transactions were eliminated. Other pools are eliminated because of the lack of timely information.

Precise loss data are available on only 77% of the pools. The loss data for the vast majority of the pools were as of June 1996. When actual loss information was available, an amount equal to the difference between initial and current support levels was used as a proxy. In most cases, the change in loss coverage will overstate actual losses.

Bond insured transactions were used where loss information was available, but excluded entirely from all calculations involving initial loss coverage. This adjustment was made to prevent the potential of the 100% covered bond insured transactions from skewing the data.

All losses are rounded to the nearest thousand. For senior/sub transactions, the subordinated levels are added to the certificate amounts to approximate the total pool size. The size of the sample, notwithstanding these adjustments, should be useful for analysis of the nonagency MBS market.

FACTORS INFLUENCING LOSS

Four major factors influence losses: economic, underwriting, loan to value, and payment structure. The economic factor is the most important of these as the above exhibits demonstrate. Standard & Poor's recently announced that its residential loss model will now adjust loss coverage based on the pool's exposure to local economic strength or weakness. A regional analysis is performed through the use of a proprietary index that measures an area's residential home price stability and vulnerability to future price declines.

The residential price stability index, designed by DRI/McGraw-Hill for Standard & Poor's, focuses on four main factors: housing price trends, housing affordability, migration, and industry concentration. Standard & Poor's and DRI/McGraw-Hill determined these factors to have the most predictive ability after an in-depth study of the nation's largest metropolitan areas. Depending on the location of the property, an adjustment is made to the assumed loss severity depending on characteristics unique to that location.

Within any given economic environment, additional factors will play a role in determining loss experience. Underwriting is one of the more influential factors. Conservative and diligent underwriting provides the best defense against future economic uncertainty. Loans underwritten to less stringent standards are more vulnerable to losses.

Poor underwriting standards were prevalent during the 1988-1991 peak loss years and made a significant contribution to the losses now being experienced from those origination years. Low document and accelerated underwriting programs became the norm. Originators tried to offset borrower quality with additional equity without success. The recent analysis performed by developers of automated underwriting systems indicate that borrower quality is a major explanatory variable in assessing future default probabilities. Income and employment should be verified, along with the source of the mortgagor's down payment. Credit scores and automated underwriting are relatively new tools available to the mortgage market and should have a positive impact on determining underlying credit quality of a pool's mortgagors.

Equity in the home can offset all other factors in mitigating or eliminating the loss potential of a mortgage. However, this is more theoretical than practical in that LTVs of less than 50% are necessary to mitigate losses in the most dire economic environments.

Loan pools composed of only 50% or lower LTVs are not a significant factor in our 1,130 pool sample. Certainly higher LTV mortgages can be found in our sample, and represent additional risk.

High LTV mortgages reduce the primary safety feature of a mortgage, which is asset protection. A 95% LTV provides a built-in loss feature if a mortgagor defaults before any significant appreciation occurs. The 5%, that is, equity is insufficient to cover foreclosure costs, guaranteeing a loss upon foreclosure. If it were not for the presence of primary mortgage insurance, there would be little incentive to originate these mortgages at all from a credit perspective.

Most pools will include a spattering of LTVs ranging from 95% to 60%. While concentrations of loans above 80% LTV is a definite indicator of risk, pools with weighted average LTVs of between 70% and 80% are not always useful in differentiating risk. The lower LTVs of loans originated under limited and no-document programs of the late 1980s turned out to be ineffective in deterring foreclosures.

Payment structures have a direct impact on future losses. Depending on the loan's payment structure, the chances of a default can be mitigated or increased. The traditional fixed-rate, fully amortizing mortgage is the safest payment structure.

The fully amortizing mortgage, along with insurance, was promoted by the Federal Housing Administration after the Great Depression to attract lenders who had left the market after incurring major losses on partially amortizing and interest-only mortgages. These balloon mortgages can still be found in the market today. Balloon mortgages increase the risk of loss by adding the risk of refinancing to the normal risk that a mortgagor will default.

The fixed-rate, fully-amortizing mortgage is structured ideally with respect to a mortgagor's income. Adjustable-rate and graduated-payment mortgages, while fully amortizing, add the additional risk that the borrower will not be able to maintain income growth that is commensurate with a rising mortgage payment.

Measuring all of the factors that influenced risk of loss can be a daunting task. To assist issuers, investors and analysts, Standard and Poor's recently introduced its residential analytic model "LEVELS™" to the market. Standard & Poor's LEVELS™ provides a loan by loan analysis with estimates of the necessary loss coverage for all rating categories.

ASSESSING FUTURE LOSSES

Investors have little information about a whole-loan pool to judge the numerous factors affecting loss. Credit protection, to cover potential risks, is based on rating agency risk assessments for loan pools. Credit protection puts all pools on an equal footing, reducing unnecessary concern with the risk of any individual mortgage pool. Knowledge about the risk factors and related loss experience can only enhance the quality of an investor's decision.

Exhibit 5 indicates S&P's experience of measuring loss coverage with risk. The amount of loss coverage has varied as a percentage of initial pool balances from a low of 7.5% to a high of 13.4%. Coverage for projected total losses fluctuates inversely with projected losses. The 1994 and 1995 data are too early in their life cycle to be considered reliable. The 1990 year projects the lowest level of coverage for projected losses of 1.80 times, is heavily influenced by Guardian Savings and Loan Association, Huntington Beach, CA loss experience. Guardian's losses account for 37% of all pools originated in 1990. In fact Guardian and the Resolution Trust Corp. account for only 5% of total issuance and 31% of total losses.

Exhibit 5: Measuring Loss Coverage with Risk

Year	Initial Pool Balance (Million $)	Initial $ Loss Coverage (Million $)	Initial Loss Coverage (%)	Projected Losses (Million $)	Ratio of Initial Loss Coverage to Projected Losses
1986*	7,437.8	600.5	8.1	97.12	6.18
1987	7,857.6	600.3	7.6	117.68	5.10
1988	8,527.2	753.5	8.8	191.88	3.93
1989	9,585.3	906.5	9.5	301.73	3.00
1990	10,180.7	866.7	8.5	481.48	1.80
1991	15,257.6	2,047.9	13.4	564.31	3.63
1992	53,053.0	5,198.2	9.7	817.53	6.36
1993	38,442.6	3,210.6	8.4	454.72	7.06
1994	41,090.6	3,097.1	7.5	189.51	16.34
1995	17,695.5	1,536.0	8.7	110.55	13.89

* Includes transactions issued prior to 1986.

Chapter 8

The Rating Agencies' Approach: New Evidence

Douglas L. Bendt
President
Mortgage Risk Assessment Corporation

Chuck Ramsey
Managing Director
Structured Capital Management
and
CEO
Mortgage Risk Assessment Corporation

Frank J. Fabozzi, Ph.D., CFA
Adjunct Professor of Finance
School of Management
Yale University

INTRODUCTION

Credit analysis of nonagency mortgage-backed securities relies upon an unusual combination of large-scale statistical aggregate analysis and micro loan-by-loan analysis. This combination arises from knowing that out of a pool of 1,000 newly originated mortgages, it is virtually certain that at least ten will be defaulted upon and go into foreclosure, but there is no way of knowing *which* ten.

The expectation that ten or more homeowners will default is based on studies of millions of mortgages conducted by private mortgage insurers, federal agencies, and the four major credit rating agencies. But not all of these studies are relevant to the default experience of mortgages collateralizing nonagency mortgage-backed securities.

The authors wish to thank Tom Gillis, Standard & Poor's; Jay Siegel, Moody's; Michelle Russell, Duff & Phelps; and, Ken Higgins, Fitch, for commenting and reviewing exhibits relating to their agencies' criteria.

For example, studies by private mortgage companies focus only on mortgage defaults on loans with high loan-to-value (LTV) ratios, as would those done on FHA/VA mortgages. And by definition, studies of mortgages that meet Fannie Mae and Freddie Mac standards are not relevant. That leaves studies by Standard & Poor's Corporation, Moody's Investors Service, Fitch, and Duff & Phelps.[1]

This chapter reviews the approach these agencies take in evaluating the loss potential of defaults of nonagency mortgages and presents new evidence about additional factors influencing losses. Rating agencies need to evaluate the magnitude of potential loss of a pool of loans to determine the amount of credit support the issuer is required to implement to achieve the desired credit ratings. Their approaches consist of four parts: (1) frequency of default; (2) severity of loss given default; (3) pool characteristics or the structure of the pool; and (4) credit enhancement or the structure of the security.

FREQUENCY OF DEFAULT

Most homeowners default relatively early in the life of the mortgage. Exhibit 1 shows the effect of seasoning assumed by two rating agencies and the Public Securities Association.[2] These seasoning curves are based on default experience of so-called prime loans — a 30-year fixed-rate mortgage with a 75% to 80% LTV that is fully documented for the purchase of an owner-occupied single-family detached house. These characteristics describe the most common mortgage type generally associated with the lowest default rates.

Loans with almost any other characteristic generally are assumed to have a greater frequency of default. Exhibit 2 summarizes the evaluation of these other risk characteristics among the four rating agencies.

Loan-to-Value Ratio/Seasoning

A mortgage's loan-to-value (LTV) ratio is the single most important determinant of its likelihood of default and therefore the amount of required credit enhancement. Rating agencies impose penalties of up to 500% on loans with LTVs above 80%. The rationale is straightforward. Homeowners with large amounts of equity in their properties are unlikely to default. They will either try to protect this equity by remaining current, or if they fail, sell the house or refinance it to unlock the equity. In any case, the lender is protected by the buyer's self-interest.

---

[1] "Moody's Approach to Rating Residential Mortgage Passthroughs", *Moody's Investors Service Structured Finance and Research Commentary* (New York, NY: Moody's Investors Service, 1990); Standard & Poor's Ratings Group, *Residential Mortgage Criteria* (New York: McGraw Hill, 1996); *Rating of Residential Mortgage-Backed Securities* (New York, NY: Duff & Phelps Credit Company, 1995); *Fitch Mortgage Default Model* (New York, NY: Fitch Investors Service, Inc.,1993).
[2] *Standard Formulas for the Analysis of Mortgage-Backed Securities and Other Related Securities* (New York, NY: Public Securities Association, 1990).

Exhibit 1: Assumed Default Frequencies

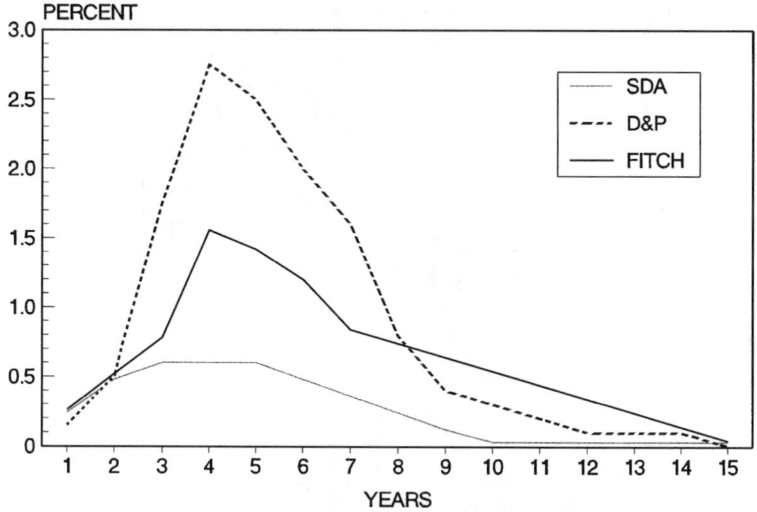

On the other hand, if the borrower has little or no equity in the property, the value of the default option is much greater. This argument is consistent with the long-held view that default rates for FHA/VA loans are much higher than for conventional loans.

Until recently, rating agencies considered the LTV only at the time of origination. Seasoning was an unalloyed good — if a loan did not default in the first three to four years, it deserved credit for making it past the hump. And many loans did not default because they were prepaid.

The recent declines in housing prices, increased volume of seasoned product, and greater emphasis on surveillance have made the *current* LTV the focus of attention. Seasoning now is as likely to be a negative for a pool as it is to be a plus. It is little comfort to own a pool of original 80% mortgages from California originated in 1990 because many of the borrowers will owe more than their houses are worth; their LTVs will exceed 100%. Moreover, the prepayment option has been taken away for these borrowers.

Mortgage Term

Amortization increases the equity a homeowner has in a property, which reduces the likelihood of default. Because amortization schedules for terms less than 30 years accumulate equity faster, all the rating agencies give a "credit" of 15% to 35% — i.e., reduced credit enhancement levels, for 15-year mortgages. Conversely, mortgages with a 40-year term are penalized up to 10%. Adjustable rate mortgages that allow negative amortization are similarly penalized.

Exhibit 2: Effect of Required Credit Enhancement for AAA Levels

Category	Standard & Poor's	Moody's	Fitch	Duff & Phelps
Loan-To-Value: AAA				
Factors				
100	4.50	N.A.	4.64	3.27
95	3.00	N.A.	3.57	3.05
90	1.50	1.70	1.79	2.41
85	1.00	N.A.	1.21	1.59
80	1.00	1.00	1.00	1.00
75	1.00	N.A.	1.00	0.91
70	1.00	0.63	0.71	0.77
65	1.00	N.A.	0.71	0.50
60	1.00	0.41	0.57	0.32
≤ 60	1.00	N.A.	0.57	0.32
Seasoning	1. 50% of home price appreciation 2. 100% of depreciation 3. Variable, depending on term, mortgage type	1. Current LTV 2. 5 years 0.68	0.9 to 0.5 for 5 to 12 years depending on payment history	1. Partial adjustments for current LTV 2. Affects timing of losses 3. Compare actual pool performance to expected performance
Term				
15-year	0.73	0.65	0.75	0.80
20-year	0.88			0.88
25-year		0.75		0.95
30-year	1.00	1.00	1.00	1.00
40-year	>1.00	1.10		1.20

Exhibit 2 (Continued)

Category	Standard & Poor's	Moody's	Fitch	Duff & Phelps
ARMS	1.05 - 1.70; additional 1.25 - 2.00 if pay cap is hit	1.20 - 1.60	1.05 - 2.00	1.15 - 1.30
Loan Purpose				
Cashout refinance	Add 5% to LTV	Add 10% to LTV	1.10 - 1.25	1.15
Rate/term refinance	1.00	1.00	1.00	0.95
New construction				1.05
Relocation				0.60
Reduced	LTV >90 2.00 - 3.00	Limited 1.05 - 1.20	1.00 - 1.50	Alternate 1.05
Documentation	80 - 90 1.50 - 2.00	Poor/None 1.50		Reduced 1.30
	75 - 80 1.20 - 1.50			Poor reduced 1.50
	60 - 75 1.10 - 1.50			None 1.75
	<60 1.05 - 1.20			Streamlined 1.30
Property Type				
Second Home	3.00	N.A.	1.25	1.10
Investor	3.00	1.48	2.00	1.40
Condo, Co-ops, Townhouses	Low-rise, 2-Family 1.20	1.14 - 1.28	1.10 - 1.25	1.25
2 - 4	Hi-rise, 3-to-4-Family 2.00	N.A.		1.40

Exhibit 2 (Continued)

Category	Standard & Poor's	Moody's	Fitch	Duff & Phelps

Credit measures	High debt ratio 1.10
	
	Delinquencies:
	2-to-5 1.10
	6+ 1.20
		1. WAC + 2 pts. 1.11 - 1.17
		   WAC − 2 pts. 0.83 - 0.89
		2. "B" quality 1.18 - 1.32
		   "C" quality 1.49 - 1.99
		3. Debt to income
		   20% 0.56 - 0.71
		   50% 1.26 - 1.60
			1. Mortgage or credit scores: 10% to 30% reduction
			2. Delinquent loans: 1.25; 100% frequency for 90+ days
				1. Interest rate above market
				2. originators "score" (A, B, C, D)
				3. credit scores

Mortgage Size/House Price	>$400,000 1.2 >$600,000 1.6 >$1,000,000 3.0	Avg/low 1.00 3 to 5 × median 2.00 6 to 9 × median 2.50 9+ × median 3.00	>$300,000 1.05[a] >$600,000 1.40[a] >$1,000,000 1.60[a]	4× median 1.22 6× median 1.34 8× median 1.48 10× median 1.63
SEVERITY OF LOSS				
Foreclosure costs	13% balance + interest	25%+/loan balance	Varies by state, coupon, and loan type; generally 23% to 28% for prime credits — higher for subprime	15% of Sale price
Market Decline	34.5%[b]	25%	32 - 45%	40%[c]

Exhibit 2 (Continued)

Category	Standard & Poor's	Moody's	Fitch	Duff & Phelps
POOL CHARACTERISTICS				
Pool Size	Minimum 100 FF = Foreclosure frequency n = pool size $FF + 2.58\left(\frac{FF(1-FF)}{N}\right)^{1/2}$ $FF + 2.58\left(\frac{FF(1-FF)}{300}\right)^{1/2}$	>500 0.95 <200 1.20	If pool size (PS) < 125, $\frac{125-PS}{125}$ plus factor for economic concentration	<110 1.50 110 1.30 200 1.10 300 1.00 400 0.98 500 0.95 1500 0.92 2500+ 0.90
Geography	High zipcode concentrations penalized; wider areas on a case-by-case basis	Economic diversity: 0.9 - 1.3 Foreclosure time: 0.9 - 1.2 Zipcode concentration Adjustments for regional economic conditions	Impact of regional economies	Volatility varies by MSA 0.80 - 1.25 Concentration factor by state, MSA, zipcode 0.90 - 1.20

[a] Adjustments to market value decline
[b] Adjusted for jumbo ~ 1.5
[c] Adjusted by region

Mortgage Type

Fixed-rate mortgages are considered "prime" because both the borrower and the lender know the monthly payment and amortization schedule with certainty. Presumably, the loan was underwritten considering this payment stream and the borrower's current income.

Both lender and borrower are uncertain about the future payment schedule for adjustable-rate mortgages (ARMs). Because most ARMs have lower initial ("teaser") rates, underwriting usually is done to ensure that the borrower will be able to meet the monthly payment assuming the rate adjusts up to the fully indexed rate at the first reset date.

Beyond that first date, however, there is uncertainty both about the future stream of payments and the borrower's ability to meet higher payments. Future payment schedules for other mortgage types such as balloons and graduated payments are known, but uncertainty about borrowers' income still exists. All non-fixed-rate mortgages carry penalties of 5% to 100% or more.

Transaction Type

Mortgages taken out for cash-out refinancings are considered riskier than mortgages taken out for purchases, chiefly because the homeowner is reducing the equity in the home. In addition, the fact that the homeowner is taking out cash may be an indication of *need*, which could indicate shakier finances, and the homeowner's monthly payment will increase. On the other hand, a no-cash refinancing — in which the rate is reduced — lowers the monthly payment and speeds the rate of amortization, so there are no penalties.

Documentation

"Full" documentation generally means that the borrower has supplied income, employment, and asset verification sufficient to meet Fannie/Freddie standards. "Low," "alternative," or "reduced" documentation means at least one form was not supplied, perhaps, for example, because the borrower is self-employed. In this case, because the income stream is likely to be more volatile, the borrower is more likely to default.

"No" documentation loans generally are made as "hard money" loans — i.e., the value of the collateral is the most important criterion in the lending decision. Typically, lenders require larger down payments for these type loans. Guardian Savings and Loan in California — seized by the RTC for insolvency — had been a major proponent of this type of program. Its collateral was put into RTC 91-9, which has a 40% serious delinquency rate, despite an average LTV of 65%.

Occupancy Status

Property owners obviously have a greater vested interest in not defaulting on a mortgage on a house in which they live. Thus, mortgages for second homes or rental property are penalized.

Property Type

Generally, single-family detached houses are the most desirable properties because they are larger, more private, and include more land. Moreover, the supply of condominiums or townhouses is more likely to become overbuilt in a local area with the addition of a single large project, potentially increasing the volatility of prices and the length of time needed to sell a property.

Mortgage Size/House Price

Most mortgages are sold into nonagency mortgage-backed securities because the dollar amounts exceed the agency conforming limits (currently $203,150). The rating agencies make the strong presumption that higher-valued properties with larger mortgages are much riskier; they impose penalties of up to 200%.

Creditworthiness of the Borrower

Although loan originators place a great deal of emphasis on borrowers' credit histories, these data are not available to the rating agencies. The Fair Credit Reporting Act restricts access to such information to parties involved in a credit extension decision.

As a result, the agencies use credit proxies such as the debt-to-income ratio, the mortgage coupon rate, past delinquencies or seasoned loans, or originators' "scores" (A, B, C, or D).

SEVERITY OF LOSS

In the case of default, foreclosure, and ultimate property sale, lenders incur two costs: (1) direct foreclosure costs, and (2) market decline. These costs may be mitigated to the extent there is equity in the property, i.e., lower LTVs will reduce the severity of loss.

Direct Foreclosure Costs Once a lender begins the foreclosure process — often as soon as a borrower becomes 60 days delinquent — it begins to incur significant direct costs.

Unpaid Interest The lender stops accruing interest on the mortgage as income, instead adding it to the unpaid balance of the loan.

Cost = coupon rate of the mortgage per year

Property Taxes The lender becomes responsible for paying taxes to preserve its first lien position.

Cost = up to 2% or more of the house price annually

Management Fees The property must be maintained so as to preserve its value for sale.

Cost = average 6% of the house price annually

Legal Fees Variable

Market Decline When a house is sold out of foreclosure, the lender is unlikely to obtain market value. Potential buyers know that the seller is distressed and know the size of the mortgage on the property. One common bidding strategy is to bid for the amount of the outstanding mortgage, figuring it is the seller's obligation to cover the out of pocket costs. The price received on a foreclosure sale depends greatly on local economic conditions and future housing prices, both of which are unknown at the time a rating agency is evaluating a loan. The range of assumed losses is 25% to 45%.

POOL CHARACTERISTICS

Rating agencies draw upon general portfolio theory that diversification reduces risk and concentration increases risk. They typically consider two characteristics of the overall pool composition in setting credit enhancement levels: (1) size of the pool, and (2) geographic composition/location.

Pool Size

Pools with fewer than 300 loans are penalized by three of the four rating agencies, while larger pools are credited. The rationale is that smaller pools are not sufficiently diversified to take account of (unspecified) desirable statistical properties.

Geography

The first kind of geographic consideration is again a question of diversification: "too many" loans concentrated in a single zip code or small local area. For example, a lender might finance an entire subdivision, townhouse development, or condominium project that might be exposed to a common, special risk such as a single plant closing or an environmental hazard.

The second kind of geographic consideration is generally broader in scope, such as a pool with a high concentration in Southern California that is exposed to risks not of a single plant but of a single industry. In special cases such as Boeing in Seattle, the risk is both industry- and company-specific.

CALCULATING CREDIT ENHANCEMENT LEVELS

Pool characteristic risks are cumulative; that is, if a loan has two or more adverse characteristics, the factors are multiplied to determine the relative degree of the fre-

quency of default. Then one calculates an expected loss equal to the discounted probability of default times the expected loss severity. After performing these calculations
on a loan-by-loan basis, the overall pool characteristics are taken into account.

Credit enhancement levels are determined relative to a specific rating
desired for a security. Specifically, an investor in a AAA-rated security expects to
have "minimal," that is to say, virtually no chance of losing any principal. For
example, Standard & Poors requires credit enhancement equal to four times
expected losses to obtain a AAA rating.

Lower-rated securities require less credit enhancement for four reasons.
First, the loss coverage ratio is lower. Second, some of the factors may be less
stringent. Third, the base case frequency of default may be lower. And fourth, the
severity of loss may be less.

NEW EVIDENCE

Default rates calculated from a data set comprised of mortgages securitized by
major issuers of nonagency MBS are particularly relevant in setting factors for the
frequency of default. The discussion is based on analysis of more than 500,000
such non-conforming mortgages.

Loan-to-Value Ratio

With current LTV now the measure, assessment of risk needs to extend above
100%. Exhibit 3 shows that delinquency/default rates for mortgages with LTVs
continue to rise. Approximate rates for 105% and 110% are 7.5 and 10, respectively, compared with 5 at 100%.

Exhibit 3: Delinquency Rates by Current LTV Range

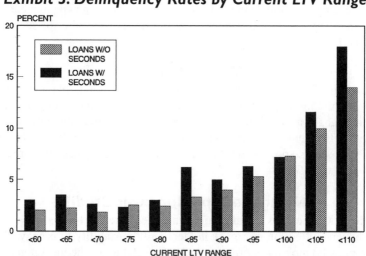

Exhibit 4: Delinquency Rates for Loans With and Without Silent Second Mortgages

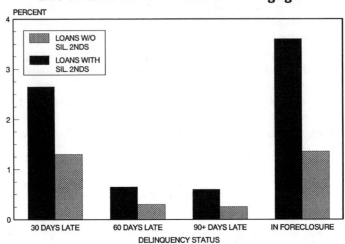

Exhibit 3 also shows that delinquency rates are higher for first mortgages whose borrowers have taken out second mortgages or home equity lines of credit even if their combined equity positions are identical. That is, if homeowner A has an 80% first mortgage, and homeowner B has a 65% first with the same coupon rate as A and a 15% second, homeowner B is a poorer credit risk. This heightened risk probably is a result of homeowner B's higher monthly payment.

As a special case of homeowners with seconds, consider borrowers who take out secondary financing as part of a purchase transaction. For example, the seller of the house — an individual if the house is a resale, the developer/builder if the house is new — may lend the buyer all or part of the down payment to facilitate the transaction. Exhibit 4 shows that the foreclosure rate for such transactions is nearly triple the rate of all transactions.

Mortgage Term

Recent experience with 15-year products has been exceptionally good, suggesting that previous credits were not generous enough. With the increasing popularity of 15-year mortgages as a liability management tool — to time the mortgage payoff either with retirement or children entering college, for example — a credit of as large as 50% seems appropriate (based on Exhibit 5) compared with the current range of 15% to 35%.

Mortgage Type/Borrower Credit

Although ARMs are considered riskier than fixed-rate mortgages, seasoning can have an adverse effect on mortgage holders and their ability to prepay. Consider homeowners who took out mortgages in 1990. A holder of the most popular ARM based on the one-year Treasury bill would have paid about 9% initially, and about 7% currently. In contrast, a fixed-rate mortgage would have cost about 10% in 1990 and about 7.75% currently.

If neither has refinanced, who's the better credit risk from this point forward? Exhibit 6 suggests that the ARM holder is the better risk because that borrower has not had an incentive to refinance, while the fixed-rate holder has had the incentive but failed to do so either because of a lack of equity or credit history deterioration. In either case, this borrower could not qualify for a new mortgage and is more of a risk.

Exhibit 5: Ratio of Current Delinquencies
15-Year versus 30-Year Fixed Rate

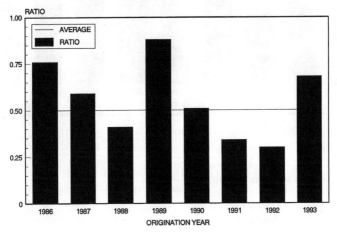

Exhibit 6: Ratio of Current Delinquencies
ARMS versus 30-Year Fixed Rate

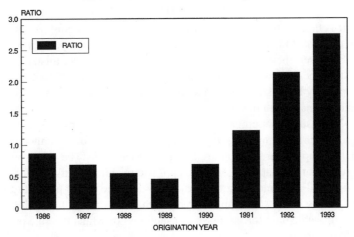

Exhibit 7: Ratio of Current Delinquencies
Cashout Refis versus Purchase Transactions

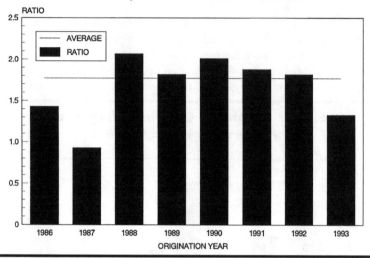

This relationship suggests a formula for calculating credits/penalties by mortgage type:

$$\text{Fixed-rate mortgage} = \frac{\text{mortgage coupon}}{\text{current coupon}}$$

$$\text{ARM's} = \frac{\text{current rate}}{\text{initial rate}}$$

For ARM's, this formula has the additional feature of explicitly increasing the penalty as the rate rises in the future.

Transaction Type

Cash-out refinancings have performed abysmally in recent years, primarily because those still in existence were taken out at or near the peak in prices in California. However, there is no reason to think that the lending mistakes of California could not be repeated in other hot markets such as Seattle. Exhibit 7 indicates that the penalty for cash-out refinancings should be 100% compared with the rating agencies' maximum of 25%.

No-cash refinancings are currently not penalized by the rating agencies, although, Exhibit 8 shows significant "appraisal bias" for refinance transactions for which the appraiser has no purchase price as a guide. The extent of the bias is measured by noting that almost all the appraised values are higher than a property value estimated from indexing the previous sale price of the property to trends in property values in the same zip code; no such bias is present in Exhibit 9, which shows comparable data for purchase transactions for which the sale price is available to the appraiser.

Exhibit 8: Evidence of Appraisal Bias
Refinance Transactions

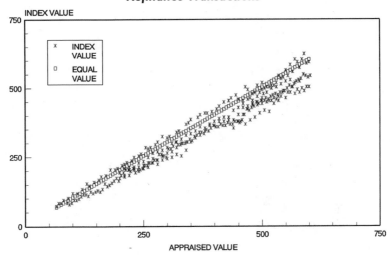

Exhibit 9: Evidence of Appraisal Bias
Purchase Transactions

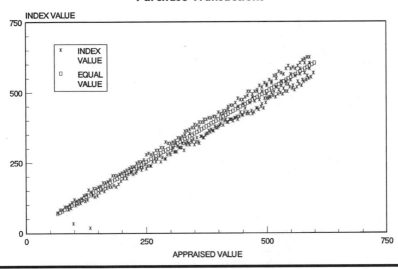

This bias probably makes its effect felt in homeowners acting according to their "true" (read: higher) LTV. Thus, instead of penalizing refinance transactions directly, it would probably be more effective to raise the stated LTV at origination by 5% to 10% to reflect this bias. The impact on the required credit support would then be greater for relatively high LTV loans.

Chapter 9

The Rating of Securities Backed by B&C Mortgages

Andrew Jones
Group Vice President
Residential MBS Group
Duff & Phelps Credit Rating Co.

Jennifer Schneider
Vice President
Residential MBS Group
Duff & Phelps Credit Rating Co.

INTRODUCTION

This chapter highlights Duff & Phelps Credit Rating Co.'s (DCR) rating approach for securities backed by residential mortgage loans to borrowers with impaired credit histories. Market participants often refer to these mortgage loans as "B&C" (or other alphabetical designations), sub-prime or home-equity loans. The securitization of these types of loans represent the fastest growing sector in the residential MBS arena.

DCR's approach to rating B&C mortgage transactions utilizes the analytical framework developed for "A" quality transactions as its underpinning, with some very important differences. DCR's model for A quality transactions focuses on a variety of mortgage characteristics, including loan type, property type, occupancy, underwriting documentation used, loan purpose, coupon, location and others, but the most important factor used to determine credit enhancement is the loan-to-value ratio (LTV). To evaluate B&C transactions, the most important characteristic of the loan is the mortgagor's credit quality, which DCR's "Borrower Credit Quality Factor" captures. These factors, described below, vary by LTV, allowing DCR to put more emphasis on the mortgagors' credit than on LTV.

Under current origination practices, B&C quality mortgage pools generally require more protection or credit enhancement than a comparable A quality pool in order to achieve the same rating. Yet many B&C transaction structures satisfy both the issuer's need for effective execution and the investors' need for adequate protection.

DEFINING B&C LENDING PROGRAMS

DCR and many market participants use the term B&C mortgages to refer to mortgage loans made to borrowers who have derogatory information in their credit histories. These derogatories could include a history of late payments on previous personal debts, a charge-off to a credit card or auto loan or a personal bankruptcy filing. The borrowers thus constitute a wide spectrum of credit quality. Some borrowers, categorized as A– (A minus) borrowers, may have just failed to qualify for agency or other A lending programs. At the other end of the spectrum, some borrowers may have such impaired credit histories that lenders make loans based solely on the value of the property. These programs are widely termed "equity" or "hard money" lending programs.

Many market participants use the terms sub-prime or home-equity to describe mortgages with comparable borrower profiles. Similarly, the securities themselves have a variety of formal names, such as mortgage passthrough certificates, home-equity loan asset-backed certificates, and mortgage loan asset-backed securities. While B&C lending includes both first-lien and second-lien mortgages, the focus of this chapter is the development of the first-lien sector of this marketplace.

Regardless of the names used to refer to this market, the borrowers and the properties are similar. B&C quality borrowers typically qualify for their mortgages at higher interest rates and higher down-payments (and, therefore, lower LTVs) than A quality mortgagors, whose loans support most private-label mortgage-backed securities (MBS). Lenders rely on the higher interest rates and lower LTVs to offset the increased credit risk of these mortgagors. B&C mortgages are closed-end,[1] generally fully amortizing mortgage loans and historically were taken out as cash-out refinancings of existing loans. While any property type may be the collateral for a B&C mortgage, most are single-family properties; nonetheless, B&C pools often contain significant concentrations of 2-to-4 family structures as well.

When DCR evaluates a pool of B&C mortgages for securitization, the Residential MBS (RMBS) Group keeps several special features of the loans in mind. First, B&C mortgagors are more likely to become delinquent and default than traditional A mortgages. Not only do these mortgagors have inferior credit histories, but the rates on their mortgage notes are higher and their debt-to-income ratios are higher than for A quality borrowers. Second, the caliber of the mortgages is particularly dependent on the accuracy of the property appraisals at origination. Third, the delinquency and loss experience on B&C mortgages is very sensitive to the quality of servicing. The servicers' collections operation must be more diligent than for A mortgages because of the tendency of these mortgagors to fall behind in their payments.

---

[1] That is, the loan was fully dispersed at origination of the mortgage, in contrast to home-equity lines of credit under which the borrower uses the line in the same way as a credit card.

History of B&C Lending

While the marketplace has characterized B&C loans as a newer mortgage product, this view is not accurate. B&C lending describes nothing more than traditional mortgage lending to risky borrowers. Traditionally, mortgage credit has been available to borrowers of different credit qualities, but the more risky the borrower, the higher the interest rate and points charged by the lender, and the more collateral or equity is required.

B&C loans typically do not conform to FNMA or FHLMC guidelines because of borrower credit history, even though the size of the loan may be within agency guidelines. Therefore, these loans can only be securitized in the private-label MBS markets.

The B&C terminology for borrowers began in the early 1980s. The naming conventions varied because the sources of the product historically were different. Thrifts and savings and loan associations traditionally originated B&C mortgage loans, while finance companies originated home-equity loans. The thrift B&C loans were typically adjustable-rate mortgages with 30-year amortization, while home-equity loans were typically fixed-rate with shorter amortization periods. B&C transactions historically contained predominantly first liens, while home-equity transactions had a significant portion (as much as 75%) of second liens.

Over time, these characteristics have changed. With the demise of the thrift industry, mortgage banks and finance companies originate most B&C mortgage loans. Most companies originate both fixed- and adjustable-rate loans and, in low interest rate environments, first liens predominate (as borrowers chose a cash-out refinancing rather than seeking a second lien mortgage). Today, there is little difference, if any, between a closed-end home-equity transaction and a B&C mortgage transaction.

B&C loans have been securitized for several years. They appear in securitizations of fully amortizing home-equity transactions dating back to the late 1980s and as B&C adjustable-rate mortgage transactions from the same time. Securitized home-equity transactions may include the whole spectrum of asset quality, from A and A– to D quality and equity loans and may include both first liens and second liens. Issuers included the Money Store, Long Beach, Southern Pacific Funding, Alliance Funding, Aames, and United Companies, among others.

SPECIAL FEATURES OF B&C MORTGAGES

There are several unique features of B&C loans that set them apart from traditional A loans. First, the underwriting guidelines establish a credit profile that differs strongly from A credits. By definition, B&C borrowers carry greater debt burdens and are more likely to become delinquent. Not only do they have inferior credit histories, but their mortgages have higher interest rates than A mortgages, adding further to their debt burdens. Also, the qualifying debt-to-income ratios for B&C borrowers are higher than for A borrowers.

To counteract these risks, underwriting guidelines often require a borrower to have more equity in the underlying property. This reliance on collateral value makes underwriting of B&C loans particularly dependent on the accuracy of the appraisals at origination. These considerations will be explored in later in this chapter.

Second, the delinquency and loss experience on B&C mortgages is very sensitive to the quality of servicing. Because of the poor quality of the borrowers, collections must be more diligent than for A loans. Because of the frequency of borrower defaults, loss mitigation policies and foreclosure and liquidation departments must be especially effective. These considerations are reviewed later.

REVIEW OF UNDERWRITING

Each lender uses the B&C quality designations in a slightly different manner; therefore, one lender's "B" product could be the equivalent of another's "C" product. To capture these differences in its transaction analysis, DCR reviews the underwriting guidelines of each originator. DCR then translates the originator's designations into appropriate codes for the residential MBS model. In this way, DCR maintains consistency in its analysis across different originators.

DCR's evaluation of underwriting guidelines for B&C programs reflects DCR's knowledge of the fundamental differences between guidelines for A programs and B&C programs. Underwriting guidelines generally address (1) the ability of the borrowers to meet their payment obligations and (2) the value and adequacy of the property as collateral for the loan. B&C programs often put less emphasis on the borrower's ability to pay than do A programs.

Categorizing Borrowers

Program guidelines group borrowers' credit histories into categories. Exhibit 1 presents DCR's designations for borrower quality based on standard underwriting variables. The A− loan category reflects data such as only one 30-day mortgage delinquency in the last year, a few 30-day late payments on consumer debt, and no prior bankruptcies. By contrast, a C designation may allow several 30-day delinquencies or a combination including one 60-day and one 90-day delinquency during the last year on existing mortgage debt, significant derogatories on consumer debt, and a bankruptcy more than one year prior.

Debt-to-income ratios in B&C programs are typically higher than for A lending programs. Many B&C borrowers are accustomed to tight budgets and have already exhibited an ability, although imperfect, to carry heavy debt burdens. It is also common for originators to allow higher debt ratios for lower LTV loans within a particular credit grade.

The borrower credit quality designations in Exhibit 1 represent "typical" guidelines, and DCR notes that guidelines can vary substantially among originators. DCR does not require that an originator conform its guidelines to these spec-ifications. To the extent that an originator's programs vary from the norm, DCR will evaluate the program and make appropriate adjustments in its analytic model. The adjustment is usually made by recoding of certain variables in the loan file DCR receives or with the originator risk factor in DCR's model, as described below in the discussion of qualitative assessments.

Loan-to-Value Ratios

LTV guidelines are another aspect of a lender's underwriting program. LTV guidelines, in combination with accurate appraisals, control the risk of loss to the lender, as well as to investors in a security, in the event of a mortgagor default. LTV guidelines for B&C loans are generally lower than for A loans. For example, most maximum LTVs in B&C programs are lower than for A loans. Few B&C programs permit LTVs above 85%, whereas 90%-LTV loans are a staple in A lending programs. In addition, the average LTV of a typical B&C quality pool is approximately 70%, significantly lower than the 77% average LTV common with A quality loans.

 Most underwriting standards provide that maximum permissible LTVs decline as the loan's riskiness increases. Inferior credit histories of the borrower, reduced documentation, or risky property types can each reduce a lender's permit-ted LTV for a given borrower. Alternatively, if a borrower of a particular credit grade takes out a mortgage with an LTV below the category maximum, some lenders may allow higher debt ratios than otherwise allowed for that credit grade.

Exhibit I: DCR's Borrower Credit Quality Definitions

Generic Borrower Credit Quality Description	Mortgage Credit	Other Credit	Recency of Bankruptcy	Debt-to-Income Ratio	Maximum LTV Ratio
A: Standard agency quality	1 × 30 last 24 months	No derogatories	5 years	36%	97%
A–: Very minor credit problems	1 × 30 last 12 months, or 2 × 30 last 24 months	Minor derogatories explained	5 years	42%	90%
B+: Minor credit problems	2 × 30 last 12 months	Moderate derogatories	4 years	45%	85%
B: Minor to moderate credit problems	4 × 30 last 12 months, or 1 × 60 last 24 months	Some prior defaults	3 years	50%	75%
C: Moderate to serious credit problems	6 × 30 last 12 months, or 1 × 60 & 1 × 90 last 12 mos., or 3 × 60 last 12 months	Significant credit problems	18 months	55%	70%
D: Serious credit problems	30-60 constant delinquency, or 2 × 90 last 12 months	Severe credit problems	12 months	60%	65%

Appraisals

The emphasis on collateral value means that accurate and reliable appraisals are essential to the success of any B&C lending program. Typically, independent, fee-based appraisers conduct the appraisals, which trained in-house[2] appraisers review. DCR reviews the underwriting department of the originator, the background of the appraisers and the quality control measures taken to ensure reliable appraisals. For example, it is prudent to track by appraiser the variance between original appraisals and any reappraisals, either during file audits or by comparison to appraisals on defaulted mortgage properties.

Originators can use different techniques to evaluate appraisals, each with a different degree of accuracy. The most accurate check on an appraisal is to obtain another full, independent fee-based appraisal on the property. This redundancy can be very expensive; nonetheless, it is important for very large loans. The next most accurate check is a drive-by appraisal, in which the review appraiser evaluates the subject property and the comparables, but without interior inspections. The desk-review appraisal is the next most accurate form of verification. It relies on a search of databases (1) to check the comparables used in the original valuation, looking for additional or more recent sales and (2) to assess the subject property's value for reasonableness given the neighborhood. The most summary review of the property value is the statistical appraisal, which uses an index of property values in an area, such as a repeat sales price index, to estimate the value of a property. Under this type of review, the person reviewing the appraisal identifies the date and amount of the previous valuation for the property and adjusts the value for changes in the index since that date.

Because wholesale operations generate most B&C mortgages today, it is particularly important for the originator to review the appraisals on the properties. If the mortgage broker submits the appraisal, the underwriter should be wary of any sign that the broker selected an appraiser that assigns higher values, thereby generating more and larger loans for the broker. Appraisal reviews are somewhat less important for retail originations under which the originator selects the appraiser based on an established and good track record.

Another important issue relates to the originator's tolerance for appraisal variance. Some originators only reduce the value on a property when the review appraisal is more than 10% below the original appraisal. Other originators adjust the value on the property if the review value is more than 5% lower. Lower tolerance levels lead to more conservative LTV ratios and less risky mortgages.

Documentation Types

Many B&C programs permit borrowers with lower LTVs to forego the submission of some documentation for their applications, such as income verification. In addition, borrowers with less reliable forms of income and employment verifica-

---

[2] That is, employed by the originator

tion are subject to additional program parameters that reduce the riskiness of those loans. Program standards typically trade off the degree of documentation against acceptable LTVs and debt-to-income ratios.

Quality Control

To ensure that loans conform to program guidelines, programs must have quality control procedures, including pre-closing reviews, post-closing audits, and monitoring loan performance by broker. DCR meets with the quality control personnel to discuss the procedures used to assure compliance with guidelines.

Underwriting Philosophy and Targeted Borrowers

DCR's review of underwriting guidelines does not entirely explain the quality of an originator's underwriting. For each program, DCR seeks to understand the philosophy behind the program with an understanding of the targeted borrowers and the reasons for lending. DCR meets with management to obtain a business overview and to explore the particular business niche of the lender. B&C lending is more of an art than a mechanical process, and therefore the experience of the underwriters and their lending focus is key.

For example, some programs focus on particular borrowers, such as those with poor consumer credit histories but with good mortgage payment histories. A borrower who habitually pays the mortgage lender first may be a good mortgage credit risk, even if the credit history on other types of receivables is poor. Other programs target "A turndowns," borrowers who barely failed to qualify for agency and other A quality programs. Rather than turn a good customer away, lenders are able to make the loan at terms appropriate to the borrower's risk.

A third type of program focuses on borrowers with poor credit histories, potentially substantial consumer debt at high interest rates, but significant equity in their homes due to property appreciation. For these borrowers, it may be beneficial to arrange a first-lien cash-out refinancing to consolidate debts or to pay other large expenses such as a child's education.

A fourth common program targets borrowers who recently encountered a single severe financial hardship. The hardship could be due to lost income related to a recession or to the burden of medical bills. With a new job or the passing of the medical condition, the individual's finances may be recovered, but a historical credit analysis may show serious derogatories. In these cases, the originator focuses on borrowers who can demonstrate that the cause of their poor credit history has been remedied.

Understanding each program's approach to developing its niche in this marketplace allows DCR to evaluate the appropriateness of the underwriting guidelines to each lender's objectives.

DCR File Review

To assess underwriting practices further, DCR's Residential MBS Group has a policy of selectively reviewing a sample of mortgagor application files. In this review, which is typically undertaken on-site at the originator, DCR will match data from documents, recalculate ratios, check file completeness, and compare mortgage/borrower data to underwriting guidelines. Errors and exceptions are subject to discussion with management.

DCR's review is not due diligence in a legal sense, and the review is not a statistical sample. DCR uses the results of the review as necessary to adjust the borrower credit quality codes to reflect the underwriting practice of the originator. The Residential MBS Group also uses the information collected from the originator and file reviews to determine an originator risk factor in the MBS model.

REVIEW OF SERVICING

For B&C programs, it is critical that the servicer has strong operations and procedures to maintain contact with delinquent mortgagors. Because of the risky nature of the borrower, borrower contact should begin before any delinquencies occur. In some cases, collectors may initiate contact prior to the first due date on the loan. Servicers must also have strong foreclosure and REO departments because of the increased frequency of mortgagor defaults

In assessing the quality of a servicer's operation, DCR meets with management and reviews the background and qualifications of the personnel. Management and staff with strong experience with B&C mortgages and similar assets is critical. For example, collectors with backgrounds in consumer finance may be well suited for collecting on B&C loans. The servicer foreclosure and REO operations should also be linked to its collections effort to enhance its ability to mitigate losses (1) by using foreclosure as a tool to accelerate cures by delinquent borrowers, and (2) acting quickly to secure and liquidate collateral on defaulted loans.

Collections

Since borrowers under these programs by definition have already exhibited poor performance, it is important that the collector be able to keep the borrower current. Methods to maintain borrower performance include the following:

1. Contacting the borrower prior to the first payment date to remind the borrower about the payment, to verify source of funds, and to specify where the payment is to be mailed (goal — removing any excuse a borrower may have for not making the first payment);
2. Building a relationship with the borrower, such as offering guidance or counseling to help borrowers budget their expenses (goal — ensuring that the borrower's ability to pay becomes a reality);
3. Making phone contact with delinquent borrowers quickly, as soon as 5-10 days after the due date (goal — avoiding initial delinquency);

4. Tracking chronic late payers, finding out what the problem is, and remedying the situation before the loan ever becomes delinquent (goal — avoiding serious delinquencies, which are difficult to cure);

5. Sending a notice of intent to foreclose when the payment is 45 days or less past due (goal — intensifying pressure on delinquent borrower to become current); and

6. Pursuing foreclosure proceedings expeditiously for mortgages that do not cure (goal — taking quick control of the property to realize its collateral value).

The purpose of these actions is to prevent 60-day delinquencies as often as possible, as it is very difficult for these borrowers with their high debt ratios to cure once they get far behind in their payments. The most successful servicers succeed in bringing a delinquent borrower current, even curing loans for which they have initiated foreclosure proceedings.

Loss Mitigation

A good B&C mortgage servicer uses loss mitigation techniques to avoid acquiring real estate whenever possible. Loss mitigation in some cases takes the form of modification of the mortgage. If the terms are materially changed, however, the servicer or other transaction party must repurchase the mortgage under the transaction documentation.

Loss mitigation may also include forbearance, in which case the servicer must report the mortgages as delinquent. DCR will question why any serious delinquencies have not entered foreclosure status, and will expect the servicer to have well founded reasons for their actions.

Another form of loss mitigation is a short-sale, in which the borrower pays off the mortgage for less than the full balance outstanding. These sales avoid the time and costs of foreclosure and liquidation of the property, thereby adding to the net recovery on the mortgage.

Alternatively, a mortgagor may relinquish title to the property to the servicer and thereby avoid foreclosure, a process called deed-in-lieu of foreclosure. This action allows the servicer to resell the property much sooner and save thousands of dollars in accrued interest and foreclosure expenses.

In addition to collections, DCR focuses on the foreclosure and REO department and related operations. In the event it is necessary to foreclose and liquidate a property, the servicer must liquidate the property promptly. The value of an accurate appraisal becomes apparent at this juncture as the servicer takes possession and markets the property. The expertise of in-house and other appraisers who are advising on the disposition of property is important to maximize the net proceeds on the property. DCR recognizes that it is often in the interest of investors that the servicers list the properties at a price low enough to ensure a speedy sale. Otherwise, the benefits of a higher price can be quickly offset by accrued interest during a long marketing period.

In evaluating the servicer's foreclosure and liquidation process, DCR assesses the average time to foreclose and liquidate a property against norms for the relevant states and property characteristics. DCR also determines the percentage of the servicer's portfolio in non-paying and paying bankruptcy status to ensure that bankruptcy levels are normal, giving consideration to regional differences.

Back-up Servicing

If the servicer of record is unable to perform servicing for any reason, the servicing must be pulled immediately and transferred to a capable institution. Any delays in the collections effort are particularly problematical in the B&C context because any interruption of diligent collections will cause delinquencies to soar. In some cases where the long term financial viability of the servicer is difficult to assess, DCR will require a third party to act as a "hot" back-up servicer. A hot back-up servicer is able to take over the servicing function quickly because it has been shadow servicing the mortgages on its own systems.

DCR'S APPROACH TO EVALUATING B&C MORTGAGES

DCR determines the protection or credit enhancement required for a rating by (1) applying its analytical model to evaluate the risk of each loan in a pool backing a security, and (2) adjusting the model's output by factors addressing qualitative considerations, such as originator and servicer quality.

The DCR Analytical Model

DCR's analytical model evaluates the riskiness of each loan in a pool backing a security. The credit enhancement level for a desired rating reflects the sum of each loan's credit enhancement requirement, which equals the product of the loan's balance and a series of factors corresponding to the particular characteristics of the loan. For B&C mortgages, DCR has a special loan level factor, the Borrower Credit Quality Factor (described in detail below), to calculate accurate credit enhancement requirements for mortgagors of any credit quality.[3]

The foundation of DCR's credit enhancement requirements is the actual performance of mortgages under stress conditions of the past 20 years. Analysts in the Residential MBS Group conducted case studies of mortgage performance in Houston during the Oil Bust of the mid 1980s and more recently in Boston and Los Angeles, among other areas. From these studies, DCR determined base credit enhancement requirements and mortgage characteristic risk factors for high quality mortgages.

---

[3] The factors for all mortgage characteristics used in the Residential MBS model are set forth for each rating category in DCR's October 1995 publication *The Rating Of Residential Mortgage Mortgage-Backed Securities*. As the DCR Residential MBS model operates by separately calculating the incidence of mortgagor default and the expected severity of mortgage loss upon default for each rating category, the presentation in *The Rating of Residential Mortgage-Backed Securities* includes loss incidence and loss severity components for each mortgage characteristic risk factor for each rating category.

These credit enhancement requirements and risk factors are important contributors to the assessment of credit enhancement requirements for B&C mortgages. To adapt the model for B&C mortgages, DCR conducted further analysis of B&C quality mortgage performance to create the Borrower Credit Quality Factors for each borrower risk grade at each rating level.

Borrower Credit Quality

The MBS model multiplies DCR's Borrower Credit Quality Factors by the credit enhancement requirement otherwise calculated for a loan given its characteristics, such as LTV, coupon, and property type. The factors apply to the expected loss incidence[4] of the mortgages because the credit concern with lower quality borrowers is their higher likelihood of defaulting relative to A quality borrowers. The model addresses loss severity once a default occurs, the second component of credit enhancement determination, through the other characteristics of the mortgages.

To demonstrate the range of DCR's Borrower Credit Quality Factors, Exhibit 2 presents these factors for 'AAA' and 'BBB' ratings. The exhibit also shows DCR's loss incidence component for its LTV risk factors and the product of Borrower Credit Quality Factors and the LTV loss incidence component. The product illustrates the impact borrower quality can have on base credit support for a transaction.

DCR's Borrower Credit Quality Factors vary by both LTV and rating category in order to achieve the correct absolute level of loss incidence for mortgagors of each credit grade. The factors vary by LTV to offset the rapidly declining loss incidence of base pool mortgages[5] as LTV declines. Low LTV A quality loans have an extremely low incidence of default, while B&C borrowers have a much higher tendency to default, even at very low LTVs. Additionally, the underwriting guidelines of B&C originators allow riskier and riskier characteristics at lower LTVs, like higher debt ratios and reduced documentation, which DCR's other risk factors may not capture. Thus, the DCR model must have higher Borrower Credit Quality Factors at the lower LTVs to reach the appropriate absolute level of loss incidence.

The factors are larger at lower rating categories to reflect the relative sensitivity of B&C mortgagors vis a vis their A quality counterparts in each rating environment. B&C borrowers are less sensitive to the economic environment because their credit positions are already impaired. Even in a strong economic environment, comparable to non-investment grade ratings, B&C mortgagors will have a much greater tendency to default than A mortgagors. By contrast, in severely stressful economic conditions, both A quality and B&C quality mortgagors are expected to default in large numbers, reducing the ratio of default frequency.

---

[4] DCR uses the term loss incidence to describe the frequency with which mortgages experience a loss to a mortgage pool. This term is similar to default frequency, but reflects the fact that many defaulting mortgages do not result in mortgage losses.
[5] The DCR base pool mortgage is a 30-year, fixed-rate, fully amortizing, full documentation mortgage to an A quality mortgagor at a market rate of interest secured by a single-family residence that is the primary residence of the mortgagor and used by the mortgagor to purchase the residence.

Exhibit 2: 'AAA' Borrower Credit Quality Factors and LTV Loss Incidence

LTV	Base Pool LTV Loss Incidence	A Quality Borrowers		A− Quality Borrowers		B+ Quality Borrowers		B Quality Borrowers		C Quality Borrowers		D Quality Borrowers	
		Factor	Adjusted Loss Incidence	Factor	Adjusted Loss Incidence	Factor	Adjusted Loss Incidence	Factor	Adjusted Loss Incidence	Factor	Adjusted Loss Incidence	Factor	Adjusted Loss Incidence
90%	29.66	1.00	29.66	1.20	35.59	1.25	37.08	1.50	44.49	1.75	51.91	2.00	59.32
85	19.77	1.00	19.77	1.20	23.72	1.25	24.71	1.50	29.66	1.75	34.60	2.00	39.54
80	12.43	1.00	12.43	1.20	14.92	1.25	15.54	1.50	18.65	1.75	21.75	2.00	24.86
75	11.25	1.00	11.25	1.20	13.50	1.30	14.63	1.50	16.88	1.75	19.69	2.00	22.50
70	9.50	1.00	9.50	1.20	11.40	1.40	13.30	1.70	16.15	2.00	19.00	2.25	21.38
65	6.13	1.00	6.13	1.20	7.36	1.60	9.81	2.00	12.26	2.60	15.94	3.00	18.39
60	4.08	1.00	4.08	1.20	4.90	2.00	8.16	2.75	11.22	3.50	14.28	4.00	16.32
55	2.48	1.00	2.48	1.20	2.98	2.75	6.82	3.75	9.30	5.00	12.40	5.75	14.26

'BBB' Borrower Credit Quality Factors and LTV Loss Incidence

LTV	Base Pool LTV Loss Incidence	A Quality Borrowers		A− Quality Borrowers		B+ Quality Borrowers		B Quality Borrowers		C Quality Borrowers		D Quality Borrowers	
		Factor	Adjusted Loss Incidence	Factor	Adjusted Loss Incidence	Factor	Adjusted Loss Incidence	Factor	Adjusted Loss Incidence	Factor	Adjusted Loss Incidence	Factor	Adjusted Loss Incidence
90%	11.77	1.00	11.77	1.25	14.71	1.40	16.48	1.70	20.01	2.00	23.54	2.25	26.48
85	7.31	1.00	7.31	1.25	9.14	1.40	10.23	1.70	12.43	2.00	14.62	2.25	16.45
80	4.23	1.00	4.23	1.25	5.29	1.40	5.92	1.70	7.19	2.00	8.46	2.25	9.52
75	3.25	1.00	3.25	1.25	4.06	1.50	4.88	1.75	5.69	2.10	6.83	2.40	7.80
70	2.28	1.00	2.28	1.25	2.85	1.70	3.88	2.10	4.79	2.60	5.93	3.00	6.84
65	1.30	1.00	1.30	1.25	1.63	2.00	2.60	2.80	3.64	3.50	4.55	4.25	5.53
60	0.78	1.00	0.78	1.25	0.98	2.85	2.22	4.00	3.12	5.25	4.10	6.00	4.68
55	0.46	1.00	0.46	1.25	0.58	4.25	1.96	6.00	2.76	7.00	3.22	8.00	3.68

In applying these factors, DCR does not use an originator's program designation as the appropriate code for a program. The originator submits a mortgage pool indicating the program or grade assigned to each borrower. DCR, having assessed each of the originator's programs or grades, applies the appropriate risk factors for the mortgage. The MBS model applies the risk factors, which may be intermediate to those in the exhibit, at the loan level to determine the appropriate credit enhancement for the pool.

Other Mortgage Characteristics

The Borrower Credit Quality Factors are only one of several variables that affect the credit enhancement levels for a B&C mortgage pool. Because there is a certain similarity among B&C mortgage transactions, there is also similarity in the various mortgage characteristics which have a strong influence on the final credit enhancement requirements for B&C transactions. The following discussion reviews how DCR's analysis responds to some of the more important characteristics.

Loan-to-Value Ratio

B&C transactions have a weighted average LTV that is approximately 5% to 10% lower than A quality transactions (65%-72% versus 70%-80%). The lower LTV ratios associated with B&C programs result in a credit enhancement reduction, which DCR's Borrower Credit Quality Factor offsets substantially. As LTVs rise in a B&C transaction, the combination of the LTV factors and the Borrower Credit Quality Factor can lead to very high credit enhancement requirements.

Coupon and Gross Margin

The coupon and gross margin on B&C mortgages are much greater than market rates for A quality mortgages. Coupons on fixed-rate loans are generally more than 4% higher than market rates, while gross margins on adjustable-rate loans average approximately 5% to 7%. DCR uses these market derived characteristics, first, as an additional indicator of an increased expectation of loss incidence and, second, to increase the interest accrual component of loss severity.

Cash-Out Refinancings

B&C transactions have very high concentrations of cash-out refinances, typically from 40% to 70%, which receive a large penalty in DCR's analysis. These borrowers' are taking equity out of their properties and are perhaps using the money for debt-consolidation. Many borrowers will pay off their debts with the cash and subsequently run up credit card balances again, causing the overall debt burden to increase. Secondly, the property values for cash-outs are determined solely by appraisals, without purchase prices acting as a check on value. Appraisal-only valuations add risk to B&C mortgages, more than A mortgages, because the underwriting relies more heavily on collateral value.

Documentation Types

Most full documentation programs at B&C lenders correspond to alternative documentation programs at A quality lenders. The B&C originators will often allow a pay stub, tax return or bank statement rather than a full Verification of Income and a Verification of Assets under their full documentation programs. In response to this practice, DCR treats most B&C "full" documentation programs as alternative documentation, which incur a modest penalty. B&C pools also tend to have high concentrations of mortgages without income or asset verification, which carry significant penalties in the DCR model.

Investor and 2-to-4 Family Properties

Pools of B&C mortgages frequently contain concentrations of other risky mortgage characteristics, such as investor properties and 2-to-4 family properties. A typical B&C transaction has approximately 15% of investor properties, compared to less than 5% for "A" quality transactions. Comparable percentages of 2-to-4 family properties are also prevalent.

Mortgage Types

While B&C programs have a variety of loan types available, one of the most common mortgages is a 6-month LIBOR ARM with 1.5% semiannual payment caps. As an adjustable-rate mortgage, DCR assigns a high penalty to these loans in its models. In addition, this loan type is riskier than a LIBOR mortgage with 1% semiannual caps, which was a popular loan from 1990 to 1995. These 1.5% cap ARMs are particularly risky because lenders underwrite the borrowers at teaser rates and with relatively high debt ratios. For example, if a borrower has an initial debt ratio of 60% based on a qualifying rate of 10%, in one year the new debt ratio, even if LIBOR stays flat, will go up to over 75%.

Other B&C mortgages today carry a fixed-rate for a period of two, three, five or seven years and then adjust based on the LIBOR index. As the initial interest rate term extends, DCR believes risk diminishes with the deferring of potential payment shock. The longer the initial period, the more the mortgage will amortize and the more the property may experience appreciation.

Location Specific Factors

The locale in which a mortgaged property is located affects the riskiness of a mortgage in two primary ways. First, state foreclosure laws and the practical aspects of their implementation define the length of time it takes to get possession of a property. Long foreclosure times lead to increased accrued interest on a defaulted property and, in a declining market, can exacerbate realized market value declines.

Second, location affects risk because local economic and housing market conditions strongly influence the frequency of mortgagor default and the severity of property value declines. DCR was the first rating agency to adjust credit enhancement requirements by the riskiness of the cities in which the property is located. Our metropolitan statistical area (MSA) risk factors reflect the nature of the local economy and trends in local housing prices. These factors increase credit enhancement in areas which may be subject to sharp price corrections or have industrially concentrated economies and reduce enhancement if housing prices are stable and the local economy is diverse.

Qualitative Assessments

Qualitative assessments enter into DCR's mortgage analysis in several ways. First, DCR's evaluation of underwriting guidelines and documentation programs require subjective assessments because most guidelines and programs do not correspond directly to the definitions used in our model. Thus, qualitative assessments enter DCR's analysis as our analysts recode data supplied by the issuer to conform to our definitions.

Second, DCR has an adjustment factor for the mortgage originator as a whole. This factor reflects how the originator implements its guidelines, how its mortgages have performed historically relative to similar loans originated at the same time, and other originator attributes that may influence the riskiness of its mortgages.

A third qualitative assessment involves DCR's evaluation of the servicing of the mortgages, which is reflected in our servicer risk factor. Of course, our examination of the servicer is paramount in this factor. DCR considers the servicer's operations, staff quality, and the historical performance of its servicing portfolio among other characteristics of the servicer. Other aspects of servicing may also impact this factor. For instance, servicing transfers often lead to an increase in mortgagor defaults as borrowers fall behind during the transfer period. DCR will increase credit enhancement if a transfer is anticipated soon after the origination of the mortgage pool.

Model Results

Taking all of the factors together, 'AAA' securities backed by B&C loans typically require 14% to 20% credit enhancement for ARM transactions and 10% to 15% for fixed-rate transactions. (See Exhibit 3.) This compares to A quality 'AAA' credit enhancement of 6.5% to 10% for ARMs and 4.5% to 7% for fixed-rate mortgages. DCR's analysis typically results in significant reductions in credit enhancement as ratings decline. However, in a transaction with securities in several rating categories, DCR may increase credit enhancement requirements to offset the concentration of losses in small classes.[6]

Exhibit 3: Credit Enhancement Requirements for B&C Mortgages

Rating	Fixed-Rate	Adjustable-Rate
AAA	10.00-15.00%	14.00-20.00%
AA	5.00-10.00%	8.00-15.00%
A	4.00-6.00%	5.00-8.00%
BBB	2.00-4.00%	3.00-6.00%

[6] See DCR's June 1994 publication *Concentration of Losses in Highly Leveraged Subordinate Classes.*

Exhibit 4: Comparison of B&C Transaction Structures

Structure	Advantages	Disadvantages
Senior- subordinate	No third-party credit risk Large senior IO strip to sell	Mortgage credit risk Unrated first loss class Investment grade classes below AAA Classes below investment grade
Subordinate IO	No third-party credit risk No unrated first loss piece necessary Small senior IO strip to sell Less total subordination than senior-subordinate structure	Mortgage credit risk Investment grade classes below AAA
Third-party Enhancement	All bonds rated AAA Investors don't need to evaluate credit risk of collateral Additional underwriting by third-party	Third-party credit risk Guaranty fee All excess spread protects guarantor No senior IO to sell

CREDIT ENHANCEMENT STRUCTURES

B&C mortgage securitizations use a variety of transaction structures. The most common structures include senior-subordinate, subordinate IO, and third-party guaranteed transactions, each of which are discussed below. Exhibit 4 summarizes the advantages and disadvantages in using each of these alternatives.

Senior-Subordinate Structures

A senior-subordinate structure apportions the cash flow from the underlying mortgages among classes or "tranches" of differing credit quality. In these MBS transactions, classes may be rated at each rating category, with an unrated class that absorbs the initial losses. Losses are first allocated to the unrated class and then are allocated to the next more senior (higher rated) class in turn. The aggregate principal balance of the subordinate classes behind each class equals the percentage amount of credit enhancement that the rating agency requires to cover losses at that particular rating category.

Historically, the senior-subordinate B&C transactions had a AAA class that was slightly over-enhanced, a large AA class (usually about 10%), a large BBB-rated class, and then a small class rated either BB or B and then an unrated first loss class. These transaction also included a AAA-rated senior interest-only (IO) class. The IO class generally received the excess interest off of the mortgage loans.

Senior-Subordinate/Overcollateralization

Many B&C mortgage transactions issued in 1995 and 1996 utilized a senior-subordinate structure in conjunction with a build up of overcollateralization (O/C). This structure creates a subordinate IO strip (sub-IO), which is available for current period losses and which is used to pay down the principal balance of the senior class thereby creating overcollateralization. The O/C is created because each dollar of interest that is used to pay down principal on the bonds, causes the amount of bonds outstanding to decrease relative to the collateral balance.

Most sub-IO structures have AAA, AA, A and BBB classes, with the sub-IO and build up of O/C as the protection for the BBB class. The sub-IO is used to build O/C until the transaction reaches a specified O/C target, usually the required BBB credit enhancement. After reaching the targeted amount, the sub-IO can be paid to the residual holder, provided that it is not needed for current losses. Additionally, these transactions often have a small senior IO strip that can be rated AAA. This class can be created because the coupons on the underlying B&C loans are very high and only a portion of the excess spread (mortgage coupon less security coupon, servicing fees and trust expenses) is necessary to achieve an investment-grade rating.

DCR evaluates the amount of spread that is available, applying both a prepayment stress and a default stress for each rating category. The same size sub-IO is worth more at BBB than it is at AAA, because the stress for AAA is much greater. DCR also allows a longer time-frame for O/C build up at each lower rating category.

Third-Party Credit Enhancement

Many B&C transactions are protected by a surety bond, also known as a wrap. In these transactions a financial guaranty company provides an insurance policy covering timely payment of interest and the ultimate payment of principal to bondholders. In these transactions, all of the bonds can be rated AAA.

In surety bond transactions, the financial guaranty company can be protected from losses with either subordination or a sub-IO structure. Most transactions utilize the sub-IO structure, such that all of the excess spread is used to build O/C up to a targeted amount. This target is usually refundable, such that if losses occur the excess spread is again diverted so that O/C will build back up to the target. The sub-IO is always available to cover losses on a current basis.

CONCLUSION

Securitization of B&C quality mortgages is of growing importance in the secondary market. In recent years, several new issuers have entered the market, including affiliates of traditionally A quality issuers. Meanwhile, many long-time participants have expanded their issuance.

In rating these securities backed by B&C quality mortgages, DCR evaluates each loan supporting the security via its loan-by-loan credit enhancement model. DCR's evaluation includes a review of the underwriting guidelines of the originator and the servicing capabilities of the servicer. DCR also analyzes the structure of the transaction to determine its impact on the securities' ratings. For securities backed by B&C quality mortgages, the most important characteristic is the borrower's credit quality. The reliance on borrower quality is a departure from A quality mortgage analysis, which relies more heavily on LTV.

Chapter 10

Evaluating Subordinate Mortgage-Backed Securities

Mary Sue Lundy
Senior Vice President
Fitch Investors Service, Inc.

Kenneth Higgins
Director
Fitch Investors Service, Inc.

With the onset of the 1990s, an evolution reshaped the speculative-grade, private-label mortgage-backed securities market. The use of pool policies as credit enhancement has lessened. Replacing it as a measure of investor protection is the senior/subordinate structure.

In 1993, over 80% of private-label transactions used this dual structure, up from 48% the previous year. Pool policies, by contrast, declined, accounting for just over 10% of new-issue volume that year.[1]

Use of the senior-subordinate structure to replace pool policies is the result of three concurrent market forces. First, pool insurers raised prices on pool policies to reduce their concentration in Southern California. Second, liquidity improved in the market for subordinate securities. Third, investors were attracted by the higher yields obtainable from subordinate mortgage-backed securities.

In response, issuers began to segment subordinate securities based on credit risk and to seek ratings on the individual subordinate tranches. Because ratings on non-investment grade securities (BB, B, CCC) are sensitive to moderate declines in current economic conditions, it is not appropriate for rating agencies to use a "worst case" scenario analysis, designed to stress high investment-grade securities. Instead, more realistic stress scenarios need to be developed to reflect the impact of current and expected regional economic changes on residential housing market performance.

---

[1] "Conduits, Mortgage Companies and Senior/Sub Structure Dominate Private-Label MBS Market in 1993," *Inside Mortgage Securities* (January 28, 1994), pp. 3-5.

The author would like to thank Greg Raab, Peter Cardinale, and Byron Klapper for their assistance and helpful comments.

The ability to forecast and use economic trends to project regional foreclosure rates and market value trends represents a significant advance in analyzing subordinate mortgage-backed securities. Credit enhancement levels should account for the expected economic activity as well as the potential volatility of the various regions.

Fitch recently introduced new rating criteria based on an evaluation of economic volatility/stability in 43 regions and its potential impact on future foreclosure rates and market values. This chapter outlines the rating methodology for calculating the required loss protection for non-investment-grade mortgage-backed securities.

REGIONAL APPROACH TO MORTGAGE ANALYSIS

Mortgage performance varies across the country. Foreclosure rates may be rising in Southern California, while declining in Atlanta. Chicago's economy reacts differently to changes in unemployment than does Houston's. New England's housing demand can't be relied upon to predict the direction of single-family home prices in Florida. Only recently have analysts begun to take these factors into account in assessing mortgage-backed securities.

The evaluation of subordinate mortgage-backed securities requires criteria that recognize how moderate changes in regional economic performance affect mortgage performance. This has been achieved by Fitch's development of a series of econometric models in conjunction with the WEFA Group.

Fitch's approach segments the U.S. into 43 distinct metropolitan, state and multi-state regions. This segmentation reflects the similarity of the underlying economies, the geographic proximity of the regions to each other, and the geographic distribution of the jumbo mortgage market, where the demand for mortgage-backed securities ratings are the greatest.

The econometric models project foreclosure rates and housing prices in each of the 43 regions. The models are based on a series of statistical analyses that determine the current and historical correlation of foreclosure rates and market value trends with six key regional economic indexes. They are: (1) unemployment rate; (2) employment growth rate; (3) personal income growth; (4) housing starts; (5) sales of existing homes; and (6) number of households (as a measure of demand for housing). The unique combination of these indicators in each region provides the foundation for forecasting foreclosure risk and changes in housing values, which in turn drive credit loss projections.

FORECLOSURE RATES

Fitch's research concludes that one of the primary determinants of foreclosures is the unemployment rate. Unemployment results in a serious disruption of personal income and few households can continue to make mortgage payments after a primary income provider becomes unemployed.

If a borrower begins to have financial difficulties in a healthy housing market, the home can be sold, avoiding foreclosure proceedings. If, on the other hand, the housing market is declining, the borrower is more likely to default. Foreclosure risk is compounded for borrowers with high loan-to-value ratios (or nominal down payments), since these borrowers have little or no equity, offering little incentive not to default.

A measure of market depth, home sales per household, is also included in the foreclosure models. Even if some current equity is retained, an owner may still be subject to foreclosure if a willing buyer cannot be found quickly enough.

Some of the regional models include a measure of labor market depth, employment per household, further capturing the effects of local economic opportunity. A family that requires the income from both spouses is particularly susceptible to defaulting if one or both wage earners is suddenly unemployed.

HOME PRICES

The unemployment rate is one of the primary drivers behind single-family home prices. As unemployment increases in a region, indicating economic distress, after a lag of roughly one to three quarters, single-family home prices tend to decline. Home sales per household, a measure of market depth, personal income per household as a measure of savings, and total employment as a measure of labor market depth all determine the effect an increase in unemployment will have on home prices.

STRESS SCENARIOS

Once the relationship of the economic drivers to foreclosure rates and single-family home prices is determined, projections based on progressively more pessimistic scenarios are developed. For each region, historical volatility of each of the underlying economic drivers is analyzed by calculating the standard deviation from the trend for each variable over the past two decades.

The stress scenarios are developed by increasing the pressure on the underlying economic drivers by one, one and one-half, and two standard deviations over eight quarters, held at that level for four quarters, and then gradually returning to the base case. The change in the underlying economic drivers and their relationship to foreclosures and home prices for each region determines the potential impact on each region's real estate market.

Forecasts are quarterly over a 5-year period, with each forecast updated as new economic data become available. The 5-year window is consistent with the historical peak default period for residential mortgage loans. Estimates are also made to capture potential foreclosures after the 5-year period.

Exhibit 1: Houston Foreclosure Rate Forecast

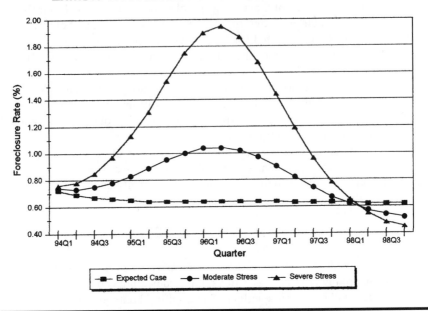

This methodology offers a consistent approach across regions, enabling comparability of pessimistic scenarios. It does not assume one scenario for the U.S., but was developed with the recognition that each region reacts to different macro stimuli, and therefore will respond differently depending on local economic conditions.

As a result, foreclosure rates and single-family home prices in historically volatile regions, whether up or down, exhibit large changes under the various stress scenarios, while well-diversified regions exhibit relatively little change. This is highlighted in Exhibits 1 and 2. Exhibit 1 indicates the baseline forecast of foreclosure rates, as well as one and two standard deviations from the baseline for Houston, while Exhibit 2 depicts the same for Chicago.

Examining unemployment (Exhibits 3 and 4), it is apparent that, although both regions have similar unemployment rates under the same stress scenarios, the foreclosure rates for each region diverge dramatically. This attests to the diversification of Chicago's economy relative to Houston's.

LOAN-BY-LOAN ANALYSIS

The rate of foreclosure and loss severity vary with the individual characteristics of mortgage loans. Key factors impacting performance are: the seasoning of mortgage loans relative to the historical default period, the loan's original loan-to-value ratio, the loan purpose, occupancy, documentation, and loan type.

Exhibit 2: Chicago Foreclosure Rate Forecast

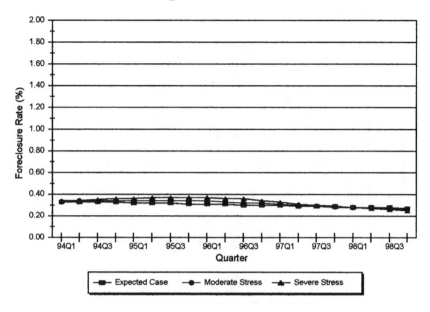

Exhibit 3: Houston Unemployment Rate Forecast

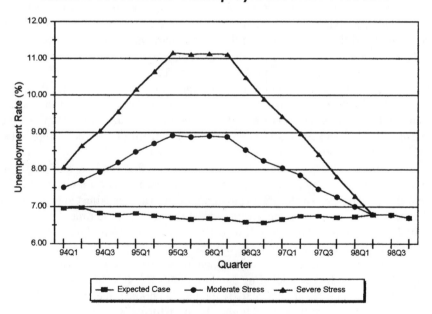

Exhibit 4: Chicago Unemployment Rate Forecast

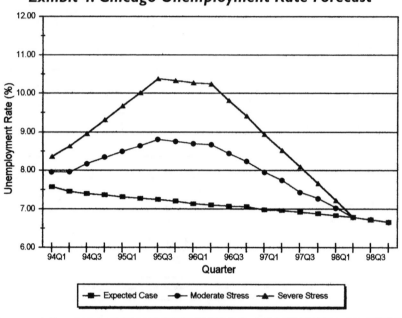

Historically, borrowers do not default within the early years of the loan. This reflects prudent underwriting standards that ensure that borrowers generally have adequate savings to see them through. Foreclosures historically increase in the second and third years, peak in the fourth year, and then tail off over the fifth and sixth years.

In the analysis, regional foreclosure forecasts are modified to reflect the age of each mortgage loan. For a new mortgage, the forecast is adjusted to reflect the increasing probability of foreclosure up to the fourth year. For a seasoned loan, the foreclosure rate curve will shift based upon the age of the loan. A 1-year seasoned loan, for example, will enter the peak foreclosure period in three years, while a 2-year seasoned loan will peak in two years.

Foreclosure forecasts are also modified to reflect the loan's original loan-to-value ratio, loan coupon, occupancy, documentation, and loan type. In addition, if the loan is seasoned, the original appraised value is adjusted to reflect any change in home price between origination of the loan and the time the security is issued. Any decline in value will directly reduce the original appraised value, while price appreciation is discounted by 50%.

The home price forecast is adjusted for loans on properties other than single-family residences, including condominiums and townhomes, as well as for homes larger than those represented by the median home price. Non-single-family detached homes as well as large homes have historically suffered larger market value declines in deteriorating markets.

Exhibit 5: Expected Losses

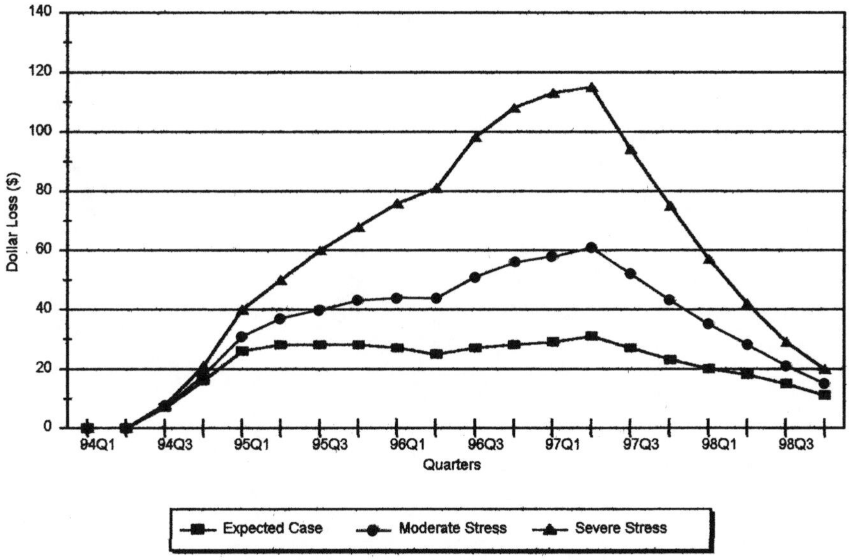

The loss severity, assuming the borrower defaults, is equal to the quarterly home price forecast less 15% in foreclosure costs, 10% in carrying costs (principal and interest advanced by the servicer while the borrower is delinquent), and a quick sale penalty of 12.5%, reflecting that less money is typically realized on a distress sale. Any recoveries due to claims under a primary mortgage insurance policy will be added to the recovery amount.

The total credit enhancement is the foreclosure percentage (a measure of the probability that the loan will default) per quarter multiplied by the quarterly loss severity, summed over a 5-year period plus an estimate of losses anticipated to occur after the 5-year period. This number is calculated for each loan in a pool and then summed to attain the total credit enhancement needed.

The expected or baseline forecast approximates the CCC rating level while the mild and severe stress scenarios approximate the B and BB rating levels, respectively.

Exhibit 5 shows the expected loss per quarter for a newly-originated loan secured by a property in San Francisco with an original loan-to-value ratio of 80% (0.371) as well as the loss under mild (0.61%) and severe (1.03%) stress scenarios. All credit enhancement levels are further adjusted to account for origination and servicing practices of the individual issuers.

Chapter 11

Evaluating Residential Subordinated Tranches

John N. Dunlevy, CFA, CPA
Director and Senior Portfolio Manager
Hyperion Capital Management

Michael Radocy
Securities Analyst
Hyperion Capital Management

INTRODUCTION

The senior/subordinated structure is now the most popular type of credit enhancement in whole-loan CMOs. According to Morgan Stanley Mortgage Research, the market share of the senior/subordinated structure rose from 51% in 1992 to 93% by the end of 1995.

Issuers have favored the senior/subordinated structure both because of its improved execution levels and investor concerns about other types of credit enhancement. Third-party credit enhancement, such as corporate guarantees, letters of credit, and pool policies, have fallen into disfavor due to concerns over downgrades and the general shortage of AAA credit enhancement providers.

Investors have been increasingly drawn to residential subordinated structures for several reasons:

- Yield advantages versus comparably rated corporates
- Excellent mortgage credit history
- Improving structural protection
- Excellent call protection with limited extension risk

In this chapter, we evaluate four important factors to consider when evaluating structural analysis. Next, we show some common methods of stress testing. Finally, other factors such as special hazard, bankruptcy, and fraud risk are analyzed.

COLLATERAL ANALYSIS

The first step in determining the relative value of investing in subordinated tranches is a detailed analysis of the deal's collateral. The collateral represents the raw material from which the deal's final structure is produced. In a typical deal, the collateral might consist of 100 to 400 loans, while for a Re-REMIC structure (a structure created by using tranches from previous deals as collateral) the number of loans constituting the collateral pool could be 1,000 to 5,000. Regardless of the complexity of the structure or the number of loans involved, the steps involved in a collateral analysis are similar.

Risk Factors

The factors to examine during a review of a deal's collateral include:

- Loan type: (fixed/adjustable)
- Loan-to-value (LTV) ratio
- Property type: (single-family, condominium)
- Loan purpose: (purchase, refinancing, equity-take out)
- Loan term: (30-year, 15-year)
- Geographic diversification
- Seasoning of loans
- Occupancy status

Because many of these factors are discussed elsewhere in this book, we highlight only some important features for analyzing subordinated tranches.

Historical analysis of static-pool data has shown that fixed-rate collateral is considerably safer than adjustable-rate mortgage (ARM) collateral. Hence, the subordinated market for deals backed by ARMs is still largely undeveloped. Therefore, this chapter's discussion focuses on fixed-rate mortgages.

A key variable in any analysis of mortgage loans is the loan-to-value (LTV) ratio. This ratio provides important information about a borrower's credit quality and net equity in a property. When analyzing a diskette or tape of loan pool information, what is particularly important is the pool's dispersion of LTV, not its weighted average LTV. Further, it is important to know the issuer's policy in pool insurance coverage for loans in excess of 80% LTV.

Another variable to examine is the percent of a pool that does not represent single-family detached homes. Single-family homes are the largest and most desirable segment of the housing market and have historically shown the best resale performance. Condominiums, townhouses, and planned unit developments do not enjoy the same record of relative price stability.

Loan purpose is another category that should be carefully examined. A potential investor should closely examine the exposure, number of loans, and individual LTVs associated with equity-take out loans (also called cash-out refinancings). The main risk associated with these loans is that the loan may be initiated to increase a borrower's leverage. This can be problematic particularly since no market transaction is evident to confirm market value; that is, these loans are made solely on the basis of an appraisal.

Loan term is another important segment in collateral analysis. Currently, however, most pools backed by 15-year mortgages are separated from those backed by 30-year mortgages. This is the case because 15-year mortgages amortize much faster than 30-year loans, and therefore present less risk due to rapidly declining LTVs. As shown in Exhibit 1, the LTV ratio is considerably different over time for these two mortgage terms.

A final important consideration is geographic diversification. Pools with the lowest level of default risk have consisted of mortgages distributed over a wide geographic area. Many investors have become particularly concerned about their levels of California exposure. This actual level of exposure should be further divided into a pool's exposure to northern and southern California. Many investors analyze a pool's exposure by zip code and overlay these zip codes by California region or county. Within California, as in the rest of the country, geographic diversification limits risk. Recent estimates show that between 50% and 60% of all nonagency borrowers are in California.

Issuer Analysis

Another important consideration in analyzing collateral risk is the credit risk originating with the issuer and servicer. In this analysis we focus on the following factors:

- Issuer
- Servicer
- Underwriting guidelines
- Written policies
- Credit approval
- Cash management/systems
- Quality control
- Collection procedures
- PMI Policies
- Property management record

Exhibit 1: Loan Balance, Market Value, and LTV Ratio for 30-Year and 15-Year Mortgages for Selected Years*

	30-Year			15-Year		
	Year 0	Year 3	Year 7	Year 0	Year 3	Year 7
Loan Balance ($)	240,000	237,003	231,677	240,000	215,080	170,786
Market Value ($)	300,000	300,000	300,000	300,000	300,000	300,000
LTV Ratio	80.0%	79.0%	77.2%	80.0%	71.7%	56.9%

* Assumes an 8% mortgage rate, full amortization, and 0% housing inflation.

• Delinquency/loss history
• Historical track record
• Financial strength

In our discussion, we focus only on the factors that are particularly important in the analysis of subordinated tranches.

The four largest nonagency MBS issuers are Residential Funding, GE Mortgage Capital, Prudential Home (NASCOR), and Countrywide. Of particular importance are the issuer's underwriting guidelines and delinquency/loss history and the servicer's ROE and collection record. In terms of underwriting guidelines, we think that full documentation or alternative documentation (when underwritten by a reputable originator/issuer) should be emphasized. Limited and no documentation loans have consistently shown a record of higher delinquencies and realized losses. Full documentation originations should fulfill the following criteria:

• Independent property appraisal
• Credit check
• Verification of income (VOI)
• Verification of deposit (VOD)
• Verification of employment (VOE)

Another factor to consider is the issuer's policy on compensating interest. Mortgage borrowers are required to make mortgage interest payments in arrears for the number of days that the mortgage is outstanding in the previous accrual period (1 month). Scheduled mortgage payments thus include 30 days interest on the previous month's balance. However, when mortgagors fully prepay a mortgage, they are required only to pay interest on the number of days the loan was outstanding, not for the entire accrual period. The lender/servicer therefore receives less interest than was scheduled, creating an interest shortfall. In a CMO structure, interest shortfalls are allocated pro-rata among the different classes. Some issuers do, however, reimburse investors for this shortfall, by paying compensating interest. Exhibit 2 shows the policies that apply among the larger issuers.

Exhibit 2: Compensating Interest Policies of the Larger Issuers
Issuer Compensating Interest Policies Reimbursement

Issuer	Curtailments?	Full Prepayment?
RFC/RALI	No	Yes, up to maximum 12.5 basis points, usually 3-8 basis points
GE	Yes	Yes, up to 12.5 basis points servicing fee
NASCOR (Pru)	No	Yes, up to 20.0 basis points servicing fee
Countrywide	Yes	Yes, up to 12.5 basis points servicing fee
RASTA	Yes	Yes, up to 12.5 basis points servicing fee

Exhibit 3: Standards & Poor's Prime Loss Coverage Statistics

Rating	Foreclosure Frequency	Market Value Decline	Loss Severity	Loss Coverage
AAA	15%	37%	47%	7.0%
AA	10%	32%	40%	4.0%
A	8%	28%	35%	2.8%

Exhibit 4: Criteria for a Prime Pool

300 or more loans
Geographically diverse
First lien
Single-family detached
Purchase mortgage
30-year term
Fully amortizing
Fixed-rate
Full documentation
Owner occupied
80% LTV
Balances less than $300,000

The value of this compensating interest will vary with the position of a bond class within a CMO structure and the degree of prepayments experience by the collateral pool. Compensating interest is discussed more fully in the structural analysis section of this chapter and in Chapter 3.

Rating Agency Analysis

The rating agencies determine the appropriate amount of credit enhancement for a given pool of collateral. For example, Standard & Poor's (S&P) developed its rating standards through analysis of the Great Depression of the 1930s and the regional recessions of the 1980s (such as in Houston, Texas). S&P's prime pool loss coverage statistics are shown in Exhibit 3. Exhibit 4 lists S&P's criteria for a prime pool.

Application of an AA prime pool rating criteria is shown below:

Home price		$300,000
Loan balance (80% LTV)	240,000	
Market value decline (32%)		−96,000
Market value at foreclosure	204,000	204,000
Loss at time of foreclosure	36,000	
Foreclosure costs (25% of loan)	60,000	
Loss	96,000	
Loss severity (96,000/240,000)	40%	
Foreclosure frequency	10%	
Loss coverage required (40% × 10%)	4%	

Exhibit 5: Impact of LTVs on Base Loss Coverage for an AA Rating

LTV (%)	Frequency Foreclosure (%)	Severity Loss (%)	Coverage Base Loss (%)
50	10	0	0.0
60	10	12	1.2
70	10	28	2.8
80	10	40	4.0
90	15	29	4.4
95	30	37	11.1

* Assumes loans over 80% LTV are covered by private mortgage insurance (PMI)

Source: Standard & Poor's

Exhibit 6: S&P's Adjustments to Base Loss Coverage

Rating	Factor Adjustment
AAA	AA Level × 1.75
AA	Established by model
A	AA Level ÷ 1.42
BBB	AA Level ÷ 2.00
BB	BBB Level ÷ 2.00
B	BB Level ÷ 2.00
NR	Sized to cover expected losses

The credit enhancement levels shown above are for prime pools as defined in Exhibit 4. Adjustments are made to the prime pool loss coverage for a variety of factors. First, the pool's loan-to-value ratios will impact a pool's loss coverage significantly. For example, assuming an AA rating is still desired, LTVs will impact base loss coverage ratios shown in Exhibit 5. Further, once an AA-level of credit enhancement is determined, S&P then scales the base loss coverage up or down depending on the desired rating level as shown in Exhibit 6. In addition to LTV adjustments, a variety of adjustments are made from the prime pool loss coverage levels to adjust for documentation standards, geographic concentration risk, property values, and occupancy status.

Finally, rating approaches vary by agency. Moody's philosophy is that ratings on mortgage securities are comparable to other types of securities (i.e., corporate and municipal bonds). Therefore, from extensive analysis of bonds that it has rated, Moody's determines expected credit losses in terms of yield impairment within each rating level. Fitch's approach is similar to S&P's, except Fitch places more emphasis on regional economics. Duff & Phelps, the newest entry in this market, has a rating philosophy most similar to Moody's.

STRUCTURAL ANALYSIS

Structural analysis involves an assessment of the type of senior/subordinated structure, class tranching, methods of allocating losses, deal triggers, clean-up calls, and compensating interest.

Exhibit 7: Shifting Interest Structure

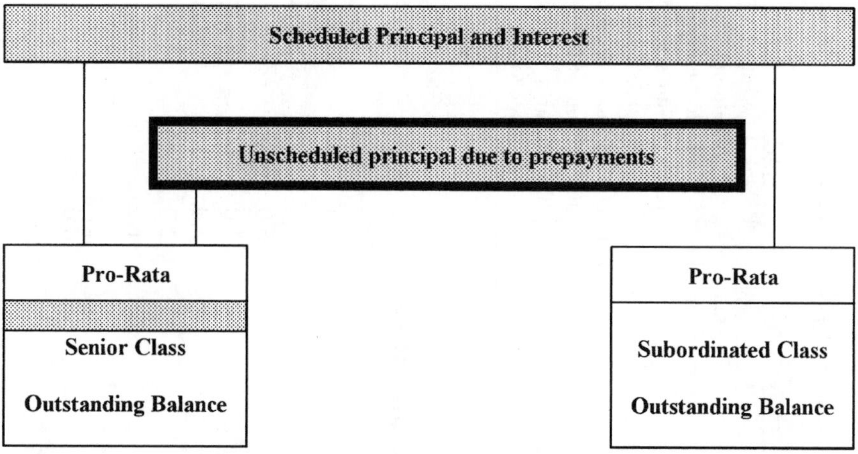

Shifting Interest Structure

A number of variations of the senior/subordinated structure have been employed since the late 1980s, but the most popular structure is the shifting interest mechanism. The subordinated classes are designed to increase a percentage of the total outstanding principal (during the early years of the transaction) and to lend additional credit support for the senior tranches.

In shifting interest structures, amortizing and interest are allocated pro-rata among all the deal's classes. Prepayments that would normally be allocated to the subordinated tranches are shifted to the senior tranches for a period of time. This is illustrated in Exhibit 7. For example, for an initial period of five years, 100% of all prepayments on the mortgage pool are allocated to the senior tranches. After the initial prepayment lockout period, a smaller percentage of the pro-rata share of the subordinated tranche's prepayment is paid to the senior classes. A typical shifting interest structure is given in Exhibit 8.

In a shifting interest structure, the junior class has a claim not on a particular amount of cash flow, but on a portion of the underlying assets. Realized losses act to reduce the lowest subordinated tranche outstanding, on a dollar for dollar basis. Hence, the first-loss tranche (also called the unrated tranche) will be reduced by losses until its principal balance is exhausted, then the next highest rated tranche will absorb losses, and so on.

Class Tranching

Originators/issuers often sell their subordinated cash flows to Wall Street dealers on a competitive basis. Therefore, the issuer is not always sure how a dealer will end up structuring a pool's cash flows. Further, the subordinated cash flows are often sold separately from a pool's senior (AAA-rated) cash flows. A typical senior/subordinated structure will often look like that shown in Exhibit 9.

Exhibit 8: Typical Shifting Interest Mechanism Allocation of Cash Flows

Year	To Subordinated Tranches			To Senior Tranches			
	Pro-rata Interest (%)	Pro-rata Scheduled Principal (%)	Pro-rata Prepayment (%)	Pro-rata Interest (%)	Pro-rata Scheduled Principal (%)	Pro-rata Prepayment (%)	Additional Prepayment
1 through 5	100	100	0	100	100	100 +	100% of Sub.'s Share
6	100	100	30	100	100	100 +	70% of Sub.'s Share
7	100	100	40	100	100	100 +	60% of Sub.'s Share
8	100	100	60	100	100	100 +	40% of Sub's Share
9	100	100	80	100	100	100 +	20% of Sub's Share
10 and up	100	100	100	100	100	100 +	0% of Sub's Share

Exhibit 9: A Typical Senior/Subordinated Structure

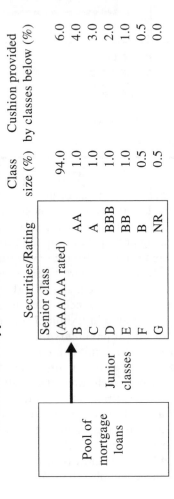

Securities/Rating		Class size (%)	Cushion provided by classes below (%)
Senior class (AAA/AA rated)		94.0	6.0
B	AA	1.0	4.0
C	A	1.0	3.0
D	BBB	1.0	2.0
E	BB	1.0	1.0
F	B	0.5	0.5
G	NR	0.5	0.0

Pool of mortgage loans

Junior classes

Exhibit 10: Information for Determining Multi-Tranche or Single-Tranche Moody's Structure

Multi-Tranche Structure			Single-Tranche Moody's Structure		
Rating	Size	10-Year Spread	Rating	1 Size	10-Year Spread
AA	8,333	135			
A	4,167	155			
BBB	4,167	195	Baa3	22,500	195
BB	4,167	425			
B	2,083	525			
NR	2,083	1,850	NR	2,500	1,850
	25,000	372		25,000	361

The dealer may consider whether to create a multi-tranche structure as shown in Exhibit 9 or the single-tranche "Moody's structure." Exhibit 10 shows some of the information needed to create the single-tranche "Moody's structure." In the example given in Exhibit 9, the dealer would have better execution using this Moody's structure.

The broker/dealer most often chooses the structure which will provide the best all-in execution. Dealers will sometimes go with the higher cost execution when there is a higher probability of successfully selling the B-pieces tranches.

It should be pointed out that the BBB bond in the multi-tranche structure is a very different bond from the Baa3 bond created in the Moody's structure. The single-tranche Moody's structures have been controversial since their introduction in 1993. Many investors argue that the Moody's structure is not of high enough credit quality to deserve Baa3 rating since there is little protection (only the first loss tranche is subordinated in the structure) against a loss of principal.

For example, in the illustration in Exhibit 9, for the BBB bond the multi-tranche structure is supported by 2.00% of the structure, while the Moody's structure is protected by only 0.60%. Advocates of the Moody's structure argue that although the risk of loss is higher, it can withstand a higher degree of losses because its size (5.5%) is substantially larger than the multi-tranche structure (BBB is 0.60% of deal). An example is given in Exhibit 11.

Methods of Allocating Losses

Losses within a senior/subordinated structure are absorbed by the most junior tranche, although the timing and allocation of cash flow can vary within a deal structure. There are two traditional methods of allocating losses within a senior/ subordinated structure: (1) the waterfall method and (2) the direct write-off method. Exhibit 12 highlights the differences between these two methods.

Several distinctions should be made between the two methods. First, under the waterfall method, multi-tranche subordinated structures can be adversely affected with the accrual of interest payments. For example, in the illustration given in Exhibit 12, the mezzanine tranche receives only $28,333 of its scheduled $67,667 interest payment. Therefore, a shortfall is created that must be repaid in later periods. If credit problems persist, the unpaid interest can amount to several months without any cash flow. This problem, which arises due to the payment of the senior's share of the loss in cash, can severely impact the liquidity of the tranche in accrual status.

These bonds have additional problems: (1) extension of average life and duration; (2) roll-up the yield curve; and, (3) no interest-on-interest potential.

Under the direct write-off method, the senior bond is entitled to the proceeds of the liquidated property, and any loss is written off against the most junior tranche. In addition, all interest and scheduled principal are allocated on a pro-rata basis.

Of the major nonagency issuers, Prudential Home and Residential Funding Corporation (pre-August 1993) use the waterfall loss allocation method. The other major issuers, including Residential Funding Corporation (since August 1993), generally use the direct write-off method.

Deal Triggers

An important component to be considered when analyzing senior/subordinated tranches is the deal's "triggers." Triggers are step-down tests that allow the subordinated tranches to be reduced as a percentage of the overall deal. For example, as illustrated in Exhibit 8, the subordinated bonds, in the standard senior/subordinated structure, are locked out from unscheduled payments (prepayments) for five years. Following this lockout period, the prepayment protection gradually "steps down" until the subordinated tranches receive their full pro-rata share of prepayments in year 10.

Exhibit II: Comparison of Two BBB Bonds
Multi-Tranche Structure

Loss %	% Deal	Level of Subordination %	% Tranche Remaining
0.0	0.6	2.0	100.0
1.0	0.6	2.0	100.0
1.5	0.6	2.0	100.0
2.0	0.6	2.0	100.0
2.5	0.6	2.0	22.3

Single-Tranche Moody's Structure

Loss %	% Deal	Level of Subordination %	% Tranche Remaining
0.0	4.0	0.5	100.0
1.0	4.0	0.5	88.8
1.5	4.0	0.5	76.3
2.0	4.0	0.5	63.7
2.5	4.0	0.5	51.1

Exhibit 12: Comparison of Waterfall and Direct Write-Off Methods

Example	
Collateral:	$200,000,000
90% Senior:	180,000,000
5% Mezzanine:	10,000,000
5% Subordinated:	10,000,000
8% Coupon	

Month 1	
Interest:	$1,333,333
Scheduled principal:	200,000
Prepayments:	800,000
Recovery:	100,000
Total:	2,433,333
Realized Losses:	150,000
Reduction Mortgage Balance:	1,250,000

Senior Bonds

	Waterfall Method	Direct Write-Off Method
Interest	$1,200,00	$1,200,000
Scheduled Principal	180,000	180,000
Prepayments	800,000	800,000
Recovery	90,000	100,000
Unrecovered Senior	135,000	0
Total	2,405,000	2,280,000
Beginning Balance	180,000,000	180,000,000
Ending Balance	178,795,000	178,920,000
Change in Balance	−1,205,000	−1,080,000

Mezzanine Bonds

	Waterfall Method	Direct Write-Off Method
Interest	$28,333	$66,667
Scheduled Principal	0	100,000
Prepayments	0	0
Recovery	0	0
Unrecovered Mezzanine	0	0
Payment Unpaid Balance	0	0
Total	28,333	76,667
Write-down Principal	0	0
Ending Unpaid Account Balance	38,334	0
Beginning Balance	10,000,000	10,000,000
Ending Balance	10,000,000	9,990,000
Change in Balance	0	−10,000

Junior Class

	Waterfall Method	Direct Write-Off Method
Interest	$0	$66,667
Scheduled Principal	0	10,000
Prepayments	0	0
Recovery	0	0
Total	0	76,667
Write-down Principal	45,000	150,000
Unpaid Interest	66,667	0
Write-Beginning Balance	10,000,000	10,000,000
Ending Balance	9,995,000	9,840,000
Change in Balance	−45,000	−160,000

Exhibit 13: Average Life at Different Speeds and Step-Down Allowances*

	Prepayment Speed (PSA)		
	250	400	600
All Step-Downs Taken	10.9	9.4	8.2
No Step-Downs Taken	16.0	15.0	13.1

* Assumes 30-year fixed-rate loans, 8.5% gross WAC, 320 WAM, and 4.50% subordinated tranche

During the initial 5-year lockout period, the subordinated bonds delever, that is, they grow as a percentage of the overall deal. These step-downs allow the subordinated bonds to delever. This delevering can occur only if a series of tests (or covenants) are met. These tests address (1) total losses and (2) total delinquencies (60+ days).

These tests are levels of credit performance required before the credit support can be reduced. The tests are applied annually after year 5, and monthly if a test is failed. Of the two tests, the loss test prevents a step-down from occurring if cumulative losses exceed a certain limit (which changes over time). The delinquency test, in its most common form, prevents any step-down from taking place as long as the current over 60-day delinquency rate exceeds 2% of the then-current pool balance.

The above step-down criteria remain in effect on older deals. However, most deals issued after October 1995 are subject to new step-down tests. Following that date new requirements were adopted by the rating agencies, particularly in the area of delinquencies. This was done largely as a result of the fact that many strong deals have performed well and have, in fact, been upgraded by the agencies, despite running delinquencies above 2% of the current pool balance. Under these new tests, the delinquency measures are less stringent and, as a result, present less extension risk for subordinated CMO tranche holders.

The following are the most recent step-down tests employed by Fitch and Standard & Poor's:

> *Fitch:* Step-down allowed if projected losses, assuming 100% default of all current 60+ day delinquencies and a 45% loss severity, do not exceed 25% of original credit enhancement.
>
> *S&P:* Step-down allowed if 60+ day delinquencies are less than 50% of current credit support AND original loss trigger tests remains unchanged.

As a result, it is important to determine which step-down test applies to a specific issue.

Although most nonagency deals in the market will currently pass the loss test, the delinquency test could be a potential problem for many deals. As the loans season and enter their peak loss years, higher delinquencies can cause a deal trigger to disallow a step-down. This occurrence can lead to a significant extension in average life and a roll-up of the yield curve, as illustrated in Exhibit 13. This potential risk should be carefully considered when evaluating securities.

Exhibit 14: Residential Funding 1993-27, Class M2

	225 PSA +100		300 PSA Base		600 PSA –100	
	Maturity	Call	Maturity	Call	Maturity	Call
Average Life	11.63	9.56	10.54	8.06	8.06	4.31
Modified Duration	6.86	6.33	6.53	5.62	5.62	3.53
Last Pay	6/23	11/05	6/23	4/03	4/23	9/98

Source: Hyperion Capital Management

Clean-Up Calls

Nonagency deals are usually subject to a 5% to 10% clean-up call; that is, the issuer has the right to collapse a deal if the deal factor is down to 0.05 to 0.10. As shown in Exhibit 14, the average life can vary significantly if run to the call date. How does this option impact subordinated tranche holders? It has two major effects on B-piece investors. First, since most subordinated tranches trade at discounts to par, it has a positive yield.

Although most deals use a 10% clean-up call, that does not necessarily mean that these deals will be called. Reasons why many deals may not be called include:

1. Advances in computer technology allow servicers to continue to maintain pool servicing functions economically.
2. Adverse selection (last loans in a pool can be the least creditworthy) may prevent the repurchase of these loans.
3. Issuer of pool often retains economic interest in pool by controlling servicing function and/or by owning the IO-tranche.

During the prepayment spike of 1993, investors were shown how negatively convex these securities can be. That is, tranches which were trading above par, were being bid by dealers to their calls, despite the 5-year prepay lockouts and the lack of first-hand experience as to the likelihood of the call option actually being exercised.

Exhibit 15 shows the likelihood of a newly issued deal being eligible for calls during the subordinated tranches' initial 5-year lockout period. For both 5% and 10% clean-up calls, if prepayment speeds are 35% CPR or below there is no interruption of the scheduled 5-year subordinated tranche lockout. If the deal prepays at 45% CPR for five years, the structure with the 5% clean-up call is unaffected, but the 10% call could be exercised in year 4. At very fast prepayment speeds (i.e., 55% to 65% CPR or faster), the calls could come into play as early as the third year after issuance.

Although most deals are structured with the 10% call option, the 5% structure can have substantially lower option costs, while trading at the same yield spreads versus the Treasury curve.

Exhibit 15: Likelihood of a Newly Issued Deal Being Eligible for Call During the Initial Five-Year Lockout Period

| | 25% CPR | | 35% CPR | | 45% CPR | | 55% CPR | | 65% CPR | |
| | 5% | 10% | 5% | 10% | 5% | 10% | 5% | 10% | 5% | 10% |
Year	Call	Call	Call	Call	Call	Call	Call	Call	Call	Call
1	No	No	No	No	No	No	No	No	No	No
2	No	No	No	No	No	No	No	No	No	No
3	No	No	No	No	No	No	No	Yes	Yes	Yes
4	No	No	No	No	No	Yes	Yes	Yes	Yes	Yes
5	No	No	No	No	No	Yes	Yes	Yes	Yes	Yes

Source: Hyperion Capital Management

Compensating Interest

Compensating interest is an important element to examine when evaluating a subordinated tranche. Compensating interest, which represents the potential make up of an interest shortfall caused by the borrower paying only interest though the date of the principal prepayment, can be reimbursed depending on the policy of the issuer. Some issuers provide compensating interest for both partial prepayments (curtailments), and full prepayments. The value of this reimbursed cash flow is a function of several factors (listed in the order of their importance): (1) the speed of prepayments on the mortgage pool, (2) the weighted average life of the subordinated tranche in question, (3) the amount of funds available from the servicer to pay compensating interest, and (4) timing during the month of prepayments.

During a period of slow prepayments, the yield impact of compensating interest can be small, but this reimbursed cash flow can be substantial during periods of prepayment spikes. For example, for a tranche with a 10-year average life, (such as subordinated tranche), the value of receiving full interest assuming a 15-day interest shortfall is as follows:

PSA speed	Basis point value
100	2.0
225	4.5
600	9.0
800	13.8

This value can also be considered in direct relation to the maturity of the bond in question. In bond classes with relatively longer average lives, any shortfall is magnified by the amount of time remaining for other shortfalls to occur. Since any shortfall negatively impacts the investor's yield, longer maturities suffer more than shorter ones. As a result, compensating interest has greater value for longer maturity classes than shorter ones. For example, assuming a 15-day interest shortfall, at a speed of 600 PSA, the value of compensating interest is as follows:

Wtg avg life	Basis point value
1.00	4.0
3.00	8.0
5.00	10.0
7.00	11.0
10.00	12.0
17.00	13.0

In addition, if insufficient funds are available in the deal for compensating interest, investors may suffer a loss of yield. This typically affects only the longest and fastest scenarios. However, in a deal with a small compensating interest allocation (e.g., 5 basis points) even a 1-year bond may suffer yield loss at 600 PSA.

Investors should remember, however, that for issuers that do reimburse, compensating interest reimbursements are usually limited to the amount of servicing fee collected during the month. Therefore, during periods of fast prepayments, interest shortfall will also occur on pools of issuers that do reimburse for compensating interest.

SUBORDINATED TRANCHE STRESS TESTING

After getting comfortable with a deal's collateral and structure, the next step is to perform stress testing to evaluate the adequacy of a tranche's credit protection.

How Do Losses Occur?

Before we can perform a meaningful stress test for subordinated tranches, we must understand how losses occur. As shown in the flowchart in Exhibit 16, before a pool loss can occur a loan must pass from current status into 30-, 60- and 90-day delinquency status before finally entering the foreclosure process. During this process, the servicer plays a very important function.

It should be pointed out that the servicer will commonly advance (principal and interest) to bondholders all the way through foreclosure. These advances, which will be reimbursed once the property is liquidated, will be paid before any pool losses are calculated.

The servicer also will work to prevent any losses from occurring to bondholders. The servicer will attempt to minimize losses, once a loan becomes delinquent, by:

1. Contacting borrower and seeking to bring balance current.
2. Providing borrower with new loan schedule (to bring balance current).
3. Encouraging owners with equity to sell the property.

If any of these strategies are successful, the servicer has prevented a delinquent loan from resulting in a pool loss.

Exhibit 16: Flowchart of the Way Losses Occur

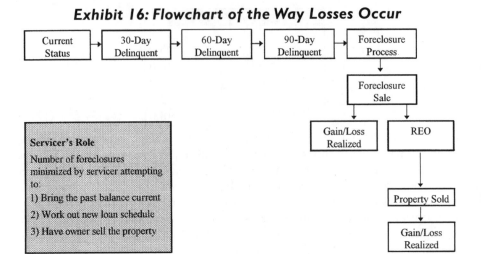

The best defense against pool losses adversely impacting the subordinated tranches is homeowner's equity in the property. That is, the homeowner's down payment or actual perceived equity in a particular property is the first line of defense against default. Defaults rationally occur only when a negative equity condition exists. Otherwise the homeowner would sell the property to prevent default.

Empirical studies on homeowners in negative equity situations show that only a small portion of this universe will default. Statistics show that it requires a period of severe borrower stress (i.e., divorce or unemployment) coupled with a negative equity condition to result in significant levels of default. Mortgage borrowers have resisted default in most negative equity situations due to: (1) the social stigma of losing one's home; (2) fear of tarnishing credit rating; and (3) the ongoing need for housing. Furthermore, negative equity/default conditions are not that common to begin with because of annual versus fixed-debt burden).

As shown in Exhibit 17, a typical loan with a 75% loan-to-value ratio, assuming no housing inflation, will decline to 71.4% after five years and 66.1% after ten years. This occurs due to normal amortization of principal over the loan's 30-year life. If any improvement in housing values is assumed (i.e., 2% housing inflation) the loan-to-value ratio will decline to 64.7% after five years and 54.2% after ten years. Thus credit mortgage pools have a normal tendency to improve with time.

Timing and Extent of Losses

The most widely accepted loss curve is the Moody's curve. This loss curve, which is shown in Exhibit 18, highlights the expected timing of losses for 30-year collateral fixed-rate single-family pools. The shape of the curve highlights the fact that losses do not typically occur during the first year (since the foreclosure process can often last more than one year), but are typically concentrated in years 3 through 7. During these years the homeowner has not had substantial time to amortize principal or enjoy the benefit of housing inflation. This is in direct conflict with the longer part of the loss curve, where losses become quite rare due to seasoning and the build-up of homeowner's equity.

Most conservative investors will perform their stress testing assuming that the allocation of a pool's total losses will be front-loaded. That is, 100% of total losses will occur between years 2 through 4 or 2 through 6.

An important factor in making new subordinated investors comfortable has always been historical pool losses. Historical pool numbers reported in a deal prospectus can be misleading, however, and we do not advocate using these statistics. An important and unbiased measure of historical pool performance is static-pool statistics, as shown in Exhibit 19. These statistics represent all losses that have occurred on all Moody's rated pools during the particular year of origination. For example, all Chase fixed-rate pools originated and rated in 1992 have suffered 12 basis points of cumulative losses through the end of 1995. Investors can use static pool data as a way of extrapolating the extent of total pool losses.

Exhibit 17: Impact of Principal Amortization and Housing Inflation on LTV

Principal Amortization: Impact on LTV

	Year 0	Year 5	Year 10
LTV	75.0%*	71.4%	66.1%

* Assumes gross weighted average coupon (GWAC) of 8.24% and 30-year weighted average maturity (WAM).

Housing Inflation: Impact on LTV

	Year 0	Year 5	Year 10
LTV	75.0%*	64.8	54.2

* Assumes gross weighted average coupon (GWAC) of 8.24% and 30-year weighted average maturity (WAM) and 2% housing inflation.

Exhibit 18: Moody's Loss Curve

Age	Losses	Cumulative
1	0.5%	0.5%
2	3.5%	4.0%
3	11.0%	15.0%
4	21.5%	36.5%
5	13.5%	57.5%
6	13.5%	71.0%
7	11.5%	82.5%
8	7.5%	90.0%
9	7.0%	97.0%
10+	3.0%	100.0%

Exhibit 19: Cumulative Loss Information

	1995	1994	1993	1992	1991
Chase	0.00	0.01	0.01	0.12	0.10
FBS	—	—	0.09	0.38	—
GECMS	0.00	0.14	0.03	0.08	0.27
Pru	0.01	0.02	0.10	0.44	1.30

Source: Morgan Stanley

Exhibit 20: Cumulative Loss Information
Standard & Poor's Historical Loss Numbers
Percent of Original Balance

Year of Origination	30-Year		15-Year		ARMs	
	Average Loss	Median Loss	Average Loss	Median Loss	Average Loss	Median Loss
1986	0.43	0.27	0.07	0.01	N/A	N/A
1987	0.50	0.44	0.19	0.12	0.59	0.47
1988	1.15	1.29	0.19	0.27	1.44	0.45
1989	0.95	0.64	0.51	0.48	1.61	1.50
1990	0.89	0.59	0.34	0.38	2.44	1.58
1991	0.36	0.23	0.15	0.06	0.85	0.14
1992	0.11	0.02	0.02	0.00	0.21	0.00
1993	0.01	0.00	0.01	0.00	0.04	0.00
1994	0.00	0.00	0.00	0.00	0.00	0.00

More recently, Standard & Poor's produced a study which contained historical loss data. S&P's numbers, however, track losses by year of origination and by product type: 30- and 15-year fixed-rate loans and adjustable-rate mortgages.

As indicated in Exhibit 20, the results show an average loss on transactions backed by 30-year fixed-rate pools, originated between 1986 to 1990, of 0.71%. Meanwhile, the loss experience of 15-year fixed-rate mortgages was 0.20%, or less than one-third of 30-year product. Finally, average losses from adjustable-rate mortgages over the same 5-year period were 1.69%, or more than twice the loss experience of 30-year fixed-rate mortgages.

The S&P study by rating category is shown in Exhibit 21. The rate of default by credit rating compares favorably with corporate defaults (as reported by a 1970 to 1994 study by Moody's). According to the S&P study shown in Exhibit 21, no tranche originally rated A or higher backed by 30-year collateral has ever defaulted. Similarly, no BB or higher-rated tranche backed by 15-year collateral has defaulted.

Exhibit 22 shows the yield impact of the default rates shown in Exhibit 21. In addition, the risk-adjusted spread of subordinated CMOs versus corporates is indicated. As shown in Exhibit 22, subordinated CMOs enjoy vastly superior risk-adjusted spreads compared to corporate bonds.

Exhibit 21: Default Occasions by Credit Tranche
Default Occasions
Percent

Credit Rating (S&P)	30-Year Fixed	15-Year Fixed	Corporates (Moody's)
AAA	0.0	0.0	0.7
AA	0.0	0.0	0.8
A	0.0	0.0	1.8
BBB	0.4	0.0	4.7
BB	8.0	0.0	18.4
B	31.7	3.6	36.7

Exhibit 22: Yield Impact of Default Rates by Credit Tranche
Yield Impact of Default Rates
Basis points

	30-year CMOs			Corporates			
Credit	Nominal Spread	Yield Loss	Loss-Adjusted Spread	Nominal Spread	Yield Loss	Loss-Adjusted Spread	Risk-Adjusted Advantage
AA	125	0	125	42	4	38	87
A	145	0	145	55	9	46	99
BBB	165	11	154	75	25	50	104
BB	430	47	383	220	110	110	273
B	900	453	447	400	249	151	296

Estimating Potential Pool Losses

In order to assess the potential risk of a non-agency pool, an investor has to address three key issues:

1. Amount of loans that will default (foreclosure frequency).
2. The amount of the loss on default (loss severity).
3. The timing of the loss.

There are two quick and simple methods to estimate what total losses will be on a pool. The first estimates expected losses using the Moody's loss curve. Assume a 1991 originated Pru-Home pool has had the following loss record:

1996 losses	Cumulative losses	Number of years seasoned
0.25%	0.15%	5

According to the Moody's loss curve, pools that are five years seasoned should have experienced 57.5% of the lifetime losses, and losses occurring during the fifth year should represent 21% of total lifetime losses. Therefore, the investor can get a range of losses based on this seasoned pool's actual performance:

Exhibit 23: Estimating Pool Losses by Assigning Cure Rates by Delinquency Category

	Delinquencies (%)					
	30-Day	60-Day	90-Day	Foreclosures	REO	Total
Status (1)	2.05	0.77	0.53	0.14	0.10	3.59
Est. Non-cured Default % (2)	5.00	15.00	30.00	50.00	100.00	
Foreclosure Frequency						
(1) × (2) = (3)	0.10	0.12	0.16	0.07	0.10	
Loss Severity (4)	30.00	30.00	30.00	30.00	30.00	
Estimated Loss						
(3) × (4) = (5)	0.03	0.04	0.05	0.02	0.03	0.17

Projected losses (cumulative) = 0.25/0.575 = 0.43%

Projected losses (5th year) = 0.15/0.21 = 0.71%

Under this method, estimated lifetime losses would range between 43 and 71 basis points.

Another popular method, illustrated in Exhibit 23, takes recent pool performance and estimates cumulative losses by assigning a probability factor to each category. In the exhibit, we are using Citicorp's estimated cure rates to calculate estimated pool losses. This example shows that loans in the 30-day delinquent category default approximately at a rate of 5%, while loans in foreclosure default 50% of the time. After coming up with a foreclosure frequency, we would apply a loss severity rate of 30%. The result is an estimated lifetime cumulative loss of 17 basis points.

This method, if used, should be updated often to reflect changes in loan categorization. That is, as a loan moves from 30 days to 60 days delinquent, the estimated losses will increase due to the lower assumed cure rate.

SDA Model

In May 1993, the Public Securities Association (PSA) came up with a benchmark default standard for evaluating the credit risk of nonagency MBS (see Exhibit 24). The model is designed along the same lines of the PSA's prepayment curve, which is used by investors to analyze prepayment risk in mortgage securities. Investors can use multiples of the SDA curve to stress test mortgage securities.

As shown in Exhibit 24, the SDA curve begins with an assumed default rate of 0.02% in month 1 and increases by 0.02% per month until it reaches a peak of 0.60% in month 30. This peak level default is maintained through the 60th month and then subsides monthly until reaching its constant level of 0.03% for the pool's remaining life.

An important point to remember is that the SDA default curve in any month is applied to the remaining balance of the performing loans at the end of the month. Therefore, the cumulative default rate over the life of the pool depends not only on the assumed monthly default rate but also on the prepayment assumption. This is illustrated in Exhibit 25. Note that the larger the assumed prepayment speed, the lower the cumulative default level for a given percentage of the SDA model.

The SDA curve's basic assumption of 100 SDA and 150 PSA produces cumulative default levels of 2.78% — which is high on a historical basis. Only high LTV loans have generally experienced this type of default levels. Most historical studies show that for loans with LTV ranging between 70% and 80%, defaults have ranged between 0.5% and 1.5%, which would equate to less than 50% SDA.

To use SDA model properly, the investor must provide input assumptions for:

• Loss severity level
• Servicer advancing
• Time to liquidation on defaults

The final step in our analysis of a subordinated tranche is stress testing to determine the impact on credit-adjusted yield. The idea is to break the collateral into different groupings that can then be stressed in different ways. The most common grouping is by LTV ratio. That is, the loans are broken into LTV clusters and stressed at different foreclosure frequencies and loss severities. One method is to apply the Texas scenario to these LTV clusters. The idea, of course, is to insure that the security in question can survive these stress testings.

Exhibit 24: Annual Default Rate, 100% SDA

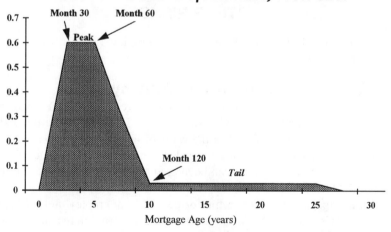

Exhibit 25: Cumulative Default Rates (%)*

	50 SDA	100 SDA	200 SDA
100 PSA	1.56	3.09	6.08
150 PSA	1.40	2.78	5.47
400 PSA	0.88	1.74	3.45

*Assume 30-year fixed loans with 360 WAM and 8% coupon.

Exhibit 26: Loss Adjusted Yield Matrix for Typical "B" Rated Subordinate Tranche

Scenario	SDA (%)	Loss Severity	100 PSA			250 PSA			400 PSA		
			Yield (%)	A/L	Cum Loss	Yield (%)	A/L	Cum Loss	Yield (%)	A/L	Cum Loss
1	0	20	14.2	15.2	0.00	15.0	11.4	0.00	15.6	9.6	0.00
2	40	20	14.1	15.4	0.37	15.0	11.4	0.24	15.6	9.6	0.16
3	50	20	13.6	16.2	0.47	14.8	11.6	0.29	15.5	9.6	0.20
4	75	20	12.0	17.8	0.69	13.8	12.4	0.43	14.8	10.0	0.30
5	100	20	10.8	19.7	0.92	12.8	13.2	0.58	14.1	10.4	0.40
6	150	20	6.7	25.8	1.36	10.9	16.0	0.87	12.9	11.3	0.60

Stress testing also involves the testing of housing values. The idea is to calculate a credit-adjusted yield on the individual tranche. Therefore, the investor will need a model that can calculate the yield impact of losses, payment delays, and "trigger' events. Most investors, when calculating credit-adjusted yields, will assume a front loading of defaults and cumulative losses.

The final step is the production of a loss matrix, which will show the credit-adjusted yield under a variety of scenarios. Exhibit 26 is a loss-adjusted yield matrix for a typical "B" rated subordinated tranche.

OTHER RISKS

Losses can also result through: (1) borrower bankruptcy; (2) borrower fraud; and, (3) special hazard risk.

Borrower Bankruptcy

When a borrower files for personal bankruptcy, there is a risk that a bankruptcy judge could reduce the borrower's mortgage debt. This debt reduction, called a cramdown, usually occurs only when the value of the borrower's home has fallen so that in the mortgage loan balance exceeds the home's market value. If a cramdown is ordered, the loan's terms can be altered by reducing the unpaid principal balance or the loan's interest rate.

A mortgage borrower can file for personal bankruptcy under Chapter 7, Chapter 11, or Chapter 13. A few cramdowns have occurred in recent years in settling Chapter 13 bankruptcy cases. Chapter 13 allows for restructuring or forgiving debts while letting borrowers retain their assets. However, the 1993 Supreme Court case of Nobelman versus American Savings ruled that a borrower filing under Chapter 13 cannot effectively reduce its mortgage debtors.

In a Chapter 7 bankruptcy filing, a type of bankruptcy that generally involves liquidation of assets to make payments to creditors, cramdowns have also been disallowed under a Supreme Court ruling.

Finally, cramdown filings under Chapter 11 are more rare than those under Chapter 7 or Chapter 13 because of their cost and complexity. Jumbo loan borrowers are more likely to file under Chapter 11 because this section can be used only when the debtor's secured debt exceeds $350,000. According to Inside *Mortgage Securities*, during 1992 Chapter 11 filings represented only 0.35% of individual filings; 71.4% filed under Chapter 7, and 28.2% under Chapter 13.

The rating agencies determine the size of the bankruptcy carve-out, based on the collateral. For example, Standard & Poor's states that for securities backed by mortgages that exceed 75% LTV, issuers must have a bankruptcy reserve of $100,000 or have cramdown coverage equal to 121 basis points.

Borrower Fraud

Another potential risk to the nonagency investor arises from borrower fraud or misrepresentation during the application process. This type of risk is often not covered by the originator/conduit/sellers' representations and warranties.

Senior/subordinated structures provide a carve-out as protection against the risk of fraud. The risk of fraud losses is front-loaded. That is, borrowers who misrepresent their income, employment, or net worth will generally run into payment problems early in the loan's life. Therefore, fraud coverage is largest at issuance — around 2%, declining to 0% by the sixth year.

Special Hazard Risk

Special hazard risk deals losses can result from properties damaged by earthquakes, mud-slides, tidal waves, volcanoes, or floods. Such losses are excluded from coverage under homeowners' and private mortgage insurance policies.

Subordinated tranches absorb special hazard losses up to a predetermined capped amount that will decline as the mortgage pool amortizes. This "capped" amount is determined by the rating agencies. Standard & Poor's requires a triple-A level of special hazard risk equal to the highest of:

- 1% of current mortgage pool balance.
- Twice the principal balance of the pool's largest loan.
- The principal balance of the highest zip code concentration within California.

Special hazard losses in excess of this capped amount are distributed among the senior and subordinated classes pro-rata.

Historically losses from special hazards are quite rare because:

- Special casualty insurance is often required on homes in high risk areas (i.e., flood insurance in flood zones, and earthquake insurance along known fault lines).
- Damage caused indirectly by an act of God, such as water damage or fire caused by an earthquake, can be covered under standard homeowners' policies.

Another important factor is land value. In costly areas such as Southern California, the value of land can represent over 50% of the value of a single-family home. Thus, if a home is totally destroyed, the land value acts as a floor in terms of the loan's loss severity.

Finally, where damage to property caused by special hazards is uninsured, the homeowner can often get access to low-cost government funds to help rebuild. Therefore, special hazards have not historically resulted in significant losses. In addition, geographic diversification can help to limit a pool's risk to special hazard risk.

CONCLUSION

In this chapter we have discussed a method of analyzing subordinated CMOs. This started with a detailed review of a deal collateral, followed by an understanding of structural risk. We discussed tranche stress testing before finally considering other risks (such as bankruptcy, fraud, and special hazard).

Of course, deciding on whether to purchase a subordinated tranche is also a function of the following:

• Relative value opportunities versus alternative products.
• Portfolio considerations (i.e., applicable benchmarks).
• Client objectives and constraints.
• Liquidity considerations.

We believe that subordinate CMOs can provide an excellent opportunity to achieve a superior risk/return profile and yet maintain a reasonable degree of liquidity within a broadly diversified portfolio.

Chapter 12

A Credit-Intensive Approach to Analyzing Whole-Loan CMOs

Edward L. Toy
Director: Private Placements
Teachers Insurance and Annuity Association

From 1987 to 1993, generally accepted estimates are that CMO issuance in the whole-loan mortgage-backed market grew from roughly $11 billion to $100 billion. A confluence of factors resulted in a winding down of the refinancing wave in early 1994. The size of the market has since declined to $31 billion in 1995 and $36 billion in 1996. Unlike agency securities, whole-loan CMOs do not benefit from any kind of government support. Investment decisions must, therefore, necessarily rely on different criteria.

The analysis of investment opportunities in the whole-loan mortgage market can be divided into two principal components: fundamental and technical. While aspects of the two components inevitably overlap at times, this chapter focuses on fundamental analysis.

WHY CREDIT ANALYSIS IS IMPORTANT

While historical experience in the mortgage market has generally been very good, it is nonetheless true that borrowers do default on their loans and losses do occur. Without the benefit of a guarantee from FNMA, FHLMC, or GNMA to cover such losses, investors must rely on the quality of the underlying collateral and other forms of credit enhancement like subordinate securities, cash reserves, and pool insurance or guarantees. Subordinate securities represent only a small portion of the overall pool and other forms of credit enhancement rarely represent a significant percentage of the pool either. A careful fundamental approach to the analysis of the collateral will lead to a basic understanding of a mortgage pool's underlying quality and an ability to forecast its future performance on the basis of reasonably rational criteria. Alternatively, developing a basic understanding of the relevant risk areas will permit the setting of logical standards for making comparisons between competing investments or avoiding certain pools altogether.

While such a credit-intensive approach is important generally, it is critical for investors in the subordinate classes. These are the at-risk securities that have a greater likelihood of being impaired. In a senior-subordinate structure, the subordinate classes, or B-pieces, act as internal credit enhancement for the senior, or class A, securities. Depending on the quality of the collateral, the subordinate classes in total will account for between 5% and 8% of the structure.

Generally, the subordinate layer is further tranched into several sub-classes. The result is very small layers with gradually smaller levels of subordination to support the given certificate. The most junior security, referred to as a first-loss piece, may be no larger than 25 basis points or 0.25% of the pool. The actual size and credit quality of the subordinate classes will be determined by the rating agencies analyzing the pool, but market acceptance of different subordination levels is also an important influence.

Analyzing a pool from the credit side is more important to B-piece investors because if the pool experiences defaults and losses on foreclosure, the subordinate classes will be allocated those losses sequentially, beginning with the lowest class, or first-loss piece. The senior bonds in any structure are allocated losses only after the subordinate classes are completely eliminated. Since the subordinate classes are allocated all of the first losses even though they represent only a small percentage of the overall structure, the subordinate classes are subject to a great deal of "negative leverage." This negative leverage will continue to be quite substantial until the pool experiences prepayments. With prepayments first allocated to the senior bonds in the typical senior-subordinate structure, gradually the subordinate classes will represent an increasing percentage of the remaining pool, thus reducing the negative leverage.

As even a relatively low level of losses can impair the value of the subordinate certificates, it is obvious that any investor considering such an investment must first develop an opinion about the likelihood of losses exceeding the level of subordination supporting the security. Even an extremely well-underwritten pool should be expected to experience some losses during its life. If the proposed investment is one of the lower classes or first-loss pieces, where little or no actual support exists in the structure, protection from losses will depend more on equity in the underlying collateral.

If one continues to assume some nominal level of losses, the emphasis shifts somewhat for these lowest classes to the timing for the losses. This is because until defaults and losses are actually experienced, even the lowest classes continue to receive a share of the interest and principal cash flow that is being generated by the pool.

A credit intensive approach to the analysis of mortgage pools will result in a strong base for estimating the likelihood and timing of losses in a pool.

THE ORIGINATOR/UNDERWRITER

The credit-intensive part of whole-loan analysis must begin with the seller of the underlying mortgages, or the entity on whose underwriting standards and abilities any investor relies. This may be the actual originator and underwriter of the mortgages. Or, it could be a conduit that is purchasing mortgages from various sources and re-underwriting those mortgages before combining them into a pool.

In this latter case, the underwriting standards of the actual originators are not relevant, because the conduit, even if it purchases packages of mortgages in bulk, will pick and choose out of that package, throwing out mortgages that do not fit its underwriting standards. The conduit will also dictate underwriting standards to its sellers so that the weeding out is not extensive. In some situations, the underwriting criteria referred to may also be underwriting guidelines of the mortgage pool insurers, to the extent a conduit program or dealer relies on pool certification by a pool insurer to package transactions. In some rare situations, the pool could involve a combination of all three. In most situations, the originator/underwriter is also the servicer or master servicer of the pool.

Historical Performance

Review of an originator begins with a basic and fairly simple quantitative approach with respect to its historical performance. Delinquency information is reviewed. Besides delinquencies, the review should include foreclosure data and segmentation of the total delinquency data into 30-, 60-, and 90-day delinquencies. Each of these should be analyzed in absolute dollar terms and as a percentage of the originator's servicing or master servicing portfolio. Generally speaking, only a fraction of 30-day delinquencies turn into unresolvable defaults. Therefore, while any delinquency may be problematic, the delinquencies of 60 to 90 days and 90 days or greater are more important.

One should view with some degree of suspicion low overall delinquency statistics, but high levels of serious delinquencies, either compared with the overall numbers or compared with other originators. This may indicate a definitional oddity that simply does not report delinquencies until they become more serious. Alternatively, a sudden increase in 30-day delinquencies, as a percentage of the overall portfolio, may be an indication of future problems. Just as for a straight corporate issuer, some degree of trend analysis can be quite revealing.

Finally, loss experience on foreclosures is also important. To the extent that an underwriter is more aggressive with respect to approving borrowers and debt-to-income levels, much of this can be offset with tighter underwriting of the collateral or enforcing tighter loan-to-value standards, resulting in lower loss levels. Of course, higher loss levels may indicate a lax underwriting approach, as opposed to just being aggressive. Housing price volatility does tend to increase with size, especially among jumbo loans. Most originators try to offset this somewhat by imposing tighter loan-to-value ratios with increased loan size, or alternatively by limiting loan size for higher loan-to-value ratios.

In looking at performance statistics, it is important to factor out distortions, both positive and negative. One factor that has led to performance statistics looking better than reality is high origination levels in a low interest rate environment. A large influx of new mortgages into a servicing portfolio will make the numbers look better than they actually are by increasing the denominator in the equation. Unless underwriting of the borrowers has been unusually weak, it would be surprising to see many newly originated mortgages going delinquent in the first year or two.

Generally speaking, one would not expect the typical mortgage pool to experience any significant defaults until the third or fourth year after origination (the "standard default curve"). Thus, in a high origination pattern, the delinquency and default numbers, which constitute the numerator in the equation, would initially stay relatively low. The easiest way to factor out this distortion is to take the current delinquency information but use the prior year's portfolio balance as a denominator, or, alternatively, use the average of the two years.

On the other side, when we see somewhat higher delinquency data, it is helpful at times to take a closer look at the reasons instead of making the automatic judgment that the underwriting is poor. For example, many originators in the late eighties were aggressive in pushing limited documentation programs to build volume. Since limited documentation loans tend to show higher defaults over time, the poor experience of these "low-doc/no-doc" mortgages may inflate the default numbers.

Current origination patterns emphasize full documentation underwriting and only permit limited documentation loans in selected situations. The shift for some originators has been from highs of 60% or 70% of originations to less than 20%. On top of this shift, today's limited documentation loans for most originators are themselves of better quality. In any case, it is only fair to note when applicable that the current profile of originations has a different breakdown and adjust historical numbers accordingly.

There are also several ways of taking a static pool approach that will reveal the true quality of the underwriting. Static pool analysis focuses on breaking down the originator's performance by origination year. The most common approach is to take the total number of loans originated in each year and determine how many loans became delinquent within 6, 12, and 18 months of origination. It can be equally informative to develop a foreclosure curve for each origination year and compare the accumulation pattern for those years. Static pool analysis is useful because overall portfolio numbers are affected by the addition of new loans and the prepayment of older loans.

Underwriting Criteria

The basic quantitative approach, of course, only gets us part of the way. Second is a thorough review of the underwriting criteria itself. While unforeseen problems can always occur, leading to a default on a mortgage, participants in the mortgage market know that certain types of loans have a higher probability of going into default. Also, loss severity can vary depending on the loan category. It would be easy simply not to make those loans, but that could also seriously limit an originator's ability to generate product. Therefore, originators set up different underwriting criteria to compensate somewhat for the additional risk of default. The task for investors is then to look at what adjustments exist for currently known risk areas.

There are four common areas of concern: documentation type, loan purpose, property type, and occupancy type. The relevant issue first is how the originator compensates for these risk areas. The most common methods are limitations on loan size or maximum loan-to-value ratios.

For example, if we accept the fact that cash-out refinancing mortgages have historically shown a higher probability of default, one would expect the maximum allowed loan-to-value to be lower, say 75%, as opposed to general restrictions for other loan types that may go as high as 90% or 95%. Also, if the usual maximum loan size is $1 million, the maximum loan size for cash-out refinancing loans might be as low as $650,000. Besides establishing specific standards to minimize known risk factors, the underwriter should also have rules that limit the possibility of loans that have cross-over risk, such as including cash-out refinancing mortgages that are also limited documentation loans. This kind of cross-over would compound the likelihood of default on the loan.

Third, and perhaps most important when reviewing originators, is the basic issue of quality control. The key is whether the establishment of underwriting criteria is a dynamic process under constant review and evaluation. The better originators will have set procedures for reassessing their approach. Many will take a regular sample of their servicing portfolio and re-underwrite the loans, looking for trends in defaults or losses.

This will likely go as far as including another appraisal. If there is a material change in the appraised value, this will be deemed suspicious, especially if the original appraisal is relatively recent. The result could be a conclusion that a given appraiser is aggressive or unreliable, and therefore no longer qualified for that originator's loan underwriting.

As discussed earlier, originators will make certain loans, notwithstanding the fact that they are recognized as having higher risk characteristics. The originator's quality control policies should include an ongoing review of the actual default rate and loss severity of such loans. If the originator concludes that the numbers are higher than expected, this should lead to adjustments for allowed loan-to-value ratios and loan sizes.

For the conduits, the statistical analysis is also key to tracking discernible patterns for defaults coming from a given mortgage originator. If a given originator shows a higher than average default pattern, that should result in the originator being put on notice, or possibly being deleted from the approved pool of originators. Generally the conduit will first look to working with the originator to determine and correct any underwriting problems.

Since in most situations the originator is also servicer or master servicer, the originator's servicing capabilities and procedures should often also be a subject of discussion during due diligence. There are several areas to focus on, such as capacity and efficiency of the servicing operation. One simple approach to getting a quick read on this is to review in some detail the mechanics of the servicing operation, specifically the procedures in place for dealing with delinquencies. For example, how quickly does the servicer react to a delinquency to get payments flowing again?

Given the substantial growth of some servicing portfolios, capacity utilization and efficiency are important issues, just as in any service-intensive industry. Many servicing operations have turned increasingly to various levels of automation to improve the effectiveness of a given group of service representatives. Just as an added level of review, it can be informative to see how and where loan files are maintained, including how much is computerized.

THE COLLATERAL

To the extent an originator/servicer passes this kind of detailed review, analyzing individual pools of collateral becomes a much more mechanical exercise. The process of reviewing individual pool characteristics can result in a sea of statistics. The easier approach is to use any anomaly as a red flag warranting further review. While it might not be possible to correct the problem by changing the constitution of the pool, any investor should at least recognize, and presumably be compensated for, pools that carry higher risk components. There are several key points that require emphasis.

Loan Type

One overall factor to be considered is loan type. The mortgage market is dominated by basic 30-year fully amortizing fixed-rate mortgages. Using that as a benchmark, there are other loan types that have tended to show different performance characteristics. Fifteen-year mortgages, another basic product type, have proven to be higher-quality collateral over time. This is because a shorter term requires higher debt service requirements. Borrowers who choose this option are, therefore, higher-income individuals who can afford to make those payments. Also, the more rapid amortization of principal results in a faster build-up of book equity. It is also true that pools of 15-year mortgages tend to have lower loan-to-value ratios to begin with as these borrowers generally bring more equity to the transaction.

One key characteristic for both of the mortgage types is that they are fully amortizing. On the opposite extreme are balloon mortgages. While there are undoubtedly many reasons for borrowers choosing a balloon mortgage, one significant one is the inability to meet higher debt service requirements under a fully amortizing one. This lower level of financial flexibility, when combined with a slower amortization of principal, results in loans that are inherently riskier. Beyond the increased likelihood of default during the life of the loan, pools that include balloon mortgages also face the potential problems that may arise in refinancing the larger final payment. The borrower's ability to do so will depend on the actual size of the balloon, the direction of home values and interest rates during the interim, and changes in the borrower's creditworthiness.

One last major product type is adjustable-rate mortgages, or ARMs. The principal concern surrounding ARM products is the potential for "sticker shock" whenever the rate adjusts. This is particularly true with the first adjustment because the initial coupon is usually an especially low teaser rate offered to entice the borrower into choosing that option. There is also the possibility that in underwriting the loan, the originator used a lower initial debt service requirement to qualify the borrower, rather than one that is more realistic for the longer term. The risk of a substantial increase in debt service, and therefore the risk of default, however, exists whenever there is a rising interest rate environment.

Geographic Concentration

The one pool characteristic recently requiring the most attention is geographic concentration. Given the historical balance of originations, this has most often evolved into a question of California concentration. Since most whole-loan packages consist almost exclusively of jumbo products, and California accounts for a very large percentage of jumbo loan originations, many pools have also been formed with exposures to California loans of 60% to 70%, and even higher. Notwithstanding the many arguments about the size and diversification of the California economy, that kind of pool concentration in most cases is imprudent.

Some have rationalized that if an investor's overall portfolio of mortgage securities is lighter in California exposure, say, 20% on average through all the individual pools, it should be possible to take a pool that is higher because the overall portfolio concentration is still low. Even though portfolio considerations are important, this logic is faulty, because the strength or weakness of one pool has no direct impact on other pools in the portfolio.

For the logic to prove out, a certain scenario would have to be true. When one pool, because of its higher California concentration experiences some difficulties, thus weakening or expending credit enhancement levels; and other pools, given their lower concentrations, maintain their credit enhancement levels or perhaps even experience improvements with loan prepayments; the first pool would have to be able to gain access to the latter's improved positions. This is, of course, not the case, since all pools are distinct legal entities with no direct link. An indirect link might occur in the marketplace to the extent that market prices for the lower concentration pools could improve at the same time that the market prices for the higher concentration pools deteriorate. This is not a very reliable link. An analogous argument is to believe that owning an IO and PO, but of different coupon collateral, represents a perfect interest rate hedge.

Unfortunately, even the most detailed and thorough economic analysis cannot fully substitute for simple diversification. Until it actually occurred, few believed that home values in California could decline as far as they did between

1990 and 1993. And if one were to rely heavily on historical experience, one would have expected defaults in California to be only a fraction of the national average. Defaults in 1993, in California, were much closer to, and in some areas of the state exceeded the national average.

This is not to say that California is the only state to be on the watch for in terms of heavy concentrations, although the focus inevitably moves there because the state accounts for so much of the jumbo loan originations in the United States. Any concentration in any one state is not wise because that pool is vulnerable to the specific economic circumstances of that state. Over time, we have also experienced varying levels of concern about the Northeast, especially Massachusetts and the tri-state area surrounding New York City. Also, lest we forget, one of the most oft-referred to disaster scenarios is, after all, the "Texas Scenario."

Geographic dispersion goes beyond just looking on a state-by-state basis. Further limitations are important since maintaining a 10% concentration maximum in California is good only to the extent that all those California loans are not located in the same zip code. A very large percentage of California's jumbo originations come in the Los Angeles area and its surrounding counties. Rules of thumb have thus evolved in terms of concentrations within individual five-digit zip code areas, three-digit zip code areas, and county concentrations. Economics notwithstanding, it is always good to know that a large percentage of a pool's loans are not within five miles of the most recent earthquake's epicenter.

One factor that has provided some limited relief on the California factor is the divergence between northern and southern California. While both are subject to the same state government influences, the size of the state and the differences in economic drivers mitigate higher California exposures with some north-south diversification.

Of some greater difficulty is looking at cross-border concentrations. Suppose a pool has 20% of its loans in Maryland and 20% of its loans in Virginia. A 20% limit might be deemed acceptable, but this profile would mean 40% between two neighboring states, plus whatever might be located in the District of Columbia. The combination is actually a relatively small geographic area. A more detailed look might also show that in fact all 40+% of the pool is located within a very narrow geographic corridor between northern Virginia and Baltimore.

This is not to say that some exceptions could not be found with more detailed analysis. It might be possible to be more comfortable with a pool that has a somewhat higher California concentration if one finds that the loans in California were underwritten to tighter standards. Beginning in 1992, many originators in fact began to hold California underwriting to tighter standards, either by management focus or outright policy. If we could break down a pool between California loans and non-California loans, this differential might become readily apparent. In one pool, for example, we might be willing to go somewhat higher if the California loans had generally lower loan-to-value ratios, especially if the differential between the California loans and the pool in general increased with increasing loan sizes. There might also be greater comfort if a larger percentage of the California loans fell into the more attractive categories of single-family detached, owner-occupied, primary residence, rate/term refinancing mortgages with full documentation packages.

Other Collateral Characteristics

Geographic dispersion is not the only area that requires detailed analysis. Other collateral characteristics warrant careful review. These include documentation type, loan purpose, property type, and occupancy type.

Documentation Type

In documentation type, a significant difference generally exists between full documentation and different limited documentation programs. A full documentation package includes a significant amount of paperwork, verifying data that the borrower has supplied about employment history, income levels, and net worth. When an originator agrees to omit some of this documentation, the potential exists that not everything is as it appears.

There are times when some amount of flexibility in documentation requirements is warranted and does not materially change the risk profile. A simple example is requiring written employment verification from someone who is self-employed.

The one form of documentation that has proven to be critical in complete underwriting is asset verification. Most will agree that having invested a substantial amount of real equity in a home is one of the prime deterrents to borrower default. To be comfortable that some amount is actually being invested by the borrower, even if the loan includes a relatively high loan-to-value ratio, originators check to see that the borrower actually had assets equal to the downpayment for at least some period of time prior to closing. This avoids late discovery that the borrower also borrowed the down payment. In that case, not only does the borrower have little or no equity invested in the property, the debt-to-income ratio is also higher, further increasing the risk of default.

Whenever written asset verification, or some other important documentation is omitted, the loan is referred to as a limited or low documentation loan. Limited documentation loans have historically shown higher incidences of default, although the differential from full documentation loans tends to vary with the originator. This is because some originators focus on other forms of verification, at least on an oral basis to compensate for the missing documentation. When verification of facts is completed through other written means, and there is at least written asset verification, loans are categorized as alternative documentation loans. An example would be accepting W-2 forms in lieu of tax returns. Generally, alternative documentation loans are seen as performing the same as full documentation loans.

Loan Purpose

Concern about default also varies substantially depending on loan purpose. In most situations, there are only three basic categories: cash-out, or equity refinancing mortgages, rate/term refinancing mortgages, and loans to fund an actual purchase of a home.

Cash-out loans are seen as much riskier than purchase loans or rate/term refinancing mortgages. A cash-out loan is in direct conflict with a prime deterrent of default. Rather than putting real equity into a home, the borrower is taking out equity. The risks of a cash-out refinancing mortgage are especially pronounced when the borrower is self-employed. Often this could mean the borrower is starting a new business, trying to expand an existing business (both risky), or trying to shore up a failing business.

While the riskier nature of cash-out refinancing loans seems readily apparent, the differential between purchase and rate/term refinancing loans is less distinct. In a rate/term refinancing transaction, the borrower can be accomplishing any one of a number of goals. The borrower could be reducing the remaining term of the loan from a 30-year to a 15-year mortgage. This will result in an accelerated amortization of the loan, thereby increasing the book equity and reducing the loan-to-value ratio. The borrower could also be keeping the same term but reducing the interest rate and therefore the monthly debt service requirements. The reduced cash requirement should mean additional financial flexibility for the borrower, therefore reducing the chances of running into cash flow problems. It also could enable the borrower to prepay a portion of the loan with the extra cash, again reducing the loan-to-value ratio at an accelerated pace. The one counterweight to these positive traits is that the appraised value in this case is not based on an arm's-length transaction, but will depend solely on comparables.

Property Type

While other factors are seen as more significant drivers for default rates on a pool, one other characteristic that can have a significant impact on recoveries when defaults do occur is property type. Property types can be broken down into very detailed categories. Generally the type recognized as cleanest is single-family detached housing. These loans are considered more desirable because they are somewhat easier to realize value on and are also less subject to loss in value due to external factors.

Second on the list is residences that are part of planned unit developments, but for which the common or shared facilities are considered de minimis. An example of not de minimis common facilities would be a golf course. In this case, the value of the residence itself is heavily dependent on the attraction of the golf course.

Miscellaneous other types are: two- to four-family homes, townhouses, condominiums, and coops. Of these, coops are considered the worst because the asset is not actually real estate, but a share ownership. There is more volatility in values for these latter categories. Loss severity can also be somewhat higher because more time may be required for resale after foreclosure, especially in a weak real estate market. During this time the servicer will in most cases advance interest on the remaining principal amount, but the servicer will then have priority for recovery of these advances from the proceeds of liquidation, thereby increasing the loss on principal to the pool.

Occupancy Type

Most properties can be defined as primary residence, secondary residence (or vacation home), or an investor-owned property. Given the overriding desire to maintain one's home, there is no question that the best occupancy type is primary residence. Vacation homes and investor-owned properties where the owner does not occupy the property for most of the year, if at all, can create difficulties because the borrower can more easily rationalize walking away from the property.

Loan-to-Value and Loan Size

Throughout the discussion of important factors that drive default rates, there has been one recurring theme — loan-to-value. This, in conjunction with loan size, is the simplest aspect of collateral analysis because these are simple numbers with little room for judgment. There is little disagreement that loan-to-value is a prime determinant of default risk. There are two reasons for this. First, a large equity investment represents a substantial incentive to continue one's mortgage payments. Second, to the extent an income problem does arise, a lower loan-to-value provides significant cushion for either the borrower or the servicer to sell the home at a price sufficient to cover the remaining principal outstanding.

For these reasons, a key consideration in any mortgage pool is the weighted average loan-to-value and the number of loans with loan-to-value ratios greater than 80%. Most pools of 30-year mortgages have weighted average loan-to-value ratios between 70% and 75%. Most pools of 15-year mortgages have weighted average loan-to-value ratios between 65% and 70%. Any pool higher than the norm should then be considered somewhat riskier.

More difficult is the extent to which the pool consists of some very low loan-to-value mortgages and some very high loan-to-value mortgages, resulting in a normal weighted average. The situation is slightly muddied by the fact that most loans with loan-to-value ratios in excess of 80% are insured down to 75% by primary mortgage insurance. While these loans are a theoretical equivalent to a 75% loan-to-value, their likelihood of default will not be driven by the existence of insurance. Therefore, investors need to decide on how comfortable they can be relying on insurers on which little if any analysis has been done.

To the extent that analyzing loan-to-value ratios is relatively straightforward, the question of loan size is also not very complicated. The simplest aspect of this factor is that the smaller the loans in a given pool, the greater the diversification for the given pool size. Larger loans, to the extent they become delinquent, will have a proportionately greater impact on the health of the overall pool. Generally speaking, higher-priced homes also tend to experience greater price volatility during cyclical swings in real estate values. The risk is also markedly greater when the price of the home is significantly above the median price for homes in the geographic area. In that case the resale process is almost certain to take significantly longer, and the likelihood of needing to accept a price that is closer to the median at resale is high.

Seasoning

One factor that can be used, on occasion, to offset some of the risk factors discussed is seasoning of the loans in the pool. The greatest likelihood of default is generally viewed to be in the early years of the loan, more specifically in years two through six. Few borrowers will default in the first twelve months of a loan. Also, after the first few years, default frequency tends to decline rapidly. This phenomenon has several explanations. The most important is the build up of book equity in the home through amortization of principal. When borrowers have more invested in the home and have more flexibility in the selling price they can accept because of their lower mortgage balance, it would be unusual for a problem to arise. A more intangible factor is the increased emotional commitment to the home.

Relying on seasoning can, however, be dangerous. To the extent an investor is considering a more seasoned pool, or a new pool that includes some more seasoned products, it is important to review in greater detail where and when those mortgages were originated. One may find that the loans were made at the peak of the market, and that home values in the area have dropped dramatically since then. This would clearly offset many of the perceived benefits of seasoning. It could also prove important to analyze the timing of the originations with changes in the originator's underwriting criteria since many originators go through cycles where underwriting standards are loosened or tightened to meet certain management objectives.

RECENT TRENDS

B & C Loans

One market trend that has made the analytical process increasingly more difficult has been the proliferation of borrower types in the marketplace. Commonly referred to as B&C borrowers, these are considered higher risk borrowers, or borrowers that are considered more likely to default on their mortgages. This assessment relies primarily on the particular borrower's past history of credit problems. As such, the range of borrower qualities has actually been more highly refined to include A–, B, C, and D. Although having more finely honed categories should be of benefit to investors, each originator and rating agency has its own definitions for these categories, thus creating potential confusion.

In general, the range of quality runs from those borrowers that have had a minor number of situations where they have been late for short periods of time on credit card, or other non-mortgage related debt payments, to those who have experienced recent bankruptcies. The time frame in which these credit problems occurred is also considered important, with more recent occurrences being of greater concern. Also, originators and rating agencies will focus on the frequency of these credit problems. On the originator's side, loan underwriters may be willing to consider reasons for these problems as mitigating factors to the extent they may be considered one-time events. Rating agencies are less likely to give credit for such considerations.

Until recently, borrowers with a less than perfect credit history went through different lending avenues to get mortgage financing. Oftentimes these lenders were considered "hard-money" lenders, or lenders who underwrote the transaction almost entirely based on the quality of the asset, giving little consideration to the quality of the borrower. This market was highly fragmented and lacked the degree of standardization necessary for securitization. Two factors have caused this to shift in recent years. First is the increased efficiency of the lending process, and therefore the ability to categorize borrowers. Second is the increased capacity of the larger originators and the desire to maintain loan volume through their origination infrastructures.

There are several reasons why B&C lending may be of concern in the nonagency market, especially for the investor in the subordinate certificates. First and foremost is the matter of disclosure. Is there sufficient information available about the quality of borrowers for investors to make an informed decision? A second concern, which was mentioned earlier, is the potential confusion over differing definitions. A B-quality borrower for one originator can be a C-quality borrower to another. This is further exacerbated by originators that may mix borrowers with different quality levels into a single pool. This makes it very difficult to determine appropriate assumptions for both prepayment expectations and default and loss assumptions. It will also potentially confuse matters when investors try to monitor and draw conclusions from actual loss experience as the transactions mature.

Another reason for concern is that some originators in their drive to enter this market may not put sufficient emphasis on the fact that the origination and servicing needs of the less than A-quality market are significantly different from what is necessary for the traditional A-quality loan. These borrowers need a great deal more guidance to avoid the credit problems that put them in this position to begin with. Also loss mitigation techniques must be much more intense and must be applied much more quickly to limit severity.

Automated Underwriting

Another aspect of loan underwriting that has caught a great deal of investor attention in recent years is credit scoring and mortgage scoring. Based on all the various factors that have proven to be predictive of the likelihood of a loan going into default, originators have traditionally used different methods to grade individual loan applications. Embedded within these grades, or scores, has been a credit score that focused specifically on the credit characteristics of the potential borrower. From here have come both different gradations of A-quality borrowers and less than A-quality borrowers. More recent innovations by both independent vendors and originators has been mortgage scoring systems that also take into account risk components associated with the other factors described earlier, such as loan-to-value and geographic location. Most scoring systems being introduced today are also based on very detailed, and highly robust statistical models. The parameters behind these models are based on the analysis of loan characteristics of both good and defaulted loans numbering in the hundreds of thousands originated over many years.

As scoring systems encourage standardization of underwriting, a positive trend has been developing. Oftentimes problems have resulted from errors in underwriting when certain potential risk factors are overlooked. Standardization should reduce the frequency of these problems. Nonetheless, scoring in and of itself should not be considered a panacea for several reasons.

First is that credit scoring and the credit component of a mortgage score focuses on the borrower's past credit history and current financial profile. As such it is only a near term predictor of the borrower's likelihood of default. It should not be assumed to be predictive for the entire life of the mortgage.

Second is the basic differential between credit scores and mortgage scores. Especially considering the short-term nature of the score, it is potentially dangerous to assume that a good credit score completely offsets other risk factors. While clearly an essential part, if not the most important part of the loan underwriting process, a borrower's ability to pay is only one aspect driving potential defaults. Taking that one step further, it is inappropriate to assume that good mortgage scores, even to the extent that they include other loan characteristics, are enough. Automated underwriting should not be mistaken for automatic underwriting. A good scoring system can be a very useful tool to the originator for determining the extensiveness of any further underwriting needs. By defining the two extremes, "easy passes" and "easy fails," a mortgage scoring system can make the process much more efficient, allowing the allocation of greater resources towards underwriting the large majority of applications that fall between the extremes. A mortgage scoring system can also give guidance on those specific areas that require more diligence. This diligence should still result in rejection for some loan applications, at least with respect to their appropriateness for certain pools.

From an investor's standpoint good mortgage scores should also not translate into an assumption that all risks have been mitigated. Loans considered to have higher risk characteristics continue to have those characteristics even if there are other factors that are considered lower risk. As an example, a cash-out loan with a high balance still represents a significant risk to investors even with a borrower that has a good credit history and a home in a good geographic area. It would not be too much of a stretch to see a dramatic decline in real estate values leading to a higher loss severity that can eliminate credit protection for the lower level tranches. Another way for investors to become overly comfortable with a pool of loans that are mortgage scored is to forget that a good average score for the pool may be a combination of some loans with better scores and some with lower quality scores. Just as with the other factors described here, detailed information on the mix of scores is important to gain full knowledge about the pool.

Assessing the reliability of any originator's scoring system also includes the same level of analysis that was necessary in reviewing an originator's underwriting criteria. One critical aspect of this is understanding and gaining comfort in how dynamic the guidelines are. Any standardized scoring system would quickly become stale and unpredictive if not continuously reviewed and adjusted to take new economic realties into account. It is important therefore to understand what management control systems exist for such regular quality control of the scoring system.

Given these provisos, investors should gain some comfort from the fact that a pool of loans has mortgage scores provided that there is still adequate information about the various loan characteristics that have been described here and the full range of mortgage scores that are represented in the pool.

SUMMARY AND CONCLUSION

The two questions of availability of information and actual benefits that can be realized inevitably must be dealt with. As to the latter issue, the potential benefits are clearly much greater for the lower rated classes in the typical senior-subordinate structure. Assuming subordination levels stay relatively robust, this level of detail has only limited value to the AAA investor. It can have some impact on potential resale prices, but only in the extreme case of an unusually constituted package will a pool actually sustain losses sufficient to impair the senior class. This may happen when there are extremely heavy state concentrations or very high levels of limited documentation loans when originators chased after market share and pure production to sustain growth in overhead.

The analysis is much more important for the subordinate classes. Especially in the early years of a pool, it does not take much in the way of delinquencies and foreclosures for stop-loss levels to be triggered. The blockage of payments, even on a temporary basis, can have a significant impact on realized yield. Further, with the very thin layers of subordination, any concentrated problem can very quickly eliminate supporting securities through allocation of actual losses in the pool.

The only way investors have of limiting this potential, since it cannot be completely eliminated, is to focus on quality of the mortgage underwriting and quality of the collateral. Alternatively, if investors are prepared to take those risks, they should be in a position to look for higher potential returns.

As to the amount of effort required, let alone the ability to access information, much of the work on originators can be done up-front in anticipation of future investment opportunities. A substantial amount can be turned into a formulaic exercise. Only where there have been substantial changes in underwriting approaches at a given originator does the process become more time-consuming.

A good collateral summary on a specific pool from a dealer will also answer the majority of questions about the characteristics of the pool, at least enough to reveal anomalies requiring further analysis. Therefore while the detail can seem daunting at first, the credit analysis side of the mortgage market is nothing that a good fundamental analyst cannot handle.

Part C: Prepayment Analysis

Chapter 13

Prepayment Analysis of Nonagency Mortgage-Backed Securities

Douglas L. Bendt
President
Mortgage Risk Assessment Corporation

Chuck Ramsey
Managing Director
Structured Capital Management
and
CEO
Mortgage Risk Assessment Corporation

Frank J. Fabozzi, Ph.D., CFA
Adjunct Professor of Finance
School of Management
Yale University

INTRODUCTION

Prepayment analysis in the past has been limited to the value of the prepayment option — determined chiefly by the gap between the mortgage coupon rate and the current mortgage rate — and to a lesser extent, the impact of loan age or seasoning along with macroeconomic variables such as GDP growth or the unemployment rate. However, analysts know that prepayment models ideally should discriminate between a homeowner's decision to refinance an existing mortgage — whether to obtain a lower rate or to obtain cash — and the decision to sell the existing home. Modeling these decisions accurately would require much more data, such as information on the homeowner's family composition, its stage in the life-cycle, and the overall financial situation. Hence, the existing "three factor" models are only proxies for the "real" model.

These model imperfections are not the result of analysts' lack of creativity, but rather the paucity of data released by Fannie Mae, Freddie Mac, and Ginnie Mae. The agencies only release aggregate information such as weighted average coupon/maturity (WAC/WAM) and quartile dispersions along with geographic concentrations at the state level, average loan age, and average loan size. Moreover, prepayments are not reported by type.

Issuers of private mortgage-backed securities (MBS) or nonagency MBS are much more forthcoming with data, generally releasing loan level detail for the collateral backing their deals. This detail makes it possible to do much more complete prepayment analysis to answer the following kinds of questions:

- Is the prepayment function for loans taken out to purchase a house different from the function for loans that refinanced a previous mortgage?
- What is the effect of homeowners' equity and changing property values on prepayments?
- Do alternate documentation or low/no doc loans prepay differently from fully documented loans?

Before answering these and other questions, however, we first compare the overall prepayment rates between agency and nonagency MBS.

TRADITIONAL AGENCY/NONAGENCY PREPAYMENT COMPARISONS

Historically, analysts have noted that prepayments for nonagency MBS tend to be faster than "comparable" agency MBS. The quotation marks denote that some analysts only control for the WAC and the WAM of the pools being compared. Among the factors cited for the faster speeds:

1. Greater variation in loan composition, such as greater WAC dispersion, can make WAC/WAM comparisons inadequate;
2. Larger loan sizes tend to prepay faster because the same size prepayment option in percentage terms is worth more in dollar terms;
3. More affluent borrowers tend to be more mobile; and
4. California — traditionally a fast-prepaying state — is overrepresented in nonagency MBS.

Other analysts correct for some of these factors. Adjusting for collateral diversity and geographic concentrations, one dealer firm finds the multipliers averaging about 1.5 except during the depths of the last recession, when nonagency securities prepaid *slower* than agency MBS.

ADJUSTED AGENCY/NONAGENCY PREPAYMENT COMPARISONS

Rather than attempt comparisons of prepayment rates between nonagency deals and agency deals, it would be preferable to make such comparisons on a loan level basis. This analysis would effectively remove the effects of WAC/WAM discrepancies and dispersions, allowing the affects of other factors to be seen more clearly.

With agency data, such comparisons normally would be impossible. However, the data provided by Dow Jones/Telerate's Advance Factor Service in Exhibit 1 clearly show the effects of analyzing prepayments by pool coupon compared to analyzing prepayments using the actual mortgage rate. Even if the pool coupon curve is shifted to the right by 75 basis points (the average servicing fee), the discrepancy is extremely large for low coupons, implying that the greatest impact of WAC dispersion is on future prepayments of relatively new collateral.

Exhibit 2 shows traditional prepayment curves for agency and nonagency collateral calculated from loan-level detail. The agency data are derived from Freddie Mac's loan file (also provided by Dow Jones/Telerate's Advance Factor Service), while the nonagency data are a composite of 6 of the 10 largest issuers. Note that the average "multiplier" for the new issue, lower coupons is about 2.5 — well above the range cited by other analysts — while multipliers for older, higher rate collateral are about 1.5 — right in the middle of the range cited by other analysts.

Exhibit 1: WAC Dispersion And Prepayments
30-Year Fixed-Rate Pools
Freddie Mac: March 1994

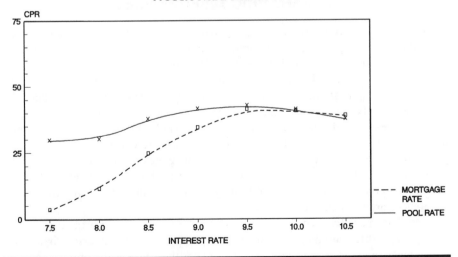

Exhibit 2: Agency versus Non-Agency Prepayments
30-Year Fixed-Rate Collateral: March 1994

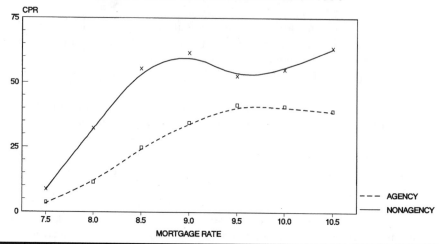

The higher multipliers for the lower coupons are measuring the effects of the refinancing wave in 1993 and 1994. For example, the barriers to refinancing have been lowered substantially with the increasing popularity of no-points mortgages. Thus, the value of the prepayment option for jumbo borrowers has increased in dollar terms relative to the value of the option for agency borrowers given the same size of rate decrease.

SEASONING, OPTION VALUE, AND GEOGRAPHIC DIFFERENCES

Prepayment data from private or agency MBS issues is generally available only from 1986, spanning only one economic cycle. Loan-level detail from the Department of Veterans' Affairs and the Federal Housing Administration is available from 1970, a time period that covers several economic cycles. Moreover, the earlier years have almost completed their life-cycle to maturity, giving an especially valuable insights into burnout and behavior near a pool's ultimate payoff.

The charts shown in Exhibit 3 show markedly different prepayment patterns for four large metropolitan areas. These charts are constructed so that each prepayment seasoning curve only includes mortgages with equal differentials between the mortgage's coupon rate and the current mortgage rate at the start of each year to create "static pools" for analysis. Several important similarities and differences are immediately apparent.

There are two similarities. First, homeowners with mortgages "in the money" (rate differentials greater than zero) prepay significantly faster than other homeowners and the speeds get faster the greater the value of the option. Second, for homeowners with no refinancing incentive (rate differential is equal to zero), there is an initial seasoning ramp-up of 4-5 years, somewhat slower than the PSA's assumed ramp-up of 30 months. There also are secondary and tertiary ramp-ups at about years 11 and 21, respectively.

Exhibit 3: Agency Prepayment Rates
A: Los Angeles, CA

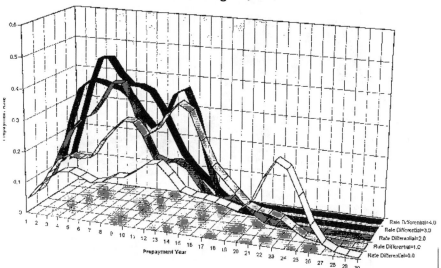

B: Dade County, FL

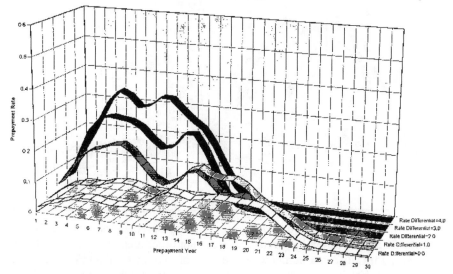

Exhibit 3 (Continued)
C: Nassau County, NY

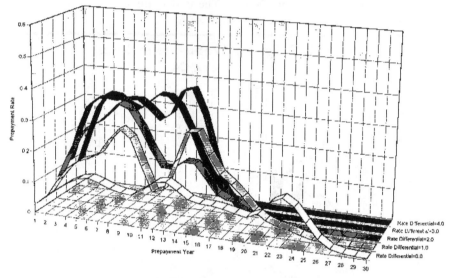

D: Cook County, IL

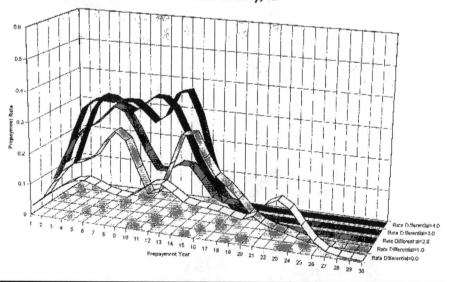

There are two major differences. First, homeowners in Dade County, Florida (Miami area) tend to prepay slower than other areas for all rate differentials. Second, California homeowners tend to prepay faster than all other areas, especially for homeowners slightly in the money (rate differential equal to 1).

Exhibit 4: Effect of LTV on Prepayments

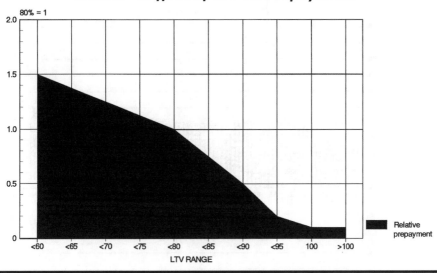

REGIONAL INFLUENCES:
THE IMPACT OF LOAN-TO-VALUE RATIO

Although the levels of prepayment rates will be significantly different for nonagency securities relative to these FHA/VA mortgages due to such structural issues as assumability and different socio-economic compositions of the borrowers, these same regional differences would be expected to be maintained in nonagency securities.

This expectation is primarily predicated on the fact that the largest single factor in determining differences in geographic prepayment rates is the behavior of home prices and their impact on the loan-to-value (LTV) ratio each borrower faces. Rising home prices create wealth, allowing homeowners to more easily trade up to bigger houses or to refinance to take cash out from the property.

Exhibit 4 shows a stylized impact of LTV on prepayment rates. Relative to a group of homeowners with 80% current LTVs, borrowers with 60% LTVs will be expected to prepay 50% faster holding other characteristics such as seasoning and rate differential constant. Conversely, those homeowners who have lost all their equity due to price declines will be expected to have prepayment rates 90% slower than the benchmark 80% LTV borrowers.

Exhibit 5 shows charts of home price change for the four metropolitan areas measured using proprietary repeat-sales methodology developed by Mortgage Risk Assessment Corporation. Note particularly that home prices in Miami showed little change throughout the last 20 years compared to the large run-up in prices elsewhere. (The higher-than-normal proportion of homeowners over 65 years of age in Miami also probably has an adverse impact.)

Exhibit 5: Home Price Trends

A: Dade County, FL

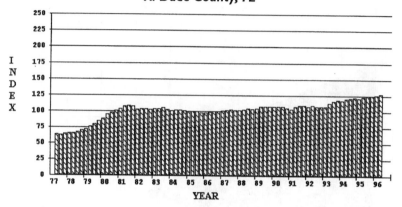

B: Cook County, IL

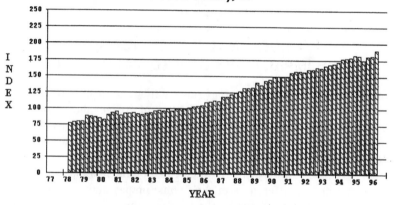

C: Los Angeles County, CA

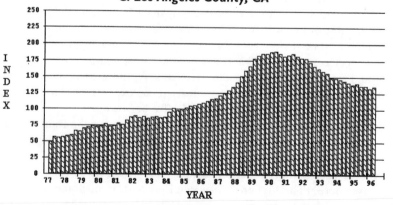

Exhibit 5 (Continued)
D: Nassau County, NY

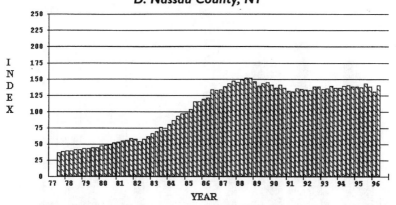

OTHER FACTORS AFFECTING PREPAYMENTS

There are four major influences on prepayment rates for nonagency securities besides coupon, seasoning, and LTV. In order of importance, they are (1) transaction type (purchase versus refinance); (2) property type (single family versus condominiums); (3) level of documentation (full, alternate/reduced, or none); and, (4) occupancy status (owner-occupied, second home, or investor). The data in the rest of this section compare prepayment rates for mortgages with certain mortgage characteristics, but always holding seasoning, rate differential, and current LTV constant.

Transaction Type

Mortgages taken out to purchase homes tend to be prepaid slower than mortgages taken out to refinance previous (presumably higher-rate) mortgages. Refinance transactions in which the homeowner takes out cash tend to be more like purchase transactions. Exhibit 6 shows this pattern clearly for mortgages at all levels of current LTV.

Homeowners who are refinancing an existing mortgage are different from homeowners who just purchased a house in two important ways. First, they already have lived in their house for some amount of time. Therefore, the chance that they have moved to a new stage in their life-cycle that requires a different type of house is greater. And second, the fact that they have refinanced their mortgage once already may make them more sensitive to future rate drops because they realize how easy the process can be. Mortgage brokers are more likely to be more aggressive with previous refinancers as well.

Property Type

Owners of condominiums consistently prepay their mortgages more slowly than owners of single-family detached homes, again holding seasoning, interest-rate differential, and current LTV constant. Exhibit 7 shows that this factor is about 50%.

Exhibit 6: Effect of Transaction Type on Prepayment

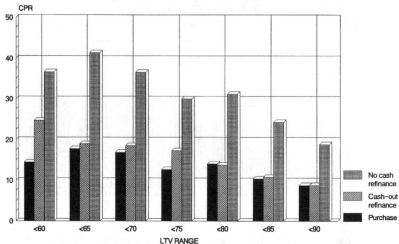

Exhibit 7: Effect of Property Type on Prepayments

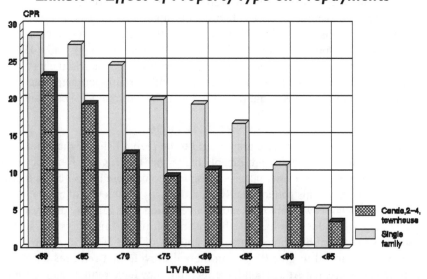

Level of Documentation

Nonagency mortgages that are fully documented are loans that are underwritten to standards that would qualify them for sale to the agencies but for the fact that the loan amount or debt ratios are higher than the agencies' limits. Borrowers are required to submit forms verifying income and employment with W-2 forms, pay stubs, tax forms, and lenders verify the sources of the assets to be used for the downpayment.

Exhibit 8: Effect of Documentation on Prepayments

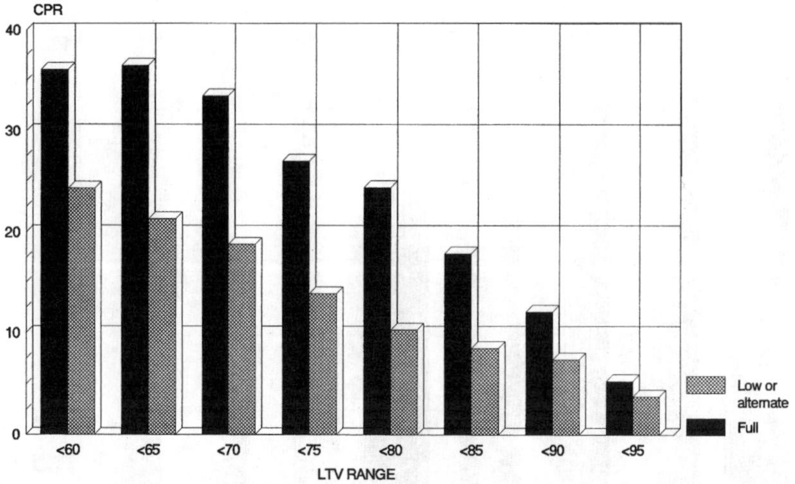

Loans that are deficient in at least one of these areas qualify under "reduced" or "low" documentation programs, usually at a slightly higher interest rate and a lower cap on the permissible LTV. In the extreme, no documentation may have been required as a trade-off for a higher rate and/or an even lower LTV.

Borrowers who did not qualify for full documentation programs have had prepayment rates that were about one-third lower (see Exhibit 8). First, the spectrum of lenders who will lend to such borrowers is wider; fewer lenders have a low or no doc program than in the past because of higher default experience. Second, borrowers who qualified under a less-than-full doc program are more likely to have fluctuations in their income — many are self-employed — that may limit their ability to refinance or trade up.

Occupancy Status

Homeowners prepay the mortgages on their primary residences much faster than they do for mortgages on their vacation homes or properties they hold as investments. Exhibit 9 shows that the speeds are reduced by a factor of one-third and one-half, respectively.

CONCLUSION

This chapter has presented analysis to show that much more detail is available to incorporate into nonagency prepayment models compared to existing agency prepayment models. Using these data to derive an explicit nonagency model will give much more accurate results than simply applying multipliers derived from WAC/WAM comparisons to the results of an agency prepayment model.

Exhibit 9: Effect of Occupancy Status on Prepayment

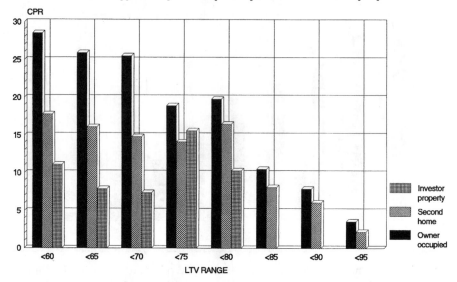

Chapter 14

Prepayments of Non-Standard Whole-Loan Mortgage Securities

Dale Westhoff
Senior Managing Director
Financial Analytics & Structured Transactions Group
Bear, Stearns & Co.

Bruce Kramer
Associate Director
Financial Analytics & Structured Transactions Group
Bear, Stearns & Co.

John Miller
Associate Director
Financial Analytics & Structured Transactions Group
Bear, Stearns & Co.

INTRODUCTION

The refinancing waves of the last several years have underscored the need to identify loan characteristics (other than coupon and age) that influence the prepayment profile of mortgage securities. Nowhere is this more important than in the nonagency (whole loan) sector, where less homogeneous loan and borrower attributes make assessing prepayment risk more difficult. However, that very difficulty creates an opportunity for investors, since some attributes that dramatically improve the convexity profile of these securities continue to go unrecognized. For example, recent data confirm the convexity advantage afforded by securities that are backed by mortgages with non-standard features (hereinafter referred to as "non-standard" loans).

To define the impact that different loan and borrower attributes have on the prepayment behavior of nonagency securities, we conducted an extensive loan-level prepayment analysis of the Bear Stearns whole loan database, which contains data on approximately 800,000 residential non-conforming mortgages. Our study had three objectives. First, we examine and quantify the impact of loan size on the prepayment profile of whole loan securities. Second, we investigate other loan characteristics that may influence the convexity of such securities. Finally, we perform a cross-sector relative value analysis comparing the risk/reward trade-off among securities backed by non-standard loans, standard jumbo loans, and agency conforming loans.

A LOAN-LEVEL ANALYSIS OF NON-STANDARD COLLATERAL

Historically, the vast majority of loans securitized in the nonagency sector were not eligible for agency securitization because they exceeded conforming loan size limits. However, beginning in 1994 certain issuers expanded their underwriting criteria to include loans that were non-standard for reasons other than loan size. In many cases, the borrowers did not meet income or employment verification guidelines (self-employed individuals or people who work on commission may fall into this category) and therefore required a "reduced-documentation" loan that might waive certain income or ratio requirements. Other non-standard features include high LTVs, loans for investor properties or loans to foreign nationals. Underwriters stress that although this new segment of borrowers does not meet agency guidelines, there is no compromise on the borrowers' credit quality as measured by credit score. This might seem surprising to some investors, considering the high subordination levels required on this type of collateral by the rating agencies. However, the rating agencies focus on the characteristics of the collateral itself (e.g., the fact that a loan might be for an investor property, or have a high LTV) rather than on the credit standing of the borrowers. A more detailed explanation of the non-standard features that characterize these new programs is provided in the appendix to this chapter.

Although non-standard whole loans have only been securitized since early in 1994, the volatility in mortgage rates during the last two years (fluctuating by over 225 basis points) has provided a rich set of prepayment observations that we can use as a basis for an empirical study. Exhibit 1 compares the loan and borrower attributes of recent originations from different segments of the mortgage market: non-standard whole loans, standard jumbo loans (represented by Capstead, Countrywide, GE Capital, Prudential and RFC), agency conforming loans (represented by FHLMC PCs), and home equity loans.

Although there are several notable differences between non-standard loans and loans from other segments of the mortgage market, the two most important differences are (1) a small average loan size and (2) a high rate premium. With respect to loan size, loans in the non-standard nonagency sector average about half the size of standard jumbo mortgages and are comparable in size to agency conforming loans. In 1995, 62% of non-standard 30-year loans were for amounts under $200,000. Less than 5% of standard jumbo loans fell into this category during the same period. As for rate premium, on average, non-standard borrowers paid about 130 basis points above the available FHLMC survey rate, compared to just 42 basis points for standard jumbo product.

Given these two distinguishing characteristics, we would expect prepayments on non-standard whole loans to be less sensitive to interest rates than both standard jumbo mortgages and agency conforming mortgages. It is well documented that a low loan balance tends to produce a more stable prepayment profile because it reduces the economic benefit of a refinancing transaction when interest rates fall. In addition, small loans are less likely to be targeted by originators since they also have less to gain from a refinancing transaction. Therefore, on the basis of loan size alone we would expect non-standard whole loan securities to possess more favorable convexity characteristics than jumbo securities. We would also expect non-standard securities to exhibit a more stable prepayment profile than agency conforming securities, despite the fact that their underlying loans are similar in size. The reason is that the non-standard mortgage market is less efficient than the agency conforming market. Borrowers in the non-standard market are offered higher rates than those available in the agency market; the rate premium is indicative of the fact that fewer funding alternatives are available to these borrowers because of their non-standard characteristics. As a result, they tend to face higher transaction (hassle) costs when refinancing, compared to the "frictionless" refinancing available to most conforming borrowers.

These expectations can now be supported by actual prepayment results in the non-standard sector. In Exhibit 2 we plot non-standard whole loan, standard jumbo and agency historical prepayments conditional on how much interest rates have risen or fallen since the loans were originated. The exhibit clearly shows that non-standard whole loans have shown more call protection than either standard jumbo or agency collateral. Furthermore, since they are similar in size to agency loans, the less responsive nature of non-standard prepayments suggests that these borrowers may indeed face more transaction/hassle costs than agency borrowers when refinancing.

Exhibit 1: Cross-Sector Comparison of Loan and Borrower Attributes

| | Non-Standard | | Standard | Agency | Home |
	1995	1996	Jumbo	Conforming	Equity
Average Loan Size	$132,000	$127,000	$260,000	$124,000	$45,000
Rate Premium	130 bp	130 bp	42 bp	0 bp	189 bp
Original LTV	74%	75%	78%	80%	70%
Documentation: Full	39%	46%	78%	ND	—
Documentation: Limited	60%	25%	12%	ND	—
Purpose: Cash-Out Refi	27%	23%	6%	11%	—
Purpose: Rate/Term Refi	18%	20%	21%	13%	—
Purpose: Purchase	55%	56%	73%	76%	—
Investor Properties	17%	27%	2%	NA	—
Geography: California	39%	32%	37%	17%	—

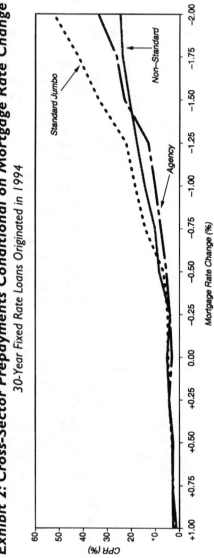

Exhibit 2: Cross-Sector Prepayments Conditional on Mortgage Rate Change

30-Year Fixed Rate Loans Originated in 1994

To further isolate the impact of loan size on non-standard whole loan prepayment sensitivity, we stratify the loans by balance range ($0-$100K, $100-$200K, $200-300K) and then measure historical prepayments conditional on how much rates have changed since loan origination. Exhibit 3 summarizes the results of this analysis. An intuitive and systematic relationship emerges between loan size and refinancing sensitivity within the non-standard sector: the higher the balance range, the more sensitive prepayments become to changes in interest rates. However, even non-standard loans with large balances offered much more call protection than standard jumbo loans. Therefore, while low balances explain some of the stability in observed prepayments, other non-standard features also contribute significantly to this behavior. We examine some of these features in the following sections.

INVESTOR PROPERTIES ARE LESS SENSITIVE TO REFINANCING OPPORTUNITIES

In addition to loan size, our research has identified two other loan/borrower attributes that contribute to the prepayment profile of non-standard collateral: investor properties and cash-out refi transactions. The non-standard sector has a much higher percentage of investor properties than the jumbo sector (17-27% versus less than 2%). The historical prepayment behavior of investor properties has been fundamentally different from that of owner-occupied homes. In a neutral to bearish environment, investor properties have a somewhat higher average speed than owner-occupied homes. The higher speeds on investor properties when the option is out of the money obviously point to a high turnover level on such properties when there is no rate-related economic advantage. It is logical to view these transactions as being motivated by the investor's long-term strategic plans (taking advantage of supply and demand trends in a particular market, for example).

The biggest difference, however, occurs as the mortgages move through the cusp and into the money. As plotted in Exhibit 4, investor property loans prepaid an average of 28% slower (11.6 CPR versus 16.2 CPR) than loans on owner-occupied properties when the mortgages were between 25 and 175 basis points in the money. These prepayment results suggest that investors in residential real estate have a qualitatively different view of their financing alternatives than do people who live in their own homes. In a bullish environment, investors appear to be unswayed by rate-related economic factors until the advantage is very large. The empirical evidence presented in Exhibit 4 suggests that, once an investor establishes a positive cash flow on a particular property, he is less likely to focus on optimizing his financing. Such concerns may be more important for people in owner-occupied homes. As a result, investor property loans have provided a substantial convexity advantage over owner-occupied properties.

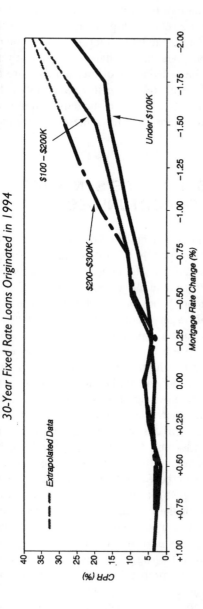

Exhibit 3: Non-Standard Loan Prepayments Conditional on Original Loan Size and Mortgage Rate Change

30-Year Fixed Rate Loans Originated in 1994

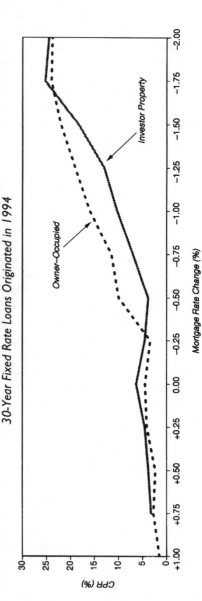

Exhibit 4: Non-Standard Loan Prepayments Conditional on Property Type and Mortgage Rate Change

30-Year Fixed Rate Loans Originated in 1994

CASH-OUT LOANS IMPROVE STABILITY AND STEEPEN THE SEASONING RAMP

Non-standard whole loan securities contain a relatively high percentage of cash-out loans (see Exhibit 1). Cash-out loans contribute to more stable prepayment behavior because they prepay faster than non cash-out loans in a flat to bearish environment. In Exhibit 5 we plot historical non-standard prepayments conditional on loan purpose (cash-out, rate/term refi, purchase) and changes in mortgage rates. In the absence of a strong refinancing incentive (less than 75 basis points in the money), loans originated as cash-out refi transactions were an average of 67% faster than purchase money mortgages and 115% faster than rate/term refinancings. In contrast, during periods when there were significant refinancing incentives present (75 basis points or more in the money), the prepayment rate for cash-out loans was midway between the rates for purchase and refi loans. Cash-out borrowers exhibit a faster base level of prepayments because they are predisposed to another cash-out transaction once their debt levels increase. This behavior is similar to our findings in the home equity sector, where prepayments tend to season more quickly and ramp to a higher level than speeds on mortgages taken out to purchase homes (see Chapter 13). Thus, cash-out loans reduce extension risk in the non-standard sector.

DEFINING THE SEASONING RAMP FOR NON-STANDARD COLLATERAL

One of the primary objectives in our analysis of historical non-standard whole loan prepayments was to define a seasoning ramp for this type of collateral. Since we have monthly loan payment histories, we were able to study prepayments as a function of loan age. The results are in Exhibit 6, which plots actual prepayments by loan age (bars) and the implied loan seasoning ramp (line). The data set for the study is 30-year fixed-rate non-standard loans issued since the beginning of 1994 (about 25,000 loans). In order to remove the effect of refinancing from the seasoning ramp, we excluded from our study any prepayment that occurred during a month in which the prevailing mortgage rate had risen or fallen more than 100 basis points since loan origination.

The definition of the seasoning ramp for a class of collateral is of paramount importance for valuation purposes. Ideally, we would prefer to have far more data than we currently have, to study the seasoning ramp in a variety of interest rate and economic cycles. Lacking that, however, we feel that the data presented in Exhibit 6 is a reasonable estimate of the seasoning ramp for non-standard whole loan collateral. As more loan history becomes available, we will continue to study prepayments as a function of age, and refine the ramp as necessary.

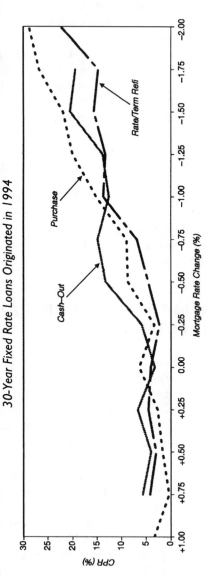

Exhibit 5: Non-Standard Loan Prepayments Conditional on Loan Purpose and Mortgage Rate Change

30-Year Fixed Rate Loans Originated in 1994

Exhibit 6: Non-Standard Loan Prepayments Conditional on Age
30-Year Fixed Rate Loans Originated in 1994

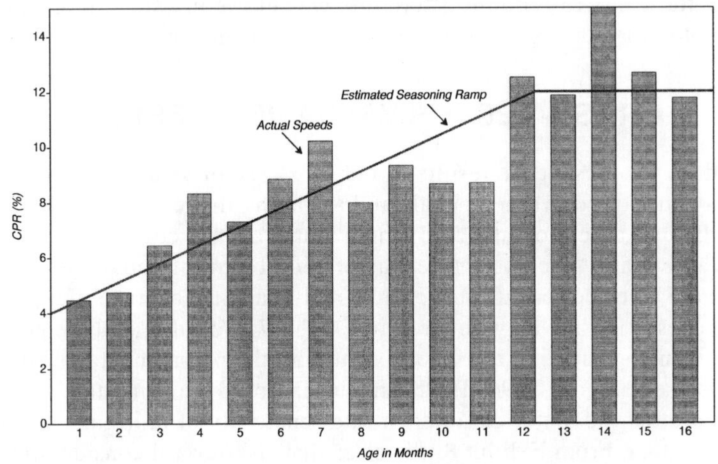

Exhibit 7: Pricing Spreads (bps)

Average Life*	Non-Standard	Standard Jumbo	Agency Plain Vanilla	Home Equity
1 year	80	90	75	62
3 year	110	115	85	78
5 year	145	160	110	100
7 year	160	165	120	125
10 year	160	165	135	145

* The 1-year average life spread for all four sectors in this exhibit is based on the 1-year Treasury bill, not the 1-year CMT.

NON-STANDARD WHOLE LOAN SECURITIES ARE PRICED COMPARABLY TO JUMBOS DESPITE A PREPAYMENT PROFILE THAT FALLS BETWEEN AGENCIES AND HOME EQUITIES

As Exhibit 2 showed, non-standard collateral has exhibited more prepayment stability (less interest rate sensitivity) than equivalent agency collateral; therefore, we would expect this type of collateral to trade at spreads equivalent to agency plain vanilla paper plus a risk premium of approximately 10 basis points for reduced liquidity and stricter risk-based capital guidelines. Nevertheless, non-standard whole loan securities trade 25 to 40 basis points wider than agencies with average lives of 3 to 10 years (see Exhibit 7) despite more favorable convexity characteristics. This suggests that they are approximately 15 to 30 basis points cheap relative to agency paper. Non-standard whole loans are penalized because they are usually traded relative to standard jumbo paper even though their prepayment behavior is more similar to (and actually preferable to) that of agency collateral. In contrast, home equity loans are not coupled to any mortgage sector and generally trade at comparable spreads to agency plain vanillas in full recognition of their better convexity profile. Therefore, we believe investors have an opportunity to exploit the convexity advantage offered by non-standard whole loans.

CROSS-SECTOR VALUATION RESULTS

In Exhibit 8, we present the results of our cross-sector valuation analysis, using identically structured synthetic deals and assuming that each is backed by a different collateral type: non-standard whole loans, agency collateral, and standard jumbo whole loans. Each structure was priced at current market spreads; since spreads were adjusted for differences in model-generated average life, the spreads will not necessarily line up with those in Exhibit 7. We calibrated the prepayment model refinancing function to be consistent with the prepayment behavior exhibited in each sector since 1994. The results in Exhibit 8 are consistent with Exhibit 2, which plotted the historical interest rate sensitivity of mortgage securities in the three sectors. From Exhibit 8 it is clear that risk/reward considerations favor non-standard whole loan securities because they have low option costs.

Two important observations can be made regarding the analysis summarized in Exhibit 8. First, convexity costs in the non-standard sector were lower than those in the agency and jumbo sectors by an average of 23% and 28%, respectively. As a direct result of lower convexity costs, non-standard collateral offered an OAS advantage of 18% over the jumbo sector and 73% over the agency sector. Second, the non-standard OAS advantage was largest in the long average life tranches, where static pricing spreads remain comparable to jumbo product.

THE IMPACT OF BALANCE IN THE
NON-STANDARD WHOLE LOAN SECTOR

To measure the impact that loan size has on the convexity characteristics of non-standard whole loan securities, we provide OAS results from three identically structured and priced synthetic deals assuming each is backed by loans that fall within a different loan size range (see synthetic deal descriptions in Exhibit 9). We calibrated our prepayment model refinancing function to be consistent with historical non-standard prepayment data within each loan size region.

OAS results confirm the convexity advantage offered by small loan balances and support the implications of the conditional prepayment analysis we graphed in Exhibit 3. The greater prepayment sensitivity seen in deals backed by larger balance loans tends to increase option costs and lower OASs. For example, while zero volatility spreads remain essentially unchanged among the three synthetic deals in Exhibit 9, convexity costs increase by as much as 17% (OASs fall by as much as 9%) in the $200K-$300K category (Deal #6) as compared to the under $100K category (Deal #4). Nevertheless, even non-standard loans with large balances exhibit a substantial convexity advantage over standard jumbo loans.

Exhibit 8: Cross-Sector Valuation Results (Synthetic Deals)

Security	Tranche	Prepayment Forecast (CPR) -200	-100	0	+100	+200	Static Analysis Price	Yield	Avg Life	A.L. Sprd to the Curve	Dur.	Convex.	Option Adjusted Spread Zero Vol. Sprd	OAS	Convex. Cost
Synthetic Deal #1		28.0	14.9	10.3	7.2	6.6									
NON-STANDARD SECTOR															
Current Coupon 30-Year Non-Standard Collateral															
	A						100.343	6.172	0.839	80	0.752	-0.178	69	55	14
	B						100.076	6.986	2.284	105	2.264	-0.419	104	65	39
	C						99.874	7.239	3.417	115	3.181	-0.634	110	62	48
	E						99.646	7.789	5.681	150	4.517	-0.518	147	78	69
	G						98.604	8.032	7.892	165	5.503	-0.516	158	91	67
	H						97.495	8.148	11.697	165	6.581	-0.207	156	98	58
Synthetic Deal #2		33.4	15.7	8.1	6.0	5.5									
AGENCY SECTOR															
Current Coupon 30-Year Agency Collateral															
	A						100.531	6.444	1.437	80	1.058	-0.359	70	38	32
	B						100.323	6.980	3.335	90	2.569	-0.644	87	35	52
	C						99.860	7.270	4.632	105	3.606	-0.560	102	39	63
	E						100.952	7.552	7.187	120	4.174	-0.827	119	35	84
	G						100.267	7.757	9.669	130	5.233	-0.590	128	46	82
	H						98.629	7.981	13.796	145	6.314	-0.378	136	66	70
Synthetic Deal #3		47.6	25.9	9.2	5.9	5.5									
JUMBO SECTOR															
Current Coupon 30-Year Jumbo Collateral															
	A						100.388	6.468	1.266	90	0.892	-0.436	77	35	42
	B						99.678	7.199	3.053	115	2.589	-0.731	109	48	61
	C						98.421	7.675	4.211	150	3.838	-0.892	139	73	66
	E						98.999	7.923	6.504	160	4.433	-0.703	153	66	87
	G						98.332	8.067	8.710	165	5.307	-0.974	156	74	82
	H						96.961	8.210	12.428	170	6.512	-0.117	157	85	72

USD Yield Curve	3mo.	6mo.	12mo.	2yr.	3yr.	5yr.	7yr.	10yr.	30yr.
Value	5.01	5.21	5.45	5.89	6.04	6.26	6.34	6.47	6.79

Assumed Pricing Date: April 15, 1996
Assumed Settlement Date: June 30, 1996
Volatility: 17.5%

Exhibit 9: Non-Standard Valuation Results (Synthetic Deals)

Security	-200	-100	0	+100	+200	Tranche	Price	Yield	Avg. Life	A.L. Sprd to the Curve	Dur.	Convex.	Zero Vol. Sprd	OAS	Convex. Cost
	Prepayment Forecast (CPR)						Static Analysis						Option Adjusted Spread		
Synthetic Deal #4	24.6	14.2	10.3	7.2	6.6	A	100.343	6.176	0.843	80	0.769	-0.167	70	56	14
NON-STANDARD SECTOR						B	100.076	6.987	2.287	105	2.299	-0.402	104	66	38
Loans Up to $100K						C	99.874	7.239	3.420	115	3.238	-0.608	110	63	47
						E	99.646	7.789	5.685	150	4.610	-0.533	147	81	66
						G	98.604	8.032	7.895	165	5.606	-0.461	158	94	64
						H	97.495	8.148	11.700	165	6.720	-0.173	156	103	53
Synthetic Deal #5	27.3	14.7	10.3	7.2	6.6	A	100.343	6.172	0.840	80	0.755	-0.176	69	55	14
NON-STANDARD SECTOR						B	100.076	6.987	2.284	105	2.271	-0.416	104	65	39
Loans Between $100K and $200K						C	99.874	7.239	3.417	115	3.192	-0.628	110	62	48
						E	99.646	7.789	5.682	150	4.533	-0.519	147	79	68
						G	98.604	8.032	7.893	165	5.522	-0.508	159	92	67
						H	97.495	8.148	11.697	165	6.605	-0.197	156	99	57
Synthetic Deal #6	31.3	15.5	10.3	7.2	6.6	A	100.343	6.167	0.836	80	0.736	-0.187	69	54	15
NON-STANDARD SECTOR						B	100.076	6.986	2.281	105	2.233	-0.438	104	64	40
Loans Between $200K and $300K						C	99.874	7.238	3.413	115	3.137	-0.645	110	61	49
						E	99.646	7.789	5.678	150	4.441	-0.507	147	76	71
						G	98.604	8.032	7.889	165	5.420	-0.566	159	89	70
						H	97.495	8.148	11.694	165	6.482	-0.250	156	94	62

USD Yield Curve	3mo.	6mo.	12mo.	2yr.	3yr.	5yr.	7yr.	10yr.	30yr.
Value	5.01	5.21	5.45	5.89	6.04	6.26	6.34	6.47	6.79

Assumed Pricing Date: April 15, 1996
Assumed Settlement Date: June 30, 1996
Volatility: 17.5%

Two other important observations can be made regarding Exhibit 9. First, the longer average life tranches (5+ year sector) tend to benefit the most from the inherent prepayment stability of small balance loans, i.e. they show the largest decrease in convexity cost between Synthetic Deals #6 and #4. Second, as a rule of thumb, for every $10,000 that the average loan size exceeds $100,000, we estimate that investors in the 5+ year sector of the curve should be compensated an additional half of a basis point in spread. We believe investors in the 1 to 5 year sector should be compensated approximately a quarter of a basis point for every $10,000 that average loan size exceeds $100,000.

CONCLUSION

Non-standard whole loans constitute an increasing percentage of the collateral now being securitized in the nonagency mortgage market. Because lenders target non-standard borrowers, the collateral now entering the secondary market is in many respects qualitatively different from both agency and traditional jumbo nonagency collateral. In many cases, it has characteristics (such as equity take-out and investor property loans) that are uncommon in the secondary mortgage market, and therefore not widely understood by investors. Some of these loan characteristics have a profound impact on prepayment behavior, and they contribute to the favorable convexity profile that we have observed in historical prepayments of non-standard collateral.

APPENDIX: SELECTED FEATURES OF NON-STANDARD LOAN PROGRAMS

The non-standard sector focuses on the needs of borrowers who have good credit, but who have had difficulty finding financing because they have non-standard borrower profiles, or because the properties have non-standard characteristics. We include examples of underwriting guidelines for several such programs. Maximum LTV, loan amount and underwriting criteria vary within each program according to the characteristics of the borrower and the property.

Unusual Features

Provides financing for high LTV loans, and for second/vacation homes and investment properties. Many combinations of qualifying ratios, liquid asset reserves, MI coverage, loan amount and LTV limits are offered to meet the needs of borrowers.

Uninsured LTV

Provides non-first time homebuyers who demonstrate a high regard for financial obligations an alternative to obtaining private mortgage insurance. A non-occupant co-borrower may be used to qualify under certain circumstances. Credit history: no late payments during the last 24 months; consumer debt no more than 1 x 30 during the past 12 months.

Self-Employed Stated Income

Designed for self-employed borrowers with established (2 year minimum) self-employment. Not for Schedule C tax filers; must file Schedules 1120 and/or 1065 and own a minimum 25% of a business. Must have complex financial structure requiring significant documentation and analysis to establish actual income.

No Income Verification

For U.S. citizens only who have demonstrated a high regard for their financial obligations as evidenced by a credit score of 680 or greater, a propensity and capability to save, and stable employment. Income ratio is not used for qualification.

International Borrower

For U.S. citizens who have been employed abroad and do not have a domestic credit history; Canadian applicants; foreign nationals; non-permanent resident aliens.

Chapter 15

Data Processing and Prepayment Modeling of Whole Loans

Yizhong Fan, Ph.D.
Quantitative Research Analyst
Global Advanced Technology

Pete Rogers
Analyst
Global Advanced Technology

INTRODUCTION

In 1994, Global Advanced Technology (GAT), in a joint effort with the Residential Funding Corporation (RFC), developed its first whole-loan prepayment model. This chapter describes recent major developments in our effort to improve upon that model. The study which is the topic of this chapter focuses on the RFC 30-year mortgages during the time period from January 1987 to December 1994. We shall use the term prepayment to include both complete and partial prepayment, refinancing to mean only complete prepayment, and curtailment to mean partial but not complete prepayment.

There are two types of mortgages, conforming and non-conforming. Government agencies which issue mortgage loans (which include GNMA, FNMA, and FHLMC) have very specific underwriting policies to which all loans they underwrite must conform, and hence, conforming loans and agency loans are synonymous terms. Whole loans, also called non-conforming loans, are different from agency loans, in that they do not conform to agency underwriting criteria. There are many reasons why a loan may fail to conform to agency criteria, the most common of these being the dollar size of the loan. Currently, conforming loans may be no greater than $207,000.

As a result of the relative uniformity and large number of agency loans, agency prepayment behavior is relatively straightforward to study and well understood, whereas whole-loan behavior has remained less understood. What has allowed for greater understanding of whole-loan behavior in this study than in

In preparing this chapter, the authors benefited from several discussions with Lori Gaberdiel, Mark Wainger, and Tom Kaehler.

previous attempts are innovations in data processing and prepayment modeling. These data processing innovations allow us to use all of the data to its best advantage in modeling and reduce errors associated with statistical noise and inaccurate or missing data.

There are several difficulties in studying whole-loan prepayment behavior. Many of these are not related to the phenomenon of prepayment per se, but to the nature, quantity, and quality of the available data. Much of our work has been involved with overcoming these practical hurdles rather than theoretical ones.

First, because the reasons that whole loans fail to conform are so diverse, their prepayment behavior is more difficult to predict than agency prepayment. Second, the sample space is much smaller than that for agency loans. Because agency loans are so great in number and uniform in attribute, they are grouped into pools for purposes of administration and securitization. For agency CMOs, a given deal is comprised of many pools, which is then sliced up into different tranches. (We use the expressions CMO, deal, and CMO deal interchangeably in this chapter.) With whole-loan CMOs, there is no intermediate pool structure. Loans are aggregated directly into CMOs and tranched. During the 8-year period that we observed, the RFC database contained 109,819 loans. That number of agency loans would comprise less than a few hundred typical pools. By contrast, during the same period the FNMA 30 database alone contained nearly 200,000 pools. This amount of data allowed us to study FNMA 30 prepayment behavior with minimal risk of bad inference due to noise.

Third, whole-loan CMO deals are much more diverse than agency deals in the scope of their major parameters, such as WAC and age. In the agency case, all loans in a given pool were generally originated in the same month. Within a given deal, the pools comprising that deal may not have originated in the same month, but generally there is no more than a 12-month difference in origination between pools in a deal. Additionally, relative to whole-loan deals, there is little variation in the coupon of the loans within an agency deal, with a range of 100 basis points (bp) or less being common. As a result, age and coupon, which are the most significant parameters, are quite uniform within a given agency CMO. Whole-loan deals are a completely different story. Recall that whole-loan deals do not have the pool level structure between loans and CMO. Even if two whole loans originated in the same month, their interest rates may be very different. Because of the limitation of low market availability, the ages and mortgage rates of the loans in a particular deal can span a wide range. We found a case in which whole loans within a single deal varied by as much as 155 months in age and 400 bp in coupon.

Fourth, the whole-loan database structure is very different from the agency database structure. Because agency data are only available at pool level, the information (issued amount, factor, weighted average coupon (WAC), etc.) has been aggregated using the weight of the outstanding balances of the loans in the pool. The whole-loan database is at loan level, that is, raw data. This structure has both advantages and disadvantages which we will discuss in detail later. Briefly, loan level data imply that every sample satisfies statistical independence assumptions, whereas pool data do not allow that assumption. On the other hand, missing or bad data have a more significant impact in loan level data than in pool data. There is also an issue of volume of whole-loan data. Because every loan produces a record every month until it matures, 100,000 loans would produce millions of records, assuming each loan's average life is several years. This is too cumbersome for most computers to handle effectively. Therefore, we must aggregate the loans before statistically analyzing the data. To aggregate, we combined similar loans into a single record in every month, which reduced the number of records to process while not appreciably diminishing accuracy. A big part of the improvement in the whole-loan prepayment modeling process involves this aggregation. We will discuss the aggregation techniques later in the chapter. Suffice it to say, we believe that this aggregation did not detract from the accuracy of the results, but did allow us to use all of the available data.

Because the prepayment behavior of agency loans has been studied far more extensively than that of whole loans, using agency prepayment behavior study methodology as a theoretical starting point, and then comparing results and conclusions is an efficient way to examine and analyze whole-loan prepayment behavior. In this chapter, we will compare the prepayment behavior of whole loans to that of agency loans. For agency loans we will discuss specifically FNMA 30-year loans. One popular method for modeling whole-loan prepayments is to use a 150% multiplier of agency prepayments as a model. We will discuss the validity of using this method. Total prepayment is composed of refinancing (total payment of the outstanding mortgage prior to maturity) and curtailment (partial prepayment of the mortgage beyond the scheduled payment prior to maturity). These have different characteristics, so our model has a refinancing part and a curtailment part, which aggregate to the complete model.[1]

DATA PROCESSING

In this section we discuss the primary whole-loan data processing difficulty, — missing data — and then present a technique to minimize this problem. Next, we go through the major whole-loan variables and how we treat them in the prepayment model. Whole-loan variables are distinguished from agency variables as that data which are available for whole loans but not for agencies. This does not preclude analysis of those factors which are common to both, but the nature of the information merits a separate discussion. Then, we discuss "bucket design." One of the important elements of the analysis is the grouping of similar data for analysis, and putting them into "buckets." The parameters of these buckets will influence the efficiency and validity of our analysis, and will be discussed. The information about bucket design may also be useful in agency data processing.

---

[1] This is also true for the model described in Vernon H. Budinger and Yizhong Fan, "RFC Whole Loan Prepayment Behavior," Chapter 13 in Frank J. Fabozzi (ed.), *The Handbook of Mortgage-Backed Securities*, (Chicago: Probus Publishing, 1995).

Missing Data

A typical difficulty in processing whole-loan data is missing data. Because whole-loan data are provided at the loan level, in any given month some current loan factors (the factor being defined as the fraction of the loan remaining outstanding expressed in decimal form) may not appear on the tape for technical reasons (late payment, data entry error, etc.). Generally, after one or two months, the valid factor returns. This problem does not exist in agency pool level data. If the factor of a loan is missing in a certain pool, the servicer simply replaces it by the scheduled factor, i.e. with zero prepayment. The error in the pool factor caused by this treatment is negligible, as most of the cases of missing data relate to data entry error or slightly late arrival of payment. Further, the overwhelming majority of payments are made as scheduled, without prepayment, so the assumption that a missing factor can be replaced with the scheduled factor is very likely to accurately reflect the actual event. On the other hand, for whole loans, missing data are not replaced with the scheduled factor. It is either blank or just a repeat of the last factor, seemingly on a random basis.

Since one month's data can affect two months' SMM calculation, neglecting missing whole-loan data could cause a significant bias. As a result, because these loans are still alive, their actual SMM is most likely to be zero. Just as in the agency case, the usual event is scheduled payment, which implies an SMM of zero. However, in the whole-loan case, if data are missing, there is no attempt to replace the data. A missing record would artificially skew the analysis, in the same way that calculating U.S. average income using information from only 49 states would. The error would be particularly biased if the left-out state's average income was far from the national mean. We believe that missing whole-loan payment data are not missing at random, but usually as a result of late, otherwise scheduled payment, and therefore missing a disproportionate number of payments with an SMM of zero. This phenomenon introduces a bias that effectively increases the measured prepayment speed.

The solution to this problem exists in the whole-loan data structure itself. In the refinancing part of our prepayment model, we use the maximum likelihood method (a non-linear regression modeling method), where the dependent variables are the total number of loans and number of refinancing loans. By definition, a loan exists from the first payment date until its factor becomes zero, since when the loan is paid off, the fraction of the loan remaining outstanding is zero. Therefore, factors do not have any effect on modeling refinancing, as either a loan refinances or doesn't — any partiality is covered in the curtailment part of this model. In doing a retrospective study, the danger of missing data is miniscule, as we can simply examine data after the last date being studied to verify whether or not the loan is alive by checking the factor. After knowing whether a given loan is surviving or refinancing, we can easily put it into a bucket according to the modeling requirement. This guarantees virtually zero data error in the refinancing part of the whole-loan model, which can not be achieved with agency pool level data.

Whole-Loan Variables

We shall define whole-loan variables as variables associated with data available for whole loans but not agency loans. Whole-loan variables merit discussion because the only useful agency variables are weighted average coupon (WAC), and age, which are also the only two useful variables common to whole-loan and agency data. These are not to be confused with environmental variables, like current mortgage or U.S. Treasury rates, which are not data dependent.

The loan level data for whole loans provides not only the complete information about refinancing but also many variables such as documentation (easy, also called limited, versus full documentation), loan to value (LTV) ratio, geography (state of origination, particularly if the loan is from California), and purpose (purchase — which means a loan taken out for the initial purchase of the house, equity refinancing — which is refinancing more than the remaining balance to take "cash out," and rate and term refinancing — which is only refinancing the outstanding balance. There are other purposes, but these three account for more than 99% of the loans.)

These and other variables are not available in agency pool level data. However, using this additional data carelessly could lead to two significant problems. First, if the sample space is small or if a given variable is not significant (or both), the result produced is noise and hence misleading. Second, to use all of the variables mentioned above in the deal prepayment forecast, we would also need to aggregate loans in every deal according to each of the categories used, and track these items to maturity in every piece of every deal. The extra memory and processing steps this requires slows down evaluation of the model, which is especially important when it is evaluated millions of times when doing option-adjusted spread (OAS) calculations. Considering that the purpose of this model is to be usable by practitioners who need to make relatively quick evaluations, processing time is a non-trivial concern.

We first consider the most fundamental question: why did these loans not qualify for agency underwriting (conform), and as a result, why do borrowers accept less favorable non-conforming mortgage rates? In recent years, non-conforming loan rates have generally been 30-50 bp higher than conforming loan rates. We think the following reasons for non-conformance are most likely. One possibility is that the size of the loan is greater than the conforming loan limit (currently about $207,000). Another possibility is that the applicant has bad credit. A third possibility is that the ratio of loan payment-to-applicant income is too high. For this reason, many applicants make a large down payment to lower the LTV and the payment to income ratio, and even so, may not qualify for a conforming loan. These measures may induce a whole-loan originator to take the loan, due to the higher interest rate which the whole-loan originator may charge. We also think the second and third reasons frequently result in the easy documentation (easy-doc) because the applicants would not pass the scrutiny of full-documentation. Based on these considerations, we use the documentation and loan size variables among the whole-loan variables discussed so far. Other variables will be discussed, and we will analyze which to use.

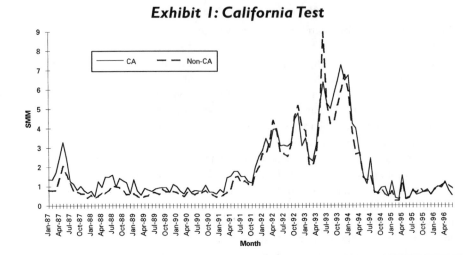

Exhibit 1: California Test

Prior to 1992, we observed that loans originated in California (CA) tended to prepay much faster than loans from other states. This phenomenon was referred to as the "California effect." Since 1992, this effect has disappeared. We came to these conclusions in an earlier study based on data from January 1987 to April 1993.[2] Tracking further to June 1996, we do not observe this phenomenon returning, and can reasonably assume that it shall not return, as the disparity between the national economy and California's economy has narrowed. This can be seen in Exhibit 1. Correspondingly, we used CA in the regression but not in the forecast. We multiply expected prepayments of all CA loans before 1992 by a constant (> 1) which is determined by the regression itself. This multiplier smoothly approaches 1, and remains equal to 1 after 1992. Therefore, to forecast prepayments, there is no difference between CA and non-CA loans.

The results of the regression lead us to believe that LTV is an important variable in our model. What we actually used is the current LTV, which we define to be the product of the original LTV and the current factor.[3] For simplicity, we assume that the value of the property is constant over the life of the loan. We believe that this assumption makes it possible to develop a model, as alternative assumptions (that is, non-constant housing value) would require predicting housing markets, which is difficult to do. Current LTV, not original LTV, is what banks take into consideration when making refinancing loans, so there is good economic sense for this variable to have an impact. This current LTV has some correlation with the age variable in our model. However, this correlation is very small in the early years for RFC loans, as the factor changes very little at first. As the rate of change for the factor increases, the correlation becomes stronger. Even though

---

[2] Budinger and Fan, "RFC Whole Loan Prepayment Behavior."
[3] In Chapter 1, the current LTV is defined in a different way.

there is a correlation between these two variables (age and LTV), we feel that using both variables is justified, as the correlation is low during much of the life of a loan, and variable over the entire loan.

We decided not to use purpose of loan as a variable for two reasons. We aggregated monthly prepayments for 96 months according to loan purpose. As mentioned above, purchase, equity, and rate-and-term accounted for the bulk of the loans, so those were the only purposes we used in the study. When doing an analysis of variance (ANOVA) to test the hypothesis that the SMM for any purpose is identical, that is, the mean SMM for each purpose is the same, we found that while purchase versus rate-term is significant, both purchase versus equity, and equity versus rate-term are insignificant. Since one pair is significantly different while the other two pairs are not, there is some ambiguity for using it as a variable. The final factor in the decision to drop it as a variable was the difficulty in designing software to track all three over the life of the loans.

Bucket Design

A bucket as used here is a grouping of similar data for processing, which has specific age, WAC, and loan size attributes. We have made two significant changes in bucket design in the new aggregation program in order to improve three things. We specifically wanted to improve *inhomogeneity* (we tried to make the number of loans in every bucket similar) and *sparseness* (we tried to increase the average number of loans in every bucket to improve its statistical properties, that is, to avoid sparseness). We also tried to make the seasoning curve, that is SMM versus age, more accurate. Not all of these goals can be simultaneously optimized, and therefore, compromise is required. Also, we needed to keep the size of the data file from becoming too large to run the regressions on our computers in a reasonable amount of time.

The first change involves seasoning. We believe seasoning is the most important part in a prepayment model. Just think about the PSA model which has one variable only — age. With this one parameter, the PSA model has remarkable efficacy. This conclusion is confirmed by our analysis. Our current model uses 107 buckets in the aggregation.[4] For age 90 months and younger, every age is a bucket. Then, each bucket spans five months for ages 91-120 months, 10 months for 121-180, 20 months for 181-240, and 60 months for the last 10 years. This provides great accuracy for most loans in the RFC whole-loan database, as for mortgages younger than 90 months, the age for each bucket is exact.

The second change involves WAC. When we quote the mortgage rate for a certain month, what we are really expressing is the average rate of the loans originated in that month. The WAC of every individual loan is distributed around that average. For whole loans, the variance from the mean rate in any given month is much greater than for agency loans. Correspondingly, when we design a WAC bucket, the width is designed so that each bucket has a similar number of mort-

---

[4] The prior model used seven age buckets (0, 10, 20, 30, 60, 120, 240, 360) in the aggregation of the data.

gages. Those buckets whose values are near the mean WAC tend to have a smaller range of WAC than those farther from that mean. However, this is only correct for loans originated very recently. Old loans peak around the rate in their originating month. Taking this into account, we now use the floating WAC bucket, tracking back the original central mortgage rate according to their ages.

These two treatments proved to be successful. Using the old aggregation, we had on average 12 loans in each bucket with a standard deviation of 44. Now we have 24 loans on average with a standard deviation of 53. Originally, more than 65% of buckets had just one or two loans. Now, this percentage is reduced to 32%.

CURTAILMENT

Up to this point, the discussion of prepayment involved only the refinancing of a loan, which is the payment of the entire remaining balance prior to maturity. Curtailment refers to the partial prepayment of a loan, which is paying down the loan faster than originally scheduled, but not total elimination of the loan in any one payment. This topic concerns an error in SMM calculation which arises when using the traditional Public Securities Association Standard Formula.[5] This calculation error systematically amplifies the SMM as it assumes that curtailment equals zero, and we will discuss this shortly. Due to the practical implications of many of the attributes of the data, this may in many ways belong in the data processing discussion of this chapter. However, we think this is important enough to be examined separately. In whole-loan data, the incidence of refinancing prepayment (SMM=100) can be calculated exactly, as we explained earlier in the chapter. On the other hand, the curtailment amplification error is not as easily eliminated, even if perfect data were available. In the agency pool level data, this error affects the overall SMM. The basic idea was mentioned briefly in the January 15, 1996 issue of *Mortgage-Backed Securities Letter*. Here we give full numerical details.

We first quote the standard formula of SMM calculation from:[6]

$$F_2 = F_1 \times (BAL_1 / BAL_2) \times (1 - (SMM / 100))$$

where 1 and 2 refer to starting and ending points in the (one month) period. With F as factor and C as gross WAC, M_0 and M are original term and WARM (weighted average remaining term M months) respectively, BAL is the amortized loan factor (as fraction of par) defined by

$$BAL = \frac{1 - (1 + C/1200)^{-M}}{1 - (1 + C/1200)^{-M_0}}$$

---

[5] *Standard Formulas for the Analysis of Mortgage-Backed Securities and Other Related Securities* (New York: Public Securities Association, 1990).

[6] *Standard Formulas for the Analysis of Mortgage-Backed Securities and Other Related Securities*, p. SF-5.

To make this calculation exact, certain guidelines need to be followed. First, WARM should be the remaining payments, not simply 360 (if a 30-year mortgage) minus ages at point 1 and 2, as WARM takes into account accumulated curtailment. Second, WARM should not be rounded off to the nearest month, but should carry as much precision as possible. However, the example quoted in the PSA implies that many users may miss these points.

In the example published in the PSA publication (page SF-6), the GNMA-I 9% passthrough issued 3/1/88 had a remaining term of 359 months. It had $F_1 = 0.85150625$ at 6/1/89 and $F_2 = 0.84732282$ at 7/1/89. From 4/1/88 to 6/1/89, 15 payments came in. Therefore, 344 at BAL_1 and 343 at BAL_2 are correct only under the assumption of zero curtailment. However, using these numbers without mentioning the zero curtailment assumption is a bit misleading, as curtailment exists.

This error will not be serious for agency pools most of the time. Among huge numbers of loans, curtailment usually should not be great enough to cause significant error in the application of the PSA formula. Assuming two months of curtailment, (that is, prepayment sufficient to reduce the life of the loan by two months) WARM at 6/1/89 and 7/1/89 were 342 and 341 respectively. The scheduled factor should be per the exact calculation. The numbers from the PSA example were calculated with a zero curtailment assumption. The exact and PSA calculations are shown below:

Exact Calculation	Calculation from PSA example
Fsched = F1 × (BAL_1 / BAL_2) = 0.85101892	0.85102709
The same calculation gives:	
Amortization = $F_1 - F_{sched}$ = 0.00048733	0.00047916
Prepayments = $F_{sched} - F_2$ = 0.00369610	0.00370427
SMM = 100 (0.00369610 / 0.85101892)	
= 0.434315%	0.435270%
CPR = 5.0891%	5.1000%
PSA = 149.68%	150%

It seems these errors are acceptable in this case, as the error is small. It is unlikely that an error of this magnitude would cause problems as a practical matter. We should keep in mind that this error will be amplified when the pool is seasoned even with no further curtailment. Let's consider an extreme case. In the above example, the last payment comes in on 12/1/2017 with the aforementioned 2-month curtailment. By definition, the last payment has an SMM of zero, and hence, the SMM in 11/2017 is always zero. However, using the formula with a zero curtailment assumption will give SMM = 100. This error begins at the first curtailment, starts small and increases to the extreme case at the terminal payment.

The situation changes for the loan level data. Also we frequently work on deals with very few loans, say 10 or so. Significant curtailment in one loan in a bucket with relatively few loans will present a phantom peak in SMM, which is not indicative of the underlying trend, but is an artifact of sparseness. As a result, the regression will include error due to its attempt to catch this peak. For an individual loan, curtailment can be huge even for very young mortgages.

Let us look at an example. RFC loan 61_309004_5 is a 30-year loan with a fixed coupon of 10.75. This loan was issued on 5/1/76, and is quite old by whole-loan standards. The factor on 2/1/87 was 0.3612. Let us assume that in actuality there was no curtailment in the 3/1/87 payment, i.e. SMM = 0. The factor on 3/1/87 would be 0.3551. Using the PSA formula we get Fsched = 0.3608. However, the corresponding calculated prepayments were SMM = 1.56%, CPR = 17.19%, and PSA = 287%. These numbers are too large to ignore. Using a formula with this sort of error may misrepresent risk at the outset of the deal. Let us assume this loan has an original balance of $100,000 and a scheduled monthly payment of $933.48. Without curtailment, the 3/1/87 payment contains $120.12 of principal payment. With the actual curtailment, it contains $609.88 of principal payment. It is this $489.76 difference that comprises the phantom SMM 1.56%.

The trouble in the above example is not a one month effect. It will continue and will be more serious until it matures. If a servicer paid investors according to this calculation, the servicer would be short of money immediately. Curiously, it is uncertain to us exactly how servicers calculate payments. Exhibit 2 is the comparison between the exact curtailment and the curtailment *calculated* with the *zero curtailment* assumption. Note that for loan level data, the SMM formula above works to calculate curtailment SMM in the following way: since prepayment is composed only of curtailment and refinancing, if a loan is alive, there is no refinancing, and therefore, the SMM formula above describes curtailment behavior. The zero curtailment assumption states simply that the curtailment calculated today is unaffected by any historical curtailment, that is, for all intents and purposes, at any point being examined there is no past curtailment. In the plot, we used a smoothing technique, as without smoothing, one or two anomalous peaks would cause the scale to be so large that for the most part the two curves would not be differentiable. The error from the zero curtailment approximation is negligible for young mortgages while more and more serious as they season. For young mortgages, accumulated curtailments are usually not too large. Furthermore, a given amount of curtailment, as measured by WARM, causes larger errors when looking at older mortgages than for younger mortgages.

PREPAYMENT MODELING

Basic Approach

Our model is fundamentally similar to the earlier reported model.[7] Based on our innovations in data processing and statistical analysis described above, we were able to more accurately utilize this framework as a foundation. We will describe it in more detail throughout this section, but first we review it briefly. Separating refinancing

---

[7] Budinger and Fan, "RFC Whole Loan Prepayment Behavior."

and curtailment in prepayment is a long time dream of mortgage industry research-ers. This has been unattainable due to the pooled nature of agency data. Loan level data are simply not available for agencies. For the reasons given earlier in this chap-ter, whole-loan data, being at the loan level, provides us with this information.

There are many advantages to this separation. First, refinancing and cur-tailment have very different patterns. To summarize the analysis in prior sections, refinancing tends to be driven primarily by current market conditions, whereas curtailment depends on the individual mortgage holder's financial situation and their expectations for the future, and thus tend to be much more random than refi-nancing. It would be highly favorable to describe them by two different models. Second, statistics requires every sample to be independent. If we consider refi-nancing only, the dollars belonging to the same loan have 100% correlation while dollars from different loans are completely independent. Because prepayment mainly comes from refinancing, it is better to use the number of loans to estimate refinancing, due to the statistical independence of loans, while using curtailment measured by dollar amount as a correction.

Different loan size could cause some problems. It can be demonstrated that different loan size just changes the variance but not the mean of the SMM. (That proof is beyond the scope of this chapter.) In agency pool level data, this separation is impossible. Fortunately, the loan size in agency pools are quite uniform so mea-suring the dollar amount and the number of loans produces about the same result. In whole-loan data, we can measure the number of loans easily and accurately. There-fore, we choose refinancing loan number and total loan number as dependent vari-ables. (We use the terms "number of loans" and "loan number" interchangeably.)

Exhibit 2: Curtailment Analysis

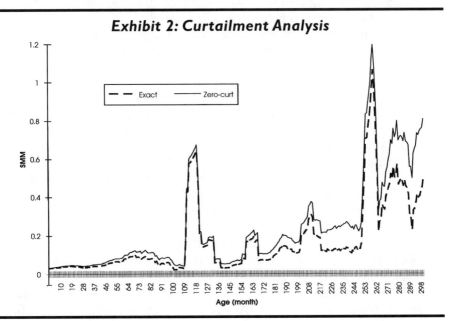

Historically, we make this decision for another reason. In agency models, we use dollar amount to measure SMM. In that model, we used a logistic function:

$$SMM = [1 + \exp(-X)]^{-1}$$

where X is the linear regressor, using the least squares method, of independent variables (see the discussion below). When we tried the same function and the same regression method for whole loans, it did not work at all because of the sparseness of the data. A significant number of our buckets contained only one loan. The X in a one-loan bucket is plus or minus infinity. We avoided this difficulty by using loan number instead of dollar amount to measure SMM and using the maximum likelihood method instead of the least squares method in regression. Apparently we are lucky again in the sense that the difficulty in the whole-loan data is overcome by the advantages inherent in the whole-loan data. We still use linear regression and dollar amount to calculate curtailment. Because refinancing and curtailment are exclusive, the surviving probability of a single dollar has the following expression:

Prob(loan surviving) = [1 − Prob(refinancing)] [1 − Prob(curtailment)]

SMM is one minus this probability, usually expressed as a percentage.

Independent Variables

The X in the logistic function is the linear combination of the following components: seasoning, refinancing incentive, seasonality, burnout, yield curve, and the specified subset of the whole-loan variables described before. Throughout this chapter and in all of the exhibits, we will use X to represent this regressor. Seasonality and burnout have some changes from the prior model reported, and will be pointed out later. Seasoning and refinancing incentive are piecewise straight lines. Taking the advantage of accurate aggregation we can locate the end points of these pieces more accurately.

Exhibit 3 provides a comparison of the seasoning curves between FNMA and RFC. Now we can see that whole loans have a PSA ramp as well, but the ramp is steeper and thus ends with a higher speed. For Exhibit 3, we set the age pieces for the piecewise function as follows: 0, 15, 25, 55, 70, 90, 120, 180, 360. Seasoning and refinancing incentive are correlated in the sense that refinancing incentive has age dependence as well. The refinancing incentive is also a piecewise straight line function. We consistently set the refinancing incentive in the same pieces.

Seasonality

In the model reported elsewhere, we used 12 constants to describe seasonality corresponding to January through December in X. For a given change in X, the change in SMM is larger for larger values of X. This is due to the concave nature of the piece of the logistic function which we use. (As a practical matter, we only involve the function for SMM < 50.) That type of change is not what we expect. We think that for loans with a WAC lower than the mortgage rate, the refinancing reasons should only be based on either relocation or otherwise irresistible circumstances, and as a result, they should have strong seasonality. Loans with a WAC greater than the mortgage rate are more likely to refinance for purely economic reasons, irrespective of other effects such as seasonality. Of course, there are lucky people who get low mortgage rates when they relocate. We simply assume they are the minority. Based on this analysis, we turn off the seasonality effect when WAC is greater than the mortgage rate.

Exhibit 4 shows the seasonality contribution to X. The peak appears in the summer. Considering the lag effect, which is simply the time between the decision to buy or sell and the actual closing, it shows that the spring is the moving season as expected. Before we made the change from constant seasonality assumption under all circumstances to seasonality equal to zero for loans with a WAC greater than the mortgage rate, the seasonality patterns for RFC and FNMA were quite different. We could not find a logical explanation for that. From Exhibit 4, we can see that these two now have very similar patterns. They have peaks and valleys at the same positions, but FNMA is smoother. One hypothesis is that because many whole loans are jumbo loans, wealthy people may have the option to move whenever they want, irrespective of market factors.

Burnout

Burnout is a measure of the excess of WAC over the mortgage rate at any given time, during the history of a loan. Essentially, it is a measure of "failure to take advantage of the opportunity to refinance cheaply in the past." The presumption is that an individual who does not take advantage of that opportunity has other reasons for not doing so, so the trend is self-perpetuating. This issue is more difficult to quantify for whole loans than for agency loans.

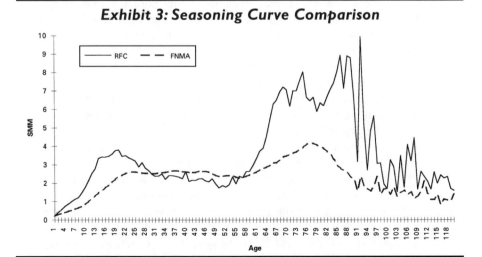

Exhibit 3: Seasoning Curve Comparison

Exhibit 4: Seasonality Comparison

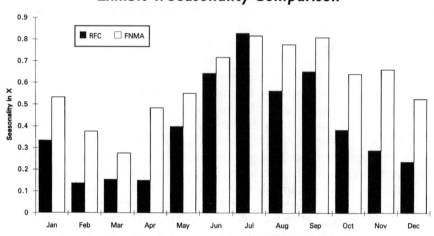

Burnout involves the sensitivity of saving money. It requires the independent sample to have some internal structure, by which we mean that the characteristics we wish to measure can be described by some distribution. In agency data, most buckets have a few hundred pools. The typical loan number at the very beginning should be several thousand per bucket, which is quite enough to have a structure. Even with our new improved aggregation program, the average RFC loan number is only 24 per bucket and we cannot say very much about its structure. It can be proven that when the bucket has only one loan, there is no further burnout accumulation in the bucket, as a loan's sensitivity is assumed to be constant for the life of the loan. Thus, the sensitivity of the bucket is defined by the one remaining loan.

We noticed that whole-loan prepayment does not have a strong burnout effect. The sample space is almost empty for age greater than 120. For the most part, before they *burn*, they are *out*. Whole loans, for a number of reasons discussed earlier in the chapter, tend to have a high propensity to refinance. But, totally ignoring burnout seems incorrect because the CMO deal level prepayment prediction certainly requires some burnout consideration. In a given deal, loans that refinance are obviously (by virtue of their having refinanced) more sensitive than loans remaining in the deal. In summary, it is more reasonable to consider burnout from the prediction point of view. However, when doing the regression, dropping burnout seems more correct, as it is a small effect, difficult to measure, and most of the buckets have a small number of loans.

To compromise the requirements of prediction and regression, we made two changes in modeling burnout. The traditional burnout measures both depth (WAC − mortgage rate) and width (number of months of exposure to any positive depth). For agency loans, depth is a necessary measure because of the "layer effect." Different depths attracts different layers of people. For example, according to a

Goldman Sachs research study,[8] some people were willing to refinance for 500 bp of savings but not for 400 bp. However, this is not true for whole loans. First, as we said before, with very few loans, there is not a great deal of internal structure, so it is unlikely that there is a significant layering effect. Second, even if the whole-loan data had as many loans as agency data, the whole-loan layer structure would be much simpler, as it seems that whole loans tend to refinance more readily than agencies. When interest rates move, refinancing may save a whole-loan borrower additional 30-50 bp beyond the whole-loan rate spread if they can qualify for an agency loan. Therefore we just accumulate width but not depth. This inference is supported by the fact that we tried to use a variable to count this layer effect, which worked in our agency models. On the other hand, we got an opposite and insignificant result from whole loans, which is certainly due to noise. In short, we think refinancing ability instead of the spread depth is the main factor for whole loans to refinance.

Another change from the previously reported model for burnout should be useful to agency models too. We think the burnout accumulation should have a decaying effect. Consider a simplified model in which there are two groups of loans. One has a constant SMM of 6% while the other has a constant SMM of 2%. Both groups have the same outstanding balance at the beginning. It can be seen that although two groups keep constant speed, the weighted average SMM is decreasing. Simple calculation shows that this decrease is not linear but concave (see Exhibit 5). This means that under the same refinancing conditions, it burns more at the beginning but less later. We have now built in this decaying effect. This decaying effect also puts a cap on the total burnout automatically. Opposite to the seasonality effect, we set burnout equal to zero when the WAC is less than the mortgage rate. When there is no money to save, and prepayment occurs for some irresistible reason, then this has nothing to do with burnout.

Exhibit 5: Non-Linearity of Burnout

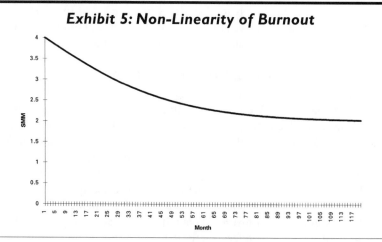

[8] Gregg N. Patruno, "Mortgage Prepayment Modeling: II," Chapter 9 in *The Handbook of Mortgage-Backed Securities*.

We summarize the whole-loan burnout effect as follows. Because whole loans tend to prepay quickly, the burnout effect is minor in a prepayment model. We think the burnout effect is more a function of a borrower's ability to qualify for refinancing than their desire to save money. In other words, whole-loan borrowers will attempt to refinance on the basis of smaller spreads than agency loan borrowers, but they will often fail to refinance due to qualification hurdles.

RESULTS AND DISCUSSION

The Pearson chi-square is a popular measure of the accuracy of a statistical model. Assume the sample space has N cells (or, in our terminology, N buckets). Every cell has N_i objects (N_i being the loan number in this case). If we have a model that says a certain event (in this case refinancing) happens in this cell with the probability p_i (p_i being predicted SMM here), where n_i is the number of objects in cell i on which the event actually happens (the observed refinancing loans), then the Pearson chi-square is defined as

$$\sum \frac{(n_i - p_i N_i)^2}{n_i}$$

If the model is perfect and there is no noise, this quantity is equal to zero. Clearly, the smaller the chi-square the better the model in general. This quantity is proportional to N. For the comparison to make sense, we should divide it by the degrees of freedom (about the same as N for large N). Although the original whole-loan prepayment model is qualitatively fine, the chi-square is about 20, which is quite large. In the present model, this is reduced to 1.275, which is within the 95% confidence level (1.459). Considering the serious inhomogeneity and sparseness in the whole-loan database, this is a great achievement.

Documentation Effect

We pointed out that we think documentation is an important characteristic for whole-loan prepayments. We think *easy*-doc is more *difficult* to refinance than full-doc. Since easy-doc is frequently a last resort, a great deal of effort has gone into the process on the part of the applicant prior to the easy-doc application process. Further, many banks do not issue easy-doc loans. Unless an applicant's circumstances have changed significantly since the original application, it will not be easy for them to get a new loan. The regression result agrees with this completely. The difference between easy- and full-doc refinancing frequency is very significant. According to our historical data, if an easy-doc group has a CPR equal to 15%, the full-doc group under exactly the same refinancing conditions would have a CPR equal to 26%.

Exhibit 6: Document Test

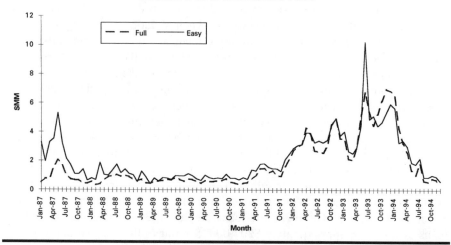

Exhibit 6 is the SMM comparison of easy-doc and full-doc in the 8-year period. The exhibit seems to indicate that easy-doc prepays faster than full-doc by about 0.3% SMM, which is the opposite of our conclusion in the prior paragraph. Upon further review, we realized that Exhibit 6 is providing a comparison in the same time scale but not the same refinancing conditions. Since easy-doc loans have their own problems, banks charge them a higher interest rate, usually by at least 30-50 bp more than full doc whole loans. As a result, for every month, easy-doc and full-doc have different refinancing incentives if their other conditions (age, LTV, location, etc.) are identical. By ignoring the time scale, that is, not comparing loans in the same month, we could find easy-doc and full-doc under a similar exposure. The full-doc refinancing advantage caught by the regression is based on that comparison.

Loan Size Effect

Loan size is one of the major reasons for which a loan becomes a non-conforming loan. Our results show that it does play a certain role in whole-loan prepayments. We found that when loan sizes are smaller than the conforming loan limit, the effect is insignificant — size is irrelevant to prepayment behavior. After that, it increases quite linearly. When the size reaches about $350,000 it becomes flat. We know that the refinancing processing fee is a constant while the money saved by refinancing is proportional to the loan size.[9] Our findings seem consistent with this.

As alluded to previously, when the size is smaller than the conforming loan dollar size limit, borrowers' major problems are bad credit and low income, so their mortgage rates are usually higher than other whole loans. Their decision to refinance may be based more upon whether they can qualify than upon how much they

---

[9] In very few states (e.g. New York and Pennsylvania), the government collects a mortgage tax, which is proportional to the loan size. In this case, the analysis is not very accurate.

can save — they want to save money, but can they qualify? The second piece, that is the group of loans from $207,000 to about $350,000, is easy to understand. These people are generally wealthier than average. Their situation is the opposite of the first piece, i.e. how much they can save by refinancing after deducting processing fees. When the size reaches about $350,000, which we shall call the third piece, our analysis suggests that mortgage holders will refinance to take advantage of any recognizable spread. At that level, every 10 bp or so can save a significant amount of money. However, a difference as small as 10 bp between an existing mortgage and an available refinancing rate is not easy to recognize in the market, due to imperfect information to the consumer. Therefore, as soon as the spread (WAC − mortgage rate) is significant (say 50 bp), refinancing becomes attractive to them.

Traditionally, it has been believed that loan size plays an important role in whole-loan prepayment. According to our findings, loan size is important, but not the sole determinant. We found that when the size effect flattens out at about $350,000 as explained above, these loans prepay 20-30% faster than the whole loans of less than approximately $207,000. Similar to the burnout analysis, we turn this effect off when the spread is negative. When the WAC is lower than the mortgage rate, the larger the loan sizes the more money they would lose if they were refinancing.

Age Distribution

We now discuss Exhibit 3 in more detail. While both curves have PSA ramps, these ramps are not identical. For FNMA, the ramp ends at 25 months and the curve flattens afterwards. For RFC, the ramp ends at 15 months with the height about 1% SMM higher than FNMA. In addition to that, it keeps the height to 25 months then drops to the FNMA level very quickly. At 55 months, both curves start speeding up while RFC has a much larger slope. Both reach peaks around 80 months and then drop. For RFC, big noise comes out after 90 months while the noise from FNMA is much smaller. The second peak (70 to 80 months) is quite universal. We observe it for all GNMA, FNMA, and FHLMC for both 15- and 30-year loans. The reason for this is easy to understand. Many life-cycle events arise after six or seven years, such as job changes, promotions and raises, children requiring more space, and the like. The first peak exists in RFC only. We think the reasons are related to the following: some whole-loan owners have temporary difficulties getting a conforming loan, while some difficulties are not temporary. Of course, most borrowers do not know if these difficulties are temporary during the application process. Temporary difficulties likely to be solved in one or two years may include unemployment (probably one person in a couple), excessive LTV, or some minor credit problems. They may have some urgent need to buy a house. Another possibility is that the price of a house is too good to pass up, and they cannot wait until they meet agency loan underwriting requirements. If these things are not overcome in one or two years, the time to resolve them tends to be quite long and random. In the case of unemployment, if it cannot be resolved in a short time, they are likely to default and also appear as a prepayment.

Exhibit 7: Life Table

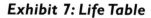

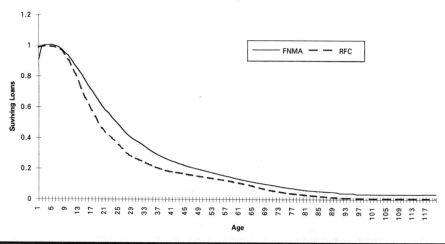

The seasoning curve is similar to, but not exactly the same as, a life table in the insurance industry. A life table measures surviving population on an absolute basis. SMM is measured versus outstanding balance on a *relative* basis, that is percentage of loans surviving. We cannot afford to track every loan from age 0 to its "death" (refinancing). Looking at the whole-loan age distribution during an 8-year period should be quite close to the "mortgage life table." Now the high accuracy aggregation allows us to analyze more details. We used five discrete points in our previously reported model. Now we have a continuous curve.

Exhibit 7 is the number of surviving RFC loans for different ages with the unit of 10,000 loans. The FNMA part is measured by the outstanding balance with unit of $600 billion. The primary reason for the small period of increase at the beginning of the period measured is that some pools are formed with loans whose age is not equal to zero, but may be 1, 2, 3 or more months. In our database, we observed one pool that started with loans with an age of 15 months. One other difference from a true life table is that at any moment during our study, new loans and pools were being added into the data. Exhibit 8 is the corresponding amortized part measured by the same units. At an age of 20 months, FNMA has 61% of principal remaining, while 46% of RFC loan principal survives. At an age of 120 months, FNMA still has 3.4% remaining, while RFC's surviving loans have been only 0.6%, or practically zero. FNMA amortizes 28% of all prepayments from an age of 1 month to 20 months. In the same period, RFC's loan number amortizes 47%. From an age of 1 month to 120 months, FNMA amortizes 92% from total, while RFC amortizes 99%. More precisely, in the history of the RFC, about 600 loans have lived for more than 10 years. With data this sparse, we cannot expect the present model to give an accurate predictions for old loans.

Exhibit 8: Death Table

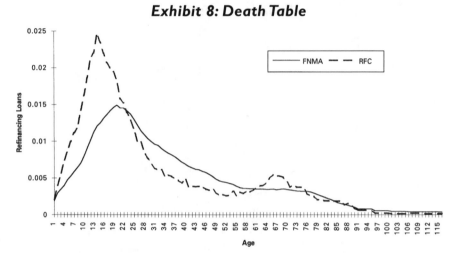

As we emphasized before, Exhibit 8 measures the absolute prepaid amount. From the seasoning curve as given in Exhibit 3, the highest peak of SMM appears around 80 months. However, less than 1% of total loans remain at that time. Therefore this peak is not important to young mortgages. This may be part of the reason that the PSA model does not include this peak.

Validity of 150% Multiplier "Whole-Loan Model"

A popular whole-loan prepayment model is the 150% multiplier model. This model takes a conventional agency (FNMA or FHLMC) mortgage prepayment model and then multiplies its speed by 150% to predict whole-loan prepayment speed. Here we discuss the validity of this approach based on the high accuracy of the aggregation.

Exhibit 9 is the seasoning curve comparison between RFC and FNMA for loans with a WAC less than the mortgage rate. Exhibit 10 is for loans with a WAC greater than the mortgage rate. In our previous reported study, we noticed that for lower coupons, RFC and FNMA had quite similar prepayment behavior. However, we did not expect them to be as similar as Exhibit 9 would indicate. The rise starting just before 60 months is due to noise, because to have a WAC lower than current rates, they must have had an anomalously low mortgage rate about five years ago, and Exhibit 9 is specifically for loans with a WAC less than the current rate. In this category, the sample space is almost empty because of the high interest rates in the middle 1980s. Clearly, a simple 100% multiplier is most proper in this case.

In Exhibit 10, we can see that for high coupon mortgages with an age of less than 20 months, a 200% multiplier does not seem bad. After that age, no certain rule can follow. Because 70% of the loans in that category prepaid before age

30 months, a 200% multiplier could be useful at least for young mortgages in that category. For loans with coupons around par, our findings in Exhibits 9 and 10 lead us to expect that a 150% multiplier of the agency model works reasonably well for quite a wide age range. Refer to Exhibit 3 again, and look at the age range from 1 to 20. In that range, we found that the 150% multiplier of the agency prepayment model is quite good. Probably, that is why people used this "model" for so many years. However, as we pointed out, using it for all coupon ranges is inaccurate, and could generate significant error.

Exhibit 9: Seasoning Curves Comparison (Lower Coupon)

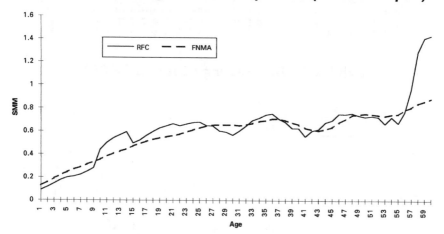

Exhibit 10: Seasoning Curves Comparison (High Coupon)

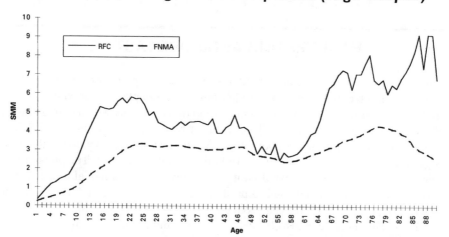

Exhibit 11: Backtesting (With all Coupons)

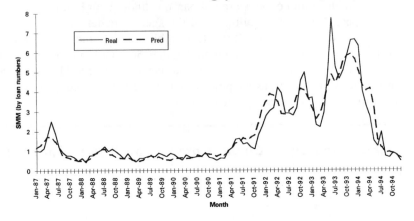

Exhibit 12: Backtesting (Coupon 8-10%)

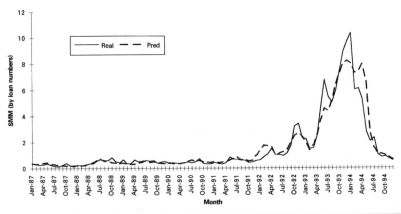

BACKTESTING AND FORECASTING

A necessary condition for a good model is that it holds up under backtesting. This involves using the model to make predictions in the sample space. Exhibits 11-14 are the backtesting plots with different coupon ranges. Loans with a coupon range of 10-12% have the best result. The reason for this is that most loans in the time period studied were in this coupon range. An interesting phenomenon is the very large spread region, which is 1993 to 1994 in Exhibits 13 and 14. The prepayment behavior has a lot of noise. We do not expect any long term model to catch that noise. However, the model tried to predict the "average," or trend, of the actual underlying phenomenon. We can see the same noise in the deal prepayment forecast later. This noise can also be seen in agency data, but is not as serious. We attribute this noise to several reasons.

Exhibit 13: Backtesting (Coupon 10-12%)

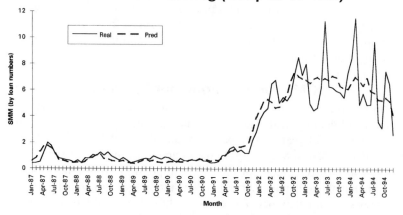

Exhibit 14: Backtesting (Coupon > 12%)

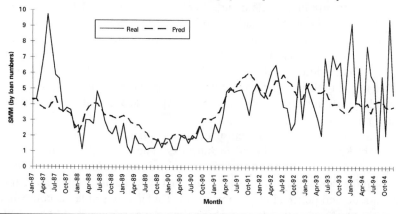

First, the sample space is quite empty, in that there are few loans with coupon rates over 10% in either whole-loan or agency data surviving beyond the early 1990s. Few whole loans stay at a large spread for very long. Of course, the smaller the number of samples, the more noise.

Second, there are many diverse reasons for a loan to be a whole loan. Different problems will require different amounts of time to approve a loan, which causes the lag effect to be more erratic. Even within a given category, for whole loans the approval time is less predictable than for agencies. According to Bear Stearns' research, about 25% of agency loans take one month to finish paper work, 40% take two months, 30% take three months, and less than 5% take more than three months. No similar results for whole loans are available, but we do not expect it to be as simple. Banks tighten or relax their loan policies according to the economic environment, which changes the approval time. This is a major component of lag. Conforming loans are not affected too much by this change in bank policies, but whole loans are. For these reasons, we think modeling whole-loan mortgage rates with a fixed lag assumption may not work well. To compensate for the uncertainty in lag, we use the average mortgage rate for the prior three months as a current mortgage rate.

CMO Deal Prepayment Forecast

We compare the monthly actual prepayment to the predicted prepayment month by month and deal by deal. This task is not easy even for very big samples. For example, FNMA 30-year 8.5s prepaid at a rate of 626 PSA in March 1996, 499 in April 1996, and 354 in May 1996. In the same three months, FNMA's lag-3 mortgage rates almost remained constant. It is impossible for a long-term model to predict such a phenomenon, that is, constant mortgage rates with significantly different prepayment behaviors. The biggest whole-loan deal has only about 2,000 loans. It has no comparison with FNMA 8.5s and therefore is more erratic.

Let us first look at a few surprising examples. First, similar deals can prepay very differently in a single month. Look, for example, at RFC Mortgage Data Report June 1996 issue. 87-4 had a 9.865 WAC and 236 WARM. 87-6 had a 9.802 WAC and 234 WARM. Besides these, their factors were 0.0740224 and 0.0705836, respectively. This implies very similar burnout. However, in July 1996, 87-4 had a 44.69 CPR while 87-6 had only a 0.26 CPR. This can be found even for very big deals. 95-S16 and 95-S17 both have about 1,500 loans and are almost identical. In the same issue, 95-S16 prepaid at a rate of 14.03 CPR and 95-S17 at a rate of 8.10 CPR.

Second, a given deal can prepay very differently in two consecutive months. 92-S20 had a 20.43 CPR in June 1996 and 2.91 CPR in July 1996. This deal had more than 200 loans left. This number is not very big as a statistical sample, but not terribly small compared with other RFC deals. During these months, the economic and political environments were relatively stable, as compared to a time period such as 1993, during which time a major recession had ended, and mortgage rates plummeted. Examples of prepayment behavior more erratic than that seen in mid-1996 could be found in 1993.

Exhibit 15 is the 18-month average CPR comparison from January 1995 to June 1996. Considering the difficulties described above, we think the predictions that resulted from our model are very good. Exhibit 16 orders errors by current number of loans in the deal, and Exhibit 17 orders them by age. In general, we can say that older and smaller deals have larger errors. This is expected. These predictions are not calculated exactly according to the model from regression analysis. When we used the model exactly, we saw a slight but overall over-prediction. When we use regression analysis in modeling, over-prediction in one area is usually the result of under-prediction in other areas. However, in Exhibits 11-14 we did not see that compensatory effect. Despite extensive testing, we could not find the reason for this over-prediction.

Exhibit 15: Deal Forecast

Deal	Count	WAC	Age	WARM	Real	Pred
86-12	7	10.09	102	257	43.70	29.21
86-15	13	10.38	101	241	22.03	30.18
87-1	52	10.27	97	256	16.84	30.58
87-3	22	10.30	97	249	14.91	32.05
87-4	59	9.87	96	256	22.86	32.22
87-6	53	9.80	96	257	10.46	30.55
87-S1	33	10.66	99	256	17.00	33.43
87-S4	52	10.26	96	259	30.18	32.06
87-S7	51	9.63	91	263	26.93	25.51
88-S1	97	10.85	88	266	16.49	26.2
89-S2	42	11.19	73	284	25.59	26.97
89-S3	31	11.41	69	288	28.79	29.33
89-S5	55	11.08	64	297	26.80	23.54
89-S6	51	11.71	63	300	32.91	25.8
90-5	94	10.94	58	300	29.09	22.65
90-S1	116	11.07	61	296	28.43	23.64
91-S30	265	9.61	38	316	20.05	17.88
92-13	157	9.02	34	323	17.00	14.85
92-S1	118	9.50	37	319	24.22	17.35
92-S11	261	9.15	33	321	16.93	16.25
92-S16	236	9.44	32	326	15.93	17.15
92-S19	202	9.10	33	322	14.43	15.52
92-S2	337	9.16	36	320	14.72	15.53
92-S20	262	9.20	32	323	15.08	16.44
92-S23	202	8.88	32	323	17.27	14.02
92-S24	362	9.16	30	327	15.76	16.07
92-S26	371	9.05	29	326	11.72	15.49

Deal	Count	WAC	Age	WARM	Real	Pred
92-S7	285	9.10	34	321	17.56	15.5
92-S9	224	8.70	35	320	12.79	13.37
93-S10	202	9.08	24	333	12.26	15.51
93-S11	581	8.66	23	333	8.90	12.63
93-S12	584	8.24	23	332	7.38	7.83
93-S14	879	8.28	21	334	8.28	8.27
93-S16	605	7.64	20	335	6.21	4.55
93-S18	1035	8.09	20	335	6.20	6.38
93-S2	456	8.71	24	330	9.17	12.59
93-S21	599	8.03	19	339	6.38	5.64
93-S22	984	7.65	19	337	3.00	4.46
93-S24	1081	7.59	18	338	4.92	4.37
93-S26	836	8.00	18	338	5.05	5.49
93-S27	523	8.11	19	336	5.90	6.62
93-S28	622	7.59	17	339	3.20	4.35
93-S3	214	8.17	25	331	5.29	6.91
93-S30	764	7.94	17	339	4.83	4.99
93-S31	1229	7.64	16	340	4.34	4.34
93-S34	637	7.54	16	340	3.50	4.24
93-S35	604	7.47	15	342	3.63	4.12
93-S37	832	7.54	15	342	2.89	4.19
93-S39	1011	7.41	15	342	3.60	4.15
93-S40	1438	7.29	14	343	5.21	4.04
93-S41	345	7.27	16	341	3.25	4.04
93-S43	907	7.28	14	344	3.85	3.97
93-S44	822	7.25	14	342	3.39	3.98
93-S45	1713	7.25	13	345	4.15	4.01

Exhibit 15 (Continued)

Deal	Count	WAC	Age	WARM	Real	Pred
92-S28	348	8.70	30	324	9.30	13.13
92-S30	436	8.57	28	326	9.02	11.32
92-S32	524	8.58	28	328	8.35	11.78
92-S33	470	8.64	27	329	11.56	11.39
92-S34	701	8.24	27	328	5.92	7.83
92-S37	522	8.53	26	330	9.09	11.23
92-S38	821	8.16	26	329	6.48	7.15
92-S43	555	8.58	25	332	9.14	11.76
92-S44	283	8.11	25	329	5.83	6.48
92-S6	392	9.18	35	322	21.50	15.96

Deal	Count	WAC	Age	WARM	Real	Pred
93-S47	1929	7.14	13	344	3.49	3.85
93-S6	519	8.73	23	331	9.35	13.87
94-S1	1724	7.22	12	346	3.60	3.81
94-S11	1430	7.44	9	349	3.44	3.77
94-S13	1392	7.62	8	350	4.64	4.28
94-S2	919	7.49	12	346	5.11	3.98
94-S3	1031	7.32	12	346	3.56	3.91
94-S5	884	7.44	11	347	3.34	3.86
94-S7	1415	7.36	10	348	4.16	3.68
94-S9	1020	7.33	10	348	4.20	3.73

Exhibit 16: Deal Forecast Errors (Ordered by Loan Numbers)

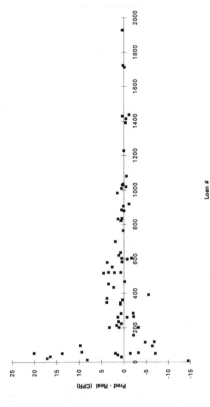

Exhibit 17: Deal Forecast Errors (Ordered by Ages)

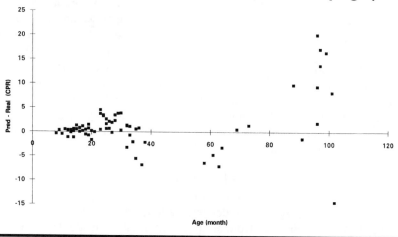

Finally, we turned our attention to the mortgage rate difference between conforming and non-conforming loans. Exhibit 18 is the rate difference between RFC (real rates, irrespective of number of points) and FNMA (rates corresponding to mortgages with zero points) in the period from July 1986 to June 1996. Before 1993, the RFC rate is at least 100 bp higher than FNMA. Starting from early 1993, the difference dropped to 30-50 bp. The period of what appears to be negative differences is an artifact of data reporting timing conventions. That is, RFC data are reported as of the last day of the month, whereas the FNMA data use the monthly average. Exhibit 18 surprised everyone, including RFC officials who reviewed these results. This seems to be the best explanation for the over-prediction. With such a large average rate difference during the majority of the time period under investigation, even if a whole loan's coupon is lower than the RFC rate, refinancing to a conforming loan is still profitable most of the time. Therefore, if the spread between WAC and mortgage rate for RFC loans remains constant over time, prepayment would be expected to be much faster prior to 1993 than it is now, due to the change in the difference between RFC and FNMA rates. This effect is not uniform to all whole loans. If the loan size is the main reason for non-conformance, this is unlikely to change for most loans in a short time. If it is a bad credit or low income problem, some could change and some not. The time for this change could also vary in a wide range. If everyone could change their qualification in a short time, the whole-loan prepayment prior to 1993 could have been much higher than it was in 1993!

The popular treatment for the problem that one part of the sample has a systematic difference from the remainder of the sample is to employ a dummy variable. Because there were record high prepayment rates for the years 1993 and 1994 (due to several factors), this method does not work in the present sample space. For many of the reasons which we have discussed, the entire sample space consists of two anomalous periods relative to 1995 and beyond. We do not plan to discuss this in mathematical detail in this chapter. Solving this problem completely requires us to wait another two or three years in order to obtain a reasonable amount of non-anomalous data. As a temporary treatment, we added a –0.3 constant in the X in the logistic function to lower the prediction. This is approximately an 80% multiplier of the SMM predicted by the exact model. This rate difference effect is actually not as large as we first thought. Let us assume the average SMM is 2%. That means only 0.4% of the borrowers, that is the over-prediction part, had the chance to change their qualification. But this has been large enough to interfere with the SMM prediction. Assuming this 0.4% stays the same, many of them will not refinance subsequent to 1995 because the rate difference between RFC and FNMA is much smaller than prior to 1993.

Final Comments

We determined that in order to properly model whole-loan prepayment behavior, we needed to use only age, WAC, documentation, original loan size, factor, and LTV as independent variables from all of the information available in the whole-loan data base. We generated seasonality, burnout, and prepayment incentive, and current LTV from this information. Then, we used this information and historical SMM based on loan number instead of the outstanding dollar amount of the loan to estimate regressions in order to build the prepayment model. While SMM based on dollar amount is traditional, we chose SMM based on loan number because it satisfies statistical independence requirements, and as it takes better advantage and avoids the disadvantages inherent in the whole-loan data. In our model we took special effort to handle the difficulty in burnout by utilization of the discovery of single loan bucket burnout problem discussed. We chose the maximum likelihood method over least squares because it overcomes the serious sparseness problems in the whole-loan database.

Exhibit 18: Rates Comparison (RFC – FNMA)

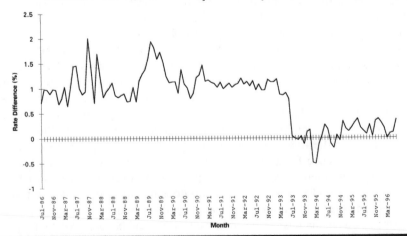

Exhibit 19: 93-S45 Prepayment Comparison

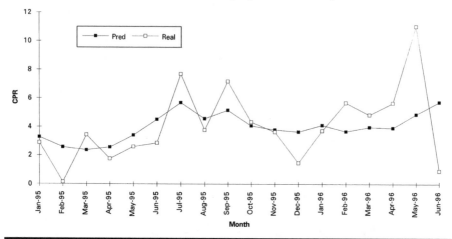

The resulting model uses the same independent variables to predict the same dependent variable, and stands up under backtesting. With the 80% multiplier, we expect this model to be useful for both qualitative and quantitative purposes. Several years from now we will have adequate data to eliminate this multiplier from the model. Exhibit 19 is the monthly speed comparison for 93-S45. We can see that even for such a large deal (about 1,700 loans), the prepayment behavior is still quite erratic. The model catches the underlying prepayment trend very well.

We think the model is excellent for providing long-term predictions. However, the reader should be aware of the model's limitations. First, it will not work well for old CMO deals. The age limit is probably about 100 months. Because that part of the sample space is basically empty, the result there is mainly the extrapolation of its neighbors. In regression analysis, extrapolation is almost not allowed; however, as a practical matter, we used it as the best possible approximation. Second, in the prediction, for most age and WAC regions, the popular scenario test involving ±300 bp shift in mortgage rates to test various CMO characteristics may not work well. There is no historical data corresponding to this large of a shift, either positive or negative. As discussed, for a large drop in mortgage rates, whole loans tend to refinance very readily. On the other hand, since large increases in mortgage rates take time to occur, whole loans tend not to survive long enough to see that sort of rate change. During the time studied, there were very few loans which experienced a negative 300 bp spread. Based on our experience, ±100 bp works fine, for the reasons discussed.

Section II:

Home Equity Loan and Manufactured Housing Loan Securities

Chapter 16

Prepayment Modeling and Valuation of Home Equity Loan Securities

Dale Westhoff
Senior Managing Director
Financial Analytics & Structured Transactions Group
Bear, Stearns & Co., Inc.

Mark Feldman
Managing Director
Financial Analytics & Structured Transactions Group
Bear, Stearns & Co., Inc.

INTRODUCTION

Understanding and valuing prepayment risk is a fundamental concern for most investors in the rapidly expanding home equity securities market. Yet conducting even a rudimentary prepayment analysis can be a difficult task because of the diversity of loan and borrower attributes at the deal level. In addition, there is often little historical prepayment information available to investors on new deals or on deals with similar collateral profiles. While the current market prepayment convention centered on issuer specific prepayment curves (similar to the PSA curve) is useful in establishing a static pricing speed assumption, it lends little insight into the underlying causes of home equity prepayments and is generally inadequate as a valuation tool. In this chapter we present a home equity prepayment model developed from historical observations on nearly 300,000 individual loans provided by leading issuers of home equity securities. The multi-issuer database used is unique in both the breadth of its coverage and in its loan-level detail, which includes information on a borrower's credit status. For the first time,

The authors would like to thank the issuers listed in Exhibit 1 for their cooperation in providing data for this study.

the underlying forces that govern home equity loan prepayments can be analyzed and statistically measured, all at the loan level. Our model, developed entirely from this new data, incorporates several innovative features:

- Given that borrowers of different credit quality exhibit fundamentally different prepayment behavior, our model is constructed as a composite forecast from three functionally independent sub-models, each representing a distinct level of borrower credit.
- Each model was estimated on a loan by loan basis using a discrete choice estimation to preserve all loan and borrower attributes (no data aggregation was performed).
- The borrower's current equity position, a key determinant of home equity prepayment behavior, is dynamically updated and measured using proprietary regional home price indices.
- Users have the ability to assess the joint effects of changes in home prices and interest rates on home equity loan prepayments.
- Borrower adverse selection, responsible for "burnout" and other path dependent prepayment behavior, is implicitly accounted for by the loan-level specification and sub-model structure of our forecasting framework.

THE LOAN-LEVEL HOME EQUITY DATABASE

A prepayment model is only as good as the data set employed in its estimation. In contrast to pool-specific data like that from FNMA/FHLMC and GNMA, loan-level information greatly enhances the precision and scope of variables available to the modeler. Bear Stearns has assembled one of the largest and most comprehensive loan-level home equity databases in the asset-backed industry. The database targets finance company fixed rate, closed-end home equity issuers and incorporates statistics on a borrower's credit status, property location, original combined loan-to-value ratio (CLTV), updated CLTV, lien position, loan size, rate, and term. The database contains ten years of historical prepayment information, including the important prepayment experience from the 1992 and 1993 prepayment cycles.

In general, there is a high level of dispersion in the loan attributes of finance company issues since the loans are made to a broad spectrum of borrowers (most with lower than A credit ratings). Home equity securities from different issuers can exhibit very different prepayment behavior owing to disparities in the credit quality of the underlying borrowers and the specific underwriting criteria imposed by an issuer. To date, most home equity prepayment studies have focused on data from a single issuer and are applicable to a relatively small universe of securities with similar collateral characteristics. By drawing our database from a representative cross-section of issuers we can minimize issuer specific effects and isolate the common loan and borrower characteristics that are responsible for the observed differences in prepayments across issuers and deals. This is particularly important given that several issuers have recently altered their product mix for strategic reasons or in response to current market opportunities. A model constructed from this data is more robust and can be applied to a wider array of securities than a model based on data from a single issuer.

The disparity in loan attributes at the issuer level is evident in the summarized issuer data shown in Exhibit 1. For example, issuers originating a greater portion of loans to higher credit quality borrowers tend to have much lower average loan rates and higher average combined loan-to-value ratios. Two observations can be made regarding the data in Exhibit 1.

First, a traditional analysis based on a stratification of home equity securities by weighted average coupon (WAC) may produce very misleading results because it ignores the substantial credit premium associated with lower credit borrowers. A high WAC often indicates the presence of credit impaired borrowers who exhibit prepayment behavior that is fundamentally different from borrowers with better credit ratings. Second, to the extent that an issuer targets loan production to a particular segment of borrowers, the prepayments of that issuer will be subject to any prepayment patterns that are unique to that sub-population.

THE DETERMINANTS OF HOME EQUITY PREPAYMENTS: IDENTIFYING THE RISKS

From the investor's perspective, the most attractive feature of home equity securities is that they are less negatively convex[1] when compared to securities backed by conventional purchase money mortgages. Indeed, historical observations indicate that finance company home-equity borrowers are relatively insensitive to changes in interest rates. For example, during the severe 1992 and 1993 refinancing cycles, most home equity securities experienced prepayments that were considerably slower (rarely above 35 CPR for more than one period) than similar mortgage-backed securities (MBS). Conversely, home equity securities did not extend as much as MBS when interest rates rose in 1994. This pattern is clearly evident in Exhibit 2, a comparison of historical prepayments between the 1990 issue FNMA 9.0% 15-year MBS and a typical B/C home equity deal (Fleet Finance 90-1). Given this experience, investors have embraced home equity issues as an attractive alternative to traditional mortgage securities since they have the advantage of limited call and extension risk. In addition, investors have found that home equity securities make a reasonable substitute for short average life CMOs since they offer PAC-like average life stability without the premium paid for a CMO structure.

---

[1] Negatively convex securities tend to shorten in duration when interest rates fall and increase in duration when rates rise.

Exhibit I: The Bear Stearns Home Equity Database

Contributing Issuer	Number of Loans	Average Loan Rate	Average Loan Size	Credit Distributions			Lien Position		OLTV Distribution			
				A	B	C	First	Second	<= 60%	60%-70%	70%-80%	> 80%
GE	55,832	10.54	54,968	88%	12%	0%	49%	51%	26%	18%	42%	14%
Conti	47,037	11.66	55,276	57%	29%	14%	66%	34%	31%	21%	42%	6%
Equicredit	101,709	12.30	39,306	46%	35%	19%	57%	43%	20%	18%	50%	12%
Advanta	69,200	13.39	33,710	49%	41%	10%	39%	61%	24%	14%	32%	30%
Alliance Funding	32,504	14.04	51,104	15%	40%	45%	47%	53%	67%	26%	6%	1%
Totals	306,282	12.31	44,601	53%	30%	17%	53%	47%	29%	18%	39%	14%

Exhibit 2: Historical MBS and Home Equity Prepayments

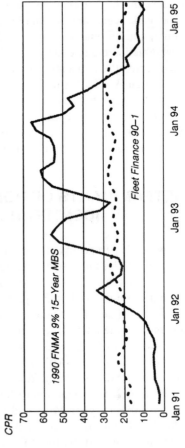

With broad investor acceptance there has been little differentiation in deal pricing speeds. The vast majority of deals have been priced to a long term speed of between 20 and 25 CPR with various permutations on the seasoning ramp. However, a comparison of the pricing speed assumptions to actual 6-month prepayments (see Exhibit 3) suggests that more deal differentiation is needed. Key loan and borrower attributes, like borrower credit quality, that influence the seasoning ramp and long-term level of home equity prepayments must be identified and accounted for at pricing. No single ramp standard (or ramp multiple) can explain the disparity evident across deal prepayments.

More importantly, within the home equity universe investors must be compensated for securities whose prepayments are more likely to be correlated to changes in interest rates. Although the market may be justified in pricing two deals to similar static long term prepayment speeds, there may still exist substantial differences in the negative convexity of the securities. Consider the extreme case of First Interstate Bank of California (FICAL) 90-1, GE 91-1 and Fleet Finance 90-1. Although all three deals were priced between 20 and 23 CPR, actual prepayments through the 1992 and 1993 interest rate cycles proved to be radically different. For example, during the period from January 1992 to December 1993 the three deals peaked at 62 CPR, 42 CPR and 30 CPR, respectively. Obviously, not all home equity securities are created equal. Nevertheless, the task of identifying deals that are more vulnerable to interest rate swings has been onerous due to the heterogeneous mix of borrower and loan attributes. In addition, the trend by finance companies to originate home equity first lien mortgages has clouded the distinction between a traditional purchase money mortgage[2] and a home equity loan. For instance, should we expect a home equity security backed by A credit borrowers with large balance, first lien loans to exhibit the same prepayment behavior as a deal backed by C credit borrowers with small balance, second mortgages? Clearly, the answer is no; however, until now valuing the impact of these disparities has been virtually impossible.

The Bear Stearns home equity model addresses the need for a prepayment forecast consistent with the underlying mix of borrower and loan characteristics present in a deal. The model inputs include six loan attributes and two exogenous variables whose independent and joint effects explain home equity loan prepayment behavior. Each of these parameters and their values as they relate to increasing prepayment risk is provided in Exhibit 4. A more detailed discussion of our findings with respect to each of these parameters follows.

STRUCTURAL CONSIDERATIONS

There are three structural factors that suppress the interest rate sensitivity of finance company fixed rate home equity loan securities: small loan sizes, short amortization schedules, and below A borrower credit quality. First, smaller average loan sizes greatly reduce the economic benefit of a refinancing opportunity. In our sample, the average loan balance was $45,000 compared to $124,000 for a

---

[2] A purchase money mortgage is used exclusively to finance the initial purchase of a home.

standard purchase money mortgage. As a rule of thumb, interest rates must fall two to four times further in the home equity market before the interest cost savings of a refinance breaks even to the interest cost savings realized from a standard purchase money refinance. It should be noted, however, that this effect is partially negated for second lien home equity loans because second liens are subject to the full refinancing risk of the underlying first mortgage.

Exhibit 3: Home Equity Pricing Speeds Versus Actual Prepayments*

| | | | Actual CPR | |
Date	Issuer	Pricing Speed	3 Months	6 Months
21-Feb-91	ADVANTA 91-1	18	21.00	20.30
31-Jul-91	AFC 91-3	20	29.40	22.20
10-Sep-91	ADVANTA 91-3	22	20.80	18.10
25-Oct-91	AFC 91-4	20	23.20	24.00
29-Jan-92	AFC 92-1	20	28.60	25.90
13-Mar-92	ADVANTA 92-1	22	19.40	17.20
26-Mar-92	OSCC 92-1	21	25.70	22.90
5-Jun-92	OSCC 92-2	25	19.90	18.70
16-Jun-92	TMS 92B	22	22.20	19.10
18-Jun-92	AFC 92-3	20	24.40	20.70
11-Sep-92	ADVANTA 92-3(14)	23	23.90	20.60
17-Sep-92	AFC 92-4	20	24.70	25.40
26-Oct-92	OSCC 92-4	25	21.50	18.80
4-Dec-92	TMS 92D	23	16.30	N/A
16-Dec-92	AFC 92-5	20	22.00	23.70
2-Mar-93	ADVANTA 93-1	23	12.30	12.30
12-Mar-93	TMS 93A	23	15.00	14.30
27-May-93	ADVANTA 93-2	23	17.90	16.20
10-Jun-93	TMS 93B	23	10.70	9.90
28-Jul-93	TMS 93C	23	14.70	N/A
16-Nov-93	First Alliance 93-2	25	29.80	22.90
16-Feb-94	TMS 94A	23	10.70	10.30
3-Mar-94	ADVANTA 94-1	23	15.60	12.20
10-Mar-94	Equicon 94-1	23	20.00	19.70
24-May-94	TMS 94B	22	13.50	11.80
25-May-94	EQCC 94-2	25	22.60	19.10
8-Jun-94	ADVANTA 94-2	22	18.90	14.90
20-Jun-94	Contimortgage 94-3 (16)	26	18.30	14.30
9-Sep-94	ADVANTA 94-3	23	20.30	16.30
13-Sep-94	EQCC 94-3	24	26.90	22.80
18-Oct-94	Equicon 94-2	23	29.00	19.30
2-Dec-94	Contimortgage 94-5	20	20.70	16.20
8-Dec-94	ADVANTA 94-4	20	12.40	9.90
8-Mar-95	ADVANTA 95-1	20	10.60	8.20

* Actual prepayments as of September 1995.

Source: Moody's Asset Credit Evaluations Report

Exhibit 4: Model Inputs and Prepayment Risk

Model Input	Lower Prepayment Risk (more prepayment stable)	Higher Prepayment Risk (more prepayment sensitive)
Borrower Credit Status	C Borrower	A Borrower
Borrower Credit Premium	High	Low
Loan Age	Seasoned Loans	New Loans
Combined Loan-to-Value	High CLTV	Low CLTV
Lien Position	Second Lien	First Lien
Loan Size	Small	Large
Level of Interest Rates (Exogenous)	Neutral	Declining
Level of Home Prices (Exogenous)	Stable/Declining	Rising

Exhibit 5: Representative Finance Company Home Equity Obligor

Age	40-45 years
Employment	8-10 years; Blue collar/light-white collar
Residence	8-10 years
Income	$40K
Credit	5-6 cards
Home Value	$100-$125K

Second, the 10-year to 15-year amortization schedule of most home equity loans limits the average life variability and price sensitivity of HEL securities. For example, a 10 CPR increase in prepayments will shorten the average life of a 30-year security by approximately 4.7 years compared to only 2.2 years for a 15-year security.[3] Third, credit impaired home equity borrowers tend to be cash-strapped and, consequently, more payment sensitive (less interest rate sensitive) than purchase money borrowers. Exhibit 5 profiles a representative finance company home equity obligor. The combination of these three factors produces a return profile that is intrinsically more stable and less interest rate sensitive than that of a standard purchase money mortgage security. Nevertheless, within the home equity universe, there still exist significant disparities in the rate of seasoning, long-term level, and interest rate sensitivity of prepayments.

BORROWER CREDIT QUALITY IS THE MOST IMPORTANT DETERMINANT OF HOME EQUITY LOAN PREPAYMENTS

Different levels of borrower credit quality expose investors to different levels of prepayment risk. The typical home equity security is backed by borrowers across a broad spectrum of credit ratings. Intuitively, the A credit borrowers are the most likely to prepay their loans when interest rates fall because they can usually qualify for a new

[3] Assuming a 9.0% gross coupon and an initial base speed of 8% CPR.

loan and are more likely to be in a financial position to pay transaction costs. Less credit worthy borrowers are less likely to refinance because they are less financially "able" to pay transaction costs and usually have fewer refinancing alternatives available to them. Lenders will generally underwrite lower credit borrowers at higher spreads and with more points and fees to offset their increased exposure to default. Moreover, during a refinancing cycle, lenders will target better credit borrowers with large balance loans before lower credit borrowers. Thus, the refinancing economics for B/C rated borrowers are usually much less attractive than for A borrowers. In effect, these constraints act as a prepayment penalty imposed on low credit borrowers.

Historical observations confirm the "credit effect" on prepayments. For example, Exhibit 6 tracks the historical prepayment experience of four separate deals, each selected to represent a different level of borrower credit quality. The highest credit borrowers populate the bank issue (FICAL 90-1) followed by A-borrowers (GE Capital 91-1), B/C borrowers (Fleet Finance 90-1), and finally D borrowers (Goldome Credit 90-1). During the refinancing waves of 1992-93, the range of prepayments across these different issues of home equity securities was extraordinary. The bank issue exhibited refinancing levels that rivaled any security in the conventional MBS market while the finance company issues, populated by more credit impaired borrowers, exhibited a much more restrained response to lower interest rates.

The degree to which prepayments were unresponsive to lower rates can be linked directly to the level of borrower credit. In the case of the Goldome issue (D borrowers) prepayments were completely uncorrelated to changes in interest rates. Moving up the credit spectrum, the Fleet Finance issue (B/C borrowers) exhibited a modest correlation to interest rates while the GE issue (A- borrowers) spiked above 35 CPR on three separate occasions; each spike was coincident with a new low in interest rates. The strong relationship between borrower credit status and prepayments was again evident in 1994 when interest rates moved higher, only this time prepayments slowed and securities extended. In the absence of a refinancing incentive, the bank home equity security became the slowest paying issue, followed by GE and then Fleet Finance. Once again, Goldome showed no response to the movement in interest rates.

The greater contraction and extension risk exhibited in securities backed by higher credit quality borrowers makes them more negatively convex than securities backed by credit impaired borrowers. Indeed, securities backed by the lowest credit borrowers remained positively convex through the prepayment cycles of 1992 and 1993. The radically different prepayment behavior evident across different credit "domains" underscores the importance of developing a sound methodology to model the influence of credit on home equity prepayments. We have accomplished this by constructing our model as a composite forecast from three independent, credit based sub-models. Loans are first stratified by credit designation, then directed to the appropriate sub-model where a separate forecast is made based on loan-level attributes. The individual forecasts are then re-combined to form the final aggregate projection. We found that this approach produced the most accurate aggregate projection for securities that are often backed by a diverse collection of borrowers. The first step in this process, however, is to identify the level of credit.

TWO MEASURES OF BORROWER CREDIT QUALITY: ISSUER RATING AND CREDIT PREMIUM

A reliable measure of credit quality is essential for an accurate prepayment fore-cast in the home equity sector. Unfortunately, generating a consistent measure of a borrower's credit quality can be problematic because of the lack of standardized underwriting criteria for each credit designation among issuers. To overcome this problem, each loan in our database is indexed in two ways: first by its credit des-ignation (supplied by the issuer) and second by a measure based on a "credit pre-mium" paid by the borrower at origination. Despite differences in underwriting guidelines, we found that the credit history criteria applied to a particular credit designation were relatively uniform. Therefore, in lieu of discarding the issuer supplied credit rating we use it as a broad indication of a borrower's recent credit standing, and account for differences in issuer underwriting limits for CLTV, loan size, etc., by directly measuring them at the loan level. Exhibit 7 summarizes the most common credit history criteria applied to each of the classifications.

Within a given credit class we further stratify the loans by calculating a credit premium. It is based on the spread between the prevailing conforming rate (we use the FHLMC commitment rate) and the home equity contract rate on the day that each loan was originated. While this measure ignores the possibility that a bor-rower "buys" the rate down, it has proven to be strongly correlated to the actual credit quality of each borrower, i.e., the higher the credit premium, the lower the credit quality of the borrower. Exhibit 8 conclusively shows that in our loan sample the average credit premium is substantially higher for lower credit classes.

Exhibit 6: Historical Prepayments on Selected Home Equity Issues

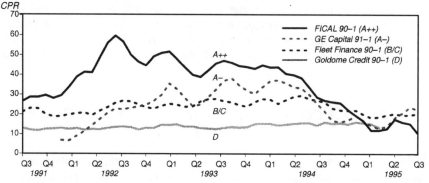

Exhibit 7: Finance Company Issuer Credit Ratings

Classification	Meaning
A	Good to excellent credit Maximum of 2 30-day delinquencies in past 12 months No bankruptcies in past 5 years
B	Satisfactory credit Maximum of 3 30-day delinquencies in past 12 months No bankruptcies in past 3 years
C	Fair/poor credit Maximum of 4 30-day and 1 60-day delinquencies in past 12 months No bankruptcies in past 2 years

Exhibit 8: Home Equity Credit Premiums

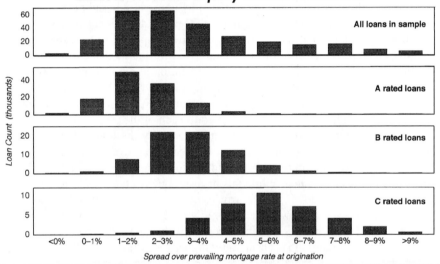

For example, the average credit premium for all A, B, and C designated loans is 1.89%, 3.32% and 5.68%, respectively. In addition, the variation in premium within a credit class, particularly the C's, indicates numerous sub-levels of credit. The credit premium provides a mechanism to statistically measure the various gradations of credit quality within a credit class. Estimation results validate the credit premium as an explanatory variable; after loan age it was the most statistically significant variable in our sub-models.

THE SEASONING OF HOME EQUITY LOANS OCCURS IN TWO PHASES

One of the most important aspects of home equity loan prepayments is how rapidly prepayments increase or "season" with loan age. Given that prepayments are less correlated to interest rates, the most common mistake at pricing is a mis-specification of the slope and leveling point of the seasoning ramp. In general, the seasoning period for home equity loans is much shorter than that exhibited in the purchase money market (measured to be 30 months by the PSA standard). Home equity deals can season in as little as 10 months or as many as 30 months depending on the credit mix of the borrowers and the loan attributes of the deal. Moreover, we have found that the aging process actually consists of two distinct phases: an initial period that is characterized by rapid seasoning and an eventual plateau in prepayments, followed by a longer second period of steadily declining prepayments.

Phase 1: Rapid Seasoning and the "Credit Cure" Effect

Our research indicates that in a neutral interest rate environment, lower credit quality loans tend to season much more rapidly and plateau at a higher level than better credit loans, all else equal (see Exhibit 9). For example, in a no-change interest rate scenario A loans season in approximately 30 months, leveling between 18 and 20 CPR; B loans season in 15 to 18 months leveling near 24 CPR; and C loans season in 12 to 15 months leveling near 30 CPR. It should be noted that the actual aging profiles shown in Exhibit 9 are conditional on age only and, thus, independent of interest rate levels. Consequently, there is some distortion in the A profile since prepayments are heavily influenced by interest rates. This will be addressed in more detail in the next section. In contrast, there is minimal interest rate distortion in the B/C aging profiles shown in Exhibit 9, since there is less correlation to interest rates. We have identified several factors that contribute to Phase 1 of the seasoning process (in order of significance):

Exhibit 9: Historical Prepayments Conditional on Loan Age and Credit Domain (All Issuers, 1988-Present)

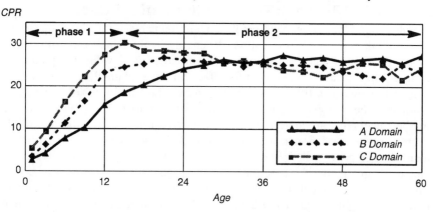

The "Credit Cure" Effect

As some of the lower credit borrowers improve the timeliness of their payments, they become eligible for a lower rate loan in a higher credit domain. Many brokers monitor the status of low credit home equity borrowers and solicit a refinance when their credit status improves. We have seen previously that there is a substantial difference in credit premium between adjacent credit domains. For example, a C rated borrower will reduce his rate by an average of 2.36% simply by qualifying for a B rated loan, while a B rated borrower will improve his rate by only 1.43% by qualifying for an A rated loan. Therefore, the lower the credit quality of borrowers in a deal, the greater the potential for a "credit cure" effect and the steeper the seasoning ramp. Furthermore, we found that once borrowers attain an A rating, credit curing is much less pronounced. The lack of a credit cure effect in the A credit domain causes a seasoning pattern that is more akin to the purchase money market (a 30 month seasoning ramp like the PSA curve). While A rated borrowers as a group remain more sensitive to interest rates, they will season at a substantially slower rate than lower credit loans when there is no incentive to refinance.

Higher Margin Loans Attract More Broker Competition

With brokers often working to originate loans 7 to 8 points above the FHLMC commitment rate, there is naturally more latitude for competition in the lower credit sector. In addition, lenders often try to offset declines in refinancing volumes by competing more aggressively in the B/C sector.

Higher Default Rates On Lower Credit Loans

While this is a marginal contribution to overall prepayments (a maximum of 2 or 3 CPR in the early months of the seasoning process), low credit domain loans experience higher default rates.

Phase 2: The "Credit Inertia" Effect

We also found that after lower credit domain loans reach their peak speed in the 10th to 20th month after origination (depending on the joint effects of credit premium, CLTV, and other factors), there is a pronounced slowdown in prepayments lasting 3 to 4 years. We believe this effect can be explained by a self-selection among borrowers in the lower credit groups. The "credit cure" effect quickly eliminates the borrowers that have the ability to improve their credit status, leaving borrowers that are more likely to remain credit impaired in the future. These borrowers have a demonstrated history of delinquency behavior that prevents them from improving their status. Unless they change this behavior there is little chance of qualifying for a better rate. The probability of a "cure" decays as a function of time so that in a period of three to four years most of the remaining borrowers are either habitually delinquent or have some other constraint (such as equity) that prevents a prepayment. We call this process the "credit inertia" effect because it characterizes the growing inability of the remaining borrowers in the population to change their status, improve their rate, or take out more equity. This puts a downward pressure on prepayments that is clearly visible in Exhibit 9 (in the B/C credit domain). The A credit domain, on the other hand, exhibits little credit inertia.

PURE INTEREST RATE EFFECTS: WHAT THE DATA TELL US

To analyze pure interest rate effects on home equity prepayments one must adjust for the higher credit premium imposed on lower credit borrowers. One common mistake made by market participants is to perform a simple WAC stratification of historical prepayments to assess the sensitivity to interest rates. Although commonly used in the MBS market, this approach can have very misleading results in the home equity market because it masks the true sensitivity to interest rates. Indeed, we often find that home equity securities behave in a manner exactly opposite to that of securities backed by conforming purchase money mortgages, i.e., prepayments from the highest WAC home equity deals are the least sensitive to low interest rates. Stratifying historical prepayments by WAC alone with no adjustment for credit premium tends to produce a flat prepayment profile and a false picture of call protection. To correct for the credit premium, Exhibit 10 plots actual home equity prepayment rates partitioned by credit domain and conditional on how much rates have risen or fallen since each loan was originated. Once these adjustments are made a more reliable picture of pure interest rate effects emerges.

Exhibit 10: Historical Prepayments Conditional on Changes in Interest Rates, and Credit Domain

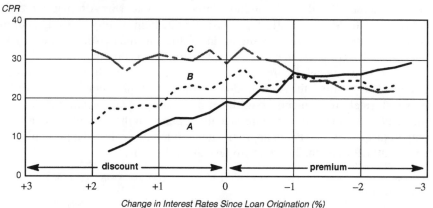

Each point on a curve in Exhibit 10 represents the average prepayment rate for only seasoned[4] loans that map to a specific credit domain and change in rates. Several well-defined trends emerge from the prepayment curves shown in Exhibit 10.

- Prepayments of A domain loans are highly correlated to the level of refinancing incentive. Loans that are deeply out-of-the money prepay on average slightly less than 10 CPR (only 2 to 3 CPR faster than the baseline level of a discount conventional MBS) while loans with the largest refinancing incentive have an average prepayment rate that is approximately 30 CPR.
- B domain loans are less correlated to interest rate changes than A loans, increasing from approximately 14 CPR on loans well out-of-the-money and leveling at around 25 CPR for loans well in-the-money.
- C domain loans range between 22 and 32 CPR but exhibit little correlation to interest rates. In fact, C loans with a positive refinancing incentive have historically prepaid modestly slower than loans with no incentive.

The curves shown in Exhibit 10 are average prepayment rates across all periods and loans within each credit domain. Actual prepayments at the deal level may be faster or slower than shown in the exhibit depending on specific loan attributes. The slightly inverted C domain profile can be explained by recent competitive forces in the B/C sector that have accelerated the discount prepayment observations in Exhibit 10. For example, in 1994 the B and C domains displayed a rapid acceleration in prepayments despite rising interest rates. A closer examination of the data in the exhibit confirms that the discount region (left side of the horizontal axis) is dominated by observations from the 1994/95 backup in interest rates, while the premium observations are more dispersed across time with burnout helping to suppress the speeds in the highest premium regions. Recent notable entrants include Residential Funding Corporation under its Alternet A program and Option One Mortgage offering adjustable rate home equity loans. In addition, when interest rates rise, refinancing business dries up and existing lenders look to other areas, like B and C loans, to offset the drop in loan production.

Another view of pure interest rate effects in A credit loans is shown in Exhibit 11. It stratifies the A credit domain by current, premium, or discount[5] and plots historical prepayments conditional on loan age. Once again, the data confirms a clear segmentation by rate incentive. Loans in the current coupon region ramp to just under 20 CPR in approximately 30 months, while the premium loans ramp to 30 CPR and the discounts to just above 10 CPR.

---

[4] For this analysis, seasoned loans in the A, B and C domains constitute loans older than 18, 15, and 12 months, respectively.

[5] The "current" sector is defined as loans with rates within 50 basis points of the actual current coupon; "premium" designates all loans with rates at least 50 basis points above current; "discount" designates all loans with rates at least 50 basis points below current coupon.

Exhibit 11: "A" Credit Home Equity Prepayments Partioned by Current, Premium, And Discount Loans

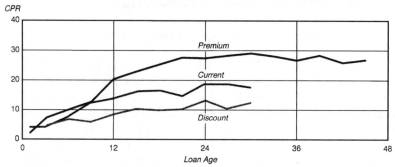

Exhibit 12: Home Equity Originations by Loan Purpose

Purpose	Percentage
Debt Consolidation	39%
Refinance	44%
Purchase Money	2%
Other	15%

A final stratification of our database by loan purpose reveals the substantial contribution to prepayments caused by either changing interest rates or credit curing. Although the population and definition of the loan purpose field varied from issuer to issuer, the general breakdown provided in Exhibit 12 confirms that home equity loans are often used to consolidate debt. However, an even higher percentage of existing loans is refinanced as a result of normal credit curing or rate and term refinancing.

COMBINED LOAN-TO-VALUE AND GEOGRAPHIC EFFECTS

After credit domain and loan age, the combined loan-to-value (CLTV)[6] ratio is the most important explanatory variable in our model. An inverse relationship exists between the CLTV and home equity loan prepayments. A low CLTV increases the probability of a prepayment for the following reasons:

- Existing home equity borrowers with substantial equity remaining in their homes are much more likely to take out additional equity in the future, whether on their own or through broker solicitation. These borrowers not only possess the necessary equity to take out a new loan but also have a demonstrated willingness to borrow against their equity.

---

[6] The CLTV is calculated by adding the balances of the first and second liens and dividing the total by the value of the house.

- Borrowers that use home equity loans to consolidate debt are predisposed to another consolidation if their debt levels continue to increase.
- A low CLTV ratio increases the likelihood that a borrower will trade-up to a new home.
- A low CLTV improves a borrower's ability to refinance.

Although a low CLTV also reduces the probability of a default, any potential decline in prepayments from lower default rates is overwhelmed by the four factors cited above. Naturally, the strength of a regional economy can have a significant impact on prepayment behavior because it changes a borrower's equity position. For example, a vigorous local economy tends to increase borrower mobility and strengthen home prices, lowering CLTVs and increasing prepayments. Conversely, a sluggish local economy lowers mobility and weakens home prices, slowing prepayments. Consider California, once the fastest prepayment state in the country, where a housing recession has severely eroded home prices and slowed prepayments to a level that is currently 15% below the national average. In general, investors should prefer geographically disperse collateral because it reduces exposure to regional economic volatility.

To account for regional loan concentrations, we dynamically update CLTVs in our home equity database by applying our proprietary regional home price indices to the original CLTV supplied by the issuer. In this way prepayment forecasts remain consistent with current home price trends across the nation. In addition, by modifying our baseline appreciation assumption, investors can assess the joint effects of changes in home prices and interest rates on the prepayment and return profile of their portfolios.

We also found that the CLTV threshold that suppresses prepayments in the home equity sector varies by credit domain. Exhibit 13 shows common CLTV underwriting limits for each credit domain followed by the approximate CLTV threshold where there is a measurable impact on prepayments. Loans with CLTVs above the thresholds listed in Exhibit 13 tended to be slower than identical loans with lower CLTVs. Bear in mind that there has been a recent trend towards relaxing CLTV standards as lenders struggle to maintain market share. It is not uncommon today for lenders to underwrite loans with CLTVs even higher than those listed in Exhibit 13. In the short term, this will put an upward pressure on prepayments as brokers canvas the existing universe of equity-rich borrowers to take out additional equity. However, the trend will ultimately slow prepayments (but increase defaults) as new limits are reached and borrowers are left with lower overall levels of equity.

Exhibit 13: Common CLTV Underwriting Limits

Credit Domain	Maximum Allowable CLTV	CLTV Threshold
A	≈ 85%	75%
B	≈ 80%	70%
C	≈ 75%	60%

CHANGES IN THE UNDERLYING BORROWER MIX AFFECT FUTURE PREPAYMENT BEHAVIOR

The unique seasoning and refinancing patterns evident in each of the borrower credit domains implies that, over time, the underlying composition of the borrowers will also change. This can have a profound impact on the future prepayment behavior of home equity securities. For example, one type of altered behavior results when lower interest rates remove the most rate sensitive borrowers from a pool of mortgages. Widely referred to as burnout, this particular type of evolution in the mix of borrowers tends to temper interest rate related prepayments in the future. From a broader perspective, the mix of borrowers at any point in time is a function of the prior interest rate path and the prepayment experience along that path. We believe home equity securities are particularly vulnerable to the "path dependent" aspect of prepayments because of the diverse mix of borrower credit quality and refinancing abilities present in most deals.

Path dependency is often the most challenging aspect of mortgage prepayment modeling owing to the complex processes at work. In the absence of loan-level data, there is no mechanism available to keep track of the remaining borrowers in a pool (modelers are forced to treat an entire pool of loans as if it were one mortgage); consequently, proxies[7] for path dependent behavior must be developed. One of the remarkable features of a loan-level model is that it automatically accounts for the borrower self-selection that is responsible for "burnout" and many other path dependent changes in prepayment behavior. Having access to loan level data allows us to model actual borrower behavior, and avoid the need to develop variables to "simulate" this behavior. We believe a loan-level model produces a superior forecast because it directly models the fundamental cause of path dependent prepayment behavior, i.e., a change in the composition of the underlying borrowers.

To the extent that borrowers are self-selected over time, our composite forecast will begin to take on the prepayment characteristics of the surviving borrowers. For example, an initially disperse credit base will shift toward B/C borrowers and more stable prepayments after a low interest rate cycle since A borrowers are much more likely to refinance out of a pool (our A domain sub-model will forecast a very fast prepayment rate, eroding the A component of the pool). Conversely, the concentration will shift toward A borrowers and more interest rate sensitive prepayments in a neutral to high interest rate cycle since B/C borrowers tend to pay faster than A borrowers in a non-refinancing environment.

LIEN POSITION AND LOAN SIZE

A significant percentage of recent home equity originations have been first liens. This trend tends to be correlated with interest rates, i.e., during low interest rate cycles many home equity borrowers prefer to refinance all of their debt (including

---

[7] Often survivorship (the percentage of a pool that has not prepaid) is used to measure the degree of burnout.

their first mortgage) at the more attractive prevailing rate. Conversely, in a rising rate environment homeowners preserve the low rate on their first mortgage by opting to take out a second lien home equity loan. A comparison of prepayments between first lien and second lien home equity loans indicates that second liens tend to prepay systematically faster than first liens in the high credit domains. Exhibits 14, 15, and 16 compare historical first and second lien prepayments in the A domain for the discount, current and premium sectors, respectively.

An important distinction between first and second lien home equity loans is that second liens are subject to the full prepayment risk of the underlying first mortgage. A second lien must always be refinanced when the first is refinanced to avoid subordination of the new first lien to the old second lien. Therefore, if homeowners elect to refinance their first mortgages when interest rates fall, second liens will exhibit a matching increase in prepayments. In addition, a borrower may elect to refinance his second lien independently of his first lien at any time.

For credit worthy second lien borrowers, the relative ease of refinancing the underlying purchase mortgage in the era of "frictionless" refinancing may have contributed to the speed differential exhibited in Exhibits 14, 15, and 16. Indeed, as Exhibit 6 illustrated, second lien borrowers with no credit impairment (represented by the FICAL issue) prepaid as fast as comparable MBS through the 1992/1993 prepayment cycle.

Exhibits 14, 15, and 16 illustrate several key differences between first and second lien prepayments.

- The prepayment difference is most pronounced in the discount sector, where second lien prepayments may be accelerated by higher turnover levels and some additional refinancing of the underlying first mortgage (which may itself be in the money).
- The prepayment difference narrows in the premium sector.
- There is more extension risk in first lien home equity loans.

Exhibit 14: Discount Sector Home Equity Prepayments Conditional on Age and Lien Position

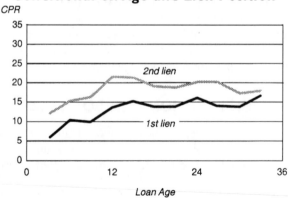

Exhibit 15: Current Sector Home Equity Prepayments Conditional on Age and Lien Position

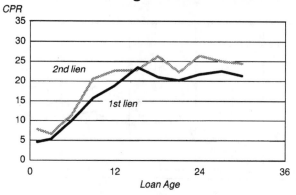

Exhibit 16: Premium Sector Home Equity Prepayments Conditional on Age and Lien Position

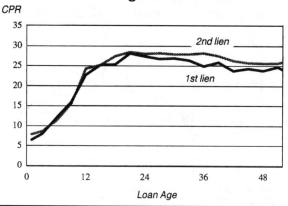

Although on the surface first lien home equity loans "look" more like traditional purchase money mortgages, we found that they do not prepay like them if (1) the borrowers have a lower than A credit rating, (2) equity is taken out of the transaction, and (3) average balances remain below standard purchase money levels. One benefit of first lien home equity transactions is that investors have complete information to determine refinancing risk. There is generally no information on the attributes of the underlying first mortgage in a second lien transaction. Our models explicitly account for the observed differences in prepayment behavior between first and second lien home equity securities. In the lower credit domains there was little systematic divergence between first and second lien home equity prepayments. Less credit worthy borrowers were probably less able and less willing to take advantage of refinancing opportunities, whether they held a first lien or a second lien home equity loan.

Exhibit 17: Historical Prepayments Conditional on Changes in Interest Rates and Original Amount

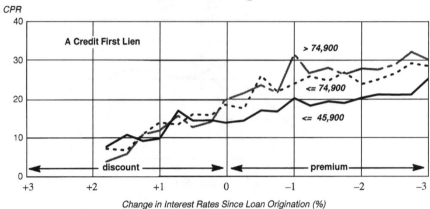

Change in Interest Rates Since Loan Origination (%)

Exhibit 18: Historical Prepayments Conditional on Changes in Interest Rates and Original Amount

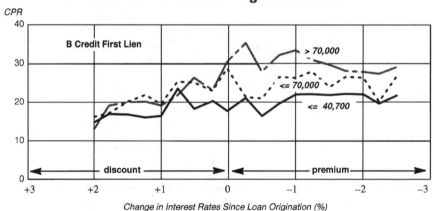

Change in Interest Rates Since Loan Origination (%)

We also found a statistically significant relationship between loan balance and prepayments, i.e., with a positive refinancing incentive large balance loans tended to prepay consistently faster than small balance loans. The influence of loan size was most apparent in A and B domain first lien loans. Second lien loans were uniformly small with an average balance of just $35,100, restricting any economic incentives to refinance. Exhibits 17 and 18 plot historical prepayments for seasoned A and B domain first lien loans conditional on loan amount and changes in interest rates. The clear segmentation evident by loan amount in Exhibits 17 and 18 reflects the greater dollar cost savings of refinancing large balance loans. In addition to the economic benefits, credit worthy borrowers with large loans are the most likely targets of broker solicitations to refinance when interest rates decline.

Exhibit 19: The Default Contribution to CPR by Credit Domain

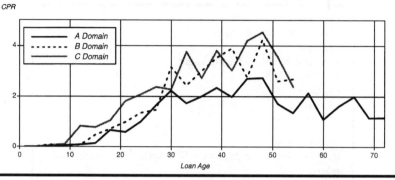

PARTIAL PREPAYMENTS AND DEFAULTS

We found that curtailments (partial prepayments) and defaults play a relatively minor role in home equity loan prepayments. Low curtailments may seem counter-intuitive given that home equity loan rates are so much higher than purchase money rates. Clearly, borrowers have an economic incentive to reduce their home equity debt service. However, by definition many of the finance company home equity borrowers are cash-strapped and unable or unwilling to make payments above the scheduled amount. This may have contributed to curtailments that were uniformly low, averaging about 1% CPR. Nevertheless, as a borrower's economic situation improves over time, we would expect higher curtailment rates to reflect a greater capacity to pay down debt over time.

Similarly, the default contribution to prepayments was relatively small but increased over time, with the maximum impact occurring between months 30 and 50 and then declining thereafter (see Exhibit 19). Lower credit domain loans experienced a higher default rate that peaked at approximately 4.5 CPR between month 40 and month 50. "A" credit domain loans exhibited a similar pattern but peaked at only 2.5 CPR. Despite these relatively low default levels, we anticipate that defaults will play a larger role in the future as increased competition pushes CLTV limits higher.

STATISTICAL ESTIMATION AND MODEL STRUCTURE

Each sub-model was developed entirely from loan level data; no data aggregation was performed. Direct measurements of WAC, age, credit rating, CLTV, and balance were available from the issuer data on a loan by loan basis. A discrete choice estimation was selected because it utilizes all loan level information, modeling the probability that a given home equity borrower will either prepay or not prepay his loan in any given period. We assumed that the probability of prepayment was a non-linear function of the independent variables with a probability distribution that follows a modified logistic curve. Prepayments were explained by the individual and joint effects of the independent variables listed in Exhibit 20.

Exhibit 20: Independent Variables

- Borrower credit rating
- Borrower credit premium
- Loan age
- Original combined loan-to-value
- Updated CLTV
- Refinancing incentive
- Loan size
- Lien position

Assuming that:
the probability of prepayment = C * exp(beta) / [1 = exp(beta)]
where:
C = Constant
beta = sum (coefficient[i] * Independent variable[i])

As previously mentioned, the impact of borrower adverse selection is implicitly accounted for by the loan level specification and sub-model structure of our forecast. Having access to loan level data allows us to model behavior at the borrower level and eliminate the need to develop variables that "simulate" behavior at the aggregate level. There are other potential variables that could be added to our home equity model; however, it is our experience that a more parsimonious approach focusing on the correct identification and specification of the key determinants of prepayments, leads to a more robust and predictive model. Furthermore, while adding variables always improves the fit, it often increases the complexity of a model with little improvement in predictive power.

The implementation of our model is straightforward, as shown in Exhibit 21. Loan level data are direct inputs and can originate from either actual deal data or hypothetical user inputs. Once loan attributes have been supplied, cash flows can be generated for various interest rate scenarios.

Projections

Exhibit 22 shows our flat rate scenario forecast for representative loans in each credit domain. Baseline loan attribute assumptions are shown in the accompanying box in Exhibit 22. As discussed earlier, under neutral interest rate conditions the forecasts exhibit seasoning profiles that are unique to each credit class. To the extent that loan attributes deviate from our baseline loan assumptions, actual forecasts may be faster or slower than those shown in Exhibit 22. In addition, the higher the concentration of A domain loans backing a given home equity security, the more sensitive it will be to a change in the interest rate assumption. For example, Exhibit 23 shows our forecasts under plus and minus 300 basis point interest rate shocks (in 100 bp increments) assuming a 100% A domain concentration. The prepayment variation caused by these extreme interest rate shocks totals approximately 26 CPR (low extreme to high extreme) in the A domain and 18 CPR in the B domain for seasoned loans with baseline attributes.

Exhibit 21: Prepayment Model Structure

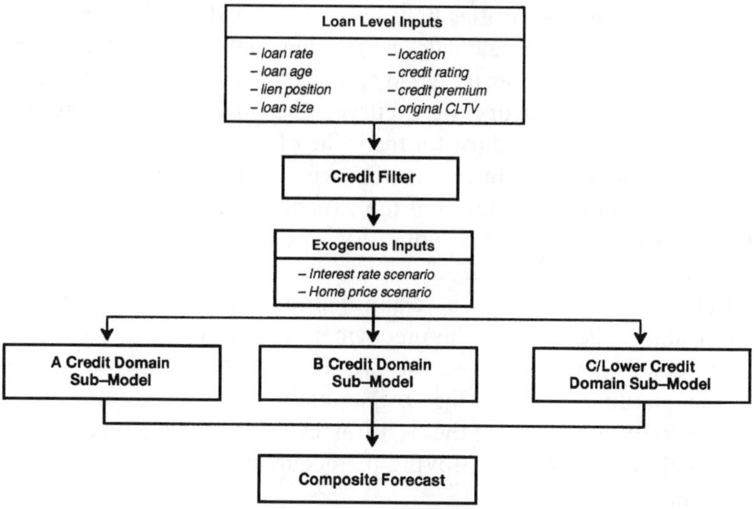

Loan Level Inputs
– loan rate
– loan age
– lien position
– loan size
– location
– credit rating
– credit premium
– original CLTV
Credit Filter
Exogenous Inputs
– Interest rate scenario
– Home price scenario
A Credit Domain Sub–Model
B Credit Domain Sub–Model
C/Lower Credit Domain Sub–Model
Composite Forecast

Exhibit 22: Baseline Forecasts for A, B, and C Domain Home Equity Loans

CPR
30
20
10
0
C
B
A
Baseline Loan Attributes
A Domain B Domain C Domain
WAC 9.75 11.41 13.81
OCLTV 70 65 55
Lien 1 1 1
Term 180 180 180
Amount 70k 60k 55k
0 12 24 36 48 60
Loan Age

Exhibit 23: Interest Rate Sensitivity Forecast for A Domain Home Equity Loans

CPR
40
30
20
10
0
Rate Shift
–300
–200
–100
0
+100
+200
+300
0 12 24 36 48
Loan Age

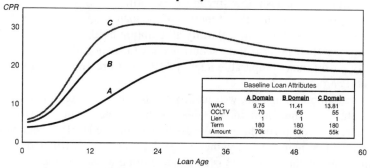

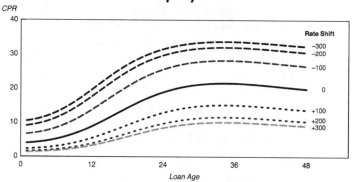

Valuation

In general, home equity securities have been priced and traded on an average life spread basis. This approach calculates a cash flow yield using a static prepayment assumption and then measures the yield spread differential to the equivalent average life point on the Treasury yield curve. The obvious disadvantage of this approach is that it does not adjust for the value of the prepayment option. A well-specified prepayment model in conjunction with an option based pricing methodology allows investors to determine the expected reduction in the static yield spread as a result of prepayment volatility. The option adjusted spread (OAS), derived from a random sample of interest rate paths, measures the expected spread over the entire Treasury curve adjusted for future interest rate and prepayment uncertainty. The value of the prepayment option, usually referred to as the "convexity cost," is measured as the difference between the static cash flow spread (0% volatility OAS) and the OAS assuming market volatilities. OAS analysis has generally proved to be the best framework to value a bond with interest rate contingent cash flows, improving the accuracy of duration, convexity and return measures.

We present two sets of complete option adjusted spread valuations in Exhibit 24 (synthetic deals) and Exhibit 25 (actual deals). In both tables, the reduction in the static cash flow spread (0% volatility OAS) measured by the convexity cost column is primarily a function of the loan and borrower-level inputs to the prepayment model and the volatility assumption used in the OAS model. Our results confirm that home equity securities have less negative convexity (lower convexity costs) than comparable agency MBS, but are more negatively convex than credit cards and autos.

In Exhibit 24 and 26, we quantify the influence of credit quality on valuation results using three hypothetical deals with identical sequential structures but with different credit distributions. We assume Synthetic Deal #1 is comprised of 100% A credit domain loans; Synthetic Deal #2 is equally distributed across A/B/C credits; and Synthetic Deal #3 is an equal split between B/C credits with 0% A concentration. Once again we assume baseline loan attributes for each credit domain. Exhibit 26 illustrates the flattening in the projected prepayment profile caused by a heavy concentration of B and C loans. Note that each point on a curve in Exhibit 26 represents the constant life speed that corresponds to the projected monthly vector of speeds at that specific interest rate assumption. In the no change scenario, Synthetic Deals #2 and #3 accelerate above Deal #1 because of the "credit cure" effect. However, Deal #1 is faster in the down 200 and 300 basis point scenarios because of additional rate refinancing.

OAS results from our synthetic deal analysis (see Exhibit 24) are intuitive and support our empirical findings. Several important observations can be made regarding the results shown in Exhibit 24:

Exhibit 24: Home Equity Valuation Results (Synthetic Deals)

Security				Prepayment Forecast (CPR)						Static Analysis				Option Adjusted Spread				
	Credit	lien	%	−200	−100	0	+100	+200	Tranche	Price	Yield	Avg Life	A.L. Sprd	Dur.	Convex.	Cash Flow Sprd	OAS	Convex. Cost
Synthetic Deal #1																		
Collateral:				26.26	23.40	18.31	12.67	9.13										
A	1	100.0	WAC 9.75	WAC	age 0	rtrm 180	size 70K	oltv 70										
									A1	99.821	5.99	1.30	84.72	1.19	−0.20	81.75	63.69	18.05
									A2	99.815	6.21	3.23	93.71	3.43	−0.32	91.05	45.15	45.89
									A3	99.733	6.54	4.92	110.76	5.19	−0.23	105.78	49.26	56.52
									A4	99.226	7.00	6.65	145.93	6.23	−0.20	145.94	87.96	47.98
									A5	98.788	7.40	10.83	163.34	7.73	0.20	158.72	134.16	24.55
Synthetic Deal #2																		
Collateral:				25.70	24.43	21.54	17.44	14.62										
A	1	33.3	WAC 9.75	WAC	age 0	rtrm 180	size 70K	oltv 70										
B	1	33.3	WAC 11.41		0	180	60K	65										
C	1	33.3	WAC 13.81		0	180	55K	55										
									A1	99.816	5.98	1.21	84.01	.89	−0.07	77.47	72.22	5.25
									A2	99.948	6.15	2.89	90.86	2.66	−0.16	89.83	66.56	23.27
									A3	99.714	6.54	4.28	116.74	4.45	−0.22	114.10	80.92	33.18
									A4	100.318	6.77	5.73	128.67	5.71	−0.09	122.27	86.73	35.54
									A5	98.915	7.39	9.56	166.80	7.74	0.25	160.20	140.00	20.21
Synthetic Deal #3																		
Collateral:				25.44	24.94	23.31	20.28	18.06										
B	1	50.0	WAC 11.41	WAC	age 0	rtrm 180	size 60K	oltv 65										
C	1	50.0	WAC 13.81		0	180	55K	55										
									A1	99.808	5.98	1.16	84.16	.82	−0.06	76.78	74.16	2.63
									A2	99.929	6.15	2.73	92.27	2.33	−0.08	91.56	78.09	13.47
									A3	99.869	6.49	3.98	114.73	3.92	−0.11	113.94	93.77	20.17
									A4	100.747	6.66	5.29	120.42	5.26	−0.04	116.63	93.29	23.34
									A5	99.072	7.37	8.85	169.23	7.58	0.25	160.47	144.77	15.70

Exhibit 25: Valuation Results For Selected Home Equity Deals

AAMES 95C

Security	Prepayment Forecast (CPR)				
	-200	-100	0	+100	+200
AAMES 95C	21.63	21.08	19.64	17.02	14.65

Collateral:

Credit	lien	%	WAC	age	rtrm	size	oltv
A	1	20.1	10.2	2	303	90K	66
	2	5.0	12.0	2	232	38K	60
B	1	17.8	10.8	2	335	86K	62
	2	3.0	12.2	2	208	27K	64
C	1	49.7	12.3	2	351	85K	62
	2	4.4	13.5	2	222	31K	61

Historical CPR speeds: 1 Mo 4.9, 3 Mo NA

			Static Analysis				Option Adjusted Spread		
Tranche	Price	Yield	Avg Life	A.L. Sprd	Dur.	Convex.	Cash Flow Sprd	OAS	Convex. Cost
AA	100.688	6.16	2.18	97.80	1.56	-0.14	80.65	64.14	16.52
AB	100.953	6.66	5.21	121.24	4.62	-0.27	123.00	89.08	33.91
AC	100.828	7.29	9.03	159.87	7.11	0.05	159.24	131.00	28.24

FNMA 95W1

Security	Prepayment Forecast (CPR)				
	-200	-100	0	+100	+200
FNMA 95W1	29.62	27.49	23.10	17.06	11.90

Collateral:

Credit	lien	%	WAC	age	rtrm	size	oltv
A	1	51.6	10.0	13	172	61K	69
	2	35.7	10.2	21	159	34K	67
B	1	8.6	10.6	17	170	64K	67
	2	4.1	10.9	19	161	32K	65

Historical CPR speeds: 1 Mo 20.1, 3 Mo 18.2

			Static Analysis				Option Adjusted Spread		
Tranche	Price	Yield	Avg Life	A.L. Sprd	Dur.	Convex.	Cash Flow Sprd	OAS	Convex. Cost
A2	101.891	6.18	1.21	103.95	0.59	-0.13	69.57	65.73	3.84
A3	103.047	6.19	1.97	102.81	1.40	-0.34	87.63	70.42	17.21
A4	103.750	6.36	2.72	113.66	2.15	-0.32	112.40	78.11	34.29
A5	104.422	6.49	3.48	119.75	3.03	-0.62	126.03	84.36	41.67
A6	105.312	6.82	5.06	137.87	4.50	-0.36	146.61	95.19	51.42
A7	105.249	7.45	9.42	173.59	6.90	0.03	179.47	145.75	33.72

FNMA 95W4

Security	Prepayment Forecast (CPR)				
	-200	-100	0	+100	+200
FNMA 95W4	27.59	25.86	22.08	16.22	10.92

Collateral:

Credit	lien	%	WAC	age	rtrm	size	oltv
A	1	60.7	9.9	6	187	70K	71
	2	28.3	10.7	12	170	31K	68
B	1	8.1	10.7	10	184	68K	70
	2	2.9	11.4	12	170	31K	67

Historical CPR speeds: 1 Mo 22.3, 3 Mo 17.5

			Static Analysis				Option Adjusted Spread		
Tranche	Price	Yield	Avg Life	A.L. Sprd	Dur.	Convex.	Cash Flow Sprd	OAS	Convex. Cost
A2	101.625	6.19	1.81	103.00	1.51	-0.29	87.20	67.39	19.81
A3	102.031	6.33	2.88	108.58	2.88	-0.37	107.08	61.43	45.66
A4	102.609	6.43	4.11	136.04	4.40	-0.47	110.09	50.05	60.04
A5	102.641	6.87	6.10	136.04	6.00	-0.35	136.27	78.37	57.90
A6	100.949	7.40	9.66	167.02	7.64	0.21	165.15	132.67	32.49

Exhibit 25 (Continued)

FNMA 95W5 — Prepayment Forecast (CPR)

-200	-100	0	+100	+200
23.80	21.27	15.53	10.97	7.33

FNMA 95W5 — Collateral

Credit lien	%	WAC	age	rttm	size	oltv
A 1	82.6	9.0	2	199	76K	72
2	17.4	10.0	4	180	29K	71

Historical CPR speeds: NA, newly issued deal

GEHEL 951 — Prepayment Forecast (CPR)

-200	-100	0	+100	+200
26.61	24.13	19.38	13.59	9.39

GEHEL 951 — Collateral

Credit lien	%	WAC	age	rttm	size*	oltv
A 1	66.7	9.2	10	180	77K	72
A 2	23.5	10.4	13	171	50K	70
B 1	8.1	10.1	9	183	77K	70
B 2	1.7	11.0	12	180	39K	70

* Non balloons only
Historical CPR speeds: 1 Mo 18.3, 3 Mo 12.1

Static Analysis / Option Adjusted Spread

Security	Tranche	Price	Yield	Avg Life	A.L. Sprd	Dur.	Convex.	Cash Flow Sprd	OAS	Convex. Cost
FNMA 95W5	A1	100.250	5.94	1.95	77.31	1.98	-0.32	71.73	31.21	40.52
	A2	100.359	6.18	3.77	85.25	4.37	-0.65	85.03	20.07	64.96
	A3	100.141	6.45	5.51	98.16	5.81	-0.44	91.55	24.53	67.02
	A4	99.844	6.85	7.89	122.89	7.27	-0.03	113.06	58.29	54.77
	A5	99.062	7.25	11.29	147.20	8.05	0.12	140.61	110.79	29.83
GEHEL 951	A1	100.422	6.17	1.02	103.46	0.65	-0.14	74.22	67.48	6.73
	A2	101.125	6.34	2.71	111.73	2.47	-0.39	104.74	64.84	39.90
	A3	101.250	6.65	4.46	125.75	4.52	-0.47	126.38	65.13	61.26
	A4	101.271	7.05	6.18	153.90	5.74	-0.39	151.49	91.59	59.90
	A5	101.270	7.40	10.09	164.72	7.42	0.09	164.72	129.50	35.21

Definitions and Assumptions:

CPR: Average Life equivalent prepayment speed projected by Bear Stearns' Econometric Prepayment Model.

Yield: Bond Equivalent Yield calculated using projected CPR.

Average Life: Weighted average time to principal return, in years, using projected prepayment speed.

Average Life Spread: Yield spread of security to interpolated Treasury with equal average life.

Duration: Price sensitivity of the security, expressed as the percentage price change, given a 100 basis point move in interest rates.

Convexity: A measure of the sensitivity of duration to changes in interest rates.

Cash Flow Spread: 0% volatility OAS.

Convexity Cost: Difference between OAS at 0% volatility and OAS with observed volatility.

Volatility: Volatility is calculated by first pricing an at the money 10 year libor cap and then solving for the implied volatility that gives the same cap price. Our implied volatility assumption is 19.8%. The volatility is *internally* translated for calculations using mean reversion. At 5% mean reversion the equivalent mortgage rate volatility is approximately 12.77%

Pricing: Bid side as of 1/12/96

Yield Curve:	3 mo	6 mo	12 mo	2 yr	3 yr	5 yr	7 yr	10 yr.	30 yr.
	5.18	5.18	5.13	5.16	5.25	5.44	5.56	5.75	6.16

Exhibit 26: Projected Life Prepayment Speeds

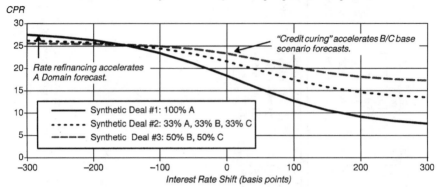

- Synthetic Deal #1 (100% A credit) has inherently more volatile prepayments than the other synthetic deals, as evidenced by substantially higher levels of convexity cost across all average life points on the Treasury curve. In the most sensitive tranche, prepayment volatility reduces the static yield spread by over 55 basis points.
- Synthetic Deal #3, backed by the most credit-impaired borrowers (50/50 B/C split), was the least negatively convex security. Convexity cost levels remained below 25 basis points even in the most volatile tranches.
- In general, finance company securities backed by the highest credit quality borrowers are two to three times more negatively convex than deals backed by the lowest credit borrowers (as measured by convexity cost). For the average deal with a relatively disperse credit profile, investors should be compensated an additional 20 to 40 basis points for prepayment uncertainty depending on the average life of the security.
- In the long average life sector, risk/reward favors the last tranche where convexity costs are lowered by the additional call protection of preceding tranches, less overall extension risk, and more stable long-dated cash flows. Convexity costs tended to drop by 30% to 40% in these issues. The most volatile tranches (highest convexity costs) tended to be concentrated in the 4 to 6 year average life sector of the curve.

We also present full option adjusted spread analytics in Exhibit 25 for 25 actual home equity securities from 5 recently issued deals. Note that differences in projected base case speeds can be explained by either a difference in seasoning or a difference in credit quality. For example, the FNMA-95W5 issue has a slower base speed than FNMA-95W1 or FNMA-95W2 since it is at the beginning of its seasoning ramp. In addition, projections for the 95W1 and 95W4 issues are propped up by today's lower interest rates (relative to when they were issued). The results in Exhibit 25 are consistent with our findings from the synthetic deal analysis presented in Exhibit 24. The reduction in static yield spread due to pre-payment volatility ranged from just several basis points in the shortest average life securities to well over 60 basis points in the 5 to 7 year average life securities backed by A credit borrowers. The most notable drop in convexity cost was evident in the AAMES issue, a result of the heavy concentration of B/C loans. In contrast, FNMA-95W5 was penalized by the heavy concentration of A domain loans and the newness of the issue. Once again, risk/reward favored the long dated tranches where convexity costs were cut by 30% to 40% relative to preceding tranches.

CONCLUSION

To address the need for a more sophisticated and robust valuation framework, we have presented the results of a comprehensive prepayment study derived from borrower level information on over 300,000 home equity loans. The result of our efforts is a prepayment model that accounts for the key determinants of home equity prepayment behavior. Linked to our option adjusted spread model, our prepayment model allows investors to differentiate and value the prepayment uncertainty inherent in home equity securities with very disperse loan and borrower attributes. Using this technology, investors can make informed and reliable cross-sector relative value decisions as well as anticipate the market response to changing interest rates and home prices. It also provides the basis for superior hedging capabilities, including option adjusted duration and convexity measurements.

Chapter 17

Manufactured Housing: Overview, Securitization, and Prepayments

Steven Abrahams
Principal
Mortgage Research
Morgan Stanley

Howard Esaki
Principal
Mortgage Research
Morgan Stanley

Robert Restrick
Associate
Mortgage Research
Morgan Stanley

INTRODUCTION

Securitization of manufactured housing loans has grown dramatically in recent years. The purpose of this chapter is to discuss this sector of the market. Specifically, we will cover the following topics: (1) the market for manufactured housing; (2) the market for the securitized loans; (3) credit risk; and, (4) prepayment risk.

THE MARKET FOR MANUFACTURED HOUSING

Manufactured homes are single-family detached homes constructed off-site and transported to an individual plot of land or to a manufactured housing community. There are eight million manufactured homes in the United States, representing about 7% of all homes and more than 10% of the housing stock in some southern states. About one-third of manufactured homes are located in manufactured housing communities,[1] with the remainder located on individually owned or rented

---

[1] See for example, Howard Esaki and Robert Restrick, "Manufactured Housing Communities: Outlook and Risk Assessment," *Morgan Stanley Mortgage Research*, October 1995 and Eric Hemel and Steve Sakura, "Manufactured Housing REITs," *Morgan Stanley U.S. Investment Research* (May 26, 1995).

plots of land. According to the Census Bureau, manufactured homes are the fastest growing type of housing, increasing by 57% in the 1980s. In the same period, the number of one-family houses increased by 13%.

Although manufactured homes are sometimes called "mobile homes," most are moved infrequently and are expensive to transport. For example, the average homeowner stay in a manufactured housing community is seven years. The home is likely to stay in the community for a much longer period. Costs of transporting a manufactured home range from $2,000 to $6,000, depending on the size of the home and location. In recent years, manufactured housing has come to more closely resemble site-built housing, containing many of the amenities of standard single-family detached homes. Newer "double-wide" homes are twice the size of older manufactured homes and are similar in size to standard homes with an average of 1,525 square feet of living space. In addition, federal government standards established in 1976 for manufactured homes have helped to improve the overall quality of this housing type.

Size, Cost and Buyer Demographics

Exhibits 1 and 2 provide cost and demographic characteristics for manufactured homes. On average, manufactured housing is less expensive and smaller than site-built housing. In 1993, the average sales price of a manufactured home was about one-fourth the cost of a site-built home, excluding land cost. The average manufactured home is about 60% of the size of the average site-built home. Since 1980, the average sales price of a manufactured home has fallen by 10% in real terms, while the price of a site-built home has risen by 13% in real terms. Manufactured housing occupants are, on average, younger and have lower incomes than site-built housing residents.

Exhibit I: Cost Comparison: Manufactured Homes versus Site-Built Homes

	1980	1993
Manufactured Homes:		
Average sales price*	$33,900	$30,500
Average square footage	1,050	1,295
Average cost/square foot*	$32.29	$23.55
Site-Built Homes:		
Average sales price*	$130,900	$147,700
Land sales price	$26,200	$36,925
Sales price without land	$104,700	$110,775
Average square footage	1,740	2,095
Average cost/square foot*	$60.17	$52.88

*in 1993 dollars

Source: U.S Department of Commerce and Bureau of the Census cited in Daniel Friedman "Manufactured Housing: It Just Keeps Rolling Along," Balcor Consulting Group.

Exhibit 2: Demographic Characteristics: Manufactured Housing versus Non-Manufactured Housing

(in percent, except for income)

	Manufactured	Non-Manufactured*
Median Household Income	$21,052	$36,785
Age:		
Under 25	5.2	0.8
25-34	22.2	13.9
35-54	33.4	42.2
55-74	28.2	32.5
Over 75	11.0	10.6
Race:		
White	92.1	89.8
Non-White	7.9	10.2

*includes multifamily housing

Source: U.S Department of Commerce and Bureau of the Census cited in Daniel Friedman, "Manufactured Housing: It Just Keeps Rolling Along," Balcor Consulting Group.

Exhibit 3: Top 10 Growth States for Manufactured Homes, 1980 to 1990

State	Percent Growth (in units)
South Carolina	91.2
Georgia	87.9
North Carolina	80.6
Texas	80.5
Alabama	75.4
Rhode Island	75.4
Mississippi	75.3
Louisiana	75.3
Oklahoma	73.9
Arkansas	70.6

Source: Bureau of the Census

Geographic Location

Almost 60% of all manufactured homes in the US are located in the South Atlantic and South Central geographical census regions. Florida alone accounts for 10% of all units nationwide. The top three growth states for manufactured housing are also in the South Atlantic, with more than 80% growth from 1980 to 1990. Exhibit 3 lists the top ten growth states for manufactured housing. Exhibit 4 shows the top ten metropolitan areas for manufactured housing, by number of units. Most of these areas are in the Sunbelt, with the exception of the Seattle and Detroit metropolitan areas.

Exhibit 4: Top 10 Metro Areas by Number of Manufactured Homes (thousands of units), 1990

Los Angeles-Anaheim-Riverside, CA	217.3
Tampa-St. Petersburg-Clearwater, FL	147.0
Phoenix, AZ	86.0
Houston-Galveston-Brazoria, TX	68.8
San Francisco-Oakland-San Jose, CA	68.1
Dallas-Ft. Worth, TX	61.8
Seattle-Tacoma, WA	59.2
Detroit-Ann Arbor, MI	58.0
Lakeland-Winter Haven, FL	51.8
Miami-Ft. Lauderdale, FL	46.5

Source: American Demographics, January 1993

Exhibit 5: Total Issuance of Manufactured Housing Securities, 1987 to 1995

Issuer	Issues	Original Balance ($ Millions)	Market Share (%)
CFAC Grantor Trust	1	306	2
CIT Group Securitization Corporation	2	279	1
Green Tree Financial Corporation	25	9,961	52
Merrill Lynch Mortgage Investors, Inc.	41	5,774	30
Oakwood Mortgage Investors, Inc.	3	468	2
RTC	3	616	3
Security Pacific Acceptance Corp.	6	919	5
USWFS Manufactured Housing Contract	1	214	1
Vanderbilt Mortgage Finance	3	539	3
Total	85	19,076	100

Source: Bloomberg

THE MARKET FOR SECURITIES BACKED BY MANUFACTURED HOUSING LOANS

Over $19 billion of securities backed by manufactured housing loans have been issued since 1987. Exhibit 5 lists the total issuance of manufactured housing securities from 1987 to 1995. About 90% of these loans are on the value of the manufactured home itself, with 10% to 20% including the land. Green Tree Financial Corporation, through Merrill Lynch Mortgage Investors, Inc. and its own shelf, accounts for about two-thirds of total issuance.

With the exception of a few early deals, the majority of manufactured housing loan asset-backed securities (ABS) are composed of AAA-rated, sequential-pay classes. Credit enhancement is usually provided by excess servicing and subordination. The excess servicing strip, which represents the difference between the weighted average coupon on the bonds and the higher coupons on the mortgages, may be 350 basis points per year or more at issue. This strip covers losses first, and allows the rating agencies to assign investment grade ratings to 100% of the bonds issued. Mezzanine and subordinate classes, rated AA, A, and BBB, or some combination thereof, provide additional enhancement for the AAA classes. The mezzanine classes are typically locked out from receiving any principal for four or more years. Many recent manufactured housing loan ABS now pay principal pro rata to the senior classes and to certain of the mezzanine classes after the initial 4-year lockout period.

Exhibit 6 shows the characteristics of the ten most recent Green Tree manufactured housing loan transactions. The average size of the Green Tree transactions was $454 million, backed by an average of more than 15,000 loans. More than 80% of the loans are on new manufactured homes. The weighted average loan-to-value ratio was 87.2%. About 42% of the loans were on single-wide homes; the remainder were on double-wides or other sizes. About one-third of the loans were on homes located in manufactured housing communities. The largest state concentrations were North Carolina (9.6%), Texas (9.5%), and Florida (6.7%). Credit support for the senior classes has averaged 19.7%. Exhibit 7 shows the characteristics of the two CIT manufactured housing loan transactions.

Indicative spread to Treasury levels as of October 15, 1995 for the asset-backed securities issued in a sample Green Tree transaction, 1995-8, are shown in Exhibit 8. Spread levels on manufactured housing loan ABS have been fairly constant over the prior year.

RATING AGENCY VIEW OF MANUFACTURED HOUSING

Rating agencies have a generally favorable view of the manufactured housing industry and securities backed by manufactured housing loans. For example, Moody's recently wrote that "the recent favorable operating environment for the manufactured housing industry — along with an improved product line and new financing options — should provide for continued growth for the industry over the short-to-intermediate term." [2]

The credit performance of securities backed by manufactured housing loans is among the best of any type of mortgage- or asset-backed security. As can be seen from Exhibit 9, of the 70 asset-backed classes upgraded by Moody's since 1986, 38 are on deals backed by manufactured housing loans. Twenty-four of the manufactured housing upgrades were based on collateral performance and 14 were because of upgrades of third-party credit enhancers or Green Tree Financial Corporation.

---

[2] Mark Stancher, "Manufactured Housing Collateral and Structural Aspects: A Solid Foundation," *Moody's Investors Service*, January 27, 1995.

Exhibit 6: Characteristics of the Ten Mid-1990s Green Tree Issues

Series	1994-6	1994-7	1994-8	1995-1
Issue Date	Sep-94	Nov-94	Dec-94	Feb-95
Original Balance ($ mil.)	463.9	353.5	523.2	378.3
Number of Loans	17,515	12,723	18,430	12,805
Average Balance ($)	26,485	27,784	28,388	29,546
WAM (Years)	18.1	18.6	18.8	19.9
WAC	11.48	11.46	11.57	11.91
Ratings (Moody's/S&P/Fitch)				
Seniors	Aaa/AAA/NR	Aaa/AAA/NR	Aaa/AAA/NR	Aaa/AAA/NR
Subordinates				
Class M-1	Aa3/AA+/NR	Aa3/AA/NR	Aa3/AA/NR	AA/Aa3/NR
Class B-1	Baa1/A-/NR	Baa1/BBB+/NR	Baa1/BBB+/NR	Baa1/BBB+/NR
Class B-2	Baa1/A/NR	Baa1/A/NR	Baa1/A/NR	Baa1/A/NR
Credit Support (%)				
Seniors	21.0	21.0	21.0	19.0
Subordinates (%)				
Class M-1	12.0	11.5	11.5	10.0
Class B-1	6.5	6.0	6.0	6.0
Class B-2	Limited Guarantee from Green Tree Financial Corporation			
Sep-95 CPR (MHP)				
1mo	7.6 (156)	6.5 (144)	7.4 (161)	6.9 (157)
3mo	7.7 (161)	7.0 (150)	6.0 (133)	6.3 (146)
Life	4.8 (111)	5.2 (122)	n/a	6.2 (149)
Loan to Value (%)				
<80	16.1	16.2	18.9	11.2
80-85	11.8	12.2	12.9	11.4
85-90	42.7	41.9	39.3	35.5
90-95	28.8	29.2	28.2	32.1
95-100	0.7	0.6	0.7	9.8
Est. Wtd Avg.	87.3	87.2	86.4	85.2
Manufactured Homes (%)				
New	82	83	83	84
Single-Wide	45	41	39	37
Double-Wide/Other	55	59	61	63
Location (%)				
Park Property	33	32	29	27
Privately Owned	51	52	55	56
Nonpark Rental	16	16	16	17
State Percentage>5%				
Texas	10.3	8.9	8.3	8.7
Florida	6.3	6.1	6.8	7.5
North Carolina	9.0	9.0	9.6	10.8
Michigan	—	6.9	5.8	6.2
Georgia	5.6	5.2	5.5	6.9
South Carolina	—	—	5.3	—
Alabama	—	—	5.2	—

Source: Morgan Stanley, Fitch, Bloomberg

Exhibit 6 (Continued)

Series	1995-2	1995-3	1995-4	1995-5
Issue Date	Mar-95	May-95	Jun-95	Jul-95
Original Balance ($ mil.)	328.3	502.2	320.0	451.2
Number of Loans	11,738	18,112	11,138	14,283
Average Balance ($)	27,966	27,727	28,730	31,593
WAM (Years)	20.5	20.8	21.2	22.3
WAC	12.10	11.67	11.19	10.65
Ratings (Moody's/S&P/Fitch)				
Seniors	Aaa/AAA/AAA	Aaa/AAA/AAA	Aaa/AAA/AAA	Aaa/AAA/AAA
Subordinates				
Class M-1	Aa2/AA–/AA–	Aa2/AA–/AA–	Aa3/AA–/AA–	Aa3/AA–/AA–
Class B-1	Baa1/BBB+/BBB	Baa1/BBB+/BBB+	Baa1/BBB+/BBB+	Baa1/BBB+/BBB+
Class B-2	Baa1/A–/A	Baa1/A–/A	Baa1/A–/A	Baa1/A–/A
Credit Support (%)				
Seniors	18.0	18.0	17.0	17.0
Subordinates (%)				
Class M-1	9.0	9.0	8.0	8.0
Class B-1	5.0	4.5	4.0	4.0
Class B-2	Limited Guarantee from Green Tree Financial Corporation			
Sep-95 CPR (MHP)				
1mo	5.3 (123)	4.8 (118)	2.7 (68)	7.5 (191)
3mo	5.4 (129)	4.6 (114)	4.5 (116)	4.0 (106)
Life	5.5 (135)	4.5 (113)	4.5 (116)	6.5 (166)
Loan to Value (%)				
<80	13.8	13.0	15.1	16.7
80-85	12.5	11.3	11.0	10.9
85-90	35.9	30.3	29.0	26.6
90-95	36.3	43.4	42.7	43.9
95-100	1.5	2.1	2.2	2.0
Est. Wtd Avg.	88.1	88.8	88.2	87.7
Manufactured Homes (%)				
New	81	80	81	83
Single-Wide	43	45	44	39
Double-Wide/Other	57	55	56	61
Location (%)				
Park Property	34	36	36	31
Privately Owned	49	45	45	54
Nonpark Rental	17	19	19	15
State Percentage>5%				
Texas	10.8	10.1	9.1	7.9
Florida	6.9	6.7	6.9	6.9
North Carolina	9.5	10.0	9.0	8.2
Michigan	5.2	—	—	7.0
Georgia	6.1	5.9	6.1	5.0
South Carolina	6.2	6.2	5.9	5.4
Alabama	5.1	—	5.1	—

Source: Morgan Stanley, Fitch, Bloomberg

Exhibit 6 (Continued)

Series	1995-6	1995-7	1995-8	Average
Issue Date	Aug-95	Sep-95	Oct-95	
Original Balance ($ mil.)	396.7	347.8	479.9	424.9
Number of Loans	12,591	10,785	14,708	15,221
Average Balance ($)	31,506	32,244	32,628	27,916
WAM (Years)	22.4	22.6	22.9	19.4
WAC	10.27	10.12	10.11	11.7
Ratings (Moody's/S&P/Fitch)				
Seniors	Aaa/AAA/AAA	Aaa/AAA/AAA	Aaa/AAA/AAA	
Subordinates				
Class M-1	Aa3/AA-/AA	Aa3/AA-/AA	Aa3/AA-/AA	
Class B-1	Baa2/BBB+/BBB+	Baa1/BBB+/BBB+	Baa1/BBB+/BBB+	
Class B-2	Baa1/A-/A	Baa1/A-/A	Baa1/A-/A	
Credit Support (%)				
Seniors	17.0	17.0	17.0	19.7
Subordinates (%)				
Class M-1	9.5	9.5	9.5	10.6
Class B-1	4.5	4.0	4.0	5.7
Class B-2	Limited Guarantee from Green Tree Financial Corporation			
Sep-95 CPR (MHP)				
1mo	7.8 (205)	—	—	
3mo	—	—	—	
Life	7.8 (205)	—	—	
Loan to Value (%)				
<80	16.5	16.7	17.4	15.0
80-85	11.3	11.2	10.8	12.0
85-90	26.8	26.5	26.3	37.5
90-95	43.8	43.7	43.9	33.0
95-100	1.6	1.9	1.6	2.4
Est. Wtd Avg.	87.7	87.6	87.6	87.2
Manufactured Homes (%)				
New	82	83	82	82
Single-Wide	39	39	37	42
Double-Wide/Other	61	61	63	58
Location (%)				
Park Property	32	31	32	32
Privately Owned	52	53	52	51
Nonpark Rental	16	16	16	17
State Percentage >5%				
Texas	7.0	6.5	5.9	9.5
Florida	6.4	5.6	6.1	6.7
North Carolina	9.1	8.3	9.3	9.6
Michigan	6.4	7.2	7.5	3.7
Georgia	5.3	5.3	—	5.8
South Carolina	5.9	6.3	5.6	3.1
Alabama	—	—	—	1.7

Source: Morgan Stanley, Fitch, Bloomberg

Exhibit 7: Characteristics of CIT Issues

Series	1993-1	1995-1[*]
Issue Date	Jul-93	Feb-95
Original Balance ($ mil.)	155.0	84.6
Number of Loans	4,598	2,152
Average Balance ($)	33,719	39,297
WAM (Years)	17.1	19.9
WAC	10.61	11.32
Ratings (Moody's/S&P/Fitch)		
Seniors	NR/AAA/NR	Aaa/NR/NR
Subordinates		
Mezzanine	NA	Aa3/NR/NR
Subordinate	NR/BBB+/NR	Aa3/NR/NR
Credit Support (%)		
Seniors	15.8	16.5
Subordinates (%)		
Mezzanine	NA	8.5
Subordinate	1.8	Limited Guarantee
Aug-95 CPR (MHP)		
1mo	12.8 (213)	7.6 (176)
3mo	10.6 (177)	7.5 (179)
Life	12.5 (210)	5.8 (143)
Loan to Value (%)		
<80	30.0	12.4
80-85	30.8	10.6
85-90	29.2	24.5
90-95	9.1	32.4
95-100	0.9	19.2
Manufactured Homes (%)		
New	84	93
Double-Wide/Other	—	74
State Percentage>5%		
Texas	—	26.4
Arizona	—	10.8
Washington	6.8	—
California	18.8	—
Nevada	6.7	—
Oregon	7.3	—

*Based on initial contracts sold to the Trust.

Source: Morgan Stanley, Fitch, Bloomberg

Exhibit 8: Pricing Spread Levels on Green Tree 1995-8

Class	Average Life (years)	Nominal Spread (bp) Over Benchmark	Benchmark U.S. Treasury
A-1	1.05	45	5.27% of 10/17/96
A-2	3.05	45	3 year
A-3	5.05	55	5 year
A-4	7.08	70	6 3/8% of 8/02
A-5	10.29	92	10 year
A-6	17.07	140	10 year
M-1	13.35	135	10 year
B-1	8.75	135	10 year
B-2	17.44	168	10 year

Source: *Asset Sales Report*, Morgan Stanley, yields as of October 15, 1995

Exhibit 9: ABS Rating Changes by Moody's, 1986-1995

	Upgrades		Downgrades	
Asset Type	#	$ (Mil)	#	$ (Mil)
Autos	17	1,087	27	14,416
Credit Cards	7	372	14	4,750
Home Equity	4	359	7	21,607
Manufactured Housing	38	3,149	2	413
Other	4	216	6	1,139
Total	70	5,182	56	42,324

Source: Moody's

Only two classes of ABS backed by manufactured housing have been downgraded by Moody's, both related to downgrades of third-party credit enhancement providers. The upgrade to downgrade ratio for manufactured housing transactions (19 to 1) is greater than for any other type of ABS. As a comparison, the residential MBS upgrade downgrade ratio is about 2 to 1 for 1995. Fitch and Duff and Phelps have also upgraded several manufactured housing transactions.

Going forward, we believe credit performance will remain strong as the rating agencies continue to maintain strict standards for ratings of manufactured housing securities. Moody's notes, "..since most securities in the asset-backed market are rated Aaa initially (and therefore cannot be upgraded), we expect that there will be relatively more downgrades in this market than in the total corporate bond market." The average rating in the corporate bond market is close to BBB/Baa, leaving more opportunities for upgrades. However, Moody's also points out that, "...given the predominance of high initial ratings and the relatively short maturities, ...relatively few of [manufactured housing] securities will end in default."[3]

---

[3] Andrew Silver, "A Historical Review of Rating Changes in the Public Asset-Backed Securities Market, 1986-1995," *Moody's Investors Service*, October 20, 1995.

PREPAYMENT RISKS

Prepayments in manufactured housing arise from the same major sources as in other mortgage-backed bonds: refinancings, housing turnover, and defaults. Because of their smaller average loan balance, manufactured housing prepayment speeds, nonetheless, tend to be lower and much more stable than speeds on mortgages on site-build homes. In fact, prepayments on manufactured housing loans are arguably more stable than prepayments on higher-balance home equity loans.

Refinancings

As in other mortgage-backed securities, refinancing of manufactured housing loans represents the most volatile component of prepayments. Refinancings can double or triple prepayments on manufactured homes within a few months, sending speeds from 6% CPR to 18% CPR. Refinancings in site-built homes, however, can generate a tenfold jump in speeds from 6% CPR to 60% CPR.

A handful of factors drive the refinancings of most manufactured housing loans:

Primary
- Interest rate incentives
- Loan size

Secondary
- Loan age
- Seasonality

Tertiary
- The economy
- Competition among lenders

Exhibit 10 summarizes the factors driving refinancing on manufactured housing loans.

Primary Refinancing Risks

Falling interest rates represent the single most important driver of prepayments. Lower rates create opportunities for borrowers to refinance their loans and capture a stream of future monthly savings. The greater the drop in financing rates below the borrower's rate, the larger the absolute stream of potential savings. Monthly savings are also directly proportional to loan size, with small and large loans producing correspondingly small and large savings. (See Exhibit 11.)

As an example, take the savings from refinancing the average 80% LTV, 15-year manufactured housing loan of $24,400. If the borrower starts with a 9% interest rate, refinancing into an 8% interest rate only saves $14.30 a month. Refinancing into a 6% interest rate only saves $41.58 a month.

Refinancing the average 80% LTV, 15-year loan on a site-built home and land, by contrast, would save much more. With an average balance of $118,160, refinancing a site-built's loan from a 9% interest rate to an 8% rate saves $69.26 a month, and refinancing to a 6% rate saves $201.36 a month — nearly five times the potential savings from refinancing the smaller manufactured housing loan.

Because mortgages on manufactured homes are roughly one-fifth the size of conventional loans for site-built homes and land, the manufactured housing loans show much less interest-rate sensitivity. For small manufactured housing loans, monthly savings from refinancing may seem small against the upfront, fixed costs of attorney's fees, title searches, and the like. Prepayments from 1992-93 suggest that prepayment rates on seasoned par manufactured housing loans would rise from 6% to 10% CPR-to-life to 16% to 20% CPR-to-life if rates dropped 300 bp. In contrast, CPR-to-life speeds on conventional par 30-year agency mortgages could rise from 6% CPR to 49% CPR, according to Morgan Stanley prepayment models.

Exhibit 10: Factors Driving Refinancings in Manufactured Housing Loans

Factor	Factor Levels	Proportional Prepayment Impact (% CPR)				
		Interest Rates Shift (bp from loan mortgage rate)				
		0	−50	−100	−200	−300
Refinancing	$18,000 balance (< avg size loan)	6	7	9	12	14
Incentive	$24,000 balance (avg size loan)	6	8	10	13	16
and Loan Size	$30,000 balance (> avg size loan)	6	9	12	14	17
Loan Age	< 24 Months	80% of average life speed				
	> 24 Months	105% of average life speed				
Seasonality	January, February	80% of average life speed				
	Other Months	105% of average life speed				
The	0.8 Million New Home Sales	Slower				
Economy	1.0 Million New Home Sales	Average				
	1.2 Million New Home Sales	Faster				
Lender	More	Raises prepayments				
Competition	Less	Lowers prepayment				

Source: Morgan Stanley

Exhibit 11: Savings from Refinancing

	Loan Size	
Monthly Payment At:	$24,400	$118,160
9% Interest Rate	$247	$1,198
8% Interest Rate	$233	$1,129
7% Interest Rate	$219	$1,062
6% Interest Rate	$205	$997
Monthly Savings From Refinancing A 9% Interest Rate Loan to a:		
8% Interest Rate	$14.30	$69.26
7% Interest Rate	$28.17	$136.41
6% Interest Rate	$41.58	$201.36

Source: Morgan Stanley

Secondary Refinancing Risks

Even in the event of falling interest rates, refinancing risk falls in the first two years of a loan made on a new manufactured home. During these two years, the underlying home typically depreciates, raising its loan-to-value ratio to levels unacceptable to many lenders. Refinancings in the first 24 months of a loan run slowly relative to their long-run average.

Seasonality influences refinancings as well. Refinancings on manufactured housing loans typically fall in January and February to 80% of their annual average. Conventional agency mortgages show the same pattern. Refinancings typically slow in January and February as borrowers recover from year-end holiday spending.

Tertiary Refinancing Risks

The economy and employment also shape prepayment risk. Robust economies with more jobs allow more applicants to build the job histories, credit, and assets to qualify for refinancing or upgrade to another home. A bad economy brings the opposite. Using new single-family home sales as an economic benchmark, an annualized pace of 1.2 million sales has coincided with refinancings running above their long-run average. A 0.8 million sales pace has coincided with speeds running well below their long-run average, and a 1.0 million sales pace typically has kept refinancings at their long-run mean.

Finally, competition among lenders can influence refinancing activity as well. To the extent that lenders get more aggressive either through lower rates or their efforts to inform borrowers of refinancing options, prepayments could become more interest-rate sensitive.

Housing Turnover

For borrowers holding mortgages with below-market rates of interest, housing turnover drives prepayments. Most of that turnover reflects borrowers trading up to larger manufactured housing units or into site-built homes, or moving out of the home to another area altogether.

A handful of factors again predict most of the pattern of turnover:

Primary
- Loan age
- Economic conditions

Secondary
- Seasonality
- Setting for the manufactured home

Exhibit 12 shows the factors driving turnover in manufactured housing loans.

Exhibit 12: Factors Driving Turnover in Manufactured Housing Loans

Factor	Factor Levels	Prepayment Impact
Loan Age	Month 1	3.7% CPR
	Months 2-23	Increases 0.1% CPR a month
	Months 24 and beyond	6.0% CPR
The Economy	0.8 Million New Home Sales	Slower
	1.0 Million New Home Sales	Average
	1.2 Million New Home Sales	Faster
Seasonality	January Low	80% of average annual speed
	July High	120% of average annual speed
Setting	On Borrower-Owned Land	Seasons over 36 Months
	In an MH Park	Seasons over 24 Months

Source: Morgan Stanley

Exhibit 13: 100% MHP

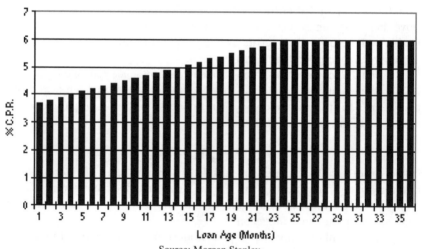

Source: Morgan Stanley

Primary Turnover Risks

As in mortgages on traditional homes, prepayments on manufactured homes rise with age. Some investors have settled on a standard *manufactured housing prepayment* curve (MHP) to describe the rising speeds. The 100% MHP curve starts at 3.7% CPR in the first month after origination and rises 0.1% CPR monthly to 6.0% CPR in the 24th month, remaining constant thereafter. This is depicted in Exhibit 13. Manufactured housing prepayment speeds can be described as multiples of the MHP curve, the same way that other sectors of the mortgage market use the PSA curve. Like the PSA curve, the MHP curve is a yardstick for prepayments rather than a forecast or a predictor. Actual seasoning can differ from 100% MHP due to changing rates of home depreciation, economic conditions, interest rates, and other factors.

The economy can have a significant influence on rates of manufactured housing turnover, beyond its already important impact on refinancing. Robust economies with strong employment tend to draw migration, raising demand for all housing. In addition, improving employment prospects for existing homeowners allow them to move easily and trade up to better homes.

Secondary Turnover Risks

Borrowers' tendency to move at the end of the school year, and with the arrival of summer weather, drives turnover toward an annual high in July, and a low in January. July's pace typically runs at 120% of its annual average, with January coming in at 80%, the same pattern as other mortgages.

The physical location of the manufactured home also helps predict turnover. Homes located on the borrower's own property turnover more slowly than homes in manufactured housing parks. The homes on owned property take roughly 36 months to fully season, rather than the normal 24. Presumably, borrowers located on owned property have a longer-term commitment to living in that area.

Defaults

Defaults constitute a larger component of manufactured housings' prepayments than of prepayments in site-built homes. Defaulted loans eventually become prepayments when the financed property is liquidated and principal returned to the investor. However, they show limited month-to-month variability. In many manufactured housing securitizations, monthly defaults constitute a steady 0.1% to 0.2% of original principal, roughly equivalent to 2% to 3% CPR a year.

CONCLUSION

The recent growth in securitized manufactured housing loans and current investor appetite for less negatively convex securities makes manufactured housing loans an attractive alternative. The small loan size, at least relative to conventional mortgage-backed securities, historically has made borrowers less sensitive to refinancing opportunities. Moreover, credit support in securitized deals has proven to be more than adequate historically, and should continue to cover reasonable credit risk.

Chapter 18

Identifying Relative Value in Home Equity Loan and Manufactured Housing Securities Using OAS Analysis

Akiva Dickstein
Vice President
Lehman Brothers

INTRODUCTION

Over the past few years, both the home equity loan (HEL) and manufactured housing (MH) markets have grown rapidly and the investor base for both products has expanded. Home equity loan issuance has grown from $7.2 billion in 1993 to approximately $15 billion in 1995, of which about $8 billion was fixed rate. Over the same period, manufactured housing securities annual issuance has more than doubled from $2.5 billion to $5.4 billion.

As the HEL and MH markets have received increased attention, investors have become more aware of the prepayment risk in these sectors. Although both sectors have exhibited more stable prepayments than agency-backed residential mortgages, the HEL sector surprised investors with the extent of the prepayment slowdown in 1994. While prepayments during 1995 for both the HEL and MH sectors were generally in line with historical experience, spreads widened in the HEL sector near the end of 1995 at least in part because prepayment risk in these securities was poorly understood. This chapter briefly reviews the prepayment characteristics of home equity and manufactured housing loans and then employs option-adjusted spread (OAS) analysis to value securities collateralized by these loans.

The introduction of OAS into the ABS market represents a significant advance and is a logical extension of the effort by market participants to understand prepayment behavior in the home equity loan and manufactured housing sectors. The use of OAS will help investors to identify relative value within a sector and to compare securities across a range of product types. Although OAS is not the only measure of value and should generally be supplemented by scenario analyses and views on interest rates, it is the best single measure of the prepayment risk-adjusted spread on a security.

We first describe prepayments in the MH and HEL sectors and address several factors that affect prepayment risk for structured securities. Then we calculate OAS for current coupon, premium, and discount securities, and make relative value comparisons. Finally, we stress our findings by using a modified model in which prepayments are more sensitive to interest rates than they have been historically.

PREPAYMENTS ON HOME EQUITY LOAN AND MANUFACTURED HOUSING COLLATERAL

Prepayments on both MH and HELs are less sensitive to interest rates than conventional agency mortgages, with home equity loans more sensitive than manufactured housing. Exhibit 1 shows the projections of the Lehman Brothers manufactured housing and agency mortgage models along with projections of home equity loan prepayments. We focus here on finance company home equity loans.

The relative stability of interest rates for both HELs and MH is due to a number of factors. Both finance company home equity and manufactured housing loans are characterized by relatively small loan sizes (averages are about $35,000 on MH and about $55,000 on HELs) and higher loan rates (currently averaging about 10% to 11%) than in the agency mortgage market. Both of these factors contribute to the relative insensitivity of prepayments for these sectors. First, smaller loans have a lower dollar incentive to refinance for a given movement in interest rates, and mortgage brokers have less incentive to refinance smaller loans. Indeed, the smaller MH loans are less sensitive than the HELs to interest rate movements. Second, in both markets the high rate paradoxically indicates that fewer refinancing opportunities exist because defaults on finance company HELs and MH have historically been higher than on conforming mortgages; fewer lenders are willing and able to originate and service these loans. In addition, the borrower base is somewhat less sophisticated in terms of refinancing.

The prepayment projections shown in Exhibit 1 are based on typical securitized home equity and manufactured housing transactions. Our research indicates that additional factors such as credit quality, loan size, prepayment penalties (on HELs), loan-to-value (LTV) ratios, and burnout also affect the prepayment behavior of these loans. All these factors are incorporated into the Lehman Brothers MH and HEL models.

Exhibit 1: Sensitivity of Prepayments to Interest Rates* (% CPR)

Asset Class	Interest Rate Move (bp from current coupon)							
	−300	−200	−100	0	+100	+200	+300	Range
Manufactured Housing	17.0	14.4	11.7	9.2	7.4	6.6	6.0	11.0
Home Equity Loans	35.0	32.0	28.0	23.0	17.5	13.0	10.0	25.0
30-yr FNMA Mortgages	62.1	48.3	20.2	8.3	6.8	5.7	4.9	57.2

* We use a single CPR that equates the outstanding balance at the end of three years to the projection of the Lehman Brothers prepayment model. For HELs and MH, the loans are assumed to be fully seasoned (12 months for HELs and 24 months for MH).

Exhibit 2: Sensitivity of Average Life to Interest Rates for Selected Collateral Types

Bond	Collateral	Interest Rate Scenario (bp)							Range
		−300	−200	−100	0	+100	+200	+300	
Green Tree 1996-1 A-3	Manufactured Housing	3.6 yrs	4.4 yrs	5.5 yrs	6.7 yrs	7.6 yrs	8.2 yrs	8.5 yrs	4.9 yrs
EquiCredit 1995-4 A-4	Home Equity Loans	5.7	6.1	6.7	7.6	8.6	10.2	11.5	5.8
FNR 1994-31 B	Agency Mtgs. (7s of 94)	1.5	1.9	4.1	7.7	9.0	10.2	11.2	9.7

PREPAYMENT RISK IN STRUCTURED SECURITIES

Almost all recent home equity and manufactured housing transactions have been structured with several bond classes of various average lives. As a result, it is important to understand not only the prepayment behavior of the underlying collateral, but also the effect of such behavior on particular classes within a structure.

One way to observe the prepayment risk of a given class is to examine its change in average life over a range of interest rates. The response of a security's average life to interest rates may be affected by a number of factors: the sensitivity of borrowers to interest rates; loan characteristics such as WAM, range of loan maturities, and percentage of balloon loans; and, structural features such as clean-up calls.

Interest Rate Sensitivity of Collateral

Securities backed by collateral with lower interest rate sensitivity will have a more stable average life profile. Exhibit 2 shows three securities with similar average lives in the base case and their average life profiles as a function of interest rates using the prepayment projections shown in Exhibit 1. The agency CMO shows the greatest average life drift, while the MH security is the most stable. This HEL security's average life is only slightly more sensitive to rates than the MH security.

Loan Amortization Characteristics

Even securities with identical prepayment sensitivities to interest rates may react differently in terms of average life drift due to different loan amortization characteristics. For example, we looked at two home equity loan securities with similar average lives, EquiCredit 1995-4 A-4 and Conti 1996-1 A-6. While the two securities behave similarly in falling rate environments, the EquiCredit transaction has significantly less extension risk than the Conti transaction if prepayments slow (Exhibit 3). The reason for this is directly related to the WAM of the two transactions: the shorter WAM on the EquiCredit transaction results in less extension of the security in a rising interest rate environment (low prepayment rates) due to the faster amortization of the underlying loans. Consequently, the EquiCredit security has less prepayment risk than the comparable Conti security. This difference would be further accentuated if the securities became discounts, with a greater possibility of a slowdown in prepayments.

In addition to WAM, other collateral characteristics affect prepayment risk in more subtle ways. For instance, a high proportion of balloons can cause more extension risk because the scheduled amortization of the loans is less than that of comparable maturity level-pay mortgages. In addition, a dispersion of WAM may have the effect of reducing extension on short classes that benefit from the shorter WAM collateral, while increasing extension risk on longer classes that are disproportionately backed by the longer WAM collateral.

Structure

Another influence on prepayment risk is the structure of the transaction. Short securities generally have less prepayment risk, since their average lives and durations are less likely to experience extreme changes due to a large move in interest rates. Very long classes also have somewhat less prepayment risk because burnout reduces call risk in the long run and scheduled amortization is a more significant portion of principal payments. However, the last class in most HEL and MH transactions is usually subject to the effects of a 10% clean-up call that gives the issuer the option to call the transaction and pay off the remaining securities at par once the outstanding balance has dropped below 10% of the original balance. Because one must assume that the issuer will call the security only in an environment where the loans could be resecuritized at a lower rate (i.e., in a low rate environment), the investor is essentially short a call option that must be valued appropriately.

USING OAS TO MEASURE PREPAYMENT RISK IN STRUCTURED MH AND HEL SECURITIES

To quantify the effect of prepayment risk in structured securities beyond simple scenario analysis, we use a full option-based framework. The traditional OAS methodology divides the nominal spread on a security with embedded options such as prepayments into a component that represents compensation for prepayment risk (the convexity or option cost) from the spread that investors receive for credit risk and liquidity. Using an OAS perspective allows us to compare relative value across various classes of MH and HEL securities as well as across ABS and mortgage sectors. We begin with an explanation of the zero-volatility spread and OAS.

Exhibit 3: Effect of WAM on Extension Risk in Home Equity Loans

Bond	WAM	CPR (%)							Range
		35	32	28	23	18	13	10	
EquiCredit 1995-4 A-4	172 mo	5.0 yr	5.6 yr	6.3 yr	7.3 yr	8.8 yr	10.7 yr	12.1 yr	7.1 yr
Conti 1996-1 A-6	205	4.5	5.0	5.8	7.2	9.2	12.2	14.1	9.6

WAM = Weighted average maturity.

Zero-Volatility Spreads

The most basic approach to valuing any security is to compare its yield with the yield of a comparable average life Treasury security; the difference is known as the *nominal spread*. However, for an amortizing security, this may not be an appropriate measure even in the absence of prepayment risk. Because the principal is paid down over a period of time, the appropriate alternative Treasury investment is not a bullet maturity bond matched to its average life, but rather a portfolio of Treasury securities with cash flows that replicate the cash flows of that security. To capture this effect, a zero-volatility (ZV) spread is used.

To a first approximation, the ZV spread is a weighted average of the spread to the par-priced zero coupon Treasury curve over the period in which the investor receives cash flows. Technically, the ZV spread is calculated using the forward curve to project a series of 1-month Treasury rates to find the spread that must be added to these rates when discounting the cash flows in order to match the current price of the security. The ZV spread gets its name from the fact that with no volatility the forward curve would have to be the realized spot curve to prevent arbitrage. The forward curve and the corresponding implied future interest rates are calculated using off-the-run Treasury securities, and ZV spreads are therefore quoted to the off-the-run Treasury curve.

The cash flows that are discounted when calculating the ZV spread are determined by a prepayment model along the path of interest rates implied by the forward curve. However, because the ABS market has grown up without prepayment models for the most part, ZV spreads have been calculated using a single prepayment assumption for the life of the security. These two approaches can produce different results since the forward path of interest rates rises when the yield curve is upward-sloping, which causes prepayments to slow along this path for many securities. In this chapter, we use the technically correct approach, allowing the model to determine prepayment rates along the ZV path.

Option-Adjusted Spreads

Although the ZV spread is an improvement over the nominal spread, it does not capture the prepayment risk inherent in a security whose cash flows may be significantly changed by the interest rate scenario. In practice, the interest rate path implied by the forward curve is only one of many possible paths that may be observed. In OAS analysis, a wide range of potential future interest rate paths is considered. The set of paths is generated using a model for the term structure of interest rates; the volatility in this model is calibrated to a robust set of options of various maturities. Along each path, a prepayment model is used to determine the response of the collateral to these interest rates and to determine cash flows. The OAS is defined as the spread that must be added to Treasury spreads so that when these cash flows are discounted to their present value, the average present value across all interest rate paths is equal to the actual price of the security today.

Mathematically,

nominal spread = zero volatility spread (ZV) + yield curve compensation

ZV spread = OAS + convexity cost (or option cost)

OAS is the compensation investors receive for credit risk, liquidity, and prepayment model risk.

OAS Evaluation of Current Coupon Securities: Longer Classes Offer Value

In both the HEL and MH sectors, nominal spreads rise significantly as the average life of the securities increases. This is principally due to two factors: a narrower investor base in the longer part of the curve and a perception that prepayment risk increases as the duration of the class rises. OAS analysis allows us to quantify the prepayment risk on various classes and reveals that the longer classes offer the most attractive option-adjusted as well as nominal spreads.

We have selected two relatively recent transactions, EquiCredit 1995-4 and Green Tree 1996-1 as representative transactions for OAS analysis (Exhibit 4).[1] The manufactured housing security has less option cost than the home equity loan due to the more stable prepayments. In both securities, with the exception of the last class, option costs tend to be highest in the 3- to 7-year sector. Securities with shorter average lives have less call risk since there is a limit to how much they may shorten, while securities in the back end of the curve have lower convexity cost because of collateral burnout and the relatively large contribution of scheduled principal payments to total principal payments. The last class in both of these examples, however, has additional option cost due to the 10% optional clean-up call. We estimate that this feature contributes 5 bp in option cost on the Green Tree transaction and 18 bp on the EquiCredit transaction.[2]

Because nominal spreads are higher on longer average life classes while convexity costs are generally lower, the highest OAS are located in the longer securities. For example, the 7-year HEL offers an OAS of 84 bp, about 40 bp wider than agency PACs and credit cards. The 16-year MH security has an OAS roughly 30 bp wider than PACs. In contrast, the OAS on the 3-year ABS securities are not significantly wider than PACs, and any difference is warranted due to credit spread, as PACs have agency guarantees while the asset-backed securities examined here are rated triple A.

---

[1] To ensure that the bonds were priced at par for our analysis, we adjusted the coupons on our securities from the actual security. In all other respects the bonds used were identical to EquiCredit 1995-4 and Green Tree 1996-1. In addition, because Green Tree 1996-1 did not include 1- and a 3-year securities, we adjusted the structure of the security by splitting the 2-year class into a 1- and a 3-year.

[2] In calculating the option cost due to the clean-up call, we took into account the rate at which the loans could be resecuritized if called as well as the step-up in coupon on the floating rate class if the EquiCredit transaction is not called.

Exhibit 4: OAS Analysis of Current Coupon HELs and MH

Avg. Life @ Model (years)	Home Equity Loans (bp)				Manufactured Housing (bp)				Agency PACs OAS	Credit Card ZV
	Nominal Sprd[a]	ZV Sprd[b]	Option Cost	OAS	Nominal Sprd	ZV Sprd	Option Cost	OAS		
1	65	58	21	37	50	41	11	30	30	30
3	85	79	38	41	50	46	18	28	35	30
5	102	95	33	62	55	52	21	31	40	34
7	125	117	33	84	73	63	20	43	45	42
10/11	150	121	40[c]	81	93	80	17	63	50	42
16	NA	NA	NA	NA	145	97	17[c]	80	50	NA

[a] Nominal spreads are quoted to the Treasury with the same maturity as the average life predicted by the model. In practice, the prepayment assumptions used in actual pricing may have a significant effect on the OAS, although option costs are not significantly affected by these assumptions.

[b] ZV spreads throughout this report are calculated using prepayment model projections along the zero volatility path. They therefore may differ from ZV spreads which assume a fixed prepayment rate.

[c] Option costs on the last classes include the cost of the optional clean-up call.

Exhibit 5: OAS Values in Home Equity Loans Depend on WAM of the Collateral

Average Life (years)	Longer WAM (Conti 1996-1), 205 months (bp)	Shorter WAM (EquiCredit 1995-4), 175 months (bp)
5	46	62
7	74	84

HEL securities backed by different WAM collateral may have significantly different OAS values. For example, ContiMortgage 1996-1 has a WAM of 205 months, compared to only 175 months for EquiCredit 1995-4. As a result, the Conti security will extend more if prepayments slow (see Exhibit 3), resulting in higher convexity costs and lower OAS values even though the two securities have the same nominal spreads (Exhibit 5).

Premium Securities: Higher Nominal Spreads More Than Compensate for Prepayment Risk

Premium HEL and MH securities are generally priced at considerably wider spreads than current coupon par-priced bonds since these bonds are perceived to have higher prepayment risk and are less liquid because some investors do not buy premium-priced securities in the secondary market. However, OAS analysis indicates that the extra spread more than compensates for the increased risk, especially in the home equity loan sector.

Using the same securities (EquiCredit 1995-4 and Green Tree 1996-1), we constructed a scenario where interest rates drop 100 bp so that the same securities would be trading at a premium.[3] The results are shown in Exhibits 6 and 7.

---

[3] We used the same securities in order to avoid complications arising from different structures with different collateral characteristics.

Exhibit 6: OAS Analysis of a Premium HEL Security

Class	Avg.Life (@ Model)	Approx. Price	Nominal Spread (bp)	ZV Spread (bp)	Convexity Costs (bp)	OAS (bp)	OAS Pickup vs. Current Coupon (bp)
A-1	0.9	$101	65	62	10	52	15
A-2	2.8	102	105	106	26	80	39
A-3	4.8	103	132	127	27	100	38
A-4	6.7	104	160	159	25	134	50
A-5	6.9	105	175	162	51	111	30
	(to call)						

Exhibit 7: OAS Analysis of a Premium Manufactured Housing Security

Class	Avg.Life (@ Model)	Approx. Price	Nominal Spread (bp)	ZV Spread (bp)	Convexity Costs (bp)	OAS (bp)	OAS Pickup vs. Current Coupon (bp)
A-1a	0.9 yrs	$101	55	51	10	41	11
A-1b	2.7	102	60	61	18	43	15
A-2	3.8	103	70	73	25	48	15
A-3	5.5	105	85	85	28	57	14
A-4	7.9	106	110	108	25	83	20
A-5	13.5	106	175	142	23	119	39
	(to call)						

In both the HEL and MH sectors, the relationship between prepayments and interest rates is fairly linear, in sharp contrast to the refinancing curve for agency and nonagency residential mortgages which steepens dramatically for cusp coupons relative to current coupons (see Exhibit 1). Therefore, although convexity costs on agency premiums are higher from those on current coupons by about 25 bp, convexity costs for premium HEL and MH securities are roughly similar to those for current coupons. For example, convexity costs are 27 bp on the 4.6-year premium HEL class and 33 bp on the 5.4-year par-priced security. In the MH sector, convexity costs are slightly higher on the premium securities, by about 4-8 bp.

Premium securities also benefit from smaller differences between the nominal spread and the ZV spread (this difference is commonly referred to as the "ZV drop"). This is because prepayments in the ZV case are based on the rising interest rate path implied by the forward curve, which tends to slow prepayments and benefit premiums. Thus, the ZV drop in the current coupon case for the 7-year current coupon HEL is 8 bp but only 1 bp for the premium.

Because the nominal spread increases on premium securities while the ZV drop falls and convexity costs remain similar, the OAS on premium HEL and MH securities are significantly higher than on current coupons. For example, in the 5-year sector, the premium HEL class offers an OAS of 100 bp, a pick-up of 38 bp in OAS over the current coupon. In manufactured housing, the pick-up is usually smaller but still significant: the 8-year premium has an OAS of 83 bp compared to 63 bp for a current coupon 9.5-year security.

Discount Securities: Convexity Costs are Related to Extension Risk

Similar to our illustration of premium securities, we analyzed discounts by examining the same HEL and MH securities (EquiCredit 1995-4 and Green Tree 1996-1) in a scenario where interest rates have risen by 100 bp.

Nominal spreads on discount HELs and MH are not substantially different from those on current coupon securities. However, on MH securities convexity costs fall in the discount sector because extension is limited. In HELs, a 100 bp rise in rates results in prepayments of about 17% to 18% CPR. Because HEL prepayments may continue to fall as rates rise, these securities still have extension risk; therefore, convexity costs are about the same as for current coupons (see Exhibits 1 and 2).

In both cases, the ZV drop is higher for a discount security, as slower prepayments along the forward path of rates tend to extend the security and cause the yield to decline. Thus, the ZV drop on the home equity loan A-3 class is 7 bp in the par case and 18 bp in the discount case.

The net result is that OAS levels on discount HEL securities are often lower than on current coupon securities while in MH the OAS on discount securities are often slightly higher than on current coupon securities (Exhibits 8 and 9).

Discount securities also are not immediately subject to the spread widening that occurs on par-priced securities when interest rates rally. This will have a positive impact on realized total return for discounts relative to current coupon securities as long premium securities trade at wider OAS.

Exhibit 8: OAS Analysis of a Discount HEL Security

Class	Avg. Life (years)	Approx. Price	Nominal Spread (bp)	ZV Spread (bp)	Convexity Costs (bp)	OAS (bp)	OAS Pickup vs. Current Coupon (bp)
A-1	1.3	99	65	48	35	16	−21
A-2	3.9	97	85	64	42	22	−19
A-3	6.5	94	120	102	36	66	+4
A-4	8.5	93	135	112	31	81	−3
A-5	12.4	92	155	114	26	88	+7
	(to maturity)						

Exhibit 9: OAS Analysis of a Discount MH Security

Class	Avg. Life (years)	Approx. Price	Nominal Spread (bp)	ZV Spread (bp)	Convexity Costs (bp)	OAS (bp)	OAS Pickup vs. Current Coupon (bp)
A-1a	1.2	99	50	39	8	31	+11
A-1b	3.6	97	50	42	12	30	+2
A-2	5.2	96	55	41	13	28	0
A-3	7.6	94	73	59	10	48	+5
A-4	10.7	93	93	65	11	54	-9
A-5	18.2	91	150	94	11	83	+3
	(to maturity)						

SENSITIVITY TO PREPAYMENT MODEL ASSUMPTIONS

Our OAS analysis is based on prepayment assumptions we believe are reasonable, but we also considered potential changes in prepayment behavior in the HEL and MH markets. Our home equity loan data extend as far back as 1988, but the market is becoming more competitive, which could change prepayment behavior. Our MH data are extensive, reaching back to the early 1970s, but changing loan characteristics, such as increasing loan size and improved borrower credit as well as increased competition, may result in prepayment responses that differ from historical experience.

In this section, we consider two types of changes in prepayment behavior: increases in "turnover" (i.e., a general rise in prepayments across all interest rate scenarios) and increases in the slope of the refinancing function. In each case, we illustrate the effect of such a prepayment change on the OAS of a 7-year security in the discount, current coupon, and premium sectors.

Increased Turnover

Over the last year, prepayments on current coupon Green Tree collateral have been higher then the historical levels of 100% MHP.[4] Prepayments on fully seasoned current coupon collateral rose to 150% MHP and pools with a weighted average coupon 100 bp lower than the prevailing Green Tree rate prepaid at about 120% MHP.[5] We have incorporated this change into our analysis above, but such a trend could continue if borrower mobility continues to improve or competition increases. For this reason, we have calculated OAS on the above securities using a variant of the prepayment model in which all speeds are higher by about 1% CPR (see Exhibit 10).

In the home equity market, we are not concerned with increasing mobility, but increasing competition among originators for new loans or a significant rise in housing prices could result in higher prepayments and easier refinancing for all home equity loans. Exhibit 11 shows a scenario in which home equity loan prepayments increase by 3% CPR. (We increased prepayments by 3% CPR in this market so that the percentage change in prepayments in the MH and HEL markets would be similar.)

Exhibit 12 shows the effect of the higher turnover on 7-year average life MH and HEL securities. In general, convexity costs are unaffected by a uniform shift in prepayments. Current coupon securities appear more attractive because the average lives of the bonds shorten, widening the spread to the comparable average life Treasury given the upward slope of the yield curve. The discount looks even more attractive since the yield on the bond rises when prepayments are higher. The premium bond appears slightly less attractive relative to the par and discount securities under this scenario due to the decline in yield when prepayments are fast. Even at these stressed levels of prepayments, however, the premium bond offers OAS values considerably wider than the current coupon security.

---

[4] MHP is the manufactured housing prepayment curve and is generally used as the standard in the manufactured housing market. It runs from 3.7% CPR in month 1 to 6% CPR in month 24 and is flat thereafter.

[5] See the Lehman Brothers report, *Manufactured Housing Prepayments in 1995*, January 19, 1996.

Exhibit 10: Higher Turnover Scenario in Manufactured Housing

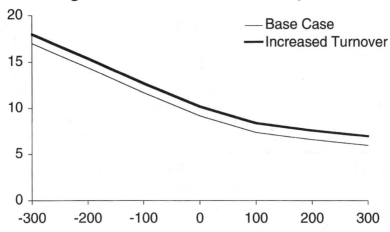

Exhibit 11: Higher Turnover Scenario in Home Equity Loans

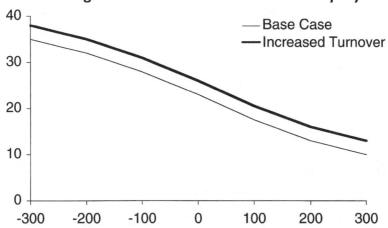

Exhibit 12: Effect of Higher Turnover on HEL and MH OAS

		Base Case		Higher Turnover		OAS
		Average		Average		
Security	Type	Life (years)	OAS (bp)	Life (years)	OAS (bp)	Change (bp)
Par	MH	6.7	43	6.1	50	+7
Premium	MH	5.5	57	5.0	56	-1
Discount	MH	7.6	48	7.0	62	+14
Par	HEL	7.5	84	6.9	100	+16
Premium	HEL	6.7	134	6.1	138	+4
Discount	HEL	8.6	76	7.9	99	+23

Increased Sensitivity to Interest Rates

Unlike increases in turnover, heightened sensitivity to interest rates directly affects convexity costs. We have stressed the above manufactured housing and home equity securities using a prepayment assumption with more sensitivity to interest rates, as shown in Exhibits 13 and 14. In both cases, we assume that the entire prepayment curve steepens significantly, so that current coupon prepayments are higher than the base case and premium prepayments increase even more. If we were to see increased competition in these markets, this is the type of change we believe would occur because increased competition would probably stimulate refinancing for current coupons as well as for premiums.

Exhibit 13: Increased Interest Rate Sensitivity Scenario in Manufactured Housing

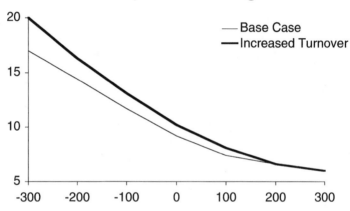

Exhibit 14: Increased Interest Rate Sensitivity Scenario in Home Equity Loans

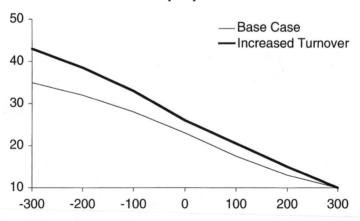

Exhibit 15: Effect of Higher Interest Rate Sensitivity on HEL and MH OAS

Security	Type	Base Case		High Sensitivity Model		OAS
		Average Life (years)	OAS (bp)	Average Life (years)	OAS (bp)	Change (bp)
Par	MH	6.7	43	6.2	37	−6
Premium	MH	5.5	57	4.9	49	−8
Discount	MH	7.6	48	7.3	41	−7
Par	HEL	7.5	84	6.8	82	−2
Premium	HEL	6.7	134	5.8	128	−6
Discount	HEL	8.5	81	7.8	80	−1

Applying these stresses will naturally generate higher convexity costs and lower OAS values. In the manufactured housing market, OAS values drop by 6-8 bp; in the home equity market, OAS values drop similarly by up to 6 bp. However, the premium securities again retain their value relative to the par-priced securities (see Exhibit 15).

CONCLUSION

Although the mortgage market has made significant strides in pricing convexity risk, the ABS market is only starting to use this methodology. This approach can reveal inefficiencies in the market in terms of OAS, and thereby suggest relative value opportunities. These opportunities may diminish, however, as market participants start relying on valuation models to price prepayment risk on the basis of convexity cost and prepayment model risk.

Chapter 19

Analysis of Manufactured Housing-Backed Securities

John N. Dunlevy, CFA, CPA
Director and Senior Portfolio Manager
Hyperion Capital Management, Inc.

Andrew Shook
Associate
NationsBanc Capital Markets, Inc.

INTRODUCTION

Manufactured housing, also referred to as mobile homes, are single-family detached homes constructed off-site and transported to a plot of land or to a manufactured housing community (park). Currently, manufactured housing is the fourth-largest sector of the asset-backed market (behind credit cards, automobiles and home equities), with over 100 deals outstanding totaling over $22 billion. In the previous chapter, the fundamentals of the manufactured housing market were presented. In this chapter we look at how to analyze manufactured housing-backed securities.

MANUFACTURED HOUSING ABS — OVERVIEW

There are two types of manufactured housing units: (1) single-section (also known as "single-wides") and; (2) multi-sections. Single-wide units, which are transported to their site in one piece, average 1,065 square feet. Multi-section units, on the other hand, are assembled at the site after being transported in pieces, and average 1,525 square feet. Exhibit 1 summarizes the manufactured housing loan characteristics.

    The typical manufactured housing loan is a 15- to 20-year fully amortizing retail installment loan. Single-section units are usually financed over 15-year terms at rates between 300 bps and 350 bps above conventional 30-year rates. Multi-section units are usually financed over 20-year terms at rates between 250 bps and 300 bps over conventional 30-year rates. Currently, only 10% of all units financed are written as mortgage loans (i.e., financed with the unit's land).

Exhibit 1: Manufactured Housing Loan Characteristics

	Single-Wide	Multi/Double-Wide	U.S. Average Site-Built
Average Home Size	1,065 Sq. Ft.	1,525 Sq. Ft.	1,945 Sq. Ft.
Average Sales Price	$26,000	$50,000	$143,000
Loan Rate vs. Conventional	+338 bps	+288 bps	—
Average Loan Term	200 mo.	240 mo.	360 mo.
Average Monthly Payment	$260	$406	$831

Source: Green Tree Financial

Exhibit 2: Total MH Issuance 1987-1995

Issuer	Number of Issues Outstanding	Percent	Dollar Value ($000) Issues Outstanding	Percent
Green Tree Financial	66	77%	15,735	82%
Security Pacific	6	7	919	5
Vanderbilt	3	4	539	3
RTC	3	4	616	3
Oakwood	3	4	468	3
Others	4	4	799	4
Total	85	100%	19,076	100%

Green Tree Financial continues to dominate the issuance of securities backed by Manufactured Housing loans. For example, during 1995 Green Tree issued $4 billion of the $5.8 billion MH securities issued. As shown in Exhibit 2, Green Tree is dominant in both number of issues outstanding as well as dollar value of securities outstanding.

Manufactured Housing Prepayment Experience

Manufactured housing has proven to be a market which is largely interest rate insensitive. We believe that this is the case due to four reasons. First, MH loans have small balances resulting in minimal saving from refinancings. (See Exhibit 3.) Even a decline of 200 basis points for a typical $35,000 MH loan would result in only a $44 monthly savings.

Second, manufacturing housing units, like cars, are subject to depreciation. In the early years of a loan's life, depreciation exceeds amortization leaving the borrower with little equity which is needed to refinance. Third, few refinancing options are currently available for used manufactured housing units. This is another reason why MH loans are insensitive to interest rate movements. Finally, MH borrowers may not qualify for alternative financings because of their limited financial resources.

Exhibit 3: Manufactured Housing Refinancing Incentive

	MH	Single-Family
Loan Balance	35,000	150,000
Term	200 mo.	360 mo.
Current Rate	11%	8%
Monthly Payment	$382	$1,100
-100 b.p.		
New Rate	10%	7%
New Payment	$360	$998
Savings	$22	$102
-200 b.p.		
New Rate	9%	6%
New Payment	$338	$899
Savings	$44	$201

Exhibit 4: Prepayment Sensitivity to Rate Movements (CPR)

	+300	+200	+100	0	-100	-200	-300	+300 BP range (CPR)
Mfd Housing ABS	6.0	6.0	6.0	6.0	11.3	13.4	15.8	9.8
Home Equity ABS	9.0	12.0	17.0	22.0	27.0	31.0	35.0	26.0
1994 FNMA 6.5	5.0	5.9	7.0	8.6	20.6	49.1	63.1	58.1

Source: Lehman Brothers

Exhibit 4 shows the interest rate sensitivity of manufacturing housing prepayments to interest rate movements. Manufactured housing have a CPR prepayment range (+300 to -300) of 9.8% CPR which was substantially lower than the 26.0 CPR and 58.1 CPR range for home-equity ABS and 30-year FNMAs, 6.5s, respectively.

Manufactured Housing ABS Credit Performance

In evaluating the credit performance of manufactured housing-backed ABS it is important to consider delinquencies, loss statistics, and rating agency upgrade/downgrade data.

In terms of delinquencies, the American Bankers Association (ABA) statistics show that total delinquencies were running at around 3% during 1995 (slightly higher than single-family mortgages) but higher than the 1% to 1.5% delinquency rates for automobiles, recreational vehicles, and boat loans. According to the Manufactured Housing Institute, delinquency levels since 1990 have ranged between 2.25% and 3.50%. Based on Green Tree static pool data, losses by cohort year are reported in Exhibit 5.

Exhibit 5: Green Tree MH Static Pool Losses

Year	Orig. Pool Size ($ billion)	Pool Factor	Loss % of Orig. Pool
1991	$0.6	0.47	4.55%
1992	1.4	0.58	2.16
1993	2.1	0.80	0.67
1994	3.2	0.90	0.16
1995	4.0	0.98	0.02

Exhibit 6: ABS Rating Changes

Asset Type	Number Upgrades	Number Downgrades	Upgrade / Downgrade Ratio
Automobiles	17	27	0.63
Credit Cards	7	14	0.50
Home Equity	4	7	0.57
Manufactured Housing	38	2	19.00
Other	4	6	0.67
Total	70	56	1.25

The default curve for manufactured housing starts off at a very low rate and peaks by year three. After year three the default rate will decline gradually until leveling off at about 50% of its peak level in year ten. Historical experience shows that loss severity ranges between 30% and 60% (double-wide units have the highest recovery rates).

Finally, the credit record for the manufactured housing sector has been excellent. For example, as shown in Exhibit 6, manufactured housing-backed securities has had more upgrades than any other ABS sector. As shown in the exhibit, the rating agency criteria for ABS appears very conservative. No single-rated ABS has ever defaulted due to performance problems. The downgrades shown above reflect third party credit-enhancement deterioration.

MH DEAL STRUCTURES

A typical structure, which is representative of late 1995 and 1996 deals is shown in Exhibit 7. The deal outlined in the exhibit was priced at a prepayment assumption of 100 MHP. MHP is a prepayment curve used for manufactured housing collateral, which assumes that prepayments start in month one at 3.7% CPR and rise 0.1% CPR per month until they reach 6% CPR in month 24, then stay constant at 6% CPR. Therefore, if a deal is priced at a 125 MHP assumption it is simply 1.25 times the 100 MHP vector (as just described).

Exhibit 7: Green Tree 1995-10 MH Structure

Class	Size ($MM)	% Deal	Rating	A/L	Window (Months)	Spread
A1	48.0	11.9%	AAA	1.05	1-24	+47
A2	63.0	15.5%	AAA	3.06	24-57	+48
A3	41.0	10.1%	AAA	5.07	41-73	+55
A4	33.0	8.1%	AAA	7.09	73-98	+71
A5	59.0	14.6%	AAA	10.25	98-152	+94
A6	92.0	22.7%	AAA	17.24	152-241	+145
M1	37.0	9.1%	AA−	12.57	63-241	+145
B1	16.0	4.0%	BBB+	8.30	63-143	+145
B2	16.0	4.0%	BBB+	17.20	143-241	+177
Total	405.0			9.25		

Collateral
No. Loans 11,805   New Unit %   83%
Avg. Size $34,134   Non-Park Unit %   72%
WAC   10.05%   WA LTV%   76%
WAM   280 M   Geographics:
                           10% North Carolina,
                           8% Michigan,
                           7% Texas

The deal shown in Exhibit 7 also assumes a 10% cleanup call. This is the same assumption used in nonagency CMOs as well as many other ABS sectors. The investor must be sure to understand that for the longer tranches, whether the tranche is priced to maturity or to the call provision.

Third, it is important for the investor to understand the deal's waterfall or cash flow priorities. The deal in the exhibit has sequential-pay priorities for classes A1 through A5 until the first crossover date. The crossover date refers to the date when the lockout period ends and the subordinated tranches (M and B1) begin to receive their pro-rate share of principal payments. Exhibit 8 shows the payment priority for Green Tree 1995-10.

As previously noted, the senior bonds pay sequentially until the crossover date, which is the latter month of 49 or when the deal's "step-down" tests (discussed below) are met. Exhibit 9 shows how losses are allocated within the structure. If losses were to exceed the first four loss priorities, then a pro-rata principal write-off would occur among the A1 to A6 tranches.

SENIOR BOND RELATIVE VALUE ANALYSIS

The structure, pricing details, Z-spreads, and OAS data for a recent deal -- Green Tree 1996-1 are in Exhibit 10.

Exhibit 8: Typical Green Tree MH Payment Priority

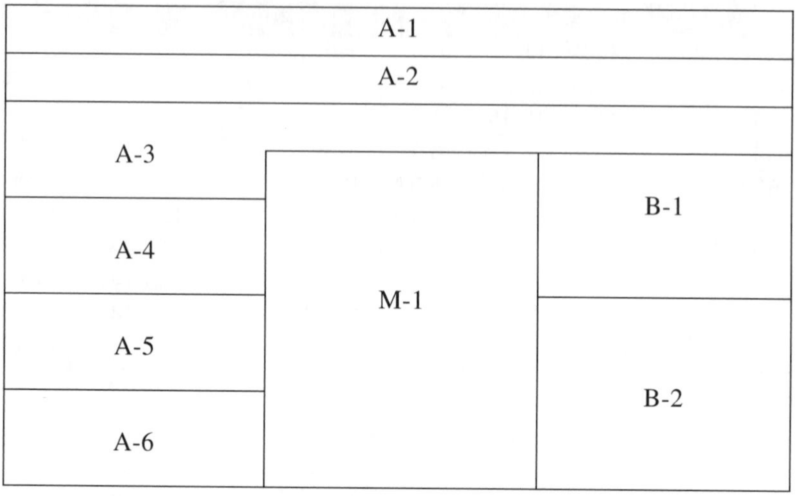

A-1

A-2

A-3		
A-4	M-1	B-1
A-5		B-2
A-6		

Exhibit 9: Typical Green Tree MH Loss Allocation

Loss Priority	Tranche	Credit Source	Credit
5th	A1-A6	Subordination	16%
4th	M1	Subordination	8%
3rd	B1	Subordination	4%
2nd	B2	Green Tree Guarantee	4%
1st	—	Excess Spread	349 bps

Exhibit 10: Green Tree 1996-1

Tranche	Size ($MM)	A/L	Window Months	Spread	Z-Spread	Option Cost	OAS
A1	120	2.1	1-48	50	42	7	35
A2	50	5.2	48-78	54	40	10	30
A3	35	7.5	78-95	71	70	18	52
A4	50	11.6	95-145	93	79	17	62
A5	76	17.5	145-309	145	101	11	90

Exhibit 11: Green Tree 1995-10 Step-Down Tests

M-1

Principal lockout until 12/99 (48 months)
Then must pass the following five tests:
1. Average 60-day delinquency ratio <3.5% of orig. pool balance
2. Average 30-day delinquency ratio <5.5% of orig. pool balance
3. Current losses <2.25% of orig pool balance
4. Cumulative losses must be less than:

48-59 months	<5.5% of orig. pool balance
60-71 months	<6.5% of orig. pool balance
72-83 months	<8.5% of orig. pool balance
84+ months	<9.5% of orig. pool balance

5. De-leveraging test

M1 + B principal	>25.5% of orig. pool balance

Based on nominal spreads, Z-spreads, and OAS analysis, the longer bonds in the senior structure seem to offer the best risk/return profile. The A4 bond, for example, at +93 versus the 10-year Treasury given the sectors stable prepayment profile is attractive versus the following alternative products:

Type	Spread	Z-Spread	OAS
MH	+93	79	62
Credit Cards	53	53	53
Corporate Industrial	35	35	35
Agency PAC	90	71	56

Finally, the senior bonds of manufactured housing ABS are both SMMEA and ERISA eligible.

Mezzanine and Subordinated Bond Analysis

Before analyzing the lower rated tranches on manufactured housing ABS, the investor must be sure to understand the priorities of cash flow which flow to these bonds. For example, the step-down tests used for the Green Tree 1995-10 deal is given in Exhibit 11. Likewise, the B1 and B2 tranches have to pass a similar series of tests in order to begin to receive principal.

The investor should know when the expected crossover date will occur. For example, Green Tree 1995-10 M1, although locked out for 48 months is not scheduled to receive any principal until month 63. This 100 MHP pricing assumption (138 MHP is needed to accelerate the principal date on M1 to month 49) is too slow to achieve step-down in month 49.

Exhibit 12: Evaluation of Subordinated Tranches of Green Tree 1996-1

Tranche	Size ($MM)	A/L	Window Months	Spread	Z-Spread	Option Cost	OAS
M1	36	11.9	49-309	145	124	13	111
B1	16	7.4	49-123	145	142	14	128
B2	16	20.0	123-309	175	130	13	117

It is therefore necessary to evaluate these tranches on an OAS basis in order to capture the extension risk in the structure. Exhibit 12 shows this evaluation for the subordinated tranches of Green Tree 1996-1.

Among the subordinated tranches shown above, we find the M1 bond is attractive versus the following alternative products:

AA Product	Spread	OAS
MH ABS	+145	111
Subordinated CMO	+150	135
CMBS	+115	90
Industrials	+50	50

Although AA-rated subordinated CMOs appear more attractive in the comparison above, MH ABS are publicly traded, increasing more liquid, and available in bigger block sizes than subordinated CMOs. However, the intermediate duration B1 tranche as shown below, does not appear attractive versus the following alternative BBB-rated products:

BBB Product	Spread	OAS
MH ABS	145	128
Subordinated CMO	230	215
CMBS	175	135
Industrials	75	75

Finally, the current attractiveness of the AA-rated M1 tranche is a relatively recent phenomenon. That is, through the end of January 1996 only five deals have been structured with this 11- to 12-year average life AA mezzanine structure. Prior to Green Tree 1995-7, the M1 tranche was a much longer bond (i.e., 17- to 19-year average life) due to a much longer principal lockout (crossover date).

SUMMARY

Manufactured housing ABS deals offer an intriguing combination of spread, prepayment stability, and growing liquidity. This chapter explains how to evaluate the relative attractiveness of manufactured housing ABS tranches.

Section III:

Commercial Mortage-Backed Securities

Introduction to Commercial Mortgage-Backed Securities

Joseph F. DeMichele
Vice President
Conseco Capital Management, Inc.

William J. Adams, CFA
Assistant Vice President
Conseco Capital Management, Inc.

INTRODUCTION

Commercial mortgage-backed securities (CMBS) are collateralized by loans on income-producing properties. The CMBS market has grown dramatically from its modest beginnings in the mid-1980s. Issuance, liquidity, and the number of investors participating in the CMBS market have all increased throughout the 1990s. This chapter gives a brief overview of the history and composition of the CMBS market. It also provides an introduction to the risks involving structure, optionality, and credit quality of CMBS that investors must be aware when allocating assets to this market sector.

HISTORY

During the 1980s, a strong economy, the deregulation of the financial services industry, and preferential tax treatment led to an explosion in the level of capital flows into the commercial real estate markets. Total commercial debt outstanding grew from over $400 billion in 1982 to approximately $1 trillion by 1990. Inevitably, extreme overbuilding caused the bubble to burst, and the boom of the 1980s was followed by a severe recession in the commercial property markets during the early 1990s. From 1990 to 1993, returns on income-producing properties fell by 28% as reported in the NCREIF Property Index.[1]

---

[1] Jonathan Adams, "CMBS Structures and Relative Value Analysis," Chapter 13 in Anand K. Bhattacharya and Frank J. Fabozzi (eds.), *Asset-Backed Securities* (New Hope: Frank J. Fabozzi Associates, 1996).

During the 1980s, the primary sources of commercial real estate funding were tax shelter syndicates, savings institutions, commercial banks, and life insurance companies. The Tax Reform Act of 1986 withdrew many real estate tax benefits and eliminated the tax shelter syndicates as a major source of funds. The severe devaluation of commercial property values in the early 1990s resulted in sizable losses among thrifts, banks, and insurance companies and led to a major retrenchment of lending activity by these traditional sources of commercial real estate funds. Two significant developments were born of this commercial real estate cycle downturn, one major and one minor, which precipitated the securitization of commercial loans.

The biggest contributing factor leading to the maturation of the CMBS market was the creation of the Resolution Trust Corporation (RTC). The RTC was created by Congress to facilitate the bailout of the ailing thrift industry. The mandate handed down from Congress was for the RTC to liquidate assets it acquired from insolvent thrifts as quickly and efficiently as possible. A large portion of the assets inherited by the RTC from the thrifts it acquired consisted of commercial mortgage loans. The RTC turned to the CMBS market to monetize its "investment." Between 1991 and 1993 it issued nearly $15 billion multi-family and mixed property CMBS. The large number of loans in each deal led to a high level of diversification much like what was found in the widely-accepted residential MBS market. The presence of an over-abundant level of credit protection through subordination, often in the form of cash, made the securities very attractive to investors.

The other occurrence, albeit minor, was the introduction of stricter risk-based capital charges for insurance companies at year-end 1993. These guidelines required insurance companies to hold larger capital reserves for whole-loan commercial mortgages than for securitized commercial mortgages, thus incentivising insurance companies to securitize their commercial mortgage holdings.

As can be seen in Exhibit 1, issuance has continued to expand since 1993, although the contribution from the RTC has fallen dramatically. As the RTC finished its job of liquidating insolvent thrifts, other issuers opportunistically stepped in to continue the growth of the CMBS market.

Witnessing the success of the RTC's foray into the CMBS market, many insurance companies, pension funds, and commercial banks began to use the CMBS market as a means of restructuring their balance sheets. Institutions began to utilize the CMBS market, as a means of liquidity for disposing of unwanted assets, to receive better regulatory treatment for holding securities in lieu of whole loans, or even simply to raise capital for underwriting more loans. As commercial real estate valuations have rebounded since the last recession, these traditional lenders have stepped up their commercial lending programs and have been a consistent source of issuance in the CMBS market.

The emergence of the commercial mortgage conduits also has fueled the expansion of CMBS issuance. Almost every major investment bank has established a conduit arrangement with a mortgage banker to originate commercial loans for the specific purpose of securitization. The number of commercial mortgage conduits providing real estate funding increased from less than five at the start of 1993 to over 30 at the start of 1995.[2] Conduit issuance has steadily grown as a percentage of total CMBS issuance (see Exhibit 2).

Exhibit 1: Private Label CMBS Issuance: 1987-1996p

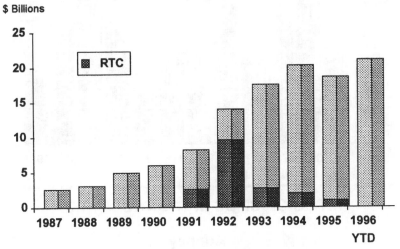

Source: Morgan Stanley, *Commercial Mortgage Alert*

Exhibit 2: Conduit Issuance: 1993-First Half 1996

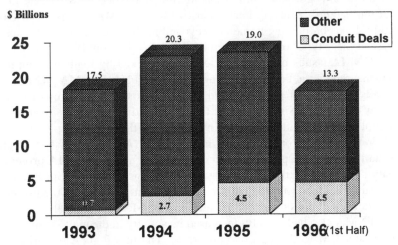

Source: Morgan Stanley, *Commercial Mortgage Alert*

[2] John Mulligan and Diane Parsley, *Commercial Mortgage-Backed Securities A Market Update* (New York: Donaldson, Lufkin, and Jenrette Securities Corp., February, 1995).

Exhibit 3: Multifamily Agency Issuance

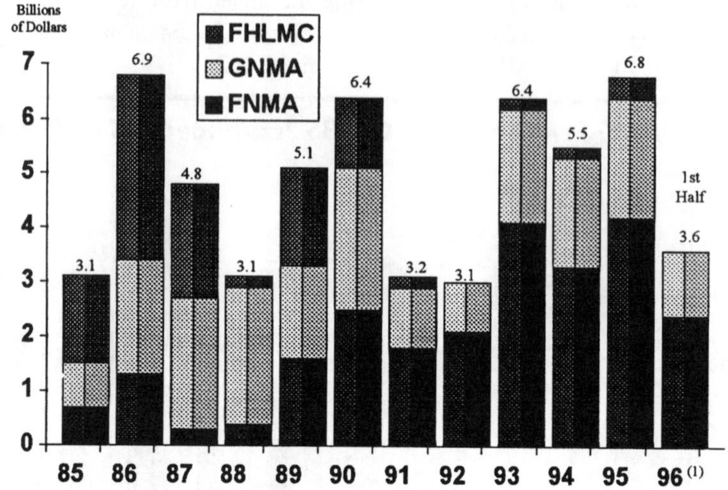

Note: (1) 1996 issuance for first six months.

TYPES OF CMBS IN TODAY'S MARKET

Agency

All three of the government's housing-related agencies (GNMA, FNMA, FHLMC) issue forms of CMBS. Because the mission of each of these agencies is to provide funding for residential housing, they have been involved in the issuance of multi-family housing loan securitizations. GNMA also issues securities backed by loans on nursing home projects and healthcare facilities. All agencies have issued these types of securities since 1985 (see Exhibit 3).

GNMA issues passthrough securities backed by loans on commercial projects insured by the Federal Housing Authority (FHA). GNMA guarantees full and timely payment of principal and interest. Most GNMA project loans are backed by a loan on a single facility, thereby negating any diversification effect that a pool of loans would provide. Any default on the underlying loan would be passed on to the investor as a prepayment. The FHA has established numerous multi-family insurance programs since its inception. Each GNMA project pool will vary depending on the underlying FHA insurance program. Specific characteristics such as project type, loan limit, prepayment features, or the presence of rent subsidies, will affect the performance of a GNMA project pool.

FNMA also has recently increased its activity in the multi-family market. FNMA issues CMBS through two programs. The first is its Alternative Credit Enhancement Structure (ACES) Program. Private lenders originate loans that qualify for this program. A senior/subordinate structure is used with a FNMA guarantee for payment of principal and interest on the senior portion, usually around 90 percent. The other, more popular FNMA securities, are issued under the Delegated Underwriting and Servicing (DUS) Program. Specific underwriting guidelines are set by FNMA for designated eligible lenders to originate loans. These loans are sold to FNMA, which then issues securities. Pools of one to five loans can be issued. The stringent call provisions have led FNMA to market these securities as substitutes for its bullet-pay agency debentures.

FHLMC issues multi-family securities through its Participation Certificate (PC) Program. The agency purchases qualifying loans and issues PCs in the same manner as its residential PC program. FHLMC was the dominant player of the three agencies before 1990. The commercial real estate recession led to a decrease in issuance from FHLMC. Recently, FHLMC issued a multi-family PC that resembles a larger, more diverse FNMA DUS pool. Backed by over 40 loans of strong credit quality, the pool provides more diversification than a DUS pool. Continued issuance of this type is expected.

Private Label

The majority of CMBS issued today are nonagency or private label securities. Some are collateralized by pools of seasoned commercial loans. The RTC deals were examples of CMBS backed by seasoned collateral. Newly-issued deals backed by seasoned collateral are generally the result of balance sheet restructuring by banks or insurance companies. As the commercial real estate market continues to rebound, the percentage of total issuance collateralized by seasoned loans will further decline. Many seasoned pools are characterized by a wide range of coupons and loan types and by widely varying prepayment protection.

Currently, more private label CMBS are backed by newly originated loans. These CMBS fall into two major categories: those backed by loans made to a single borrower, and those backed by loans made to multiple borrowers. Single borrower deals can involve one property or a group. Single property deals represent a small portion of the CMBS market (see Exhibit 4), and many are done as private placements. Usually, they are backed by large properties such as office buildings or regional malls. Although the transactions obviously lack diversity, information is generally more current and comprehensive. Insurance companies are the most common buyer, since many have the necessary real estate lending expertise to evaluate these deals. The attractiveness of the lower reserving requirement for CMBS over commercial whole loans also entices insurance companies.

Single borrower deals with a variety of properties are more common (Exhibit 4). Properties are run by a single management company. Real Estate Investment Trusts (REIT) sometimes issue this type of CMBS. Typically all the properties backing a particular deal are *cross-collateralized* and *cross-defaulted*. Should one property in the pool experience an impediment to cash flow, the cash generated from the other properties is used to support it. Should one property experience a default, all the remaining properties are defaulted. This is a strong disincentive against defaulting, preventing the borrower from walking away from lower quality properties. In essence, this feature allows the cash flow from stronger properties to support weaker ones. Another important characteristic of single borrower pools is the presence of release provisions. A *release provision* requires a borrower to prepay a percentage of the remaining balance of the underlying loans if it wishes to prepay one of the loans and remove the property from the pool. Thus the bondholders are protected from the borrower being able to remove the strongest properties from the pool.

The most common type of private label CMBS is backed by loans underwritten by more than one unrelated borrower on various property types (Exhibit 4). Conduit deals are the most prevalent example of multiple borrower deals in today's market. Because the loans are underwritten with the intent of securitization, conduit deals possess certain characteristics that are favorable to investors. Loan types tend to be more homogeneous, and call protection is strong. They also have more uniform underwriting standards, and information on credit statistics is generally readily available.

Another kind of CMBS deal found today is one backed by leases on a property. These *triple-net lease* or *credit tenant loan deals* are collateralized by lease agreements between the property owner and a tenant. As long as the lease cannot be terminated, the CMBS created have the same credit as any debt obligation of the underlying tenant. Additionally the bonds are secured by the property. The majority of these securities have been collateralized by mortgages on retail stores with lessees, such as Wal-Mart and Circuit City, who are rated by one of the nationally recognized rating organizations. Recently, mortgages on large office buildings with publicly rated tenants such as Merrill Lynch and Chubb have also been securitized.

Exhibit 4: Borrower Type: First Half 1996

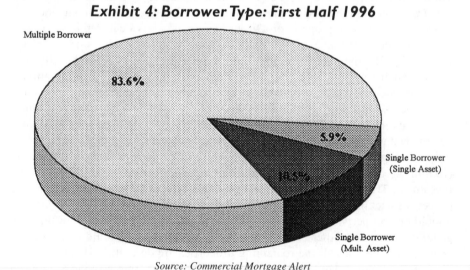

Source: Commercial Mortgage Alert

STRUCTURE OF CMBS

Senior/Subordinate Structure

The majority of private label CMBS created today utilize a *senior/subordinate structure*, whereby the cash flow generated by the pool of underlying commercial mortgages is used to create distinct classes of securities. Monthly cash flow is first used to pay the class with the highest priority, the senior classes. After interest and scheduled principal is paid to the senior classes, the remaining classes are paid in order of stated priority. Should cash flow collected from the pool be insufficient to pay off the bonds designated senior, the loss will be incurred first by the class with the lowest priority.

In a senior/subordinate structure the lower priority classes provide credit enhancement for the senior securities. The amount of subordination is determined in conjunction with the rating agencies in order to obtain the desired rating on the senior securities. Exhibit 5 shows an example of a hypothetical CMBS structure with subordination levels typical in the market as of the end of 1996. Note that the majority of securities created are senior classes. Subordination levels are set to attain a AAA credit rating on the senior class. This is the highest rating given by the rating agencies, and signifies bonds deemed to have minimal credit risk. Issuers set subordination levels such that the senior classes will receive this rating, thus being more attractive to investors. Rating agencies determine the appropriate amount of credit enhancement based on an analysis of the credit quality of the pool of commercial loans. This will be discussed in more detail later in the chapter.

In industry jargon, those non-senior securities receiving investment grade ratings are known as *mezzanine bonds*. Those rated non-investment grade are known as subordinate or "B" pieces. The class with the lowest payment priority is called the *first loss piece*. Any shortfall of cash flow on the commercial loan pool would affect this class first, thus putting it at the highest risk of a loss of principal. The risk profile of the other classes changes inversely to the priority of payment schedule.

Exhibit 5: Hypothetical CMBS Structure

Class	Rating	Size ($MM)	Description	Credit Support (%)	WAL (Years)	Principal Window
A1	AAA	343.00	Senior	32.55	7.00	1/97-7/05
B1	AA	30.60	Mezzanine	26.50	9.70	7/05-8/06
B2	A	30.60	Mezzanine	20.50	9.80	8/06-9/06
B3	BBB	25.50	Mezzanine	15.50	9.90	9/06-10/06
B4	BBB-	12.70	Mezzanine	13.00	9.90	10/06-10/06
B5	BB	30.60	Subordinate	7.00	10.00	10/06-11/06
C	B	17.80	Subordinate	3.50	10.00	11/06-11/06
D	NR	17.77	First Loss	NA	13.70	11/06-11/16
IO	AAA		IO			

Exhibit 6: Hypothetical CMBS Structure with Sequential Pay

Class	Rating	Size ($MM)	Description	Credit Support (%)	WAL (Years)	Principal Window
A1	AAA	130.00	Senior	32.55	5.70	1/97-7/05
A2	AAA	213.00	Senior	32.55	9.40	7/05-7/06
B1	AA	30.60	Mezzanine	26.50	9.70	7/06-8/06
B2	A	30.60	Mezzanine	20.50	9.80	8/06-9/06
B3	BBB	35.50	Mezzanine	15.50	9.90	9/06-10/06
B4	BBB-	12.70	Mezzanine	13.00	9.90	10/06-10/06
B5	BB	30.60	Subordinate	7.00	10.00	10/06-11/06
C	B	17.80	Subordinate	3.50	10.00	11/06-11/06
D	NR	17.77	First Loss	NA	13.70	11/06-11/06
IO	AAA		IO			

A unique feature of the senior/subordinate structure is the fact that credit enhancement can grow over time. Since principal is paid to the senior classes first, if no losses occur these classes will pay down faster than the mezzanine or subordinate pieces. This has the effect of increasing the amount of non-senior classes as a percentage of the entire deal and thus providing more enhancement to the remaining senior classes.

Additional forms of credit enhancement are available. For some deals, such as the RTC originated transactions, a cash account, known as a *reserve fund*, will be maintained to absorb losses and protect investors. *Overcollateralizing* is another form of credit enhancement. It refers to the excess of the aggregate balance of the pool of commercial loans over the aggregate balance of the bond classes created. Like a reserve fund, losses would be absorbed by the amount of excess collateral before affecting any of the bond classes.

Paydown Structures

The most common principal paydown method used in CMBS is the *sequential-pay method*. All principal paydowns, both scheduled and prepaid, are allocated entirely to the most senior class outstanding. Occasionally, a variant of the sequential-pay structure is used. The pool of loans may be segregated into loan groups with each loan group collateralizing a specific set of bond classes. In either pay down structure, principal payments can be designated further to create different bonds within the same class. In Exhibit 6, we have altered slightly our hypothetical CMBS to illustrate this technique. The senior class has been further tranched to create two bonds, A1 and A2. Principal is allocated to A1 before A2, thus creating two senior bonds with different average lives.

Interest Payments

In a CMBS structure, all interest payments generated by the underlying commercial loans can be used to pay either interest or principal payments on the created securities. One alternative is to have all the interest received used to pay interest on the bonds. The principal weighted-average coupon on the bonds can be set to equal the principal weighted-average coupon on the pool of loans. In this case, as different loans with different coupons in the pool pay down, the principal weighted-average coupon on the pool will change. In turn, the amount of cash flow available to pay interest on the bonds will vary. Thus, the coupons on the bonds will be variable. CMBS classes from this structure are said to have *WAC coupons*.

In order to create fixed coupon bonds, the most common method used in CMBS structures is to set the highest coupon on the securities lower than the lowest coupon of the underlying loans. This will ensure that there will be a sufficient amount of interest payments generated by the pool to make all interest payments on the securities. This will lead to a higher level of interest cash flow from the pool of loans than is required to pay interest on the bonds. This extra cash flow is known as *excess interest*.

In some cases excess interest is used to paydown principal on the most senior bonds outstanding. Under this type of structure the more senior classes will amortize at a rate faster than the junior classes, thus leading to overcollateralization and providing additional credit enhancement for the deal.

More frequently, the excess interest is used to form an *interest-only* or *IO class*. The IO class receives no principal. Its yield is determined solely by the interest cash flow generated by the pool of loans. If the principal balance of a loan is paid prior to its maturity, the yield of the IO will fall. Should a principal payment extend beyond maturity for a loan, the yield will rise.

Underlying Mortgage Type

There are several mortgage loan types that back CMBS deals. The most common are fully amortizing loans, amortizing balloon loans, and interest-only balloons. All else being equal, the faster the amortization of the loan, the faster equity is built up in the property, and the less risk of default. Fully amortizing loans provide the best credit profile. Balloon mortgages also introduce the notion of extension risk, which will be discussed later.

Commercial mortgage loans may have fixed or variable interest rates. If variable rate loans are uncapped, and rates rise substantially, the income generated by the property may not be enough to service the debt. Also, if variable rate mortgages are used to structure CMBS with fixed rate classes, basis risk will exist, and interest on the loans may not cover coupon payments on the bonds.

OPTIONALITY

Prepayment Risk

As with most mortgage-backed securities, CMBS have inherent prepayment risk. The underlying commercial mortgages may be prepaid by the borrower. Prepayments on CMBS will affect the yield and average lives of the bonds issued, particularly interest-only securities. Fortunately for investors, most commercial mortgages have explicit provisions that preclude borrowers from prepaying.

The most onerous to a borrower is the *prepayment lock-out*. Written into the loan agreement, a lock-out is a provision preventing any prepayments for a set time period. The time may vary, but generally will range from three to five years.

Another form of prepayment protection in CMBS structures is called *yield maintenance*. The yield maintenance provision is designed to create a disincentive for the borrower to prepay. If the borrower chooses to prepay, the lender must be compensated for any lost yield. If market interest rates are lower than when the loan was originated, the borrower must reimburse the lender for any lost interest income. The yield maintenance penalty would be equal to the income that would have been earned by the lender less what would now be earned by reinvesting the prepaid proceeds at the risk-free Treasury rate.

A third form of prepayment protection is the prepayment penalty in the case of a prepaid loan. This will typically take the form of a fixed percentage of the remaining principal balance of the loan. The most common penalty in today's market is the "5-4-3-2-1" penalty. During the first year of the penalty period, the prepayment penalty would be equal to 5% of the unpaid principal balance of the loan. In year two, the penalty would decline to 4%, and so on.

Today, most commercial mortgages backing CMBS possess some combination of these three prepayment provisions. However, many loan agreements allow for prepayment penalties to decrease over time with the loans becoming freely prepayable during the last six to nine months of the life of each loan.

During the time that these prepayment provisions are in place, the predominant cause of prepayments will be defaults. After these provisions have expired the prevailing interest rate environment will become a determinant of prepayments as in the residential mortgage market. Other factors, such as retained equity, will affect the level of prepayments. If capital improvements are needed and cheaper financing cannot be found, the owner will most likely prepay the loan in order to refinance. If the property has appreciated sufficiently in value or net operating income has grown enough to cover additional leverage, the owner will most likely do an equity take-out refinancing.

Unfortunately, the amount of data available on prepayments in the CMBS market pales in comparison to the residential mortgage market. Data available are mostly from the RTC deals. Underwriting standards as well as the current real estate market environment are much different today and bring the validity of comparisons on prepayments into question. Additionally, the lack of a dominant, measurable variable such as interest rates makes option analysis much more difficult than with residential mortgage-backed securities. Fortunately, the call protection provided by the various prepayment provisions in CMBS helps to significantly offset these factors.

Extension Risk

The majority of CMBS issued today are collateralized by balloon mortgages. In order to meet the balloon principal payment the borrower will have to either sell the property or refinance the loan. Should neither be possible, the servicer usually has the option to extend the loan beyond the balloon date. The extension option varies but typically cannot exceed three years. Rating agencies generally require the stated final maturity of the bond to be four or five years beyond the maturity of the underlying loans. This would allow time for foreclosure and workout should refinancing be unavailable.

Factors that affect extension risk are loan-to-value (LTV) and the interest rate environment at the balloon date. Should property values fall, LTV will rise, and refinancing will be more difficult, thus increasing extension risk. Likewise, if interest rates are high enough such that the income produced by the property does not generate an acceptable debt service ratio, refinancing may not be obtainable.

EVALUATING CREDIT QUALITY IN COMMERCIAL MORTGAGE-BACKED SECURITIES

As the commercial mortgage-backed securities market continues to grow in both dollar amount and investor acceptance, a move toward an acceptance of standardization appears evident. This may prove to be an alarming trend if investors in these securities are lowering credit standards or reducing their level of analysis in exchange for yield and favorable regulatory treatment. Prudent investors must remember that these securities require a consistent level of credit and cash flow analyses, well beyond that of standardized structured collateral. The best analysis for the securities must combine elements of both structured finance and fundamental collateral and credit analyses. Therefore, in this section, we attempt to build a basic, analytical framework for CMBS transactions, which starts with the previously discussed development and appreciation of the forces which created this market. Next, the inherent volatility and cash flow variability of the underlying commercial mortgages are described. Finally, a means of dealing with the unique characteristics of the collateral, including underwriting standards and structural features, is presented. The point of this section is to focus investor attention on relative value and issues affecting the quality of various CMBS transactions in the market.

Earlier, we discussed the development of liquidity in the CMBS market from direct real estate lending to securitization. Readily available capital for the asset class led to excessive development which culminated in the early 1990s real estate recession. The RTC was created to monetize problem commercial real estate. It did so through structured securities, thereby broadening the investor base and creating many of the structural and legal features of the market today. During this time, a black cloud formed over commercial real estate as an investment. Traditional real estate investors left the market, creating both a liquidity crisis for any new and/or existing financing and an over-supply of additional product due to a reduction in exposure to the asset class. In this void, Wall Street's expertise and capital was required, thereby fueling the CMBS market as we know it today.

The current commercial real estate market combines the two elements described above: the RTC's structure and Wall Street's capital. In the mid-1990s, commercial real estate appears to have recovered from its recent problems. The RTC's role is diminishing to zero, fewer banks and insurers are selling the asset class (in fact, many traditional long-term real estate investors have returned to the market), and, most important, Wall Street's capital remains in the market in the form of conduits. Conduits are now the (re)financing vehicle of choice for real estate owners and developers starved for regular sources of capital. Conduits originate and then securitize real estate loans, rather than maintain the credit risk on their own balance sheet. Typically, conduits take the form of mortgage brokers/bankers backed by an investment bank or commercial banks. Mortgage brokers originate and underwrite commercial mortgages using the capital, warehousing, and distribution channels of the investment bank. A commercial bank provides all such functions, thereby offering it a viable commercial real estate operation, while maintaining significantly lower levels of direct real estate exposure on its balance sheet.

As the CMBS market has evolved, the commercial mortgage market has taken an interesting turn (or return, in this case). With traditional real estate lenders returning to the market along with the capital provided by real estate investment trusts, the highest quality properties (Class A) are rarely available for conduit programs. As such, most commercial real estate underwritten by conduits is average, at best, typically Class B and C quality. Historically, this asset class was the domain of the S&Ls. Wall Street's capital, therefore, is filling a financing void left by the S&Ls, while securitization is transferring risks. These two points are key. It is important to understand the issues and reasons why S&L collateral became RTC collateral and avoid those mistakes again. By structuring commercial real estate mortgages, investors best suited to manage real estate risks are those investors getting paid for it, while investors without the necessary real estate analysis capabilities receive the benefits of the asset class without having to staff a complete real estate operation.

While this brief description of the evolution of commercial real estate lending is clearly simplified, we discuss the nature and role of conduits to raise specific points about evaluating CMBS. This is a highly competitive business involving many constituencies with conflicting interests. The competition is likely causing both spread compression (cheaper capital) and lower quality underwriting standards and/or property quality; these are two inconsistent forces. However, demand for the securities from the investment community remains strong, and, as such, issuance is likely to continue its current rapid pace. Therefore, within this environment, it is even more important to provide a proper framework for credit analysis for CMBS.

THE UNDERLYING COMMERCIAL
REAL ESTATE MORTGAGES

If Wall Street's conduit programs have truly replaced S&L's historical financing role, obviously the historical performance of this class of commercial mortgage assets should be assessed when analyzing today's conduit product. However, the lack of historical information on the CMBS market is problematic. The traditional real estate asset is far from standardized, varying significantly by property type, market, transaction, and ownership structure. As such, consistent and standardized historical performance information is not available to the market, and, therefore, credit ratings and valuation decisions are often driven largely by generalizations about the collateral, near-term performance of the assets, and analysis of small, non-uniform portfolio characteristics. While this market is often standardized under the CMBS heading, it is crucial to consider the significant differences amongst the variety of assets found in a pool, as well as the resulting differences in underwriting criteria demanded. Thus, investors will have a better sense of the differences found in today's CMBS pools and the stability of the individual cash flows and valuations.

Multi-Family

Multi-family housing generally is considered to be a more stable real estate investment. Cash flows typically are quite consistent, and valuations are much less volatile than other types of income producing properties, due to the stable demand for rental housing. However, the asset also is tends to be the most commodity-like income-producing property type, making it more susceptible to competitive pressures and rapid changes in supply and demand. Multi-family properties are unique in that they combine elements of both commercial, income-producing real estate, and residential housing. As such, the traditional analysis of commercial real estate (location, property quality, market dynamics, etc.) is an important consideration for the properties, while the impact of its residential characteristics also needs to be recognized.

The primary difference between multi-family properties and other types of income-producing properties involves the lease term of the typical tenant, and the diversification provided by the large number of available units for rent relative to office or retail space. Residents in multi-family properties are obligated on short-term leases, ranging from six months to two years. This is a positive characteristic of the projects in that it permits the property to adjust quickly to improving market conditions, and also provides owners with regular opportunities to pass through increased operating costs. However, the inverse is also true, as multi-family properties are susceptible to increased supply or competitive pressures and weakening economic or demographic trends within market. This is especially true in strong multi-family markets, as the barriers to entry are low enough for multi-family developers to quickly bring supply into any given market.

These characteristics demand an understanding of key housing trends in the local geographic areas, and the age and condition of the individual property, as well as its ability to remain competitive within its market. Property owners and underwriters must allocate money for maintenance spending. Absent such upkeep, apartments can quickly deteriorate and show significant underperformance of cash flows. Also, consider historical performance of the market (boom/bust versus conservative capital allocation) as well as the outlook for markets in which the pool is heavily weighted. One year's operating performance is the typical underwriting period for multi-family properties, often completed with little sense of the past or expected market conditions going forward.

Retail/Shopping Center

Retail real estate ranges from large super-regional malls to smaller neighborhood shopping centers. As implied by the names, this space is differentiated by its size. Regional and super-regional malls are typically enclosed structures, ranging from 500,000 square feet to upwards of 3 million square feet. These properties generally are well-known, high quality shopping centers within the property's given market and surrounding area. The malls are anchored by nationally-recognized department stores and retail tenants, and maintain significant fill-in, small shop space. The assets are primarily the domain of long-term, direct real estate investors (such as insurers or pension funds) or equity REITs, and are rarely found in pooled CMBS transactions; those assets in the CMBS market primarily are in the form of single asset transactions. Given the unique positioning and retail exposure of most large malls, as well as high barriers to entry, cash flows are often quite stable for this asset class.

Community and neighborhood shopping centers are more likely to be found in today's conduit transactions, and these properties' cash flows can prove to be more volatile. The properties are usually an open-air format, ranging in size from under 100,000 square feet to 500,000 square feet, serving a smaller market area than the larger malls. The properties often are anchored by necessity-based retailers, such as national and regional discount chains, grocery markets and drug stores. Smaller centers are sometimes unanchored. The anchors serve as a drawing point for customer traffic to the smaller, in-line stores, which also are often characterized by necessity shopping and convenience (banks, dry cleaners, video rental, small restaurants, for instance). The properties are standardized, nondescript neighborhood convenience centers, which implies that an accessible location is a key valuation feature. Also, the properties are susceptible to competition and new development, so regular maintenance spending is important in keeping the centers competitive.

When evaluating retail real estate, an investor should consider the following: the age and quality of the property, the presence and quality of anchors tenants in the center, location and accessibility, sales volume on a square foot basis, competitive development, sales trends, and occupancy costs in relation to sales volumes. Recognize the excessive growth in retail real estate space over the past ten years. According to some national surveys, the growth of retail space in the United States over the past decade increased almost 40%, exceeding annualized population growth by more than a full percentage point. Certainly, some space has been removed from service over this time as well. However, the growth trends remain striking. Of particular interest for conduit investors is the above-average growth of neighborhood and community centers. As stated earlier, retail exposure in today's conduit transactions is typically neighborhood and community centers in the Class B and Class C quality range.

Office

Office space is a unique component of the commercial real estate market. Office buildings comprise over 25% of real estate space in the United States, but the exposure is highly fragmented and diverse. Significant differences between various classes of space exist, ranging from renowned Class A landmarks to poorly located, aging Class C space in need of both deferred maintenance spending and capital improvements. Properties are also classified by location, ranging from the central business district (CBD) to suburban space. CBD settings are tightly grouped on small parcels of land, typically representing the "downtown" business districts of the representative market. Suburban space, on the other hand, is more widely dispersed on larger areas of land often grouped in the business park setting. During the past decade nearly 70% of office space constructed in the United States was built in a suburban setting, due in part to cheaper construction and lower priced land costs, as well as the continued "suburbanization" of corporate America. These facts along with excellent, decentralized distribution locations will likely keep suburban office space competitive over the long term.

The office sector also presents unique credit issues to analyze. The sector experienced significant overbuilding in the 1980s and also proved susceptible to corporate downsizing. Rental rates are extremely volatile and occupancy levels can swing dramatically. The properties typically are subject to longer-term leases and require significant spending for maintenance and improvements, tenant build-outs, and leasing commissions. Information regarding lease rollover schedules, tenant quality and retention rates, down time between leases, and rental stream forecasting (effective rent versus straight line rents in periods of free rent and over/under market rent conditions) are necessary to understand the performance of office properties. Future market conditions are also important to consider, since markets can change dramatically with the addition of new, large projects. Given this cash flow volatility, both investors and rating agencies continue to demand strong debt service coverage ratios and adequate credit enhancement for office properties within conduit pools.

Other Operating Properties

Recent CMBS transactions are beginning to include other non-traditional real estate investments, characterized by higher cash flow volatility, as well as an operating/business component. Hotels, for instance, continue to represent a growing component of transactions, as do self-storage centers and health care facilities. While a detailed description of these commercial assets is not appropriate for this analysis, some description of the issues affecting property quality and volatility is important. These properties maintain a high correlation with the macro-economic forces shaping property performance, are very susceptible to increased competition and supply, and possess high operating leverage. Volatility of the cash flows can be as high as 30% to 50%, from peak to trough; therefore, rating agencies and investors demand higher underwriting standards and credit enhancement for these assets. Additionally, the operating business component results in volatile income due to typical real estate forces affecting commercial properties, but also as a result of management's ability to operate and maintain the property's competitiveness.

UNDERWRITING CRITERIA

One method analysts use to evaluate cash flow volatility among different property types and property qualities is mortgage underwriting standards. Clearly, the credit quality of any commercial mortgage pool is determined by the underlying collateral's ability to function as an income producing, debt servicing property over a defined time period. Several financial ratios are available for determining the credit quality of the property, including a ratio of cash flow to the required debt service (DSC) and a ratio of the mortgage loan amount to the value of the property (loan to value or LTV).

In many ways, debt service coverage is a more important credit analysis tool available for real estate securities than is valuation. This cash flow ratio compares a property's net operating income (NOI) to its required debt service payments, with NOI defined as income less property operating expenses and an allowance for maintenance capital spending or replacement reserves. Typically, NOI also will include other recurring expense items demanded by an individual property, such as leasing commissions for retail properties or tenant buildout costs for office properties. The data are often calculated on a trailing 12-month basis. However, shorter reporting periods are annualized or longer reporting periods averaged. Whatever the case, a true picture of normalized operating performance is required to understand the property's ability to service its debt load. More often than not, a reporting period may overstate NOI due to above-market leases, stronger than expected occupancy levels, or leasing commissions/tenant buildout costs not commensurate with the existing lease rollover schedule. In such a case, it is imperative to normalize operating cash flow, and consider its impact on the credit profile of the individual property or collateral pool.

The credit rating agencies attempt to quantify the process of normalizing cash flow by reporting the agency's variance figure. Expressed on a percentage basis, the variance figure calculates the rating agency's re-underwritten (or normalized) cash flow figure relative to the cash flow reported by the mortgage originators. Recently, the rating agencies have "haircut" reported NOI for a variety of reasons, including above-market rents and occupancy levels, below-market mortgage interest rates, normalized amortization, management fees, tenant buildout costs, leasing commissions, replacement reserves, and deferred maintenance. Potentially volatile cash flows derived from a property or the pool must be accounted for in the initial valuation of the CMBS transaction. Additionally, when armed with both underwritten and normalized NOI, investors can determine the appropriate level of DSC for a given property or pool to account for volatility in the cash flows and its ability to service debt. This figure can be as low as 1.1× to 1.15× for stable properties with a positive outlook to 1.6× to 1.7× for properties subject to highly volatile cash flows.

Loan to value is another analytical tool used to compare the property's debt level to its current valuation, as well as its loan balance at maturity. While third-party appraisals are used in this process, which are subject to significant interpretation, a general sense of a property's or pool's loan to value ratio allows one to address refinancing risks. Clearly, lenders and investors should require equity, in line with the property's quality and cash flow volatility. Equally important is an acceptable level of debt amortization over the life of the loan. In doing so, investors protect themselves from shifts in valuation, whether driven by true changes in cash flows or the required rate of return demanded for the asset class. The equity portion of a property's capitalization also tends to incent property owners to properly maintain the asset. Finally, investors protect themselves at maturity by reducing the LTV ratio over the life of the loan through amortization, thereby increasing the likelihood of refinancing the property when the loan is due. If refinancing at maturity is unlikely, then investors must factor in principal shortfalls or extension risks. To repeat, standards for LTV ratios vary by property type with stable multi-family units pressing the 75% level and riskier hotels or offices sometimes as low as 50% to 55%.

Portfolio Issues

CMBS investors also must focus on a number of portfolio issues, especially those involving the composition of the total collateral pool. The benefits of the CMBS structure derive from an ability to make real estate investments without the risks associated with direct mortgage or equity placements (i.e., diversification by property type, loan size and type, geography, borrower, and tenant). As discussed, diversification by property type should be evident, as a well-mixed pool clearly will overcome the cash flow volatility of any one property type. Geographic diversification is also important, because commercial real estate performance is a function of local and regional economics, demographics, and employment conditions. Higher state concentrations increase the correlation amongst properties, thus offsetting the benefits of diversification. Loan size and borrower/tenant concentration are also important features of a well-diversified mortgage pool, as greater loan diversity by size or borrower diminishes investor reliance upon and exposure to any one property, set of properties, or individual borrower or tenant performance.

STRUCTURING — TRANSFERRING RISKS AND RETURNS

We have attempted to provide a continuum of stability amongst the various property types typically found in today's CMBS transactions, as well as the resulting underwriting issues created by cash flow variability. As discussed, the standard structure in today's conduit deals is a senior/subordinate structure which transfers significant risk to the underlying equity and support bonds. This risk is typically borne by the master or special servicers or some other real estate professionals, which will be discussed in more detail later. On a portfolio level, these issues are manifested by the level of credit enhancement demanded by the rating agencies for any given rating category. Therefore, one must recognize that varying levels of credit enhancement and the subsequent differences in valuation from one security to the next represent the ratings agencies' and investment community's attempt to cope with the cash flow and valuation variability of the underlying collateral. As such, excessive credit enhancement for a pool is not necessarily a good investment characteristic, but could indicate high expected cash flow volatility and/or poor property quality.

Compare standardized residential mortgage pools requiring 6% to 8% credit support at the AAA level, versus 28% to 34% credit support often found in commercial mortgage pools. The CMBS level of credit support is designed specifically to recognize the lack of standardization of the underlying collateral, cash flow volatility, and the higher default frequency and loss severity on commercial mortgage securities. As stated, some commercial properties require DSC ratios as high as 1.6× to 1.7×, indicating cash flow variability in excess of 40%. The property's ability to service its debt load is driven by any number of controllable and non-controllable factors. Residential housing, on the other hand, is owned by its occupants and holds a much more meaningful position to its occupants, other than holding a put option on the property. As such, volatility is significantly higher for commercial mortgages, and the level of credit support required to protect senior investors is more substantial.

Default frequency and loss severity are also important issues to consider when investing in commercial mortgage securities. Typically, individual assets are structured in bankruptcy-remote entities or some other type of isolation from third-party bankruptcy risks. Therefore, there is no recourse to the borrower's assets beyond the equity in the property. While low LTV ratios alleviate some risks in this scenario, maintaining equity value when a commercial mortgage has reached the point of default is often futile. Often, property level cash flows have fallen, and, for properties underwritten with a low DSC ratio, debt service requirements may exceed cash flow. Additionally, property cash flow problems which are driven by macro-economic issues (over-building or weakening economic conditions, for instance) will have a substantial impact on valuations. In this environment, equity withers and properties that do not cover debt service become uneconomical. Borrowers without a contractual obligation, incentive and/or an ability to fund losses are forced to default, and the decision to do so is certainly easier than that of a residential mortgage.

Loss severity on the typical commercial real estate default is also impacted in this scenario and is often higher than residential mortgage losses. Valuation drops as the property's performance weakens. However, this loss is exacerbated by market forces which demand either higher rates of return on the asset class and/or stronger equity coverage (i.e., more mortgage losses on the original loan balance). Finally, the costs of liquidating commercial mortgages exceeds those of residential mortgages. The assets are large and unique, and often in need of capital improvements or deferred maintenance. The investor population is smaller, more sophisticated and specialized, while there are costs associated with the property (taxes, insurance, etc.) that must be carried often for extended marketing periods. As such, loss severities approaching 60% or 70% are not unreasonable. Clearly, for this asset class, the original cash flows, debt service coverage, and loan to value ratios are the mitigant to these risks, and, therefore, must be thoroughly analyzed and understood when the transactions are originated.

Master and Special Servicers

A final important structural feature of CMBS transactions is the presence of both master and special servicers. Master servicers manage the routine, day-to-day administration functions required by all structured securities or collateralized transactions, while special servicers are used to handle delinquent loans and work-out situations. Assigned the task of maximizing the recovery on a defaulted loan, special servicers play an important role in CMBS transactions as both defaults and work-outs are frequent and specialized. Often, the servicer's interests are aligned with investors as servicers are now investing in non-rated and subordinate bonds within the deals they service. Thus, it is important to assess the quality and competency of the servicer. Investors should consider the level of latitude and advancing capabilities provided the servicer in a work-out situation, its financial condition, historical performance and experience within the commercial real estate asset class (and in work-out situations, if applicable), and the monitoring, reporting and servicing capabilities (including cash management and collections operations). Investors must be comfortable with the servicer's ability to function effectively in that role, as well as the outlook for the servicer's continued viability.

Regulatory Issues

Increasingly, CMBS have been afforded favorable regulatory treatment. The National Association of Insurance Commissioners (NAIC) recognizes CMBS as securities rather than real estate. This allows for a capital reserve requirement ranging from 0.03% to 1.0% for investment grade fixed-income securities compared with 3.0% for commercial mortgages. Bank regulators currently are considering lowering the risk-based capital weighting on AAA rated CMBS to 20%. Currently, the risk weighting is 100%. The Department of Labor also is continuing to study the possibility of granting an ERISA exemption to CMBS. Should this change occur, ERISA-guided pension plans would be able to purchase investment grade CMBS. Clearly, the growing CMBS market would benefit from these new investors, as new capital would support the securities, increase coverage and improve liquidity.

CONCLUSION

In this chapter, we presented an overview of the development of the CMBS market and a discussion of the current issues facing investors today. Commercial real estate lending is evolving into sophisticated, structured securities that represent a growing portion of the fixed income market. Despite trading under the general CMBS heading, the securities and the underlying collateral are specialized and unique, thereby presenting investors with new challenges, as well as potentially higher return. As pointed out, the securities must be recognized for the individual characteristics which differentiate them, thereby demanding prudent analysis. If recent issuance is any indication, this market should continue to expand, and new investors will continue to enter the market. With the continued expansion of available securities and investors, as well as new performance data, the market likely will differentiate the securities by quality. This chapter presents an introduction to those issues and security types which affect the quality of CMBS transactions and the market's investment potential going forward.

Chapter 21

Rating of Commercial Mortgage-Backed Securities

Joseph C. Franzetti
Senior Vice President
Duff & Phelps Credit Rating Co.

INTRODUCTION

The ratings of commercial mortgage-backed securities are opinions of credit worthiness. There are four major rating agencies currently involved in providing ratings for these types of securities. While there are a great many areas of similarity, there are unique aspects to each rating agency's approach. This chapter attempts to deal with the major rating issues, but is written from the view point of Duff & Phelps Credit Rating Company.

For over a decade rating agencies have been assigning ratings to commercial mortgage-backed securities. The structures are usually either bond type securities in which a mortgage and note on a cross-collateralized package of loans is pledged as collateral, or pass-through certificates in which the securities rated represent ownership in a trust that, in turn, owns certain mortgage loans.

The property types collateralized are normally retail, office, multifamily, industrial and other income-producing properties. The rating agency approach is to analyze the cash flow and value of the collateral as well as the mortgage and security structure. Issuers, their counsel, accountants and investment bankers present the collateral information, mortgage and security documents to be reviewed for the rating. Rating agencies rely on this information as well as other due diligence reports (i.e., appraisals, engineering and environmental reports) and legal opinions. Except as needed to disclose certain information in support of the analytical conclusions reached in the rating process, the information is usually kept confidential.

The rating process is comprised of four steps:

This chapter was compiled from various reports produced by the Commercial Mortgage Backed Securities group at Duff & Phelps Credit Rating Co. Additional contributions were made by Patrick Sargent of Andrews & Kurth LLP.

- preliminary assessment of the transaction based on a term sheet, financial statements and other relevant data,
- site visits, cash flow analysis and review of other outside due diligence information,
- review of deal structure, legal documents and legal, and
- Credit Rating Committee review and assignment of rating.

UNDERWRITING APPROACH

This section describes the rating approach to individual property analysis and underwriting. The main areas of analysis in the rating process are: (1) discussion of the market area and economy in which the property is located, including an examination of the competition, (2) analysis of the property's physical quality and location, and (3) analysis of the property's lease structure and financial attributes.

Market and Site Area

Location is the most important factor to the current and long-term viability of real estate. Site inspections are performed for the majority properties in the transaction, with the exception of large pool issues. In such cases, a statistical sampling determines the properties to be visited. The site inspection considers issues such as visibility and accessibility (ingress and egress), as well as convenience to major thoroughfares, transportation centers, employment sources, retail areas, hotel and hospital services, and educational and recreational facilities. Other factors that affect real estate marketability include compatibility with the surrounding neighborhood, recent and proposed development, and the strength of local real estate values.

The market area is defined on an individual basis and requires a broader analysis than the specific site review. The market area review includes an evaluation of competitive properties, supply and demand characteristics, and a review of nearby land use development for the defined market area. The market analysis also involves contacting local real estate professionals for current rental and sales information, vacancy levels, new construction and absorption.

For all property types, historical rental rates and occupancy levels, average lease terms and rent concessions are reviewed for the property as well as the market. The current demand, including historical and current absorption data, is reviewed. The corresponding supply, including projected additions along with the historical market occupancy, is also analyzed. The property's lease terms, including concessions, are compared with those currently prevalent in the market before real estate cash flow projections are developed. Information about property expenses is derived from the subject and competitive properties.

This information is compared with market averages found in industry reports such as those issued by the Building Owners and Managers Association

(BOMA), the Institute of Real Estate Management (IREM), or the Urban Land Institute (ULI). Additional demographic data are collected from local and national sources. Where available, specific local or property type market surveys provide additional information on market characteristics. All information collected in the field is compared with information provided in the appraisal and/or other information submitted.

The market and site analysis is the most important component in analyzing a property. The demand for and marketability of the property are the primary determinants in analyzing its potential for continuous occupancy. While the site and market area review criteria apply to all property types, there are differences in the focus of review for various property types. The following paragraphs outline those unique property issues.

Office Properties

There is a wide range of office property types, with different qualitative considerations for each. Space in a central business district has significantly different site and market characteristics than a suburban office building. Similarly, the definition of "market area" for these property types would be substantially different.

Generally, office properties depend on the strength and stability of the market area as a desirable business location. The success of the location will depend on the area economy, which impacts the ability to attract stable tenants on a consistent basis. Construction in most markets peaked in about 1986 and declined rapidly to a halt thereafter. The supply moratorium has begun to have an impact. Vacancies have stabilized in most markets, though there remains a huge oversupply. However, recent demographic trends in unemployment suggest office users are requiring less space, which has slowed the absorption of the oversupply and may impact the future demand for space.

There recently has been a trend toward bifurcation in the office markets of most central business districts into those that are technologically capable of accommodating the modern business user and those that are not. The latter continue to suffer physical and functional obsolescence and may never return to competitiveness. Floor plate sizes and layout will affect marketability, as will access to transportation and similar business users. Replacement cost currently exceeds economic value, therefore, new construction is neither justified nor anticipated in the near term.

Office properties require significant cash infusion over time to provide for general capital expenditures and to provide for tenant improvements and related costs of re-leasing space. In fact, the owner's ability to access capital for these needs has proven to be an effective, competitive tool in attracting new tenants. The attendant volatility in office cash flow is directly accounted for in the underwriting process, by stabilizing the cash outflows and including them in our base-year cash flow estimate. Depending on the lease rollover pattern, this may result in the required build-up of some reserves over time, in anticipation of these costs.

Retail Properties

Retail properties include regional and super-regional malls, strip centers, power centers, free-standing stores, neighborhood shopping centers and specialty centers. Of primary concern to the success of retail properties is site visibility, access and area demographics. Most retail properties rely on automobile traffic for accessibility to the customer base. To draw tenants, the property must be well located with easy access to attract this customer base. For large shopping malls, a good location is identified by reference to the surrounding residential quality and density and traffic patterns. Small retail centers must be well positioned in comparison with other retail centers and also must have an adequate residential base.

Single-property retail financings are typically feasible only when the property dominates its location, has three or more good-quality anchors and when opportunities for new competition are limited by the absence of developable land. Particular attention is given to "dark anchor" risk, which pertains to the likelihood of an anchor closing down its operations while maintaining its lease obligations. This would have an obvious deleterious affect on the property, and is avoided by the inclusion of operating covenants or recapture provisions in the anchor lease with respect to conditions under which operations must be maintained.

The physical condition and layout of the property should be adequate for the modern retail user, with respect to its larger shop space requirements and parking needs. Sales and occupancy costs per square foot are the primary indicators of the property's performance. Trends over time are examined and comparisons with competitive properties and published sources such as the ULI publication "Dollars and Cents of Shopping Centers" are made. With respect to percentage rent, an analysis is conducted on historic sales numbers to ascertain their volatility. This is then used to determine a base-year sales number upon which to calculate an appropriate percentage rent estimate.

Industrial Properties

The qualitative review focuses on building clear heights, column spacing, bay depths, divisibility, truck-turning radius, and overall functionality and accessibility. Vital to industrial properties are local labor sources, proximity to supply sources and customers, major employers in the market area, and accessibility to rail lines and major roadways.

Quoted rents for industrial properties commonly include a significant portion of specialized amortized tenant improvement costs. When developing an underwriting cash flow it is important to calculate the "shell rent," or rent net of these costs, to perform similar comparisons. In general, flex space is considered less desirable collateral than light manufacturing or warehouse due to its significant office component, which renders this asset type susceptible to dramatic swings in rental rates.

Multifamily Properties

Multifamily properties are the most commodity-like of the income-producing property types and can experience supply changes in a relatively short period of time. An apartment market with historically low vacancies may experience substantial new construction, which could quickly create an oversupply. These new properties can be extremely competitive and may offer the latest in amenity packages that older properties cannot provide. Multifamily residents are typically on short-term leases and can easily "trade up" to new properties. Other factors, such as zoning changes and local economic trends may also significantly affect the stability of a market.

The barriers to entry for multifamily properties remain low, and this points toward increased competition in this market. The key factors in underwriting are the age and condition of the property, which will be partly affected by the adequacy of ongoing maintenance, and overall management quality.

The results of the qualitative market and site review are used to develop quantitative assumptions for market growth (supply and demand), expected turnover, rental rates and expense factors, and vacancy factors. The qualitative market and site analysis is used to evaluate the current and future marketability of the property. These calculations directly affect the assessment of a property's sale or refinancing risk.

Construction Quality

The construction quality of a property affects its current and future marketability as well as the ongoing cash flow stream. Factors such as age, functionality, efficiency of rentable space, energy systems and usage of space all contribute to required maintenance costs and capital expenditures. A property that requires significant amounts of operating expenditures or excessive repairs will have a decreased income stream, reducing cash flow and property value calculations. Properties requiring capital improvements or other nonrecurring capital expenditures are required to provide evidence of adequate reserve balances.

A property must appeal aesthetically and functionally to current and prospective tenants. A property's amenities, architectural design, parking, landscaping, utilities and security systems contribute to the attractiveness of the property for tenants and may affect potential marketability.

Management Quality

The management company is analyzed from the perspective of its historical performance and its financial strength.

In terms of the management track record, the following factors are considered: 1) the number of square feet of property under management of the same asset class as the collateral, 2) the qualifications and experience of the management team, including the leasing agents, 3) the ability to attract and retain high-quality tenants, 4) the ability to maintain a proper tenant mix and avoid excessive concentration of lease rollovers, 5) the ability to maximize the property's bottom line cash flow without sacrificing tenant credit quality or permitting deferred maintenance and 6) the adequacy of the accounting systems and capital expenditures budgeting.

A face-to-face meeting is conducted with the management team to ascertain their strengths or weaknesses in the categories listed above. With respect to financial stability, the industry is characterized by small, often thinly capitalized entities. Many management companies are the reincarnation of development companies that went bankrupt in the previous real estate recession. Consequently, a number of controls are required. For example, the management fee should represent adequate compensation for the services rendered. In the event that a replacement manager is sought, the fee should be high enough to attract competent interested parties. The subordination of this fee to the mortgage payment potentially accelerates the property's demise, due to lack of financial incentive for the property manager. On the other hand, this subordination puts creditors ahead of management.

Control over the cash flow from the tenants should be instituted. The most secure form is to set up a lock box account to which the tenants send all payments, thus circumventing the financial risk associated with management. The disadvantage of this is that it may hamstring the management from performing its usual functions. An alternative is to establish a "modified lock box," which is an account held by the trustee. The manager has access only in the amount exceeding the payment of principal and interest on the mortgage, property taxes, insurance and replenishment of any reserves that have been set up. This compromise method meets the dual objectives of maintaining cash control, and allows the manager the much-needed flexibility of access to the funds.

Insurance

Hazard Insurance should be provided by a creditworthy third party. Additionally, business interruption insurance will be required. This is to mitigate interruptions that could arise in cash flows to the bondholders, from events including a partial or full condemnation or casualty, or the necessity of structural work for any number of reasons. The same credit standards apply to this insurance provider as to casualty insurance, as described above.

Additional comprehensive public liability insurance should be provided, including blanket contractual and personal injury coverage.

If the property is located in an area identified by the U.S. Secretary of Housing and Urban Development as having special flood hazards and in which flood insurance has been made available under the National Flood Insurance Act of 1986, then coverage should be provided for this risk. Any other insurance, as may reasonably be required by the mortgagee to protect its interests, should be provided.

Leases/Tenants

Another important factor in determining the credit quality of commercial real estate is the quality and diversity of the leases and tenants. Diversity of leases refers primarily to variety in user and a variety of expiration dates. A mix of lease terms reduces the turnover risk at any one time during the term of the security. A diversity of tenants refers to the size and type of the business conducted by the tenants. Tenant diversity helps to protect the property from economic downturns or cycles in any specific industry. The credit quality of the tenants affects timely rent payments and lease renewals.

To make qualitative assessments regarding tenant profiles, rating agencies analyzes current leases and, where available, leases under negotiation. The rent roll submitted to rating agencies should include the following major provisions:

(1) number and identity of the tenants,

(2) amount, type (e.g., storage, penthouse) and location of space occupied by each tenant,

(3) rental rates (including percentage rent and escalation provisions),

(4) lease terms, including expirations,

(5) expense payment provisions, and

(6) renewal and/or cancellation options.

Where possible, lease abstracts should present this information in detail and disclose other lease requirements, such as free rent or early occupancy utility payments, security deposits, tenant improvements required, and brokerage commissions. In addition to the actual lease information, a payment history on a tenant-by-tenant basis is useful. All major tenants are analyzed on the basis of credit quality and payment reliability. This analysis often requires the submission of financial statements from key tenants and review of the full lease documents, including any operating agreements, main covenants, reciprocal easement agreements, etc.

A re-leasing vacancy period is assumed to occur in addition to appropriate leasing fees and concessions. The information analyzed during the lease and tenant review is used to develop the cash flow projections for the property. Quantifiable factors include rental rates and escalation provisions, free rent concessions, current and projected vacancy factors, operating expense allocations and tenant improvement requirements.

Renewal options are discussed with current management to determine realistic lease expirations. Leases with contractual rental increases or expense stops (caps) are considered favorable because they make cash flow projections more predictable.

QUANTITATIVE ANALYSIS

The maximum amount of mortgage debt for a given rating level will vary depending on a number of quantitative factors. These include the debt service coverage ratio, the loan-to-value ratio at commencement, the loan-to-value ratio at balloon date, fixed versus variable interest rate, and lease provisions including escalation clauses and rollover dates. There are also numerous security structure provisions that bear upon the debt amount including extension features.

Cash flow is a more reliable indicator of commercial property performance than value. The appraised value is nonetheless an important benchmark in the underwriting parameters. Current third-party appraisals should be provided on single-property financings. However, property value is subject to errors of estimation due to the unavailability of arm's length transaction data. Hence, there is the requirement of subjective determination of appropriate capitalization ("cap") rates. For this reason, rating agencies frequently will adjust the third-party approximation of the cap rate to reflect the uncertainty element in this key number and will recalculate the value on this basis. Likewise, the cash flow projection for the determination of value is internally reviewed and adjusted.

For all properties with medium- to long-term leases (generally retail, industrial and office), gross rental income used in the annual cash flows is calculated as the contract rental payments currently in place (as marked to market). Partial credit will be given to leases that are expiring in the coming year by assuming a probability of renewal. This probability assumption is also applied to the costs associated with rollover, namely tenant improvements, leasing commissions and downtime between leases. Leases that are at above-market rental rates will be adjusted down to market for this calculation. Industrial leases (flex space) will be adjusted to shell rents. Contractual increases are accounted for only when a specific dollar or percentage amount is stipulated if the amount does not exceed market rents or if the tenant is investment grade. Adjustments tied to the consumer price index or similar benchmark will not be given credit. The occurrence of a recent high inflation period, which will be imminently adjusted for under the terms of the lease, will be considered on a case-by-case basis. The overriding objective is to arrive at a representative stabilized estimate, not to reflect an above- or below-average inflationary environment.

A lease-by-lease analysis is performed for tenants representing greater than or equal to 20% of the total gross leasable area. Current rental income from all other tenants is calculated and projected over the holding period. In either case, annual lease rollover is estimated and tenant improvement, leasing and other costs are estimated based on a conservative renewal probability. In general, properties with occupancy levels above the market average are assumed to stabilize at market levels upon lease rollovers. Market rent and lease term, for the purpose of estimating revenue from new and renewal tenants, are based on recently signed leases in the building and/or competitive properties (if available) or reliable local market statistics. The year-one operating statement or pro forma is used as the base year for all projections. Other income is based on historical collections and industry statistics.

All general operating expenses including property taxes, insurance, administrative, utilities, repairs and maintenance, and management fees are estimated. Estimates are taken from the property's historical operating results and/or industry standards for the market. When examining market data, expense-to-revenue ratios are compared to market averages. Properties with ratios higher than market are assumed to remain at the year-one level during the period of analysis. Properties with ratios below the market average are increased to the market average over the period of analysis. This is to reflect the loss of any operating efficiencies relative to the market due to the negative effect of the foreclosure process. Further increases may be warranted depending on the age of the property, level of occupancy and condition of the property and the market. Properties with below-average expense ratios are subject to escalation of operating expenses at a rate of not less than 5% per year.

The analysis examines the age, occupancy, size and type of the property in determining appropriate levels of reserves. Actual levels are taken from industry averages. Tax rates are assumed to remain constant. Unless otherwise indicated, a management fee ranging from 2%-5% of annual income is assumed.

It is assumed that stabilized properties remain at the lower of current or market occupancy levels. Absorption for properties that require lease-up to reach stabilization is based on the expected rate of the market absorption. The market's current overall occupancy is taken as the level for stabilized occupancy. In addition to this overall vacancy, lag vacancy is estimated based on lease rollover, the renewal probability, lease term and expected number of months of downtime between leases. A collection loss relating to the property type and tenant quality is also applied.

A stabilized occupancy number will be utilized by comparing the property's current occupancy with the market occupancy. This will be judged against historical tenant retention and the current lease structure.

Tenant improvements and leasing commissions are estimated and deducted from net operating income. Tenant improvement costs are projected based on the estimated renewal probability and degree of current build-out. Leasing commissions are based on the local commission structure and the renewal probability of leases.

Additional reserves are deducted for replacing or repairing capital items such as the roof, HVAC systems or parking lots. The amount varies depending on property condition, quality and type. Capital expenditures for upgrading or repositioning the property are only assumed to be incurred when the need is substantial. Such deferred maintenance must be taken into consideration and deducted from current cash. The amount deducted is based on engineering reports, appraisals or other sources. When such information is not available, estimates are made from industry cost estimating manuals.

CROSS-COLLATERALIZED STRUCTURES

The analysis of cross-collateralized and cross-defaulted loans includes elements of single-asset and pool analysis. The diversification of the pool is the primary determinant of the rating levels. However, most cross-collateralized pools have, to date, fallen short of the minimum size in terms of the number of loans to attain pool status. They frequently consist of fewer than 30 properties and commonly have concentration of a single asset type. This is due to the fact that these pools are primarily issued by medium- to large-sized developers that are seeking to refinance a portion of their overall portfolios, and that developers of this size have usually specialized in one or two property types. Their development expertise is usually limited to particular property types. This compares with non-crossed pools, the source of which is usually a portfolio lender, such as a life insurance company, conduit or other institutional lender, which are typically diverse across borrower, property types and geographic regions. For convenience, cross-collateralized and cross-defaulted pools are referred to here as simply "crossed." Non-cross-collateralized and non-cross-defaulted loans will be referred to as "non-crossed."

The critical distinction with crossed pools is the impact this has of significantly reducing the probability and severity of default, because each property's cash flow before debt service supports every other property in the pool. If, for example, there are 20 properties in the pool and there is currently a 2.0X debt service coverage (fixed rate), before a default becomes likely, cash flow would need to drop 50% or more *on a portfolio basis*. This contrasts with multiple-borrower pools whereby individual loans will default as cash flow deteriorates. There are therefore likely to be fewer defaults in a crossed structure, all other things being equal. In a non-crossed pool, individual loan defaults will result in losses if the liquidation price of the real estate falls short of the outstanding principal balance, including accrued interest and all related expenses allocated to each loan. However, in a crossed pool, the total liquidation proceeds from each and all of the properties are available to repay the outstanding principal.

Conversely, with a crossed pool, as individual properties deteriorate to the point where they would otherwise default if they were non-crossed, they are likely to be neglected by the owner/manager, thus exacerbating the diminution in real estate value. Certain early warning provisions may be included in the structure to mitigate this. Examples include debt coverage triggers to remove or substitute individual properties, or triggers to replace the management by vote of some predetermined percentage of the bondholders.

A properly structured cross-collateralized pool will require lower subordination levels. The rationale is that the pool benefits from diversification, and some of the losses that occur due to individual loan foreclosures are avoided. Also, no unrated subordinate piece will be required if the total LTV and DSCR are adequate on a pool basis to meet the minimum required for the rating. This contrasts with multiple-borrower, non-crossed pools, wherein even though the weighted-average LTV and DSCR may meet the target for the rating category, some subordination will be required. For this reason, it is far more common to see unrated subordinate tranches in non-crossed pools.

DIVERSIFIED-BORROWER MORTGAGE POOLS

Mortgage pool securities are generally certificates that represent ownership interests in a trust. The trust owns a number of loans from individual borrowing entities that, generally, are not cross-collateralized. These loans are either a subset of a lender's loan portfolio or an aggregation from a conduit. In either case, the approach taken incorporates the following steps:

- evaluate the credit quality of the individual loans,
- determine the quality of the origination,
- assess the competence and financial capacity of the servicing function and
- review the aggregated pool statistics for mitigating circumstances or pool-wide exposures.

Loan Credit Quality

In evaluating the credit quality of each loan, rating agencies attempt to discern any unique strengths or weaknesses in the loan due to either specific property or loan features. These include among others: market conditions, location issues, physical construction, lease rollover and secondary financing. This analysis is achieved by:

- reviewing loan files or "long form" due diligence reports, including appraisals or market studies,
- analyzing financial statements and lease reviews,
- sensitivity analysis of cash flows,
- performing site inspections,
- reviewing tenant quality,
- adjusting cash flows to achieve a "marked-to-market" scenario,
- adjusting LTVs based on current cash flow and cap rates, and
- reviewing engineering and environmental reports.

Depending on the pool size, rating agencies will perform a detailed analysis and site visit on either the entire pool or a statistical sample. (For example, the sample is usually employed in loan pools in excess of 50 loans. The minimum sample is targeted to be 33% of the dollar amount of the pool with 50 properties being visited. The selection is based upon the pool diversity as well as potentially volatile asset types and geographic locations. In a pool of more than 50 loans, at least 75% of the loan pool due diligence information is reviewed in depth and 100% of the loan profile information.)

Quality of Origination

Rating agencies will review the circumstances of the loan originations to ascertain any potentially adverse selection situations. For a loan held in portfolio, the following questions will be asked, among others: Why is the loan being sold? What was the purpose for originating? What situations have changed in the organization? What competitive issues influenced the underwriting? What was the level of analytical rigor documenting the credit approval?

For loans from a conduit, rating agencies review the underwriting guidelines, decision-making process and incentives of the originators. The quality control and compliance issues must be reviewed to ensure that a consistent, thorough approach is taken by the conduit. Since these originations are designed particularly for third-party sales, rating agencies need to ascertain what risk-sharing proposals are in place to keep the conduit's focus on credit quality and compliance.

The representation and warranties a seller makes are critical to the rating process. While these may be provided in a variety of forms, overtime many have become commonplace. Aside from the actual representations and warranties made, rating agencies review how they are made. Did the seller go through a detailed analysis to make sure those "reps" are true? What procedures did they employ? This can be proven through third-party due diligence or other documentation. In cases where comfort cannot be achieved from the seller on the "reps," a highly rated entity would need to back up the seller's position.

Servicing Capabilities

The amount of flexibility the servicer/special servicer has in modifying defaulting loans can have a significant impact on the amount of loss mitigation for any particular pool. Modifications generally deal with the following:

- extending the maturity date,
- adjusting the amortization schedule,
- deferring interest payments,
- adjusting the interest rate,
- forgiving debt, and
- releasing or accepting collateral.

The most obvious situations are balloon loans that have good debt service coverage, but the borrower is unable to obtain a refinancing at maturity. Clearly, giving the borrower more time or restructuring to a fully amortizing loan would be appropriate. However, deciding on forgiving debt or deferring interest with the hope that the borrower can turn around a troubled property is a more difficult task.

The assessment of servicer flexibility must be governed by two issues. The first is the ability of the servicer to evaluate trouble situations and recommend courses of action that will result in maximizing net present value to certificateholders. The second is that their decision-making process and conclusion is fully documented and supplied to the trustee, not for affirmation, but to document the various alternatives entertained and that the optimal alternative was chosen.

Pool Analysis

Once the loan credit quality, origination quality and servicer quality have been assessed, an expected loss for the pool of loans is calculated. This loss is based on both the rating category and the factors discussed above. However, the higher the rating category the greater the loss tolerance that a pool of loans should be able to sustain. In other words, the pool should have a larger subordinate first loss piece or cash reserve in order to get a higher rating on the more senior certificates.

In sizing the loss expectation for any pool at a given rating category there are two primary factors:

- Probability of Loss: The probability that any particular loan will go into default, be foreclosed upon and liquidated.
- Loan Loss: The loss realized upon liquidation of that loan.

The conclusions reached in the analysis of the credit quality of the loan, the quality of its origination, the pool aggregation and the servicer, will be manifested in the determination of the probability and loan loss.

Probability of Loss

The elements that will have a material impact on whether a loan goes into default and is foreclosed upon and liquidated are:

- LTV/DSCR,
- property type,
- loan structure (i.e., balloon)
- fixed/floating interest rates,
- loan quality,
- seasoning of property and loan,
- management,
- ownership structure,
- barriers to entry/loan to replacement cost,
- cash flow volatility and
- recourse.

Loan Loss

The actual loss sustained by any mortgage loan upon liquidation will be affected by three major items:

- Obtaining the asset
    recourse
    state law
    foreclosure period
    ownership structure

- Time to sell
    location
    property type

- Costs to sell
    liquidation (cost to carry, legal fees, commissions, property protection
        expenses, improvement expenses, asset management fee)
    loan size

The loss expectation on any portfolio of loans is simply the summation of the products of each loan's probability of loss and anticipated principal loss.

There are then a number of macro issues (poolwide adjustments) that will impact the pool's performance, which are addressed through overall adjustments to the loss expectations. These are as follows:

- geographic diversification,
- overall environmental exposure,
- seismic exposure,
- servicer/special servicer flexibility capabilities,
- loan diversification,
- origination quality,
- information quality,
- cash control and
- reserves.

There are a number of items which, will have negative or positive impacts on the loss expected. These adjustments are outlined below.

Amortizing

Fully amortizing loans that obviate the need to refinance the property reduce the risks associated with a volatile credit market. However, fully amortizing transactions are generally of a longer term, which introduces the risks of changing neighborhoods, physical obsolescence and the need for capital improvements.

Seasoning

Seasoning represents the period of time that the borrower has been paying on the loan. A payment history, in and of itself, is neither positive nor negative. An unblemished payment history by a borrower is positive. What mitigates some of this positive, however, is that depending upon the year of origination, the property value and cash flow may have declined. Therefore, the quality of current information is critical when looking to assess the impact for seasoning.

Servicer/Special Servicer

The specific assessments of the servicer and special servicer will impact credit enhancement. If a servicer/special servicer used is deemed unacceptable, the transaction is probably not ratable. There is still a wide variety of quality differential even if the overall assessment is acceptable. Given this wide variety of quality and the ability to modify loans, credit enhancement can increase or decrease depending on the operational capability and financial capacity of the servicer and special servicer.

Origination Quality

Origination quality refers to the rigor of the individual underwriting. This includes the way that cash flows and value are assessed. Additionally, it deals with the strengths of legal documentation and covenant restrictions. While differentiation between excellent versus very good underwriting may not significantly change the quality of the collateral, poor underwriting can have a devastating impact, particularly when it comes to preservation and control of the asset. Similar to origination, determining information quality is a subjective analysis. We look for the information provided to be complete, recent, insightful and analytical.

Cash Control

Cash control is the ability of the lender to effectively get its hands on the property cash flow. This provides not only the ability to reduce the loss of collateral, but it is an effective tool for bringing a recalcitrant borrower into a more cooperative posture. This function ranges from sweeping accounts periodically to having tenants make payments directly to the servicer.

Reserves

Reserves are established at a loan level to make cash available to the property owners and lender for particular needs. These range from maintenance and capital items to tenant improvement and commissions. Additionally, reserves can be established for debt service in the event of significant tenant rollover. The reserves will reduce defaults due to short-term cash flow problems and act to preserve asset quality in the long term.

Floating Rates

Floating-rate loans that have caps will be tested assuming increasing rates over time. The specific analysis will be determined based upon the index used, the adjustment frequency and amortization adjustments. Typically, the stressed index rate used is its highest level over several business and economic cycles. The resulting adjusted debt service coverages will then be used in the tabular calculation of credit enhancement.

Asset Quality

The assessment of the differences among class A, B, C and D properties cannot be done in isolation. Superior/inferior asset quality differential should be measured within a particular submarket. The balance of existing stock of different asset classes versus the potential for new development potential needs to be measured. Generally, class A property is viewed more favorably because even in depressed economic situations, there is a trend to upgrade by tenants who remain in the market. Class A is also more accepted by institutional investors who would be purchasing or refinancing.

Barriers to Entry

Each market and submarket will be reviewed to determine the likelihood of new construction. This is done by property type. The determination of whether a market and property type have significant barriers to entry will not necessarily result in changes to credit enhancement since amortization and lease structure interrelate on this issue.

Cash Flow Volatility

Suffice it to say that properties with erratic cash flows due to tenant rollover or high expense ratios will require greater credit enhancement levels. The subjectivity in addressing this topic is due to a specific analysis of lease structure and whether current rents are below market rents. The level of reserves established will also positively contribute to mitigating cash flow volatility.

Loan Size

The particular dollar amount of a loan is not significant. However, the benchmark credit enhancement levels incorporate liquidation costs. Recognizing the fixed portion of the costs to foreclose and liquidate property, smaller loans may experience disproportionately higher losses. Therefore, for loans less than $3 million, the loss expectation will be increased because liquidation costs will be a higher percentage of the loan. Conversely, loans greater than $5-7 million should see some reduction as liquidation costs represent a smaller percentage of the loan.

Location

It is impossible on a poolwide basis to assess particular credit enhancement attributable to location. Generally, in-fill locations are more desirable given a supporting population base and a lack of available land. Differentiation between suburban and urban is only significant given the property type and the local market demographics and submarket supply/demand.

Concentration

Generally, state concentration of should be avoided. However, certain markets are more resilient than others. Concentration in any market is a risk. Diversifying into markets that are considered substandard will not positively impact credit enhancement. Individual loan or borrower concentrations in excess of 5% of the pool are analyzed on a loan-by-loan basis. Issues of importance are borrower structure (single-purpose entity) and property quality. Generally, the more concentrated (more than 5% in any category) the greater the credit enhancement needed. Depending on loan quality, the adjustment can be significant.

STRUCTURAL AND LEGAL CONSIDERATIONS

In commercial MBS programs, the primary structural goal is to isolate the assets or collateral that will generate the cash flow to investors. Outside credit risks or exposure should be removed to the greatest extent possible.

Typically, assets are transferred to a bankruptcy-remote special-purpose vehicle (SPV or Issuer) that is limited to only business relating to the assets to be acquired (an SPV may be a corporation, partnership or trust). Consequently, the SPV should not be able to incur additional debt or obligations that might enable a creditor to bring action against it that could interfere with payments to the investors.

The SPV should also be structured to reduce the possibility that a bankruptcy court, in a proceeding involving the parent or other affiliate, would order substantive consolidation of the assets of the SPV with those of its parent or affiliate. Assuming the SPV is bankruptcy remote, the transfer to the SPV should further be structured to be a true sale so that the assets will not be deemed a part of the transferor's estate (in the event of the transferor's bankruptcy) pursuant to Section 541 of the United States Bankruptcy Code (the Bankruptcy Code).

The focus of this section will be on debt obligations using commercial mortgages as collateral, although many of the points will apply to certain aspects of pass-through transactions as well.

Issuer/SPV Criteria

A nonconsolidation opinion of counsel will generally be required stating that, in the event of a bankruptcy proceeding involving the parent, the assets of the SPV will not be substantively consolidated with those of the parent. The issuer/SPV (or, in the case of passthrough securitizations, the seller or depositor) should satisfy certain criteria:

- The corporate charter, partnership agreement or trust document, as the case may be, should limit the business and operations of the issuer to activities related to acquisition and holding of the specific assets, issuance of the securities and other activities necessary and appropriate to carry out the foregoing.

- The issuer should be restricted from incurring additional debt unless (1) the debt would not result in a reduction of the current rating, (2) the debt is fully subordinate to the rated debt (provided rating agencies approve LTV and coverage limits) or (3) the debt is rated at the same or higher level as the existing rated debt and would not impair the current rating.

- So long as the securities are outstanding, the issuer should not be able to (1) change the limitations set forth in the charter or other governing instrument, (2) dissolve or liquidate prior to payment in full of the securities or (3) merge with any entity, or transfer or pledge any of its property or assets, except under certain limited conditions. (See "Transfer Restrictions.")

- The SPV and, where applicable, parent or other affiliate, should provide the following "separateness" undertakings:

  1) SPV should be adequately capitalized.
  2) SPV should maintain its books and records separate from its parent and affiliates. It should prepare separate tax returns, or if part of a consolidated group, it should be shown as a separate member.
  3) The SPV should utilize its own letterhead and telephone and should maintain an office distinct from its parent.
  4) All transactions with the parent or any affiliate should be on an arm's-length basis and pursuant to enforceable agreements.
  5) SPV should be held out to the public by SPV and its parent as a separate and distinct entity. There should be no commingling of assets or funds with any other entity.
  6) At least one director of the SPV should be an outside director not affiliated with the parent or any of its affiliates.
  7) Regular board meetings should be held to approve SPV activities; transactions with affiliates must be approved by the outside director(s).
  8) The transfer of assets to the SPV should be adequately disclosed to transferor's creditors.
  9) The parent and identifiable creditors should agree not to voluntarily place the SPV into bankruptcy proceedings. The SPV should be restricted from filing a voluntary bankruptcy or other insolvency proceeding unless it is approved by all directors, including the outside director.
  10) The SPV should not guarantee or pay debts or other obligations of the parent or any other entity; the parent will not guarantee obligations of the SPV other that indemnification of certain limited obligations to underwriters.
  11) Any common employees or overhead shared with affiliates should be appropriately allocated and charged.

In mortgage conduit programs, the SPV criteria and substantive consolidation concerns arise at two levels: 1) at the seller/depositor level where the mortgage assets are being pooled and 2) at the borrower level where each mortgage is originated. A pool of loans from a single owner or small group of owners merits close attention to the SPV criteria and delivering of a nonconsolidation opinion. As the pool increases in size and diversity, the severity of the impact of substantive consolidation with respect to a single borrower on the pool as a whole diminishes.

True Sale versus Pledge

A transaction should be structured to ensure that the SPV has complete and absolute ownership of the assets used to secure the securities issued. Accordingly, the transfer of the assets from the parent/affiliate to the SPV should be treated as a true sale or, if made as a capital contribution, as an absolute conveyance. In the case of a pass-through transaction, the seller/depositor must convey all right, title and interest in the assets to the trustee for the benefit of the certificateholders. An opinion of counsel to the issuer generally will be required to the effect that the assets will not be deemed property of the transferor under Section 541 of the Bankruptcy Code. The courts often look to the intent of the parties and the true nature of the transaction. Factors considered by the court in determining whether or not the transferor retains any equity ownership in the assets transferred to the SPV include:

- The amount of recourse to the transferor; any amount in excess of historical losses may cause the transaction to be viewed as a secured pledge.
- A determination of which party bears the risks and enjoys the benefits of ownership of the assets.
- The relation between the fair value of the assets and the price paid.
- Whether or not the seller retains any rights in the assets (e.g., right of substitution, redemption or repurchase).
- Whether or not collections from the transferred assets are segregated from any other assets that may be held by or retained by the transferor. If the transferor act as servicer, detailed servicing agreements should be included and segregated accounts used.
- How the parties treat the transaction for tax, accounting and regulatory purposes.
- The intent of the parties, particularly as indicated by the language of the documents.

Fraudulent Conveyance/Transfer

In some instances, it will be necessary to ensure that the transaction will not be deemed a fraudulent conveyance or fraudulent transfer under applicable state law or Section 548 of the Bankruptcy Code. Section 548, which is similar in many respects to the various state fraudulent conveyance or fraudulent transfer codes, provides that the trustees may avoid any transfer if the debtor: (1) made the transfer with actual intent to hinder, delay or defraud any creditor or (2) received less than a reasonably equivalent value in exchange for such transfer and either (a) was insolvent at the date of the transfer or became insolvent as a result of the transfer, (b) was engaged in business for which its remaining capital was unreasonably small or (c) intended to incur debts beyond its ability to pay. A legal opinion may be required, which may rely on extrinsic evidence of solvency and value, such as MAI appraisals and independent fair value certificates.

Other Legal Opinions

Opinions of counsel to the issuer generally must be rendered to the rating agencies regarding the following matters:

Legality/Enforceability All documents relating to the transaction must be legal, valid, binding and enforceable in accordance with their terms. They should have been duly authorized, executed and delivered by the issuer (and the parent or other transferor, with respect to the transfer of assets to the issuer). They should not conflict with or violate the issuer's organizational documents, bylaws or any agreements or orders by which the issuer is bound, or any applicable laws or regulations. Such documents include the following:

> Trust Indenture
> Sale/Transfer Agreement
> > Pooling and Servicing Agreement
> Mortgages/Leases
> > Other Security or Collateral Agreements

Security Interest/Perfection In the case of a debt transaction using an indenture, an opinion that the trustee will have a first perfected security interest in all assets comprising the trust estate that are pledged or transferred to the trustee for the benefit of the investors is required.

Issuance of Securities In the case of a debt transaction, an opinion that the notes or bonds are validly issued and entitled to the benefits provided for in the indenture is required. In pass-through transactions, an opinion that the certificates are legally issued and created pursuant to the terms of the pooling and servicing agreement or trust agreement and are entitled to the rights and benefits set forth should be provided.

Credit Enhancement Similar opinions also are required from appropriate counsel with respect to any credit enhancement documents, such as letters of credit, interest swap and cap agreements, insurance policies, surety agreements, master leases or guarantees.

Trust Indenture/Trustee

Minimum requirements necessary in the indenture are:

- Eligible investment criteria for investment of trust funds will be established. All investments should be 'AAA' rated instruments or U.S. government securities (i.e., cash equivalents).

- All funds held in a corporate trust account must be segregated from other accounts. Funds held in trust should be adequately collateralized pursuant to Office of the Comptroller of the Currency regulations.The indenture should require immediate investment of funds into eligible investments.
- Cash flow of funds within the indenture will be reviewed and determinations made as to:

> Priority of distributions: principal, interest, fees, expenses and subordinate classes.
>
> Release of funds from the indenture.
>
> Receipt of investment income, and whether such income will first replenish a reserve account or similar accounts.

Indemnification of Trustee/Limits on Liability Standard provisions generally are acceptable; however, a "gross negligence" standard is not. The trustee will not be relieved from liability for, or indemnified against, its own action or inaction that constitutes negligence.

Provision of Reports Trustee must take notice of defaults with respect to failure of issuer to provide timely reports, statements and certificates required by the transaction documents. Also, trustee should affirmatively check compliance with minimum ratings of insurance company, servicer or other entities on a regular basis.

Requirements of Trustee A minimum long-term debt rating of 'A' is required if trustee is obligated to make advances directly or as back-up to servicer, otherwise a rating of 'BBB' is required. Back-up servicing or advancing function may be required. Minimum capital surplus of $50 million is required.

Bondholder Vote In many instances a majority or super-majority is acceptable for major decisions. However, a 100% vote is required to reduce interest rate, change the term/maturity or reduce the principal and change voting percentages. Other items may require full bondholder approval.

Redemption Provisions Whether or not there will be any requirements for or limitations on early, optional or mandatory redemptions will be determined.

Defeasance of Securities Requires deposit of collateral with appropriate maturities and a ratings equivalent to or better than the securities being defeased (as described in "Eligible Investments" under Trust Indenture/Trustee).

Pooling and Servicing Agreement/Master Servicer

In the case of pass-through securities where a pooling and servicing agreement is utilized, many of the considerations under "Trustee Indenture/Trustee" above will apply, together with an evaluation of the master servicer and the following points:

- Representations and warranties as to mortgage loans/assets conveyed to trustee will be confirmed. Seller/depositor should have a cure or repurchase obligation as to any material breach.
- Trustee/custodian should review mortgage file(s) to determine completeness within 30 to 120 days after closing.
- If the master servicer will have any advancing functions (e.g., principal and interest payments, taxes and insurance), they should be through foreclosure and liquidation.
- Detailed servicing and accounting records must be maintained; 30-, 60- and 90-day delinquency and default status reports and certifications should be provided quarterly.
- Collections should be remitted to the trustee on at least a monthly basis. A segregated account must be utilized.
- Master servicer may not resign or be removed until a qualified substitute servicer has been appointed.
- Property inspections should be performed on a regular basis (e.g., once per year and after 60 days delinquency).
- Special servicers may also be required to handle defaulted and troubled loans. Limits on servicer's authority to modify and reform loans should be established.
- Amount and source of compensation will be considered along with the priority in distribution of trust funds.
- Servicer should monitor borrowers' compliance with minimum insurance carrier rating policy coverage requirements.
- In general, the same criteria regarding financial statements will apply as in "Trust Indenture/Trustee" above, except that property operating statements, audited for each property, should be provided in a pool of fewer than 20 loans. If all properties are owned by the same borrower, then the statements should be provided for each property, but audited only as to the pool.

Forms of Credit Enhancement

Various types of credit enhancement are involved in rated transactions, including letters of credit, senior/subordinate structures, master leases, surety bonds, insurance policies, reserve funds and over collateralization. Consideration will be given to the legal and other criteria required for each of these types of credit enhancements.

SERVICER

The servicer's capabilities and knowledge are critical to the performance of a pool. The following section describes the analysis of the servicer.

The general areas of analysis include the servicing history; financial condition; quality of originations; breadth and depth of experience in categories such as loan size, property type, geographic regions and problem loan issues; administrative capabilities; and systems and personnel of the servicer. This policy lists the information required to be provided to rating agencies. In some cases, the servicer under review is also the originator of the loans. In these situations, the term "servicer" also refers to originator and all areas of origination and servicing are evaluated by rating agencies in their review.

The ability of the servicer to facilitate timely payment of interest and principal, especially in the event of collateral shortfalls, is factored into the structured finance rating. The servicer assessment should not be misconstrued as a securities rating. The servicer assessment indicates that specific conditions have or have not been met to allow the servicer to participate in a structured finance transaction.

Historical Experience

It is important that the servicer be able to demonstrate that it has gained the broad depth of experience needed to adequately service a commercial real estate structured finance transaction. The evaluation includes an analysis of the servicer's historical performance in order to assess previous performance and to determine whether there are any developing trends that may effect future performance. The historical growth of the portfolio, both on a total and annual basis, and the resulting impact on performance is reviewed to determine the company's flexibility and potential capacity.

The length of time that a servicer has been in operation provides an indication of the company's experience through various business and market cycles. Companies with a minimal history must be carefully evaluated to determine the viability of the operation. Taken into consideration are such situations in which the servicer is a subsidiary of a larger company or when senior management consists of a group of professionals with substantial combined experience. While the current business organization may have limited operating experience, points such as the prior experience of a seasoned senior management team and the support of a strong parent entity are factored into the assessment process.

Performance of the servicer's own portfolio or portfolios serviced on a contract basis is analyzed with an emphasis on delinquencies, gross and net loss experience, foreclosures and recoveries as a percent of the outstanding principal balance serviced. It is important to factor in changes such as growth or decline in portfolio balances that may skew the statistics in a misleading way. Static pool data are preferred. Growth or declines in portfolios will be reviewed when determining trends in statistics.

Consistency in performance indicates that a portfolio is performing well during times of various economic stress. Anomalies caused by individual loans or borrowers will be reviewed when analyzing the statistics. The current mortgage loan portfolio of the servicer will be analyzed along various parameters. The servicer will be required to have maintained a servicing portfolio size of at least

$100 million in commercial mortgage loans over the past 12 months. The required level of expertise by loan size, property type and geographic region must be commensurate with the pool(s) to be serviced. While limited levels of experience will be considered for specific pools with corresponding loan characteristics, a lack of broad expertise will be reflected in the assigned assessment

The historical performance of the portfolio is analyzed by reviewing delinquency and default reports. The adequacy of tracking procedures is determined. The procedure for handling delinquencies is reviewed to assess timeliness of response, level of consistency regarding follow-up on open items, evidence of uniform adherence to procedures and overall effectiveness of the system. Levels of delinquency and amounts recovered will be reviewed for consistency and trends.

The servicer's policy for the loan workout process is analyzed. Levels of authority and procedures for decision making are reviewed. Unlike single-family mortgage loans, commercial loans involve more options when loans become delinquent, including the ability to extend maturities, forgive interest or provide equity infusions. The servicer must exhibit flexibility as well as the ability to recognize and evaluate the available alternatives within the context of the parameters of the pooling and servicing agreement. The servicer must clearly demonstrate a track record of negotiating successful outcomes to delinquent loan situations and the ability to maximize loan recoveries.

Operations

The quality of a servicer's personnel is measured in terms of experience, knowledge and commitment. The support of senior management is evaluated during the review process. Interaction with management, supervisors, collectors, credit analysts and other operational personnel provides a basis for our qualitative assessment.

The familiarity of management with the portfolio assets is vital to the proper planning for systems, policies, procedures and the hiring of competent staff. Management's prior experience is important in order to anticipate potential problems and to create plans to address those difficulties. In addition to its experience, management must demonstrate its competence and its commitment to the business. The size of the servicing staff relative to the number of accounts and level of complexity of the accounts serviced is an indication of the effectiveness of the operations.

Management should be focused on the business of servicing commercial mortgage loans. To the extent that the servicer is engaged in servicing of other lines of business, these will be reviewed as to their performance. In addition, the management and future business plan of the other lines of business are reviewed to insure that the other businesses will not detract from the overall business plan of the servicer to be rated.

Financial Condition

The financial condition of servicers varies substantially and plays an important role in the ability of the servicer to continue to perform its contractual obligations over the extended period of time involved in a structured financing. Overall financial condition will be reviewed to determine long- and short-term financial stability.

Some servicers have support from a strong parent, while others may be start-up operations with limited working capital. Although a new servicing operation may be managed by professionals with extensive experience, limited capital resources may restrict its ability to properly staff and equip operations in order to expand or to remain competitive. During the review, management should address future expansion and staffing needs that will require additional capital and the proposed sources of that capital.

A financial analysis of all lines of business will be performed if the company is a multiline business in which commercial real estate servicing is a part of the overall company business plan. The chief financial officer should discuss the financial condition of the corporation and the corporate business objectives.

Analysis of the servicer's financial statements indicates its ability to make servicer advances, if required, and demonstrates its immediate viability. A servicer must exhibit the ability to remain in existence for the life of a transaction. If there is a possibility that the servicer may not continue operations or may become unable to fulfill its obligations under securitization documents, provisions must be included to provide for a substitute or back-up servicer. If the servicer is not yet earning a profit, then the financial statements should disclose the source of working capital. If the servicer is supported by a strong parent, management should be prepared to discuss the reliability of capital infusions, advances and other types of financial support as well as the potential for a severance of the relationship and covenants involving intercompany borrowing and dividends of income. A business plan should outline a start-up servicer's projection of growth and profitability.

The financial viability, as well as the servicing capability, of a new servicing operation is very unpredictable. Such servicers may be required to submit periodic financial statements to rating agencies in order that any deterioration may be detected immediately.

Long-term viability is, in part, reliant upon diversification of income sources. Rating agencies view the servicer's viability as at risk if a significant portion of the servicer's income is earned from a single client.

INFORMATION GUIDELINES

The following exhibits provide general guidelines as to what information should be provided. These items are particular to Duff & Phelps Credit Rating Co. However, there are numerous similarities with other rating agency formats. The timely and accurate provision of this information helps to facilitate the rating process.

Each transaction is unique, therefore, some of these exhibits may not apply to all transactions. Additionally, there may be other information needs that present themselves during the rating process.

Exhibit 1: Submission Package

The following information and documents are to be submitted as part of the rating. This information will vary depending upon whether the transaction involves a large pool, small pool, single property, new loan or existing loan.

(1) A term sheet from the underwriter explaining the financing structure of the transaction. This explanation should include the bond structure, identification of the principal parties in the transaction, identification of the underlying credit enhancement and description of the mortgage loan structure.

(2) Information concerning the servicer.

(3) A market analysis.

(4) Information concerning the property management and leasing company will include the track record and depth of experience in managing and leasing the property in the market area. A history of the property management and leasing company should be included along with an organizational structure, financial reporting and record keeping for projects managed. A history of the on-site management and management turnover at the projects should be supplied. Information on property maintenance and prior and anticipated capital expenditures for replacements and improvements is required.

(5) An engineering report is required showing the adequacy of the utilities of the property at full capacity, the structural condition, foundation, framing, roof and floor strength, and condition of all services such as the heating, ventilating, air conditioning, fire and safety systems. The engineering report also should discuss compliance with all zoning and building codes and other appropriate governmental requirements (including environmental and waste disposal) and an overall evaluation of the construction quality, design and appearance. There should be an evaluation of rehabilitation work or capital improvements planned, expected or needed.

(6) The property's historical operating results for the past five years with an audited report for at least the most recent year and pro forma 10-year cash flow projections. Market support for all assumptions underlying the projections concerning lease turnover, rental rates and expense increases should be included.

(7) Copies of all executed commercial leases or lease abstracts. The location of each tenant in the property should be supplied. The lease abstract should show the tenant's name, space occupied, location of space, rental rate, lease term and types of expense payments and options (extension, expansion, renewal termination and the rights and options of tenants, and right of first refusal). Other information that should be provided to the rating agency includes rental concessions provided in the leases, side letters, broker's commission requirements, tenant improvement payments, percentage rents, and security deposits.

(8) Insurance policies.

(9) Representations and warranties from the servicer and issuer as described in Exhibit 3.

(10) Environmental reports

Upon receipt of all of the above information, the rating agency will perform a property site inspection and analysis of the proposed transaction. The rating agency relies on the accuracy and completeness of the information supplied and assumes no responsibility for verification.

Exhibit 2: Portfolio Submission Package

In order to process mortgage pool transactions, the following data items should be submitted to the rating agency in spreadsheet form.

- Property Address
- Property Type
- Gross Square Footage
- Net Rentable Square Footage
- Number of Units
- Property Age
- Owner/Borrower
- Property Manger
- Lien Status
- Property Valuation
- Date of Property Valuation
- Source of Property Valuation
- Three years historical operating information including at a minimum:
    Total Revenues (net of vacancies, credit losses, etc.)
    Occupancy %
    Total Expenses (excluding capital expenditures)
- Capital Expenditures
- Date/Period of NOI Compilation
- Source of NOI Compilation
- Next ten years of scheduled lease rollover (commercial properties only, expressed as % of GLA)
- Original Loan Amount
- Loan Origination Date
- Payment History
- First Payment Date
- Payments Frequency
- Current Loan Amount
- Loan Maturity Date
- Remaining Term to Maturity
- Original Amortization Period
- Remaining Amortization Period
- Loan Balance at Maturity
- Loan Interest Rate
- Loan Interest Rate Index
- Loan Interest Rate Margin
- Loan Modification Details, if applicable
- Any additional loan information required to accurately calculate expected loan payment schedule, such as rate caps, floors or reset information
- Current and original DSCR and LTV

Exhibit 3: Representations and Warranties

The following comprise certain basic representations and warranties to be delivered in connection with commercial mortgage securitizations. This list is not all-inclusive and may be modified or expanded depending on the specific terms and structure of a given transaction. This list is intended only as a general guideline for the scope and substance of typical provisions.

1. Mortgage Loan Schedule
The information with respect to each mortgage loan is true and correct in all material respects at the date or dates the information is given.

2. Ownership of Mortgage Loans
Immediately prior to the transfer and assignment of the mortgage loans to the purchaser, the seller is the sole owner of each mortgage loan and transfers the lease free and clear of all liens. Additionally, each mortgage loan should be a whole loan and not a participation interest in a mortgage loan.

3. Ratios
The debt-service-coverage ratio and loan-to-value ratio with respect to each mortgage loan are not to be less than *XXXX* and *XXXX*, respectively, as of the cut-off date.

4. Payment Record
No mortgage loan is delinquent beyond any applicable grace period nor more than 30 days delinquent at any time subsequent to origination, without giving effect to any applicable grace period.

5. First-Lien Mortgage
Each mortgage is a legal first lien on the mortgage property, subject only to (a) the lien of the current real property taxes, ground rents, water charges and sewer rents, and assessments not yet due and payable, (b) exceptions and exclusions specifically referred to in lender's title insurance commitment or policy (including rights of way and easements), none of which materially interferes with the current use of the mortgaged property or the security intended to be provided by the mortgage, and (c) other matters to which like properties are commonly subject, none of which materially interferes with the current use of the mortgaged property or the security intended to be provided by such mortgage (collectively, "permitted encumbrances").

6. Assignment of Leases and Rents
The mortgage file contains an assignment of leases or an assignment of rents (assignment of leases) either as a separate instrument or incorporated into the related mortgage, which creates, in favor of the holder, a valid, perfected and enforceable lien of the same priority as the related mortgage, in the property and rights described; provided that the enforceability of such lien is subject to applicable bankruptcy, insolvency, reorganization, moratorium, and other laws affecting the enforcement of creditors' rights generally, and by the application of the rules of equity. The seller has the full right to assign to the purchaser such assignment of leases and the lien created thereby as described in the immediately preceding sentence. No person other than the mortgagor owns any interest in any payments due under the related leases.

7. Valid Assignment
Each assignment of mortgage and related assignment of leases has been duly authorized, executed and delivered by the seller in recordable form, in order to validly convey the seller's interest to purchaser.

Exhibit 3 (Continued)

8. Waivers and Modifications

None of the terms of any lease, mortgage note, mortgage or assignment related to a mortgage loan have been impaired, waived, altered or modified in any way, except by written instruments, all of which are included in the related mortgage file (and, to the extent necessary, all such waivers, alterations and modifications have been filed and/or recorded or submitted for record in all places necessary to perfect, maintain and continue the validity and priority of the lien of the mortgage). The related lessee, mortgagor or guarantor, if any, has not been released, in whole or in part, from its obligations related to the mortgage note, other than pursuant to releases previously approved in writing by the seller or any affiliate, copies of which are included in the related mortgage file.

9. No Offset or Defense

There is no right of rescission, offset, abatement, diminution, defense or counterclaim to any mortgage loan (including the defense of usury). The operation of any terms of the mortgage note or the mortgage, or the exercise of any rights under the agreement, will not render the mortgage note or the mortgage unenforceable, in whole or in part, or subject to any right of rescission, offset, abatement, diminution, defense or counterclaim (including the defense of usury or the violation of any applicable disclosure or consumer credit laws). No right of rescission, offset abatement, diminution, defense or counterclaim has been asserted with respect thereto.

10. Mortgage Status

Neither the seller nor any prior holder of any mortgage loan has satisfied, canceled, rescinded or subordinated the mortgage in whole or in part, released the mortgaged property in whole or in part from the lien of the mortgage, or executed any instrument that would effect any such satisfaction, cancellation, rescission, subordination or release. The terms of the mortgage do not provide for a release of any portion of the mortgaged property from the lien of the mortgage.

11. Condemnation

To the best of the seller's knowledge, there is no proceeding pending for the total or partial condemnation of any mortgaged property.

12. Legal Compliance-Origination

All requirements of relevant federal, state and local law, rules and regulations have been satisfied or complied with in all material respects as they relate to the origination, funding servicing and the terms of the mortgage loans, including, without limitation, usury, truth in lending, real estate settlement procedures, consumer credit protection, equal credit opportunity or disclosure.

13. Title Insurance

The lien of each mortgage is insured by an ALTA lender's title insurance policy (or a binding commitment) or its equivalent, as adopted in the applicable jurisdiction. The policy insures the seller, its successor and assigns, as to the first priority lien of the mortgage in the original principal amount after all advances of principal, subject only to permitted encumbrances, none of which, individually or in the aggregate should interfere with the current use of the mortgaged property or materially detract from the benefit of the first priority lien of the mortgage. The seller or its successors or assigns are the sole named insured of the policy, and the policy is assignable to the purchaser without the consent of or any notification to the insurer.

14. No Holdbacks

The proceeds of each mortgage loan have been fully disbursed, or, in cases of partial disbursement, there is no requirement for future advances. To the best of the seller's knowledge, all requirements imposed by the originator to completion of any on-site or off-site improvements and to disbursements of any escrow funds have been complied with. Construction of the improvements on the mortgaged property are complete.

Exhibit 3 (Continued)

15. Mortgage Provisions
The mortgage note, mortgage and assignment of leases for each mortgage loan contain customary and enforceable provisions for commercial mortgage loans secured by properties such as the mortgaged properties, so as to render the rights and remedies of the holder adequate for the realization against the mortgaged property of the benefits of the security, including realization by judicial, or if applicable, non-judicial foreclosure subject to the effect of bankruptcy and similar laws affecting the rights of creditor and the application of principles of equity.

16. No Mortgage Default
There is no default, breach, violation or event of acceleration under the mortgage note, mortgage or assignment of leases, and no event that, with the passage of time or the giving of notice, or both, would constitute a default or event of acceleration, nor has the seller waived any such default. No foreclosure action or other form of enforcement has been threatened or commenced with respect to any mortgage.

17. Other Collateral
Each mortgage note does not, and has not since the date of origination of the related mortgage loan, secured by any collateral except the lien of the related mortgage, as assignment of the related leases, and any related security agreement. The mortgaged property does not secure any other mortgage loan not represented by the related mortgage note. No mortgage loan is cross-defaulted with any other mortgage loan nor is any mortgage loan secured by the mortgaged property that secures another mortgage loan.

18. Trustee Under Deed of Trust
In the case of any mortgage that is a deed of trust, a trustee, duly qualified under applicable law to serve as such, is properly designated and serves in accordance with applicable laws. No fees or expenses are payable to the trustee under the deed of trust, except in connection with a trustee's sale after default by the mortgagor or in connection with the release or the mortgaged property or related security for the mortgage loan following the payment of the mortgage loan in full.

19. Leases
The seller has delivered the purchaser a complete schedule of all leases with respect to each mortgaged property as of a date not more than 30 days prior to the closing date set forth in the attached schedule (XXX). Based on mortgagor representations, tenant estoppel certificates and other documents obtained by the seller, (i) the information contained therein is true and correct in all material respects, (ii) such leases are in full force and effect, and (iii) no default by the mortgagor or the lessees has occurred under such leases, nor, to the best of the seller's knowledge, is there any existing condition which, but for the passage of time or the giving of notice, or both, would result in a default under the terms of such lease. (Applicable to commercial loans with anchor tenants; multifamily properties may refer to attached rent roll.)

20. Lease Termination
No lease may be amended, terminated or canceled, and the lessee may not be released from its obligations, except under are certain limited events relating to material damage to, or destruction of, the mortgaged property, or condemnation of less than the entire mortgaged property, which, in any case, the lessee in good faith determines will render its continued occupancy and use of the remainder of the mortgaged property economically unsound, or condemnation of all the mortgaged property. (Applicable to retail/office loans.)

21. Condition of Mortgaged Property
Each mortgaged property is in good repair and condition, free of any material damage.

Exhibit 3 (Continued)

22. Local Law Compliance

Each mortgaged property is in compliance with all applicable laws, zoning ordinances, rules, covenants and restrictions affecting the construction, occupancy, use and operation of such mortgaged property. All inspections, licenses and certificates required, including certificates of occupancy, whether by law, ordinance, regulation or insurance standards to be made or issued with regard to the mortgaged property, have been obtained and are in full force and effect.

23. Environmental Compliance

In each mortgage, the mortgagor represents and warrants that it has not and will not use, cause or permit to exist on the related mortgaged property any hazardous materials in any manner that violates federal, state or local laws, ordinances, regulations, orders, directives or policies governing the use, storage, treatment, transportation, manufacture, refinement, handling, production or disposal of hazardous materials. The mortgagor agrees to indemnify, defend and hold the purchaser and its successors and/or assigns harmless from and against any and all losses, liabilities, damages, injuries, penalties, fines, expenses, and claims of any kind whatsoever (including attorney's fees and costs) paid, incurred, or suffered by, or asserted against, any such party resulting from a breach of any representation, warranty or covenant given by the mortgagor under the mortgage.

24. Opinion re Mortgage Enforceability

Each mortgage file contains an opinion letter(s) from counsel to the mortgagor which opines that, among other things, (A) the mortgage note, the mortgage, the assignment of leases, the UCC-1 or UCC-3 financing statement and all other documents and instruments evidencing, guaranteeing, insuring or otherwise securing the mortgage loan are genuine, and that each is the legal, valid and binding obligation of the maker, enforceable in accordance with its terms, except as the enforcement may be limited by bankruptcy, insolvency, reorganization, receivership, moratorium or other laws relating to or affecting the rights of creditors and by general principles of equity (regardless of whether such enforcement is considered in a proceeding in equity or at law) (B) all parties (other than the originator) to the mortgage note, the mortgage, the assignment of lessee, the UCC-1 and UCC-3 financing statement and each other document and instrument evidencing, guaranteeing, insuring or otherwise securing the mortgage loan have legal capacity to enter into the mortgage loan and to execute and deliver the mortgage note, the mortgage, the assignment of leases and other documents and instruments, (C) all necessary approvals, consents and authorizations required to be obtained by any party (other than the originator) have been obtained, and (D) the mortgage note, the mortgage, the assignment of leases and other documents and instruments have been duly authorized, executed and delivered by the parties (other than the originator).

Exhibit 3 (Continued)

25. Insurance

Each mortgaged property and all improvements are covered by insurance policies providing coverage against loss or damage sustained by (i) fire and extended perils included within the classification "All Risk of Physical Loss" in an amount sufficient to prevent the mortgagor from being deemed a co-insurer, and to provide coverage on a full replacement cost basis; and the policies contain a standard mortgagee clause naming mortgagee and its successors as additional insureds; (ii) business interruptions or rental loss insurance, in an amount at least equal to 12 months of operations of the mortgaged property; (iii) flood insurance (if any portion of the mortgaged property is located in an area identified by the Federal Emergency Management Agency as having special hazards); (iv) comprehensive general liability insurance in amounts as are generally required by commercial mortgage lenders, and in any event not less than $2 million per occurrence; (v) workers' compensation insurance; and (vi) other insurance as applicable to specific circumstances and criteria. The insurer in each case is qualified to write insurance in the relevant jurisdiction and has a claims paying ability rating from the rating agency of lot less than 'A'. The insurance policies contain clauses providing they are not terminable and may not be reduced without 30 days prior written notice to the mortgagee, and all premiums due and payable through the closing date have been made. No notice of termination or cancellation with respect to any such policies has been received by the seller.

26. Loan Underwriting

Each mortgage loan complies with all of the terms, conditions and requirements of the seller's underwriting standards in effect at the time of origination of such mortgage loan.

27. Status of Mortgage Documents

The mortgage note, related mortgage, any guaranty, assignment of leases and/or rents, security agreement, and chattel mortgage, each instrument delivered and all other documents evidencing, securing, guaranteeing, insuring or otherwise relating to the mortgage loan are genuine and the legal, valid and binding obligation of its maker, enforceable in accordance with its terms, except as such enforcement may be limited by bankruptcy, insolvency, moratorium or other laws affecting the enforcement of creditors' rights, or by the application of the rules of equity.

28. Inspections

The seller has inspected or caused to be inspected each related mortgaged property within the last 12 months.

29. Taxes and Assessments

There are no delinquent or unpaid taxes or assessments (including assessments payable in future installments), or other outstanding charges affecting any mortgaged property which are or may become a lien of equal or coordinate or higher priority than the lien of the mortgage.

30. Liens

There are no mechanics' or similar liens or claims that have been filed for work, labor or material. There are no claims outstanding that under applicable law could give rise to such lien, affecting the related mortgaged property which are or may be a lien prior to, or equal or coordinate with, the lien of the related mortgage.

31. Mortgagor Bankruptcy

To the best of the seller's knowledge, no mortgagor is a debtor in any state or federal bankruptcy or insolvency proceeding.

Exhibit 3 (Continued)

32. Fee Simple Interest
Each mortgaged property consists of an estate in fee simple in real property and improvements owned by the mortgagor. The buildings and improvements on the mortgaged property are owned by the mortgagor and used and occupied for commercial purposes in accordance with applicable law.

33. Loan Terms
No mortgage loan has a shared appreciation feature, other contingent interest feature or negative amortization.

34. Transfers and Subordinate Debt
The mortgage contains a "due on sale" clause that provides for the acceleration of the payment of the unpaid principal balance of the mortgage loan if, without the prior written consent of the holder, the property subject to the mortgage, or any interest therein, is directly or indirectly transferred or sold. The mortgage prohibits any further pledge or lien on the mortgaged property, whether equal or subordinate to the lien of the mortgage, without the prior written consent of the holder. (Any exceptions must be approved by the rating agency.)

35. Financial Statements
Each mortgage requires the mortgagor to provide the holder with quarterly and annual operating statements, rent rolls and related information. Annual financial statements must be audited by an independent certified public accountant upon the request of holder.

36. Escrow Deposits
All escrow deposits and payments relating to each mortgage loan are in the possession or under the control of the seller, and all amounts required to be deposited by the applicable mortgagor under the related mortgage loan documents have been deposited, and there are no deficiencies regarding them. All such escrows and deposits have been conveyed by seller to purchaser and identified as such with appropriate detail.

37. Selection Process
The seller has taken no action in selecting the mortgage loans for sale, assignment and transfer to the purchaser which, to the seller's knowledge, would result in delinquencies and losses on mortgage loans being materially in excess of delinquencies and losses on the seller's actual portfolio of commercial mortgage loans.

38. Borrower Concentration
As of the closing date, not more than 5% of the aggregate outstanding principal amount of the mortgage loans have the same mortgagor or, to the seller's best knowledge, are to mortgagors which are affiliates of each other. (Exceptions should be noted. Indicate whether non-consolidation opinions have been provided.)

Exhibit 3 (Continued)

39. Single-Purpose Entity

Each mortgagor is either a corporation or a limited partnership whose organizational documents provide that it is, and at least so long as the mortgage loan is outstanding will continue to be, a single-purpose entity. (For this purpose, "single-purpose entity" shall mean a person, other than an individual, which is formed or organized solely for the purpose of owning and operating a single property, does not engage in any business unrelated to such property and its financing, does not have any assets other than those related to its interest in the property or its financing, or any indebtedness other than as permitted by the related mortgage or the other mortgage loan documents, has its own books and records and accounts separate and apart from any other person, and holds itself out as being a legal entity, separate and apart from any other person.) If the foregoing entry is a limited partnership, (i) one general partner must be a single-purpose entity, and (ii) the partnership agreement must provide that the dissolution and winding up or insolvency filing of such limited partnership requires the unanimous consent of all general partners.

40. Servicing

No other person has been granted or conveyed the right to service the mortgage loans to receive any consideration in connection therewith.

In the event representation (32) regarding fee simple interest cannot be made, the substance of the following representations regarding ground leases should incorporated and approved by the rating agency.

Chapter 22

Commercial Mortgage Default Rates and Loss Severity

Pamela T. Dillon
Director
Fitch Investors Service, L.P.

Donald S. Belanger
Associate Director
Fitch Investors Service, L.P.

INTRODUCTION

As the commercial mortgage-backed securities (CMBS) market has matured, performance data on loans in many of the early transactions have become available and meaningful. In this chapter we report the most recent findings regarding CMBS performance. In this study, Fitch examines both default rates and loss severity. Moreover, Fitch examines in detail the extent to which certain characteristics — debt service coverage ratio (DSCR), property type, geographic location, loan size, interest rate type, and loan type — affect commercial mortgage loan default and loss severity. Fitch examines the components of loss severity and as well as compares loss rates by transaction. We then discuss how Fitch incorporates the results into the rating process and what areas are most important for future study.

DATA AND BASIC METHODOLOGY

Although $1 trillion in size, the commercial mortgage market has eluded study because historical performance data have been quite limited. As the CMBS market has matured, performance data on loans in many of the early securitized transactions have become available.

The authors thank Jeffrey T. Kennedy for his contribution in preparing this chapter.

A database containing 17,702 loans in 22 transactions with a total principal balance of approximately $11.7 billion was analyzed. This sample includes multi-borrower, performing transactions rated by Fitch that were issued between 1991-1995. These transactions contain loans with diversified loan and property characteristics. Transactions with special characteristics, such as those with loans backed exclusively by credit leases, were not included. Fitch acknowledges both the relatively short time and mild economic climate over which it has observed data.

Most of the loans in these transactions are of thrift quality because many of the earliest securitizations were issued by the RTC. Fitch's sample, which is summarized in Exhibit 1, includes thrift quality loans in non-RTC transactions as well, such as those in Merrill Lynch 1994-M1 and SASCO 1993-C1. Other transactions are composed of somewhat higher quality loan product, such as those in New England Mutual Life 1993-1 and Phoenix Real Estate Securities.

Fitch has used standard statistical methodology to compute and test its results. The period studied was 1991 through mid-1996. Defaults are reported as average annual rates of each of the independent variables, including DSCR, property type, geographic location, loan size, interest rate type, and loan type. These default rates are a function of the time the loans had been securitized. Loss severities are reported as average loss rates for each of the independent variables. In addition, average loss rates are provided for components of loss and on a transaction basis. In reporting its results, Fitch has noted which default and loss rates were determined not to be statistically significantly different from one another. A lack of significant difference between the means indicates either equality of results or a sample size too small to resolve any difference.

DEFAULT RATES AND LOSS SEVERITY

The average annual default rates reported in this study are a function of the number of actual loan defaults and the time the loans were securitized. Fitch defined a default as a loan that was 60 days or more past due on a debt service payment or 90 days or more past due on a balloon payment. Even if a loan became current at a later date, it was still considered to be a defaulted loan to avoid double counting. Of the sample of 17,702 loans, Fitch observed 2,364 defaults, representing approximately 12% of the total loan balance. The average annual default rate was 4.3%.

Fitch emphasizes that the default rates reported are the average annual rates observed from 1991 through mid-1996. These default rates are not cumulative and, as such, do not project the percentage of loans that default over time.[1] Future average default rates could be either higher or lower.

---

[1] For a discussion of cumulative rates of default, please refer to Fitch Research on "Commercial Mortgage Stress Test," dated June 8, 1992.

Exhibit 1: Multiborrower Commercial Mortgage-Backed Securities Database

Transaction Name	Securitization Date	Number of Loans	Geographic Concentration*	Property Type Concentration*
RTC 1991-M6	December 1991	391	75% CA; 7% AZ	100% Multifamily
RTC 1991-M7	December 1991	591	27% OH; 9% FL	100% Multifamily
RTC 1992-M3	April 1992	1,432	18% MN; 13% FL	100% Multifamily
RTC 1992-C4	June 1992	2,694	13%PA; 12% NJ	18% Office; 17% Retail
RTC 1992-C5	July 1992	3,591	12% CO:9% KS; 9% OH	21% Retail; 18% Office
RTC 1992-CHF	October 1992	1,763	77% CA; 6% FL	47% Multifamily;14% Office
SASCO 1993-C1	March 1993	683	61% CA; 6% MI	34% Retail; 31% Multifamily
KPAC 1993-M1	May 1993	57	43% CA; 6% 10% CO	100% Multifamily
Mortgage Capital Funding 1993-C1	September 1993	61†	62% NC; 15% TX	47% Multifamily; 33% Retail
Salomon Brothers Mortgage 1993-C1	September 1993	19	17% PA; 13% MO	100% Retail
New England Mutual Life 1993-1	December 1993	193	15% CA; 10% PA	37% Office; 25% Industrial
Phoenix Real Estate Securities	December 1993	102	22% CA; 16% NY	39% Retail; 24% multifamily
RTC 1993-C3	December 1993	984	23% CA; 13% AZ	43% Multifamily; 14% Office
Merrill Lynch 1994-M1	April 1994	83	27% CA; 15% TX	100% Multifamily
Commercial Real Estate Securities 1994-1	July 1994	263	58% WA; 19% CA	26% Multifamily; 20% Retail
FDIC 1994-C1	August 1994	1,806	21% NY; 11% TX	29% Office; 20% Retail
ACP Mortgage, L.P.	November 1994	23	87% CA; 5% UT	52% Multifamily; 29% Mixed Use
Nomura Asset Securities 1994-C3	November 1994	55	14% TX; 12% FL	61% Multifamily; 11% Manufactured Home
RTC 1994-C2	November 1994	1,566	33%CA; 13% NJ	38% Multifamily; 18% Office
American Southwest 1994-C2	December 1994	39‡	23% NY; 18% MI	35% Multifamily; 30% Office
SASCO 1995-C1	January 1995	208	27% CA; 25% PA	34% Retail; 28% Multifamily
RTC 1995-C1	June 1995	1,109	31% CA; 20% FL	65% Multifamily; 9% Retail
Total		17,702		

Exhibit I (Continued)

Transaction Name	Fixed-Rate Loans (%)*	Balloon Loans(%)*	Comments
RTC 1991-M6	22	98	60% of loans originated by FarWest
RTC 1991-M7	43	71	27% of loans originated by Mid-America Federal
RTC 1992-M3	62	63	Loans originated by 93 institutions nationwide
RTC 1992-C4	43	70	14% of loans originated by Great American Federal
RTC 1992-C5	43	60	Loans originated by 46 institutions nationwide
RTC 1992-CHF	23	95	All loans originated or purchased by HomeFed Bank
SASCO 1993-C1	63	92	Loans purchased from the RTC by Lehman Brothers
KPAC 1993-M1	100	100	Loans acquired by Kidder Peabody
Mortgage Capital Funding 1993-C1	64	96	78% of loans acquired from 1st Home Federal savings & Loan
Salomon Brothers Mortgage 1993-C1	100	22	Loans acquired by Salomon from Aetna Life
New England Mutual Life 1993-1	100	89	Originated by New England Mutual Life; 8% restructured
Phoenix Real Estate Securities	87	94	Loans originated by Phoenix home; 11% restructured
RTC 1993-C3	61	82	Loans originated by 237 institutions nationwide
Merrill Lynch 1994-M1	97	96	Loans originated by American Savings and Loan; 35% restructured
Commercial Real Estate Securities 1994-1	70	64	Loans acquired by Gentra Capital from Pacific First; 15% restructured
FDIC 1994-C1	66	80	24% of loans originated by American Savings Bank; 12% subperforming
ACP Mortgage, L.P.	13	56	Loans acquired by Argo from CalFed; 19% restructured
Nomura Asset Securities 1994-C3	100	83	30% of loans originated by Arbor National and 28% originated by Nomura
RTC 1994-C2	51	75	26% of loans originated by the RTC
American Southwest 1994-C2	100	100	Loans acquired by DIJ from Connecticut Mutual
SASCO 1995-C1	82	85	57% of loans originated by Westinghouse; 40% acquired by Lehman Brothers
RTC 1995-C1	70	89	40% restructured and modified loans

* As a percentage of principal balance. † Including two mortgage participations. ‡ Effectively 30 loans.

Exhibit 2: Average Annual Default Rate
by Debt Service Coverage Ratio (x)

DSCR (×)	Default Rate (%)
≥ 2.10	1.8
1.75-2.09	2.9
1.40-1.74	3.9
1.20-1.39	4.1
1.00-1.19	5.2
0.80-0.99	7.1
0.50-0.79	7.2
<0.50	7.1

One of the variables on commercial loan performance that Fitch studied was DSCR. The default rates were measured using DSCR at securitization. Fitch computed DSCRs for only those loans with reliable cash flow information. The DSCRs reflect stressed refinance rates and amortization terms. While loan-to-value ratio (LTV) may also explain the performance of the loans, such data were largely unavailable or unreliable, particularly with respect to loans in RTC transactions.

Fitch defined a loss to be a function of the loan balance at securitization, the loan balance at default, property sales proceeds, property income, property protection expenses, and interest advanced. Fitch computed the average loss rates as a percentage of the loan balance at securitization rather than at default because Fitch's ratings, which are intended to be long-term in nature, reflect the subordination levels at securitization. Fitch included only those losses incurred on loans that have been completely resolved. Fitch observed a total of 547 losses, representing approximately 4.5% of the total loan balance. The average loss rates are indicative of the sample and the period studied, and future average loss rates could be either higher or lower.

Debt Service Coverage Ratio

As expected, DSCR influenced commercial loan defaults. The higher the margin between property income and loan debt service, the higher the probability the borrower will meet the debt service payment. As shown in Exhibit 2, loans with relatively high DSCRs defaulted much less frequently than loans with lower DSCRs. The average annual rate of default ranged from a low of 1.8% for loans with DSCRs of more than 2.10 times (×) to 7.1% for loans with DSCRs of less than 0.50×. Moreover, the spread between the annual averages is among the widest of any property or loan characteristic studied, suggesting that DSCR is a factor that strongly influences loan performance.

Fitch's results also show there was no "cliff" at a DSCR of 1.00×. Not all borrowers immediately exercise their default option when property income falls below that needed to pay debt service. These borrowers will support, at least temporarily, a property that they view to have the long-term ability to pay debt service. The average annual rate of default of 4.1% at a DSCR between 1.20×–1.39× indicates the inherent riskiness of commercial real estate as an asset class, especially considering the mild economic climate between 1991 and mid-1996.

Not only did loans with relatively low DSCRs default more frequently, preliminary results show that average losses were higher as well. Higher losses result from the implied negative equity in a property when the loan has a DSCR below 1.00×. The results are presented in Exhibit 3; however, Fitch emphasizes that DSCR does not have a statistically significant influence on the loss rates. Fitch currently assumes higher default frequencies and loss severities for loans with a DSCR below 1.00× and will continue to study the effect of DSCR to refine its assumptions.

Property Type

Loans secured by warehouses had an average annual default rate of 1.9%, lower than loans secured by multifamily, industrial, office, nursing home, retail, or lodging properties (see Exhibit 4). Warehouses are more general purpose buildings, often requiring less capital investment than industrial and office properties and, therefore, experience less risk due to rollover expense. Warehouses, unlike office buildings, were not prone to the overbuilding of the 1980s.

Exhibit 3: Severity of Loss by Debt Service Coverage Ratio

DSCR (×)	Average Loss (%)
<0.50	55.3
0.50-0.79	51.6
0.80-0.99	45.3
1.00-1.19	47.5
1.20-1.39	47.7
1.40-1.74	30.7
1.75-2.09	15.1
≥2.10	12.8

Exhibit 4: Average Annual Default Rate by Property Type

Property Type	Percentage
Warehouse	1.9
Multifamily	3.9
Industrial	4.4
Office	4.7
Nursing Home	5.0
Retail	5.1
Lodging	5.6

Exhibit 5: Severity of Loss by Property Type

Property Type	Percentage
Industrial	19.2
Nursing Home	19.2
Lodging	22.4
Warehouse	30.7
Retail	32.8
Office	34.5
Multifamily	44.8

While preliminary results suggest default rates for multifamily properties were relatively low, the average loss rates were fairly high. Fitch found the average loss rate for multifamily loans was 45%. However, many of the multifamily loans in the RTC transactions are of particularly poor quality, although not necessarily worse than many multifamily loans in conduit transactions. Industrial loans were found to have a much lower average loss rate of 19% (see Exhibit 5). While Fitch reports the average loss rates for loans secured by other property types, Fitch notes that these property types do not have a statistically significant influence on the loss rates.

Fitch believes once certain risks are addressed, diversity of property type in a transaction is generally a strength because performance cycles vary by property type. Property type risks are addressed by applying certain criteria to underwriting cash flow. For example, office properties typically require considerable investment in tenant improvements, leasing commissions, and capital reserves just to maintain a stable cash flow. Consequently, in underwriting the cash flow of office buildings, as well as other properties, Fitch subtracts capital items to determine the cash flow available for debt service. In addition, Fitch assumes a higher default frequency for loans secured by certain property types, such as hotels and unanchored retail.

Geographic Location

Loans secured by properties in the Pacific Northwest defaulted less than loans secured by properties in any other region (see Exhibit 6). The average annual default rates for Oregon and Washington loans were lower than any other state studied and were much lower than the default rates for either Massachusetts or Connecticut loans. In fact, Massachusetts loans defaulted five times more often than Oregon or Washington loans. Unlike other areas, the Pacific Northwest did not become as overbuilt during the 1980s, which almost certainly contributed to the relatively low rates of default.

Geographic diversity is generally a strength in a transaction, since different regions of the U.S. tend to experience economic difficulties at either different times or to varying degrees. Fitch ordinarily assumes a higher default frequency for loans secured by properties in the state or region with the greatest concentration to allow for the effects of an economic downturn. Fitch also assumes a higher default frequency for loans secured by properties in a state or region about to or already experiencing economic difficulties.

Exhibit 6: Average Annual Default Rate by Geographic Location

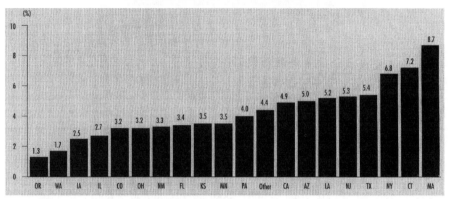

Loss Severity on Foreclosed Loans

As shown in Exhibit 7, loans secured by properties in New Jersey and Pennsylvania suffered much lower average loss rates than loans secured by properties in California or Texas. These lower loss rates seem to be less indicative of the economic climate than of how the loans were resolved. However, these lower loss rates were not the result of nonjudicial foreclosures, which are typically less time consuming and expensive; foreclosures in both New Jersey and Pennsylvania are handled judicially. Most of the properties securing the loans were simply not foreclosed upon, which avoided the process altogether. The lower loss rates were a result of loan restructurings, loan sales, or obtaining deeds in lieu of foreclosure.

Further analysis revealed that historical average loss rates across the U.S. were a result of the method of loan resolution. The average loss rate of loans secured by properties foreclosed on was 56%, while loans resolved without foreclosure proceedings suffered an average loss rate of only 30%. Loans secured by properties foreclosed on suffered losses almost twice as high as loans that were otherwise resolved.

Loan Size

Two contradictory schools of thought exist on how loan performance is likely to be affected by loan size. Some believe that a large loan is less likely to default because it is secured by a large property with more professional operations about which considerable due diligence has been done. Also, larger properties are often able to attract institutional financing and higher quality tenants. Others assert that a small loan is less likely to default because the livelihood of the borrower often depends on its performance, and that refinancing is easier because less proceeds are required. Currently, Fitch does not adjust default frequency based on loan size in its CMBS default model.

Exhibit 7: Severity of Loss by Geographic Location

State	Average Loss (%)
New Jersey	13.2
Pennsylvania	13.6
New Mexico	20.2
Other	24.3
Arizona	25.7
New York	29.1
Colorado	35.5
Oregon	40.1
California	42.4
Illinois	43.3
Minnesota	43.9
Massachusetts	45.3
Texas	45.4
Kansas	49.6
Florida	50.6
Ohio	59.9
Connecticut	62.6
Louisiana	73.6
Iowa	74.2

As shown in Exhibit 8, relatively large loans defaulted more frequently than smaller loans. The average annual default rates for loans with principal balances exceeding $750,000 ranged from 5.6%-7.8%. Loans with principal balances of between $125,000-$249,999 experienced an average annual default rate of 4.7%.[2] However, defaults on the smaller loans were not at the low rate historically experienced by residential loans. Although default rates are somewhat influenced by loan size, preliminary analysis showed that average loss rates seemed unaffected by loan size. The average loss rates are shown in Exhibit 9. However, Fitch emphasizes that loan size does not have a statistically significant influence on the loss rates.

Additional analysis showed that recourse to the borrower did not explain the lower default rate for smaller loans. The percentage of recourse loans that defaulted was about the same for smaller loans as it was for larger loans.

Interest Rate Type

Even during a period of relatively stable and low interest rates, floating-rate loans defaulted much more often than fixed-rate loans. Fitch's analysis shows that the

---

[2] Fitch does not report the default rate or loss severity for loans below $125,000 because Fitch considers much of those loan balance data to be unreliable.

average annual default rate for floating-rate loans was 5.2%, which is notably higher than the average annual default rate of 3.6% for fixed-rate loans. Not only did floating-rate loans default more often than fixed-rate loans, they had higher average losses as well. The average loss rate for floating-rate loans was 41.2%, greater than that of fixed-rate loans which was 31.1%.

Although interest rates over the period studied were relatively low, Fitch's results show that even a modest increase in rates can create a stress event for the loan. Default can occur because debt is generally sized based on interest rates at origination. Fitch would expect default rates for loans with floating interest rates to be still higher during a high interest rate environment. Fitch addresses the risks of floating-rate loans by calculating the DSCR based on a stressed interest rate of the lower of 13% or the interest rate cap.

Exhibit 8: Average Annual Default Rate
by Loan Size ($)

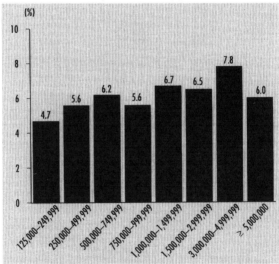

Exhibit 9: Severity of Loss by Loan Size

Loan Size ($)	Average Loss (%)
125,000-249,999	32.8
250,000-499,999	30.7
500,000-749,999	42.4
750,000-999,999	32.8
1,000,000-1,499,999	41.1
1,500,000-2,999,999	39.1
3,000,000-4,999,999	49.3
≥ 5,000,000	34.8

Loan Type

Fully amortizing loans defaulted much less often than balloon loans. Fitch's analysis shows that the average annual default rate for fully amortizing loans was 2.4%, which is much lower than the average annual default rate of 6.7% for balloon loans. While fully amortizing loans defaulted less than balloon loans, balloon loans had lower average loss rates. The average loss rate for balloon loans was 30.1%, lower than the average loss rates of 51.3% for fully amortizing loans. Higher average loss rates for fully amortizing loans may suggest that a borrower does not default on a fully amortizing loan unless the property is especially distressed, or that the balloon dates force borrowers to confront their subperforming properties sooner.

The balloon date is a critical point for the performance of a loan, as in the absence of an extension granted by the special servicer it will either pay off or default. Fitch addresses the risks of balloon loans by calculating DSCRs based on hypothetical refinance rates that consider loan and property type. In addition, Fitch views full servicer flexibility, including the ability to extend or modify defaulted loans, to be critical in offsetting balloon risk. Full servicer flexibility is especially important in conduit transactions, where the balloon loans tend to have grouped maturities.

LOSS SEVERITY AND COMPONENTS OF LOSS

The overall performance of a CMBS transaction depends on not only the defaults experienced by the pool of loans but also the loss severity associated with each of those defaults. Of the 2,364 loans in Fitch's sample that defaulted, 547 have resulted in losses to date. The losses were due to advanced interest on the loans, property protection expenses, and, in the vast majority of cases, a decrease in the value of the property. These losses were offset by property income and, in some instances, an increase in the value of the property. The losses were due to loan restructurings, loan sales, or liquidations following property foreclosures or obtaining deeds in lieu of foreclosure.

Fitch has defined a loss to be the loan balance at default plus advanced interest and property protection expenses less property sales proceeds and property income. Loss severity was computed as a percentage of the loan balance at securitization rather than at default because Fitch's ratings reflect the subordination levels at securitization. Fitch included all loss observations in its analysis of loss severity. Fitch noted only a few situations where the value of the property was sufficiently high to result in a "negative" loss, or a gain in the case of real estate owned.

Over the period 1991 through mid-1996, the average loss rate was 36.9% of the loan balance at securitization. One-quarter of the observed loss rates were greater than 64%, and one-half were greater than 27% (see Exhibit 10). The average loss severity had three components — loss due to a decrease in property value, advanced interest, and property protection expenses. The average loss due to a decrease in property value was 32.5%, advanced interest was 8.7%, and property protection expenses was 2.0%, for a total loss severity of 43.2%. Partial amortization on the loans reduced the average loss severity to 36.9%.

Exhibit 10: Loss Distribution

Number of Losses	547
Mean Loss (%)	36.9
First Quartile (%)	1.4
Median (%)	27.0
Third Quartile (%)	63.7

The average loss severity of approximately 37% of the original loan balance is surprisingly high considering the mild economic climate during which the loans were resolved. This high loss rate may reflect the property quality and the quality of underwriting that was characteristic of the thrift industry. Indeed, 477 of the 547 loss observations are on loans in RTC transactions.

Other commercial loan studies have found lower loss rates.[3] Snyderman reported a loss severity of 36% for foreclosed loans and estimated the loss severity of restructured loans to be 18%, one-half of that for foreclosed loans. Snyderman's estimate of loss severity for restructured loans of one-half that for foreclosed loans is consistent with Fitch's results. However, the implied overall loss rate is clearly lower than the loss severity that Fitch observed. This lower loss severity resulted probably because Snyderman studied insurance company loans, which tend to be higher quality product. Also, Snyderman's loss rate may be understated to the extent that the insurance companies loaned to facilitate the sale of foreclosed properties.

LOSS SEVERITY BY TRANSACTION

Of the 22 transactions studied, 16 have suffered losses from loans resolved by mid-1996 (see Exhibit 11). Both the average loss rates and the range of loss rates varied considerably among the transactions. Fitch's analysis shows that the average loss rates experienced in RTC 1992-C4, RTC 1992-CHF, and RTC 1994-C2 are comparatively lower than the average losses experienced in any of the RTC multifamily transactions, FDIC 1994-C1, or SASCO 1993-C1. The comparatively lower average loss rates are due to the very large number of small losses in RTC 1992-C4, RTC 1992-CHF, and RTC 1994-C2. While the loss rates for the sample ranged widely from less than 1% to 219% of loan balance at securitization, the average loss severity was skewed downward by the large number of very small losses (see Exhibit 12). The spike in the data reflects legal and other costs incurred after a loan resolution.

---

[3] Mark P. Snyderman, "Update on Commercial Mortgage Defaults," *The Real Estate Finance Journal* (Summer 1994), pp. 22-32; and Brian A. Ciochetti and Timothy J. Riddiough, "Loss Severity and Its Impact on Commercial Mortgage Performance," Unpublished Manuscript, University of North Carolina and Massachusetts Institute of Technology's Center for Real Estate, 1994. Note that Ciochetti measures loss severity only through foreclosure of the loan and not through the sale of the property.

Exhibit 11: Severity of Loss by Transaction

Transaction Name	No. of Losses	Average Loss (%)	Special Servicer	Servicer Flexibility
New England Mutual Life 1993-1	1	4.9	Lennar	Yes
RTC 1995-C1	4	9.3	Banc One	Yes
RTC 1994-C2	28	15.9	AMRESCO/CPC	Yes
RTC 1992-C4	181	16.9	J.E. Robert	Yes
RTC 1992-CHF	63	21.0	AMRESCO	Yes
ACP Mortgage, L.P.	1	30.4	AMRESCO	Yes
Commercial Real Estate Securities 1994-1	1	31.3	Gentra	Yes
KPAC 1993-M1	2	37.4	Bankers Trust*	Moderate
RTC 1993-C3	25	52.6	Banc One	Yes
FDIC 1994-C1	21	53.2	Banc One	Yes
RTC 1992-M3	39	53.6	AMRESCO**	Yes
RTC 1992-C5	78	53.7	AMRESCO**	Yes
SASCO 1993-C1	41	55.9	Banc One	Yes
RTC 1991-M6	37	62.8	GECAM	Limited
Merrill Lynch1994-M1	2	69.5	AMRESCO	Yes
RTC 1991-M7	23	74.3	Bank of America	Limited

* Master servicer with ability to extend loans.
** Equitable sold the contract to AMRESCO in October 1995.

Exhibit 12: Distribution of Losses

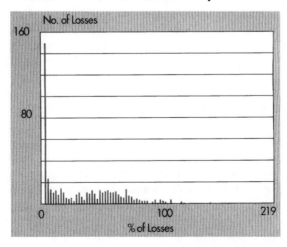

In addition, transaction structural characteristics may have affected the average loss rates. Limited servicer flexibility in the pooling and servicing agreements for RTC 1991-M6 and RTC 1991-M7 may explain, to some degree, their relatively high loss rates. Also, the pooling and servicing agreements for these RTC transactions do not have the recoverability standard that is typical of other transactions. In addition, the special servicers do not own the first-loss piece on these RTC transactions, which may have affected the servicers' performance.

CONCLUSIONS AND APPLICATIONS

The default and loss rates reported in this chapter reflect the performance of only those loans studied over the period 1991 to mid-1996, and future average rates may be higher or lower. Consequently, extension of these results to the default frequency and loss severity assumptions Fitch makes in estimating subordination would be premature. First of all, the performance of the loans studied may not be indicative of the performance of other loans. Other property and loan characteristics may also explain loan performance, or several characteristics considered together may explain more than the characteristics considered individually. In addition, performance of the loans would have been different in a more stressful environment. Nevertheless, Fitch's results provide valuable insight into the variables that influence default and loss of commercial loans.

Fitch found that loans with low DSCRs, floating-rate loans, and balloon loans all had relatively higher average annual rates of default. Fitch currently assumes higher default frequencies for loans with lower DSCRs, and calculates DSCR for floating-rate loans based on stressed interest rates. Fitch addresses the risks of balloon loans by calculating DSCRs based on hypothetical refinance rates, which consider loan and property type. In addition, Fitch views full servicer flexibility to be critical in offsetting balloon risk. Smaller loans tended to default less than larger loans, but recourse to the borrower did not explain the lower default rate. However, smaller loans did not show lower average losses than larger loans. Currently, Fitch does not adjust default frequency or loss severity based on loan size, but will continue to study the influence of loan size on loan performance.

The average loss severity of approximately 37% of the original loan balance was high considering the mild economic climate during which the loans were resolved and is likely due to the weak underwriting standards in the thrift industry during the 1980s when many of these loans were originated. While the quality of underwriting on today's conduit pools is better, the loans in the conduit pools are secured by properties that are of the same "B" and "C" quality. Consequently, similar loss rates could result. Of course, the overall performance of conduit transactions will be influenced significantly by economic conditions at the time the loans mature, especially since conduit loans tend to have grouped maturities.

Chapter 23

Structural Considerations Impacting CMBS

John N. Dunlevy, CFA, CPA
Director and Senior Portfolio Manager
Hyperion Capital Management

INTRODUCTION

Commercial mortgage-backed securities (CMBS) are a rapidly growing segment of the fixed-income market. This growth has been spurred by the ability of Wall Street to securitize real estate and loans of real estate, and transform equity into real estate investment trusts (REITs) and debt into CMBS (see Exhibit 1). This chapter will focus on the structural considerations impacting CMBS investments. There are five basic types of CMBS transactions; however, we will concentrate on the three types of CMBS deals which are greatly impacted by structure.

BASIC CMBS STRUCTURE

A CMBS transaction is formed when an issuer places commercial loans into a trust which then issues classes of bonds backed by the interest and principal of the underlying mortgages. The basic building block of the CMBS transaction is a commercial loan which was originated either to finance a commercial purchase or to refinance a prior mortgage obligation.

Exhibit 1: Transformation of Real Estate and Real Estate Loans

	Equity	Debt
Private	Direct Investments Commingled Funds	Whole Loans
Public	REITs	CMBS

Exhibit 2: Commercial Loan Disposition after Origination

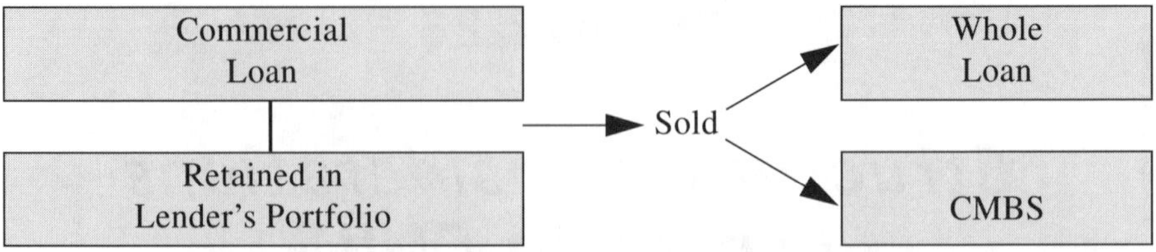

Many types of commercial loans can be either sold by the originator as a commercial whole loan or structured into a CMBS transaction (see Exhibit 2). The whole loan market, which is largely dominated by insurance companies and banks, is focused on loans between $10 and $50 million issued on traditional property types (multifamily, retail, office, and industrial). CMBS transactions, on the other hand, can involve loans of virtually any size (from conduit loans as small as $1 million to single property transactions as large as $200 million) and/or property type.

The CMBS transaction structure takes shape when the owner of the commercial loans has a potential transaction "sized" by the rating agencies. This sizing will determine the necessary level of credit enhancement to achieve a desired rating level. For example, if certain *debt service coverage* (DSC) and *loan-to-value* (LTV) ratios are needed, and these ratios cannot be met at the loan level, then subordination is used to achieve these levels. In Exhibit 3, a simple example demonstrates how a CMBS transaction can be structured to meet the rating agencies required DSC and LTV ratios. For example, Duff & Phelps requires a 1.51× coverage to achieve a single-A rating on a regional mall deal. Since that level cannot be obtained at the collateral level (coverage of 1.25×) a CMBS structure with 17.2% subordination is created.

Paydown Priority

The rating agencies will require that the CMBS transaction be retired sequentially with the highest rated bonds paying off first. Therefore, any return of principal caused by amortization, prepayment, or default will be used to repay the highest rated tranche.

Interest on principal outstanding will be paid to all tranches. In the event of a delinquency resulting in insufficient cash to make all scheduled payments, the transaction's servicer will advance both principal and interest. Advancing will continue from the servicer for as long as these amounts are deemed recoverable.

Losses arising from loan defaults will be charged against the principal balance of the lowest rated CMBS bond tranche outstanding. The total loss charged will include the amount previously advanced as well as the actual loss incurred in the sale of the loan's underlying property.

Finally, the investor must be sure to understand the cash flow priority of any prepayment penalties and/or yield maintenance provisions, as this can impact a particular bond's average life and overall yield.

Exhibit 3: How a CMBS Transaction can be Structured to Satisfy Required DSC and LTV Ratios of Duff & Phelps

Loan Information	
Assume $100 million Regional mall loan	DSC 1.25×* LTV 75%*
Market value	$133.3 million
Debt service	$10.0 million
NOI	$12.5 million

CMBS Structure	Required Subordination (%)*	Tranche Size	Tranche LTV (%)	Tranche DSC
AAA	31.4	68.6	51.5	1.82×
AA	23.3	8.1	57.5	1.63×
A	17.2	6.1	62.1	1.51×
BBB	12.0	5.2	66.0	1.42×
BB	6.6	5.4	70.1	1.34×
B	2.6	4.0	73.1	1.28×
NR	0.0	2.6	75.0	1.25×
		100.0		

* Source: Duff & Phelps.

Structural Call Protection

The degree of call protection available to a CMBS investor is a function of the following two characteristics:

1. call protection available at loan level
2. call protection afforded from the actual CMBS structure

At the commercial loan level, call protection can take the following form:

1. prepayment lockout
2. prepayment penalty
3. yield maintenance penalties

The strongest type of prepayment protection is prepayment lockout. A lockout is a contractual agreement that prohibits all prepayments during the period of the lockout.

Prepayment penalties are predetermined penalties which must be paid by the borrower if the borrower wishes to refinance. For example, 5-4-3-2-1 is a common prepayment penalty structure. That is, if the borrower wishes to prepay during the first year, he must pay a 5% penalty for a total of $105 rather than $100 (which is the norm in the residential market). Likewise, during the second year, a 4% penalty would apply, etc.

Exhibit 4: Sequence of Principal Paydowns

CMBS Structure	Principal Paydowns
AAA	
AA	
A	
BBB	
BB	
B	
NR	

Losses

Yield maintenance penalties, in their simplest terms, are designed to make investors indifferent as to the timing of prepayments. The yield maintenance provision makes it uneconomical to refinance solely to get a lower mortgage rate. The simplest and most restrictive form of yield maintenance (Treasury flat yield maintenance) penalizes the borrower based on the difference between the mortgage coupon and the prevailing Treasury rate.

The other type of call protection available in CMBS transactions is structural. That is, because the CMBS bond structures are sequential-pay (by rating) the AA-rated tranche cannot paydown until the AAA is completely retired, and the AA-rated bonds must be paid off before the A-rated bonds, etc. (see Exhibit 4). However, as mentioned earlier, principal losses due to defaults are impacted from the bottom of the structure upward.

Balloon Maturity Provisions

Many commercial loans backing CMBS transactions are balloon loans which require substantial principal payment on the final maturity date. Although many investors like the "bullet bond-like" paydown of the balloon maturities, it does present difficulties from a structural standpoint. That is, if the deal is structured to completely paydown on a specified date, an event of default will occur if any delays occur. However, how such delays impact CMBS investors is dependent on the bond type (premium, par or discount) and whether or not the servicer will advance to a particular tranche after the balloon default. Another concern for CMBS investors in multi-tranche transactions is the fact that all loans must be refinanced to pay off the most senior bond holders. Therefore, the balloon risk of the most senior tranche (i.e., AAA) may be equivalent to that of the most junior bond class (i.e., B).

Currently, there are three types of structural provisions that can be present in CMBS transactions. The provisions are summarized in Exhibit 5.

The first provision — *time matched method* — is no longer used in CMBS transactions because it often results in actual defaults upon balloon maturity. This method was common prior to the real estate recession which began in the late 1980s. Prior to this national real estate downturn, extension risk was not a primary concern for traditional lenders (i.e., insurance companies and banks). However, the real estate recession caused a rapid decline in property values which in turn caused many loans to be non-refinanceable under the original loan terms. Many of these deals did contain default rate provisions. That is, an extension could be granted in exchange for an increase in the interest rate. Further, many deals of this type also had a "cash-trap" mechanism which captured all excess cash flow and used it to paydown debt.

The second type of balloon loan provision is the *internal tail*. The internal tail requires the borrower to provide ongoing evidence of its efforts to refinance the loan. For example, the following procedures would have to be undertaken within one year of the balloon date:

- appraisals on all properties
- Phase I environmental reports
- engineering reports

Finally, within six months prior to balloon maturity, the borrower must obtain a refinancing commitment.

The third type of balloon loan provision is the *external tail*. This method is preferred by the major rating agencies since it gives the borrower the most time to arrange refinancing while avoiding default on the bond obligations. The external tail method, as shown in Exhibit 6, sets the maturity date of the CMBS issue longer than that of the underlying loans. The difference between these two dates acts as a buffer to arrange loan refinancing. Further, the CMBS investor does not suffer an interruption in cash flow during this period since the servicer advances any missing interest and scheduled principal (but not the balloon payment).

Exhibit 5: Types of CMBS Balloon Provisions

Method	Description	Examples
Time matched	Balloon maturity and bond maturity are the same	CMBS deals pre-RTC
Internal tail	Balloon maturity and bond maturity same but provisions for refinancing begin 1 to 2 years prior to maturity	DLJ 1992 and 1993 "M" series
External tail	Balloon maturity occurs before bond maturity	Most 1995 conduit deals and secured REIT debt transactions

Exhibit 6: External Tail Time Line

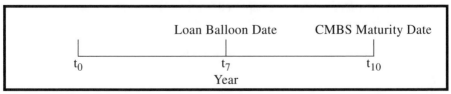

Loan Balloon Date   CMBS Maturity Date

t_0 t_7 t_{10}

Year

Exhibit 7: Diagram of Principal Payment Windows

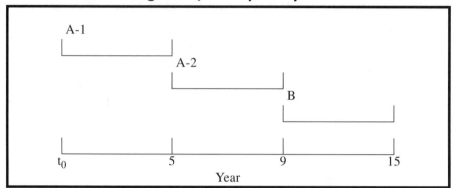

Evaluating the Timing of Cash Flows

Similar to mortgage-backed and asset-backed securities, CMBS structures can experience principal amortization throughout the life of the underlying loans.

As shown in Exhibit 7, the investor must evaluate CMBS cash flows occurring across the varying principal payment windows. The traditional evaluation uses yield to maturity to evaluate a bond's relative attractiveness. However, yield to maturity assumes each cash flow received over the life of a security can be reinvested at a constant rate. This implies that the yield curve also remains unchanged or flat over time. The "flat" scenario is highly unlikely over extended periods of time. When, for example, the yield curve is steep, the actual total return to maturity should be less than the yield to maturity for amortizing classes.

This is the case because in a steep yield curve environment it is not possible to reinvest at a yield to maturity level without sharply increasing duration. Therefore, a better way to evaluate these securities is to use the bond's *Z-spread*. Z-spread refers to the bond's option-adjusted spread (OAS) at a zero interest rate volatility. Z-spread allows the investor to quantify the cost of the amortization period, and achieve an apples-to-apples comparison between a bullet bond and an amortizing security.

Another key component in evaluating a security's overall attractiveness is the bond's default-adjusted yield. This calculation can only be performed after the necessary time and resources have been committed to building a default model. The recently announced Equitable Real Estate/Hyperion Capital joint venture has built such a model. The key elements to building such a model are as follows:

- 20+ years experience captured with regard to all *actual whole loan experience*

- Database of actual *NOI volatility* by: property type, geographic location, and point in real estate cycle

- Generation of 1,000 interest rate and NOI paths to estimate foreclosure frequency

- Ability to use actual experience as RTC servicer to generate loss severity estimates by: property type and state

- Ability to estimate losses and calculate yield impact on tranches by overlying deal structure

- Ability to calculate standard deviation of defaults and estimate confidence intervals

- Ability to calculate above on a loan-by-loan basis rather than using simplifying assumptions

Servicer's Role

The servicer on a CMBS deal can play a key role in the overall success of the transaction. The key responsibilities of the servicer are:

- collect monthly loan payments
- keep records relating to payments
- maintain property escrows (taxes and insurance)
- monitor condition of underlying properties
- prepare reports for trustee
- transfer collected funds to trustee for payment

There are different types of servicers, and their roles can vary from deal to deal. In general, we will discuss three types of servicers: the sub-servicer; the master servicer; and the special servicer. These different servicers are highlighted in Exhibit 8.

Exhibit 8: Types of Servicers

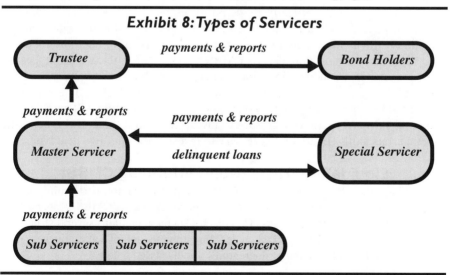

The *sub-servicer* is usually the originator of the loan in a conduit deal who has decided to sell the loan but retain the servicing. All payments and property information will then be sent by the sub-servicer to the *master servicer*. The master servicer oversees the deal and makes sure the servicing agreements are maintained. In addition, the master servicer must facilitate the timely payment of interest and principal. That is, when a loan goes into default, the master servicer has the responsibility to provide for servicing advances. This role is critical to the success of a deal; therefore, it is important for an investor to be comfortable with both the financial strength and the overall experience of the master servicer.

A *special servicer* also plays a vital role within a CMBS transaction. The special servicer is usually engaged whenever a loan becomes more than 60 days past due. The special servicer usually has the following powers:

- extend the loan
- make loan modifications
- restructure the loan
- foreclose on the loan and sell the property

The special servicer is important to subordinated buyers because the timing of the loss can significantly impact the loss severity, which in turn can greatly impact subordinated returns. Therefore, first loss investors usually want to either control the appointment of the special servicer or perform the role themselves.

DIFFERENT TYPES OF CMBS DEALS

Exhibit 9 shows the five types of CMBS deal structures. The first three types — liquidating trusts, multi-property single borrower, and multi-property conduit — will be discussed in detail in this section. These three deal types, which allow investors to focus more attention on structural aspects, have been the focus of most fixed-income money manager's CMBS activity. The latter two deal types — multi-property non-conduit and single-property single borrower — have been the focus of real estate money manager activity within CMBS. The recently announced Equitable Real Estate/Hyperion Capital joint venture will combine the structural skills (Hyperion) necessary to invest in the first three deal types with the real estate skills (Equitable) necessary to invest in the later two deal types.

Liquidating Trusts (Non-Performing CMBS)

A small but interesting segment of the CMBS market is the non-performing or liquidating trusts. This segment, as the name implies, represents CMBS deals backed by non-performing mortgage loans. This market segment contains several structural nuances which must be analyzed when deciding upon the relative attractiveness of a particular bond tranche. Some of the features are discussed below.

Exhibit 9: CMBS Deal Structures

	Liquidating Trusts (Non-Performing)	Multi-Property Single-Borrower	Multi-Property Conduit	Multi Property Non-Conduit	Single-Property Single-Borrower
Sample deals	-RTC N-Series -Lennar -SKW -Kearny Street	-Belaire -Factory Stores	-Nomura -Megadeal -DLJ Conduit	-RTC C-Series -New England	-Danbury Mall -Freehold Mall
Key risks	Structural	Structural/Credit	Structural/Credit	Credit	Credit
Loan age	Seasoned	New	New	Seasoned	New
Available ratings	AA-B	AAA-NR	AAA-NR	AAA-B	AAA-NR

Fast Pay Structure

The so-called *fast-pay* structure requires that all cash flows from both asset sales and ongoing debt service, after bond interest payments, be used to retire the most senior bond class outstanding. The fast pay structure prevents the equity holder from receiving any cash flow until all bond classes are retired. Since equity holders are highly sensitive to internal rate of return (i.e., they want to retire the bond classes quickly), the bondholder's interests are aligned with those of the equity holder.

Over Collateralization

Liquidating trusts are structured so that the debt obligations (bond classes) are less than the actual receivables outstanding (loan note amount). This creates a level of over collateralization which can be used to offer discounted payoffs in order to accelerate the retirement of the bond classes. As an example, the first non-performing CMBS transaction — RTC 1992-N1 — had the following attributes:

- Estimated market value: $155.3 million (DIV)
- Bond classes issued: $110.0 million
- Original loan balances: $345.8 million
- Equity contribution: $61.8 million

These transactions have proven to work well since structurally the acquisition price or derived investment value (DIV) is often 60% or less of the current balance of the mortgage collateral. In this case the DIV was 45% of the original loan balances ($155.3/$345.8), while the bond classes issued were only 71% of the estimated market value or DIV.

Servicer Flexibility

Liquidating trust structures generally allow the servicer maximum flexibility to liquidate the pool's underlying assets. Non-performing loans are generally grouped into three categories: performing, sub-performing, and real estate owned (REO).

Exhibit 10: Asset Disposition Strategy by Servicer

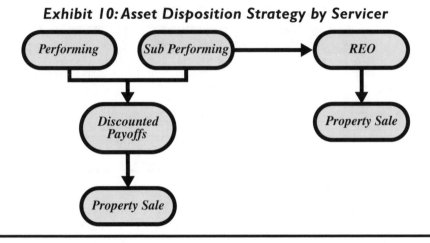

As shown in Exhibit 10, the servicer (who is often also the transaction's equity holder) will work to carry out an asset disposition strategy which was designed at the deal's inception. The servicer's ability to dispose of property is paramount to maximizing value for bondholders. To help ensure that bondholder values are maximized, incentives are built in for the servicer.

Generally, the servicer can use one of two disposal strategies: discounted pay-offs or take title of a property through foreclosure, then sell the property from REO. The method employed is a function of where the loans are currently situated. That is, if a high percentage of loans are already in REO, the investor will expect a shorter average life and less potential extension risk. Deals with a higher percentage of performing loans are expected to have longer average lives and more extension risk.

Furthermore, performing loans can only be liquidated using the discounted payoff method, as they have the right to continue through the maturity of the loan. The sub-performing loans can be liquidated either by using the discounted payoff method or by initiating foreclosure proceedings. Foreclosure can be a difficult and expensive undertaking, but when it is successful and the title to the property is obtained, the trust can then liquidate the underlying property to retire the mortgage debt.

Reserve Funds Another important structural feature found in liquidating trust transactions are reserve funds. Reserve funds are necessary in these transactions since it is difficult to project the timing of asset dispositions and their resulting cash flows. These reserve funds are established at the time of closing and are used to protect bondholders. The two common types of reserve funds are summarized in Exhibit 11.

Usually the asset expenditure reserve can be used to back up the liquidity reserve and make interest payments in the event of interest shortfalls to the investment-grade bonds. However, the asset expenditure reserve is not used to accelerate bond class paydown after the investment-grade bonds are retired.

Exhibit 11: Types of Reserve Funds

	Liquidity	Asset Expenditure
Purpose	Cash flow used to prevent interest shortfalls to investment-grade bonds	Cash flow used to pay taxes, legal fees and property maintenance
Used for Acceleration	Yes	No

Required Principal Payments

Non-performing CMBS are structured with relatively short average lives that receive cash flows from some loans while others are being disposed of. Therefore, the deal will be structured to achieve certain principal pay-down targets. In the event these targets are not achieved, often the fixed rate coupon is scheduled at a preset date (i.e., increased from 10% to 12%). This motivates the borrower not to allow extension on the lower rated bond classes.

Single-Borrower/Multi-Property Deals

The second type of CMBS deal which contains important structural considerations is the single-borrower/multi-property transaction. The following are important structural features which are often contained in these deals:

- cross-collateralization and cross-default feature
- property release provisions
- lock-box mechanism
- cash-trap features

Each of these features are discussed below.

Cross Collateralization and Cross-Default

Cross-collateralization is a mechanism whereby the properties that collateralize the individual loans are pledged against each loan. Cross-default, on the other hand, allows the lender to call each loan within the pool, when any one defaults. Thus, by tying the properties together, the cash flow is available to meet the collective debt on all the loans. Therefore, from a credit standpoint, an individual loan should not become delinquent as long as there is sufficient excess cash flow available from the pool to cover this shortfall.

Exhibits 12 and 13 show a simplified example of the power of the cross-collateralization cross-default mechanism. In our example, we assume that all properties have the same debt service coverage (DSC) ratio and loan-to-value (LTV) ratio, except for one distressed loan. In Exhibit 12, we calculate the breakeven DSC ratio possible before a default would be likely to occur.

For example, if a single loan pool had a DSC ratio of 1.30× (that is, it can cover debt service by 1.30 times), then the coverage ratio could decline by 23%

before a breakeven level is reached. A further decline could lead to a loan default. However, if the same loan was within a pool of five cross-collateralized, cross-defaulted loans it could experience a complete loss of cash flow (100%) and a second loan could also experience a 15% decline in the cash flow before a similar breakeven point is reached. As can be seen from Exhibit 12, the stronger the overall DSC of the pool and the larger the overall pool, the greater the cushion against a single distressed loan. Similarly, Exhibit 13 shows the buffer of protection available on cross-collateralized, cross-defaulted pools by LTV.

As shown in Exhibits 12 and 13, a five loan pool with an initial LTV of 75% could have a single distressed loan decline in value to zero and have a second loan decline in value by 25% before a zero equity position in the pool is reached.

Property Release Provisions

Another structural feature often present in single-borrower/multi-property transactions is property release mechanisms. The investor should be concerned about the ability of the lender to prepay or otherwise remove the stronger properties from the pool. Various property release provisions will protect the investor against this risk. These provisions usually take the following form:

- If any properties are sold, the borrower must retire *125% of the initial allocatable mortgage amount*;
- Resulting *DSC ratios cannot be lower than before sale*; and,
- No collateral substitutions are permitted.

Exhibit 12: Breakeven DSC Ratio

Number of Properties	DSC Ratio (%)				
	1.15 ×	1.25 ×	1.30 ×	1.35 ×	1.50 ×
1	13	20	23	26	33
3	39	60	69	78	100
5	65	100	115	130	167
10	130	200	230	259	333
15	196	300	345	389	500

Exhibit 13: Breakeven LTV Ratio

Number of Properties	LTV Ratio (%)				
	90%	80%	75%	70%	60%
1	10	20	25	30	40
3	30	60	75	90	120
5	50	100	125	150	200
10	100	200	250	300	400
15	150	300	375	450	600

Exhibit 14: Lock-Box Structure

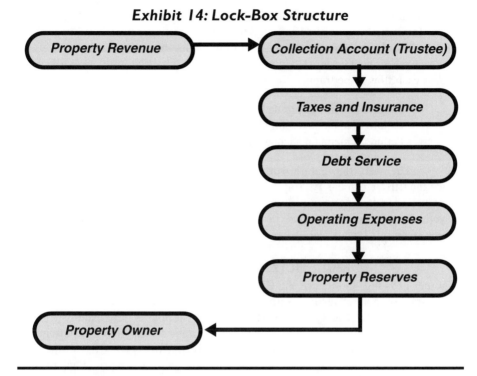

These property release provisions are important in order to maintain adequate structural protection in single-borrower transactions. Again, these provisions are to protect the investor from the borrower stripping the pool of its best properties.

Lock-Box Structures

Another structural feature often found in single-borrower transactions is the lock-box mechanism. The lock-box mechanism gives the trustee control over the gross revenues of the properties. (See Exhibit 14.)

Just as the cash flow of a CMBS deal flows through a waterfall payment mechanism, the property cash flow in a lock-box structure flow through a waterfall. As shown in Exhibit 14, the owner only has claim to excess cash flow after taxes, insurance, debt service, operating expenses, and property reserves. Likewise, management fees are often subordinate to debt service and operating expenses. The intent of the lock-box structure is not only to insure payment of debt service but also to provide a strong incentive for owners and property managers to operate the properties efficiently since they have a subordinate claim on cash flow.

Cash-Trap Feature

Another structural feature sometimes found in single-borrower/multi-property transactions is the "cash-trap." The cash-trap is the CMBS equivalent of "early amortization" within the asset-backed market. The intent is to penalize the borrower for something he/she has failed to do by amortizing the CMBS debt ahead of schedule. In the process, the cash-trap prevents the borrower from receiving excess cash flow. The most common triggers — which would cause all of the excess cash flow to be trapped for debt reduction — are:

- Failure to maintain pre-determined DSC ratio
- Failure to maintain required minimum debt ratings
- Failure to maintain adequate property reserves

The cash-trap feature works particularly well with a lock-box structure, since the trustee can easily "trap" all of the deal's excess cash. Cash-trap features have not been that common in recent deals (i.e., 1995 vintage) since borrowers have had more funding options (i.e., traditional lenders have returned and REITs which issue this type of debt have recently used unsecured debt issuance).

Multi-Borrower/Conduit Deals

Another growing segment of the CMBS is conduit-originated transactions. Conduits are commercial-lending entities that are established for the sole purpose of generating collateral to securitize. Most Wall Street houses have established conduits to originate collateral to be used in CMBS transactions. Some important factors when analyzing conduit deals are: origination standards, number of originators, pool diversification, and degree of loan standardization. Each of these considerations will be further discussed below.

Origination Standards

A key consideration in analyzing a conduit CMBS product is understanding how the loans were originated. This analysis must address the following standards:

- Key DSC and LTV ratios
- Cash flow assumptions used in underwriting
- Standards for property reserves
- Method of arriving at appraised values
- Loan terms offered (i.e., amortizing/balloon and call protection terms)
- Geographic and property type diversification
- Timing of loan originations (i.e., month and year of origination)

Analyzing the origination standards are important in understanding how the loans were originated.

Number of Originators

Many conduit deals have had more than one originator. This is usually done to speed up the funding period and to accumulate a larger critical mass. Most analysts agree that a minimum issue size of $100 to $125 million is desirable to effectively price a CMBS deal (given the fixed expenses of issuance). However, because multiple lenders may have originated the product, the investor has to get comfortable with the fact that a different lender underwrote the loans in a consistent manner. This can usually only be determined by carefully analyzing the mortgage loan files. It is for this reason that most investors prefer conduit deals originated by a single entity.

Pool Diversification

Another important factor to consider in conduit-originated deals is the diversification of the underlying loans. That is, how geographically and numerically diversified are the loans? Most investors like to see loan originations across several states without any major loan concentrations. One recent conduit deal had a single loan which comprised nearly 15% of the pool. A concentration such as this or a group of similar loans could severely impact the default-adjusted yields of the underlying securities.

Furthermore, the rating agencies have recently given lower overall levels of credit-enhancement to deals which contain diversification across property types. The theory being that because one cannot predict which property type will enjoy the best performance going forward, it is better to be adequately diversified.

Degree of Loan Standardization

It is important to analyze just how "cookie-cutter" a particular mortgage pool is. The higher the homogeneity, the greater the comfort that investors can look to the deal's structural features. For example, if a deal has a large concentration of 10-year balloon maturities with seven years of prepayment lockout, then the deal will usually appeal to crossover corporate buyers. Moreover, a highly standardized deal will more easily accept tranches such as bond-IOs (interest only strips). However, a deal which enjoys a high degree of standardization with regard to loan terms may not appeal to below investment-grade buyers. This is because the rating agencies have tended only to upgrade deals due to retirement of debt or deleveraging. In the example above, the balloon term usually implies interest only (i.e., no debt amortization), while the long lockout period would prevent voluntary prepayments. Thus, the below investment-grade bonds would not be candidates for upgrade.

SUMMARY

This chapter has focused on the structural considerations impacting MBS investments. We first looked at the basic CMBS structure: paydown priority, structural call protection, balloon maturity provisions, cash flows, and servicers' role. We then discussed the different types of CMBS deals focusing on three types: liquidating trusts, single-borrower/multi-property deals, and multi-borrower/conduit deals.

Chapter 24

Understanding Prepayments in CMBS Deals

Da Cheng
Development Associate
Wall Street Analytics, Inc.

Adrian R. Cooper, Ph.D.
Vice President
Wall Street Analytics, Inc.

Jason Huang
Structuring Associate
Wall Street Analytics, Inc.

INTRODUCTION

One of the most important and least understood aspects of CMBS deals is their behavior under prepayments. In residential deals the bondholders are protected against prepayments solely by the cash flow distribution structure. For commercial deals, call protection at the loan level leads to a greater cash flow certainty, and this has led some investors to grossly misprice CMBS tranches by ignoring the allocation of prepayment risk. Within a rising rate environment, which is often coupled with a booming real estate market, a thorough analysis of the prepayment risks become especially important.

The prepayment protection in commercial deals comes from both the call protection available at the loan level, and also from the CMBS structure. The call protection is provided by a combination of prepayment lockouts, prepayment penalties, and yield maintenance, so it is important to understand the way that these interact with the structure of the deal. The purpose of this chapter is to provide a comprehensive catalog of the methods commonly used for prepayment protection in CMBS deals.

LOCKOUTS AND PREPAYMENT PENALTIES

The simplest method of affording call protection is to require that for some period after the loan is originated, no prepayments be allowed to occur. This is known as a *lockout*, and has the advantage that it is simple to model and provides complete protection against prepayments. A lockout typically only covers the first few years of a loan, and CMBS deals that use them almost invariably combine them with at least one other method.

The next simplest form of call protection is a *prepayment penalty*. This represents an additional penalty that the borrower must pay when he chooses to prepay the loan. It is expressed as a percentage of the prepayment amount, and generally declines over time. Prepayment premiums are often substantial, and may be used in conjunction with lockouts. A commonly used schedule is shown in Exhibit 1.

In a typical CMBS deal, the prepayment penalties will be distributed separately from other funds. The rules by which they are allocated are obviously crucial for assessing the risk exposure of various bonds. There is a common misconception amongst investors that prepayment premiums are a relatively ineffective means of providing call protection. However, as we will see below, in a rising rate environment they may significantly outperform yield maintenance.

YIELD MAINTENANCE

In addition to lockouts and prepayment premiums, most CMBS deals also use a far more complex form of call protection. This is known as *yield maintenance* (YM), and perhaps represents the most misunderstood aspect of commercial deals. At the current time there is a peculiar stratification of the CMBS marketplace. On the one hand, since yield maintenance is generally too complex to be modeled on spreadsheets, many buyers are forced to ignore it. Those with more sophisticated systems, however, are able to correctly price even the most volatile tranches, giving them a significant investing advantage. More surprisingly, perhaps, even issuers are finding that their in-house systems are able to handle only the simplest methods of yield maintenance. In fact, one major investment bank was recently embarrassed when they discovered that the language in their prospectus didn't agree with their own yield maintenance model. At this point — long after issuing the deal — they were forced to invent a new type of yield maintenance to match the prospectus, and to acquire a new analytical system that allowed them to model it.

Exhibit 1: Commonly Used Prepayment Penalty Schedule

Year after lockout	Prepayment Penalty
1	5% of prepayment amount
2	4%
3	3%
4	2%
5	1%
6 and after	no penalty

Yield Maintenance Defined

The basic concept behind yield maintenance is quite simple: When a borrower prepays his loan, he must pay the lender an additional *yield maintenance charge* (or *make-whole charge*). The amount of the charge is calculated so that the lender becomes indifferent to prepayments. So the question is, what is a fair compensation to the lender for receiving a prepayment?

To illustrate this point, imagine that we make a loan in January with a maturity date in May. The first couple of months go by without event and we receive our principal and interest payments as scheduled. Suddenly in March the borrower informs us that he wishes to prepay. How much should we charge him for this privilege? A fair approach would be to require that the total check that we receive in March be equal to the value of all the remaining payments we were due to receive in order to "make us whole." In other words, he must pay us a yield maintenance charge given by

YM charge = Value of future scheduled payments − Amount prepaid

Our intention is that by reinvesting the prepayment amount and the yield maintenance charge, we could reproduce the future cash flow that we'd been scheduled to receive from the original bond. At this level, the concept of yield maintenance is very simple. The complexity comes from determining exactly how the value of future scheduled payments should be computed, or equivalently from deciding how the prepayment proceeds can be reinvested. In the following sections we shall explore the rather daunting variety of yield maintenance methods in the marketplace today. These have generally evolved from differing assumptions about the available reinvestment options, although some of their variants have arisen as mere historical accidents.

Having decided on the YM penalty that should be paid by the borrower, a further complication arises when we realize that the prepaying loan is part of a CMBS deal. Even after the YM charge has been computed, the question remains as to how it should be distributed amongst the bondholders. We shall discuss the various allocation methods that are currently used, and describe in particular how *bond yield maintenance* is used to make whole the individual tranche holders.

The Importance of Analyzing Yield Maintenance

Before discussing the details of yield maintenance, we give a brief example of the magnitude of its effects. These will generally be most significant for an IO strip. To illustrate this, we take an actual CMBS deal and plot the yield of the IO against prepayment speed both with and without the effects of yield maintenance. The results are shown in Exhibit 2.

It is important to stress that the beneficial effects to the bondholder of yield maintenance may be either less than or greater than those of a simple prepayment lockout, depending on the precise form of YM used and the scenario under consideration.

Exhibit 2: Class I-I Pre-Tax CBE Yield* Without and With Yield Maintenance

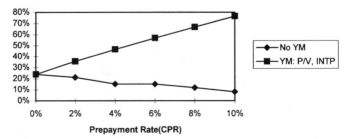

* From Mortgage Capital Funding, Inc., Multifamily/Commercial Mortgage Pass-Through Certificates, Series 1994-MC1

COLLATERAL YIELD MAINTENANCE

In the following, as is typical in CMBS deals, we assume that when a loan prepays it prepays completely, so that *prepaid amount* is equal to the outstanding balance of the loan at the date of prepayment. It is a simple matter to allow partial prepayment of loans instead. The basic philosophy behind all the methods is to compare the value of the cash flow that would have occurred in absence of prepayments to the value of the cash flow after the prepayment has occurred. Although the details of many of the methods may seem rather convoluted and artificial, they have all been used in actual CMBS transactions, and so must be understood and modeled by anyone wishing to accurately price commercial deals.

The Simple Model

The most straightforward form of yield maintenance (generally referred to as the *simple model*) estimates the value of future scheduled cash flows by adding up future scheduled payments. The YM charge then becomes

$$\sum \text{Future scheduled payments} - \text{Prepaid amount}$$

or equivalently

$$\sum \text{Future scheduled interest payments}$$

The lender in this case will clearly be overcompensated since there is no discounting of the future value of cash flows. For this reason it is not commonly used in today's deals.

The Bullet Model

A slightly more complex variant of the previous method is the *bullet model*. For this, the YM charge is given by

Prepaid amount × Remaining term × (Loan coupon − YM coupon)

where *loan coupon* represents the coupon of the loan at origination, and *YM coupon* is a prevailing interest rate at the prepayment date. The interpretation behind this is that at the date of prepayment we pretend that the loan represented a single bullet that would come due on its maturity date, and in the meantime paid interest at the *loan coupon* rate. We next assume that the prepaid amount can be invested in a similar bullet bond, bought at par, and paying interest at YM coupon. As in the case of the simple model, we ignore discounting and take the difference between the two cash streams to give the *YM charge*.

The bullet method ignores both the loan amortization and the discounting of future cash flows. For loans with a short balloon period, this assumption will be less inaccurate.

The Single Discount Factor Model

The *single discount factor model* is a little more sophisticated and gives the YM charge as

$$\sum_t \frac{\text{Future scheduled payment}_t}{(1 + \text{YM yield})^t} - \text{Prepaid amount}$$

where the summation index t represents the number of months after the prepayment date. The model computes the net present value of the future scheduled cash flows discounted back at a constant rate of *YM yield*. This rate will typically be chosen as the yield of a Treasury of comparable maturity, plus some hand-picked spread. If there were no spread, then the YM charge would allow the lender to exactly reproduce the future scheduled cash flow with a risk-free Treasury portfolio, which is clearly an overcompensation.

The Multiple Discount Factor Model

The *multiple discount factor model* is similar to the single discount factor model, but the discounting of future cash flows is taken with respect to the Treasury spot curve and gives the YM charge as:

$$\sum_t \frac{\text{Future scheduled payment}}{(1 + \text{Treasury spot rate}_t + \text{YM spread})^t} - \text{Prepaid amount}$$

Again the summation index t represents the number of months after the prepayment date.

With *YM spread* set to zero, this model is known as *Treasury flat yield maintenance*, and provides a sufficient charge for the lender to reproduce the future scheduled cash flow by purchasing a Treasury portfolio. This is clearly an overcompensation, since a Treasury portfolio would be risk free. With a non-zero value of YM spread, the charge would be sufficient to allow the lender to reproduce the scheduled cash flow by purchasing a portfolio of investments with a spread *YM spread* over the Treasury curve. Its value is therefore chosen to represent the expected spread of bonds with a similar risk profile to the original loan. With YM spread of 150 basis points, this model is generally known as a "T+150" yield maintenance premium.

In many ways this model represents the most sensible definition of yield maintenance, and the others described here can be thought of as approximations to it.

The Interest Difference Model

For the interest difference model, the YM charge is given as the present value of the difference between the scheduled interest payments, and the scheduled interest payments that would have been due with the same amortization schedule but with the coupon of the loan replaced by the coupon of a Treasury bond of comparable maturity. More precisely it is

$$\sum_t \frac{\text{Scheduled interest}_t - \text{Scheduled interest at YM yield}_t}{(1 + \text{Treasury spot rate}_t)^t}$$

where *YM yield* is chosen as the yield of a Treasury bond of comparable maturity to the loan, plus a possible hand-picked spread. The justifying assumption behind this approach is that upon receiving the prepayment, the lender can reissue bonds with an identical amortization schedule. The (fixed) coupon of these new loans will equal some spread over a comparable Treasury. The difference between the present value of the two cash flows produces the YM charge.

As a slight variant of this method, YM yield is occasionally based upon the yield of a Treasury bond whose maturity is comparable to the remaining average life of the loan at the prepayment date, rather than its remaining term. In another variation, the Treasury spot rate in the denominator is replaced by a single discount factor.

The Truncated Interest Difference Model

Unfortunately, the preceding model has spawned a rather confusing mutation in which the YM charge is given by

$$\sum_t \frac{\text{Max}(\text{Scheduled interest}_t - \text{Prepaid amount}_t \times \text{YM yield}, 0)}{(1 + \text{YM yield})^t}$$

where again YM yield is chosen as the yield of a Treasury bond of comparable maturity to the loan, plus a possible hand-picked spread. Roughly speaking, the assumption behind this is that the prepayment can be reinvested in a non-amortizing bond that pays YM yield for some period of time (however, the duration of this period has no sensible interpretation). The resulting cash flows are discounted at a single rate of YM yield.

Yield Maintenance Floors

For most of the methods described above, the YM charges will decrease in a rising interest rate environment. In order to provide additional protection to lenders, they are often supplemented with *yield maintenance floors*. These impose a minimum value for the YM charge as follows:

YM charge = Max (Raw YM charge, Prepaid amount × YM floor rate)

where *Raw YM charge* represents the charge before the floor is taken into account.

ALLOCATION OF YIELD MAINTENANCE CHARGES

In the previous sections we have discussed various methods of implementing Yield maintenance on the collateral side. It is now necessary to consider how the resulting YM charges will be allocated amongst the bondholders of a CMBS deal.

It is important to realize that under many circumstances although the YM charge is computed so as to protect the whole loan against prepayments, it may be insufficient to protect all of the bonds. In other words the sum of the make-whole amounts for the bonds will not equal the make-whole amount for the collateral. Given this discrepancy, it is obviously extremely important to model the allocation of the YM charges completely. To further illustrate this point, Exhibit 3 shows how switching between some commonly used allocation methods may dramatically affect the yield of a bond.

Exhibit 3: Different YM Allocation Rules

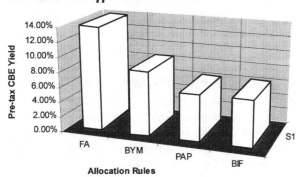

This IO certificate is part of the Nationslink Funding Corporation, Commercial Mortgage Pass-Through Certificates, Series 1996-1. Its price is 3% excluding accrued interests. All mortgage loans balloon 60 month from the cut-off date.

> FA   Full Allocation of yield maintenance to IO certificate
> BYM   Bond Yield Maintenance method
> PAP   Principal Allocation method
> BIF   Base Interest Fraction method

Source: Statistical results generated by the Structured Financing Workstation by Wall Street Analytics, Inc.

The Principal Allocation Percentage Method

The simplest method used for the allocation of the YM charge is the *principal allocation percentage method*. For this, the YM charge is paid to the bonds in proportion to the amount of prepayment principal that they receive. Specifically, a bond X receives as its share of the YM charge

$$\frac{\text{Prepayment paid to } X}{\text{Total prepaid amount}} \times \text{YM charge}$$

This method has the advantage that it is simple to implement, although it tends to undercompensate the holders of bonds that are structurally locked out. Moreover, a discount bond would tend to be overcompensated since it would generally benefit from a prepayment, while the converse would be true of a bond bought at a premium. As an extreme example of this consider the case of a PO strip. If the entire collateral prepaid one month after the deal had been issued, then the PO holder would obviously be delighted. There is obviously no reason to compensate him further with a portion of the YM charge.

The Base Interest Method

The base interest method provides a far more complex, though somewhat arbitrary, means of distributing the YM charge. When a mortgage M prepays, the amount of the YM charge distributed to a bond X is given by

$$\frac{(\text{Principal paid to } X)}{(\text{Total principal paid})} \times \frac{\text{Max}(\text{Coupon of } X - \text{YM coupon}, 0)}{\text{Net coupon of } M - \text{YM coupon}} \times \text{YM charge}$$

with all excess YM charge being distributed to the IO strip.

This method has an advantage over the previous method in that it treats premium and discount bonds more fairly. In particular, a PO strip will receive no portion of the YM charge. A complete analysis of the deal would be required to tell whether a particular bond was fairly compensated.

Bond Yield Maintenance Method

Perhaps the most logical method for allocating the YM charge is to use *bond yield maintenance*. This is somewhat analogous to the process of calculating collateral yield maintenance. The concept is that a bondholder should be "made whole" for the disruption in cash flow that he suffers for receiving a prepayment. For a particular bond, the fair value for this is

$$\text{Bond YM amount} = \sum_{t} \frac{\text{Scheduled bond payment}_t - \text{Actual bond payment}_t}{(1 + \text{Bond YM yield})^t}$$

where *Scheduled bond payment$_t$* represents the total payment that the bond would receive at time t if the prepayment had not occurred, and *Actual bond payment$_t$* is the total payment that the bond would receive at time t after taking into account the effects of the prepayment (but ignoring any YM distributions). *Bond YM yield* is set equal to the Treasury spot rate for a maturity comparable to the bond, plus a spread. This spread may be the same as the current bond spread at the time of prepayment. Alternatively, if it is expected that the bond will be upgraded, a lesser spread might be used. (This will generate a higher bond YM amount, which is obviously reasonable if the bond has become more valuable.)

As an extension to this method, if the prepayment has the effect of changing the bond's risk profile, then different discount spreads may be used for computing the two present values. In other words,

$$\text{Bond YM amount} = \sum_t \frac{\text{Scheduled bond payment}_t}{(1 + \text{Bond YM yield}_1)^t} - \frac{\text{Actual bond payment}_t}{(1 + \text{Bond YM yield}_2)^t}$$

where *Bond YM yield*$_1$ is the Treasury rate corresponding to the scheduled maturity (or average life) of the bond, plus a spread appropriate to the scheduled term and risk profile. Similarly, *Bond YM yield*$_2$ is the Treasury rate corresponding to the scheduled maturity of the bond after taking into account the prepayment, plus a spread appropriate to this term and risk profile. The exact values of these spreads will be negotiated between issuer and buyer.

The bond YM amount computed above would give the bondholder a fair compensation for receiving a prepayment. However, as we have mentioned before, there is no guarantee that the total YM charge collected from the borrowers will be sufficient to pay each of the bondholders their fair bond YM amount. Instead, a bond X will receive as its share of the YM charge an amount equal to

$$\frac{\text{Bond YM amount for } X}{\sum_{\text{all tranches}} \text{Bond YM amounts}} \times \text{YM charge}$$

This is effectively the "best that we can do" with the available YM charge.

From a purely practical standpoint, the correct modeling of bond yield maintenance can prove extremely difficult. For a scenario with n prepayments, the deal must be run n+1 separate times. However, a good structuring or modeling tool should be able to perform these calculations automatically.

Defeasance

For completeness, we should also mention the most precise form of call protection. This is known as *defeasance*. From the point of view of the borrower, it is equivalent to Treasury-flat yield maintenance. However, the proceeds generated from the YM charges are not distributed directly to the bondholders, but are instead invested by the servicer in a Treasury portfolio. By design, this generates the same future cash flows that would have been obtained in absence of prepayments, and these are distributed to the bondholders as if no prepayments had occurred. This has the advantage of imposing no extra taxes due to the distribution of YM charges, and also maintains a higher level of credit on the remaining assets.

SPECIAL CONSIDERATIONS FOR IOS

While prepayment considerations are important for all bonds in a CMBS deal, their most dramatic effect can generally be seen on the IO. In this section we briefly review the necessity of the IO strips, and discuss their risk profiles in more detail.

Typically, a CMBS deal will contain collateral with a wide range of coupons. Since different loans will amortize at different rates, and some may prepay or default, the weighted average coupon (WAC) for the collateral will tend to change over time. The presence of this *coupon dispersion* obviously makes it impossible to structure a deal with only fixed rate bonds. Sometimes this is dealt with by creating one or more *WAC bonds* whose coupon changes with the collateral. In effect, the dispersion is passed through to the bondholders. An alternative approach is to allocate any excess interest payments over some specified cutoff to an IO strip, thus giving the collateral a constant effective passthrough rate. This strip may be taken either directly from the collateral, in which case the technique is referred to as *ratio stripping*, or it can be taken from the bonds.

An IO that has been stripped directly from the underlying loans will obviously be influenced the most by high coupon loans. These loans will have a higher coupon either because they were originated earlier when rates were higher, or because they are loans on riskier asset types. The former type will be particularly subject to prepayment risk, while the latter will be subject to credit risk, so it may seem that such an IO would be at high risk from both defaults and prepayments. In a well structured deal, however, the allocation of prepayment premiums will protect it against calls. Moreover, since the servicer is generally required to advance principal and interest, prepayments and defaults will tend to affect this type of IO similarly.

In contrast, an IO that has been stripped from a senior bond will be affected very differently by prepayments and defaults. Because of the subordination structure, it will be relatively insensitive to defaults risk. However, the same subordination structure will cause it to be highly sensitive to prepayment risk.

When investing in IOs, it is especially important to realize that a deal using yield maintenance does not always provide the best call protection. For many of the methods discussed in this chapter, the YM charge may be reduced to zero in an upward rate environment. A prepayment could then cause the IO to disappear, without any distribution of YM charges to compensate. In contrast, a lockout or prepayment premium would provide far better protection. This highlights the point that when analyzing an IO, there is no substitute for thoroughly modeling the entire yield maintenance provisions of the deal, and performing analysis runs for multiple scenarios.

CONCLUSION

In this chapter we have provided a catalog of the different techniques that are used to provide prepayment protection in CMBS deals, and have illustrated the dramatic effect that they can have on the risk-return profiles of bonds. This emphasizes the importance to investors of completely modeling the call provisions of a CMBS deal and performing analyses under several scenarios.

Within residential CMOs, it is the payment structure of the deal that protects tranches against prepayments. This is often achieved with considerable complexity and may involve multiple layers of PAC classes and accrual bonds. In contrast, CMBS deals typically have a far simpler bond structure. They instead achieve call protection by imposing various prepayment lockouts and fees on the collateral, the most complex of which is yield maintenance. In this, a borrower who chooses to prepay is subject to an additional charge that is intended to fairly compensate the lender for any loss of investment yield. This penalty is then distributed to the bondholders in such a way as to render them indifferent to the prepayment.

We have examined the different ways in which the yield maintenance charge may be defined, and have also listed the current methods for allocating it amongst tranches.

As the market evolves, it seems inevitable that the methods of CMBS call protection discussed in this chapter will become supplemented by some of the techniques used in residential deals. In this case we can look forward to deals that combine PAC bonds, Z bonds, and bond yield maintenance within a single structure. It is obviously important that anyone building a CMBS structuring or analysis model designs it with enough flexibility to allow for this future expansion.

Chapter 25

Commercial Mortgage Prepayments

Jesse M. Abraham, Ph.D.
Director, Servicing Division
Federal Home Loan Mortgage Corporation

H. Scott Theobald
Senior Financial Analyst, Finance Division
Federal Home Loan Mortgage Corporation

INTRODUCTION

Prepayments are the primary focus when it comes to the valuation of single-family securities. Virtually all of the market volume is in agency or highly rated private issues which are subject to little or no risk to ultimate repayment of principal. The risk of early retirement of collateral because of mortgage borrower prepayments therefore becomes the key to valuation of those types of securities.

But that is not the case with commercial mortgage-backed securities (CMBS). In this market the prime determinant of pricing is the depth of credit protection required by the rating agencies. That is the case because there are virtually no whole loan issues fully guaranteed by the government (RTC, GNMA) or government sponsored enterprise (FNMA, FHLMC) being done today, while the magnitude of credit risk is much greater than with single-family mortgages.

It is also true that contract features of commercial mortgages lend themselves to greater predictability of prepayment behavior than 30-year single-family mortgages: typically there are prepayment disincentives immediately after funding, which discourage early payments, together with short maturities of only 5, 10, or 15 years that together reduce the uncertainty about the timing of prepayments. Still, any payment uncertainty in an investment needs to be understood and priced. And with commercial pools composed of generally fewer loans than single-family passthroughs, the behavior of each individual loan takes on added importance.

We appreciate the comments of our colleagues in Freddie Mac's Financial Research Department, and of Mark Buono of Goldman Sachs. George Wisniewski assisted in the early stages of this research. The opinions expressed in the paper reflect only those of the authors and not of other employees or the Board of Directors of the Federal Home Loan Mortgage Corporation.

Exhibit I: Comparative Conditional and Cumulative Prepayment Rates (%) Multifamily and Single-Family 1984 Originations

Year	Single-family		Multifamily	
	Conditional	Cumulative	Conditional	Cumulative
1985	15.7	15.7	1.0	1.0
1986	51.3	58.9	1.7	2.7
1987	36.9	74.1	0.0	2.7
1988	18.2	78.8	6.5	9.0
1989	14.8	81.9	34.6	39.9
1990	13.8	84.4	36.3	60.1
1991	19.3	87.4	29.7	70.1
1992	26.7	90.8	22.1	75.1
1993	24.2	93.0	14.0	77.4
1994	21.1	94.5	39.5	83.1

In this chapter, we present prepayment data from a sample of multifamily mortgages, and review the issues that differentiate commercial mortgage activity from single-family behavior. The relative importance of theoretical issues for valuation are then brought out through the discussion of a prepayment model estimated with the sample presented earlier.

We assume the reader is familiar with single-family prepayment issues. Therefore, we start in the first section pointing out reasons why single-family experience is not directly transferable to the CMBS market. The second section confronts the data with our now increased sensitivity to features of commercial mortgages. The final section presents a prepayment model and estimation results.

HOW COMMERCIAL DIFFERS FROM SINGLE-FAMILY

An assumption that CMBS and MBS pools of similar vintage should behave in a like manner would be convenient, but inaccurate. Despite gross similarities between these two mortgage instruments, they have markedly different contract features. In addition, the personal incentives of mortgagors are different between (largely) owner-occupied 1-4 unit dwellings and investor-owned, multi-unit rental businesses.

This simple point is driven home by Exhibit 1, which reports conditional and cumulative prepayments for Freddie Mac's single-family and multifamily mortgage loans originated in 1984. For one thing, the average coupons are different, with an average multifamily coupon of 13.41%, and 13.10% for the single-family. The left two columns show that most of the single-family loans prepaid in 1986-87; conditional rates were lower during the subsequent four years, rising again in the refinancing boom of 1992-1993. In contrast, in the right-hand columns multifamily loans did not really get started until some 40% prepaid in 1989, and another 20% the next year, followed by successively smaller conditional rates, even as interest rates crashed in 1992-93, before turning up in 1994.

A useful starting place for investigating the source of these differences is the virtual identity commonly cited in single-family analysis to decompose dollars of prepayments into four components:

$$total\ prepayments\ =\ relocations\ -\ assumptions\ +\ curtailments\ +\ refinances$$

In single-family prepayment behavior, relocation is important because home sales typically lead to mortgage termination, except when assumptions occur as is allowed with FHA loans securitized by Ginnie Mae. Curtailments, or partial prepayments, are quite small in magnitude but need to be accounted for. The research emphasis is appropriately put on refinances, which are the greatest source of volatility in prepayment behavior.[1]

Commercial loans, if anything, exhibit an even greater sensitivity to refinances. Curtailments are virtually nonexistent (less than 1% of principal in our dataset), as borrowers look to maximize leverage rather than make extra principal payments. In addition, there is a lower frequency of sales in commercial than in single-family properties, including assumptions, as performing real estate is a valuable asset for both its cash flow and for its use as collateral to obtain increased financing.

The conditions which motivate and ultimately enable borrowers to accomplish a refinance require quite different modeling between these two markets. Below we discuss five sources of potential difference between single-family and CMBS loan behavior: the optimization rule; the degree of ruthlessness; the metric for measuring loan quality; extension risk; and, call protection provisions.

The Optimization Rule

In idiosyncratic ways, households seek to manage their portfolio of assets — human capital, physical capital, financial assets, and real estate — to maximize their utility. The impact of maximizing the return on one, e.g. health and well-being, may be only tangentially related to the management of another, such as finances. Some connections, such as seeking the best job to maximize the return on education and housing, are widely recognized. But sorting through this problem is very complex, it suffers from incomplete data and promises little reward.[2]

The problem is much more straightforward with a commercial property owner who is expected to be a wealth maximizer, and who in every period is looking to increase his portfolio's expected return. An owner's decisions regarding

---

[1] An accessible explanation of each component is provided in Gregg N. Patruno, "Mortgage Prepayments II," Chapter 9 in Frank J. Fabozzi (ed.), *Handbook of Mortgage-Backed Securities* (Chicago: Probus Publishing, 1995).

[2] A good discussion of this issue is provided in Wayne Archer, David C. Ling, and Gary A. McGill, "The Effect of Income and Collateral Constraints on Residential Mortgage Terminations," *Regional Science and Urban Economics,* forthcoming.

any given loan may be made for financial reasons that are specific to that property, but could also go beyond that one property to his entire portfolio. In addition, there exist a wider variety of financial options available to a commercial borrower than to a single-family borrower, making terms that are familiar to the single-family borrower like "refinance" and "default" too crude to capture the richness of the choices faced by a commercial property owner.

An example of portfolio concerns would be an owner who has cross-collateral agreements from one property to another, or other covenants that restrict his ability to maximize the profit from each property as a separate entity. Reputation effects could well come into play when it comes to capital improvements or a default decision.

That "refinance" is too crude a term for commercial property owners becomes clear when one considers the importance of the preferred degree of leverage to maximize a return-on-equity. Should the property appreciate in value, a refinance (or a second mortgage) lets the owner take money out to fund other investments. But the ability to do that depends upon current interest rates and market liquidity. Tax code changes at the national and local levels — which change periodically for commercial property — can affect whether an owner prefers ordinary income or capital gains, which in turn would drive a "hold or sell" strategy. Whether the investor receives current cash flow or future income can be managed, at least in the short term, by varying capital expenditures.

While conceptually important, fully addressing these issues is beyond the scope of current data and research. The model discussed later will assume that in refinancing borrowers seek to minimize the expected value of payments necessary to retire their outstanding obligation, anticipating that they will continue to own the property for the foreseeable future.

Degree of Ruthlessness

A now commonplace framework for analyzing single-family mortgage behavior is options pricing, in which a borrower is seen to be issued, in addition to a fully amortizing loan, a put option which may be exercised when the property value falls below the par mortgage value, and a call option which may be exercised when the market value of current mortgage payments exceeds the par mortgage value. Clearly, the focus here is on the call option.

Essential to the application of the option pricing formula is the ruthless exercise of an option given the right circumstances. This does not necessarily mean that the option is exercised immediately upon entering "into the money," only that there is a clear set of rules the holder "ruthlessly" follows to maximize wealth.[3]

---

[3] This methodology is followed in James B. Kau, Donald C. Keenan, Walter J. Muller III, and James F. Epperson, "Pricing Commercial Mortgages and Their Mortgage-Backed Securities," *Journal of Real Estate Finance and Economics*, 3, 1990, pp. 333-356; and Sheridan Titman and Walter Torous, "Valuing Commercial Mortgages: An Empirical Investigation of the Contingent-Claims Approach to Pricing Risky Debt," *Journal of Finance* (June 1989), pp 345-373.

Exhibit 2: The Probability of Prepayment for Single-Family and Commercial Mortgages

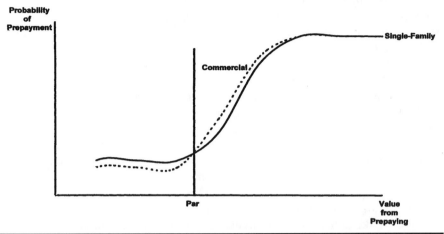

The elegance of the application of a pure option pricing solution is belied by observed experience: mortgage holders of a single vintage and coupon never act in concert. Capturing the heterogeneity of borrower experience (and hence behavior) without violating the theoretical insights from the options framework becomes a challenge as soon as the model becomes tested empirically.

Commercial investors should be expected to more ruthlessly exercise wealth maximization options than owner-occupants. This point is illustrated in Exhibit 2, which plots the probability of prepayment against the value from prepaying. The familiar "S" shape arises because single-family loans will have an irreducible prepayment rate from relocations, even when the market value of the mortgage is below par. As interest rates decline and the market value rises, the probability of single-family prepayment rises rapidly, then asymptotes towards 100%. In contrast, we should expect the commercial loan to have a lower autonomous rate, because of fewer relocations. As mortgage rates decline, the probability of refinance should increase faster with commercial mortgages than with single-family mortgages.

Since real world data are net of investor portfolio concerns, and the variety of other possible influences mentioned earlier, estimation results could be more equivocal than this discussion suggests. Still, one would expect the theoretical differences between owner-occupants and investors should be born out in the data.

LOAN QUALITY METRIC

In the single-family prepayment literature it is widely recognized that models need to include measures of loan quality. In part, this is because loan defaults in investor pools become prepayments. But more importantly, researchers recognize that current investor guidelines require positive equity to refinance a loan. During the 1992-93 bond rally, when interest rates dropped considerably and many borrowers failed to refinance, it became abundantly clear that the likelihood of prepayment is highly correlated with the credit quality of the outstanding loans. The sensitivity of loans that remain in a pool to house price changes is critical for anticipating prepayments.

A reliable measure of loan quality for single-family loans is the loan-to-value (LTV) ratio, so it is used as an explicit threshold for approval for refinancing, with investors such as Freddie Mac requiring refinances to be no greater than 90% LTV. Appropriately, virtually all simulation models that project prepayments therefore include house price appreciation as a key determining "state" variable.

Measuring the credit quality of a commercial property is much more complex than with single-family properties. Not only are there no good measures of property value trends, but it is almost impossible to measure *quality* along a single axis, since a property's cash flow and equity are both important, as well as possibly a host of qualitative factors.

Unlike in the earlier discussion on portfolio effects, in this area we have attempted to reflect this complexity in the modeling work below. The quality measure used for individual properties is a measure of cash flow, the debt coverage ratio (DCR). It is calculated as a property's net operating income — less expenses — divided by debt service payments.[4] A DCR of 1.00 will be close to default, since the cash flow is then only just enough to cover debt service, while a property generating a 1.50 DCR is in good shape, and positioned to be able to absorb several adverse shocks to its cash flow before potentially becoming a problem.

Extension Risk

Single-family loans are typically fully amortizing, over 15- to 30-years, with no penalty assessed should a borrower choose to pay off part, or all, of the loan early. In contrast, commercial loans are typically balloons, may or may not amortize, and almost certainly carry provisions which limit prepayments.

The risk that a borrower will be unable, or unwilling, to refinance a loan when a balloon payment is due is termed *balloon risk* or *extension risk*. At the end of the contracted term the loan technically becomes "in default" and could be taken over by the lender.[5] Only credit-impaired loans will fall in this category, since no borrower with positive equity would welcome this loss of control. However, lenders are rarely eager to become landlords. Industry practice is to engage

---

[4] A cash flow model of property performance is motivated, developed, and analyzed in Jesse M. Abraham, "On the Use of a Cash Flow Time Series to Measure Property Performance," *Journal of Real Estate Research, 11 (1996), pp. 291-308*. This model is used as the basis for a credit model of multifamily performance in Jesse M. Abraham, "Credit Risk in Commercial Real Estate Lending," Mimeograph, December 1993.

[5] Single-family loans can also be restructured, but restructurings occur at a much lower frequency than with commercial properties. Additionally, workout processes at the agencies are not important to single-family passthrough holders since investors get paid off 120 days into a delinquency.

in workouts or loan modifications, in the hope of avoiding a borrower's milking the property before being forced out, as well as avoiding the deadweight costs of foreclosure proceedings. With loan securitization, investors with different credit exposures can have conflicting interests in how impaired loans should be resolved. Therefore these structures include explicit agreements covering the rights and obligations of all investors, the servicer, and the special servicer.

The financial implications of this practice — and in particular the effect on loan payoffs — are a challenge to evaluate and model. In this chapter, we only examine prepayments during the contract term, since the incentives of both the mortgagor and mortgagee change considerably after the balloon date.

Investor Call Protection

Another feature that is common with commercial, but infrequent in single-family, loans is terms discouraging early prepayment. These could be as modest as a 1% fee, but often are much more complex and costly for a period of time right after origination. Our data cover the gamut from absolute *lockouts* that prohibit prepayments during an initial period, to so called *yield maintenance agreements* (YM) which are less legally restrictive, but meant to have the same effect.

A single YM formula is now commonly used by insurance companies, Freddie Mac, and Fannie Mae. The objective is to remove the borrower's incentive to prepay prior to a designated date by imposing a fee roughly equal to the savings from the (presumably) new lower mortgage rate. It is the present value, over the remainder of the YM period, of the difference between the note rate and a U.S. Treasury yield at prepayment, multiplied by the principal amount to be prepaid.

Our data also include some loans with an even simpler structure. The penalty follows a 5-4-3-2-1 pattern for the first five years of a mortgage. A prepayment in the first year after origination would precipitate a 5% fee, in the second year a 4% fee, etc.

It should be noted that the incentive to prepay is not eliminated, only reduced with these fees. A borrower might be willing to pay the fee if he thought interest rates were going to rise from their current levels, and be much higher after the yield maintenance period was over. Alternatively, it may be well worthwhile to incur some added costs towards the end of the YM period, if low mortgages rates are available to be locked in for an extended period of a new mortgage.

A LOOK AT THE DATA

There are very little data publicly available with which to fashion expectations about commercial loan behavior. The highest volume issuer of CMBS securities, the Resolution Trust Corporation (RTC), conveniently separates its securities by property type. However, their loans are of uncertain credit quality, have unknown prepayment disincentive features, and uncertain extension provisions. Freddie

Mac and Fannie Mae factors are another potential source of data, but their total volume to date has been limited. Compared to single-family, loan defaults will have a significant impact on security prepayments, while origination credit quality is not part of the disclosure package.

The data presented here provide one of the first publicly available, systematic reviews of commercial prepayment experience. Before proceeding directly to the modeling, it is helpful to understand the characteristics of this data, and to see the extent to which the data confirm or refute expectations in the market.

Freddie Mac has been in the multifamily market since 1973. However, purchase volume did not become significant until the end of 1983 with the introduction of Plan A and Plan B programs, and in 1989, Plan C. Plan A purchases included a wide variety of contract structures and (now) suffer from incomplete data. The data summarized here are from 7,769 Plan B and C loans originated between 1984 and 1990. Plan Bs are fixed rate, level payment, with 10- or 15-year terms with 15- to 30-year amortization and 4.5-year lockouts; they comprise 87% of the sample. Plan C loans have 5- to 15-year terms, with 30-year amortization, and various prepayment disincentive features. In each year, DCR at origination ranged from just over 1.00 to over 2.00.

Interest Rate Effects

For a given economic environment, one would expect high coupon mortgages to prepay faster than low coupon mortgages. This standard behavior is confirmed in Exhibit 3, which shows Freddie Mac's cumulative multifamily prepayment rates, by origination year, through 1994. For each origination book, coupons less than the sample median were assigned to the low-rate category, while loans with coupons greater than the median were assigned to the high-rate category. The rates reported for each category are the first and third quartile values, respectively.

Exhibit 3: Cumulative Multifamily Prepayment Rates
High and Low Coupons Through 1994

Origination Year	Low Coupon		High Coupon	
	Median Coupon	Prepayment Rate	Median Coupon	Prepayment Rate
1984	13.02	82.4	13.75	83.8
1985	11.62	64.1	12.47	78.8
1986	10.38	48.7	11.03	57.2
1987	9.91	24.7	10.82	34.9
1988	10.74	20.9	11.29	14.9
1989	9.72	13.2	10.69	17.0
1990	9.97	11.8	10.73	10.5

Looking at the data across origination years, we note that the 1984 and 1985 books have distinctly higher coupons than the remaining books, and they appropriately have prepaid more completely to date. Within origination years, with the exception of the 1988 and 1990 books, more loans have prepaid in the high-rate category than in the low-rate category. Note there is less difference in spread (55 basis points) between the categories in the 1988 book than any of the other books. The 1990 book is not yet completely out of the yield maintenance period.

Credit Quality Effects

As discussed in the first section, the credit quality of the collateral securing the loan is important to the ability to obtain funds to refinance, or equivalently, the ability to maximize the leverage of the property. Exhibit 4 shows prepayments for the 1984 and 1985 books broken into four ranges of origination debt coverage ratio. Higher rates of debt coverage at origination, which ought to be correlated with higher ongoing coverage levels, exhibit higher rates of refinancing. (Note that refinancings here do not include loan defaults.)

There is likely a similar story of credit quality behind the Exhibit 5 data, which show that for the 1985 and 1986 books, California loans prepaid at faster rates than New York/New Jersey mortgages. The strong California market in the late-1980s provided plenty of liquidity and opportunities to refinance or sell; the ailing Northeast market battered property values, reducing owners' ability to find new funds, and drove some owners towards assumptions. (This regional breakout used the 1985 and 1986 books since they had the heaviest volume.)

Both Exhibits 4 and 5 look like hockey sticks, illustrating the potent impact of prepayment restrictions. Prepays are virtually nonexistent during the first 4.5 years of the mortgages.

THE PREPAYMENT MODEL

In this section we summarize both the theoretical features and the results of a regression model we have developed. Details of variable construction and model estimation are reported elsewhere.[6]

The possibility of an event of significance to a mortgage loan is the result of environment risks that develop over time from four potential sources: market, property, borrower and contract.[7] By *market risk* we mean changes in financial markets, federal tax policy, and other variables that are national in scope and affect all financial markets. In our model, these are captured through interest rate changes. Beyond macroeconomic uncertainty, there are risks specific to *property* markets such as cash flow and valuation volatility, which we represent through

---

[6] See Jesse M. Abraham and H. Scott Theobald, "A Simple Prepayment Model of Commercial Mortgages," forthcoming, *Journal of Housing Economics*.

[7] A similar characterization of risks is discussed in the Appendix to Jesse M. Abraham, "On the Use of a Cash Flow Time Series to Measure Property Performance."

changes in property income and expense, and local vacancy rates. *Management actions* also play a part in property-specific realization of this type of risk. The financial circumstances of the borrower — the borrower's portfolio position and strategies or reputation — can evolve in a way that affects the exercise of the mortgage call and put options. And finally, features of the lending *contract* can mitigate or create risks in tandem with the stochastic influences.

Exhibit 4: Cumulative Prepayment Rates by Origination DCR
1984 Originations

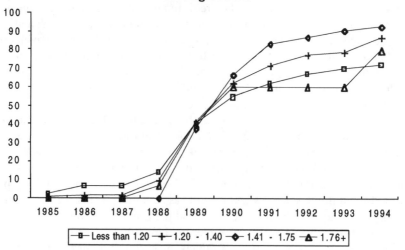

Cumulative Prepayment Rates by Origination DCR
1985 Originations

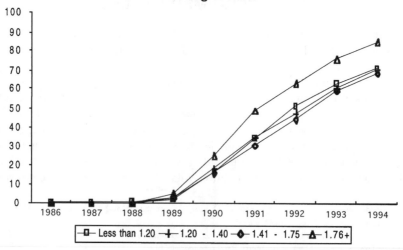

Exhibit 5: Cumulative Prepayment Rates by Property State
1985 Originations

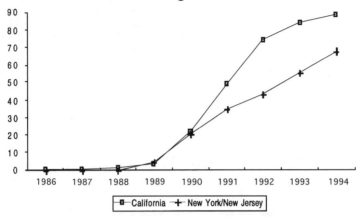

Cumulative Prepayment Rates by Property State
1986 Originations

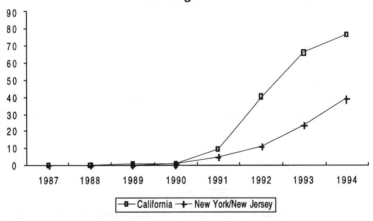

A model of borrower behavior is necessary to bring order to this sea of stochastic events to explain mortgage prepayments. A useful framework comes from option pricing theory. Our conceptual view of prepayment of a commercial mortgage is of a borrower exercising a call option: if the expected present value of an available new source of funds, net of contractual constraints (lockouts) or pre-payment fees, is lower than on the existing obligation, the borrower will refinance and terminate the existing contract.[8]

---

[8] See Patric H. Hendershott and Robert Van Order, "Pricing Mortgages: An Interpretation of the Models and Results," *Journal of Financial Services Research*, Volume 1, 1987, pp. 77-111 for a good overview of this approach.

Exhibit 6: Translation of Environment Risks into Eligibility and Willingness

	Eligibility	Willingness
Market risk	Level of refinance debt service relative to origination Prospective lender DCR standards	Borrower payback period requirements
Property and management risk	Property's current NOI	Appreciation permits re-leveraging
Borrower and portfolio risk	—	—
Mortgage contract features	Lockout forestalls early prepayment	Yield maintenance and prepayment fees affect loan-specific incentives

Commercial borrowers face contractual and market constraints which limit their opportunities to pay in full before the end of a loan's term. This suggests thinking of the prepayment action as the result of two related, but still behaviorally separate states. First, borrowers may be "eligible" or "not eligible" to prepay. Second, the financial incentives may or may not exist for a prepayment.[9] The conditions under which these two criteria are met are considered next.

The fundamental risks identified above are mapped into the behavioral concepts of the option model in Exhibit 6. There is little to say about borrower risk as regards the prepayment option — it is more important in exercise of the default option than in the prepayment option — so that line is left blank. But the other entries indicate how the fundamental risks identified above affect the two prepayment concepts that are useful to measure, and become important in our empirical results used below.

Eligibility

Not all loans, at any given point in time, are candidates for a refinance. To the extent one can segment existing borrowers into eligible and ineligible borrowers, an estimation model will have improved discriminatory powers.

A loan's eligibility to be prepaid depends on the current borrower's ability both to escape from the existing contract and to obtain financing for a new contract. Canceling the existing contract may not be an option if the contract is written with a lockout provision.[10]

---

[9] The empirical approach followed here was originally developed in Chester Foster and Robert Van Order, "FHA Terminations: A Prelude to Rational Mortgage Pricing," *AREUEA Journal*, 13(2), 1985, pp. 24-36.

[10] Some loans in our sample are affected by this, but in practice lockouts have since been replaced with yield maintenance provisions.

A prepayment is also possible only if a lender, which could include the current mortgagee, is willing to provide new financing. Reasonably, lenders require a borrower to have positive equity and a healthy cash flow to be eligible for mortgage funds. While minimum equity and debt service levels may vary from one lender to another, too little equity, or too low a DCR, together with certain property characteristics, can make it virtually impossible for an owner to refinance (without putting more money into the property). The ability of a property to satisfy those lenders' conditions changes over time from movements in local housing markets, as well as the national capital markets. Lender standards can also change over time, such as loosening in a period of excess supply of capital (mid-1980s), toughening in a credit crunch (early 1990s), or loosening when new lenders enter the market (the entry of conduits in 1993).

The model presented below measures credit quality using cash flow rather than equity, making our credit threshold a constant debt coverage. In our favored specification, a borrower needs to achieve a DCR in excess of 1.20 using the refinance rate. That is, using our loan level data, in each period during our estimation, a property's prospective debt coverage ratio is compared against the threshold: DCRs exceeding the threshold are deemed "eligible." The prospective DCR is calculated by dividing the property's updated net operating income by the debt service of the outstanding loan balance at refinance rates. Thus eligibility becomes determined both by property-specific cash flow conditions as well as market trends.

An example of the effect of imposing the eligibility criteria in our estimation for the 1984 and 1989 high-coupon books is shown in Exhibit 7. The clear bar shows the percentage of original loans outstanding at the beginning of each exposure year; the shaded bar shows what happens to eligibility. The 1984 book is subject to lock-outs, so all loans remain ineligible until 1988. As they emerge from lockout, most, but not all, benefit from the roughly 350 basis point drop in interest rates since origination.

With the 1989 book, with yield maintenance provisions, loans become eligible to refinance much earlier. A relatively low percentage of loans are eligible early on because 78% of the book's originations (compared to 58% of 1984's originations) started with a DCR at or below 1.20. As interest rates declined, and the debt service of the prospective refinanced loan declined, increasing numbers of loans became eligible, while few actually prepaid because of yield maintenance provisions.

Willingness

Not all eligible borrowers will be have incentive to prepay. What we have termed borrower "willingness" to prepay is sensitivity to changes over time in market conditions, property risk, and initial contract features, as indicated in Exhibit 6. The most straightforward way to see this is to calculate the value of PREPAY in the equation below, which is the market value of the existing payment obligation relative to the book value of the existing obligation:

$$PREPAY = (MVUPB - TRNSCOST - PREPFEE)/UPB$$

Exhibit 7: Original and Eligible Loans Outstanding
1984 Originations – High Coupon

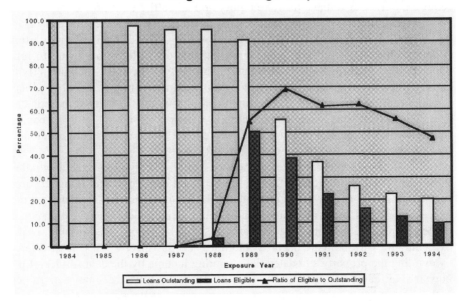

Original and Eligible Loans Outstanding
1989 Originations – High Coupon

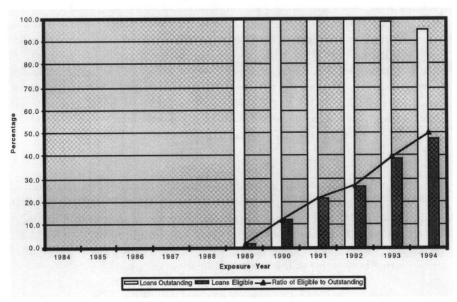

where

MVUPB	=	the present value of the principal and interest payments, plus the balloon, of the outstanding mortgage, discounted at the current market (mortgage) rate.
TRNSCOST	=	the transactions costs of originating a new loan. We assume they are a fixed 2.5% of the outstanding loan balance. However, at the balloon date, transactions costs are not discretionary to the borrower (unless the property is sold), so they should not act as a disincentive to payoff of the loan at that time. What makes transactions costs important is the extent to which they are accelerated from the balloon date. Therefore, in our calculations this variable is set equal to zero at the balloon date, with a 2.5% cost increased in proportion to the time value of refinancing early (with the one-year Treasury bond rate).
PREPFEE	=	the prepayment fees specific to each loan program. In the Freddie Mac programs, there were no fees to pay off the loan during the last six months of the term. Prior to that, there was a 1% fee, a yield maintenance provision, or a lockout.
UPB	=	the modeled unpaid principal balance of the loan.

If there is no change in interest rates, the PREPAY variable will remain generally below 1.0 because of the fixed costs associated with a refinance transaction. As interest rates rise, MVUPB falls in value since the same cash flow is now discounted at a higher interest rate. Conversely, as rates decline, PREPAY will exceed 1.0, indicating that the borrower is in-the-money for the refinance option. In other words, the present value from refinancing exceeds the present value of remaining with the current obligation. The variable PREPAY will generally have values in the range from 0.80 to 1.30.

Crucial to the calculation of PREPAY are the assumptions one makes regarding the current market mortgage rate and the payback period required by the borrower to make the transaction viable. Two extremes are defined by borrower views of the current risks and rewards of utilizing financial leverage. An aggressive borrower, seeking to maximize leverage, considers the new loan to be only a substitute for (roughly) the remaining term of the existing loan, financed for the shortest term and with the cheapest source of funds around. A conservative borrower, seeking to minimize leverage, considers the new loan to be a mechanism for retiring the existing loan, financed for a longer term and with a more expensive source of funds. Our empirical testing slightly favored the short term view, with those equations being the source of the results we report later.

Exhibit 8: Value of PREPAY Variable
1984 Originations – High Coupon

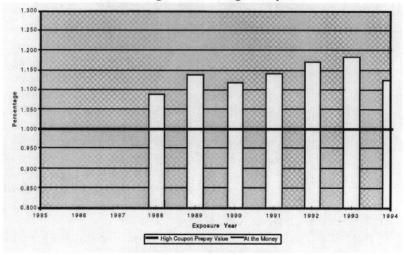

Value of PREPAY Variable
1989 Originations – High Coupon

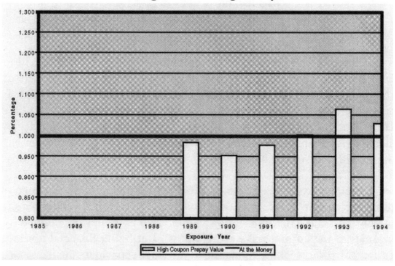

The value of the PREPAY variable — averaged across all eligible loans in our sample — is shown for the high-coupon 1984 and 1989 books in Exhibit 8. The horizontal line at a value of 1.0 occurs when the market value, net of transactions costs, equals the book value, putting values exceeding one in the money to prepay. The top panel shows that with a decline in the 10-year Treasury rate of

350 basis points from origination in 1984 to 1988, borrowers can realize a gain of over 10% of their loan value by refinancing. As cash flows improved and declined further through 1993, the gain from a refinance grew to approach 20%.

The 1989 book shows a different picture. Even with interest rate declines through the subsequent years, PREPAY does not move decisively higher. This is the result of disincentives from the yield maintenance provisions and other transactions costs, as well as weak gains in property cash flows.

Model Results

These two measures — eligibility and willingness — have been calculated using loan level Freddie Mac multifamily data, grouped by origination year and exposure year. We then estimated a nonlinear, least squares regression to explain prepayments as the product of these measures. A logistic transformation was performed to capture the shape shown in Exhibit 2. The standard goodness of fit measure, R squared, was 0.75.[11]

The fitted values for the 1984 and 1989 high-coupon book years are shown in Exhibit 9. Actual prepayments are shown with bars, and fitted values are illustrated with the line. These fits are consistent with those observed for the other book years in our sample data set. Under prediction in the 1989 and 1990 exposure years and over prediction in the 1992 and 1993 exposure years suggest changes in lender standards and borrower expectations not yet captured in the current model. Unfortunately, attempts to capture these impacts using readily observed or calculated data series yielded higher R squares and lower residuals but also yielded counterintuitive coefficients that defied reliable interpretation. As a result, these alternative specifications were rejected in favor of the current model.

With the fitted equation, we can now return to Exhibit 2 and compare the derived sensitivity to interest rate movements of multifamily prepayments with single-family prepayments. This is shown graphically in Exhibit 10 with the value of the probability of prepayment for eligible loans plotted against the prepayment incentive, (PREPAY). The commercial coefficients come from the model discussed above, while the single-family coefficients come from the identical model estimated with single-family 30-year fixed-rate loans.[12]

We can see that the commercial specification is more sensitive to interest rates than the single-family model. The relevant range along the horizontal axis goes from being out of the money by 10% (0.90) to being in the money by up to 30% (1.30). Multifamily goes from being similar to single-family when both are out of the money, to a prepayment rate of nearly 60% versus less than 40% when both are in the money by 30%.

---

[11] For a full explanation of what was done, see Abraham and Theobald, "A Simple Prepayment Model of Commercial Mortgages."

[12] See Chester Foster and Robert Van Order, "Estimating Prepayments," *Secondary Mortgage Markets*, (Winter 1990/91), pp. 24-26,

Exhibit 9: Incremental Prepayment Rates
High Coupon Originations

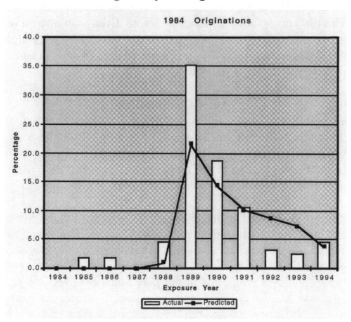

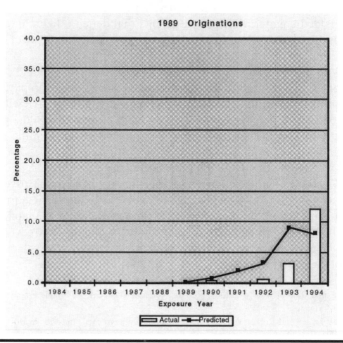

Exhibit 10: Fitted Graph of Multifamily versus Single-family Prepayment Probability Curves

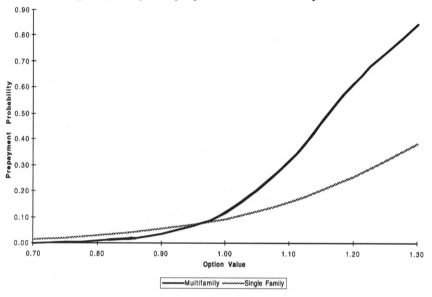

CONCLUSION

When it comes to the prepayment behavior of commercial mortgage-backed securities, investors currently rely on dealer judgements that CMBSs are "slow prepays" because of contract restrictions. That qualitative assessment is borne out by comparing the cumulative prepayment data reported in Exhibit 1. There are little data or research yet available to support more detailed hypotheses or quantitative assessments. The reasoning and modeling reported here start to fill that void.

We have shown that contract restrictions are effective in limiting prepayments in the early years of a commercial mortgage. Conditional rates can then accelerate sharply when the contract restrictions are removed. However, the eligibility to refinance for a number of loans will remain impaired due to credit quality. Falling interest rates help, but do not remove this problem. Once loans breech the eligibility threshold, however, they have faster prepayments than single-family loans.

Chapter 26

An Option-Theoretic Approach to the Valuation of Multifamily Mortgage Loans and Securities

Michael D. Youngblood, Ph.D.
Managing Director — Mortgage Research
Chase Securities Inc.

INTRODUCTION

Issuance of multifamily and commercial mortgage securities accelerated briskly in the 1990s, from a meager $5.7 billion in 1990 to $20.3 billion in 1994, before slipping to $19 billion in 1995. However, issuance has rebounded and should set a new record in 1996. Renewed issuance of mixed-collateral commercial securities by dealer conduits, which totaled $12.7 billion, or 60.9% of the total, has led this rebound. Such vigorous issuance has provided investors with a wide range of opportunities, spanning virtually all investment grades (from AAA to NR), intermediate and long maturities, fixed and floating interest rates, and property types. In addition, it has enlarged the secondary market for multifamily and commercial mortgage securities, although the intemperate demand for new securities usually produces odd-lot allocations that impede subsequent secondary trading.

Nevertheless, the proliferation of multifamily and commercial mortgage securities should not obscure the risks to which they expose investors. Greater liquidity does not necessarily mean lower risk, as the markets for high-yield securities and syndicated bank loans attest. The primary risks facing investors are prepayment or default of one or more of the underlying mortgage loans. These events could result in reinvestment of principal at lower interest rates and/or in outright loss of expected interest or principal, or both. Even if a subordinated class or cash reserve fund should absorb any loss, the elevated cash flow variability or the reduction in available credit enhancement could widen yield spreads and undermine performance. These are, obviously, the primary risks of single-family mort-

I wish to express my gratitude to my colleagues, Dr. Eugene Xu and Sangam Pande, for their expert assistance in the preparation of this chapter.

gage securities as well, although the much larger size of the underlying loans and the much smaller number of them magnify these risks for multifamily and commercial mortgage securities.

Consider the most salient examples of the risk of prepayment and default of these securities in recent years:

- One $122 million privately-placed floating-rate multifamily security, issued in June 1993 and maturing in August 1998, was refinanced two years later. Ironically, in July 1996 the borrower used the same collateral to support a new $125 million fixed-rate security, maturing in 2015.
- Cumulative losses have exhausted the $122.2 million reserve fund of Resolution Trust Corporation, Series 1991-M2, leaving a single $51.9 million subordinated class to protect $151.6 million of senior classes from future losses (as of the July 1996 remittance report). In light of the vulnerability of the senior classes, Moody's Investors Service and Standard & Poor's Rating Group have sliced the original ratings from Aa1/AA or Aa2/AA to Baa3/B.
- The first two non-RTC multifamily securities issued in the 1990s have effectively failed. The rating of the very first security tumbled from AA in 1991 to D (Standard & Poor's) in July 1996, as the most senior class incurred losses of $1.7 million, or 3.1% of the unpaid principal balance, after the utter depletion of the subordinated classes. To forestall potentially huge investor losses, the issuer of the second nonagency security of 1991 repurchased all of its senior classes in 1994. The ratings on this security and one other, which was also repurchased, were withdrawn before they could be cut.

The poor performance of these landmark issues, three of which contributed prominently to re-establishing the nonagency multifamily market in 1991, after its virtual dissolution in the late 1980s, highlights the risks inherent in multifamily and commercial securities.

In this chapter, we show how to evaluate the risks of prepayment and default of multifamily mortgage loans and securities through the same option-theoretic approach that has evolved to evaluate them for single-family mortgage loans and securities. This approach has evolved from the seminal work of Black and Scholes, Merton, and Cox, Ingersoll, and Ross, and from continuous refinements by practitioners over the past decade.[1] We focus here on prepayment and default of multifamily mortgage *loans* rather than *securities* because the former necessarily leads to the latter. And the operation of nonagency credit enhance-

---

[1] See Fischer Black and Myron Scholes, "The Pricing of Options and Corporate Liabilities," *Journal of Political Economy*, 81 (1972), pp. 637-54; Robert Merton, "Theory of Rational Option Pricing," *Bell Journal of Economics and Management Science*, 4 (1973), pp. 141-83; and J.C. Cox, J.E. Ingersoll, Jr., and S.A. Ross, "A Theory of the Term Structure of Interest Rates," *Econometrica*, 53 (1985), pp. 385-407.

ment in absorbing losses on the loans underlying multifamily securities requires no explanation to institutional investors. While using a common option-theoretic approach, we need to adjust for certain fundamental differences between multi-family and residential loans, borrowers, and properties. By adjusting for these differences, we can specify the multifamily (and, without loss of generality, commercial) prepayment and default functions that allow optional valuation under Monte Carlo or binomial simulation of an interest rate process.

DIFFERENCES BETWEEN MULTIFAMILY AND SINGLE-FAMILY LOANS

Multifamily and residential mortgage loans differ fundamentally in their terms and conditions. Multifamily mortgage loans generally amortize over terms of 240 to 360 months, with a final balloon payment of principal due in 60 to 240 months. Some loans amortize fully over terms of 300 to 360 months, with no balloon payment. Some loans do not amortize at all, but pay only interest until the final maturity date. Most loans have significant constraints on prepayment before maturity, which can take many forms:

- Lock-out periods which absolutely prohibit prepayment and which may be succeeded by further constraints.
- Yield maintenance premiums that require the borrower to pay the present value of the change in the yield of a specified Treasury note between closing date and prepayment date, depriving the borrower of any pure interest-rate incentive to refinance; variations in calculating these premiums may reduce the borrower's disincentive.
- Prepayment penalties, expressed as a percentage of the unpaid principal balance of the loan, which typically decline as the loan approaches maturity.

Loans that do allow the borrower to prepay, subject to constraints like these, usually require payment in full and explicitly prohibit partial payment. In contrast, the huge majority of single-family mortgage loans, whether fixed-rate or adjustable-rate, amortize over 15- or 30-year terms. (Of course, the comparatively small number of residential balloon loans amortize over 360 months, with final payments of principal due in five or seven years.) Single-family loans generally permit prepayment in full or in part at any time without penalty.

THE OPTION TO PREPAY WITH TRANSACTION COSTS

The multifamily borrower has invested equity in and raised debt on the security of the apartment property solely to obtain the after-tax real financial returns that it generates, in the form of periodic income and ultimate proceeds from sale. In maximizing the return on equity, the borrower, who is rarely an individual and usually a partnership or corporation, will act rationally to prepay or to default on the mortgage loan. In contrast, residential borrowers usually derive housing services as well as financial returns from the equity and debt invested in a house; the physical or emotional value of housing services may outweigh the investment returns. Hence, the residential borrower may not act rationally to maximize return on investment. Moreover, individuals generally lack access to the full information about alternative returns from investment or costs of debt that institutional borrowers generally possess, which ignorance may contribute to evidently irrational actions.

The multifamily borrower will generally prepay the mortgage loan, subject to the constraints set forth in the related note or deed of trust, when the present value of the scheduled payments exceeds the present value of payments on a new loan under whatever terms may prevail in the future, plus transaction and other costs. If the borrower seeks to prepay when yield maintenance or prepayment penalties are required by the note, then these payments will effectively increase the present value of the alternative loan. Similarly, the borrower will incur substantial upfront costs in refinancing a multifamily mortgage loan, which will overtly increase the present value of the alternative loan.

These expenses include (1) the fees to the commercial loan broker who located the lender of the new loan (1% to 3% of the new loan amount); (2) commitment fees and other "inducements" to the lender (2% to 5%); (3) the title insurance policy or its equivalent (1%); (4) fees for a FFIEC-eligible appraisal, engineering report, and Phase I environment assessment; and, (5) legal fees, including those for recordation. The last two typically represent 0.50% of the new loan amount. One estimates that borrowers incur transaction costs, on average, of 5% of the new loan amount. These average transaction costs are roughly equivalent to an additional 1% on the annual interest rate of a 10-year non-amortizing balloon mortgage loan. In sharp contrast, residential borrowers can obtain new loans for average points and fees of 1.50%, or less, of the loan amount.

Furthermore, the engineering report and Phase I environment assessment may reveal deferred maintenance, or violations of building codes, or environmental hazards. These may range from the innocuous, i.e., potholes in the parking lot, to the pathological, i.e., friable "popcorn" asbestos sprayed on a significant proportion of the interior surface of an apartment building. If these conditions impair the current or future value of the building, then the lender will routinely require the borrower to cure these conditions. The lender will always require cure of building code violations, without which the borrower cannot obtain a certificate of occupancy. The lender may not agree to advance any or all of the funds needed to cure these conditions, which would present the borrower with additional upfront expenditures, further inflating the present value of alternative credit. Together, prepayment penalties, transaction costs, and deferred maintenance expenditures set a high threshold on prepayment that can deter the borrower from prepayment.

Prepayment Function

In light of these considerations, we can define the *prepayment function* as the relationship between the present value of the existing loan under the terms set forth in the mortgage note, and the present value of an alternative mortgage loan under whatever terms lenders may offer in the future. The prepayment function discounts the principal and interest payments scheduled under the original loan by current interest rates, plus the average risk premium or yield spread that lenders currently charge for comparable loans. Mathematically this is expressed as follows:

$$\Pi_0 = \sum_{i=0}^{T} (P_i + I_i)\left(1 + \frac{r_0 + s}{2}\right)^{-2t_i} \tag{1}$$

where

Π_0 = the original loan amount
P_i = the scheduled principal payment of period i
I_i = the scheduled interest payment of period i
T = the final period
r_0 = the base rate at origination (month 0)
t_i = the time to receive principal and interest payments of period i
s = the risk premium

The prepayment function also discounts the principal and interest payments scheduled under the alternative loan by the interest rates that prevail in the future, plus the same risk premium, and then adds prepayment penalties, transaction costs, and deferred maintenance expenditures as shown below:

$$\sum_{i=0}^{T} (P_i + I_i)\left(1 + \frac{r_{i0} + s}{2}\right)^{-2(t_i - t_{i0})} > \Pi_{i0} + PP_{i0} + PTC_0 + DM_0 \tag{2}$$

where:

r_i = the discount rate at i_0
Π_{i0} = the alternative loan amount at i_0
PP_{i0} = the prepayment penalty at i_0
PTC_0 = the prepayment transaction cost
DM_0 = deferred maintenance expenditures

and T, t_i, s, P_i, and I_i are as defined in equation (1).

If the value of first term of the inequality, the existing loan, exceeds that of the second term, the alternative loan, then the borrower should prepay, presumably in the following month.

The rationality of the borrower simplifies this part of the valuation of multifamily loans relative to that of residential loans. One does not need to introduce an econometric model to estimate the likelihood or rate of non-rational prepayment as one does with residential loans. One need only to solve the prepayment function in conjunction with an appropriate interest-rate process.

THE OPTION TO DEFAULT WITH TRANSACTION COSTS

Unlike the residential borrower who acquires a house as a shelter and as an investment, the multifamily borrower acquires an apartment property only as an investment. He or she acquires the property, with a mixture of equity and debt in order to receive the monthly net operating income and the proceeds from eventual sale that it will generate. Net operating income is the cash that remains after deducting the opportunity cost of vacant units and the operating expenses of a property from its gross possible income.[2] It does not include deductions for accounting depreciation or debt service payments. Most real estate investors calculate the expected return on equity and debt from net operating income and sale proceeds using one of the many forms of *the discounted cash flow approach.*

However, the borrower does not receive net operating income, but rather the residual cash that remains after payment of scheduled principal and interest and of escrows for property taxes, insurance premiums, replacement reserves, and other impounds. Indeed, multifamily loans sometimes require the apartment manager to remit all rents, late payment penalties, deposit forfeitures, and other collections directly to a lock box which the lender controls. The lender will remit to the borrower only the residual amount that remains after payment of all amounts due. Similarly, the borrower does not receive all of the proceeds from the eventual sale of the property, but rather the residual cash after repaying the unamortized loan amount. No lender will release the title on sale of a property until payment of the remaining loan amount, any interest accrued but not yet paid, and any late payment penalties outstanding.

Therefore, the borrower should expect to receive the present values of the monthly net income from the property and the net proceeds from sale. The present values of the net income and the net proceeds will jointly determine the borrower's decision each month over the life of the mortgage loan either to make principal and interest payments, and other mandatory payments, or to default. Understanding this monthly decision is essential to the analysis that follows: *the valuation of the borrower's option to default depends on both the net income and the net proceeds.* Unless net income falls below zero (when net operating income is less than principal and interest payments), the borrower will not default, even if the present value of net proceeds is negative (when the market value of the property is less than the loan amount). Monthly net income must fall below zero *and* the market value of the property must fall below that of the loan balance.

---

[2] See Charles Wurtzebach and Mike Miles, *Modern Real Estate* (New York: John Wiley, 1991), pp. 206-211.

Furthermore, the borrower will include transaction costs in the monthly decision to pay or to default on the loan. Whereas one can quantify the transaction costs incurred in the prepayment decision, one cannot precisely quantify those incurred in default because they include the following three components that vary widely among borrowers: (1) decreased availability and increased cost of future debt and equity; (2) lender recourse to the borrower; and, (3) federal income tax liability.

First, some lenders do not extend credit to real estate borrowers with a history of uncured defaults. Those who do extend credit to such borrowers routinely impose more stringent terms; these terms may become onerous for borrowers with a history of opportunistic default. Second, fewer loans originated in the 1990s than heretofore allow recourse to the borrower in the event of default. The declining popularity of recourse provisions belongs, in part, to fierce competition from conduits and other non-traditional lenders and, in part, to the legal form of many borrowers. If the borrower takes the legal form of a limited partnership or a special purpose corporation, the mortgaged property may be the only asset. Where recourse provisions exist, the borrower must weigh the likelihood of the loss of other assets in addition to those explicitly pledged in the mortgage note. One cannot measure the value of these assets, or the lender's ability to locate and attach them. Third, the borrower will incur a federal income tax liability equal to the difference between the loan amount and the property value. The value of this difference to the borrower depends upon his or her marginal income tax rate and other considerations, which one does not know.

Nevertheless, one can estimate the loss of operating funds, the forfeiture of property, and certain expenses. The expenses include (1) operating income from the property until definitive foreclosure; (2) working capital, accounts receivable, and escrows; (3) furniture, fixtures, and equipment used to furnish or manage the property; (4) management fees for operating the property; and (5) legal fees, which increase if the borrower also files for bankruptcy. Offsetting these costs, the borrower may retain rents, late payment fees, and other miscellaneous income collected over several months until the lender can accelerate the mortgage note and take control of the property. We estimate that these transaction costs average 7% of the loan amount.

Default Function

In light of these considerations, one can define the *default function* from two simultaneous relationships:

(1) monthly net operating income less scheduled principal and interest, and other payments over the term of the *loan*.

(2) the present value of monthly net operating income over the life of the *property*, plus transaction costs, less the present value of scheduled principal (including the final balloon) and interest, and other payments over the term of the loan.

As long as the first relationship remains positive, the borrower will not default. He or she has sufficient income to pay monthly debt service, and, bolstered by the endemic optimism of real estate investors, will continue to make scheduled payments even if the second relationship has turned negative. As long as the second relationship remains positive, the borrower will not default. He or she retains the excess of the property value over the loan amount, or positive equity. If the first relationship turns negative, then he or she can sell the property, repay the outstanding loan, thereby avoiding default, and realize the amount of positive equity. This relationship reveals an important aspect of the default option on mortgage loans: the loan amount represents the price at which the borrower can sell, in effect, the property to the lender at any time in the future, should equity become negative. When the first and second relationships turn negative, the borrower will default. He or she lacks the income to pay scheduled monthly principal and interest, while the future value of the property, plus transaction costs, has fallen below the loan amount, leaving negative equity.

Rents, Vacancies, and Operating Expenses

The default function of the first relationship compares net operating income to scheduled payments of principal and interest, and escrows. Hence, it requires projection of net operating income as the sum of gross possible rents, the opportunity cost of vacant units, and operating expenses, for each month over the term of the loan. We project future rents as a function of employment growth, income growth, population growth, household formation, housing affordability, net change in the stock of apartments, the natural vacancy rate — all from the housing sub-market in which the property is located — and future 10-year Treasury rates. We estimate the opportunity cost of vacant units from the *natural vacancy rate*, as developed by Rosen and Smith as an equilibrium function of historical rents and operating expenses.[3] Last, we project future operating expenses from their historical correlation with rents. Like the prepayment function, the default function discounts the scheduled principal and interest payments, and other payments, on the loan by the interest rates that prevail in the future, plus the initial risk premium or spread charged by the lender. Therefore, we can project both the net operating income from the property, over the life of the property, and the scheduled payments, over the term of the loan, given an interest rate process.

Similarly, the default function of the second relationship discounts monthly net operating income over the life of the property by the interest rates that prevail in the future, plus the multifamily risk premium. We project net operating income as before over the expected *economic life* of the property, which we obtain the from the mandatory FFIEC-eligible appraisal or engineering report. A

---

[3] Kenneth Rosen and Lawrence B. Smith, "The Price-Adjustment Process for Rental Housing and the Natural Vacancy Rate," *American Economic Review*, 73 (1983), pp. 779-786, and Lawrence B. Smith, "A Note on the Price Adjustment Mechanism for Rental Housing," *American Economic Review*, 64 (1974), pp. 478-481.

new apartment property has an expected economic life of 50 years, assuming that rehabilitation does not extend it, but most of the apartment properties underlying multifamily (and mixed-property commercial) securities are not new, which reduces the term over which they can generate net operating income.

The default function of the second relationship discounts the net operating income by the interest rates expected to prevail in the future, plus a multifamily risk premium. The multifamily risk premium is the entrepreneurial return that the borrower requires for investing equity and debt in the apartment property. We measure it by the spread between the yield capitalization rate of the property and the interest rates that prevailed at origination of the mortgage loan. The yield capitalization rate is the internal rate of return that equated the appraised or sales value of the apartment property, at the time of the origination of the mortgage loan, to the future net operating income that it may generate over its economic life, assuming no rehabilitation.[4]

Therefore, default occurs in any month i_0 over the term of the mortgage loan, if both of the following relationships are satisfied:

$$NOI_{i_0} < P_{i_0} + I_{i_0} + E_{i_0} \tag{3}$$

$$\sum_{i=i_0}^{EL} NOI_i \left(1 + \frac{r_{i_0} + ycr}{2}\right)^{-2(t_i - t_0)} + DTC_0$$

$$- \sum_{i=i_0}^{T-1} (P_i + I_i + E_i) \left(1 + \frac{r_{i_0} + s}{2}\right)^{-2(t_i - t_0)} < 0 \tag{4}$$

where

NOI_{i0}	=	a (future) payment of net operating income, from the rent process, at period i
r_{i0}	=	the discount rate at period i_0
ycr	=	the discount mortgage risk premium
P_i	=	the scheduled principal payment of period i
I_i	=	the scheduled interest payment of period i
T	=	the final period in the term of the mortgage loan
EL	=	the final period in the economic life of the property
r_0	=	the base rate at origination (month 0)
t_i	=	the time to receive principal and inters payments of period i
s	=	the risk premium
DTC_i	=	default transaction costs at period i

Alternatively, we can rewrite equation (4) such that default occurs if the following inequality obtains:

---

[4] See Kenneth M. Lusht and Jeffrey D. Fisher, "Anticipated Growth and the Specification of Debt in Real Estate Value Models," *AREUEA Journal*, 12 (1984), pp. 1-11.

$$\frac{\displaystyle\sum_{i=i0}^{EL} NOI_i \left(1 + \frac{r_{i_0} + ycr}{2}\right)^{-2(t_i - t_0)} + DTC_0}{\displaystyle\sum_{i=i_0}^{T-1} (P_i + I_i + E_i)\left(1 + \frac{r_{i_0} + s}{2}\right)^{-2(t_i - t_0)}} < 1 \tag{5}$$

If the ratio of present value of the property, plus default transaction costs, to the present value of the mortgage loan falls below 1 and if the relationship in equation (3) is less than zero, then the borrower will default.

INTERPRETING PREPAYMENT AND DEFAULT FUNCTIONS

The default and prepayment functions assume the same interest rate process, which generates the future interest rates that discount both the principal and interest payments of the mortgage loan and the net operating income of the apartment property. For the interest rate process, we employ a proprietary variant of the one-factor model proposed by Cox, Ingersoll, and Ross. Our variant precludes certain extreme results, for example, negative interest rates.

We begin with the discount rate of the on-the-run 1-month Treasury bill and generate a series of 1-month arbitrage-free forward rates that extend over the entire Treasury yield curve, i.e., over 360 months. We calibrate these rates so that they recover, or produce the exact prices of, the on-the-run Treasury coupon curve. These are the future interest rates described in the prepayment and default models described earlier. Generating these rates requires the on-the-run Treasury yield curve and a measure of interest-rate volatility for each of the 360 months. To provide the monthly volatilities, we interpolate the term structure of volatility from the series of average implied volatilities of puts and calls on (U.S. dollar) interest rate swaps, which range from one week to ten years in term. Furthermore, we can generate a full path of 360 arbitrage-free riskless discount rates for any sequence of 360 monthly volatilities that we may produce with Monte Carlo or other methods.[5]

By applying the default and prepayment functions simultaneously to the path of forward discount rates generated by this process, we can simulate the borrower's decision to default on or prepay any multifamily loan in the present or any future month. Indeed, we can value the borrower's options to default and to prepay by simulating these decisions over all possible paths of forward discount rates. While this comprehensive simulation would require infinite calculations, we can achieve equivalent valuation of the borrower's options by simulating a finite set of

---

[5] See Frank J. Fabozzi, *Valuation of Fixed Income Securities and Derivatives* (New Hope, PA: Frank J. Fabozzi Associates, 1995), pp. 131-154.

paths of forward discount rates that achieves a lognormal distribution, using established tests with appropriate size and power for the lognormal distribution.

To value the options to default and to prepay, we simulate the borrower's rational decisions over a sufficiently large set of discount rate paths in the following sequence:

- Decompose the loan amount into its scheduled monthly payments of principal and interest over months (t) of its remaining term, and its balloon payment, if any, at term (T);
- Reprice the loan, using the appropriate on-the-run Treasury note, plus a risk premium, which is the average yield spread charged by lenders on comparable loans for the same term;
- Solve for the zero-volatility spread (Z-spread) of the loan using current forward discount rates;
- Calculate the present value of the loan over every month in its term with the associated forward discount rate plus the Z-spread;
- Over every path, calculate the present value of the loan over every month with the associated forward discount rate plus the Z-spread;
- Compare the present value of the loan, obtained using current rates, with the present value of the loan (plus prepayment penalties, prepayment transaction costs, and deferred maintenance expenditures) in each path, using path-specific rates; if the conditions of equations (1) and (2) obtain in any month in any path, prepay the unamortized principal balance;
- Decompose the property value into its projected net operating income over months (t) of its expected economic life (EL);
- Solve for the yield capitalization rate and the related Z-spread of the mortgaged property, using the contemporary appraised value or sales price, and current forward discount rates;
- Calculate the present value of the property over every month with the associated forward discount rate plus the Z-spread;
- Compare the present value of the property, obtained using current rates (plus default transaction costs) with the present value of the loan in each path, using path-specific rates; if the conditions of equations (3) and (4) or (3) and (5) obtain in any month in any path, default the mortgage loan;
- Integrate the principal and interest payments over every month and every path and then solve for that risk-adjusted spread to the discount rates in every path that produces an average loan price equal to price of the loan.

CREDIT-ADJUSTED OAS, EFFECTIVE DURATION, AND CONVEXITY

This approach to the simultaneous valuation of the borrower's options to prepay and default enables us to solve for the option-adjusted spread (OAS) or, more precisely, the credit risk option-adjusted spread (CROAS) of a multifamily mortgage loan. Solution of CROAS requires only two steps, assuming the prior simulation of arbitrage-free forward discount rates along a sufficiently large number of paths.

First, we integrate the principal and interest payments that result from allowing rational prepayment and default in every month over the term of the loan and over every path of forward discount rates. One series of payments, from origination to termination of the loan, corresponds to each path of discount rates. Second, we solve iteratively (by trial and error) for the *spread*, that added to the forward rates along each path, will discount each series of monthly payments to its present value, the average of which equals the current price of the loan (plus accrued interest). The semiannual bond-equivalent of this spread is the CROAS. This is expressed mathematically as follows:

$$P + I = \sum_{i=0}^{N} \sum_{j=0}^{T} (PF_{i,j} + IF_{i,j}) \times D_i \times \prod_{i=d}^{i+d} \left(1 + \frac{r_{i,j} + s'}{12}\right)$$

$$s = 2 \times \left[\left(1 + \frac{y' + s'}{12}\right)^6 - \left(1 + \frac{y}{2}\right)\right]$$

(6)

where

P	=	the price
I	=	the accrued interest
N	=	the number of paths;
T	=	the number of months to maturity
$PF_{i,j}$	=	the principal cash flow in ith path and jth month
$IF_{i,j}$	=	the interest cash flow in ith path and jth month
D_i	=	the extra discount factor in ith path due to fractional month of the cash flow's timing
$r_{i,j}$	=	the 1-month Treasury rate (30/360) in ith path and jth month
y'	=	the mortgage-equivalent 10-year
s'	=	the CROAS expressed in mortgage equivalent terms (12 month compounding)
y	=	the bond-equivalent 10-year Treasury yield
s	=	the CROAS expressed in bond equivalent term (semi-annual compounding)

This CROAS is directly comparable to the OAS of any mortgage or non-mortgage security evaluated using the same interest rate process.

Furthermore, we can calculate the first and second derivatives of the price and CROAS of the multifamily loan with respect to the term structures of interest rates and volatility: *effective duration, convexity, volatility sensitivity, volatility convexity,* and so on. We calculate these additional parameters of value by numerical methods, changing the term structures of interest rates or of (average implied swaption) volatility.

For *effective duration*, we increase the term structure of discount rates by any arbitrary magnitude, for example, 25 basis points, for all paths and solve for the average price that results. We then decrease the term structure by the same magnitude for all paths and solve for the average price that results. The difference between the two average prices that result, scaled by the change in basis points and the current price, is the effective duration of the mortgage loan. Effective duration measures the sensitivity of the price of the loan to a change in the term structure of interest rates.[6] The second derivative of price with respect to the term structure of interest rates, *convexity*, follows directly from this calculation. It is the effective duration scaled by the current price multiplied by the square of the same change in interest rates.[7] We calculate the volatility sensitivity and the volatility convexity of the mortgage loan in the same way.

The formulas for duration and convexity are given below.

$$D = \frac{\Delta P}{2P\Delta y} = \frac{P_+ - P_-}{2P\Delta y} \tag{7}$$

$$C = \frac{\Delta^2 P}{100 P \Delta y^2} = \frac{P_+ - 2P + P_-}{100 P \Delta y^2} \tag{8}$$

where

D = the duration
C = the convexity
Δy = shift in yield curve
P = the current price
P_+ = the projected price when the yield curve is up by Δy
P_- = the projected price when the yield curve is down by Δy

VALUING A MULTIFAMILY MORTGAGE LOAN

Consider the example of a representative multifamily mortgage loan, which was underwritten to FNMA DUS standards and originated in August 1996. FNMA's underwriting standards for the DUS program are representative of those employed by most institutional lenders; indeed, most conduit lenders have openly embraced these standards for their multifamily programs for the expedient reason that the rating agencies and institutional investors generally accept them. The lender furnished the following limited information about the loan and the related property:

---

[6] Effective duration differs from modified duration in that the latter does not allow for how changes in the term structure affect a security's cash flow.
[7] Andrew Kalotay, George Williams, and Frank J. Fabozzi, "A Model for Valuing Bonds and Embedded Options," *Financial Analysts Journal* (May-June 1993), pp. 35-46, and Fabozzi, *Valuation of Fixed Income Securities and Derivatives*, pp. 93-130.

Property city, state, and zip code	Houston, TX 77077
Principal balance amount	$8,000,000
Mortgage interest rate	8.42%
Maturity date	8/1/2006
Original amortization term	30 years
Prepayment premium option	Yield maintenance
Yield maintenance period	7.0 years
U.S. Treasury yield rate	5.625%
Security due date	2/1/2006
Total number of units	436
Annual net operating income	$951,904
Loan-to-value ratio	79.21%
Appraised value	$10,100,000
Occupancy	92%
Debt service coverage ratio	1.29x

From our own analysis of the Briar Forest sub-market, where this property is located, and our econometric models of the apartment market in metropolitan Houston, we add the following to FNMA's information:

Risk premium of DUS Tier II loans	1.67%
Yield capitalization rate	13.00
Long-term rent growth rate	3.26
Long-term rent volatility	6.86
Natural vacancy rate	11.20
Prepayment transaction costs	5.00
Default transaction costs	7.00

From this information and our projections of rent growth, rent volatility, and the natural vacancy rate for the apartment property, we calculate the following parameters of risk and value:

Frequency of prepayments	11.3%
Average months to prepayment	83
Average prepayment price	107-04 (32s)
Option cost	9 b.p.
Frequency of defaults	20.7%
Average months to default	82
Average loss severity	27.1%
Option cost	45 b.p.
Z-spread	166 b.p.
Prepayment and default option cost	54 b.p.
CROAS	112 b.p.
Effective duration	6.08 years
Convexity	0.30

This multifamily mortgage loan has an 11.3% probability of prepaying and a 20.7% probability of defaulting over its 10-year term. The probabilities of prepayment and default combine to reduce the nominal and Z-spreads of this mortgage loan by 54 basis points to a CROAS of 112 basis points. Similarly, the effective duration of the loan, which reflects the combined risks, is 6.08 years, whereas the modified duration of the loan, which assumes neither prepayment nor default, is somewhat longer, 6.25 years.

It is striking that the frequency of default and the average severity of loss projected on this multifamily loan, which was underwritten to common institutional standards, fall within the ranges of default and loss experienced historically by mainstream institutional lenders. From his most recent study of the historical performance of commercial mortgage loans originated by life insurance companies in the years 1972-1991, Synderman finds a aggregate lifetime rate of default of 13.8%.[8] However, Synderman concedes that the historical default rate is artificially low, because many of the loans in the insurance company sample remain outstanding — they have yet to default or mature. After adjustment, he projects an 18.3% lifetime default rate. Similarly, on reviewing Synderman's first two studies, Fitch Investors Service noticed that the widespread restructuring of loans by life companies reduced the frequency of default.[9] Based on this review and a separate study of the commercial mortgage portfolios of 11 life companies, Fitch projects a much higher lifetime default rate of 30%. This level forms the baseline for its rating of commercial mortgage securities. It is also consistent with the default rate projected on the representative multifamily mortgage loan.

In addition, Synderman finds that the severity of loss of commercial mortgage loans (measured as a percentage of the unpaid principal balance) varies widely by the origination year, from a low of −7% in 1972 to a high of 96% in 1984. He concludes that the severity of loss averaged 33% in the 1970s and 45% in the 1980s; the average yield cost of default was 50 basis points. Fitch adopts the average loss severity of the 1980s, projecting a loss factor of 40% to 50% for defaulted commercial mortgage loans. As with default frequency, the loss severity projected on the representative multifamily loan is consistent with the historical experience of mainstream commercial lenders. Indeed, Synderman's estimate of the yield cost of default of 50 basis points is virtually the same as the yield cost of default of 45 basis points on this multifamily loan.

THE PARAMETERS OF CROAS

We can explore the risks of this multifamily mortgage loan in greater depth by calculating the sensitivity of the CROAS to its salient parameters: loan-to-value ratio, debt service coverage ratio, term to maturity of the loan, long-term rent

---

[8] Mark Snyderman, "Update on Commercial Mortgage Defaults," *Real Estate Finance Journal* (Summer 1994), pp. 22-32.

[9] Fitch Investors Service, Inc., "Commercial Mortgage Stress Test," *Structured Finance* (June 8, 1992), pp. 1-12.

growth rate, long-term rent volatility, and natural vacancy rate. By exploring the partial derivatives of these parameters to CROAS, we expose the influence on the likelihood of prepayment and default of the underwriting criteria, the terms and conditions of the loan itself, and the local property market. (See Exhibit 1.) Accordingly, we vary each parameter across a wide, but arbitrary, range of values and record the CROAS that results, in terms of basis points and price. We hold all other parameters and the price of the loan constant. We find that:

- Increases in the loan-to-value ratio (LTV), by diminishing the borrower's equity and increasing his or her leverage, decrease CROAS modestly. A decline in LTV from 79.8% to 55% increases CROAS from 112 basis points to 136 basis points. Decreases in LTV increase CROAS symmetrically.
- Increases in the debt service coverage ratio (DSCR) increase CROAS slightly less than the given changes in LTV. An increase from 1.29× to 2.5× DSCR would increase CROAS from 112 basis points to 131 basis points. Decreases in DSCR also affect CROAS symmetrically.
- Term to maturity affects CROAS inversely: the longer the term of the loan, the lower the CROAS. This inverse relationship reflects the operation of volatility; the longer a loan remains outstanding, the broader the range of rental growth rates, including negative rates, that may occur. Term to maturity affects most options in this fashion, especially the short-term exchange-traded financial options that the Black-Scholes or Black futures model evaluate accurately. Indeed, given the unambiguously positive influence that shorter terms have on CROAS, its is paradoxical that the four rating agencies penalize loans with them, requiring more credit enhancement than for otherwise identical loans with longer terms.

Exhibit I: Sensitivity of Parameters and Terms of Multifamily Mortgage Loan Expressed as CROAS
(In Basis Points and Price in 32s)

					Base					
LTV (%)	100	95	90	85	79.8	75	70	65	60	55
CROAS (bp)	83	91	99	106	112	120	125	129	133	136
CROAS (32s)	4-24	4-10	3-27	3-15	3-05	2-21+	2-14	2-05	1-30+	1-25
DSCR	0.90	1.00	1.10	1.20	1.29	1.40	1.50	1.75	2.00	2.50
CROAS (bp)	94	102	109	110	112	116	117	122	126	131
CROAS (32s)	4-02+	3-21	3-09	3-07	3-05	2-30	2-27	2-19	2-12	2-03+
Term (Years)	30	25	20	15	10	7	5	3	2	1
CROAS (bp)	52	54	59	76	112	128	130	143	184	229
CROAS (32s)	5-24+	5-21+	5-11	4-18+	3-05	2-17+	2-11	1-19	0-23+	0-08+
Rent Growth (%)	−1.0	0.0	1.0	2.0	3.3	4.0	4.5	5.0	5.5	6.0
CROAS (bp)	42	64	81	98	112	123	127	131	134	137
CROAS (32s)	15-28+	5-20+	4-25+	3-28	3-05	2-16	2-08+	2-02	1-29	1-22+
Rent (Vol.)	25.0	20.0	15.0	10.0	6.9	5.9	4.9	3.9	2.9	1.9
CROAS (bp)	−8.3	−35	11	77	112	128	137	144	150	154
CROAS (32s)	12-21	10-14	8-08	5-00	3-05	2-07+	1-23+	11-10+	0-29+	0-23+

- The long-term rent growth rate affects CROAS strongly and asymmetrically. An increase from 3.26% to 6.0% increases CROAS from 112 basis points to 137 basis points, but a decrease to −1% drops CROAS to 42 basis points. It is noteworthy that the rent growth rate crosses a threshold of sensitivity below 2%. From 2% to 0%, the rent growth rate cannot overcome the influence of the projected 6.9% volatility, which propagates enough simulated negative growth rates to render CROAS consistently negative. Of course, below 0%, negative growth rates predominate with commensurate effects on CROAS.
- Long-term rent volatility affects CROAS even more strongly than the rent growth rate. It governs the range of potential growth rates associated with the simulated forward discount rates, in effect, raising or lowering the influence of interest rates on rents. High levels of volatility will propagate over time broader ranges of rent growth rates, including negative rates, that ultimately turn CROAS negative.
- The natural vacancy rate acts asymmetrically on CROAS. Increasing vacancy rates diminish CROAS more than increasing this rate inflates CROAS. It is particularly striking that CROAS declines very rapidly once the vacancy rate exceeds 25%.

The influence of these parameters on CROAS reveals its acute vulnerability to the initial equity and leverage of the borrower, and to the conditions of the local market. Investors will need to scrutinize carefully loans with LTVs above 85% or DSCRs below 1.2%, and loans with underlying properties located in volatile real estate markets.

VALUING A MULTIFAMILY MORTGAGE SECURITY

The analysis of the representative multifamily mortgage loan discussed in the previous section leads directly to that of nonagency multifamily and, by extension, commercial mortgage securities. It enables one to quantify the risks of prepayment and default of the underlying mortgage loans, and to measure the adequacy of the credit enhancement provided by the security.

Consider a truly exemplary multifamily mortgage security, the Evans Withycombe Finance Trust, which was issued in August 1994 by a special purpose Delaware limited partnership, which is, in turn, wholly-owned by Evans Withycombe, Inc., a publicly-held real estate investment trust. The multifamily security consists of four classes, one senior (A-1) and three subordinate (A-2, A-3, and A-4), all totaling $131 million. (See Exhibit 2.) The three subordinated classes, which total $29 million and represent 22.1% of the principal balance, protect the senior class against loss from default on the underlying mortgage notes. Each class receives payment of interest sequentially at a 7.98% annualized rate; class A-1 receives interest, then class A-2, and so on. The securities do not amortize and mature in August 2001; they cannot be prepaid in whole or in part until March 2001. Unusually, the servicer has no obligation to advance interest in the event that the borrower fails to pay on any due date.

Exhibit 2: Structure of Evans Withycombe Finance Trust, August 1994 (Dollars in Millions)

Class	Amount	Coupon (%)	Maturity	Call Date
A-1 (Senior)	102.0	7.98	8/1/2001	3/1/2001
A-2 (Sub.)	15.0	7.98	8/1/2001	3/1/2001
A-3 (Sub.)	9.0	7.98	8/1/2001	3/1/2001
A-4 (Sub.)	5.0	7.98	8/1/2001	3/1/2001

The underlying collateral consists of 22 apartment properties which are located in the Phoenix and Tucson metropolitan areas. They incorporate 5,380 apartments units, with 4.88 million square feet of rentable space. The average apartment size is roughly 907 square feet. The borrower describes the properties as "oriented to upscale residents seeking high levels of amenities, such as clubhouses, exercise rooms, tennis courts, swimming pools, therapy pools, and covered parking." The units rented for an average of $606 a month in the 12 months ending May 31, 1994, subject to a 92% economic occupancy rate. The apartments units were constructed between 1984 and 1990, leaving little scope for economic or functional obsolescence. A subsidiary of Evans Withycombe. Inc. manages the properties on behalf of the special purpose partnership. The underwriters estimated a debt service coverage ratio of 1.68× and a loan-to-value ratio of 54% at issuance of the security. After updating this information for current apartment market conditions in Phoenix and Tucson, we project a long-term rental growth rate of 2.3% on these properties, a long-term volatility of the rental growth rate of 4.3%, and a natural vacancy rate of 10%.

Assuming that dealers would offer the senior class A-1 at a nominal spread of 75 basis points over an interpolated Treasury note with a 4.7-year maturity, we calculate a CROAS of 74 basis points. (See Exhibit 3.) We estimate a zero probability of prepayment, given the absolute prohibition against it until March 2001, and a zero probability of default, given the high DSCR, low LTV, and favorable rental growth and volatility rates of the properties. Arbitrarily reducing the initial DSCR to 1.20× and raising the initial LTV to 80% would produce a 17.7% probability of default and an 11% expected loss rate; the CROAS of class A-1 falls by six basis points to 68 basis points. Under this scenario, losses of 1.95% of the principal balance of the mortgage notes, or $2.55 million, would result. Losses of this magnitude would eliminate 51% of the A-4 subordinated class, but leave classes A-2 and A-3 intact. Arbitrarily reducing the initial DSCR to 1.0× and raising the initial LTV to 100% would produce a 47.5% probability of default and a 12.3% expected loss rate; the CROAS of class A-1 would fall by 106 basis points to −32 basis points. Under this scenario, losses of 5.84% of the principal balance of the mortgage notes, or $7.65 million, would result. Losses of this magnitude would eliminate the A-4 subordinated class entirely, and 29.5% of the A-3 class, but leave the A-2 class intact. The senior class would not suffer actual loss, but rather an erosion of relative value such that it would yield substantially less than a comparable Treasury note. Since extreme conditions must occur to undermine the performance of class A-1 to such an extent, we conclude that the credit enhancement for class A-1 more than compensates for the likely risk of default and may render class A-1 a candidate for upgrading from AA by Standard and Poor's.

CONCLUSION

The approach to joint valuation of the prepayment and default options of multi-family loans that we developed in this chapter offers important advantages over other approaches. First, it unifies the valuation of multifamily and commercial mortgage loans and securities with that of single-family mortgage loans and securities by means of a common interest rate process. The simulation of arbitrage-free forward discount rates using the term structure of (average implied swaption) volatility along a sufficiently large number of paths by Monte Carlo methods provides the framework for discounting all monthly (or other periodic) future cash flows, whatever their source, commercial or residential, by appropriate risk premia. Hence, one can directly compare the usual first and second derivatives of price, rate, and volatility across the various types of loans and securities.

Second, the approach unifies the valuation of the mortgage loan and the related apartment property, by a more complex application of the common interest rate process. It discounts all future monthly cash flows, from loan or from property, by the same set of forward discount rates, plus respective risk premia. It offers thereby a framework capable of valuing a wide variety of financial instruments, not only mortgage loans and securities. Furthermore, it simulates the future net operating income from an apartment property as a function of economic and demographic variables, drawn from the local real estate sub-market, and the yield of the 10-year Treasury note. It creates thereby a direct link to forward 10-year discount rates and an indirect link through dynamic covariance coefficients for each economic and demographic variable to the 10-year rate. These coefficients will vary in size, sign, and lag. Hence, we can simulate the future net operating income for a property consistently with the simulation of future interest payments on alternative mortgage loans, which could lead to prepayment. In contrast, most other approaches simulate the value of the loan separately from the value of the property, using distinct stochastic processes. Accordingly, they may randomly associate future states of the property with future discount rates, propagating potentially aberrant relationships; one could find a very high growth rate or high variability of property price inflation associated with a very low discount rate.

Exhibit 3: Scenario Performance of Evans Withycombe Finance Trust, Class A-1

Scenario (DSCR / LTV)	Nominal Spread	CROAS	Loss Frequency (%)	Loss Severity (%)
1.68 / 54	75	74	0.0	0.0
1.20 / 80	75	68	17.7	11.0
1.00 / 100	75	-32	45.7	12.3

Third, the approach estimates the value of the property by the function described above for each month of the term of the related loan, including the final balloon payment. Thus, it avoids recourse to an externally-specified value of the property at maturity of the loan. The continuous internal determination of property value overcomes a critical weakness in the discounted cash flow approach that many lenders, borrowers, and appraisers use to value multifamily loans and properties: the arbitrary choice of the value of the property at maturity of the loan. Amid its countless variations, the discounted cash flow approach generally applies a constant discount rate, usually the yield of a comparable Treasury note plus a risk premium, to the projected annual net operating income and to the final sale price or market value of property, as of the maturity of the loan. This value is determined by capitalizing the projected net operating income in the last year at a projected rate. The projected capitalization rate is seldom derived by any methodology; rather, appraisers and others often use a rule of thumb, adding 1% or more to the initial capitalization rate, which is itself an average of capitalization rates sampled from recent sales or loans.[10] The discounted cash flow method, thus, founders at a critical point in any valuation by arbitrary, if not randomly, selecting terminal property value.

The fourth advantage is that the continuous internal determination of the value of a specific property overcomes a critical weakness in the valuation of multifamily properties: the arbitrary choice of the rate of return or "building-payout rate." Those who evaluate the property by a pure stochastic process often assume that it will offer the same rate of return as did equity real estate investment trusts (REITs), i.e., 8%, over some arbitrary period of time such as 1980-1987. This choice of rate of return invites numerous objections. REITs provide investors with valuable *liquidity*, which permits a higher valuation and lower rate of return on the properties that they own. REITs represent many different property types, so that any average return will not reflect a return specific to apartment properties. REITs own different types of properties in different markets, allowing a smoothing of return by the natural covariance of returns across property types and markets, which again leads to imprecision in valuing an individual apartment property. REITs typically use much less debt than other real estate investors; lower leverage implies lower risk and, appropriately, lower returns to investors. Also, REITS provide professional management of income-producing properties that small apartment properties (36 units or less) may not, which would motivate investors generally to require higher returns and expect higher variance of returns from them. In contrast, our approach infers the yield capitalization rate of a specific property and the risk premium to current interest rates implied by this rate. It then adds the property-specific risk premium to the forward discount rates across all paths, which produces a different series of capitalization rates for each path. Therefore, our approach provides greater specificity as well as greater flexibility in the valuation of mortgaged properties.

---

[10] See D. Richard Wincott, "Terminal Capitalization Rates and Reasonableness," *The Appraisal Journal* (April 1991), pp. 253-260.

The fifth advantage is the approach estimates the incidence of default and loss on foreclosure by the same function. Default occurs when the two conditions of the default function occur simultaneously. The number of paths on which default occurs automatically furnishes the frequency of default. The delay between default and final foreclosure and sale, which we obtain by random draws from a normal distribution that assumes an average of 24 months and variance of five months, permits calculation of the accrued interest foregone. (To the accrued interest, we add additional foreclosure costs of 5% the loan balance, and deduct net operating income received from the property over the foreclosure period.) The loss on foreclosure of the property derives from the difference between the property value, 24 months or so after default, and the unpaid principal balance of the loan. Hence, the magnitude of loss arises from the internal operation of our approach to value. Of course, one can compare the incidence of default and severity of loss projected on any loan to the historical experience of comparable loans originated by life insurance companies, RTC-administered financial institutions, or agency multifamily portfolios.

Finally, our approach offers a compromise in the persistent debate on the subject of *ruthless* versus *non-ruthless* default. Some contend that a borrower will rationally default on a property whenever its present value falls below that of the related mortgage loan, without consideration of transaction costs — hence, ruthless default. Any delay by the borrower in defaulting on the loan arises from his or her unwillingness to forego the persistent value of the option to default in the future, since the property value may continue to decline. (This decline magnifies the borrower's implicit gain and the lender's loss, because the loan amount fixes the strike price or tacit sales price of the property to the lender.) However, others contend that a borrower will rationally default on a property whenever its present value falls below that of the related loan, but will include transaction costs in assessing its value; hence, non-ruthless default. The borrower will not default as soon as the present value of the property falls below that of the loan, eliminating equity, but waits until negative equity should accumulate to the amount of observable and unobservable transaction costs.

While our approach clearly incorporates transaction costs in anticipating the borrower's rational decision, it also tenders a compromise to the opponents in the debate. We contend that the borrower should default in any month when two conditions occur: when net operating income falls below scheduled debt payments and when property value falls below loan amount, eliminating the borrower's equity. In practice, the second condition occurs before the first. The present value of expected net operating income falls below the present value of scheduled mortgage payments before income falls below scheduled payments. Property value declines faster than loan value, in part, because net operating income is discounted with a much higher risk premium than is the mortgage payment. Accordingly, the borrower may have sufficient cash flow to make scheduled payments even though the property value has fallen below the loan amount, plus transaction costs. He or she will rationally delay default as long as net operating income continues to exceed scheduled monthly payments, even though equity is negative. Therefore, the future option to default consists only of the option to default before these cash flows decline to zero. Our approach conflates the value of the present and future options to default.

Furthermore, those who conclude that the borrower has an option to default in the present and in the future must ignore the presence of the lender, who should act as rationally as the borrower. While few mortgage notes give the lender the ability to act unilaterally when the borrower's equity turns negative, all lenders have the legal right to accelerate the note and begin foreclosure as soon as the borrower fails to pay. The separate assignment of rents enhances the lender's ability to collect rents as soon as default occurs. Indeed, the lender will attempt to take possession of the property in order to forestall the borrower from optimizing the value of the option to default! The lender endeavors to obtain the property before its value falls below that of the loan, minimizing the value of default to the borrower. In most states, within three months of the first failure to pay scheduled principal and interest, the lender can obtain possession of, if not title to, the property and begin to receive net operating income. In conclusion, if a value to default in the future does exist, it consists either of the option to receive cash flow until it turns negative, or an option on property value from the month that cash flow turns negative until the lender assumes control of the property. These options have little time or intrinsic value, and we already incorporate them within our approach to valuation.

Chapter 27

Understanding and Managing the Balloon Risk of Commercial Mortgages in CMBS

David P. Jacob
*Managong Director and
Director of Research & Securitization
Nomura Securities International, Inc.*

Peter Fastovsky
*Associate
Nomura Securities International, Inc.*

INTRODUCTION

Unlike the residential mortgage market, where fully amortizing loans make-up the majority of the market, commercial mortgages most often are amortizing loans (20-30 year amortization schedules) with a balloon payment between 7 and 12 years. Whereas the scheduled principal and interest during the term of the loan is paid from the cash flow generated by the property, the balloon payment is usually made by refinancing the mortgage. This event can cause financial stress to the borrower, which may require the lender to take a variety of actions. The risk of a borrower not being able to meet a balloon payment is reasonably well understood by the traditional lenders. However, many investors in CMBS are relative new-comers to the commercial mortgage market and are not yet aware of the potential impact of balloon risk. Even traditional lenders, such as insurance companies, who are allocating more money to CMBS, do not understand the interaction between the CMBS structure and the underlying pool of balloon mortgages. Moreover, with the advent of loans originated for securitization, many innova-tions have appeared which mitigate the effects of balloon risk on bondholders.

    In this chapter we review balloon risk of commercial mortgages, with an emphasis on understanding the impact on CMBS. We review some of the features which help reduce the risk, and how investors can minimize the risk from a port-folio perspective. An understanding of what a lender and the servicer can do at the balloon date provides a guide to CMBS investors as they attempt to analyze this risk. Finally, in the appendix we analyze how balloon risk has been handled in some of the recent CMBS deals.

BALLOON RISK

Borrowers prefer balloon loans when the yield curve is positively sloped since they should be able to borrow at a lower rate. Investor appetite for short- to intermediate-term bonds also tends to favor balloon mortgages as collateral. However, balloon mortgages are considered more risky than fully amortizing commercial mortgages since there is more uncertainty about the repayment of principal at the balloon date. In the case of fully amortizing loans (and balloon loans during the term), as long as the net income from the property is sufficient to pay the scheduled principal and interest, the lender will receive the promised payments. Since loans are originated with coverage ratios above 1.0×, the property's income has some room to decline from the origination date, and still be able to make the required payments. If the borrower defaults during the term of the loan, it is likely due to serious problems with the property which led to a precipitous drop in the property's income. On the other hand, most borrowers will have to make their balloon payment by refinancing their mortgage. The risk that a borrower may be unable (or unwilling) to make his balloon payment is known as *balloon risk*.

A borrower's ability to refinance will be a function of the loan-to-value at the balloon date, as well as the coverage ratio at that date. There can be a variety of reasons why a borrower might be able to make principal and interest payments, but not be able to refinance. For example, income may have dropped, and lenders may not feel the coverage ratio is sufficient for the amount to be borrowed. Alternatively, income may have stayed the same or even risen, but interest rates may have increased even more, leading to an insufficient coverage ratio. Thus, the balloon date can represent a crisis point for a borrower.

In a recent study by Fitch Investors Service in which they report the results of their analysis of over 17,000 loans, balloon mortgages defaulted about *2.8 times as often* as fully amortizing loans.[1] In the Fitch study the average annual default rate for balloon loans was 6.7% compared with 2.4% for fully amortizing loans. This supports the view that the balloon date represents a potential crisis for the borrower. Fitch also found that loss rates for loans that defaulted at the balloon date were 41% *less* than loss rates on fully amortizing loans that defaulted. This supports the notion that a default at a balloon date does not imply that the property cannot support the current debt service.

It is not completely obvious how the risk changes as a function of the remaining time to the balloon date. There are several competing factors. On the

---

[1] This study is reported in Chapter 22.

one hand, for a given amortization schedule, the further away the balloon date, the lower the mortgage balance at the time of the balloon date (since the mortgage has had time to amortize). All else equal, this clearly lowers the risk. On the other hand the more time passes the greater the possibility that NOI, interest rates, and DSCR can deviate from the current level. (This leads to the possibility of declining NOI and property value.) Therefore, perhaps, a 2-year balloon loan is less risky than a 5-year balloon loan.

From a theoretical standpoint we find validity to both of these statements. In Exhibit 1 we graph the option-adjusted spread (OAS) of a balloon loan with a 30-year amortization schedule and a spread over Treasuries of 200 basis points (bp), as a function of increasing maturity date.[2] (The x-axis measures time in years to the balloon date.) The OAS measures the effective spread of the loan over Treasuries after adjusting for default risk. Initially, the spread is high, but drops as the maturity increases. This is because for a very short balloon, the likelihood of being able to refinance is high since NOI and interest rates did not have much time to deviate too much from the initial conditions. However, as time to maturity increases, the OAS drops as the balloon risk becomes evident. Eventually, as the balloon date is pushed further out, the risk (more accurately, the potential effect on yield) decreases. This occurs for two reasons. First, because the amortization of the loan balance begins to lower the risk of default. And, second, because the discounted present value of a default becomes less significant. By comparing the three lines one can see the impact of more highly leveraged loans. The higher the leverage the more significant the effects.

Exhibit 1: OAS versus Time to the Balloon Date

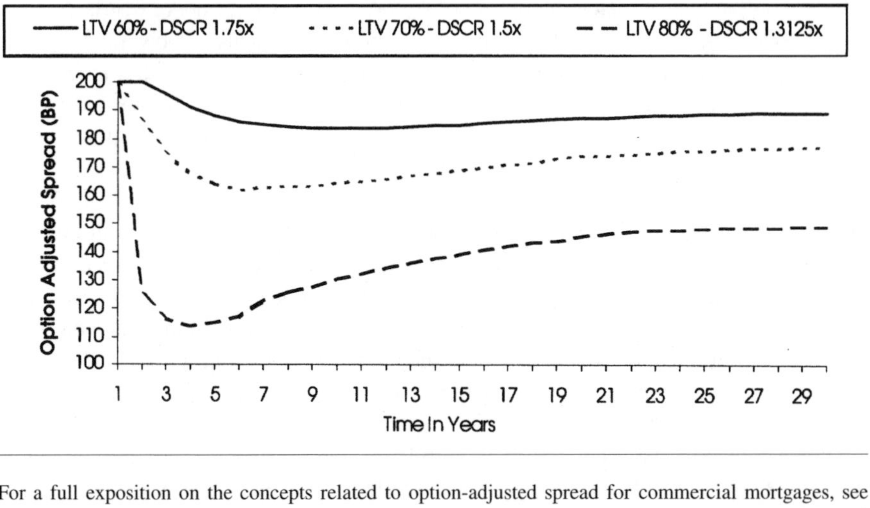

---

[2] For a full exposition on the concepts related to option-adjusted spread for commercial mortgages, see David P. Jacob, Ted Hong, and Laurence Lee, "An Options Approach to Commercial Mortgages and CMBS Valuation and Risk Analysis," *The Handbook of Commercial Mortgage-Backed Securities*, Frank J. Fabozzi and David P. Jacob (eds.) (New Hope: PA, Frank J. Fabozzi Associates/Nomura Securities International, 1997).

For analytic purposes it is useful to separate balloon defaults into those situations that occur because the borrower truly is unable to refinance a loan, from scenarios where borrowers are able to refinance, but instead are attempting to extract better terms from their current lender by threatening non-payment. It is obviously impossible to insure that the first circumstance does not occur. However, as discussed below, there are techniques for guarding against savvy borrowers who realize that lenders do not want to go through a foreclosure and try to take advantage of their position.

LOAN MODIFICATION

When the borrower fails to make the balloon payment, he is in default. The lender can begin foreclosure proceedings and, depending upon the jurisdiction, the speed and results of this process can vary significantly. Foreclosure is an expensive process. Therefore, the lender may choose not to foreclose immediately. In the past, many insurance companies would just roll the loan over. Alternatively, the lender often chooses to modify the loan. The modification may allow an extension of the maturity date and/or a change in the interest rate (In some cases the servicer in a CMBS deal can forgive principal).

While on the one hand, permitting a flexible approach may sound reasonable for the lender who wants to avoid the foreclosure process, it may not lead to the best result. From the borrower's perspective, the modification is nearly always favorable, which without some restrictions appears to give the borrower a free option. The borrower would appear to have the option of trying to improve things or just keep paying debt service and earning income on the property. As we discuss below, new loan originations include significant features which remove this option. This is important because, studies have shown that modified loans that eventually default have significantly higher loss rates. This occurs because the borrower will likely defer maintenance of the property, thus allowing the property to further decline in value.

For the traditional lender such as an insurance company, the impact of a balloon default is not simply the potential for losses, but also the risk that can arise from the mismatch of assets and liabilities. These lenders attempt to match the duration of their assets and liabilities. If the balloon payment is not made, the lender has to pay the liability by selling other assets. If the mismatch due to a balloon extension were to occur in a high interest rate environment the lender would suffer a loss. While balloon extension does not occur exclusively in a rising interest rate environment, one would expect to see more balloon defaults in a high rate environment. This implies there is negative convexity associated with balloon loans which needs to be priced by lenders. In almost all cases, a loan that has been extended is payable without penalty. Thus, at this point, the lender is actually short a call option to the borrower.

Adjusting the coupon down is another modification that is sometimes made in the event of a balloon default. Obviously, from an economic standpoint, the lender would only agree to this if he expects that this will produce greater proceeds on a not present value basis versus foreclosure. Lenders realize that not only can foreclosure be time consuming and costly, but in bankruptcy, the court could force the lender to accept a lower rate (cramdown) on the mortgage.

LOAN FEATURES THAT REDUCE BALLOON RISK

There are several loan features that are used in practice which reduce balloon risk. The first line of defense lies in the underwriting standards. Lenders adjust for the added risk of balloon loans by essentially requiring higher NOI. Rating agencies do this through the use of a constant, which, for a given NOI, has the effect of lowering the DSCR and thus requiring greater subordination in a CMBS deal. The constant is generally a function of the type of property, the level of interest rates, and the length of the loan. The constant used for balloon loans is 70bp-90bp higher than that used for fully amortizing loans.

Loans where the initial LTV is low are also less likely to experience problems at the balloon date, since there is more of a cushion to start with. Analysts often calculate the loan balance at the balloon date to gauge how low the property value could drop and yet have an LTV that is reasonable for refinancing.

A very powerful deterrent to the threat of extension by the borrower is the hyperamortization feature combined with a lock box. Under these provisions, the borrower/property owner is not permitted to receive any income until the loan is fully paid. Any net cash flow over and above that which is necessary to pay scheduled P&I, insurance, and reserves, must be used to pay down the remaining principal on the loan. The lock box mechanism prevents the borrower from getting at the cash flow. This feature not only serves as a deterrent, it also limits the extension. At some point, one can assume that the LTV is low enough that the borrower will be able to refinance.

Another feature that can be used to serve as a deterrent to a borrower who might try to force an extension in a high interest rate environment is a step-up in the coupon rate of the loan. The rate should be tied to the level of interest rates so that it is punitive even in a rising rate environment.

Borrowers with alternative financing options such as REITs or other publicly traded entities may be more likely to be in a position to pay off their balloon loan. On the other hand these sophisticated borrowers may, if not appropriately disincented, be in a strong position to bully their lenders. Therefore, in our view the loans with the least balloon risk are those made to strong borrowers, where the loan has the hyperamortization and lockbox feature and step-up rate provision. REIT borrowers would most likely do all they can to make their balloon payment in order to avoid having their cash trapped and used to hyperamortize their loan. REITs, in addition, have a requirement that they pay out most of their income in dividends. The cashtrap/hyperamortization feature could make this difficult to do.

EFFECTS OF BALLOON DEFAULT/EXTENSION AND COUPON MODIFICATION ON CMBS

The effect of a balloon extension on CMBS can vary greatly depending upon the bond class and its interaction with the collateral as dictated by the algorithm which governs the payment priorities. If a borrower does not pay on the balloon date, there will be a shortfall in cash flow available to pay bondholders. While the servicer is generally required to advance scheduled principal and interest payments in the event of a default, they are not required to advance the balloon payment.

In the case of the whole loan lender or a single class deal, only one investor has to weigh the trade-off between losses that might be exacerbated by foreclosure versus the impact on yield due to a loan modification. In the case of a multiclass senior-sub structure, a sharp division can arise between the interests of the senior and junior bond classes if a balloon default occurs. From a credit perspective, the senior class usually views an extension as a negative event (unless there is little or no subordination left) since the real estate collateral could continue to deteriorate and thereby lessen the proceeds at foreclosure. From a performance (total rate-of-return) perspective, the senior bondholder could be better off if the extension were to occur in a falling interest rate environment. On the other hand, an extension in a rising rate environment would negatively impact the performance of the senior bondholder.[3]

The junior bondholder may prefer an extension. If the property value has deteriorated to the point where in foreclosure the proceeds would be less than the mortgage balance (plus unpaid interest), the junior class would surely suffer a loss. In this case the junior class prefers that the borrower be granted an extension. On the other hand, if the property value in foreclosure is large enough to fully pay the junior class, the junior class would likely align himself with the senior class to push for foreclosure as quickly as possible. One would not expect the latter situation to occur often, since if this were the case, the borrower might do better to sell the property and pay off the mortgage. (Of course, if there were significant prepay penalties the borrower may not benefit from this and instead allow the foreclosure to take place.)

In the event a balloon extension is granted, at a minimum all bond classes that were expecting to receive a principal payment on that date could be affected. In the simple case of a single class deal and a single loan, this result is obvious. However, when there are many loans and many classes, the results are not always obvious. It is clearly possible that one or several loans may extend and a bond class receiving principal on that date will be unaffected since its expected cash flow on that date may come from other loans or from scheduled amortization. Less obvious is the situation where a bond that is not expecting principal cash flow on that date gets extended as a result of the balloon extension. This can occur if the first bond that was expecting to be paid has to get its payment from a later loan payment, which in turn

---

[3] If the bonds were purchased at a premium, the extension could be beneficial up to a point.

was expected to pay the second bond class. This can be seen in Exhibit 2. In this case we show two loans structured into two bond classes. If the first loan gets extended beyond the balloon date of the second loan, the second bond class has to extend. The number and concentration of balloon loans affects the impact the extension will have on a bond class. The greater the concentration, the larger the potential impact.

As discussed earlier, another common modification of loans that miss their balloon payments is the lowering of the coupon. This obviously lowers the available cash. The effect on bond classes will depend on their priority position as well as whether or not they are fixed-rate bonds or weighted average coupon (WAC) bonds. From a priority standpoint, naturally the most junior class will suffer first. In addition any WAC bonds will suffer as well. A less well understood point is that even without the reduction in the coupon rate of a loan, the coupon on a WAC bond can be affected by a loan extension. The coupon may increase or decrease depending on whether the extended balloon loan has a coupon rate which is higher or lower than the weighted average.

Interest-only (IO) classes, which are structured in order to create bond classes with prices close to par, are particularly sensitive to balloon risk. Since, in almost all deals, the IO classes are priced to the balloon date (i.e., they assume no extension), extension is usually a positive event since the investor receives extra cash. Of course, this assumes that the loan extension leads to an extension of the IO and that the servicer is advancing and/or the borrower is still paying. For an IO investor, even a few years of extension can add several hundred basis points in yield. However, a subtle point often missed by investors is that a WAC IO can be negatively impacted by an extension if the balloon loan falls inside the IO bond's payment window and the coupon on the loan is below the WAC. In this case the interest payments can go down.

Exhibit 2: The Effects of Balloon Extension on Bonds

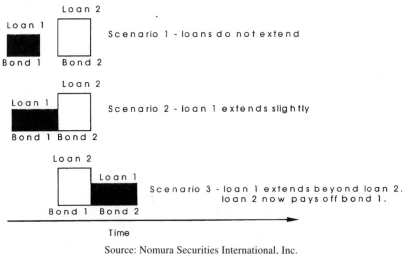

Source: Nomura Securities International, Inc.

Exhibit 3: Sample CMBS Structure

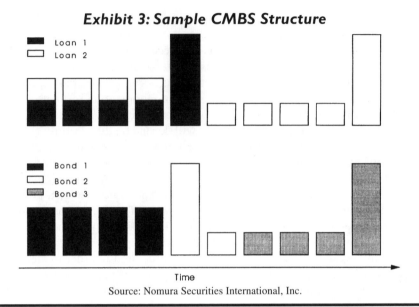

Time

Source: Nomura Securities International, Inc.

Since the effect on the performance of a bond class due to the extension of a loan depends on many factors, the only way to properly analyze the impact is to run many scenarios including changes in NOI, property value, and interest rates.

STRUCTURAL FEATURES OF CMBS WHICH REDUCE BALLOON RISK

Any feature which reduces the balloon risk on the loans acts to reduce the balloon risk for bondholders. Thus, conservative underwriting, hyperamortization, and step-up coupon rates all provide protection to bondholders. In addition, there are structural characteristics which can create further protection against balloon risk. A straightforward form of protection is to create a bond whose principal is paid strictly from amortization of loan principal. Exhibit 3 shows an example of such a bond. In the first panel of this exhibit we depict the principal paydown of two balloon loans. In the second panel the loans are structured into three sequential bond classes. The first bond class receives its principal from the scheduled amortization of the two loans. If either loan gets extended at its balloon date or even if both loans get extended, this bond does not extend.[4]

A second structural feature that is evident from Exhibit 3 is that the second class is somewhat protected from extension in that even if the first loan gets extended, it has first claim on the balloon cash flows from the second loan. This

---

[4] For structuring aficionados, there is actually a scenario where this bond could extend, but it is too unlikely to mention.

serves to limit the extension period. Similarly, the hyperamortization also benefits the second class over the third class.

In a CMBS deal the pooling and servicing agreement specifies the rights and responsibilities of the servicer. Among the rights is the power to modify the loans. In modifying loan terms the servicer is guided by his duty to maximize the proceeds of the loan on a net-present-value basis.[5] This, can put him at odds with the varying interests of the different bond classes. Many deals put added constraints on the servicer should he desire to extend the loan. Some deals allow a maximum of three years of extension, and permitting extensions of one year at a time. Other deals couple this with minimum coverage ratio tests and required property appraisals. In some cases the servicer can be forced to foreclose through a majority vote of the certificate holders.

A more recent innovation is the use of an extension advisor. The extension advisor is elected by a majority (based on the outstanding balances) of certificate holders (excluding the most junior outstanding class). Unlike the servicer, the extension advisor looks after the interests of the most senior classes. The extension advisor can overrule the servicer and not permit an extension. Often, the extension advisor is not appointed until after several extensions have already been made.

SURVEY OF BALLOON EXTENSION IN RECENT CMBS DEALS

In this section we review the balloon extension issues in nine recent CMBS deals. The deals are described in Exhibit 4. We summarize the points which we feel exhibit the strengths/weaknesses of these CMBS deals.

On the loan side of the deal, we examined the cash trap, lock box (cash management system), step-up rates, default rates, balloon ltv's and balloon periods.

1. The cash trap is used to catch excess NOI to help pay down the principal of a loan. This creates the "hyperamortizing" style loan and its strength is that it dissuades borrowers from missing their balloon payment. At this point, very few deals have these types of loans. In the deals summarized here the Chase deal is the only one that has this loan structure and of the 84 loans in the deal only one is using this cash trap.

2. Lock boxes are used to make sure that the borrower does not receive cash until debt service is paid. This is an important feature to maintain the cash flow to the loan and to prevent the borrower from tampering with the cash. Loans in two of the deals, CS First Boston and Lehman Brothers, use this structure.

---

[5] The servicer clearly has a fiduciary responsibility to the certificate holders. His own interest would be to extend the loan since in an extension he would keep earning his servicing fee.

3. The step-up rate and default rate are both used to deter borrowers from extending their balloon loans. The step-up rate is an increase of the current rate at the point of the balloon extension and the default rate is another rate increase at the point where a loan defaults. None of the deals examined use step-up rates, but this can be found in other deals in the marketplace. The default rate is only being used by CS First Boston, but as with the step-up rates, there are other deals in the marketplace that utilize this feature more often than the deals examined here.

4. The balloon LTVs and the balloon periods are very important factors for analysis. The balloon LTV ratios are unfortunately not disclosed with every deal. Examination of the balloon periods of these deals shows that there are many deals with 10-year balloons that are ballooning in the 2004-2006 period. If the LTV ratios and interest rates are high during this period, the borrowers could have problems refinancing.

On the deal side, important factors are the extension advisor, DSCR level checks, property checks, coupon protection and principal protection.

1. The point of the extension advisor (or operating advisor) is to create an independent party/office to maintain a check on the special servicer. All of the deals except DLJ have either an extension advisor or an operating advisor. The problem that should be examined is that six of the eight deals have clauses allowing the special servicer to make modifications to the loan if the advisor's position is vacant. The election of the advisor is dependent on the certificate holders.

2. DSCR level and property value checks are also important. Many of the deals will only allow extensions on loans if the DSCR levels are above a certain point and that the property value has been recently examined by appraisals, rent rolls, and operating statements. These are all checks to make sure that the loan has the possibility to refinance at a later date and, therefore, should be granted the extension. If not, the extension should not be granted and foreclosure procedures should begin. From the loans examined, the Nationslink, Aetna, and DLJ deals have the strongest requirements for balloon extensions.

3. Coupon protection and principal protection are also very important to a deal's strength. Modification of the coupon is very significant and deals should protect the bonds from it. Four of the deals do try to protect the bonds, but many of them only protect the fixed-rate bonds ignoring the IOs and WAC-based bonds. Also important is principal protection and once again four of the deals make an effort to protect the principal.

Exhibit 4: Summary of Nine CMBS Deals Examined

Deal Name	Cash Trap/ Lock Box	Step-Up Rate/ Default Rate	Balloon LTV	Largest % of Ballooning and Date	Extension Advisor	DSCR Checks	Appraisals/ Rent Roll Checks/ Operating Statements	Coupon Protection	Principal Protection (forgiveness, deferral, substitution)
JP Morgan 1996-C3	None/ None	None/ None	54.9%	62.7% of pool, 2005-2006	Is required on all extensions greater than 3 years	None	None/None/ None	None	None
Merrill Lynch 1996 C-1	None/ None	None/ None	58.38%	56.18% of pool, 2005-2006	Is required on all extensions greater than 3 years	None	None/None/ None	None	None
Nations Link 1996-C1	None/ None	None/ None	Not Available	48.5% of pool, 2005-2006	Extensions can be granted if Extension Advisor's Office is vacant	>1.25×	Yes/Yes/Yes	Yes - protects fixed rate bonds	None
Mortgage Capital Funding 1996-MC1	None/ None	None/ None	Not Available	57.69% of pool, 2005 2006	Extensions can be granted if Extension Advisor's Office is vacant	None	None/None/ None	None	None
Aetna 1995-C5	None/ None	None/ None	Not Available	15.99% of the pool, 1996-1997	Extensions can be granted if Extension Advisor's Office is vacant	>1.25×	Yes/Yes/Yes	Yes - protects fixed rate bonds	Yes - Operating Advisor must approve.
DLJ 1996 CF-1	None/ None	None/. None	Not Available	58.6% of pool, 2005- 2006	No Extension Advisor	DSCR > 1.10×	Yes/Yes/Yes	None	Yes - limited
Chase 1996-1	Yes/ None	None/ None	Not Available	69.07% of pool, 2005-2006	Extensions can be granted if Extension Advisor's Office is vacant	None	None/None/ None	Yes - protects fixed rate bonds	Yes but limited
CS First Boston-1995 WF1	None/ Yes	None/ Yes	Not Available	37.72% of pool, 2004-2005	No Extension Advisor - Operating Advisor instead - position can be vacant	None	None/None/ None	Yes - rate can't be reduced	Yes - Operating Advisor must approve.
Lehman Brothers 1996-C2	None/ Yes	None/ None	66.01%	37.72% of pool, 2004-2005	No Extension Advisor - Operating Advisor instead - position can be vacant	>1.25×	None/None/ None	None	None

Section IV:

Municipal Housing Revenue Bonds

Chapter 28

Single Family Mortgage Revenue Bonds

Michael Marz
Vice Chairman
First Southwest Company

Frank J. Fabozzi, Ph.D., C.F.A.
Adjunct Professor of Finance
School of Management
Yale University

INTRODUCTION

In 1968, Congress passed legislation permitting the use of tax-exempt bonds to obtain proceeds that would finance low- and moderate-cost housing. To obtain funding, most states created state housing finance agencies to issue tax-exempt housing bonds. The first issuance of housing bonds by state agencies was done in the early 1970s. In 1978, local governments began issuing housing bonds. Local government issuers include counties, cities, towns, and villages. These bonds are called *single family mortgage revenue bonds*, although they have been issued under other names such as residential mortgage revenue bonds, home ownership development bonds, and single family mortgage purchase bonds.

Historically, single family mortgage revenue bonds have been structured as either a mortgage purchase bond or a loans-to-lender bond. In the former structure, the proceeds from the bond issue are used to buy mortgages from lenders who have agreed to originate loans on behalf of the issuer. In a loans-to-lender bond, the proceeds from the issue are used to make collateralized loans to approved lending institutions that must use the borrowed funds to make mortgage loans. Today, a mortgage purchase bond is the most common structure used by state housing finance agencies and local issuers.

An *official statement* describing the issue and the issuer is prepared for new offerings. Municipal securities have legal opinions which are summarized in the official statement. The importance of the legal opinion is twofold. First, bond counsel determines if the issuer is indeed legally able to issue the securities. Second, bond counsel verifies that the issuer has properly prepared for the bond sale by having enacted various required ordinances, resolutions, and trust indentures and without violating any other laws and regulations.

When market participants first attempt to evaluate mortgage revenue bonds, it is common to try to use the extensive research available from the taxable mortgage-backed securities market. Investors should resist this temptation. Although it is common for tax-exempt "qualified mortgage bonds" to be backed by Ginnie Mae, Fannie Mae or Freddie Mac, there are a lot of basic tax issues which make the analysis of these securities quite difficult. Because of their structural complexity and because much of the information needed for analysis of these securities is unavailable, the evaluation of mortgage revenue bonds even today is more art than science. In this chapter we will discuss the structure of these bonds and the difficulties associated with analyzing their cash flows.

THE COLLATERAL

First, let's review the collateral which backs these bond issues. The basic requirements of qualified mortgage bonds fall under Section 143 of the Internal Revenue Code. To be a "qualified bond" a single family bond must: (1) be a "qualified mortgage bond," (2) obtain a volume cap allocation under Section 146, which includes "private activity bonds," and (3) meet certain other requirements including a public approval process.

In qualified mortgage revenue bond issues, the individual loans must satisfy two types of requirements. First they must satisfy mortgage eligibility requirements. These include the residence requirement, first time home buyer requirement, the purchase price limitation, mortgagor income limitation, and the new mortgage and assumption requirement. Second, the individual loans must satisfy non-mortgage eligibility requirements. These are the special arbitrage rules for qualified mortgage bonds, the targeted area requirement, and the mortgage subsidiary recapture provisions.

Mortgage eligibility for these types of bond issues requires that in addition to real property, a residence may include stock in cooperative housing and mobile homes if they are permanently affixed to real property. The "principal" residence requirements may normally be satisfied by the execution of an affidavit by the mortgagor to the effect that the borrower intends to use the residence as a principal residence within at least 60 days after closing of the mortgage. The first time home buyer requirement generally states that mortgages under the bond program may not have had a mortgage interest deduction on their tax return in a principal residence within a 3-year period prior to the date the mortgage (for the bond program) is executed. Certain exceptions may exist for targeted areas which fulfill a special public purpose and for certain qualified home improvement or rehabilitation loans.

Virtually all single family mortgage revenue bonds provide that the "acquisition cost" of a residence may not exceed 90% of the "average area purchase price." The total costs are included in this consideration, and applied against the "statistical area" during the last 12 months for which such data exist. Mortgages under Section 143 programs have income limitations which state that family income may not exceed a certain percentage of an areas "applicable median family income." This is specific to any geographical region and thus can extenuate the regional aspects of the prepayment rate of all mortgages financed under an issuer's indenture.

The last point to be made in respect to mortgage eligibility requirements for tax-exempt bond issues is the most powerful. The IRS Code requires that a portion of the "subsidy" provided to mortgagors through qualified mortgage bond programs be "recaptured." A basic generalization of this requirement is that the mortgagor must rebate to the Treasury up to 50% of the gain, if any, realized on the disposition of the bond-financed residence for up to nine years or as a result of the mortgagor's death. The bond issuer is required to provide notice to the borrower at the closing settlement and within 90 days following the loan closing notifying the mortgagor of the federally subsidized amount of the loan.

The loans purchased by an housing agency will consist of loans insured by the Federal Housing Administration (FHA), Veterans Administration (VA), or Rural Housing Service (RHS), or conventional loans (i.e., those not insured by one of these entities). For conventional loans, there may be private mortgage insurance. For example, to be included in the mortgage loan portfolio of the Texas Department of Housing and Community Affairs, the trust indenture requires: "Mortgage Loans must (i) be federally insured or guaranteed, (ii) have a principal balance not exceeding 80% of the lower of the appraised value of the purchase price of the property securing the Mortgage Loan (the "Value"), or (iii) be insured by a private mortgage insurer approved by the Department in an amount by which the loan exceeds 80% of the Value."

The composition of the mortgage loan portfolio for the Texas Department of Housing and Community Affairs as of 1996 was:

Loan type	No. of prior loans	Outstanding principal amount	Percent of total (%)
Conventional	3,045	$134,711,226	44.02
FHA	2,967	155,907,174	50.94
VA	333	14,792,645	4.83
RHS	9	641,573	0.21
Total	6,354	$306,052,618	100.00%

EMBEDDED CALL OPTIONS

The non-mortgage eligibility requirements relate more to issuers than to bondholders. As investors attempt to analyze the properties of single family mortgage revenue bonds, the primary consideration usually relates to the wide variety of call options embedded in a given structure. Mortgage revenue bonds can be more complex than some of the most complicated classes of collateralized mortgage obligations. Unlike a generic passthrough security, mortgage revenue bonds tend to have serial maturities. Thus, based on stated final maturities, bonds are redeemed first from scheduled principal payments on the underlying mortgages and then usually called with the proceeds of prepayments. The effect of this serialization of maturities means that most of these bond structures resemble sequential CMOs. For total-rate-of-return investors, option adjusting the duration and convexity of these type bonds is particularly difficult because of the large uncertainty in the speed of prepayments on the underlying collateral.

Prepayments

It is a widely accepted practice to use the GNMA market as a starting point for making a prepayment assumption. It is important to remember that the unpredictability of this class of mortgages is due to their relatively small size and the significant geographical bias inherent to an issuer. Investors will find that the lag in prepayments to corresponding levels of interest rate movements are greater in tax-exempt mortgage bonds than in their taxable counterparts. Primarily the difference is the true passthrough nature of typical taxable mortgage bond structures. Single family mortgage revenue bonds commonly have semiannual redemption cycles, as well as provisions which require notice of call redemptions as far as 30 to 60 days in advance. The lengthy intervals between prepayment calls also has a smoothing effect on prepayment redemption activity. Market participants can attempt to translate information about how many bonds from a given issue have been called into an estimate of what the prepayment rate on the underlying mortgages has been.

The use of municipal prepayment indexes can be a good relative value analysis tool for investors. Using an index can be an easy measure of estimating prepayments and will help rule out the trends of small pools which may exhibit random aberrations. Geographic bias is a significant factor in any mortgage pool. Insight into state prepayment differentials are provided in the *Kenny Housing Call Report* published by J.J. Kenny and the *Merrill Lynch Municipal Prepayment Redemption Index*. Prepayment differentials among various bond structures are often not reflected in municipal bond pricing. The use of index analysis can aid in active management and help portfolio managers exploit opportunities.

Conclusions drawn from this type of analysis must take into account the specific structure of each bond issue and each indenture under which a specific issuer operates.

Other Call Features

Aside from prepayments, other call options which may be specific to single family mortgage revenue bonds are unused proceeds calls, surplus calls, cross calls, and optional redemptions.

Unused Proceeds Call

Since 1989, federal law has required a mandatory redemption of any unused bond proceeds within 42 months of the date of issuance. Once a new money bond issue is priced the mortgage origination period is limited and any unspent proceeds must be used to redeem a corresponding amount of bonds.

The conventional market assumption is that unused proceeds calls are unavoidable consequences of interest rate declines which might follow the issuance of a mortgage revenue bond. Investors should review the program's underwriting guidelines, who the specific mortgage originators are, and what the historical issuer originations have been. Although the market does not consistently discriminate between different bond issues based on unused proceeds call risk, investors may find value in the substantial differences which do in fact exist due to the wide range of issuer origination efficiency. Municipal bond pricing does not distinguish between single family mortgage revenue bonds on the basis of unused proceeds call risk. Historically, redemptions have exhibited interest rate cyclical behavior. These calls reached record levels following the sharp decline in interest rates in 1993.

Although interest rate declines following the issuance of a single family mortgage revenue bond are virtually a prerequisite for an unused proceeds call to exist, it does not explain the disparate levels of call that have been made. Issue size, continuous origination pipeline, and ability to warehouse loans in advance of bond sales will produce results which can be contrary to conventional wisdom.

Surplus Calls

Under Section 143, a primary rule which applies to the mortgages originated under the bond program is that the "effective rate of interest" may not exceed the yield (true interest cost) on the bond issue by more than 1.125%. The result of this allowable excess is surplus calls. Surplus exists from the spread between the net mortgage rate and the bond rate. Other structural items such as over-collateralization, interest earnings, and excess reserve funds can provide the dollars to trigger surplus calls.

Cross Calls

Another element which exists as a call option on single family mortgage revenue bonds is the *cross call option*. Cross calling is a practice followed by some state housing finance agencies, in which repayments from lower interest rate loans financed by one "issue" are applied to pay bonds of a different "issue." The appendix to this chapter provides an example of this option from the official statement of the Department of Housing and Community Affairs Single Family Mortgage Revenue Bonds 1996 Series D and Series E.

Here again is where investors are forced to do all their homework. Although it is more common for state issuers than local housing agencies, an authority with bonds issued under the same master bond indenture or resolution, commonly referred to as "open indentures," will cross call their bonds. That results in more interest savings to the issuer than if it had called a lower interest rate bond of the issue that originated such lower interest rate mortgages. Thus, investors should initially assume that the issuer will use or not use its cross call option in the worst possible way from the bond buyer's point of view. Under an open indenture, although unlikely in the market environment at the time of this writing, issuers sometimes retain the right to "recycle" funds by making new mortgage loans with the proceeds of prepayments. Recycling works only if new mortgages will pay a high enough rate to service outstanding bonds. Given all these uncertainties, bondholders dealing with bonds issued under open indentures would be wise to make very conservative assumptions in estimating effective redemption dates.

Optional Redemption

The last major call option generic to single family mortgage bonds is optional redemption. The municipal market standard is that housing bonds are sold with 10-year 102 calls against optional redemption. Over the last 20 years, the bulk of the outstanding housing bond new issue volume was created between 1980 through 1985. It was not until the bulk of outstanding single family mortgage revenue bonds reached their optional call date and became eligible for current refundings that empirical evidence could evaluate the importance of optional call behavior. A variety of motives can exist for the exercise of an optional refunding, some of which are not particularly sensitive to the levels of interest rates.

An overview of what some mortgage revenue bondholders have experienced reveals a wide array of justifications, all of which have caused rapid amortizations of their bonds. Issuers often are motivated to provide deeply discounted loans which can be achieved by blending these loans with higher coupon mortgages to pay the debt service on a refunding bond while remaining within legal arbitrage limits. Another reason for optional redemption is transferring mortgages to restructure new indentures and bolster asset/liability ratios. Restructuring can also allow outdated indenture language to be removed. Needless to say, buyers of single family mortgage revenue bonds cannot focus solely on prepayment options. In fact, the list of characteristics and considerations may seem unbearable. Invariably, proper analysis will tend to produce an even shorter average life than an estimate which is based upon any single embedded call.

CREDIT RISK

While municipal bonds at one time were considered second in safety only to U.S. Treasury securities, today there are concerns about the credit risks of municipal securities. Concern about credit risk came out of the New York City billion-dollar financial crisis in 1975. On February 25, 1975, the state of New York's Urban

Development Corporation defaulted on a $100 million note issue that was the obligation of New York City; many market participants had been convinced that the state of New York would not allow the issue to default. Although New York City was able later to obtain a $140 million revolving credit from banks to cure the default, lenders became concerned that the city would face difficulties in repaying its accumulated debt, which stood at $14 billion on March 31, 1975. This financial crisis sent a loud and clear warning to market participants in general — regardless of supposedly ironclad protection for the bondholder, when issuers such as large cities have severe financial difficulties, the financial stakes of public employee unions, vendors, and community groups may be dominant forces in balancing budgets. This reality was reinforced by the federal bankruptcy law that took effect in October 1979, which made it easier for the issuer of a municipal security to go into bankruptcy.

The nationally recognized statistical rating organizations assign ratings to single family mortgage revenue bonds. In addition, to the guarantees by the insurers of individual mortgages, these bonds can be credit enhanced — municipal bond insurance or state appropriation provision.

Insured Bonds

Insured bonds, in addition to being secured by the issuer's revenue, are also backed by insurance policies written by commercial insurance companies. Insurance on a municipal bond is an agreement by an insurance company to pay the bondholder any bond principal and/or coupon interest that is due on a stated maturity date but that has not been paid by the bond issuer. Once issued, this municipal bond insurance usually extends for the term of the bond issue, and it cannot be canceled by the insurance company.

Most insured municipal bonds are insured by one of the following insurance companies that are primarily in the business of insuring municipal bonds: AMBAC Indemnity Corporation; Capital Guaranty Insurance Company; Connie Lee Insurance Company; Financial Guaranty Insurance Company; Financial Security Assurance, Inc.; and, Municipal Bond Investors Insurance Corporation.

Appropriation-Backed Obligations

Housing agencies or authorities of several states have issued single family mortgage revenue bonds that carry a potential state liability for making up shortfalls in the issuing entities obligation. The appropriation of funds from the state's general tax revenue must be approved by the state legislation. However, the state's pledge is not binding. A debt obligation with this nonbinding pledge of tax revenue is called a *moral obligation bond*. Because a moral obligation bond requires legislative approval to appropriate the funds, it is classified as an *appropriation-backed obligation*.

An example of the legal language describing the procedure for a moral obligation bond that is enacted into legislation is as follows:

In order to further assure the maintenance of each such debt reserve fund, there shall be annually apportioned and paid to the agency for deposit in each debt reserve fund such sum, if any, as shall be certified by the chairman of the agency to the governor and director of the budget as necessary to restore such reserve fund to an amount equal to the debt reserve fund requirement. The chairman of the agency shall annually, on or before December I, make and deliver to the governor and director of the budget his certificate stating the sum or sums, if any, required to restore each such debt reserve fund to the amount aforesaid, and the sum so certified, if any, shall be apportioned and paid to the agency during the then current state fiscal year.

The purpose of the moral obligation pledge is to enhance the creditworthiness of the issuing entity. The first moral obligation bond was issued by the Housing Finance Agency of the state of New York. Historically, most moral obligation debt has been self supporting; that is, it has not been necessary for the state of the issuing entity to make an appropriation. In those cases in which state legislatures have been called upon to make an appropriation, they have. For example, the states of New York and Pennsylvania did this for bonds issued by their Housing Finance Agency.

Moody's and Standard & Poor's appear to have a different view of moral obligation bonds. Moody's appears to view the moral obligation feature as more literary than legal. Therefore, it does not consider this feature a credit strength or enhancement. Standard & Poor's appears to view moral obligation bonds as being no lower than one rating category below a state's own general obligation bonds. Its rationale is based upon the implied state support for the bonds and the marked implications for that state's own general obligation bonds should it ever fail to honor its moral obligations.

ALTERNATIVE MINIMUM TAX

Tax-exempt municipal bonds are not treated uniformly with respect to federal income taxes. *Taxable income* is the amount on which the tax liability is determined. For an individual, it is found by subtracting the personal exemption allowance and itemized deductions (other than those deductible in arriving at adjusted gross income) from adjusted gross income. The *alternative minimum taxable income* (AMTI) is a taxpayer's taxable income with certain adjustments for specified tax preferences designed to cause AMTI to approximate economic income. For both individuals and corporations, a taxpayer's tax liability is the greater of (1) the tax computed at regular tax rates on taxable income and (2) the tax computed at a lower rate on AMTI. This parallel tax system, the *alternative minimum tax* (AMT), is designed to prevent taxpayers from avoiding significant tax liability as a result of taking advantage of exclusions from gross income, deductions, and tax credits otherwise allowed under the Internal Revenue Code.

Some municipal issues are subject to the AMT, while others are not. Those issues subject to the AMT will trade at a higher yield to compensate for the tax effect. For the Texas Department of Housing and Community Affairs Single Family Mortgage Revenue Bonds, the 1996 Series D was subject to the AMT while the 1996 Series E was not.

CONCLUSION

Local governments have been issuing single family mortgages revenue bonds since 1978. Traditionally, single family mortgage revenue bonds have taken one of two forms: loans-to-lender bond structures and mortgage purchase bond structures. Mortgage purchase bonds are the prevalent form today. Single family mortgage revenue bonds are usually secured by the mortgages and mortgage loan repayments on single-family homes.

Collateral for single family mortgage revenue bonds must meet both mortgage and non-mortgage eligibility requirements. Along with having both personal income and residential cost limitations, mortgage eligibility requires not only a first time home buyer, but that this first home be the buyer's principal residence. Non-mortgage eligibility requirements include: limited origination period, the special arbitrage rules for qualified mortgage bonds, the targeted area requirement, and the mortgage subsidiary recapture provisions. An additional and important requirement is the government subsidy recapture which induces the mortgagor to rebate to the government up to 50% of the gain realized on the sale of a mortgage assisted residence if liquidated within nine years of purchase.

In evaluating single family mortgage revenue bonds, one must remember several points: (1) do not use taxable mortgage-backed valuation techniques; (2) compare insured bonds with uninsured equivalents; (3) consider alternative minimum tax implications; (4) with respect to appropriation bonds, one must consider S&P and Moody's rating concerns along with the mortgage eligibility requirements; (5) be aware that single family mortgage revenue bonds are riddled with esoteric call options which compound in complexity as a direct function of maturity serialization; and, (6) the rating effects.

The structure and the difficulties that result in analyzing the cash flows of single family mortgage revenue bonds present numerous problems. Given the number of variables involved and the intricacy of their relationships, it is easy to see why valuation of mortgage revenue bonds is still considered more of an art than a science.

APPENDIX

Example of a Call Cross Option: Department of Housing and Community Affairs Single Family Mortgage Revenue Bonds Series D and Series E

Prior Mortgage Loans

The proceeds of certain Single Family Mortgage Revenue Bonds and certain other moneys have been used to purchase Mortgage Loans (including Mortgage Certificates representing Mortgage Loans). All Mortgage Loans acquired to date under the Trust Indenture are fixed rate loans with terms not exceeding 30 years. The following table summarizes certain information regarding the Mortgage Loans (including Mortgage Certificates representing Mortgage Loans) acquired with the proceeds of the Single Family Mortgage Revenue Bonds. For a more detailed examination of the Mortgage Loans, the portfolio of Mortgage Loans, delinquent Mortgage Loans and information regarding Mortgage Loan insurance, see "APPENDIX F-1 -- DEPARTMENT'S MORTGAGE LOAN PORTFOLIO." Unless otherwise specified, all information is as of July 31, 1996.

Series	Mortgage Loan Rate	Original Amount of Mortgage Loans Purchased	Mortgage Loans Outstanding
1980 Series A	11.20%	$133,937,742	$21,816,414
1982 Series A	13.93	14,212,374	495,828
1983 Series A	10.79	216,229,754	42,579,408
1984 Series A/B	12.10/9.75	171,555,575	22,743,819
1985 Series A	9.75	118,045,235	38,379,542
1985 Series B	9.70/9.55	29,176,697	8,163,934
1985 Series C	8.20	27,726,038	13,179,728
1986 Series A	8.70	73,021,140	36,617,156
1986 Series B	7.99/7.90	81,998,265	46,549,484
1987 Series B	7.99/8.05/8.70	69,454,306	41,452,419
1995 Series A-1/B-1	6.65	34,147,391	34,074,886
Total		$969,504,517	$306,052,618

As of September 30, 1996, $38,837,260 of monies remained in the Mortgage Loan Fund relating to the 1995 Series A-1/B-1 Bonds to purchase Mortgage Certificates bearing an interest rate of 6.65%. Except for that amount reserved for targeted area loans, substantially all of such remaining moneys have been committed to the origination of Mortgage Loans for specified borrowers. In addition, $15,595,000 of lendable proceeds were deposited in the Mortgage Loan Fund relating to the 1996 Series A Bonds and 1996 Series B Bonds on October 1, 1996 and will be used to originate Mortgage Loans evidenced by Mortgage Certificates. Such funds are designated for certain limited geographic areas in the State for a period of eighteen months. Such proceeds will be used to purchase Mortgage Certificates bearing an interest rate of 6.95%. Although the Department expects that all of the remaining lendable proceeds relating to the 1995 Series A-1/B-1 Bonds and the 1996 Series A Bonds and 1996 Series B Bonds will be used to purchase Mortgage Certificates, it can give no assurance that the availability of such monies will not affect the ability of participating Mortgage Lenders to fully originate the lendable proceeds of the Series D/E Bonds. Failure to fully originate the lendable proceeds of the Series D/E Bonds could result in their early redemption at par. See "THE SERIES D/E BONDS -- Redemption Provisions."

Since the inception of the Department's Program, the Department has foreclosed on approximately 2,888 Mortgage Loans having an outstanding principal balance, at the time of foreclosure, of $149,972,948. The Department continues to hold title to property securing 23 of such Mortgage Loans. In an effort to maximize its return on real estate owned by the Department as a result of foreclosures, the Department has entered into a contract with outside contractors to manage, maintain and arrange for sales, in conjunction with real estate brokers, of such real estate owned. See APPENDIX F-1 -- DEPARTMENT'S MORTGAGE LOAN PORTFOLIO for information concerning the Department's current delinquency and foreclosure rates with respect to the Mortgage Loans.

Source: Page 16 of Official Statement

INDEX

Coverage You Can Count On.
Accuracy You Can Trust.

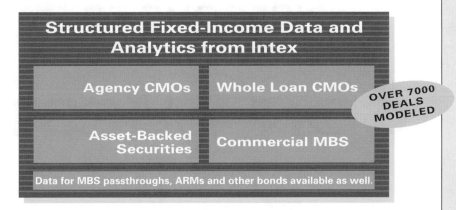

Structured Fixed-Income Data and Analytics from Intex

Agency CMOs | Whole Loan CMOs

Asset-Backed Securities | Commercial MBS

OVER 7000 DEALS MODELED

Data for MBS passthroughs, ARMs and other bonds available as well.

Before you build or buy your next fixed-income system, call Intex first. Intex provides the industry's most accurate and complete database of deal models for residential CMOs, asset-backed securities and commercial mortgage-backed securities of any complexity. All models are updated in a timely manner with information gathered from a variety of independent sources.

Intex clients have a choice of data interfaces and analytics including flexible **C++/C-Callable Subroutines**, ready-to-use applications like **Intex Trader**™ and **CMO Analyst**™, built-in access from a variety of well-known **third-party products**, and the **Intex Structuring Tool**™ for deal creation. So whether you wish to build your own system or buy an existing one, Intex has a solution that's right for you.

Intex has long been recognized as the premier provider of structured data and analytics to the fixed-income market. In fact, most leading broker/dealers, issuers, banks, insurance companies and money managers rely on Intex for their essential fixed-income applications.

For bond administration, trading support, portfolio management, risk management, structuring and a host of other front- and back-office applications, make Intex a part of your solution.

Intex is an independent company located near Boston, MA. For over a decade, Intex has provided high quality products and support to the fixed-income industry.

For more information, call or write:

Intex Solutions, Inc.

35 Highland Circle
Needham, MA 02194
Tel: 617 449-6222

Fax: 617 444-2318
E-mail: desk@intex.com
Web: http://www.intex.com

INTEX SOLUTIONS, INC.

WELCOME TO

A CMBS Pricing and Analysis Service

offered by

CHARTER RESEARCH CORPORATION

www.cmbs.com

By subscribing to Conquest, CMBS buyers receive constantly updated financial information on bonds and underlying mortgage loans, reverse-engineered bond models, and the ability to run any combination of pricing scenarios.

Conquest is dedicated to CMBS. Charter built Conquest from the ground up to model only CMBS transactions, using conventions familiar to any CMBS trader. From collateral summaries to bond structuring to individual monthly loan flows, Conquest supports CMBS investors.

Conquest uses superior analytics. Charter has developed *BondScript*,^{SM} a bond modeling language that describes structured securities clearly and simply. Conquest publishes each model's *BondScript*^{SM} — so subscribers need not guess how Charter modeled a transaction.

Subscribers can create their own scenarios by setting any combination of loans to prepay and/or default.

➤ Conquest's prepayment and default mechanics model the behavior of commercial loans, including prepayment lock-outs, yield maintenance penalties, balloon or payment defaults, and partial recoveries. Subscribers can compare a traditional CPR analysis to an analysis that respects lock-outs and includes yield maintenance penalties.

Likewise, Conquest generates traditional CDR analysis but also allows complete control over the timing of defaults, timing of disposition, and magnitude of loan losses.

➤ From an individual loan to an entire pool. Conquest tracks master servicer advances (including interest), distinguishes actual and recognized losses, tracks master servicer indebtedness and computes fees (master servicing, special servicing, and trustee). By manipulating master servicer behavior, subscribers can better price interest-only strips and junior bonds.

Conquest is an easy-to-use Internet application. Charter publishes Conquest over the World Wide Web. Subscribers do not install dedicated software or manage error-prone periodic data updates; they simply access Conquest through Netscape Navigator.

Address questions about Conquest to Hal Haig at Charter Research, 617-227-0933.

CHASE

WHY CLIENTS TURN TO CHASE FOR EXPERTISE IN MORTGAGED-BACKED FINANCE

This announcement appears as a matter of record only.   March 1997

Kmart CMBS Financing, Inc.

$335,000,000
Commercial Mortgage Pass-Through Certificates

Secured by a first mortgage on 81 retail properties which are leased to Kmart Corporation.

Co-Lead Manager
Chase Securities Inc.

 CHASE

The announcement appears as a matter of record only.   December 1996

 World Financial Properties, Inc.

$434,346,000
Commercial Mortgage Pass-Through Certificates

Secured by a mortgage lien on Tower D in the World Financial Center, New York City

Issuer
World Financial Properties Tower D Finance Corp.

CHASE

 1996

Chase Commercial Mortgage Banking Corp.

$800,000,000
Fixed-rate Mortgage Loan Production
174 Multi-family and Commercial Properties

 CHASE

1996

Chase Commercial Mortgage Securities Corp.

$700,000,000
Commercial Mortgage-Backed
Securities Issued

CHASE

Chase is a leader in mortgaged-backed securitization offering customized solutions and superior execution.

CHASE. The right relationship is everything.℠

MORTGAGERISK

Mortgage Risk Assessment Corporation

1011 Highway 6 South, Suite 105
Houston, Texas 77077
Tel: (281) 368-1600
(800) 227-1601
Fax: (281) 368-1633

Chuck Ramsey
Anay Srivastava

30 Montgomery Street, Suite 1200
Jersey City, New Jersey 07302
Tel: (201) 413-1900
(800) 990-6722
Fax: (201) 432-7850

Doug Bendt
Ted Wahlstrom

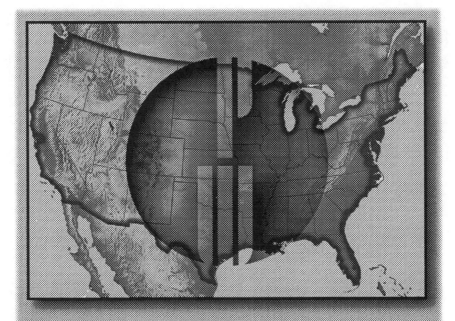

Don't go back to the drawing board to develop your risk management system

Don't waste your time and resources trying to replicate GAT's team of PhD researchers, C language software developers, CMO reverse engineers, and data collectors.

Founded in 1987 by Dr. Thomas S.Y. Ho, GAT today provides fixed-income OAS models to hundreds of customers.

Now you can incorporate these time-tested models in your applications. Whether you're a vendor marketing a risk management system, or an institution working on developing an in-house system, you can leverage GAT's expertise in implementing complex research into tractable software routines.

Contact us at (212) 785-9630 for information on how to license GAT's subroutine libraries of fixed-income models.

GAT's research is widely published and available in the public domain. Don't forget to ask us for copies of the papers that detail the intricacies of these models.

Our callable C libraries include:

Call-adjusted spot curve estimation

Interest rate models: Ho-Lee, Black Derman Toy

Backwards substitution routines for path-independent securities

Path simulation using Linear Path Space for path-dependent securities

Prepayment models

4000 CMO structures

Whole loan CMO cashflow generation

Agency CMO cashflow generation

OAS model for CMOs

Analytics · Consulting · Research

"All-Pro"

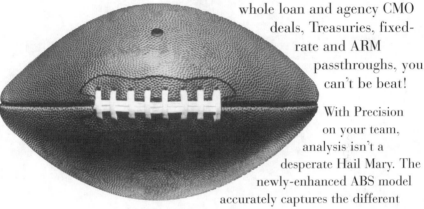

Why punt when you can score a touchdown? GAT Precision™ gives your team the power and ability to get the ball into the end zone. With over 4100 asset-backed structures, whole loan and agency CMO deals, Treasuries, fixed-rate and ARM passthroughs, you can't be beat!

With Precision on your team, analysis isn't a desperate Hail Mary. The newly-enhanced ABS model accurately captures the different collateral types. Prefunding mechanisms, excess servicing, draws on lines of credit, and revolving period structures: it's all part of Precision's game plan.

You're the quarterback. Generate three-dimensional graphs, mark a portfolio to a market, analyze the average-life volatility of a portfolio, and generate option-adjusted durations and convexities. Apply Precision's powerful analytics to mortgage pools.

As a Precision user, you'll make decisions with more confidence. Our contacts in the industry help us gather timely and accurate data. Our experts reverse-engineer even the toughest ABS structures. Our client support staff is responsive and dependable. Count on Precision. We're on your team.

Our Business is Helping Yours®
Find A Way.

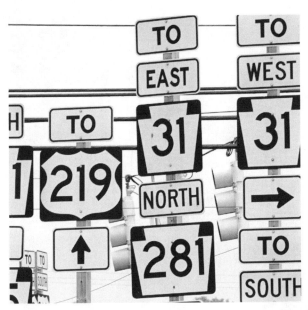

Successful commercial real estate financing depends on access to competitive financing solutions.

The GE Capital Access program gives you simplified access to the CMBS market with competitive priced fixed rate loans of $1-$10 Million on most general purpose real estate. Underwriting and due diligence are controlled in–house by a culture committed to responsiveness. Qualifying applications are reviewed and approved quickly with loan commitments direct from the lender. Plus, customers are eligible for the Power Buyer Service, which helps you obtain top-quality products and services such as HVAC Equipment, Roofing and Insurance.

Give us a call to explore commercial real estate deals over $1 million.

GE Capital
Commercial Real Estate Financing & Services
Our Business is Helping Yours®

GE Capital Commercial Real Estate Financing & Services
(888) GE FIRST
• Atlanta, GA • Boca Raton, FL • Boston, MA • Charlotte, NC • Chicago, IL • Cincinatti, OH • Denver, CO • Dallas, TX • Irvine, CA •
• Kansas City, MO • Nashville, TN • New York, NY • Phoenix, AZ • Philadelphia, PA • San Francisco, CA • Seattle, WA • Washington, DC •
• London, England • Mexico City, Mexico • Toronto, Canada •

For mortgage and asset securitization services, you need a team of pros.

Cash Flow
Analysis

Pool
Analysis

Tape Cracking &
Collateral Review

Payment Date Accounting

GAAP & RAP
Accounting

Mathematical
Verification

Original Issue
Discount
Reporting

CMBS Due
Dilligence

CMBS Portfolio
Surveillance

Transaction Structuring

Residual Costing
& Valuation

Strategic Tax
Analytics

Portfolio Dispositions
& Valuations

The
Ernst & Young
Team

Good students of ABS and MBS deals know...

where to get the most thorough Securitization Service...

Deloitte & Touche brings our size and experience to work for you.

As the largest securitization practice, we have worked on literally thousands of securitized transactions involving more than a trillion dollars in aggregate principal.

We currently serve most of the leading issuers and other participants in the securitization market, and offer a full range of consulting and technology services.

New York
(212) 436-2159

Los Angeles
(213) 688-3218

Deloitte & Touche LLP

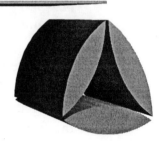

Deloitte & Touche works with issuers of all asset types to achieve their securitization goals.

We're there from start to finish, and then some.

Because of our up-to-date knowledge of the industry, we can help you identify potential problems faster and recommend better solutions.

Our commitment to the asset securitization market doesn't stop with the transaction closing. We offer consulting support at every phase of the process, and our market presence allows us to respond quickly and effectively to your needs.

We're with you for the long run. The systems we've developed for clients reflect our market knowledge and are designed to meet your needs in the future as well as the present.

New York
(212) 436-2159

Los Angeles
(213) 688-3218

Why gamble with fixed income valuations?

Accurately evaluating thinly traded securities is a tough game. But Interactive Data helps put the odds in your favor.

Get accurate fixed income valuations

At Interactive Data, we pride ourselves on unbiased valuations. Our professional fixed income analysts monitor each market sector throughout the trading day. Our staff and market contacts are located in the major global financial markets.

We integrate up-to-date market information with our proprietary financial models to give you accurate, objective valuations. For example, we use an Option Adjusted Spread (OAS) model to evaluate bonds with early redemption features, and we generate additional valuations from models that incorporate relative spreads and prices from multiple dealers.

Boston   Chicago   Hong Kong